Oman
Live·Work·Explore

Get FRiENDi mobile,
provider for expats in Oman."

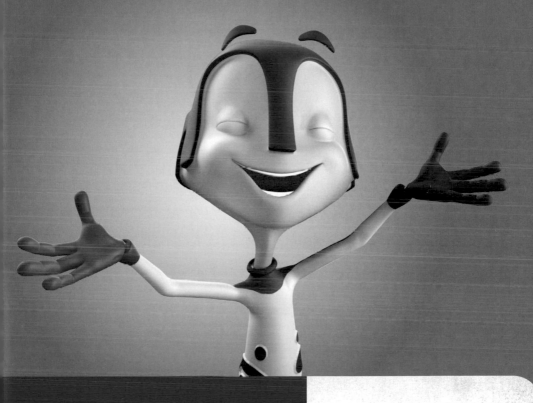

Oman Explorer
4th Edition ISBN 13 - 978-9948-03-386-8

Copyright © Explorer Group Ltd 2009
All rights reserved.

Front Cover Photograph – Pete Maloney

Printed and bound by Emirates Printing Press, Dubai, United Arab Emirates.

Explorer Publishing & Distribution
PO Box 34275, Dubai
United Arab Emirates

Phone	+971 (0)4 340 8805
Fax	+971 (0)4 340 8806
Email	info@explorerpublishing.com
Web	www.explorerpublishing.com

Welcome

By simply buying this fantastic book, you've just made moving to Oman a whole lot easier. The following pages are packed full of information that will help make this vibrant country your home. As you pack up your belongings, look for new accommodation or venture out into Oman's great outdoors, this book will provide all the information you need to get things done and take advantage of all that's here.

The **General Information** chapter (p.1) provides a background into Oman's culture, covering history, geography and environment. You'll also find handy information on places to stay and the best way to get around. The **Residents** chapter (p.55) is packed with practical information and useful tips so you'll be armed with all the facts you need to battle through the bureaucracy and set up shop.

When you are ready to investigate your new home, the **Exploring** chapter (p.145) will give you tips on where to start and what not to miss. Whether it is lounging around on the beach, camping in the desert or soaking up some culture in Oman's souks and museums, it's all covered here. When you're ready to venture further out there are also a few suggestions of great places to visit for a weekend break or a longer adventure.

If you can't wait to get the adrenaline pumping, there are several ways to keep active in Oman and it's all covered here. From daring watersports to caving, the **Activities** chapter (p.211) has the details. You'll have enough ideas to keep your free time packed with adventurous things to do, whether it's clambering over dunes, diving along Oman's coastline or kicking back in its luxurious spas.

When it's time for some retail therapy, arm yourself with the **Shopping** chapter (p.257), which is dedicated to guiding you straight towards all you could possibly need. You'll find details of the best places to furnish your home, buy groceries and peruse high fashion – not to mention how to bargain like a pro in the souks. Don't use up all your energy running around the malls though, as the **Going Out** chapter (p.303) points out the best spots to let your hair down in Muscat, with a full listing of the city's restaurants, bars and clubs.

You'll find the **Maps** section (p.345) at the back of the book, with detailed maps of Muscat and the surrounding area, ensuring you know where you're going and how to get there.

So now there's nothing left to stop you. When you've had the chance to familiarise yourself with Oman, keep us up to date on your adventure, or simply fill us in on your fortuitous finds – log on to www.liveworkexplore.com and share your expertise with your fellow explorers.

The Explorer Team

Stay Beside The Beach

Beach Hotel is Located on a quiet, palm lined street in the heart of Shatti Al-Qurum the architecturally fascinating Beach Hotel is known as one of Muscat's best kept secrets. From the friendly and skilled reception staff to the luxurious rooms and suites to the tranquil courtyard and pool, the Beach Hotel aims to exceed expectations at every turn. Hotel offers exclusive privacy, unbeatable value, skilled service, and uncompromising luxury.

Contact Details:
 P.O. Box: 678, P.C: 116 Mina Al Fahal, Sultanate of Oman
 Tel : **(+968) 24695119, (+968) 24695495**   Fax: **(+968) 24697686**
 E-mail: **beach@motifoman.com**

Managed By Motif Hospitality and Investment Management
E-mail: info@motifoman.com, Web: www.motifoman.com

MOTIF BEACH CAFE

Food and Beach
A Delicious Combination

Location:
Jawharat Al-Shatti
Behind Oasis Complex
Contact Details:
Tel: (+968) 24603992
E-mail: info@motifoman.com

Managed By Motif Hospitality and Investment Management

THE

Now available
Oman

For more information call us on
+971 4 364 2900

TIMES

daily across

visit us: www.thetimesme.com

Contents

Contents

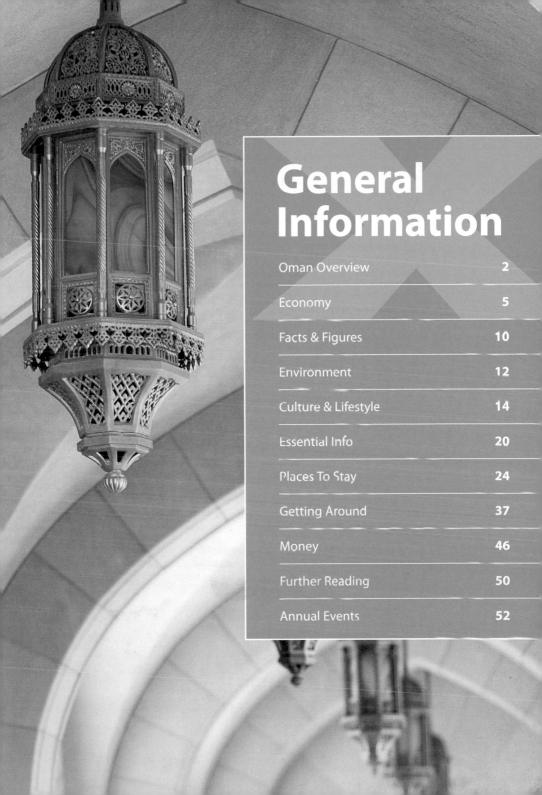

General Information

General Information

Geography

Situated in the south-eastern quarter of the Arabian Peninsula, the Sultanate of Oman is bordered by the Kingdom of Saudi Arabia to the west, Yemen to the south-west and the United Arab Emirates (UAE) to the north-west. Estimates of its total land area vary but the official figure is 309,500 square kilometres, making it the third largest country in the peninsula. Mountain ranges (15% of the land) and a narrow strip of coastal plains (3%) break up a topography that is predominantly made up of valleys and deserts (82%). Oman's coastline, which is about 2,000km long, extends to the Gulf of Oman and the Arabian Sea as well as the Indian Ocean. The geographic coordinates for Oman are 21 00N, 57 00E.

The country is divided into eight administrative regions: three governorates (Muscat, Dhofar and Musandam) and five regions (A' Dakhliyah, A' Dhahirah, Al Batinah, Al Wusta and A' Sharqiyah). Each region is further divided into smaller 'wilayats' (districts) headed by a 'wali' (district governor). The capital of the country is Muscat.

Musandam, known as the 'Norway of Arabia' because of its majestic fjords, lies at the furthest east point of the Arabian peninsula and is separated from the rest of the country by the United Arab Emirates (UAE). This is an area of great strategic importance, lying south of Iran and controlling the main navigable stretch of the Strait of Hormuz, through which 90% of the world's crude oil passes. An Omani enclave also lies in the village of Al Madha in the UAE.

Off the coast there are several islands, the largest of which is Masirah Island in the south-east. It is a strategic entry point from the Arabian Sea to the Gulf of Oman, and houses military facilities used by the United States.

Oman's countryside is among the most stunning and varied in the Gulf region. It features 'sabka' (salt flats), 'khwars' (lagoons), oases, and stretches of sand and gravel plains dominated by stark mountains of rock and brownish-green ranges of ophiolites. The Hajar Mountains are the largest range, stretching from Musandam, through the UAE, to northern Oman, and rising to 3,000 metres at Jebel Shams, the highest peak in the country. The countryside is crossed by 'wadis' (riverbeds), which are formed by the force of torrential water during the rainy season.

Oman is home to a large part of the seemingly endless Rub Al Khali (Empty Quarter) desert, which continues into Saudi Arabia and the UAE. The other main desert is the Ramlat Al Wahaybah (Wahiba Sands), home to nomadic Bedouin tribes, where dunes can rise to a spectacular 200 metres.

In contrast, the Dhofar region in the south is renowned for its green, tropical appearance and monsoon season with relatively high rainfall. It is one of the few places in the world

The corniche at Mutrah

where the frankincense tree grows; ancient trade in this resin features prominently in Oman's history.

Most of the population lives along the coast, on the Al Batinah plains and in the Muscat metropolitan area. You can discover more about Oman's landscapes in the Exploring section of this book (p.145).

History

Archaeological evidence suggests that an early form of civilisation existed in Oman at least 5,000 years ago. The name 'Oman' is said to come from the Arab tribes that migrated to the area from a place in Yemen called Uman. The Omanis were among the first Arabs to embrace Islam, back in 630AD, and Oman became an Ibadhi state ruled by an elected religious leader, the Imam.

Sultan Qaboos Bin Said

In the 1960s a serious new threat arose from Dhofar. By 1965, the Dhofar rebellion was underway, led by the Dhofar Libération Front and aided by South Yemen.

On 23 July 1970, a day henceforth celebrated as Renaissance Day, Sultan Qaboos bin Said assumed power. He was only 30 years old at the time but already had a strong vision for his country. Born in Salalah on 18 November 1940, he is the only son of the late Sultan Said bin Taimur and is eighth in the direct line of the Al Busaidi Dynasty. He spent his youth in Salalah, where he was educated until he was sent, at the age of 16, to a private school in England. In 1960, Sultan Qaboos entered the Royal Military Academy at Sandhurst as an officer cadet, where he reputedly discovered a love for classical music. After military service in Germany he studied local government administration in England and went on a world tour, before returning to Salalah for six years. He devoted this time to studying Islam and Omani history. The Sultan married in 1976 but later divorced. He has no children.

History Of Trading

Oman's geographical position on some of the world's most important trade routes between Africa and Asia has given it a unique dimension. From the first to third centuries, the southern part of the country was one of the wealthiest regions in the world due to the ancient trade in Arabian horses and the world's purest frankincense. Oman became a prosperous seafaring nation, sending dhows to Africa, India and the Far East.

A Struggle For Power

The Portuguese arrived by force in 1507, with a view to protecting supply lines to the east and constraining Oman's trading power. They were driven out of their main bases, first from Hormuz in 1622, and eventually from Muscat in 1650, by Sultan bin Saif Al-Ya'arubi. This event marked the start of full Omani independence, making the country the oldest independent state in Arabia.

From the 1600s to the 1800s Oman vied with both Portugal and Britain for trade in the Gulf and the Indian Ocean. During the Ya'aruba Dynasty (1624–1744), Oman entered an era of prosperity and many of its great buildings and forts were built. But tribal warfare over the election of a new Imam halted this expansion and Persian forces invaded the coastal areas.

The history of Oman has always been a struggle for economic and political power between the interior (ruled by an Imam), and the coastal areas and Muscat (ruled by a Sultan). In 1744, Omani tribes elected Imam Ahmed bin Said, founder of the present Al Busaidi Dynasty. He expelled the Persian invaders, united the country, restored Oman's fortunes and moved the capital from the interior to Muscat. He

Sultan Qaboos
Sultan Qaboos bin Said came to power on July 23, 1970. Under his rule, Oman has enjoyed a period of peace and prosperity that can be credited to the wise and gentle leadership of the sultan.

Oman Fact Box
Coordinates – 21°00′ North 57°00′ East.
Borders – 410km with UAE, 676km with Saudi Arabia and 288km with Yemen
Total land area – approx. 212,460 sq km
Total coastline – 2,092km
Highest point – 2,980m (Jebel Shams)
Time Zone – UTC + 4

also adopted the title of Sultan, which remains to this day.

Government treaties in 1798 and 1800 furthered links with Britain. These gave Oman British protection while maintaining its independence. In return, Britain could maintain the supply route with its empire further east.

The Development
Of Oman
Using the new oil
wealth, Sultan Qaboos
immediately set about
transforming Oman
and modernising the
infrastructure.
In 1970, Oman had
only three primary
schools, 10 kilometres
of paved roads, two
health centres, no
infrastructure to speak
of, and a per capita
income of less than
$50 a year. Today it is
peaceful, stable and
relatively prosperous.
The Sultan is a strong
yet benign leader,
drawing his people
into the modern world
but at the same time
preserving much of the
character and heritage
of his country, making
Oman a unique place
to visit.

Significant Leadership

The Omani empire reached the height of its power in the mid 19th century under Sayyid Said bin Sultan. He extended control all the way to Zanzibar and Mombassa in Africa, and to parts of Persia, Pakistan and India. (Oman only withdrew from Gwadar in 1958 when Sultan Said bin Taimur, father of the current ruler, allowed it to be reintegrated into Pakistan). Sayyid Said established political links with France, Britain and the United States, making Oman the first Arab state to establish relations with the USA. When Sayyid Said bin Sultan died the empire was split between his two sons. One became the Sultan of Zanzibar and the other, the Sultan of Muscat and Oman. Zanzibar became the nation's capital until it was declared an independent sultanate in 1861. Sultan Said bin Taimur came to power in 1932. He was able to enforce his rule over the interior, partly with the backing and encouragement of the British who needed stability in order to search the interior for oil. However, after establishing his rule, the Sultan became progressively more isolated, closing the nation's borders and shielding his country from the influences of the outside world. Eventually the only contacts were through the Sultan's mainly British advisors and certain well established trading families. Although Oman began commercialising oil in the late 1960s, the people spent much of the 20th century living as they had for centuries, under various restrictions.

Oman Timeline

1508	Oman falls under Portuguese control
1659	The Ottoman Empire takes control of Oman
1744	Ottoman Turks are overthrown by Ahmed bin Said of Yemen, who becomes Imam and starts the leadership of the Al Busaidis, which remains to this day
1890	Oman becomes a British Protectorate
1962	Oil is discovered in Oman
1970	Sultan Qaboos comes to power as the Sultan of Oman
1971	Oman becomes a member of the United Nations and the Arab League
1981	Oman joins with other Gulf countries to form the Gulf Cooperation Council (GCC)
1984	The first branch of Oman International Bank opens its doors
1986	Sultan Qaboos University opens
1996	Sultan Qaboos issues a decree clarifying the laws of royal succession and granting basic human rights for all citizens of Oman
1997	Two women are elected to the Consultative Council
1999	Oman and the United Arab Emirates settle their border disputes
2000	Oman joins the World Trade Organisation (WTO)
2003	All Omani citizens over the age of 21 are given the power to vote
2004	The first female government minister is appointed
	A royal decree grants foreigners the right to purchase freehold property in certain developments in Oman
2006	Oman signs a free trade agreement with the USA
2007	Cyclone Gonu hits Oman causing the death of more than 50 people and creating damage costing approximately $4 billion
2009	First residents move into The Wave
2010	Muscat holds the Asian Beach Games

Oman Overview

The Sultanate's economic strategy is based on a series of five-year plans. In 'Vision 2020', Oman aims to become a 'Newly Industrialised Economy' and to double gross domestic product (GDP) per capita.

The situation in the Sultanate is radically different from that of 40 years ago when Oman was an economically poor nation. It is now a middle-income developing country with the 18th most liberal economy in the world, free universal welfare services and impressive infrastructure. Real GDP growth has been averaging 5% annually over the past 20 years. In recent years Oman has experienced deflation thanks to government subsidies and lower import prices in local currency terms.

Oil

At around 40%, oil remains the largest contributor to GDP. The GDP for 2008 soared to approximately $45 billion, from $30 billion the previous year. Petroleum Development Oman (PDO) – a consortium between the government (60%), Royal Dutch Shell (34%), Total-Fina-Elf (4%) and Partex (2%) – contributes more than 90% of total oil revenues and accounts for nearly 95% of oil production. Most of Oman's estimated recoverable oil reserves (5.5 billion barrels) are located in the northern and central regions. At current production levels of about 760,000 barrels per day, there should be enough for another 20 years. Oman's only oil refinery and terminal is at Mina Al Fahal, near Muscat.

Other Industries

Endowed with modest oil reserves, Oman aims to create a viable non-oil economy by shifting economic emphasis to tourism, agriculture, fisheries, mining and light industry, while continuing aggressive development of natural gas to offset depleting oil production. Oman's main export partners are Japan, South Korea, China, Thailand, Taiwan, Singapore and the USA. The main import partners are the UAE, Japan, the UK, the USA and Germany.

Omanisation

Efforts to diversify the economy also include 'Omanisation', or a gradual replacement of the expatriate workforce with Omani nationals. This means that all companies must employ a certain percentage of Omanis. Around 40,000 young Omanis enter the job market each year, some with skills and some without. Government training schemes are in place to give nationals the necessary skills. By 2020, the government aims to have at least 95% of public sector jobs filled by Omanis, and at least 75% of private sector jobs. When the Omanisation laws were first passed in 1994, minimum levels were set according to industry. Private sector companies in various industries were compelled to employ the following percentages of Omani staff: transport and communication (60%), finance and real estate (45%), hospitality (30%), retail (20%), industry (35%) and contracting (15%). Since then, these percentages have been increased on a regular basis. This presents a challenge for some companies, who have to comply with the law, but who also face a shortage of skilled Omanis in particular industries.

Trade

Oman belongs to the World Trade Organisation, the International Monetary Fund and various pan-Arab economic groups, like the Arab Gulf Cooperation Council (AGCC) and the Indian Ocean Rim Association (IORARC) – Oman is a founding member of both. It is not a member of the Organisation of Petroleum Exporting Countries (OPEC) – although its pricing policy tends to follow that of OPEC fairly closely. In 2006, the US Senate approved a free trade agreement with Oman. This means that duties on goods traded between the two countries will be eliminated.

Really Tax Free?
Taxes. Do they exist in Oman? Well, yes and no. You don't pay personal income or sales tax except when you buy pork, tobacco and liquor, in which case the price you pay includes the 100% import tariff. The main taxes that you will come across in your hotel or restaurant bill are a 5% municipality tax, a 6% tourism levy, and occasionally, a service charge of 5% or more, pushing up the bill by a whopping 17%. The rest are hidden taxes in the form of 'fees', such as your car registration renewal and visa or permit fees.

Tourism

Oman has much to offer tourists; stunning and unspoiled landscapes, rich marine life, a stable political climate, a low crime rate, an ancient culture, and most importantly, genuinely hospitable people.

After years of seclusion from the world, Oman started welcoming tourists in the mid 1980s. There were 1.3 million tourists in 2003, mostly coming from the UAE, UK, Germany and France. Many come to visit family and friends or to enjoy the country's rugged landscape. Expatriates and nationals from surrounding Arab countries also see Oman as an alternative to foreign travel.

In 2003 the government earned RO 58.1 million from tourism (a mere 0.7% of GDP). The aim is to double this rate by 2010 and further increase it to 5% by 2020. With about 50% of the population under the age of 18, the tourism sector is expected to absorb the waves of young Omanis who enter the job market annually.

In contrast to neighbouring Dubai, which encourages visitors of any background, Oman has repeatedly stressed its desire to develop this sector only to the extent that it does not conflict with the values of a traditionally conservative society. It is keen to promote upmarket tourism, focusing resources on adventure tourism, eco-tourism, cultural and heritage attractions, and coastal resorts. Backpackers will remain a rare sight for the foreseeable future.

The slow growth in this sector has given more time to expand services and hotels to meet the demands of the modern traveller. To realise its full potential, the government engaged International Development Ireland (IDI) in July 2002 to perform the same miracles it did for Ireland's tourism sector.

A new Ministry of Tourism was created in June 2004, underscoring tourism's importance in the new economy. Primary target markets have been identified as the UK, France, German-speaking parts of Europe and the GCC states. Travel restrictions have been eased, and visitors from 75 countries may now get a visa, valid for one month, on arrival at Oman's air, land or sea entry points. Oman has a joint visa facility with Dubai and a cross-border agreement with Qatar. The government undoubtedly hopes to attract some of Dubai's 4.7 million visitors, particularly during the summer months when the cooling mists of the Dhofar region provide a refreshing respite from the searing heat that blankets the region.

Seeb International Airport is set to undergo major redevelopment, including construction of a new terminal which will increase its capacity to 12 million passengers per year. The international airport in Salalah will be upgraded to handle more inbound charter flights.

Oman Air, the national airline, has acquired new planes and expanded its destinations. Almost all well-known hotel chains are present. There are currently over 60,000 beds, but this is set to increase to 100,000 by 2010. Hotels are continually upgrading their offerings to better attract business travellers. The luxurious Al Bustan Palace InterContinental Muscat reopened in early 2009 following closure to repair damage caused by Cyclone Gonu.

Oman's landscape is dotted with over 500 castles, forts and towers, of which about 70 have been restored. These have become popular tourist attractions, along with the traditional souks. Oman's forts are systematically being restored under the The Forts and Castles Restoration Project.

To increase its global presence, Oman hosts international dune rallies, yacht races, and annual festivals like the Muscat Festival and the Khareef Festival in Salalah.

Oman is a successful example of how modernisation can be achieved without giving

In The Pipeline

A new convention centre is being built in As Seeb, called Seeb Corporate Park, at an estimated cost of RO 100 million, and incorporating three hotels, 150 serviced hotel apartments and a shopping mall. Plans for three new airports (Ras Al Hadd, Nizwa and Sohar) were announced in January 2006. Nine abandoned mountain hamlets are being transformed into B&B-style lodgings. Several new trekking routes have been charted in the mountains north of Oman, and there are three new caving projects on the cards (besides the one at Al Hoota). Watch this space.

up a country's cultural identity. Muscat is one of the region's most attractive capital cities: clean and unexpectedly green, modern yet architecturally traditional. To visit Oman is, to use today's tourism slogan, to experience 'the Essence of Arabia'.

Key Projects

Fast-paced development is a regional phenomenon in the Middle East, and Oman is no exception. There are some exciting building and development projects already underway in the sultanate, and many more at the planning stage.

Musanah
Barka
Map 1 B2

Asian Beach Games 2010

www.muscat2010.org.om

Oman is set to play host to this major sporting event in 2010, which is held every two years in a different country. Several new facilities are being prepared ahead of the games at Musanah, 70km from Muscat, and the venue will become an attraction in itself with hotels, an Olympic village, sporting arenas and a 400 berth marina. The games consist of both modern and traditional events, with teams from all over Asia taking part.

Al Sawadi
Map 1 B2

Blue City

www.almadinaalzarqa.com

This ambitious project will create a whole new city over 32 square kilometres. The resort city will integrate tourism and residences, and will be home to around 200,000 people. Facilities will include a golf course, a tourist village and heritage museum, a sports stadium, luxury hotels, two hospitals, a university, a harbour for cruise ships and plenty of shopping opportunities.
Completion date: construction began in 2006 and will be completed in phases over the next 15 years.

Duqm
Salalah
Map 1 F3

Duqm

In a bid to attract tourists and citizens, the industrial oil town of Duqm is undergoing massive development. The project will include an airport, hotels, residential complexes, refinery, free trade zone, power station, health facilities, shops, schools, recreational facilities, dry dock, commercial port and a shipbuilding yard. This coastal town also benefits from pleasant weather so it is hoped the area will develop into a maritime getaway destination. The development will open in phases.

As Seeb
Map 1 B1

Muscat Hills Golf & Country Club

www.muscatgolf.com

Muscat's first green golf course opened in early 2009 with 18 holes and a state of the art clubhouse. This RO 20 million development will also incorporate luxury residential villas that will be available for freehold purchase. Call 24 51 0065 for more information.
Completion date: 2010

Al Khawd
Map 1 B2

Oman Botanic Garden

www.oman-botanic-garden.org

Oman Botanic Garden, an impressive 420 hectare project run by the Diwan of Royal Court, will be an education and conservation attraction showcasing over a thousand species of Oman's plants. Divided into huge plots which reflect the climate and landscape of various areas in Oman, visitors will experience everything from arid desert to cool forests. There will also be a mini village that demonstrates local skills, plus exhibitions, displays and education facilities. Currently a building site, the garden welcomes booked groups only to view its progress; the project will open to visitors over the next three years.

Salalah
Map 1 E3

Salalah International Airport

www.omanairports.com

New runways will be constructed to improve facilities at this airport, which is used predominantly for cargo but also used for passenger flights, particularly during the khareef season. The upgraded airport will have the capacity for two million passengers a year.

Completion date: work on the runways began in 2006 and the first phase is expected to be complete by 2012.

As Seeb
Map 1 B1

The Wave

www.thewavemuscat.com

This multi-million dollar venture will see the staggered completion of four zones of entertainment, leisure and residential facilities. The development involves significant land reclamation and will eventually spread for over seven kilometres along Oman's coastline near Muscat. Facilities will include a golf course, hotels and spas, conference facilities, a marina, a shopping centre, and a range of residential options available for purchase by both Omanis and expats.

Completion date: phase one is complete; construction is scheduled to finish by 2012.

Yiti
Map 1 C1

Yenkit

www.yenkit.com

This 9.4 square kilometre area, approximately 20km south-east of Muscat, will be a hub for visitors to Oman. The $2 billion project, with its unique coastal location, will offer several hotels, an eco-friendly resort, 18 hole golf course, beaches, diving destinations and a hilltop residential village with traditional architecture.

Completion date: unpublished.

Apartments at The Wave

Oman Botanic Garden

International Relations

In its foreign relations Oman maintains a stance of non-alignment and non-interference in the affairs of other countries, but is committed to Arab unity. Since taking power in 1970, Sultan Qaboos has managed the extremely tricky task of maintaining friendly relations with just about everyone. In 1993 he became the first Gulf leader to welcome an Israeli Prime Minister to his country, and was one of only two Arab leaders who did not break off diplomatic ties with Egypt after it signed the peace agreement with Israel in 1979. In recent years Oman has developed into a backroom mediator in solving the more politically volatile issues of the region. It was testimony to the Sultan's unique position on the world's stage when, in October 1998, he was presented with the International Peace Award by former US president Jimmy Carter, and in 2001, the Peace Prize from the Jewish-American Committee.

Oman is a member of the main international organisations, including the United Nations, IMF, WTO, Interpol, Arab League and the Arab Gulf Cooperation Council (GCC). Most of the major embassies or consulates are located in the Shati Al Qurm area and the Al Khuwayr diplomatic area. A few are in the Ruwi commercial business district (CBD). For a list of embassies and consulates, see p.21.

Government & Politics

Oman's system of government is an absolute monarchy and hereditary through the male line of Sayyid Turki bin Said bin Sultan of the Al Busaidi Dynasty, the great great-grandfather of the present ruler, Sultan Qaboos bin Said. He is the Head of State and Supreme Commander of the Armed Forces. He is also Prime Minister, Defence Minister and Foreign Minister, although the day-to-day running of these and various other ministries is performed by a Council of Ministers. The political and economic capital, and seat of government, is Muscat.

Given Oman's history of warring factions, it would have been difficult to put in place any kind of long lasting economic, social and political reforms without some form of constitution. In November 1996, Sultan Qaboos passed the Basic Laws of the State. It is not actually a constitution in the official sense, but it does outline a series of basic human rights for Omani citizens. More importantly, it defines the rules of succession, as the Sultan has no children.

The Basic Law provides for a bicameral legislature presided over by the 'Majlis Oman' (Council of Oman). It consists of the 'Majlis A'Shura' (Consultative Council) whose members are elected by Omani citizens to represent the various wilayats, and the 'Majlis Al Dawla' (State Council) whose members are appointed by the Sultan.

Oman's legal system is based on Islamic Shariah law and English common law, with ultimate appeal to the Sultan. Capital punishment is rare and subject to review by judicial and religious authorities.

The Sultan has reportedly said that his country is not yet ready for full parliamentary democracy, implying that he considers this as the way forward. Nothing has been publicly finalised, although in November 2002 every Omani citizen over 21 years was granted the right to vote.

In his 39 years of rule, Sultan Qaboos bin Said has been an extremely capable, far-sighted and benign leader, held in high regard by his people. This is most apparent in their reactions when he travels around the various wilayats on his annual 'Meet the People' tour.

Workers' Rights

In 2006, Oman made some much-needed changes to its labour law, perhaps triggered by concerns over the free trade agreement with the USA. Workers are now permitted to form labour unions and carry out peaceful strikes. Oman will also punish employers who are found guilty of labour law violations or employing forced labour.

Population By Area

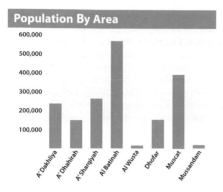

Population Age Breakdown

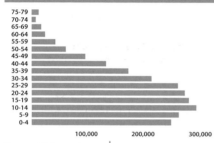

Source: Ministry of Plannning

Population

A national census is taken every 10 years and the last one was held in December 2003. The Ministry of National Economy put the population of Oman at 2,340,815, of which 76.1% are Omanis and 23.9% are expatriates. The population growth rate is 1.84%, comparing favourably with the rate of 3.5% in developing countries. There are 1.02 Omani males to every female, an indication of a demographically stable community. However, in respect of the total population, due to the dominance of male expatriates who outnumber female expatriates by three to one, there are 1.28 males to every female.

In 1970, the life expectancy was 40 years. Today Omani males have a life expectancy of 72.2 years and females of 75.4, compared to the global life expectancy of 68 years for males and 72 years for females.

Muscat Governorate has seen great progress in education over the last 10 years. Illiteracy among Omanis (10 years and above) has dropped from 22.8% in 1993 to 11.6% in 2003. The average size of an Omani household in Muscat is 7.3 members.

National Flag

The flag of Oman comprises three equal horizontal bands of white (top), red (middle) and green (bottom) with a thicker vertical red band on the hoist side. White stands for peace and prosperity, red for the battles fought against foreign invaders, and green for the fertility and greenery of the land. Centred at the top of the vertical band (in white) is the nation's emblem, an Omani 'khanjar' (dagger) and belt, superimposed on two crossed swords.

Local Time

The Sultanate of Oman is four hours ahead of UCT (Universal Coordinated Time, formerly known as GMT), and there is no summer time saving. When it is midday in Muscat it is 08:00 in London, 13:30 in Delhi and 17:00 in Tokyo, (not allowing for any summer time saving in those countries).

Social & Business Hours

Social hours vary in Oman – some people get up early, some stay up late, and some do both. Some businesses still close for a long afternoon break – this is known as 'split shift'. Standard split shift hours are from 08:00 to 13:00 and then from 16:00 to 19:00 (for offices) or 22:00 (for some shops). However, most private sector offices will work a straight shift, usually 08:00 to 17:00 or 18:00. The weekend is traditionally Thursday afternoon and Friday (the holy day), but a few organisations close all day Thursday and Friday.

Government offices are open from 07:30 to 14:30, Saturday to Wednesday. Bank hours are usually 08:00 to 12:30, Sunday to Thursday.

Smaller shops and souks are generally closed between 13:00 and 16:00 and usually remain closed on Friday mornings. The Mutrah Souk closes at 20:00 (although some shop's start closing from 19:30). Many shopping malls also close for a long lunch, although Markhaz Al Bahja and Muscat City Centre both remain open throughout the day. Supermarkets are generally open all day, seven days a week.

Working hours at embassies and consulates vary but are generally 08:00 to 13:00 or 14:00. Most are closed on Thursdays and Fridays, but leave a contact number on their answering machines in case of emergencies.

Ramadan

During Ramadan, work hours in most public and private organisations are reduced by two to three hours per day, and business meetings may be difficult to arrange. Muslims in the private sector may work only six hours per day and government offices close at 14:00 or earlier. Many private offices start work an hour or so later and shops are open until 22:00 or 24:00. Most restaurants are closed during the day. The Ruwi district in Muscat and more popular shopping malls are usually crowded, even at night, and parking can be hard to find.

Photography

Normal tourist photography is allowed and in some parts of the country, actively encouraged. However, taking photographs near government buildings, military installations, ports and airports is not allowed, and you will see signs banning photography in certain areas. Always ask permission when taking photos of local citizens – the Arabic phrase 'mumkin shura, min fadlak' means 'may I take your picture please?' Children and men will usually oblige but local women may not, especially if the photographer is male.

Public Holidays

The Islamic calendar starts from the year 622AD, the year of Prophet Muhammad's migration (Hijra) from Mecca to Al Madinah. Hence the Islamic year is called the Hijri year and dates are followed by AH (AH stands for Anno Hegirae, meaning 'after the year of the Hijra').

As some holidays are based on the sighting of the moon and do not have fixed dates on the Hijri calendar, Islamic holidays are more often than not confirmed less than 24 hours in advance. Most companies send an email to employees the day before, notifying them of the confirmed holiday date. Some non-religious holidays are fixed according to the Gregorian calendar. It should be noted that the public sector often gets additional days off for holidays where the private sector may not (for example on National Day the public sector gets two days of official holiday, whereas private sector companies take only one day). This can be a problem for working parents, as schools fall under the public sector and therefore get the extended holidays, so your children will usually have more days off than you do. No problem if you have full-time home help, but if not then you may have to take a day's leave.

Public Holidays (2010)

Holiday	Date	
New Year's Day (1)	1 Jan	Fixed
Prophet Muhammad's Birthday (2)	26 Feb	Moon
Lailat Al Mi'raj (1)	09 July	Moon
Renaissance Day (2)	23 July	Fixed
Eid Al Fitr (3/4)	11 Sep	Moon
Eid Al Adha (3)	17 Nov	Moon
National Day (2)	18 Nov	Fixed
Islamic New Year (2)	18 Dec	Moon

The table above lists the holidays and the number of days they last. This applies mainly to the public sector, so if you work in the private sector you may get fewer days per holiday.

The main Muslim festivals are Eid Al Fitr (the festival of the breaking of the fast, which marks the end of Ramadan) and Eid Al Adha (the festival of the sacrifice, which marks the end of the pilgrimage to Mecca).

Mawlid Al Nabee is the holiday celebrating the Prophet Muhammad's birthday, and Lailat Al Mi'raj celebrates the Prophet's ascension into heaven.

Climate

Oman's climate varies considerably with the different regions, but sunny blue skies and warm temperatures can be expected most of the year. The best time to visit Oman is in winter, between October and April, when temperatures average between 25°C and 35°C during the day and about 18°C at night.

The north is hot and humid during the summer, with temperatures reaching 48°C during the day in June and July, and averaging about 32°C at night. Humidity can rise to an uncomfortable 90%. The 'gharbi' (western) wind from the Rub Al Khali can raise coastal town temperatures by another 6°C to 10°C.

The interior is usually hotter than the coastal area, often reaching 50°C in the shade. In the mountains, night temperatures can fall to -1°C with a light dusting of snow.

Rainfall is infrequent and irregular, falling mainly between November and March. Average annual rainfall in the Muscat area is 75mm, while rainfall in the mountains can be as high as 700mm.

The southern Dhofar region usually has high humidity, even in winter. Between June and September the area receives light monsoon rains, from the Indian Ocean, called the 'khareef'. The area around Salalah is lush and green and at certain times of the year is swathed in a cooling mist – it's hard for visitors to reconcile this image with the usual Arabian landscapes of forbidding deserts and rocky, inhospitable mountains.

Information on local weather and meteorological conditions is available by dialling 1102 (Arabic) or 1103 (English).

Fantastic Falaj

The UN Economic & Social Commission for West Asia has done a study on Oman's falaj systems, which have been in operation for centuries. The study report found that agricultural farmers depend on falaj for as much as 60% of their total water supply.

Flora & Fauna

Flora

Oman has around 1,200 native plant species. Of the indigenous flora, date palms provide oases of green covering about 49% of Oman's cultivated area. The deserts are fairly barren but after a bout of rain they are dotted with wild flowers. Coconut trees, banana trees and other tropical fruit trees thrive well in the subtropical climate of Salalah.

Oman is home to the frankincense tree (Boswelia sacra), which grows only in Dhofar, the Wadi Hadhramaut in Yemen, and Somalia. They are short trees with a gnarled trunk and silver-green leaves. Incisions are made on the bark to collect the aromatic resin. For hundreds of years, frankincense was more valuable than gold and Dhofar frankincense was said to be the finest and purest in the world. It was used not only as a fragrance, but also to embalm corpses and as a medicine. The frankincense trade brought immense wealth and importance to southern Arabia – even Alexander the Great had plans to invade the area in order to control the trade at its point of origin.

Mangrove trees (Avicennia marina) used to cover large stretches of Oman's coast but have been threatened with extinction in many areas. Some of the most beautiful and dense mangrove forests today are found in the Qurm Nature Reserve in the heart of Muscat, and at Mahawt Island, 400km south of the capital. The Qurm Nature Reserve contains an important site where prehistoric fishermen exploited mangrove resources, and a nursery that produces seedlings for replanting. Thanks to urgent conservation measures, mangrove forests now cover about 1,088 hectares of Oman's coastline.

Fauna

Oman has a wide variety of indigenous wildlife which includes many endangered species such as the Arabian oryx, Arabian leopard, Arabian tahr (a mountain goat now found only in Oman), Nubian ibex and humpback whale. Realistically though the only large animals you are likely to see are camels, donkeys and goats, often roaming dangerously close to the road.

Environment

Marine Life

Several new varieties of seashells have been discovered on Oman's beaches. Around 150 species of commercial shell and non-shell fish, 21 species of whales and dolphins and other assorted marine creatures are found in Omani seas. The humpback whale feeds and breeds in the rich waters off central and southern Oman.

There are four breeds of sea turtle that come ashore to lay their eggs. The huge leatherback turtle is known to swim in the waters offshore but there are no records of it nesting in Oman. The more popular nesting sites are Ras Al Hadd for green turtles, Masirah Island for the world's largest population of nesting loggerheads and the Daymaniyat Islands Nature Reserve – Oman's only marine reserve – for hawksbill turtles. Be aware that collecting live shells, turtle eggs and shellfish is forbidden in Oman.

Birds

Some 460 species of birds (of which 80 are resident) are found at different times of the year – an impressive number considering that Oman has vast areas of desert and no real forests. Millions of birds wintering in East Africa pass over Oman on their spring or autumn migration to Central Asia. For more information on birds in Oman, contact the Oman Bird Group (www.birdsoman.com).

Environmental Issues

Oman is one of the world's top 10 environmentally committed countries and is party to international agreements on biodiversity, climate change, desertification, endangered species, hazardous wastes, marine dumping, Law of the Sea, whaling and ozone layer protection. In 1984, it became the first Arab state to create a ministry dedicated to environmental issues; environmental protection laws have been in place since 1974. At the Earth Summit in 1989, Sultan Qaboos established the biannual Award for Environmental Conservation, the first Arab prize to be awarded in this area. In 1990, a new hybrid of rose was named in the Sultan's honour, in recognition of his commitment to the environment and his support for human rights.

Various organisations have been formed to protect the environment, as well as to educate the people on the importance of environmental issues and the protection of human health. 2001 and 2002 were declared Years of the Environment. The 2003 Law on Nature Reserves and Wild Life Conservation reinforced Oman's policies on biodiversity and environmental management.

The Sultan has always been committed to an extensive 'greening' programme of his cities. Highways are lined with colourful bougainvillaea, grassed areas, palm trees and flowers, all maintained by an army of workers who also pick up the litter on the roadside. It's no surprise then that Muscat Municipality received the UN Public Services Award for cleanliness in June 2003.

The Sultanate aims to protect endangered wildlife species by establishing nature reserves, while working together with local communities to ensure their success. The turtle breeding beaches at Ras Al Hadd and Ras Al Jinz are protected sites, as are the Daymaniyat islands, which are a bird sanctuary to which entry is restricted during the breeding season. The Arabian Oryx Sanctuary on the Jiddat Al-Harasis is a Unesco World Heritage Site. Wadi Al Sarin, one of Oman's oldest reserves, is home to the Arabian tahr, while Jebel Samhan in Dhofar is a refuge for the Arabian leopard. Saleel Park is a nature reserve inhabited by gazelles and rare trees. Hunting and killing of any wildlife is strictly prohibited and carries stiff penalties.

Despite these efforts there are still some serious threats to the environment facing the Sultanate, such as groundwater pollution, rising soil and water salinity, desertification and beach pollution from oil spills. For more information on and what you can do to help, contact the Environment Society of Oman (www.environment.org.om).

Face To Face
Omanis greet profusely on meeting and parting, and it would be polite to return the gesture with a friendly remark (master those greetings) or a handshake. Unlike the firm western handshake (a sign of aggressiveness), the handclasp is light and may be followed by placing the hand over the heart to show sincerity. Some Muslims prefer not to shake hands with the opposite sex, so when meeting an Omani man or woman, wait until they offer their hand before you go in for the handshake. Light cheek-to-cheek kissing between men is also common, but reserved for family and close friends. Avoid bad and forceful language and discussing local politics with casual acquaintances. It is considered impolite to ask someone about their origin or birthplace.

Culture

Oman's distinctive culture is influenced by Islamic traditions and regional heritage. Islam is more than just a religion: it is a way of life that governs everyday events, from what to wear to what to eat. Unfortunately Islamic fundamentalism and its links to terrorism has caused some misunderstanding of this hugely popular religion, and of Muslim countries and culture in general. In reality, Islam is a peaceful and gentle religion that is followed by millions of faithful Muslims around the world.

Due to Oman's position on many historical trade routes, the local citizens (Omanis) have been exposed to different cultures for centuries, and as a result are tolerant, welcoming and friendly. Foreigners are free to practise their own religion, alcohol is served in hotels and the dress code is relatively liberal. Women face little discrimination and, contrary to the policies of some neighbouring countries, are able to drive and walk around unescorted.

Among the most highly prized virtues are courtesy and hospitality, and visitors are sure to be charmed by the genuine warmth and friendliness of the people.

Visitors are generally able to roam freely in the souks and villages, and may be pleasantly surprised by genuine offers of coffee. Perhaps the only exceptions are mosques and the Lewara quarter, adjacent to the Mutrah Souk in Muscat, where many Shi'a Muslims live.

As you travel deeper into the interior the people become more conservative but no less hospitable. The forbidding mountains and formidable deserts have kept them isolated from external influences so a foreign face becomes a welcome diversion.

To get a quick overview of Oman, its traditions and its people, spend some time in one of the many excellent museums in the Muscat area (see p.171).

Language

Other options **Learning Arabic** p.136, **Language Schools** p.236

The official language of the country is Arabic, but English is widely spoken. Other commonly heard languages include Urdu, Baluchi, Swahili, Hindi and other Indian dialects. Most road signs, shop signs and menus are in both Arabic and English. The further into the interior you go, the more Arabic you will find, both spoken and on street signs. See p.15 for a quick list of useful Arabic phrases to get you around the country.

Arabic isn't the easiest language to pick up (or to pronounce), but if you learn the usual greetings you're more likely to receive a warmer welcome. Most Omanis appreciate the effort and will help you with your pronunciation. Just give it a try – it certainly won't hurt and it definitely helps when dealing with officials of any sort.

Religion

Islam is the official religion of Oman, with most Omanis following the Ibadhi sect, named after its founder Abdullah bin Abadha. Ibadhism is regarded as 'moderately conservative' and a distinguishing feature is the choice of a ruler by communal consensus and consent. Some Omanis are Sunni Muslims and live primarily in Sur and the surrounding areas, and in Dhofar. The Shi'a minority live in the Muscat-Mutrah area. The basis of Islam is the belief that there is only one God and that the Prophet Mohammed is his messenger. There are five pillars of the faith (the 'hadith'), which all Muslims must follow – the Profession of Faith (a statement of the belief, as above), Prayer, Charity (giving of alms), Fasting (during the holy month of Ramadan) and Pilgrimage. Every Muslim, if possible, is required at least once in their lifetime to make the pilgrimage or 'Hajj' to the holy city of Mecca (or Makkah) in Saudi Arabia. Additionally, a Muslim is required to pray five times a day, facing Mecca. The times

Culture & Lifestyle

Basic Arabic

General

Yes	na'am
No	la
Please	min fadlak (m) / min fadliki (f)
Thank you	shukran
Please (in offering)	tafaddal (m) / tafaddali (f)
Praise be to God	al-hamdu l-illah
God willing	in shaa'a l-laah

Greetings

Greeting (peace be upon you)	as-salaamu alaykom
Greeting (in reply)	wa alaykom is salaam
Good morning	sabah il-khayr
Good morning (in reply)	sabah in-nuwr
Good evening	masa il-khayr
Good evening (in reply)	masa in-nuwr
Hello	marhaba
Hello (in reply)	marhabtayn
How are you?	kayf haalak (m) / kayf haalik (f)
Fine, thank you	zayn, shukran (m) / zayna, shukran (f)
Welcome	ahlan wa sahlan
Welcome (in reply)	ahlan fiyk (m) / ahlan fiyki (f)
Goodbye	ma is-salaama

Introductions

My name is...	ismiy...
What Is your name?	shuw ismak (m) / shuw ismik (f)
Where are you from?	min wayn inta (m) / min wayn inti (f)
I am from...	anaa min...
America	ameriki
Britain	braitani
Europe	oropi
India	al hindi

Questions

How many / much?	kam?
Where?	wayn?
When?	mataa?
Which?	ayy?
How?	kayf?
What?	shuw?
Why?	laysh?
Who?	miyn?
To/for	ila
In/at	fee
From	min
And	wa
Also	kamaan
There isn't	maa fee

Taxi Or Car Related

Is this the road to...	hadaa al tariyq ila...
Stop	kuf
Right	yamiyn
Left	yassar
Straight ahead	siydaa
North	shamaal
South	januwb
East	sharq
West	garb
Turning	mafraq
First	awwal
Second	thaaniy
Road	tarlyq
Street	shaaria
Roundabout	duwwaar
Signals	ishaara
Close to	qarib min
Petrol station	mahattat betrol
Sea/beach	il bahar
Mountain/s	jabal/jibaal
Desert	al sahraa
Airport	mataar
Hotel	funduq
Restaurant	mata'am
Slow Down	schway schway

Accidents & Emergencies

Police	al shurtaa
Permit/licence	rukhsaa
Accident	haadith
Papers	waraq
Insurance	ta'miyn
Sorry	aasif (m) / aasifa (f)

Numbers

Zero	sifr
One	waahad
Two	ithnayn
Three	thalatha
Four	arba'a
Five	khamsa
Six	sitta
Seven	saba'a
Eight	thamaanya
Nine	tiss'a
Ten	ashara
Hundred	miya
Thousand	alf

vary according to the position of the sun. Most people pray at a mosque, although it is not unusual to see them kneeling by the side of the road if one is not near. It is not considered polite to stare at people praying or to walk over prayer mats.

The modern call to prayer, broadcast through loudspeakers on the minarets of each mosque, ensures that everyone knows it's time to pray. Prayer timings are also published in local newspapers. Friday is the holy day. Other religions are recognised and respected, and followers are free to practise their faith.

Forecast By Phone

If you subscribe to Oman Mobile, you can get a weather forecast sent to your mobile phone. Just send a text message with the name of the area you are in, preceded by f., to 90023 (so if you were in Muscat, you would type in f.Muscat and send it to 90023).

Ramadan

Ramadan is the holy month in which Muslims commemorate the revelation of the Holy Quran, the holy book of Islam. During Ramadan, Muslims fast during daylight hours (while fasting, they abstain from eating, drinking and smoking). In the evening, the fast is broken with the Iftar feast. Iftar timings are listed in the daily newspapers.

The starting date of Ramadan is not fixed in terms of the western calendar, but each year it occurs approximately 11 days earlier than the previous year. For most Muslim countries the start of Ramadan depends on an actual sighting of the moon. Out of respect non-Muslims should not eat, drink or smoke in public places, even in their cars, between sunrise and sunset. Office business hours are usually cut short, while shops and parks open and close later. Small restaurants may be closed during the day and hotels provide screened rooms for those not fasting. Bars are closed and the sale of alcohol is banned. Ramadan ends with a three day celebration and holiday called Eid Al Fitr, or 'Feast of the Breaking of the Fast', followed 70 days later with Eid Al Adha, or 'Feast of the Sacrifice', which marks the end of the pilgrimage season to Mecca. For Muslims, Eid has similar connotations as Diwali for Hindus or Christmas for Christians.

A Mosque With A Difference

There are prescribed washing rituals for both Muslim men and women that must be completed before entering a mosque. Non-Muslims with cameras, intent to gawk are generally not allowed in mosques and signs prohibiting entry may be posted at the entrance. The exception to this is the majestic and architecturally pleasing Sultan Qaboos Grand Mosque in Al Ghubrah (Muscat). It is open to visitors Saturdays to Thursday from 08:30 – 11:00. It is closed on Fridays and public holidays. Ladies' night is on Mondays from 16:00 – 21:00. Women must wear loose fitting, long sleeved shirts, long trousers or skirts (an abaya will be perfect), and headscarves. Men should not wear shorts. Children under the age of 10 are not allowed to enter. Photography is allowed. There is also a prayer hall for ladies, a public library and an information centre.

Places Of Worship

Catholic Church Of Sts Peter & Paul	Ruwi	24 701 893	Catholic
Holy Spirit Catholic Church	Ghala	24 590 373	Catholic
Krishna Temple	Darsayf	24 798 546	Hindu
The Protestant Church In Oman	Ruwi	24 799 475	Protestant
Salalah Christian Centre	Salalah	23 235 727	Catholic
Shiva & Bajrangbali Temple	Muscat	24 737 311	Hindu
St Anthony's Church	Sohar	26 841 396	Catholic
St Francis Xavier's	Salalah	23 235 727	Catholic

National Dress

Most Omanis wear traditional dress during work and social hours. Men wear an ankle length, collarless gown with long sleeves (dishdasha). It is usually white, although beige, lilac, black and navy are also sometimes worn. The neckline has a tassel called a furakha, which is sometimes scented with perfume. A plain cloth (wuzar) is worn under the dishdasha from the waist down. On their heads men usually wear a brimless embroidered hat (kumah). Sometimes a square of finely woven cotton is wound around the head, over the kumah, to make a turban (muzzar). On formal occasions, men may wear a black or beige cloak edged in silver or gold thread (bisht). A traditional dagger (khanjar) often hangs from the waist, secured by a belt of leather and silver (sapta) or a strip of cloth.

Traditional Omani dress

Some men also carry a stick (assa or baakora) as an accessory. Omani men wear sandals, even on formal occasions. Traditional women's costumes are very colourful and vary from region to region. The main components are a pair of loose trousers (sirwal), a long-sleeved tunic and a headdress (lihaf). The tunics are often extremely colourful, with bright greens, reds, purples, and oranges, intricately woven together in embroidered patterns. The lihaf covers the head and shoulders and is black or the same fabric as the tunic. In northern and coastal Oman, women tend to wear a full-length, caftan-style dress (khandoura), which is embroidered in different patterns.

In public, women cover their normal clothes with a full-length, black cloak-dress (abaya). The abaya is usually made of sheer, flowing fabric, sometimes open at the front. Modern women will often wear trousers or a long skirt underneath.

You can still see women, usually in the interior but also in Muscat, wearing the 'burkha' (mask) that covers the brow, cheekbones and nose. It is often dyed gold or indigo. Some older women also pierce their noses on both sides and wear a carnelian stone or a gold flower stud. In Dhofar, indigo is sometimes rubbed on the face to give a bluish tint that complements the robes.

Made In Oman?
Authentic Omani souvenirs include silver items, pottery, weaving, textiles, fragrances, copper and sweets. Of particular interest is the intricately crafted traditional dagger, the khanjar. The curved dagger is traditionally attached to a belt and hung around the waist. The best place to hunt for authentic souvenirs is in the souks – just be on guard for new 'Omani' silver items that are actually made in Indian antique factories.

Food & Drink
Other options **Eating Out** p.304

You can eat your way around the world in Oman – there is a huge choice of international cuisines thanks to the cosmopolitan mix of nationalities living here. Not only can you feast on exotic foods in the numerous five-star hotels, but you can also find cheaper options at the many street cafes and independent restaurants. You'll also find all the obligatory fastfood outlets such as McDonald's, KFC and Pizza Hut. Browse through the Going Out section (p.304) for some pointers on where to find the kind of cuisine you love.

Arabic Cuisine

Arabic cuisine is similar in some respects to Omani cuisine, using many of the same ingredients and styles of cooking. It is basically a blend of many types of cooking, such as Moroccan, Tunisian, Iranian, Egyptian and Afghani, although in general terms modern 'Arabic cuisine' invariably means Lebanese food. The cuisine is excellent for meat eaters and vegetarians alike.

Shawarmas (lamb or chicken carved from a rotating spit, then rolled in flat bread with salad) are sold in small shops throughout Oman. If you don't eat meat, you can try a vegetarian version of this delicious, inexpensive snack made with foul (a paste made from fava beans) or falafel (deep-fried balls of mashed chickpeas). Salads like fattoush and tabbouleh are cheap and healthy.

Don't miss out on trying the ultimate Arabic dessert – umm ali (similar to British bread and butter pudding) is made with milk, bread, nuts and raisins and it is delicious.

Social Visits

When travelling in Oman, the opportunity to visit a local home for some traditional Arabic coffee may arise. The coffee is usually bitter, but is often served with dates to sweeten things up. If you don't want a second helping, shake your cup lightly next time the coffee pot comes around. When entering a local house, you should remove your shoes. Men may gather in a different area to women. Seating may be on carpets or low cushions – another good reason to dress modestly. Make sure the soles of your feet (or shoes) are not facing anyone.

Omani Cuisine

Traditional Omani cuisine is fairly simple, with rice as the main ingredient cooked together with beef, mutton, goat, chicken or fish. The meat is roasted, grilled or baked after marinating in a variety of spices, including cardamom, cinnamon, cumin, ginger, pepper, turmeric and saffron. This is not surprising considering Oman's position on the ancient trade routes. However, the food is rarely 'hot and spicy' since the flavours are used in a subtle manner.

Traditional Omani meals are eaten with the right hand. The main meal is usually eaten at midday, while the evening meal is lighter. Salads are quite simple – lettuce, cucumber and tomatoes served with a slice of lime for dressing. Maqbous is a saffron coloured rice dish cooked over spicy meat. Skewered meats (kebabs) are often served with flat bread (khoubz). Harees is a staple wheat-based dish with chicken, tomato, seasoning and onion. Fish and shellfish are used widely in dishes such as mashuai – whole spit-roasted kingfish served with lemon rice.

Favourite local drinks are laban (heavy, salty buttermilk) and yoghurt, which is often flavoured with cardamom and ground pistachios. Fresh juices, made on the spot from fresh fruits (mango, banana, pineapple, pomegranate), are delicious and very cheap. In particular, the mixed fruit cocktail should not be missed.

Omani 'halwa' is a popular dessert made of eggs, palm honey sugars, water, ghee and almonds, flavoured with cardamom and rosewater. These ingredients are blended and cooked to form a sweet, dense block with a delicious flavour and consistency. Traditionally, the making of halwa is very much a male preserve, with recipes being handed down from generation to generation.

It is during Ramadan that one can sample Omani food at its best. Dishes, such as shuwa, arsia (lamb with rice) and mishkak (similar to kebabs), are mainly served during Eid celebrations. Shuwa is elaborately prepared by

Coffee on the streets

seasoning a large piece of meat (often lamb) and wrapping it in banana leaves, sacking and then burying it in a pit on top of red-hot coals. The meat is left to cook slowly over a couple of days in the embers and when unwrapped, is tender and succulent.

Many hotels set up a Bedouin-style tent outdoors in the winter months – this is an ideal opportunity to sample authentic Omani cooking. However, the Bedouins themselves enjoy a far more limited diet, depending on where they are travelling. Their standard fare is usually camel meat (dried or boiled), served with rice.

The serving of traditional coffee (kahwa) is an important social ritual in the Middle East. Local coffee is mild with a taste of cardamom and saffron, and is served black without sugar. It is served with dates, to sweeten the palate between sips. It is considered polite to drink about three cups of the coffee when offered (it is served in tiny cups, about the size of an egg cup).

Arabic Family Names

Arabic names have a formal structure that traditionally indicates the family and tribe of a person. Names usually start with that of an important person from the Ouran or someone from the tribe. This is followed by the word 'bin' (son of) for a boy and 'bint' (daughter of) for a girl, and then the name of the child's father. The last name indicates the person's tribe or family. For prominent families Al, the Arabic word for 'the', comes immediately before it. For instance, the ruler of Oman is Sultan Qaboos bin (Al) Said. When women get married, they do not change their name. Family names are very important here and extremely helpful when it comes to differentiating between the thousands of Mohammeds, Ibrahims and Fatimas.

Pork

Pork is taboo in Islam. Muslims should not eat, prepare or serve pork. In order for a restaurant to serve pork on its menu, it should have a separate fridge, preparation equipment and cooking areas. Supermarkets also require pork to be sold in a completely separate area. You can buy pork mainly from Al Fair supermarkets, but you have to find the walled-off pork section first. All meat products for Muslim consumption have to be 'halaal' – this refers to the method of slaughter. As pork is not locally farmed you will find that it is more expensive than many other meats. However after a few Friday brunches with chicken sausages and beef bacon you will be surprised how easy it is to have a fry up without pork.

Alcohol

The attitude to alcohol in Oman is far more relaxed than in some other parts of the Middle East. The government grants alcohol licences to hotel outlets and independent restaurants, plus a few clubs. Alcohol cannot currently be purchased in local supermarkets. Permanent residents who are non-Muslims can easily get liquor supplies under a permit system from their embassy. However, it is illegal to carry alcohol around, the only exception being when you are taking your purchases home directly from the liquor shop or airport duty free. Keep your receipt as this gives you the right to transport alcohol. It is also illegal to resell alcohol to others. If you have an accident while driving under the influence of alcohol, the penalties are high and in addition, your vehicle insurance will be invalid. Alcohol is not served during Ramadan, even in hotels.

Shisha

Smoking the traditional shisha (water pipe) is a popular and relaxing pastime enjoyed throughout the Middle East. It is usually savoured in a local cafe while chatting with friends. They are also known as hookah pipes or hubbly bubbly, but the proper name is nargile. Shisha pipes can be smoked with a variety of aromatic flavours, such as strawberry, grape or apple, and the experience is unlike normal cigarette or cigar smoking. The smoke is 'smoothed' by the water, creating a much more soothing effect. Smoking Shisha is one of those things that should be tried at least once while you're in Oman, especially during Ramadan, when festive tents are erected throughout the city and filled with people of all nationalities. You can buy your own shisha pipe from the souks, and once you get to grips with putting it all together you can enjoy the unique flavour anytime you want. See Shisha Cafes (p.336).

In Emergency

Expats and tourists are not entitled to use government hospitals but must instead register with one of the private hospitals or clinics. Muscat Private Hospital and Al Shatti Hospital are clean and well-staffed with English speaking professionals but can lack the specialist equipment of the government hospitals. If you have a medical emergency while in Oman, you can just turn up at the Al Shatti Hospital accident and emergency department to be seen by a doctor. You may then be transferred to one of the government hospitals for further specialist treatment if required. Charges depend upon what kind of treatment you receive, but are not cheap, regardless of which medical centre you choose. A consultation with a doctor will set you back around RO 20, even before any medication or treatment is dispensed. Medical insurance is a must.

Emergency Numbers		
24 Hour Pharmacies		
Muscat Pharmacy	Al Khuwayr	24 487 980
	Ruwi	24 702 542
Scientific Pharmacy	Ruwi	24 702 850
	Al Qurm	24 566 601
Emergency Services		
Electricity Emergency	Various Locations	24 714 300
Municipality Emergency Number	na	800 777 222
Royal Oman Police	na	9999
Water Emergency	na	1 442
Medical Emergency		
Al Shatti Hospital	Shati Al Qurm	24 604 263
Hatat Polyclinic	Wadi Adai R/A	24 563 641
Muscat Private Hospital ▶p.119	Bawshar	24 583 600
Qurm Medical Centre	Al Qurm	24 692 898
Traffic Incidents		
Royal Oman Police HQ	Various Locations	24 560 099

Before You Arrive ◀

Oman's health sector is good and you should be able to get adequate treatment for most conditions. However, if you require regular medication for something, it is a good idea to stock up at least a year's supply before leaving your home country, on the off-chance that you will not be able to get your medication (or a substitute) in Oman.

Health Requirements

No health certificates are required for visitors to Oman, except for people who have recently been in a yellow fever infected area. However, it is always wise to check with an Oman diplomatic mission or your travel agent before departure as health restrictions may change. If you are travelling from a yellow fever area, you will need a certified vaccination at least 10 days before arriving in Oman. Travellers from Africa may be tested for malaria on arrival.

Malarial mosquitoes are rarely a problem in the cities. They are sometimes found around wadis and pools in the mountains, but they are not found in the desert or at altitudes above 2,000m. Long-term residents do not usually take malaria tablets. As of 2001, the World Health Organisation declared Oman malaria-free and taking preventive medication is no longer required. However, certain short-term visitors (such as elderly people or people with compromised immune systems) are advised to take the necessary precautions. Check requirements a month or so before leaving your home country.

Rabies has not been eradicated in Oman, so if you are bitten you should seek medical attention immediately. Vaccinations for Hepatitis A and B, and typhoid are recommended.

Oman's climate can be harsh, particularly in summer. Drink plenty of water and cover up when out in the sun. Try to avoid too much exposure to the sun between 10:00 and 15:00 and use the appropriate factor of sunscreen – sunburn, heat stroke and heat exhaustion can be very unpleasant and in some cases, dangerous.

The risk of contracting avian flu (bird flu) when travelling is very low, and Oman has had no reported cases so far. However, it is sensible to avoid direct contact with any birds (alive or dead), and undercooked poultry and egg dishes. It is a good idea to check the hygiene standards of any food outlet before you eat there. Visit www.fco.gov.uk for updated travel information on Oman and other countries.

Health Care

Other options **General Medical Care** p.117

The quality of medical care in Oman is quite high and visitors should have little trouble obtaining appropriate treatment, whether privately or from government-run hospitals. Towns in the interior have at least one health centre. Tourists are strongly encouraged to arrange private medical insurance before travelling since private medical care is fairly costly.

If you need medical assistance you may have to rely on friends, family or even a taxi to get you to a hospital since ambulance services are limited. In the case of life-threatening emergencies you can dial 9999 throughout Oman, and the Royal Oman Police will arrange appropriate transport. There are also many opticians and pharmacies in Muscat that provide excellent service.

Travel Insurance

All visitors to Oman should have travel insurance – just in case. Choose a reputable insurer with a plan that suits your needs and the activities you intend to do while in Oman, especially if they are extreme sports such as diving or mountain climbing. There is every chance that no accidents or illnesses will befall you during your visit, but this is one of those things in life where it is better to have it and not need it, than need it and not have it.

A good travel insurance policy will not only cover you for illness and injury, but also for loss or damage to your luggage. Just be sure to read the small print – many policies don't cover costs if you injure yourself while under the influence of alcohol or while partaking in extreme sports.

Female Visitors

Women should face few, if any, problems while travelling in Oman. It is generally safe to walk unescorted in well-lit and well-populated areas in Muscat and Salalah. Travelling alone in the interior or taking a public taxi on your own is not recommended. Single female travellers who don't want extra attention should dress modestly and avoid lower-end hotels. When travelling to the interior, always keep on hand a long-sleeved shirt and long skirt or an abaya, in case you have to cover

Embassies & Consulates

Name	Phone	Map Ref
Australia (Saudi Arabia)	+966 1 488 7788	na
Austria	24 694 127	7 E1
Bahrain	24 605 074	7 D1
Canada	24 791 738	12 E2
China	24 696 698	8 B4
Czech Republic (Saudi Arabia)	+966 1 450 3617/9	na
Denmark	24 526 000	10 A3
Egypt	24 600 411	7 C1
France	24 681 800	7 D1
Germany	24 832 482	12 D3
India	24 684 500	7 D1
Iran	24 696 944	7 C1
Ireland	24 701 282	12 E2
Italy	24 695 131	7 E1
Japan	24 601 028	7 D1
Jordan	24 692 760	7 C1
Korea (South)	24 691 490	7 D2
Kuwait	24 699 627	7 C1
Lebanon	24 695 844	7 E2
Mexico (Saudi Arabia)	+966 1 480 8822	na
The Netherlands	24 603 706	7 D1
New Zealand	24 794 932	9 L4
Norway	24 703 289	10 A4
Pakistan	24 603 439	7 F2
Philippines	24 605 140	7 E1
Qatar	24 701 802	7 C1
Russia	24 602 894	7 D1
Saudi Arabia	24 601 744	7 C1
Singapore (Saudi Arabia)	+966 1 480 3855	na
South Africa	24 694 793	7 E1
Spain (Saudi Arabia)	+966 1 488 0606	na
Sri Lanka	24 697 841	7 E2
Sweden	24 708 693	12 E2
Switzerland	24 568 202	11 E1
Thailand	24 602 684	7 E1
United Arab Emirates	24 400 000	7 C1
United Kingdom	24 609 000	7 D1
United States of America	24 643 400	7 C1

up quickly. No matter what, most foreign females receive some unwanted stares at some point, particularly on the public beaches, but it tends to be out of mere curiosity rather than anything more threatening or sinister.

Travelling With Children

Oman is a very family-friendly place and kids of all ages will have a great time. Although there are few parks and amusement centres, there are endless activities, particularly in the winter, for those who love nature and adventure. Many families go out at weekends to camp and explore Oman's many wadis, beaches and mountains. The Muscat Festival (p.52) also offers all sorts of fun-filled activities for the whole family. The Activities (p.212) and Exploring (p.146) sections of this book will give a better idea of what there is to do for kids.

Hotels and shopping malls (p.294) are generally well geared up for children, offering everything from babysitting services to kids' activities and small play centres. Restaurants (p.308), on the other hand, have children's menus but tend not to have many high chairs; it's best to ask when making reservations. Discounted rates for children are common.

Meeting The Challenge

Hotels with specially adapted rooms for guests with disabilities include the Al Bustan, Grand Hyatt, Muscat InterContinental, Golden Tulip Resort (Khasab), Radisson BLU, Shangri-La's Barr Al Jissah Resort and Crowne Plaza. The Chedi in Muscat will arrange the necessary facilities on request.

People With Disabilities

Most of Oman's hotels have wheelchair access and toilet facilities for people with special needs. However, when it comes to catering for people with special needs, Oman has a long way to go. Some places do have wheelchair ramps, although these are often really nothing more than delivery ramps, hence the steep angles. There are reserved parking spaces for disabled people, and drivers tend to leave these open as the police carry out regular inspections.

Dress Code

Although Oman is a Muslim country, there is no need for women to wear headscarves or veils or dress in floor-length, long-sleeved garments. However, respect for local customs is recommended and it is better to dress a little bit more conservatively than you might in your home country.

Short, revealing or tight clothing can be worn, but it will attract a lot of unwelcome attention. It is always best to keep shoulders and knees covered in public, but you can show some more skin in hotel bars, clubs and restaurants. Topless sunbathing is a definite no-no. Attitudes in rural areas are a lot more conservative than in the cities. You will have to dress appropriately if you visit the Sultan Qaboos Grand Mosque (p.190) – long skirts or trousers and long-sleeved shirts for ladies, with neck and chest covered, and long trousers for men.

Lightweight summer clothing is suitable for most of the year, but something slightly warmer may be needed in the evening for the winter months. In winter and summer, be sure to take some sort of jacket or sweater when visiting hotels or the cinema, as the air conditioning can reach arctic temperatures. During the day, good quality sunglasses, hats and buckets of sunscreen are needed to avoid the lobster look.

Photography

Normal tourist photography is allowed and in some parts of the country, actively encouraged. However, taking photographs near government buildings, military installations, ports and airports is not allowed, and you will see signs prohibiting photography in certain areas. Always ask permission when taking photos of local citizens – the Arabic phrase 'mumkin shura, min fadlak?' means 'may I take your picture please?'. Children and men will usually oblige but local women may not, especially if the photographer is male.

Crime & Safety

Other options **In Emergency** p.20

While street crimes are uncommon in Oman and violent crimes rare, a healthy degree of caution should still be exercised. Keep your valuables and travel documents locked in a safe. Don't leave valuables or tempting items like mobile phones or portable computers in plain sight in a parked car, particularly in hotel carparks. When in crowded areas, be discreet with your money and wallet. As with anywhere in the world (no matter how safe), just remain vigilant and know what's going on around you. Ladies are strongly advised not to get into the orange and white taxis if they are alone – while there are many upstanding and honest taxi drivers around, there have been many reports of women being harassed in taxis.

With a variety of driving styles converging on Oman's roads, navigating the streets either on foot or in a vehicle can be challenging. There are few pedestrian crossings and overpasses but don't be tempted to make a run for it, particularly across the main Sultan Qaboos highway (and while driving, be on the lookout for those who do). Omanis are generally polite and will stop to let you cross, but do make eye contact and make sure their vehicle has completely stopped. Learn the rules of the road before getting behind the wheel, and drive defensively. Needless to say, make sure you have insurance.

Tourist Information	
Desert Discovery Tours	24 493 232
Gulf Leisure	99 819 006
Mark Tours	24 782 727
National Travel & Tourism	24 660 300
Orient Holidays	24 478 902
Zahara Tours	24 400 844

Tourist Information

The official online tourist service for Oman is www.omantourism.gov.om. There are no tourist information centres as such in Muscat, but you can find information from a number of private tour operators. You can also enquire in your hotel which operators they recommend as many will have a deal set up with a particular company.

Oman Tourist Information Abroad

Oman participates regularly in major tourism fairs and has recently obtained backing to open representative offices in the UK, Germany, Spain, Switzerland, the United States and Hong Kong. Details of these offices can be found at www.omantourism.gov.om.

Sultan Qaboos Grand Mosque

Al Bustan Palace InterContinental Muscat

Places To Stay

Visitors to Oman can be assured of a reasonable choice of places to stay, from hotels to hotel apartments, rest houses, officially approved campsites and even desert camps for tourists. The range of good quality, cheap hotels is limited, but there are some youth hostels that have opened recently.

With new emphasis on tourism as an income generator for the country, the number of hotels and resorts is expected to increase, and the facilities and services to get better and more competitive. Visitors can expect attractive promotions during the summer months as hotels strive to fill unused capacity. On the other hand, at certain peak times of the year it can be difficult to find an available room, such as during the Khareef in Salalah or in Muscat at festival time.

Hotels

Other options **Weekend Break Hotels** p.209, **Landmark Hotels** p.28

Most of the top hotels in Muscat are located in Qurm Heights and Shati Al Qurm, with good locations near the beach. However, there are also some hotels with city locations, such as the Radisson BLU in Al Khuwayr, and right at the eastern end of Muscat you will find the regal grandeur of the Al Bustan Palace InterContinental Muscat and the luxury of Shangri-La's Barr Al Jissah resort.

There are some less fancy hotels along the Mutrah Corniche and in other city locations – while they might not be five-star hotels, they are still clean and functional. If you want to stay right near the beach in one of the most prestigious areas of Muscat, without spending a fortune, the Beach Hotel has an enviable location right in the heart of luxurious Shati Al Qurm.

It takes around 20 minutes to reach the hotels in Qurm from the airport, and a further 20 minutes to reach the Al Bustan Palace InterContinental Muscat or the Shangri-La. The larger hotels offer an airport shuttle service, sometimes for a minimal charge and sometimes on a complimentary basis.

As with anywhere in the world, you can usually negotiate for a discount on the 'rack rate' (published rate). Check the internet or local press for special discounts at certain hotels. If you are travelling outside of Muscat, you will find plenty of good hotels in Salalah, Nizwa, Sur, Sohar and Khasab.

Hotels

Five Star	Phone	Website	Map Ref
Al Bustan Palace InterContinental Muscat ▶ p.29	24 799 666	www.albustanpalace.com	15 A1
Al Nahda Resort & Spa ▶ p.161	26 883 710	www.alnahdaresort.com	1 B2
The Chedi Muscat	24 524 400	www.chedimuscat.com	6 E2
Crowne Plaza Salalah ▶ p.29	23 235 333	www.cpsalalah.com	1 F3
Crowne Plaza Sohar ▶ p.29	26 850 850	www.crowneplaza.com	1 B2
Grand Hyatt	24 641 234	www.muscat.hyatt.com	7 E1
Hilton Salalah	23 211 234	www.salalah.hilton.com	1 F3
InterContinental Muscat ▶ p.344	24 680 000	www.intercontinental.com	8 A4
Shangri-La's Barr Al Jissah Resort & Spa ▶ p.309	24 776 666	www.shangri-la.com	15 E3
Six Senses Hideaway Zighy Bay ▶ p.33	26 735 555	www.sixsenses.com	1 A2

THE PERFECT LOCATION
FOR BUSINESS OR PLEASURE

The Crowne Plaza Muscat's high standards of service complement the hotel's luxuriously appointed facilities. Its very unique cliff top location includes beach access and boasts the most breathtaking views of the Gulf of Oman. The hotel enjoys 200 elegantly appointed rooms.

- Set in 10 acres of landscaped gardens
- 7 international Restaurants and Bars
- Crowne Club Rooms with dedicated lounge
- Extensive conference facilities
- Outdoor dining and product launch venue
- Fitness Centre with Tennis and Squash courts
- Private beach

P.O. Box 1445, Ruwi 112
Muscat, Sultanate of Oman
Tel: +968 24660660, Fax: +968 24660600
e-mail: cpmuscat@cpmuscat.com

cpmuscat.com

CROWNE PLAZA®

MUSCAT

Hotels (Contd.)

Four Star	Phone	Website	Map Ref
Al Buraimi Hotel	25 642 010	na	1 B3
Al Falaj Hotel Muscat	24 702 311	www.omanhotels.com	12 D1
Al Sawadi Beach Resort	26 795 545	www.alsawadibeach.com	1 B2
Al Wadi Hotel	26 840 058	www.omanhotels.com	1 B2
Coral Hotel	24 692 121	www.coral-international.com	7 E1
Crowne Plaza Muscat ▶ p.25	24 660 660	www.cpmuscat.com	8 C3
Golden Tulip Resort Khasab	26 730 777	www.goldentulipkhasab.com	1 A2
Golden Tulip Seeb	24 510 300	www.goldentulipseeb.com	4 E4
Haffa House Hotel	24 707 207	www.haffahouse.com	12 D2
Holiday Inn Muscat Al Madinah ▶ p.29	24 596 400	www.holiday-inn.com	6 B4
Holiday Inn Muscat	24 502 190	www.holiday-inn.com	7 A2
Hotel Muscat Holiday	24 487 123	www.muscat-holiday.com	7 C2
Nizwa Hotel	25 431 616	www.nizwahotel.net	1 C2
Radisson BLU Hotel Muscat ▶ p.321	24 487 777	www.muscat.radissonsas.com	7 C3
Ramada Qurum Beach Hotel	24 603 555	www.ramadamuscat.com	8 A4
Ramee Guestline	24 564 443	www.ramee-group.com	8 D3
Sohar Beach Hotel	26 841 111	www.soharbeach.com	1 B2
Sur Plaza Hotel	25 543 777	www.omanhotels.com	1 C1
Three Star			
Al Burj International Hotel	24 798 008	na	9 D3
Al Diyar	25 412 402	na	1 C2
Al Jabal Al Akhdhar Hotel	25 429 009	na	1 C2
Al Sharqiya Sands Hotel	25 587 000	na	1 C1
Beach Hotel ▶ p.vi	24 696 601	www.omanbeachhotel.com	8 A4
Falaj Daris Hotel ▶ p.165	25 410 500	www.falajdarishotel.com	1 C2
Hamdan Plaza Hotel	23 211 025	www.hamdanplaza.com	1 F3
Hotel Golden Oasis	24 811 655	www.hotelgoasis.com	13 A4
Ibri Oasis	25 689 955	na	1 B2
Khasab Hotel	26 730 271	www.khasabhotel.net	1 A2
Marina Hotel	24 714 343	na	10 A3
Park Inn	24 507 888	www.parkinn-muscat.com	7 A2
Ruwi Hotel	24 704 244	www.omanhotels.com	12 D2
The Treasure Box	24 502 570	www.treasureboxhotels.com	6 E4
Two Star			
Al Hanna Hotel	23 290 274	na	1 F3
Dhofar Hotel	23 292 300	na	1 F3
Mina Hotel	24 711 828	na	10 A3
Muttrah Hotel	24 798 401	na	12 F1
Qurum Beach Hotel	24 564 070	na	8 D3
Safari Hotel	25 432 150	na	1 C2
Seeb International Hotel	24 543 800	na	3 B3
One Star			
Abha Hotel	25 654 700	na	1 B3
Al Qurum Resort	24 605 945	na	8 A4
Al Raha	24 701 655	na	12 E3
Corniche Hotel	24 714 707	na	10 A3
Ras Al Hadd Beach Hotel	99 376 989	na	1 C1

Landmark Hotels

Shangri-La's Barr
Al Jissah Resort
& Spa
Off Al Jissah St
Al Jissah
Map 15 E3

Al Bandar ▶ p.309

24 776 666 | www.shangri-la.com

Apart from the 195 rooms (all with balcony or terrace), Al Bandar also has eight dining outlets, 11 meeting rooms, and a huge ballroom. This is the business travel option of Shangri-La's Barr Al Jissah Resort, and has a souk area selling upmarket brands, art and crafts. There is a large swimming pool snaking around the hotel, sunbeds immersed in water, a Jacuzzi and a kids' pool.

Al Bustan St
Nr Al Bustan R/A
Al Bustan
Map 15 A1

Al Bustan Palace InterContinental Muscat ▶ p.29

24 799 666 | www.albustanpalace.com

This award-winning hotel of palatial proportions nestles in a coastal oasis of 200 acres fronting rugged mountains. The elegant Arabic theme of the imposing lobby carries over to its rooms and suites, all with private balconies. There are five international restaurants, including the spectacular Vue by Shannon Bennett (p.322) and an impressive concert hall.

Shangri-La's Barr
Al Jissah Resort
& Spa
Off Al Jissah St
Al Jissah
Map 15 E2

Al Husn Hotel ▶ p.309

24 776 666 | www.shangri-la.com

Resembling an Omani fort and built with luxury in mind, Al Husn is the most exclusive section of the Shangri-La. Each of the 180 bedrooms has a balcony or terrace and bathrooms are designed to ensure you can see the sea from your bath (which your butler can run for you). Al Husn has a private gym, a beach, an infinity pool and a library, as well as some excellent restaurants and bars.

Sayq Plateau
Nizwa
Map 1 C2

Al Jabal Al Akhdhar Hotel

25 429 009 | jakhotel@omantel.net.om

This hotel makes an ideal base for those wishing to explore the stunning scenery of the 'green mountain.' The hotel has 26 rooms and a coffee shop/restaurant serving international cuisine. The hotel itself is basic rather than luxurious, but it provides a perfect place from which to explore the mountain.

Nakhal Rd
Barka
Map 1 B2

Al Nahda Resort & Spa ▶ p.161

26 883 710 | www.alnahdaresort.com

The lovely Al Nahda Resort& Spa is perfect for both family getaways and personal relaxation trips. The spa offers several distinct therapies, including Ayurveda, hot stone therapy and yoga. The hotel section includes one and two bedroom villas as well as a bar and live entertainment and there's plenty going on for the children too.

Explore spectacular Oman with IHG

Al Bustan Palace
InterContinental Muscat

Reopened in its full original splendor, this world renowned hotel is the chosen place to stay of presidents and princes. 1km private beach, infinity pool, leisure facilities and a selection of Oman's finest restaurants.

Tel: +968 24 764205
reservations@albustanpalace.com
www.albustanpalace.com

Crowne Plaza Muscat

One of Muscat's most popular and lively hotels in a spectacular setting. High standards of service complement the hotels friendly atmosphere. Relax on the private beach and enjoy great food and extensive leisure facilities.

Tel: +968 24 660660
reservations@cpmuscat.com
www.cpmuscat.com

Crowne Plaza Salalah

Situated in 45 acres of lush tropical garden, overlooking the Indian Ocean and on a long stretch of pristine white sandy beach. Great leisure facilities including diving centre and four swimming pools.

Tel: +968 23 235333
reservations@cpmuscat.com
www.cpsalalah.com

InterContinental Muscat

Five star luxury hotel with resort character in the heart of Muscat. Enjoy a variety of trendy restaurants or the English pub. Beautifully landscaped gardens with direct access to the beach. Extensive fitness & leisure facilities, including shaded kids' pool & playground.

Tel: +968 24 680680
reservation@icmuscathotel.com
www.intercontinental.com

Holiday Inn Muscat
Al Madinah

This great value hotel is located midway between the airport and the city centre. It offers a health and fitness club, tennis courts and a swimming pool.

Tel: +968 24 529700
reservations@cpsohar.com
www.holidayinn.com

Crowne Plaza Sohar

The perfect place to spend the weekend, or to break the journey from Dubai to Muscat. With 2km outdoor swimming pool children's pool, bowling alley, floodlit tennis courts, volleyball, snooker, billiards, table tennis, baby football and darts.

Tel: +968 26 850777
reservations@cpsohar.com
www.crowneplaza.com

www.ihg.com

Al Sawadi Beach Resort

9km from
Al Sawadi Jct
Barka
Map 1 B2

26 795 545 | www.alsawadibeach.com

Guests have the option of staying in one of the chalet-style rooms, or using one of the tents and camping on the private beach. Facilities include a pool, gym, tennis, squash and mini-golf. Available watersports include windsurfing, waterskiing, jetskiing and kayaking. The dive centre offers PADI courses, and organises regular trips to dive sites at the nearby Daymaniyat Islands.

Al Waha Hotel ▶ p.309

Shangri-La's Barr
Al Jissah Resort
& Spa
Off Al Jlssah St
Al Jissah
Map 15 E3

24 776 666 | www.shangri-la.com

This is the largest of the hotels in Shangri-La's Barr Al Jissah Resort and has been built for families. Kids will love the 'Little Turtles' club, where they can play in air-conditioned comfort or outdoors. The hotel has numerous swimming pools, including a rubber-cushioned toddlers' pool and a kids' pool in the shape of a mushroom. Babysitting services are available.

The Chedi Muscat

Nr Lulu Hypermarket
Al Khuwayr
Map 6 E2

24 524 400 | www.chedimuscat.com

One of the most luxurious hotels in the Gulf, The Chedi is a magnet for lovers of modern comfort. With a calming mix of traditional architecture and zen-like symmetry, it is ideal for escaping the city even if just for a meal in The Beach Restaurant (p.330) or an afternoon in the spa (p.253). Guests can opt for a room or suite and also enjoy the adults-only infinity pool or 370 metre private beach.

Crowne Plaza Muscat ▶ p.25

Bldg 1730 Qurm St
Qurm Heights
Map 8 C3

24 660 660 | www.cpmuscat.com

On a cliff overlooking Al Qurm, this hotel has one of the best viewpoints in Muscat. The outdoor pool seems to spill onto the beachfront below, which is accessed by steps from the gardens. Its location makes dining alfresco in its three international restaurants, including the excellent Iranian restaurant Shiraz (p.328), a real pleasure. There is also a popular health club in the hotel.

Crowne Plaza Salalah ▶ p.29

Al Khandaq St
Salalah
Map 1 F3

23 235 333 | www.cpsalalah.com

Set in a private garden beside the sea, the Crowne Plaza features 153 rooms and 19 three-bedroom family chalets. There are three pools, kids' facilities, health and fitness facilities and a miniature golf course. Guests have three restaurants to choose from, including the new Dolphin Beach Restaurant offering alfresco dining with stunning views of the white sands and Indian Ocean.

Khasab Main Rd
Khasab
Map 1 A2

Golden Tulip Resort Khasab

26 730 777 | www.goldentulipkhasab.com

This hotel is situated in a small cove at the foot of the mountains. Visitors can choose from guest rooms and suites or chalets with mountain views. Dining options include a coffee shop, pool terrace, restaurant, the Oriental Café tent and Darts, an English-style pub. There's a swimming pool and children's play area, and the hotel organises diving, fishing, and dhow cruising trips.

Exhibition St
As Seeb
Map 4 E4

Golden Tulip Seeb

24 510 300 | www.goldentulipseeb.com

This handy hotel is located 1.5km from Seeb International Airport and next door to the Oman International Exhibition Centre. Guests can enjoy the private beach (across the road), and other leisure facilities within the hotel. There are 177 rooms, including six luxurious suites. Le Jarden restaurant serves international buffet cuisine and there is a bar with a live band.

Way 3032
Shati Al Qurm
Map 7 E1

Grand Hyatt

24 641 234 | www.muscat.hyatt.com

The decor is often described as 'Disneyland meets Arabia', but most of the Hyatt's rooms have sea views. The hotel has a delectable range of dining options. Tuscany (p.323) for tastes from the Mediterranean; Mokha Café (p.320), for all-day dining; Marjan (p.312) for alfresco dining, and the lively Copacabana and Safari nightclubs (some of Muscat's most happening nightspots)

Sultan Qaboos St
Salalah
Map 1 F3

Hilton Salalah

23 211 234 | www.salalah.hilton.com

This five-star establishment has a simple Omani-style exterior which hides a luxurious domed lobby and mirror-like marble floors. Its beachfront location, 12km from Salalah centre, allows guests to truly get away from it all. There are three restaurants, two entertainment outlets, a health spa and a doctor on call. If you're off to enjoy the Khareef, here's where you can do it in style.

Al Kharijiyah St
Shati Al Qurm
Map 8 A4

InterContinental Muscat ▶ p.344

24 680 000 | www.intercontinental.com

The InterCon continues to be popular for its outdoor facilities, international restaurants, Al Ghazal Pub (p.339) and entertainment from dinner theatres and visiting bands. Alfresco restaurant, Tomato (p.324), is a must-try. Trader Vic's, with its legendary cocktails, is perennially popular as is Senor Pico's (p.325), a buzzing Mexican restaurant. The health club is one of the best in Muscat.

Nizwa Hotel

20km from Nizwa
Btn Hajar Mountains
Birkat Al Moaz
Map 1 C2

25 431 616 | *www.nizwahotel.net*
Located a few kilometres from the centre of Nizwa, on the main road to Muscat, this hotel benefits from a picturesque setting with landscaped gardens and views of the Hajar Mountains. There are 40 guest rooms and all have private access to the central swimming pool. The Birkat Al Mawz restaurant serves international cuisine and the hotel has two comfortable bars and a nightclub.

Park Inn

Sultan Qaboos St
Al Khuwayr
Map 7 A2

24 507 888 | *www.parkinn-muscat.com*
Park Inn caters to business travellers and its location, close to the embassy area and 15 minutes from the airport, is handy. It offers a gym and spa, various conference rooms and two restaurants, including the RBG Grill. The interior is bright with a stunning central atrium, but the star of the show is the spacious rooftop pool area which offers privacy and waiter service.

Radisson BLU Hotel Muscat ▶ p.321

Way 209
Al Khuwayr
Map 7 C3

24 487 777 | *www.radissonblu.com/hotel-muscat*
Just 12 minutes from the airport, this hotel stands out in the Al Khuwayr business district. Some of its 156 rooms have views of the mountains. The Tajin Grill, Muscat's legendary steakhouse, will satisfy any serious meat cravings, and Olivo's is a delightful venue for a bright and breezy lunch. The health club is well-equipped and there is a complimentary shuttle to the Muttrah Souk.

Sheraton Oman Hotel

Street 40
Ruwi
Map 12 F2

24 772 772 | *www.starwoodhotels.com*
This hotel dominates the Ruwi skyline and is ideal for business travellers or serious shoppers. It offers all the comforts of a Sheraton, plus internet access in every room. The culinary theme nights, particularly Seafood Night on Wednesdays, make it an enduring favourite. There are four restaurants and three entertainment outlets, including a popular bowling alley.

Six Senses Hideaway Zighy Bay ▶ p.33

Zighy Bay
Musandam Peninsula
Dabba
Map 1 A2

26 735 555 | *www.sixsenses.com*
Surely one of the most incredible getaways in the region, Six Senses was built using local, natural materials. The seaside complex revolves around the world class spa and every aspect of the resort is geared to relaxation and tranquility. The food outlets are equally impressive. It's not cheap but worth the trip, especially when you have the option of arriving by paragliding into the grounds.

SIX SENSES
HIDEAWAY
ZIGHY BAY

Six Senses Hideaway Zighy Bay
brings a new level of innovative
and natural luxury to the Middle
East. Located on Oman's dramatic
Musandam Peninsula - a 90-minute
drive from Dubai, the spectacular site
provides the perfect retreat for residents
of Oman and Dubai and is an ideal
destination for guest coming from
abroad. The setting has mountains on
one side and a 1.6-kilometre
sandy beach on the other.

Six Senses Hideaway Zighy Bay is
designed with 82 pool villas, including
the two-bedroom Retreats and the
four-bedroom Reserve – all with butler
service. It offers a choice of dining
alternatives – from a hilltop restaurant
serving international cuisine to a central
restaurant featuring regional specialties
and a Chef's Table.

The Six Senses Spa focuses on holistic
wellness and rejuvenation. It offers a full
menu of treatments delivered by skilled
international therapists.

Guests have a choice of arrival
experiences which include a scenic
drive down from the top of the hill,
a 15 minute speed boat ride or the
choice to travel as a companion
passenger with the Hideaway's
professional paraglider!

Zighy Bay, Musandam Peninsula
Sultanate of Oman
T: +968 26735 555 F: +968 26735 556
reservations-zighy@sixsenses.com
www.sixsenses.com

Sallan Beach
Sohar
Map 1 B2

Sohar Beach Hotel

26 841 111 | www.soharbeach.com

With its whitewashed exterior in the style of an Omani fort, this is something of a landmark. Five kilometres from Sohar centre, it offers 41 luxury guest rooms, suites and chalets (all with balconies) and a choice of dining options including the Sallan, for international cuisine. Leisure facilities include a swimming pool, gym, tennis court, and the pristine sandy beach right on the doorstep.

Sur Main Road
Sur
Map 1 C1

Sur Plaza Hotel

25 543 777 | www.omanhotels.com

Located a few kilometres from the centre of Sur, this is a perfect base from which to explore the surrounding area including the turtle nesting sites at Ras Al Hadd and Ras Al Jinz. The hotel offers 108 guest rooms, and has a swimming pool, health club and gym. Dining options include Oysters Restaurant for international cuisine, and three bars with live entertainment each evening.

Hotel Apartments

A cheaper alternative to staying in a hotel is to rent furnished accommodation. This can be done on a daily, weekly, monthly or yearly basis. While it may not be as luxurious as a five-star hotel room, a hotel apartment can feel more like home. Usually the apartments come fully furnished, from bed linen to cutlery, plus maid service. There is normally a range of sports and leisure facilities, such as a gym, swimming pool and possibly even a restaurant or cafe, in the building.

Hotel Apartments

Al Khuwair Hotel Apartments	Al Khuwayr	24 789 199	www.safeerintll.com
Al Noorah Gardens Guest House	Madinat As Sultan Qaboos	99 322 247	www.noorahgarden.com
Al Shorouq Darsayt	Mutrah	24 789 900	www.shorouqhotels.com
Al Waffa Hotel Flats	Ruwi	24 786 522	na
Arabian Palms Apartments	Al Khuwayr	24 488 563	www.arabianpalmsapartments.com
Asas Residence	Qurm Heights	24 568 555	na
Beach Hotel Apartments ▶ p.vi	Shati Al Qurm	24 696 601	www.omanbeachhotel.com
Dhofar Park Inn International	Salalah	23 292 272	na
Haffa House Salalah	Salalah	23 295 444	na
Hala Hotel Apartments ▶ p.35	Ruwi	24 810 442	www.halahotelapartment.com
Isra Hotel Apartments	Khasab	26 730 562	www.khasabtour.com
Majan Hotel	Al Khuwayr	24 592 900	www.majanhotel.com
Manam Hotel Apartments	Al Wutayyah	24 571 555	www.manamhotel.com
Naseeb Hotel Flats	Wadi Kabir	24 811 782	na
Noos Hotel Apartments	Al Khuwayr	24 483 314	na
Nuzha Hotel Apartment	Bayt Al Falaj	24 789 199	www.safeerhotel.net
Safeer Hotel Suites	Al Khuwayr	24 691 200	www.safeerintll.com
Samharam Tourist Village	Salalah	23 211 420	na
Seeb International Hotel	As Seeb	24 543 800	na

Rest Houses & Motels

Visitors who travel to Salalah and the interior by road can break their journey at one of the Arab Oryx rest houses on the highways out of Muscat. These are located at Ghaba (319km from Muscat), Ghaftain (626km) and Qitbit (765km) on the Muscat-Salalah highway, and at Al Qabil (172km from Muscat) on the road to Sur. The rest houses each have about 10 simple, clean, air-conditioned rooms and a basic restaurant, with a filling station and fastfood outlets. The Al Qabil Rest House is perfect for visiting the Wahiba Sands or the Turtle Beach in Ras Al Hadd.

Prices at the rest houses vary, but you can expect to pay in the region of RO 15-20 for a single room and RO 20-30 for a double room. Some of these establishments have a limited number of rooms available so it's a good idea to book as far in advance as possible – particularly during peak times.

Rest Houses & Motels		
Al Ghaftain Rest House	Al Ghaftain	99 485 881
Al Qabil Rest House	Al Qabil	25 581 243
Ghaba Rest House	Ghaba	99 358 639
Majan Guest House	Salalah	25 431 910
Qitbit Rest House	Qitbit	99 085 686

Hostels

There are three youth hostels in Al Kamil town and the Al Wusta and Dhofar regions. Another hostel is planned in Al Dakhiliya. However, these hostels are primarily aimed at encouraging Omani youth to explore their country and should not be seen as 'backpacker' accommodation. For those travelling on a budget, some of the smaller hotels and the rest houses are good options.

Campsites

Other options **Camping** p.215

Good weather and beautiful landscapes make camping a good option for accommodation in Oman. In the mountains or desert you can set up camp wherever you find a suitable spot, as long as it isn't on private or cultivated land and not too close to habitation. If you are not too sure about camping 'in the rough', there are also official camping grounds with full amenities.

It is possible to camp at many of the various beaches around Muscat, the most private and sheltered being the beaches that can only be reached by boat. Just look for the tide line before you set up camp! You can also try camping along Azaiba beach, but be prepared to share your space with quad bikes, speeding 4WDs, fishermen and, if you're lucky, a glimpse of the Sultan's horses being taken for their morning exercise. Please respect the environment and take any rubbish away with you.

You can camp in the Arabian Oryx Sanctuary in Jaaluni, which is more than six hours from Muscat by car. There are no facilities. It is very important that you contact them in advance, as they are very strict on poachers and you wouldn't want to be mistaken for one. Check their website (www.oryxoman.com) for requirements.

There is also The Desert Camp, situated in the Wahiba Sands, 220km from Muscat. This is definitely a more luxurious version of camping however, with excellent facilities and a number of leisure activities. For more information, visit www.desert-camp.com.

Campsites		
Al Raha Tourist Camp	99 343 851	www.alrahaoman.com
Arabian Oryx Sanctuary	24 693 537	www.oryxoman.com
Desert Camp	99 311 338	na
Desert Nights Resort	92 818 388	na

Desert & Wadi Driving

As you travel out of Muscat, camels and goats wandering onto the roads are the major hazards, particularly at night when they are hard to see until it's too late. Camels often do not move out of the way, and some are hobbled which slows them down, so do not rely on them moving to let you by. If you hit one you'll do serious damage, not only to the camel but to yourself and your car. Some of the roads cross wadi beds (shown by red and white poles). While these are dry for much of the year, more care should be taken in the wetter months as water levels can rise very quickly.

Getting Around

Other options **Exploring** p.146

The most popular way to get around Muscat and to the interior cities of Nizwa, Sur and Sohar is by car. If you don't own a car, you can hire one (p.42) or make use of the many taxis available. There is a reasonable public bus service in Muscat, but because of the heat very few people walk or cycle. Motorcycles are used only by those few brave souls prepared to face the traffic. There are no trains or trams, but Oman Air links Muscat to Salalah and Khasab, cutting down a day's drive to an hour's flight.

Oman's highways are of an excellent standard and international traffic symbols are in use. Major roads usually have two to four lanes, with intermittent roundabouts (traffic circles) at busy intersections. If you are new to the roads, be aware that drivers on the inside lane have priority over those entering the roundabout, so don't be surprised if someone jumps from the inside lane to the exit, cutting you off in the process. Further into the interior, the quality of roads is reduced to graded tracks that often seem to branch out in every direction. These tracks are often bumpy, hence the popularity of 4WDs.

Road signs are almost always in both English and Arabic, as are street and house numbers. However, people tend to rely on landmarks rather than road names to give directions. Landmarks are usually shops, hotels, petrol stations or distinctive buildings. To confuse matters further, places are sometimes referred to by a nearby landmark, rather than their real name.

At the back of this book you'll find a comprehensive map section. The maps are easy to use and should help you head off in the right direction. Other useful maps are the *Muscat Map* and the *Muscat Mini Map* from Explorer Publishing. If you are going somewhere by taxi, it is a good idea to ask someone to write the address for you in Arabic, just in case your driver speaks little English.

Air Travel

Muscat is located at the crossroads of Europe, Asia and Africa, so it is an easily accessible city. Most European cities are only seven hours away. However, Muscat's proximity to larger Middle East hubs like Dubai, Abu Dhabi and Doha mean that you have to connect via another Gulf city. There are some direct flights to London (on British Airways, Gulf Air and Oman Air), and you can fly direct to India, Pakistan and numerous Middle East countries. Gulf Air now offers direct flights from Muscat to Paris.

Seeb International Airport is located 35km, or about 20 minutes, from the main part of Muscat. It is a comfortable, modern airport that also offers domestic flights to Salalah and Khasab (Musandam). The Salalah and Khasab airports handle limited international flights. When leaving the country, there is a departure tax that you will have to pay (RO 5), but this should be included in the cost of your ticket. All flights to and from Seeb International Airport are listed in the daily newspapers.

Oman In A Package

Oman Air offers a variety of holiday packages that include flights, accommodation and activities to help you make the most of your time away. It currently covers Oman, UAE, Egypt, Lebanon and India. Get more info at www.omanair.aero.

The country's national carrier is Oman Air, but Oman also has part ownership in Gulf Air along with Bahrain. Abu Dhabi recently withdrew from the partnership to concentrate on its national carrier, Etihad. This follows the withdrawal of founding partner Qatar, in 2002, to concentrate on Qatar Airways. Oman Air operates direct flights to various regional destinations. To contact Oman Air, call 24 531 111 (24 hours) or visit their website at www.omanair.aero.

Abu Dhabi's national carrier, Etihad, has started a direct route from Muscat to Abu Dhabi (operating daily). Log on to www.etihadairways.com for more information.

Flying to Salalah and Khasab (Musandam) cuts down a full day's journey from Muscat to 90 minutes and is the quickest option if you don't plan to camp or visit the many attractions along the way. Oman Air offers three daily flights from Muscat to Salalah. The cost for a return economy class fare from Muscat to Salalah is in the region of RO 68. Flights to Khasab are on Sunday, Tuesday, Thursday and Friday and cost around RO 40 return. Oman Air also flies directly to Khasab and Salalah from Dubai.

> **Duty Free Allowances**
> - Two bottles of alcohol per non-Muslim adult (maximum two litres)
> - 100ml of perfume
> - 400 cigarettes

A duty-free shop is located in the departure area at Seeb International Airport and outbound travellers have a chance to win cash prizes or luxury cars with a raffle ticket. The arrivals hall has two Travelex exchange counters (one before immigration for visa payments), a smaller duty free shop, a tourist information counter, car rentals and hotel reservations.

Oman National Transport Company (ONTC) runs a bus service from the airport at various times during the day.

Mapping Muscat & Oman

For a good overview of Oman, refer to the maps at the back of this book to orientate yourself. Explorer has also produced the Muscat Mini Map, a handy foldout colour map of the city, with major roads, hotels, hospitals, parks and attractions marked. Alternatively, see the Tourist Map of Oman that includes visitor information.

E-tickets, Electronic Check-in & E-Gate Cards

E-ticketing is a fairly new concept in Oman and is practised by a few airlines – currently Gulf Air, Oman Air (selected destinations), British Airways, Emirates and Air Arabia. An e-ticket is an electronic ticket, which means that you are no longer issued with a conventional paper ticket (one less document to lose) and all your booking and ticketing details are held in the airline's central reservation system. Bookings are made through the usual channels – through a ticket office or online. Electronic self check-in, however, is only offered by Gulf Air and usage is very limited, although this is set to change in the near future.

To cut back waiting times further, E-gate cards are now in use via the new residents' card which has a chip. There is a separate queue (usually very quiet) where you simply swipe the card and place the requested finger on the screen to match the print.

> **The Airport**
> If you're lucky enough to have friends, family or a hotel shuttle to collect you from the airport, you'll avoid the hassles of bargaining for the taxi fare, most probably in broken English, with the driver. You can approach the 'Airport Taxi' desk to get an idea of a reasonable fare. If you need of cash there are Travelex counters in both the departures and arrivals areas. There is no official airport bus but to get to the airport go to Ruwi Station on Al Jaame Street. Buses depart to Ibri, Sur and Buraimi and cost 400 baisas. For more information see the ONTC website, www.ontcoman.com, or call 24 490 046.

Meet & Greet

The Ahlan Lounge, based at Seeb International Airport, provides a 'Meet & Greet' service. Staff will greet and assist new arrivals and then clear all visa formalities for them, while passengers wait in the comfort of the lounge, with Omani coffee. They will guide clients through a separate immigration counter (no waiting in line) and facilitate baggage collection in around 20 minutes or less. They also give general information, will hold visas for collection and can arrange welcome bouquets of flowers and hotel transport. This extremely useful service is perfect for unaccompanied minors or those who require special assistance when travelling.

The cost varies according to the service required, but the basic service costs RO 12 per person. Holding a visa for collection costs an additional RO 6. Assistance with onward travel booking is also available.

For more information or to book the service, ask your travel agent or call 24 601 758 (09:00–13:00 and 16:00–19:00, Saturday to Wednesday) or the 24 hour Seeb hotline (24 519 026).

Customs

No customs duty is levied on personal effects brought into Oman. It is against the law to import narcotics, firearms (including toys and replicas) and pornography. There is no restriction on the import or export of any type of currency, although Israeli currency is prohibited.

If you enter the country by air, your bags are x-rayed before you leave the airport and opened if there are suspect items. Up to five videos or DVDs can be brought into the country although they may be temporarily confiscated for the material to be checked. You will be given a receipt to collect them at a later date and anything offensive will be erased (unless it's the whole thing, in which case you won't get it back). If you enter Oman by land, which means driving in from the United Arab Emirates, your bags may be searched at the Oman customs post. It is illegal to bring any alcohol into the country by road.

It is not advisable to bring your pets on holiday with you, as there are strict quarantine rules – various vaccinations and health certificates from the Department of Health and from your own vet may be required. Your pet may be subject to a six-month quarantine period although, strictly speaking, this is not required when coming in from a rabies-free country.

Mini Magic

The *Oman Explorer* is the ultimate resource for residents so you won't want to part with it – tricky when your out-of-town guests want to take it on their sightseeing tours. Avoid the tussle and give them a copy of the *Oman Mini Visitors' Guide* instead: it fits neatly in a pocket and contains all the essential tourist info on Oman.

Airlines

Air Arabia	24 700 828	www.airarabia.com
Air France	24 562 153	www.airfrance.com
Air India	24 818 666	www.airindia.com
British Airways	24 568 777	www.britishairways.com
EgyptAir	24 630 759	www.egyptair.com
Emirates Airline	24 510 060	www.emirates.com
Etihad Airways	24 823 555	www.etihadairways.com
Gulf Air	24 482 777	www.gulfair.com
Indian Airlines	24 791 864	www.indian-airlines.nic.in
Jet Airways	24 813 321	www.jetairways.com
KLM Royal Dutch Airline	24 566 737	www.klm.com
Kuwait Airways	24 701 262	www.kuwait-airways.com
Lufthansa	24 708 986	www.lufthansa.com
Oman Air	24 531 111	www.omanair.aero
Pakistan International Airlines	24 792 471	www.piac.com.pk
Qatar Airways	24 771 900	www.qatarairways.com
Royal Brunei Airlines	24 784 933	www.bruneiair.com
Royal Jordanian	24 796 693	www.rja.com.jo
Saudi Arabian Airlines	24 789 485	www.saudiairlines.com
Shaheen Air	24 817 021	www.shaheenair.com
Singapore Airlines	24 791 233	www.singaporeair.com
SriLankan Airlines	247 845 45	www.srilankan.aero
Swiss International Air Lines	24 787 416	www.swiss.com
Thai Airways	24 705 934	www.thaiair.com
Turkish Airlines	24 703 033	www.thy.com

Speeding Tickets
If using a rental car, tickets for speeding and parking offences may be charged to your credit card, sometimes weeks after your departure.

Bicycle

Other options **Cycling** p.220

While you won't see many tourists cycling their way around Oman, it can be an enjoyable way to see the country. There are no designated bike lanes, so the busiest parts of Muscat and the highways are best avoided if you're on two wheels. However in the quieter areas there are some good riding spots, and you'll probably see parts of Oman that you might miss in a car. In the hotter months there is a higher risk of heat exhaustion, dehydration and sunburn, so take the necessary precautions.

Boat

An increasing number of cruise ships are calling into Muscat as part of their itinerary. However, there are no scheduled passenger services from Muscat to other countries. There is a ferry service running between Muscat and Musandam. The two catamarans that make the trip are incredibly fast, completing the journey in less than five hours. At the time of writing, the ferry runs from the Mina Qaboos port in Muscat to the Khasab Port in Musandam. That will change, however, when the port in Shinas is finished sometime before 2010, at which time the ferry will run from Shinas to Khasab. For more information, contact the National Ferries Company (800 72000, ww.nfcoman.com).
At various points along the coast it is possible to hire fishing boats or dhows for daytrips to hidden bays or, for instance, along the coast of Musandam. If you are just looking for a quick boat ride, head for Bandar Al Jissah Beach (p.176), where you will find a crowd of crusty old seafarers touting for willing passengers – for about RO 3 they will take you on a half-hour trip around the coastline. It's a good way to get a different perspective of Shangri-La's Barr Al Jissah Resort.
There is a daily ferry from Shanab to Masirah Island (this is the only way that travellers can get to the island). The ferry only leaves at high tide (so you might have to wait a while) and the crossing takes around 90 minutes.

Bus

The state-operated Oman National Transport Company (ONTC) runs a national network of buses and coaches all over Oman and to the UAE. Buses operate to all areas of the capital and timetables, destinations and route numbers are found at bus stops (marked with a red bus on a green sign) at the side of the road. Most trips cost a few hundred baisas, making this the cheapest method of getting around. Fares are paid to the driver when you board, so try to have the correct change ready.

Marina Bander Al Rowdha

Coaches leave from the bus station in Ruwi (just off Al Jaame Street, along from the Sheraton Hotel) and Mutrah Fish Market for long distance trips to Salalah, Al Buraimi, Sinaw, Yankul, Ibri, Sur, Fahud-Yibal, Marmul, Dubai and Abu Dhabi. They are comfortable, air conditioned and generally on time. The bus service to Salalah (four times a day) costs RO 12 return and RO 7.500 one way, and takes a bottom-numbing 12 hours. There are also daily buses from Ruwi to Dubai and Abu Dhabi, and from Salalah to Dubai. Tickets from Muscat to Dubai cost around RO 9 return and RO 5 single, and the journey takes five hours each way. Check the daily newspapers or the ONTC website (www.ontcoman.com) for coach schedules.

Zero Tolerance

The Royal Oman Police exercise a strict zero tolerance policy on drinking and driving. It is illegal even to transport alcohol around Oman, except from the airport or liquor shop directly to your home. If you have had ANY alcohol to drink take a taxi or appoint a non-drinking friend as your designated driver. If you are pulled over and found to have consumed alcohol you are likely to find yourself enjoying the hospitality of the police station overnight – at the very least. If you are involved in an accident, whether it's your fault or not, and you are found to have been drinking and driving, your insurance is automatically void. Penalties are severe, so the message is simple: if you're going to drink, don't even think about driving.

Other contacts: Oman National Transport Company (24 490 046), Ruwi ticket office (24 708 522 or 24 701 294), head office hotline (24 492 948), Salalah (23 292 773).

A private bus company, Comfort Line (24 702 191), offers a service from Muscat to Dubai in the morning and evening. Its buses are not air conditioned. Tickets cost around RO 5 one way and RO 9 return, and the ticket office is located behind the Sultan Qaboos mosque in Ruwi.

Car

Other options **Transportation** p.137

Considering that in 1970 there was only 10km of tarmac road in the whole of Oman, the country's present road network of over 10,000km is excellent and drivers should have few problems while out and about. A dual carriageway links Muscat to Salalah (12 hours), Nizwa (two hours), Sur (three hours) and Sohar (two and a half hours). Driving to Khasab involves exiting Oman, entering the UAE, then exiting the UAE at Tibat and crossing into Musandam. The whole journey may take as long as a day. Secondary roads go to virtually every town in the interior, even crossing the Rub Al Khali and the Ramlat Al Wahaybah.

Driving Habits & Regulations

The golden rule for being a happy driver in Oman is to drive defensively. The legal driving age is 17, and the driving conditions can be described as immature, with lots of young, macho drivers fighting for their space on the tarmac. According to the Royal Oman Police (ROP), there are about 28 deaths per 100,000 people due to traffic related incidents. While this figure may be low compared to other developing countries, the combination of high speeds, poor driving skills and inexperience on the roads remains lethal. Drivers often seem to be completely unaware of other cars on the road, and the usual follies of driving too fast, too close, swerving, pulling out suddenly, not using the indicator lights and lane hopping happen far too regularly. Try to keep a reasonable stopping distance between yourself and the car in front. Ultimately it also helps to have eyes in the back of your head.

Road Safety

If you are involved in an accident, call 9999 for police assistance. The Royal Oman Police website (www.rop. gov.om) offers further information on traffic violations and road safety. You can also check and pay for your traffic fines online.

The burgundy and white striped cars seen around are for learner drivers, so give them a wide berth. It is also a good idea to keep a lookout for pedestrians who frequently attempt to cheat death by crossing busy roads and major dual carriageways.

Driving is on the right hand side of the road, and it is mandatory to wear seatbelts in the front seats. Children should be in the back, and the use of handheld mobile phones while driving is banned. These rules apply countrywide, even though you'll still see people driving with their child on their lap or happily chatting on their phones. The fine for these violations is RO 10. Drivers should pay the fine as directed by the police and not attempt to pay or negotiate a payment at the time of the violation.

The ROP are active in policing the roads and will even stop you to point out if your car is dirty! It is actually illegal to drive a dirty car in Oman, carrying a stiff penalty of RO 50, but if you're lucky you'll get away with a warning. This applies even to rented cars and off road vehicles, so there is invariably a queue at the car wash at the end of weekends. On the whole, the police are courteous and helpful (especially if you break down) and fairly stringent in applying the law. Carry your vehicle documentation card and driving licence at all times.

Speed Limits

The speed limits are clearly marked and are usually 60, 80 or 100kph within the Muscat area, and can be 120kph on roads to other parts of the Sultanate. When entering a built-up area the speed limit can drop suddenly from 120kph to 80kph, so keep your eyes peeled for signs and speed traps. The roads have both fixed and moveable speed traps which are activated by travelling over nine kilometres above the speed limit. If you go more than 40kph over the speed limit the potential penalty is a year's ban from driving and a three-day prison sentence. In most cases you won't even know you've received a speeding fine until you renew your vehicle registration. You can check your traffic offences online at the ROP's website (www.rop.gov.om).

Driving Licence

You can drive a rental vehicle for three months with either an international driving licence or a licence from your country of origin. If you wish to drive a private vehicle, you must first convert your licence to an Oman licence. Citizens of some countries (see p.66) can convert their licence directly, after taking a blood test. Unless you have an Oman driving licence you are not insured to drive a private vehicle.

Accidents

If you are involved in a traffic accident, however minor, you must remain with your car at the accident scene, call 9999 to report the incident to the ROP, and wait for them to arrive. Under no circumstances should you move your vehicle until instructed by the ROP. Unfortunately, in Oman, when you have an accident you become the star attraction as the passing traffic slows to a crawl with rubberneckers. In the event of a road accident where medical assistance is required, the ROP will arrange an ambulance to the nearest hospital.

Non-Drivers

In addition to dealing with the speed freaks in cars, you will find that pedestrians and cyclists also seem to have a death wish. The few cyclists who do brave the roads will often cycle towards you on the wrong side of the road, invariably without lights if it is dark. Pedestrians often step out dangerously close to oncoming traffic and the lack of convenient, safe crossings makes life for those on foot especially difficult.

Car Rental Agencies

Al Masky Rent-A-Car	24 595 241	na
Avis Rent A Car	24 202 582	
	24 601 224	www.avisuae.com
Budget Rent A Car ▶ p.43	24 794 721	
(Crowne Plaza Salalah)	23 235 160	www.budget.com
Europcar	24 700 190	www.europcar.com
General Automotive Co	24 500 849	na
Global Car Rental	23 289 323	
	24 697 140	na
Hertz Rent A Car	24 566 208	www.nttoman.com
Sixt	24 482 793	
	23 294 665	www.sixt-oman.com
Thrifty	24 489 248	www.thrifty.com
Toyota Rent-A-Car	23 290 908	
	24 561 427	na
Value Plus Rent-A-Car	24 817 964	www.valueoman.com
Xpress Rent A Car	24 490 055	www.sunnydayoman.com

Parking

In most cities in Oman, parking is readily available and people rarely have to walk too far in the heat. Increasing numbers of pay and display parking meters are appearing around Muscat. These areas, mostly around Qurm and Mutrah, are clearly marked with a blue signboard and cost 50 baisas for every half hour. Meters operate from 08:00 to 13:00 and 16:00 to 21:00, Saturday to Thursday. Parking is free on Fridays and public holidays. If you haven't purchased a ticket, you don't display it properly or you fail to renew an expired ticket, you may be unlucky enough to receive one from the

Discover

Oman

with the right wheels

Oman is full of delightful surprises. The best way to discover them is with Budget Rent A Car.

With six branches across the country, we offer you a 1100-strong fleet of European, American and Japanese cars, from 4WDs to luxury vehicles and practical cars. And an equally diverse range of services, to fulfil all your needs on the road. For the right car at the right price, call us. Explore Oman in top gear!

| Short-term rental | Long-term lease | Chauffeur service | Guided tours |
| Trips to the interior areas | International car hire reservations at special prices |

police for RO 3. Try to have loose change (25 and 50 baisa coins) with you since there are no automatic change machines available.

Safe & Sound
The number of deaths on Oman's roads is above international averages; between January and April 2009, 300 people were killed on the roads and another 3,100 were injured in road accidents. Oman's 'Salim and Salimah, Safe and Sound' campaign aims to reduce these statistics by educating drivers in safer practices, such as wearing a seatbelt or restraining children in the correct kind of seat. By logging on to its website, you can watch some hair-raising videos of what can happen to a child sitting unrestrained on the back seat if your car is involved in a head-on collision. You can also print out leaflets on road safety and get updated statistics of traffic accidents in Oman. For more information, visit www. salimandsalimah.org.

Petrol/Gas Stations

Petrol stations in Oman are numerous and are run by Shell, Omanoil and Al Maha. Most offer extra services, such as a car wash or a shop selling the usual necessities like bread and milk, cigarettes and newspapers. Most visitors will find petrol far cheaper than in their home countries – prices range from 120 baisas per litre for Super (98 octane), 114 baisas per litre for Regular (95 octane) and 102 baisas per litre for diesel.

Car Hire

You'll find all the main car rental companies, plus many locally owned ones, in Muscat and Salalah. Some have counters open 24 hours at Seeb International Airport. The larger, more reputable firms generally have more reliable vehicles and a greater capacity to help in an emergency (an important factor when handling the administrative aftermath if you are unfortunate enough to have a car accident). Depending on the agency, cars can be hired with or without a driver, and the minimum hire period is usually 24 hours. Daily rates range from approximately RO 14 for smaller cars to RO 35 for 4WDs. Child seats are available on request. Comprehensive insurance is essential and is usually included in the rental price. If you plan on exiting the country, you'll need to pay for extra insurance at the time of car hire.

Road Permits

To leave Oman by road, you need to have a valid road permit. There are four kinds of road permit: all are multiple entry, but they have different validity periods and the cost varies. Your sponsor should be able to help you get a road permit, but for the procedure you will need to provide a 'Request for Road Permit' form (available from ROP), two passport photos, a copy of your resident card, a copy of your passport, and an NOC from your sponsor.

Taxi

Apart from cars, taxis are the most common way of getting around and they will often hoot to attract your attention if you are on foot. All taxis have distinctive orange and white stripes. Each taxi is privately owned by an Omani National, who may or may not speak good English and might not provide you with a seatbelt. Taxis are not metered so always agree on a price before you get in. The usual fare from As Seeb airport to Madinat Qaboos is approximately RO 7, but this can be reduced if you have good negotiating skills! Shared taxis and the small 14-seater mini vans are cheaper and a more popular option, especially for longer journeys. They have set routes and fares and to board one of these, just flag them down at the

Taxi Companies	
Allo Taxi	24 697 997
City Taxi	24 603 363
Hello Taxi	24 607 011

side of the road. A short ride from Ruwi to Muscat can cost as little as 200 baisas. There are three private taxi firms which you can phone for a taxi at any time of the day or night. You can make an advance reservation but it is wise to remind them of your reservation nearer the time to make sure they know your location and will arrive on time. Taxi companies are not too fastidious about timekeeping, so be sure to specify if you have an urgent appointment to keep. The drivers are registered and in radio contact with a controller and the vehicles are clean and safe. These are highly recommended for women travelling alone, especially during evening hours. Because these cars are metered, you will often end up paying less than if you try to haggle down the price of an orange and white taxi.

Walking

Other options **Hiking** p.231

Muscat is spread out over a long, thin area between the mountains and the coast, and therefore is not the easiest place to explore on foot. However, if you limit your exploring to specific 'pocket' areas, you can cover quite a lot of ground on foot. A walk around Qurm Park or along Qurm Beach is highly recommended for some beautiful sights in this tranquil and picturesque suburb. During low tide hordes of people walk or jog along the stretch of beach between the Crowne Plaza and the Grand Hyatt. You can also explore the Mutrah area on foot, taking in the corniche, the famous Mutrah Souk and the port. A wander around the old town of Muscat is fascinating for its insight into life in simpler times – the ramshackle houses and narrow streets are a huge contrast to the turquoise and gold splendour of the Sultan's palace. The roads in this area follow a confusing and convoluted one-way system, so exploring on foot is easier than by car.

If you don't mind doing some walking of a slightly more serious nature you could always tackle the trekking paths through Oman's mountains. The *Oman Trekking Explorer* features 12 spectacular trekking routes of varying degrees of difficulty, and with a little bit of effort (and a good pair of boots), you'll be rewarded with some amazing views of the country. Most of the routes follow trails through the Hajar mountains, but there is a route from Riyam to Mutrah that is easy to follow. Obviously the heat in summer, with daytime temperatures of over 40°C, makes walking a sweaty experience. After sunset it does cool down and a walk can be pleasant, but still a bit on the warm side. From October to March the temperatures are perfect for being outdoors.

Blood Money

If you are driving and cause someone's death, you may be liable to pay a sum of money, known as 'blood money', to the deceased's family. The limit for this has been set at RO 5,000 per victim and your car insurance will cover this cost (hence the higher premiums). However, insurance companies will only pay if they cannot find a way of claiming that the insurance is invalid (such as if the driver was driving without a licence or, for example, under the influence of alcohol). The deceased's family can, however, waive the right to blood money if they feel merciful.

Park life

Money

Cash is the preferred method of payment in Oman, although credit cards are accepted in larger department stores, restaurants and hotels. Cash and traveller's cheques can be exchanged in licensed exchange offices, banks and international hotels – as usual a passport is required for exchanging traveller's cheques. To avoid additional exchange rate charges, take traveller's cheques in US dollars if possible. Local cheques are generally accepted in business but not for personal purchases. If you are taking a lease for accommodation, it is likely that you will need to pay by cheque and supply post-dated cheques for the remaining period of the rent. There are no restrictions on the import or export of any currency. Israeli currency is prohibited. For an idea on what basic items cost in Oman, compared to your home country, see the Cost of Living table on p.79.

Hot Tip

Tipping practices are similar at all hotels, bars and restaurants around Muscat. The tips are probably shared among all the staff working, although it is unclear if this ever sees the inside of your waiter's pockets! The usual amount to tip is 10%, despite the fact that most places have already added 17% under the guise of service charge, tourism tax or other charges. It is however entirely up to the individual whether to tip and it is not a fixed expectation like in some countries. You will not be expected to tip your petrol attendants or bag packers, but hairdressers and taxi drivers will appreciate the gesture of a tip (usually around 10%).

Local Currency

The monetary unit is the Oman rial (RO or OR). It is divided into 1,000 baisas (also spelt 'baiza'). Notes come in denominations of rials 50, 20, 10, 5, 1, 1/2 (500 baisas) and 100 baisas. Coin denominations are 50, 25, 10 and 5 baisas. Denominations are written in Arabic and English. It is best to take a few minutes to familiarise yourself with the currency, although shopkeepers are generally honest when giving you your change.

The way prices are written can lead to some confusion. An item may be marked 'RO/OR.1,500' – the price could be one thousand five hundred rials or one rial and five hundred baisas. The value of the item will usually be obvious. For clarity in this book, prices are shown in a standard way: one rial and 500 hundred baisas will be shown as RO 1.500 and one thousand five hundred rials as RO 1,500, while 15 rials will be RO 15.

The rial is tied to the US dollar at a mid-rate of approximately US$1 to RO 0.385, which has basically remained unchanged for a number of years.

Banks

The well-structured and ever-growing network of local and international banks, strictly controlled by the Central Bank of Oman, offers the full range of commercial and personal banking services. Transfers can be made without

Exchange Rates

Foreign Currency (FC)	1 Unit FC = RO x	RO 1 = x FC
Australia	0.33	3.01
Bahrain	1.02	0.98
Bangladesh	0.005	179.45
Canada	0.36	2.78
Denmark	0.07	13.37
Euro	0.56	1.80
Hong Kong	0.05	20.13
India	0.008	126.21
Japan	0.004	239.21
Jordan	0.54	1.84
Kuwait	1.34	0.74
New Zealand	0.27	3.72
Pakistan	0.005	215.40
Philippines	0.008	125.59
Qatar	0.11	9.46
Saudi Arabia	0.10	9.73
Singapore	0.27	3.70
South Africa	0.05	19.53
Sri Lanka	0.003	298.18
Sweden	0.05	18.28
Switzerland	0.37	2.72
Thailand	0.01	87.77
UAE	0.10	9.54
UK	0.64	1.57
USA	0.39	2.60

*Rates are correct as of September 2009

difficulty as there is no exchange control and the Oman rial is freely convertible to other currencies. Bank headquarters are clustered in Ruwi, Muscat's central business district. There are branches all over Muscat and Salalah, and in major towns such as Nizwa, Sur and Sohar.

Banking hours are usually 08:00 to 13:00 or 14:00 (Sunday to Thursday).

Main Banks

Bank	Location	Phone	Website
Bank Dhofar	Muscat	24 790 466	www.bankdhofar.com
	Salalah	23 294 886	
Bank Muscat SAOG ▶ p.77	Muscat	24 795 555	www.bankmuscat.com
Bank Sohar ▶ p.49	Muscat	24 730 000	www.banksohar.net
Banque Banorabe	Muscat	24 704 274	na
Central Bank of Oman	Muscat	24 702 222	www.cbo-oman.org
Habib Bank	Muscat	24 817 142	www.habibbank.com
HSBC Bank Middle East Limited ▶ p.IFC	Muscat	24 799 920	www.oman.hsbc.com
National Bank of Abu Dhabi	Muscat	24 761 000	www.nbad.com
National Bank of Oman (NBO)	Muscat	24 811 711	www.nbo.co.om
Oman Arab Bank	Muscat	24 706 265	www.omanab.com
	Salalah	23 292 005	
Oman International Bank	Muscat	24 682 500	www.oiboman.com
	Salalah	23 291 512	
Standard Chartered Bank	Muscat	24 773 666	www.standardchartered.com

ATMs

Most banks operate automatic teller machines (ATMs) that accept a wide range of cards. Common systems accepted around Muscat include MasterCard, Visa, American Express, Global Access, Plus System and Cirrus. ATMs can be found in shopping malls, at the airport, and various street locations in Muscat.

Exchange rates used in the transaction are normally competitive and the process is often faster and easier than traveller's cheques.

Oman Central Bank

Why Pay Full Price? ◀

Bargaining is a traditional part of doing trade in Oman and it is still widely used today, especially in the souks. You can sometimes end up paying half of the original asking price. A discount of 10% is usual, even in appliance stores, but not in supermarkets or department stores. It can also be a fun way to do business; vendors will square up to 'do battle', courteously offering their customers some kahwa (coffee), and in return customers should bargain hard. Start your negotiations by asking for the 'best price' and go from there.

Money Exchanges

Money exchanges are found all over Muscat and Salalah, offering good service and exchange rates (often better than the banks). Exchange houses are usually open from 08:00 to 13:00 and 16:00 to 19:00, and often operate in the evenings and at weekends. Alternatively, hotels will usually exchange money and traveller's cheques at the standard (non-competitive) hotel rate. At Seeb International Airport, there is a Travelex counter before immigration to facilitate visa payments.

Exchange Centres	
Abu Mehad	24 566 123
Al Barzah Money Exchange	24 487 444
Gulf Overseas	24 834 182
Hamdan	23 296 903
Laxmidas Tharia Ved	24 700 065
Modern Exchange	24 832 133
Oman & UAE Exchange Centre	24 584 358
Oman International Exchange	24 832 197
Oman United Exchange	24 794 305
Purshottam Kanji Exchange	24 713 338

Credit Cards

Larger shops, hotels and restaurants in Muscat and Salalah accept major credit cards (American Express, Diners Club, MasterCard and Visa) and they will often have the card logos displayed at the entrance. However, if you are travelling in the interior, or are shopping at souks and smaller shops, cash is usually the only form of payment accepted.

Tipping

An increasing number of hotels and restaurants automatically include a service charge of at least 5% (check the bottom of your bill), although it is unlikely to end up with your waiter. Tipping is optional although a few hundred baisas are greatly appreciated, particularly in smaller restaurants.

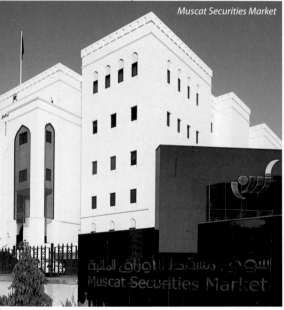
Muscat Securities Market

Oman Development Bank

Finger On The Pulse
*For a real insider's
point of view on what's
happening in Oman,
take a look at some
of the blogs written
by local residents.
For starters check
out http://muscati.
blogspot.com.*

Newspapers & Magazines

Newspapers and magazines are available from bookshops, supermarkets, petrol stations, grocery shops and hotel shops. There are no street sellers at present. You will probably be provided with one of the local papers or a copy of Oman 2day in your room if you are staying in a good hotel.

The *Oman Daily Observer*, the *Times of Oman* and the *Oman Tribune* (200 baisas each) are the three daily English newspapers. You'll usually find various colour supplements in the Thursday editions. *The Week* is a free tabloid published every Wednesday and distributed from branded stands that can be found in various locations around Muscat. You'll almost always be able to find a copy at your nearest Starbucks or Al Fair. While these newspapers aim to keep Oman's English-speaking residents abreast of news and events in the region, the editorial quality can be somewhat dubious. As is the case across the region, Oman's newspapers operate under the heavy hand of censorship. Censorship means that you will rarely read anything negative about the country, which can result in a false sense of security regarding crime and personal safety.

Foreign daily tabloid newspapers, mainly American, Asian, British, French and German, are available in hotel bookshops and supermarkets, although they are usually a lot more expensive than they are back home and a few days out of date. They will also be without extras like supplements and gifts. Hobby magazines, such as computing, photography, sports and women's magazines are also available, but are very expensive. Although the Press Act supposedly allows freedom of speech, the public media exercise rigorous self-censorship. The internet is monitored and any site deemed offensive to the religious, moral, cultural or political principles of the country will be inaccessible. Publications are also censored for political, moral, religious and cultural reasons, and you'll often find that certain images or articles have received the infamous 'black marker' treatment. Many expats stock up with glossy magazines every time they travel, and then distribute them among their friends upon their return.

There are a number of decent publications available in English. Many are published in the UAE and cover a variety of topics: *ID* is an interior design magazine, *Oman 2day* covers lifestyle, *Al Mara*, *Emirates Woman* and *Hello! Middle East* cover women's interests, and *Oman Economic Review* and *Business Today* cover business. These regional magazines cost a fraction of the inflated price of imported magazines, and are definitely worth a look.

Books

Other options **Websites** p.51

There is a huge range of books available about Oman, from glossy coffee-table books showcasing the natural beauty of the country to specialist hobby books and travel guides.

If you have an interest in the history of the region, which has grown from barren desert to rapidly developing cities over a relatively short period of time, you will appreciate *Arabian Sands* by the great explorer Wilfred Thesiger. It is a pictorial account of his crossing of the Empty Quarter with a group of Bedouins in the early 60s. *The Maverick Guide to Oman* by Peter Ochs is an excellent travel guide if you are visiting Oman independently (not as part of a tour group).

To find your way around the less well-travelled areas of Oman, and see things that not all visitors get to see, get a copy of the *Oman Off-Road Explorer*. It is the ultimate accessory for any 4WD, and contains trip plans and maps for over 20 adventurous routes (all marked with GPS coordinates and points of interest). If you prefer to do your off-roading by foot, the *Oman Trekking Explorer* features 11 trekking routes (each with a separate route card), a trekking handbook and an area map.

Websites

With internet usage becoming more and more popular in Oman, there is an increase in the number of local websites available. The table lists websites that are particularly useful – if you regularly use a website that is not listed here, you can send feedback via www.liveworkexplore.com.

Websites	
Business & Industry	
www.buinessdirectoryoman.com	Business directory for Oman
www.chamberoman.com	Oman Chamber of Commerce and Industry
www.gcc-sg.org	What the GCC is all about
www.kom.om	Knowledge Oasis Muscat – Oman's IT park
www.mctmnet.gov.om	Muscat Municipality
www.mocioman.gov.om	Ministry of Commerce and Industry
www.moneoman.gov.om	Ministry of National Economy
www.muscatmall.com	Online shopping
www.nawras.om	Internet and telephone services provider
www.oeronline.com	Oman Economic Review
www.oite.com	Oman International Trade Exhibitions Centre
www.omanet.om	Ministry of Information
www.omantel.net.om	Internet and telephone services provider; search for phone numbers
www.omantel-yellowpages.com	Online Yellow Pages
www.omantourism.gov.om	Ministry of Tourism
www.tenderboard.gov.om	Details of tender announcements
Embassies	
www.embassyworld.com	Details of Omani embassies abroad and foreign missions in Oman
www.oman.org/gov90.htm	Details of embassies in Oman
Sports	
www.motorsport.com	Motor sport rallies in the Middle East
Oman Information	
www.arab.net	News of the Arab world
www.destinationoman.com	All about Oman and getting there
www.freetheweek.com	Weekly newspaper
www.liveworkexplore.com	Essential info on living in Oman from Explorer Publishing
www.myoman.com	Information and pictures
www.newsbriefsoman.info	News and comments about Oman
www.nizwa.net	Environment and culture, plus many links to Oman websites
www.omanaccess.com	Up-to-date community guide to Oman
www.omanforum.com	Interactive forum on a variety of topics relevant to Oman
www.omanglobe.com	News about the Middle East
www.omannews.com	Oman news agency; daily updates
www.omanobserver.com	Daily newspaper
www.oman-radio.gov.om	Oman radio broadcasts schedule
www.omantoday.co.om	Oman Today – the essential leisure guide
www.omantourism.gov.om	Official online tourist service
www.oman-tv.gov.om	Oman TV programmes schedule
www.outpostoman.com	The Outpost Network – information for expats living or relocating abroad
www.rop.gov.om	Royal Oman Police – visa information and traffic fines
www.timesofoman.com	Daily newspaper

Annual Events

Throughout the year, Oman hosts a number of well-established annual events, some of which have been running for years. The events described below are some of the most popular regular features on Oman's social calendar.

Year round
Oman International
Exhibition Centre

Exhibitions
www.omanexhibitions.com

With the increasing importance of MICE (Meetings, Incentives, Conferences, Exhibitions) tourism to Oman, the government-owned Oman International Exhibition Centre has seen a full calendar lately. It is located a stone's throw from the Seeb International Airport and is adjacent to the Golden Tulip Seeb Airport Hotel. See their website for a monthly listing of exhibitions.

**Public
holidays and
National Day**
Various Locations

Camel Racing

Time spent watching this traditional sport is an extraordinary experience. Races are spread over several days, with different sprints organised daily for different age groups of camels. The camels are bred and trained for racing; those with Omani bloodlines are the most coveted. Winners can fetch up to RO 250,000. Camel races are held at tracks in As Seeb, Salalah, the interior and Batinah regions during public holidays and National Day celebrations. Admission is free.

Winter
Various Locations

Bullfighting

In the true sense of the word, two gargantuan Brahmin bulls butt heads and lock blunt horns sumo-style until one of them stumbles, flees or is knocked out of the arena. Human handlers restrain over-aggressive bulls rather than incite them. The bulls are bred for fighting and winners can fetch up to RO 2,500. Matches start at around 16:00 during the winter months in Barka and As Seeb. Admission is free.

Winter
Oman Auditorium
of the Al Bustan
Palace Hotel

ROSO Concert Series

Although Oman has no tradition of classical music, the Sultan's passion for it led to the creation of the Royal Oman Symphony Orchestra in 1985. It is composed entirely of young Omanis trained locally by foreign experts. A lively series of public concerts is held in the winter season at various locations. Check the local press for concert schedules.

Winter
Muscat

Horse Racing & Show Jumping

Oman is famous for its pure-bred Arabian horses, which originate from Zad-ar-Raakib, the stallion given by the Prophet Solomon to the Azd tribe. The Oman Equestrian Federation (24 490 424) organises the Annual Royal Meeting national show jumping competitions every winter, and the Royal Equestrian Show every five years, at the Enam Equestrian Grounds in As Seeb.

January/February
Various Locations

Muscat Festival

This 22 day event is designed to showcase Oman's vibrant history and culture, in order to boost tourism. It is organised by Muscat Municipality in January and February. Traditional dances, camel races, concerts, sporting and educational events, and various activities for adults and children are held in different venues throughout Muscat. Some hotels and commercial centres offer discounts.

March/April
Maidan Al Fateh

Rally Oman
www.rallyoman.com

Oman's premier motorsport event is usually held in March or April over three days on 260km of timed gravel special stages around Muscat, with a three kilometre timed spectator stage at Maidan Al Fateh in Wattayah. International rally teams compete with local talent for pole position. Family entertainment is also on offer including a freestyle motorcross competition, music concert and parachutists. Entrance is free.

May
Fahal Island

Fahal Island Swim
www.pdo.co.om

Petroleum Development Oman has been hosting this challenging, yet fun, competition every May since 1989. Brave competitors get up at 06:00 to swim four kilometres from Al Fahal Island to the Ras Al Hamra Recreation Centre beach. Anyone can participate; swimmers just need to fill in the entry form, pay the fee of RO 5 and organise boat support.

June
Various Locations

Musical Events
www.ifacca.org

Fete de la Musique, a traditional French festival of music organised by the French Embassy, is held every year on June 21. The Ras Al Hamra Music Ensemble, composed of PDO employees and their families, hosts a number of concerts each year including ensemble concerts (one in a wadi) and children's concerts. Contact Sheila Neal (Secretary), on 24 601 681 or 99 37 8529, or RAHRC (PDO club) office (24 677 321) for timings. Admission is free.

July
Salalah

Khareef Festival
www.salalahfestival.com

This festival is held in Salalah each year, from 15 July to the end of August, to celebrate the monsoon season. There are music and dance performances from different regions of Oman, the exhibition and sale of Omani handicrafts, and sports events. It is a chance to witness rare performances such as the Zanooj dance, which involves a cast of thousands.

July
Various Locations

Renaissance Day

Held on 23 July, this day commemorates the accession of His Majesty Sultan Qaboos to the throne. The event is marked by a variety of festivities and a holiday for both the public and private sector.

September
Enam Equestrian Grounds in As Seeb

Terry Fox Run
www.terryfoxrun.org

Each year, millions of people around the world gather to raise money for cancer research in the Terry Fox Run (named after the courageous Canadian, Terry Fox, who lost a leg to cancer and attempted to run across Canada to raise funds and awareness). Terry Fox Runs are casual affairs, and you can complete the run on a bike, with a pram, or even on rollerblades. The date of the Oman Terry Fox Run changes each year so check the website for details and organiser's contact details.

October/November
Wahiba Sands

Wahiba Challenge
www.rah-orac.org

Usually held in early winter, this motor sports event involves crossing the Wahiba Sands from east to west in a 4WD. The organiser, PDORC Land Rover Adventure Club, emphasises that it is not a race, but rather a test of skill and endurance – you will have to cross about 31 dune ridges in 60km! More information is available online.

December
Muscat

Reunion d'Adventures Bike & Run
www.authentiqueaventure.com

Reunion d'Aventures is the only major adventure-nature endurance competition which brings together contestants of different levels in a single event, but who share the same passion for nature, sport, exertion, team work and unexpected, unpredictable situations.

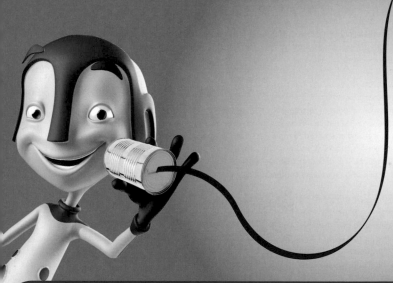

"Call FRiENDi mobile to FRiENDi mobile for only

39 Bz

per minute
ANYTIME."

Talk more and save more with FRiENDi mobile

*For more information, visit www.friendimobile.om or call Customer Service
98400000 to talk in Arabic, English, Malayalam, Hindi, Urdu and Bengali.*

www.friendimobile.om

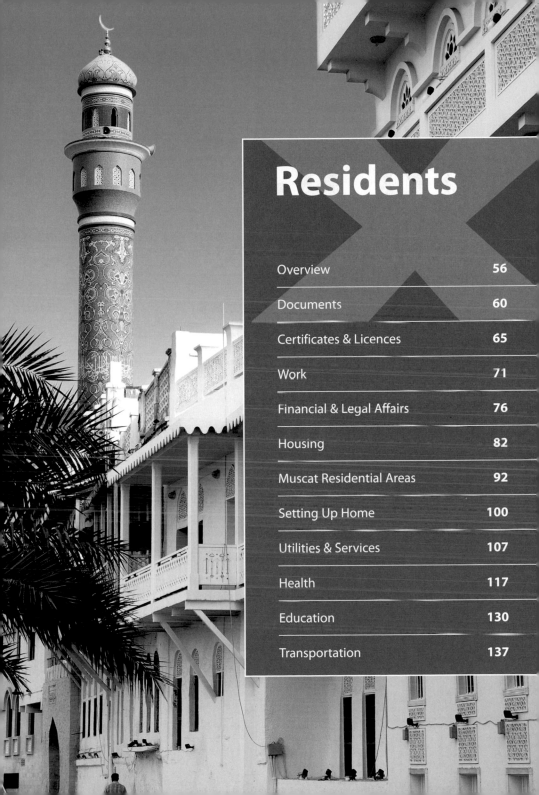

Residents

Residents

Not The Best, Not The Worst
The Economist Intelligence Unit conducted a survey in 2005 of the world's best countries to live in, and ranked Oman at number 67 (that's two points ahead of the United Arab Emirates). The survey was based on a number of factors including security, infrastructure, and the availability of goods and services. The world's most desirable country was Ireland, while Zimbabwe was the least.

Overview

There's no doubt that living in Oman (or any other Middle Eastern country) will be vastly different to living in your home country, and you will experience a steep learning curve in the few months after your arrival. Moving to a new country always involves an element of stress, and moving to a country with such a different culture can be particularly challenging. However, once you get over the initial culture shock, most expats discover that it is a relaxed and friendly country, it is modern (and developing all the time), and yet it still retains a certain charm from the past that is unique to the region.

One of Oman's greatest assets is its people, who are warm and welcoming, and who have a long history of fascinating traditions. You'll also find a large group of friendly expats, and before you know it you'll meet loads of people.

This chapter contains all the information that you'll need to make your transition to life in Oman as smooth as possible. Remember that rules and regulations change frequently in this part of the world, so keep your eye on the local press and be prepared for the unexpected.

Considering Oman

Although the nature of work contracts taken up by expats in Oman are often for a fixed term, there are many thousands of foreigners who stay for much longer periods, and are in no hurry to move. And it's not hard to see why: sunshine almost every day of the year, great leisure facilities, a beautiful mix of scenery (ocean, mountain, desert, greenery), luxurious hotels and their top-notch in-house restaurants, and a pace of life that is neither too hectic nor too boring. And to top it all, the salaries are tax-free. Of course there are a few hassles and annoyances associated with life in Oman, but on the whole the negatives are far outweighed by the positives.

Although Oman strives to build a national workforce powered mainly by its own citizens, there are still plenty of opportunities available for expats – particularly in the fields of oil, education, construction and tourism. And unlike Dubai (where there are so many expats that employers can be choosy, which has driven down the average wage package), Oman's expats still have access to that sought-after 'expat package', which includes housing, schooling, medical insurance and possibly even leisure benefits (like health club membership).

View of Mutrah Corniche

If you are seriously considering moving to Oman, there is lots of paperwork to be taken care of but your employer will almost always do this on your behalf – leaving you to worry about more important things like whether you've got enough summer clothes in your wardrobe.

Before You Arrive

It is unusual for people to arrive in Oman on a visit visa to look for work – most people already have jobs lined up before they arrive. If you have accepted a job offer in Oman, most of the administrative tasks will be taken care of by your employer, but you might still want to visit the country before you take up your post to look at houses and schools.

Some people love expat life but there are those that hate it from the beginning and never manage to adjust. Therefore it is not always a good decision to cut all ties with your home country (like selling your property and closing your bank accounts) before you've tested the waters for a year or so. However, you will need to get your financial affairs in order, particularly if you have to continue paying tax in your home country.

If you have children of school-going age, you will need to start investigating schools straight away. There are not many schools to choose from and with Muscat expanding all the time, some schools are running out of places in certain age groups. See p.130 for a rundown of the nursery, primary and secondary schools in Muscat.

If you negotiate your contract well, you will have made provision for shipping costs – both for when you arrive and when you leave. If you are staying for more than a year, it is probably well worth it to ship out some of your belongings, as this can make you feel at home sooner.

If you are coming to Oman to look for work, do your research before you arrive. Contact recruitment agencies and sign up with online job sites as far in advance as possible. There may also be agencies in your home country that specialise in overseas recruitment. The Work section (p.72) should give you some handy info.

When You Arrive

The list of things you'll have to deal with in the first few weeks can be a little daunting, and you may well be in for a lot of form filling, queuing, and coming and going. Try not to let it spoil your first impressions of the country though, because hopefully you'll soon be a fully fledged resident enjoying your new life, and all that boring bureaucracy

will be a distant memory. Here are some of the key issues you should be covering:

- Residency visas – your sponsor should arrange everything for you, but you will need to get a health certificate from your home country, stating that you are free from illness and not carrying any communicable diseases. For more information on residency permits and what you can do to make the process smoother, see p.62.
- Furnish your new home and get connected – for advice on home furnishings and how to get your water, electricity, satellite TV and phone connected, see p.107 and p.108.
- Buy a car – for advice on what's available, and how to complete the purchase and registration process, see p.138.
- Licences – you'll need to transfer your local driving licence into an Oman one, and if you want to buy alcohol you'll need a liquor licence. Find out how on p.65.
- Register with your embassy – it's always worthwhile letting your embassy know that you are living in Oman. You'll find a list of embassies on p.21.
- Get acquainted – meet like-minded people by taking up a hobby, joining a sports team, or finding a support group. The Activities chapter (p.212) will point you in the right direction, and support groups are listed on p.129.

Combat Culture Shock

Knowing as much about Oman as possible before you get here is a good way to help reduce culture shock. This book, of course, is one of the most comprehensive sources of information, but you may also find the websites listed on p.51 and social groups on p.244 of some interest.

Essential Documents

For many procedures you'll have to produce your 'essential documents'. At the very least, these are:

- Original passport
- Passport copies (including photo page and visa page)
- Passport photos
- Copy of labour card (if you are working)
- Copy of sponsorship certificate for non-working residents

You will need countless passport photos over the coming months, as just about every procedure requires at least one. To save time and money, ask for the negative or a CD with the digital image. Then duplicate photos can be made easily. You'll also need plenty of passport copies.

When You Leave

Rather than just jetting off, there are certain things that have to be wound up before you leave. You will have to disconnect your electricity and water supply (p.107) and get your security deposit back from your landlord (minus any damages). You will have to sell your car – not always an easy task, and used car dealers can smell a departing expat a mile away, so be prepared for some very low offers. For a list of used car dealers, see p.139.

You will need to ship your household contents back home, and sell whatever you are not taking with you. The more notice you can give the shipping company, the better. For a list of companies, see p.100. If you are selling loads of stuff, you can put a notice up on the community noticeboards (they can be found near Al Fair supermarkets in MSQ centre and Sarooj Centre), have a garage sale or list your items on www.omanbay.com.

Entry Visa

A passport (valid for at least six months and with enough blank pages) is required for all visitors, except nationals of Bahrain, Kuwait, Qatar, the United Arab Emirates and Saudi Arabia who hold national identity cards, and holders of a Macau (SAR) Travel Permit.

Visa requirements have been greatly simplified as the country welcomes increased tourism. However, regulations should always be checked with your Oman Embassy or Consulate before travelling, especially if you plan to get a visa on arrival. Refer to the website of the Royal Oman Police (www.rop.gov.om) to get the latest information on visitor visas, residence permits and other visas (employment, investor, student).

A joint visa facility exists between Qatar and Oman, under which citizens of 33 countries can apply online for a one-month visa that allows free travel between the two countries. After paying with a credit card, you print the confirmation and receipt, and present these papers to the entry port in either country. Visit www.gov.qa for more information.

If you have sponsorship from an Oman entity, make sure they fax you a copy of the visa before the flight. The original should be lodged at Seeb International Airport for you to collect at the pre-booked visa collection counter before passport control (assuming you haven't already received the original).

Tourists wishing to enter Oman are grouped, depending on their nationality, under either List (1) or List (2), for which different procedures and terms of the visa apply. There are five types of visa that are of interest to visitors – single entry, multiple entry, express, 'short', and the common visa facility with Dubai.

Visa application forms are available before passport control, and there is a Travelex counter to ease visa fee payments. Verify the expiration date on your visa before you leave the immigration counter.

For all visas, there is a stiff penalty of RO 10 per day if you overstay your welcome. This will be charged at the control point when you leave the country. In extreme cases you may not even be allowed to leave Oman until you have applied for an extension.

Single Entry Visa

Nationals in List 1 (see p.62) can get this visa upon arrival at all air, land or sea entry points or through an Oman diplomatic mission, after filling in an application form and payment of RO 6 or its equivalent. The passport must be valid for at least six months. The visa is valid for one month and can be used within six months from date of issue. It can be extended for another month by personally applying to the Directorate General of Passport and Residency (DGPR) and paying a fee of RO 6.

Nationals in List (2) should be part of a tour package from a government-approved tour operator. The package should include accommodation and return air tickets on Oman Air or Gulf Air. Visitors must apply for the visa at least two days before arrival; the tour operator usually helps to arrange visas. The completed form is sent to the DGPR who will process the application within two days from date of receipt. The visa is valid for one month and can be used within six months from date of issue. It can be extended for another month by personally applying to the DGPR and paying a fee of RO 6. This visa is valid for entry at the airport only.

Multiple Entry Visa

Nationals in List 1 may get this visa on arrival at all land, sea or air entry points or through a diplomatic mission, after filling in an application form and paying RO 10 or its equivalent. The passport must be valid for not less than one year at the time of applying. This visa is valid for one year. The holder can stay for three weeks at a time, but a minimum of three weeks must elapse between each visit. This visa cannot be

Royal

EVENTS & WEDDINGS

WEDDINGS
LADIES EVENTS
VIP EVENTS
THEME EVENTS

www.royalevents.com • e-mail:info@flyingelephant.com

A DIVISION OF FLYING ELEPHANT

Do You Need A Visa?

List 1

Europe: *Andorra, Austria, Belgium, Bulgaria, Croatia, Czech Republic, Cyprus, Denmark, Estonia, Finland, France, Germany, Greece, Hungary, Iceland, Ireland, Italy, Latvia, Liechtenstein, Luxembourg, Macedonia, Maldavia, Malta, Monaco, Netherlands, Norway, Poland, Portugal, Romania, San Marino, Slovakia, Spain, Switzerland, Sweden, Turkey, United Kingdom, Vatican Republic*

South America: *Argentina, Bolivia, Brazil, Chile, Colombia, Ecuador, French Guyana, Paraguay, Peru, Suriname, Uruguay, Venezuela*

Other Countries: *Australia, Brunei, Dar as-Salaam, Canada, Hong Kong, Indonesia, Japan, Lebanon, Macau, Malaysia, New Zealand, Seychelles, Singapore, South Africa, South Korea, Taiwan, Thailand, Tunisia, Turkey, United States*

List 2

Albania, Belarus, Bosnia-Herzegovina, China, Egypt, India, Iran, Jordan, Morocco, Russian Federation, Syria, Ukraine

extended but you may reapply for another multiple entry visa following the same procedure. For nationals in List (2) the same conditions and procedures as for single entry visa apply. The visa fee is RO 10.

Express Visa

This visa is for nationals who are not in List (1) or List (2). It is issued within 24 hours through the Directorate General of Passport & Residency by applying directly at an Oman diplomatic mission abroad or through an Oman commercial or tourist establishment on your behalf. The processing fee is RO 7 or its equivalent. The passport should be valid for at least six months. The visa is valid for two weeks and cannot be extended.

Common Visa Facility

Nationals on List (1) who are arriving from Dubai, with a Dubai tourist visa or entry stamp, do not need a separate visa to Oman if a joint facility form is completed. Forms are available at airports, sea ports and at the Hatta Fort Hotel for those arriving from the Al Wajaja terminal. Visitors are allowed to stay for the period specified in the Dubai visa or up to a maximum of three weeks. This visa may not be extended. They may return to Dubai via the same route without needing a second UAE visa. A reciprocal visa agreement also exists with Qatar.

Short Visit Visa

This 14 day visa is available to people from most countries in List (1). It costs RO 7 and can be picked up at Seeb International Airport for RO 3 for a foreign national in a GCC state. You can apply online at www.rop.gov.om.

Health Card

There is no health card as such in Oman. You will need to undergo a medical test as part of your residency process. This involves a blood test, taken at the Ministry of Health clinic in Ruwi, where they will test for infectious diseases (such as HIV and hepatitis) and blood type. Your sponsor will advise you on the procedure and perhaps even accompany you to the clinic to assist. When you get to the clinic you will find a very long queue, so to avoid waiting all morning you should get there as early as possible.

Some nationalities are required to produce a health certificate from their home country if they are entering Oman on an employment visa. This test will be a comprehensive report including x-rays and blood tests. Your sponsor should be able to advise you, or you can check www.rop.gov.om (the website of the Royal Oman Police) for more information according to your nationality.

Residence Visa

Before getting a visa you must get a no objection certificate (NOC). This is an official document stating that neither your Omani sponsor nor the government has any objection to your entering the country.

There are two types of residence visas – one for employment (when you are sponsored by your employer) and one for residence only (when you are sponsored by a family member). Normally, you or your employer will apply for a residence visa at the Oman embassy in your country of origin, before you leave for Oman. Your sponsor should organise everything related to your visa, including payment. On arrival, your company's PRO or your sponsor will take you to the Royal Oman Police (ROP) station on Death Valley Road to be fingerprinted. Those working must have labour clearance and an employment residence visa; spouses and family members are each issued with a 'joining family' residence visa. It is illegal to work on a joining family residence visa, even part time. If you wish to work you must get an employment visa. If you are working for the same sponsor as your spouse, exchanging the visa is usually a simple process. If you obtain a job elsewhere, you must transfer sponsorship to your new employer and go through the whole process from the beginning. Your new sponsor will do what's necessary.

It is advisable, if possible, to try to avoid doing this (or anything which requires the involvement of government departments) during Ramadan, when everything tends to slow down until after Eid, by which time there will be a huge backlog. The ROP is located near Muscat Private School on Madinat A'Sultan Qaboos Street (Death Valley Road), and the phone number is 24 600 099.

Most expats seeking employment or applying for residency in Oman must have a health certificate from their home country, stating that they are free from illness and not carrying any communicable diseases. UK citizens are currently exempt, although this could change at any time.

Sponsorship By Employer

Your employer should handle all the paperwork, and will usually have a staff member (who is thoroughly familiar with the procedure) dedicated to this task alone. This staff member is usually called the PRO, which stands for public relations officer. After your residency is approved, they should then apply directly for your labour clearance. You will need to supply the essential documents (p.58) and your education certificates. You must have all your certificates attested by a solicitor or public notary in your home country and then by your foreign office to verify the solicitor as bona fide. The Oman embassy in your country of residence must also sign the documents. While this sounds like a runaround, it is much easier if you get this done before you arrive in Oman.

Family Sponsorship

Full-Time Maids
If you want to hire a full time maid, you are required to sponsor her and provide accommodation. If you would rather hire a part-time maid, you can do so through an agency. See p.104 for more information.

Once you are sponsored by your employer, you can then arrange sponsorship for your family members. Many employers will help you with this task. If yours doesn't, the process can be lengthy and tedious. There are two family sponsorship options available – a family joining visa or a family residence visa.

A family joining visa is for your spouse and children only (children cannot be older than 28 years). The family residence visa is for relatives that do not fall into the family joining visa category, such as siblings or elderly parents. Brothers and sisters of the resident must be younger than 18 years, and a document must be provided stating that there is no other family income outside Oman. People on family sponsorship may not work in Oman, paid or unpaid. Once a visa has been granted, the holder has up to six months from the date of issue to enter Oman. The visa is valid for two years from the date of entry. This visa is renewable and allows multiple entries.

No Objection Certificate (NOC)

Once the NOC has been issued, a number will be sent by telex or fax to the airline from the Oman Immigration Department, authorising them to board you on the flight to Muscat. If the airline does not have this authorisation, you will not be allowed to board the plane. On arrival at the airport in Muscat you must go to the NOC counter where you will receive a small piece of paper, which you take to passport control and exchange for your visa.

The NOC can only be collected from Seeb International Airport. Most hotels can arrange an NOC in about a week. You just need to make a reservation and send a copy of your passport, a list of the countries you have visited in the past year and, in some cases, photos. The hotel will usually charge a small fee for the service and ask for your commitment to stay with them for a minimum of three nights. Some people, for example journalists or Palestinians, find it more difficult to get an NOC; women travelling on their own usually find it easy.

Pregnant & Single?
While it is possible for single parents to sponsor their children here, having a baby out of wedlock in Oman is against the law. If you find yourself in this situation, you will need to make arrangements to have the baby outside of the country, or get married as soon as possible. For more information, see p.67.

Sponsoring A Maid

The regulations for sponsoring a housemaid vary slightly for locals and expats. Your salary should meet minimum requirements, you need to get labour clearance, and then you need to get a work visa for the maid from the Immigration Department. You must ensure that you provide life insurance for your maid, and a return air ticket every two years.

Sole Custody/Single Parents

There are no problems for a single parent wanting to bring their child into Oman as long as their passport and documentation is in order.

If you have sole custody of your child and wish to sponsor him or her, you may need a letter from the other parent stating the child's name, passport number and nationality, and that they have no objection to the child living with you in Oman. The letter must be endorsed by the legal authority that issued the sole custody, and attested. If you have no way of contacting the other parent (or if they are deceased), then the attested divorce or sole custody paperwork (or death certificate) should suffice.

Labour Card

The old labour card, issued by the Labour Department, was a legal document certifying the employment status of an individual. If your employer is arranging your residency, your labour clearance should be processed directly after your residency has been approved. If you are on family residency and decide to work, your employer (not your visa sponsor) will need to apply for your labour clearance. Your sponsor should supply an NOC. Women on their husband's or father's sponsorship are not allowed to work unless they have a work visa.

ROP Information
Memorise the website address for the Royal Oman Police – the site is packed with essential information on what documents you will need for various procedures (www.rop.gov.om).

In 2005 the government began replacing labour cards with resident cards. The resident card uses biometric recognition and is multi-functional, holding personal details, driving licence, and emergency medical information. It can be used for electronic validation at immigration checkpoints, and can even serve as an electronic cash card for transactions at government organisations.

Cards are issued by the Directorate General of Civil Status. You will need a completed application form, passport, medical certificate, labour clearance from the Ministry of Manpower (private sector workers) and two photographs. Non-working residents (family members) need a completed application form, passport, birth certificate, medical certificate and two photographs. Further information can be requested from the Directorate General of Civil Status, located on the Seeb Airport Roundabout.

Free Zones

Free zones are not as prevalent in Oman as they are in other Gulf states, but there are two developments. A technology park called Knowledge Oasis Muscat (www.kom.om) is situated in Rusayl Industrial Estate (near Sultan Qaboos University) and offers 100% foreign ownership of businesses. You pay no personal income tax, you are exempt from foreign exchange controls, and you pay no tax on your company profits for the first five years.

Salalah Free Trade Zone (www.sfzco.com), built around the Salalah Port, offers attractive incentives to foreign and local businesses. It boasts office buildings, warehouse units and plots of land (developed and undeveloped) for long-term leasing.

No Oman Licence?
The traffic law permits expatriates on a visit visa to drive rental cars for up to three months. Expats on employment visas should have Oman driving licences.

Driving Licence

Other options **Transportation** p.137

Compared to some other countries in the region, the driving on Oman's roads is fairly calm. However, there are still a lot of motorists who drive recklessly and with scant regard for the safety of pedestrians and other road users. The government promotes road safety with a number of high-profile campaigns such as the Salim & Salimah – Safe & Sound campaign (see www.salimandsalimah.org for more information).

If you are a new arrival in Oman and find the road conditions scary, the best advice is to get behind the wheel as quickly as possible. Your first few drives will be stressful but it won't take long to get the hang of defensive driving.

The roads are monitored closely by the Royal Oman Police (ROP). Drinking and driving is illegal – there is a zero-tolerance policy, so even if you've only had half a shandy or a bowl of trifle laced with sherry, don't get behind the wheel. Road blocks (where police pull drivers off the road and make them do a breathalyser test) are infrequent, but if you have an accident and you have any alcohol in your bloodstream, you are in very hot water. Not only will your insurance be invalidated, but you could face a hefty fine or even jail time.

Using your mobile phone while driving is prohibited, unless you are connected to a hands-free device. If caught, your fine could be as much as RO 70 (that's one expensive phone call).

Always carry your driving licence with you. Failure to produce it in a spot check will result in a fine. If you have any queries on driving licences or traffic regulations, contact the ROP Directorate of Traffic on 24 600 099 or visit the website (www.rop.gov.om).

Driving Licence Documents

- Licence Exchange form with signature and stamp of sponsor
- An NOC from your sponsor/company (in Arabic)
- Two photographs
- Passport and resident visa copy
- Original driving licence along with a photocopy (and translation, if requested by the Traffic Police)
- Blood Group Certificate

Additional Requirements For Female Applicants:

- NOC letter addressed to the Director of Licensing, brought in person by the guardian or substitute
- If married, marriage certificate or birth certificate of a child
- If unemployed, a copy of husband's labour card and a letter from his sponsor/company

Visitors

Visitors do not need a temporary Oman licence to drive in Oman. All they need is a valid international licence or a licence from their home country (GCC and European nationalities only).

Permanent Licence

To drive a light vehicle in Oman you must be over 17 years of age (you have to be over 21 to drive heavy vehicles or trucks). Residents from many countries, including the UK and the US, can simply exchange their driving licence from their home country for an Oman licence. The only condition is that they have had the licence for one year or more. It costs RO 20 to transfer the licence, which can be done at the traffic police headquarters on Death Valley Road (near Muscat Private School). Take along essential documents (see p.58) and you will need to have an eye test done before you go. Strangely, married women have to take their marriage certificate and a letter of no-objection from their husband. Your company's PRO will usually go with you to help you through the process.

If you do not have a driving licence from one of the 'automatic exchange' countries, you will need to take a driving test. The first step is to obtain a learning permit – start by picking up an application form from the traffic police headquarters. To do this you'll need to take your essential documents (p.58) and RO 5. You will be given an eye test at the Traffic Police. Your next step is to find a good driving school. There are a few schools, but many instructors work individually and you will find them by word of mouth. They often operate out of Death Valley Road police HQ, although some will come to your house. They drive white cars with easily recognisable red diagonal stripes. There are female driving instructors for women, although no female test inspectors. When your instructor feels you are ready to take the test, you will have to sit a three-part driving test, consisting of a reversing test, a road test and a highway code test. The first involves reversing between oil drums placed in two parallel rows barely wider than your car; you have to get it right first time and you can't take the road or theoretical tests until you've passed this test (known, with fear and loathing, as 'the barrels'). Once you've passed all three tests, you have to apply for your licence through the authorised driving school. The police are known to be strict in issuing new licences and this process can take several months. You'll need perseverance.

> **Automatic Licence Transfer**
>
> The following driving licences are transferable in Oman without taking a driving test: GCC countries, Australia, Belgium, Brunei, Canada, Denmark, Finland, France, Germany, Ireland, Italy, Japan (after translation), Jordan, Lebanon, Luxembourg, Monaco, Morocco, the Netherlands, New Zealand, Norway, Spain, Sweden, Tunis, Turkey, United Kingdom and United States.

Driving Schools

Al Farsan Driving School	As Seeb	24 565 776
Morning Star Driving School	Al Khuwayr	24 478 506
Muscat Driving School	Various Locations	24 781 123
Oman Driving Institute	Various Locations	24 596 921
Safety Line Institute	Various Locations	24 568 919

Oman driving licences are valid for 10 years and can be renewed at the traffic police headquarters. To renew your licence you will need a driving licence renewal form (stamped by your sponsor), your expired licence, a copy of your labour card and a passport copy. If you need to get an international driving licence, take your Oman licence to the Oman Automobile Club (24 510 239) and they will help you through the procedure. You also need to take two passport photos and RO 10.250.

Behave Or Be Blamed
Rowdy, lecherous behaviour might seem like a good idea with eight pints inside you, but it is punishable with fines, prison time or (in extreme cases) deportation. So if you are drinking, do it nicely or you may have more than your hangover to worry about the next morning.

Liquor Licence

Other options **Alcohol** p.262

Attitudes to drinking in this region are a bit stiffer than you might experience back home (popping into your corner shop for a six-pack is a definite no-no). However, compared to some of the other GCC countries, Oman has a fairly relaxed view of alcohol. Non-Muslims can drink in licensed bars and restaurants, at private clubs, and at various social events that are generously sponsored by major alcohol retailers. Muscat is not famous for its buzzing nightlife, but some hotel bars have extended their opening hours to 03:00 (thus brightening up the social scene a bit).

However, drunk and disorderly behaviour in public is frowned upon and fortunately most expats seem to respect this.

If you want to buy alcohol for consumption at home, you need to apply for a liquor licence. Only non-Muslim residents with a labour card are allowed to apply. If you are married, only the husband can apply, and his wife cannot use the licence to buy alcohol unless he works in the interior. Licences are valid for two years, but can't be used outside of the city in which they were issued.

Your liquor licence permits you to buy a limited amount of alcohol each month. Your allowance is calculated based on your salary, and is usually not more than 10% of it. You can apply for a larger allowance on certain conditions (for example, if your job entails corporate entertaining).

You can't 'bank' your allowance – you must either use it or lose it. Many expats have learned the benefits of stockpiling alcohol, particularly in the lead-up to Ramadan when liquor stores are closed for a whole month and bars do not serve any booze. It is illegal to drive around with liquor in your car, with the exception of transporting it from the liquor store to your home.

New liquor licences and renewals are available from the liquor licencing office (located in the ROP station at the end of Ruwi Street). You will need an NOC in Arabic and English, a copy of your passport and labour card, a copy of your employment contract, a copy of your labour card statistical form (issued by the Directorate of Labour Affairs), two passport photos and the fee (3% of your monthly salary). For renewals, you also need to submit your previous permit as well as a copy of the front page.

The liquor licensing office is open from 07:30 to 12:30, Saturday to Thursday. Contact the office on 24 704 666 for more information.

Birth Certificate & Registration

Citizenship

Even if your baby is born in Oman, it does not get Omani citizenship. It will take the citizenship of the mother or the father (or both). Speak to your embassy regarding citizenship rules for your baby.

The birth of an expat child should be registered within two weeks of the date of delivery. It is important to get all paperwork relevant to your new baby in order, particularly if you are planning to travel in the near future.

You'll get an official birth certificate from the hospital where your child was born (it costs RO 6), and you then need to have this certificate stamped at the Ministry of Foreign Affairs Attestation Office (consular section – 24 699 500) in Qurm. Then you need to go to your embassy, where your baby will be issued with a passport, before applying for your baby's residence visa through the usual channels. If you are British you can register your child's birth with the British Consulate – this is not compulsory but it means your child will have a British birth certificate and will be registered at the General Registry Office in the UK. You do not have to do this immediately after the birth, but you should try to do it before you leave Oman for good. If you don't, and you subsequently lose your child's birth certificate, you can only get a replacement from the British Consulate in Oman. But if you do complete this procedure, you will be able to get a replacement birth certificate from the UK. Before the birth, it is worth checking the regulations of your country of origin for citizens born overseas (see p.21 for a list of embassies and consulates in Oman).

To register your child with the Oman authorities, you will need a completed application form, birth notification from the Ministry of Health (birth certificate), resident cards or passports of both parents, and the parents' marriage certificate. Legal responsibility for registering the child's birth rests with the father, although in his absence it may also be done in the order of their listing by any adult relative present at the birth, any adult residing with the mother, the doctor or any midwife who attended the event.

Marriage Certificate & Registration

There are Catholic and Protestant churches in Muscat (Ghala and Ruwi) and Protestant churches in Salalah and Sohar. Protestants should contact the pastor at the office in Ruwi for an appointment (24 799 475/24 702 372). Both partners should be resident in Oman and must provide proof of their marital status, which can take the form of a letter from their sponsor or embassy. Partners from different countries must provide evidence from their respective embassies that they are free to marry. Widowed or divorced people must produce appropriate original documents indicating they are free to marry. Four witnesses, two from the bride's side and two from the groom's, must attend the wedding ceremony. Copies of the passport information page and visa of each partner must be provided. The church requires at least one month's notice to perform the ceremony and premarital counselling is recommended. The marriage certificate must be attested by both the Ministry of Foreign Affairs (consular section) Attestation Office and by the couple's respective embassies. There is no fee for the ceremony but a donation is welcomed. To marry in the Salalah or Sohar protestant churches, contact the pastors (23 235 677 in Salalah or 26 840 606 in Sohar).

Catholics should contact the priest at the Catholic Church of Saints Peter & Paul in Ruwi (24 701 893) or at Holy Spirit Catholic Church in Ghala (24 590 373). The couple is expected to take instruction before the wedding ceremony takes place. You will need your original baptism certificates and a no objection certificate from your priest stating that you have not previously been married in a church. A declaration of your intent to marry is posted on the public noticeboard of the church for a period, after which, if there are no objections, the priest will fix a date for the ceremony. The parish priest will advise you of his fee accordingly.

Dynamic Decorator
Giovanni D Cannavo of Haila Trading decorates weddings with flair and style. Call him on 24 489 930 or 99 356 756, or email him on duiliocannavo@ hotmail.com for more information.

Getting Married In Oman

Since Oman law is governed largely by Islam, it is actually illegal for an unmarried couple to live together. It is even illegal to share a house with flatmates of the opposite sex who are not related to you. However, many couples do end up living together without getting into trouble – as long as you are discreet and stay out of trouble, you should be left alone to co-habit in peace.

The singles scene is not exactly swinging in Muscat and if you are single you may find yourself doing the rounds at endless family barbecues where everyone is married with children. But you never know – true love may be round the corner. It is not common for expats to stay in Oman to get married – the expense of flying all your family and friends out for a posh party in one of the many five-star hotels puts most people off. However, if you choose to have an Oman wedding, there are numerous options at your disposal. If you've got the cash, and can scrape together the minimum requirement of 200 guests, you could have your wedding at the Al Bustan Palace InterContinental Muscat – the bridal package includes two nights' stay in an Arabian Suite (including dinner and breakfast), flowers, cake, hairstyling and a Bentley to transport you in style. If you'd rather save your money for the honeymoon, you can have a civil service at your embassy or consulate and a more modest reception in a hotel ballroom or restaurant (depending on number of guests). To compare prices and services, contact the following: Ms Fahima Al Adwi (Al Bustan Palace InterContinental Muscat, 24 164 110), Nina Macao (Chedi Muscat, 24 524 400 ext 6202), Christina Grama (Crowne Plaza Muscat, 92 191 389), Omeir Al Hinai (InterContinental Muscat, 24 680 000 ext 8402) or Deserie Armenio (Radisson SAS, 24 487 777). To find out about wedding packages at Shangri-La (24 776 241) or the Hyatt (24 621 234), ask to be put through to their banqueting departments.

Word of mouth is a good way to find your wedding photographer – you might be lucky enough to find a talented fellow expat who is an enthusiastic amateur photographer and would be happy to use your big day as an opportunity to practise. Alternatively, you could call I K Sadanandan from Risail Photo Laboratory (99 349 204) or Anirudh Bhosle from Photocentre (99 269 121) for a quote.

If you decide to get your wedding stationery made, there are several options, all of which can provide lovely designs to coordinate with the colours and theme of your choice. Call Lucie (99 479 618), Caroline (92 835 530), Rahwanji Cards (24 810 744) or email Habibi on habibioman@yahoo.co.uk.

When it comes to finding the perfect dress, there are literally hundreds of tailor shops dotted around Muscat. The best way to find a good one is to ask around, and it's always a good idea to try them out with a smaller job before you hand over your priceless fabric. See p.101 for a list of tailors.

Most florists will be able to make the necessary floral arrangements for your wedding, but The Flower Shop in Sabco Centre (24 560 043) and Caesar Flowers & Gifts (24 484 899) specialise in wedding flowers.

There are several excellent hair and makeup salons around Muscat. The following salons specialise in bridal packages: Star Salon in the Hyatt Hotel (24 601 255), Raz Hair & Beauty in Qurm (24 561 669), Diva Hair & Beauty in MSQ (24 693 011), and Lucy Beauty Salon in Qurm (24 571 757).

The Paperwork

All marriages should be registered at the Department of Notary Public in Al Khuwayr, within 30 days. To register your marriage, you will need a completed application form, and the marriage notification (from the Ministry of Justice) or a marriage certificate authenticated by the Oman diplomatic mission in the country where the marriage took place (if not in Oman).

Wedding Venues

Crowne Plaza Muscat ▶ p.25	24 660 660
InterContinental Muscat ▶ p.344	24 680 633
Al Bustan Palace InterContinental Muscat ▶ p.29	24 764 193
Radisson BLU ▶ p.321	24 487 777
Shangri La Barr Al Jissah ▶ p.309	24 666 241
Grand Hyatt Muscat	24 641 127

If one of the newly-weds is an Omani, they should produce their resident card or passport and ID card, as well as an approval letter from the Ministry of Interior. A marriage can be registered by the husband or the wife, or by their fathers.

Although the Department of Notary Public is part of the Ministry of Justice, it is not located in the same building in Al Khuwayr. The Ministry of Justice is located on Ministry Street, but the Department of Notary Public is located in Dohat Al Adab Street, one street down from the Radisson SAS Hotel. The phone number is 24 485 795, although not many employees speak English, so it might be better to go down there in person. The opening hours are 07:30 to 14:30.

Muslims

Two Muslims wishing to marry should apply at the marriage section of the Shariah Court in Wattayah. You will need two witnesses, both of whom should be Muslims. The woman does not need the permission of her father or brother to marry, unlike in some other Middle East countries. Passports and passport photocopies are required and you may marry immediately. The Shariah Court is located just off the Wattayah Roundabout, next to the Royal Oman Police (ROP) football stadium.

Civil Weddings

Couples wanting a non-religious ceremony should contact their local embassy or consulate, as they may have regulations and referrals to arrange for a local civil marriage, which can then be registered at their embassy. See the list of embassies and consulates on p.21. Many people opt to hold their wedding receptions in Oman's plush hotels. Several hotels offer facilities for hosting weddings (see the table opposite for contact details).

Hindus

Hindus can be married through the Shiva Temple (24 737 311), the Darsait Temple (24 798 548) and the Indian Embassy (24 814 274). Contact the Indian Embassy for further details.

Local Weddings
If you get the opportunity to attend a local wedding, grab it! Local weddings in Oman are traditionally grand affairs, especially in terms of size – it is not uncommon for the guest list to reach figures of 200 or more. The ceremony takes place over two days, and includes traditional singing and dancing, as well as vast quantities of favourite local dishes.

Divorce

All divorces occurring in the Sultanate need to be reported within 30 days from the date of the event. You will need a completed application form, divorce notification from the Ministry of Justice or divorce certificate authenticated by the Oman Diplomatic mission in the country where the divorce took place. If one of the married couple is an Omani citizen, their resident card or passport and their ID card should be produced, along with an approval letter from the Ministry of Interior. Divorces are finalised at the Department of Notary Public (24 485 795). See Marriage Certificates & Registration (p.67) for location details. See p.70 for more information on divorcing in Oman.

Death Certificate & Registration

In the unhappy event of the death of a friend or relative, the Royal Oman Police (ROP) must be informed immediately. The ROP will make a report and you must also inform the deceased's sponsor, who is responsible for registering the death with the authorities. Death registration must be done within two weeks. To register the death, the sponsor should produce a completed application form (which you get from the ROP), a notification from the Ministry of Health, the ID of the deceased, the resident card or passport, and a letter from an official authority notifying that the burial has been carried out or that the body has been sent out of the country. Remember that in Muslim societies, bodies must be buried as soon as possible (in some cases, before sunset on the day of the death), so things can happen very fast. If there are any suspicious circumstances, the ROP will take photographs of the body. Post mortems, which are carried out at the ROP hospital in Wattayah, are only performed in the event of a suspicious or accidental death.

In the case of an accident, doctors in the hospital will release the death certificate unless there is a post mortem pending, in which case the ROP will do so. The certificate is usually released to the sponsor. There is no charge for the death certificate, although it will not be released until all hospital bills are settled. Ensure that the cause of death is stated on the death certificate. From hospital, the deceased is taken to the mortuary. In order to release the body, you or your sponsor must obtain a letter from the relevant embassy authorising the removal of the deceased from the hospital. This letter should be taken to the ROP, who will issue a letter for the hospital. You or your sponsor must arrange transport for the body, so you will need to buy a coffin and hire an ambulance. If you can't afford an ambulance, the deceased can be transported in your car.

If desired, you can transport the deceased to their home country. To do this you should talk to the relevant airline to enquire about their procedures (see the airlines table on p.39). You will need a release letter from your embassy, and the body will need to be embalmed. The ROP hospital charges RO 120 for embalming, and Khoula Hospital charges RO 100.

If you wish to perform a burial in Oman, you should get a letter to that effect from your embassy. Give this to the ROP, who will supply you with a letter for the hospital to release the body. Contact the church of your choice to perform the funeral service (see a list of churches on p.16). Your embassy will contact the municipality. For non-Muslims, there is a cemetery at PDO.

On a precautionary note, if you intend to stay in Oman for some time you should seriously consider making a will under Shariah law, particularly if you are married. If one partner dies, it is so much easier for the remaining partner to sort out legalities quickly. Otherwise, it can take a long time to resolve questions about the inheritance of items that are in your partner's name – and you can't leave the country until this has been resolved.

Working In Oman

Expat workers come to Oman for a number of reasons – to advance their careers, for higher standards of living, to take advantage of new career opportunities, to escape negative aspects of living in their home countries (such as crime), or just for the experience of living in a new culture.

Some people are seconded to Oman by companies based in their home countries, and some actively seek out opportunities for a new job that includes a place in the sun. The expat lifestyle is pretty good, although it's not all coffee and sunshine. Setting up a new life in a strange country and forming new social networks is still hard work. And you only have developing labour laws to protect you in the instance of a dispute with your employer.

One of the main differences about working in Oman, as opposed to your country of origin, is that you need to be sponsored by an employer, which leave some people feeling tied or uncomfortably obligated to their employer. If you leave the company your current visa will be cancelled and you have to go through the hassle of getting a new residency permit (for you and your family, if they are on your sponsorship).

While Omanisation has closed off certain sectors of industry to expat job seekers, you will still be able to find a job fairly easily in sectors like oil, medicine and education.

Setting Up A Business In Oman

Setting up a business in Oman can be a lengthy and arduous task. Firstly, you will need to find a suitable Omani sponsor, which is easier said than done. Obtain professional legal advice throughout and ensure all agreements are written down, not just verbal. It may be easier to set up in Knowledge Oasis Muscat (www.kom.om) or in Salalah Free Zone (www.sfzco.com).

Networking

While Muscat is still a relatively small city, networking is critical, even across industries. Everyone seems to know everyone and getting in with the corporate 'in-crowd' certainly has its benefits. Business acumen can, at times, be more important than specific industry knowledge and therefore it pays to attend business events and meetings. Make friends in government departments and this will often land you in the front line for opportunities. Because bad news is rarely made public in the newspapers here, staying tuned in to the business grapevine helps prevent wrong decisions.

Business Culture & Etiquette

Although it is an up-and-coming modern city, Muscat is still an Arab city in a Muslim country, and this affects every aspect of daily life, including how business is done. Even if your counterpart in another company is an expat, the head decision maker is often an Omani who could possibly have a different approach to business matters. Your best bet when doing business in Muscat for the first time is to watch closely, have loads of patience, and make a concerted effort to understand the culture and respect the customs. Don't underestimate your business contacts or assume that you have a better way of doing things than them – Omanis can smell an arrogant expat a mile away and you'll soon find many business opportunities passing you by.

Banning

Until recently, if you wanted to change jobs within Oman you would require a release letter from your employer stating that he had no objection to you finding work with another company in the Sultanate. This was more often than not impossible to obtain and you would be forced to find work either in the neighbouring UAE or back in your home country. It is worth staying on the good side of your current employer if you want to switch jobs. Be aware that you are generally not permitted to live in Oman if you are not employed, because you must have sponsorship, and that sponsorship normally ends when your employment does. You will be required to obtain an alternative visa immediately or you will be staying in the country illegally.

Working Hours

If you've never worked in this region before, you'll quickly get to know of a new work phenomenon: the split shift. Across the GCC, many companies prefer to start work a little earlier, break for a long lunch (usually three hours), and return to work for a late-afternoon session. Split-shift timings are usually 08:00 to 13:00 and 16:00 to 19:00. Not all companies follow these hours however, and many work a 'straight shift' with a short lunch break. Most private sector companies work straight shifts, as do government organisations. Straight-shift hours are usually 07:00 to 14:00 for government organisations, and 07:00 to 16:00 for private companies (although hours do vary from one company to another).

Independent shops normally work the split shift, and many big shopping malls also close for an extended period at lunchtime. Most supermarkets remain open from 08:00 to 21:00, and some of the bigger malls (like Muscat City Centre and Markaz Al Bahja) are open from 09:00 to 22:00.

The official weekend is Thursday and Friday, although some people also have to work on Thursdays until 13:00 and some sectors are moving towards a Friday-Saturday weekend. Public holidays are declared by the government. Most public holidays are religious holidays and therefore are governed by the Hijri calendar (and the moon). The holiday can't be declared until the new moon has been seen by the Moon Sighting Committee. As a result, it is hard to plan ahead for long weekends because you never know the exact day or duration of the holiday until the moon is sighted the night before.

During Ramadan, all Muslims and people working in government organisations have reduced working hours as stipulated by Article 69 of Oman's labour law. The normal working day is normally reduced to six hours instead of eight. Some private sector companies reduce working hours for all staff, including expats.

Business Councils & Groups

For in-depth information about business in Oman, refer to your local business group or the commercial attache at your embassy or consulate. The contact numbers can be found in the table below.

Finding Work

Expat workers come to Oman for various reasons, primarily because the salaries are great and there is no personal income tax. As an added bonus, the weather is sublime, it is a relatively safe country, and the lifestyle is easy. When weighing up the pros and cons of accepting an offer in Oman, don't be too blinded by the lure of paying no tax –

Business Councils & Groups		
British Council	24 681 000	www.britishcouncil.org/me
Ministry of Commerce & Industry	24 810 209	www.mocioman.org
Ministry of Social Affairs, Labour & Vocational Training	24 645 000	www.mone.gov.com
Muscat American Business Council	24 797 623	www.abcgc.us
Oman Chamber Of Commerce & Industry	24 707 674	www.chamberoman.com
Omani Centre for Investment Promotion & Export Development (OCIPED)	24 812 344/24 817 600	www.ociped.com
United Media Services	24 700 896	www.oeronline.com

remember that the rial is pegged to the US dollar, which has not been performing too well over the last 18 months or so. You might find that currency fluctuations decrease the actual value of your salary package when you compare it to what you would earn in dollars, sterling or euros back home.

Nevertheless, a good expat package in a good company in Oman is a golden opportunity to experience a different culture in a country where the sun always shines. The main setback to finding a good expat posting in Oman is the highly successful Omanisation programme. Some organisations have achieved over 90% Omanisation, so less than 10% of their workforce are foreigners.

Nationality Counts ◀

Some nationalities may have trouble getting a work or residence visa for certain categories of employment. For example, a Bangladeshi male is not eligible for a work visa, unless he is employed as a gardener.

Finding Work Before You Come

It is better to have a job lined up before you come to Oman, as with a sponsor lined up all your paperwork will be taken care of on your behalf. If you fancy living in Oman for a few years and are on the lookout for a good opportunity, contact some reputable recruitment agencies in your home country who may have jobs available in this region. If you want to do the legwork yourself, you have a number of options. You can 'cold-call' companies by sending out unsolicited CVs to targeted industries, although this is rarely the path to success. If you have friends or acquaintances in Oman, you can send them some copies of your CV and ask them to put out feelers for you. Or you can do some research on the internet to find out more about job vacancies in Oman. Try visiting the following websites: www.gulfjobsites.com, www.careermideast. com, www.overseasjobs.com, www.smartgroups.com/groups/oman-skillpool, www. oclped.com, and www.monster.com. Alternatively, you could visit the websites of some of Oman's larger organisations to see if they have any vacancies. Try Petroleum Development Oman (www.pdo.co.om), British School Muscat (www.britishschool.edu. om), Al Shatti Hospital (www.alshattihospital.com), Muscat Private Hospital (www. muscatprivatehospital.com), Omantel (www.omantel.net.om), Nawras (www.nawras. com.om), or American British Academy (www.abaoman.edu.om). If you are in the hospitality industry, try contacting the individual hotels directly (see a list of hotel websites on p.24).

If you get a job offer, you will need to negotiate your employment package carefully to cover all bases. A good package covers housing, medical insurance, transport (a company car or a car allowance), shipping or relocation costs, and education for your children.

Finding Work While You Are In Oman

Unless you have excellent contacts lined up before coming to Oman, don't expect to find work while you are on a visit visa. The slow pace of life means that decisions are not always made quickly.

There are no newspaper supplements for appointments, and any classified ads in the papers are usually targeted at Omanis or at labourers. When you arrive, pick up a copy of the Apex Business Directory of Oman, which contains information, addresses and phone numbers of most companies. You can find a copy at the Apex office in Ruwi (24 799 388). If you have come to Oman with your spouse who is working and you wish to find a job for yourself, the options are limited unless you are in the teaching or medical professions. To find a job in these sectors, it's best to ask directly at schools, hospitals and clinics. The rigorous Omanisation programme does not permit an expat to hold a job that an Omani is qualified to do, which cuts out most administrative jobs and many others. If you are a well-qualified English teacher, then you should be able to find work as a teacher of English as a second language. There are several institutes offering English courses to non-native speakers. Try the Polyglot Institute (24 831 261), Khimji Training Institute (24 783 997); the Centre for British Teachers (24 685 290) and the British Council (24 600 548). The latter two also offer CELTA courses if you wish to train.

Recruitment Agencies

Virtually non-existent, recruitment agencies generally cater for manual labourers from Asian countries. The only agencies that might offer more interesting expat jobs are those listed in the table.

To register, check with the agency to find out if they take walk-in applicants. Most accept CVs via fax or email these days and will then contact you for an interview. The agency takes its fee from the registered company once the position has been filled. It is illegal for a recruitment company to charge job seekers for their services.

Recruitment Agencies		
CFBT Education Services & Partners	24 481 938	www.cfbt.com
Ideas Management Consultants	24 791 876	www.ideas-consulting.com
Light House Consultancy	24 484 638	www.tlhglobal.com
Modern Centre for Business Services	24 482 283	www.mcbsglobal.com
National Training Institute	24 472 121	www.ntioman.com

Voluntary & Charity Work

There are several opportunities to do charity work in Oman, and the organisations listed below are always on the lookout for committed volunteers:

BSO (British Scholarships Oman)

Sends gifted students who could otherwise not afford it to study at universities in England. The students are strictly vetted and chosen by a committee. BSO also works with Sultan Qaboos University and sends medical students to the UK to complete their studies. Usually around 12 students can be helped each year, depending on the amount raised by fundraising. Funds are raised at a number of events in Muscat and through British government assistance. Go to www.britishcouncil.org for more details.

Down Syndrome Support Group

A support group (affiliated to the Association of Early Intervention for Children with Special Needs) for parents of children with Down Syndrome. Meetings are held weekly at the Early Intervention Centre in Al Athaiba, with the aim of providing practical and emotional support for the children and their parents. The group is always on the lookout for volunteers to help them keep the children busy and stimulated. If you have some extra time on your hands, you can pick up a volunteer application form from the Early Intervention Centre. For more information, call 24 496 960 or email earlyint@ omantel.net.om.

National Association For Cancer Awareness

In many parts of the world cancer is still taboo and, to a certain extent, Oman is no different. The Association aims to work hand in hand with the healthcare providers in the field of cancer management as a patient support group, while supporting continuous medical education. They assist in research, particularly through fund raising to support the association programmes, and they reach out to people who are not in close contact with tertiary medical facilities. Email smith@aroundoman.com for details.

Whale And Dolphin Research Group

The Whale & Dolphin Research Group is part of ESO (Environmental Society of Oman) and consists of a group of volunteer scientists and interested parties working together to collect and disseminate knowledge about Oman's cetaceans. With support from local businesses, the group has been able to acquire equipment needed to carry out research on whales and dolphins off the coast of Oman. Funds are needed to cover costs of repairs, supplies and equipment, and donations of goods and services are also

extremely valuable. Volunteers to help with activities are always welcome. Contact Ross Rosenquist on 92 689 505 or log onto www.whalecoastoman.com for more information.

Know The Law
The labour law benefits employees more than employers. You should be able to get a copy from your employer, but if not, you can get one from the Ministry of Manpower (24 794 175).

Employment Contracts

Accepting an expat posting can have its pitfalls, so before you sign your contract pay special attention to things like probation periods, accommodation, annual leave, travel entitlements, medical and dental cover, notice periods and repatriation entitlements. Once you accept your offer, you will be asked to sign both an English and an Arabic copy of your contract. The Arabic copy is the one that will be referred to

Public square in the CBD

in any legal dispute between you and your employer, so if you have any doubts about the integrity of the company, ask a lawyer or Arabic-speaking friend to look through it. However, if there was ever a legal dispute, the court would want to know why there was any discrepancy between the English and Arabic versions in the first place.
It is worth reading through a copy of the Oman labour law before you sign your contract. The contract takes precedence over the labour law, so if your contract reads differently from the labour law and you have signed it, then the terms of the contract are binding (not the law).
If you are sponsored by your spouse and want to work, you need to get an NOC from his employer before you can sign a contract with your new employer. Your employer will then apply for your labour card.

Labour Law

The current version of the Oman labour law was promulgated in 2003. The law outlines everything from employee entitlements (end of service gratuity, workers' compensation, holidays and other benefits) to employment contracts and disciplinary rules. The labour law is considered fair and clearly outlines the rights of both employees and employers. Labour unions and strikes are illegal, but adherence to the law is rigorously policed and disputes are adjudicated by the Labour Board. Copies of the labour law can be obtained from the Ministry of Manpower (24 794 175) or viewed at www.directory-oman.com.

Changing Jobs

It is unusual for expats to change jobs while in Oman. Cushy expat packages mean that people generally don't leave to seek out better opportunities in other companies; they just work out their contract and leave Oman at the end of it (or renew). If you do decide to change jobs while in Oman, you have to get a release letter from your employer (in English and Arabic), confirming that you have no obligations to them and that they have no problem with you working elsewhere. A release letter is not guaranteed and whether you get one depends on your relationship with your employer. Without this letter, you are obliged to leave the country and may not return (even as a visitor) for a period of up to two years (but usually the minimum period is six months).
Changing jobs while in Oman depends solely on the release letter from your current employer, so it is in your best interests to remain on good terms with them at all times.

Financial Planning – The Basics
The minimum requirements for a good financial plan are: an emergency cash buffer (three to six months' salary), a retirement income, a retirement home, and adequate insurance (life, household and medical).

Bank Accounts

There is a good range of international banks in Oman, all of which offer standard facilities such as current, deposit and savings accounts, ATM facilities, chequebooks, credit cards and loans. Keep your eyes on the banking sector over the coming year, as with the property market opening up to expats, you should see a great deal of development in terms of mortgages and finance.

With all the great shopping to be done in Muscat, you'll find you're never too far from your nearest ATM – if you can't find one of your own bank's ATMs, you can access funds through most other ATMs using a central network, but you may be charged. Some ATMs offer global access too, so you can withdraw money from your foreign accounts. Before you can open an account in Oman, you need to have your residence visa sorted out (or at least you should have your application underway). You will need a copy of your passport, showing your personal information page and your visa page, as well as your original passport.

Bank timings vary, but they generally open by 08:30 and close at 12:00 or 13:00, Saturday to Wednesday. Most are also open from 08:00 to 11:30 on Thursdays. None of the banks are open in the evenings or on Fridays.

Banking Comparison Table

Name	Phone	Web	Tele-Banking
Bank Dhofar	23 294 886	www.bankdhofar.com	800 766 666
Bank Muscat SAOG ▶ p.77	24 795 555	www.bankmuscat.com	24 795 555
Bank Sohar ▶ p.49	24 730 000	www.banksohar.net	24 730 000
Habib Bank	24 817 139	www.hbl.com	na
HSBC ▶ p.IFC	24 799 920	www.hsbc.co.om	800 774 722
National Bank Of Oman (NBO)	24 811 711	www.nbo.co.om	800 770 077
Oman Arab Bank	24 706 265	www.oman-arabbank.com	na
Oman International Bank	23 291 512	www.oiboman.com/OIB-Main.html	800 707 888
Standard Chartered Bank	24 773 666	www.standardchartered.com/om	24 773 535

Capital Gains Tax
Even though you are no longer resident in your home country, you may still be liable for capital gains tax on any profit you make from the sale of assets in that country. Check with the revenue service of your country – the following websites may be helpful: UK (www.hmrc. gov.uk), USA (www. irs.gov), South Africa (www.sars. gov.za), Australia (www.ato.gov. au), Canada (www.cra-arc.gc.ca), New Zealand (www.ird.govt.nz).

Financial Planning

The big advantage of working for a few years on an expat package is the opportunity to earn more money and be able to put a little something away for the future. Unfortunately, despite their best intentions, many expats get caught up in the consumer-driven lifestyle and don't manage to save much at all. If you're serious about financial planning, make it a priority from the time you arrive in Oman. If your idea of saving is to squirrel money away in a shoebox under the bed, you might want to consider enlisting the services of a good financial planner.

When choosing a financial planner, consider whether they have an international presence – if you leave Oman you still want to be able to contact the company easily and enjoy the same access to advice and information. It may be better to use an independent company or adviser who is not tied to a specific bank or savings company, and therefore can objectively offer you a full range of savings products. Many expats set up offshore accounts in places like the Isle of Man, Jersey and Guernsey. They are seen as preferable to Oman-based accounts as they allow easier access to your money if you leave the country, or in the event of your death. They are also tax-free, whereas any interest from an account in your home country could be subject to tax. With an offshore account you will usually be able to choose the currency (US dollars, sterling or euro).

Before leaving your home country to take up an expat posting, you should contact the tax authorities to ensure that you are complying with the financial laws there. Most

Financial Advisors		
AGN Mak Ghazali	24 794 158	www.agnoman.com
The Financial Corporation Co (FINCORP)	24 816 655	www.fincorp.org
Financial Services	24 825 600	www.finserve.net
Gulf Investment Services	24 790 614	gisoman.net
HC Shah & Co	24 707 654	biznesstools.com
International Investment Company	24 489 789	www.ohigroup.com

countries will consider you not liable for income tax once you prove that you are not resident in that country. But you might still have to pay tax on any income you are getting from your home country (for example if you are renting out your property or earning interest on a bank account).

Taxation

Oman levies no personal taxes and withholds no income tax of any sort. However, the IMF is advising many Middle Eastern countries to introduce tax reforms to diversify their resources.

Currently, the only taxes you are obliged to pay as an expatriate are as follows: an obligatory 8% service tax in hotel food and beverage outlets, a 4% tourism tax, a 5% municipality tax, and a 3% municipality tax on rental accommodation. There is also a tax on alcohol bought at retail shops, and on pork (six slices of bacon costs RO 5, the equivalent of filling your car up with petrol).

Legal Issues

Keeping It Rial
If the costs listed in the Cost of Living table mean nothing to you, refer to the Currency Exchange Table on p.46 to work out the equivalent in the currency of your home country.

Oman is an absolute monarchy with a bicameral system. The Head of State and Supreme Commander of the Armed Forces is His Majesty Sultan Qaboos Bin Said. Laws in Oman are issued by Royal Decree as primary legislation, or by Ministerial Decisions as secondary legislation. Oman has the following court system – Supreme Court, Appellate Courts, Courts of First Instance and Courts of Summary Jurisdiction. Each court is able to deal with matters relating to civil, commercial, labour, tax and personal (Shariah) law. Although judges can practise either secular law or Shariah law, Shariah is the basis for all legislation as set out in the basic law (Royal Decree 101/96), which is in effect the constitution of Oman.

Court proceedings are conducted only in Arabic. All official documents issued by the courts and used in proceedings must also be in Arabic.

The main legal issue likely to affect expats is property ownership. As a foreigner, this is limited to purchasing property within integrated tourist complexes only, such as The Wave and Muscat Golf and Country Club. Other issues where you might land on the wrong side of the law are linked to the rules of Islam: gambling is forbidden, and although you can drink under certain conditions you are inviting trouble if you get drunk and disorderly in public places. Living with a member of the opposite sex who is not a family member is illegal.

Divorce

Unless you are married to an Omani, you may find it simpler to get divorced in your home country. Whether you choose to carry out the divorce in Oman or back home, you should contact your embassy first for guidance on the procedures and laws that apply to separation of assets, custody of children and legal status. While they may be able to provide some guidance, you should also contact a good lawyer in your home country, who will be able to advise on all aspects (for a fee, of course).

Making A Will

Just like having savings, getting household insurance and contributing towards some kind of pension scheme, having a valid will in place is one of those essential things that everybody should do. As an expat, it is strongly advisable to make your will in your

Cost Of Living

Apples (per kg)	RO 0.800
Bananas (per kg)	RO 0.500
Bottle of house wine (restaurant)	RO 12.000
Bottle of wine (off licence)	RO 6.000
Burger (takeaway)	RO 0.500
Bus (10km journey)	RO 0.500
Camera film	RO 1.000
Can of dog food	RO 0.400
Can of soft drink	RO 0.100
Cappuccino	RO 1.500
Car rental (per day)	RO 15.000
Carrots (per kg)	RO 1.500
CD Album	RO 7.000
Chocolate bar	RO 0.500
Cigarettes (per pack of 20)	RO 0.750
Cinema ticket	RO 3.000
Dozen eggs	RO 1.000
Film developing (colour, 36 exp)	RO 3.600
Fresh beef (per kg)	RO 5.000
Fresh chicken (per kg)	RO 2.500
Fresh fish (per kg)	RO 1.500
Golf (18 holes)	RO 5.000
House wine (glass)	RO 2.500
Large takeaway pizza	RO 7.000
Loaf of bread	RO 0.700
Local postage stamp	RO 0.050
Milk (1 litre)	RO 0.500
Mobile to mobile call (local, per minute)	RO 0.055
New release DVD	RO 7.000
Newspaper (international)	RO 0.800
Newspaper (local)	RO 0.200
Orange juice (1 litre)	RO 0.800
Pack of 24 aspirin/paracetamol tablets	RO 0.600
Petrol (gallon)	RO 0.120/Ltr
Pint of beer	RO 3.000
Postcard	RO 0.100
Potatoes (1kg)	RO 0.500
Rice (1kg)	RO 0.700
Salon haircut (female)	RO 20.000
Salon haircut (male)	RO 7.000
Shawarma	RO 0.250
Six-pack of beer (off licence)	RO 3.000
Strawberries (per punnet)	RO 1.200
Sugar (2kg)	RO 0.450
Taxi (10km journey)	RO 2.500
Text message (local)	RO 0.010
Tube of toothpaste	RO 1.000
Water (1.5 litres, restaurant)	RO 1.500
Water 1.5 litres (supermarket)	RO 0.200
Watermelon (per kg)	RO 0.600

country of residence so that local laws do not adversely affect it. If you become a property owner in Oman, you must make sure that you have changed your will accordingly as Shariah law has a very different view on who inherits your possessions in the event of your death. A good Oman-based law firm will be able to assist you with a locally viable will.

Adoption

There are some orphanages in Oman but it is not clear whether expats are permitted to apply to adopt any of these children or not – it depends on who you speak to. Many couples find it relatively easy to adopt from outside Oman, for example from Asia or the Far East. Once you have successfully met all the requirements in your adopted child's home country, you should have little trouble bringing your child back to Oman and applying for a residence visa. Check the regulations involved in securing your citizenship for your adopted child; your embassy will be able to help with this matter.

Crime

Crime levels are not openly reported in the media, so it is hard to evaluate the true safety situation. However, compared to many countries, Oman is considered to have a very low crime rate. Theft seems to be the main problem, although in most cases it is petty theft without violence or much forward planning. Although rumours and gossip can't be trusted completely, there have been some murmurings of more serious crimes like rape. If you are out walking alone and somebody starts 'trailing' you, do not enter into any form of conversation with them. It is always a good idea to carry your mobile phone and a camera (if you don't have one on your phone), so that you can call for help if necessary and take pictures of the offender. You should report such cases to the ROP immediately. The golden rule is to never let your guard down, even though your surroundings seem safe. And many people who have lived in Oman for a while would definitely advise women travelling alone to use private taxi services rather than the orange-and-white cabs.

Muggings are not widely heard of in Oman, but it is always wise to keep a tight hold on your handbag when out shopping in crowded areas. If you leave any personal possessions in a local taxi you will be unlikely to receive it back. If this happens in a registered taxi from a private taxi company though, you needn't worry as the drivers are usually trustworthy and will even drop your phone or bag back to you the next day. Giving the driver a tip to show appreciation for their honesty is a good idea in this situation.

There is one prison near Mabella and a new one is being constructed in Nizwa. Oman's prisons are best described as basic. Facilities are poor and hygiene is questionable. Your personal items (including shoes and belt) will be taken from

Myths & Truths

• If you write a cheque that bounces, you will be given around a week to pay the amount (if it is your first offence). If you can't pay, you will be taken into custody.

• Be careful what stickers you place on your car – car stickers featuring donkeys (even if it is a national mascot of a particular region in your home country) are apparently illegal because the position of the sticker on the car indicates that anyone passing the sticker is a donkey themselves. You will receive a fine.

• Flogging does not happen in Oman.

• Pregnancy outside wedlock will result in deportation if you are caught.

• Smoking, eating or drinking in public places during Ramadan is considered highly offensive and can carry a jail term of up to three months.

• Unmarried men and women are not permitted to live together unless they are related (brother and sister, for example). However, before you rush down the aisle, rest assured that this law is rarely enforced. Just be discreet, and you should be fine.

you when you enter the prison and only returned when you leave. You may be allowed to make a phone call, or the prison may inform your sponsor or company PRO officer that you are in custody. For a first offence, bail can be paid after 48 hours – the bail amount is usually somewhere between RO 50 and RO 75. If you can't afford the bail then you have to remain in custody. Your embassy will not be able to offer financial or legal assistance.

Drinking & Driving

If you are caught driving under the influence of alcohol, you will spend 48 hours in jail and receive a fine of up to RO 75. On your second offence, the jail time increases to 72 hours and the fine to RO 150. If you get caught a third time you will be given a RO 300 fine and deported to your home country.

Being drunk and disorderly in public carries similar charges to drinking and driving. Thankfully, taxi drivers are unlikely to report your inebriated state to police as long as you don't cause any trouble. If you are involved in a fight, there is a possibility you will have to appear in court (depending on the circumstances and whether there are any medical expenses involved).

Drugs & Fraud

Drug offences usually result in serious sentences, and your time in prison can be anywhere from one month to 25 years, depending on the amount you were caught with, the type of drugs and the circumstances surrounding the arrest. In addition, your fine could be up to RO 20,000 and the court can even sentence you to death in severe cases. If you are caught with forbidden prescription medicines, it is important that you can produce the actual doctor's prescription for them. It will depend upon the judge's decision for what sentence you will receive, but it will again be severe.

If you are involved in a crime relating to fraud, or drugs or anything relating to large sums of money, your bank account will be frozen for investigation by the ROP.

Traffic Offences

If you are involved in an accident involving a fatality, you will be required to hand over RO 7,000 to the ROP, RO 5,000 of that being 'blood money' which will go to the deceased's relatives. The other RO 2,000 will be used for any medical bills or repatriation in case of an expat. It will be up to your insurance company to decide whether or not your insurance will cover the cost of this blood money. The court could take up to six months to finalise the sentence, so you may be allowed to continue working until your sentence is given. You will not however, be allowed to leave the country while your court case is pending.

Law Firms

Al Busaidy, Mansoor Jamal & Co	24 814 466	www.amjoman.com
Curtis, Mallet-Prevost, Colt & Mosle	24 564 495	www.curtis.com
Denton Wilde Sapte	24 573 000	www.dentonwildesapte.com
Dr Abdullah Alsaidi Law Office	24 799 755	www.omanilaw.com
Hamad Al Sharji, Peter Mansour & Co	24 780 333	na
Jihad Al Taie & Associates	24 478 282	www.jihadtaie.com
Said Al Shahry Law Office	24 603 123	www.saslo.com
(Salalah)	23 289 833	www.saslo.com
Trowers & Hamlins	24 682 900	www.trowers.com

Finding A Killer Villa ◀

Check for proximity of mosques (all of which are fitted with loudspeakers), schools, the airport flight path or rubbish bins. Keep an eye open for buildings under construction, and get yourself on the waiting list. A secluded villa surrounded by empty ground is peaceful at first, but if the area is marked for development you might find yourself surrounded by building sites as time goes by. Construction work usually starts at around 06:00 and finishes at around 22:00, with the occasional midnight concrete pour, six days a week.

Housing

Although foreigners have recently been given the legal right to purchase property on certain developments in Oman, none of these developments are near completion and therefore renting is still the only option for accommodation. If you drive around Muscat you'll see several 'To Let' boards hanging up outside available properties, so if you have a preferred area in mind this is a good way to look for a house. A reliable estate agent can save you a lot of time and effort by arranging viewings of suitable properties. Muscat is spread out into distinct residential areas, mostly divided by mountains, valleys or highways. The main areas are Muscat, Mutrah, Ruwi, Wattayah, Qurm, Shati Al Qurm, Madinat As Sultan Qaboos (MSQ), Al Khuwayr, Ghubrah, Azaibah and As Seeb. If you are arriving in Oman on a full expat package then accommodation is usually included in your employment contract. Some companies provide a cash allowance to spend on rent, some let you choose a property and then they liaise directly with the landlord and make the payment on your behalf, and some companies provide staff accommodation on a compound.

Renting In Oman

Depending on which company you are joining in Oman, you will either be given company accommodation, an annual accommodation allowance, or an additional amount included in your monthly salary to be used for accommodation.

In Oman, rent is paid annually and not monthly. This is good news for the landlord, but bad news for tenants who often have to come up with a sizeable lump sum to cover their rent for the whole year. If your company provides you with an annual accommodation allowance, then they will usually cover your rent upfront. However, if you get a monthly allowance, it is often up to you to put aside a certain amount each month to cover your next rent payment. Some landlords demand one payment, although some may be more flexible and let you pay in two or three cheques.

Even with vigorous Omanisation policies, expats are still relocating to Muscat in large numbers and so there remains a steady demand in the rental market (especially for better quality properties). The golden rule is that if you see a house you love, you should sign on the dotted line as soon as possible or it will get snapped up by someone else. On the other hand, don't jump into anything: the yearly rent payment means that if you cut your lease short you could lose your money, so make sure that the place you choose is the place you want to stay in for at least one year.

If you are allowed to choose your own accommodation (if you are not provided with accommodation on the company compound), you will need to do some research into Muscat's residential areas. Consider access to roads, schools and leisure facilities. Muscat is relatively small (you can drive from one end to the other in around 40 minutes), so you can benefit from lower rents and bigger villas if you move to one of the less central areas, without feeling as though you are stuck in the middle of nowhere.

Finding A Home

There are a number of ways to find suitable accommodation, the most obvious of which is by using the services of a real estate agent. Alternatively, you can drive around your desired area keeping your eyes peeled for 'To Let' signs – often this is a good way to rent directly from the landlord and therefore avoid paying agents' commission. Look out also for properties nearing completion. Although they may not have a sign outside, try and find the watchman who will give you the landlord's number. You can also browse the classified ads in the local newspapers, or keep an eye on supermarket noticeboards.

If you do use an agent, you have the choice of local agencies or internationally recognised ones. Reputable agencies (see table on p.86) will not only show you a

selection of suitable properties, they will also assist with the paperwork and ensure that the required municipality procedures are followed.

It is possible that your company will have arranged meetings on your behalf with an agent, but it is always good to check that this agent is a registered real estate broker, who is authorised to conduct leasing procedures in Muscat. Landlords should pay the agent's commission and you should bear no cost or 'finder's fee'.

You will sometimes come across an agent who doesn't drive, and you will have to pick them up to go to house viewings.

The Lease

Your lease is an important document and will state, in addition to the financial terms, what you are liable for in terms of maintenance and what your landlord's responsibilities are. It is important that you (or your company PRO, who may have more knowledge about the pitfalls of rental contracts) read through the lease and discuss any points of contention before you sign it. You may be able to negotiate on certain clauses in your contract, such as how many cheques you can use to pay your annual rent, who is responsible for maintenance, and how much security deposit you should pay.

The entire leasing process in Muscat is governed by well-drafted legislation and the lease is prepared on a standard municipality form. The standard lease, which can have minor changes made to it, is normally for one year but is automatically renewable unless three months' notice is given before expiry by either the landlord or the tenant.

To take out a personal lease (in your name, not your employer's name), you need to be a resident. The landlord will need a copy of your passport (with visa page), a no objection letter (NOC) from your employer, a copy of your salary certificate, a signed rent cheque and up to three post-dated cheques covering the remainder of the annual rent (the number of cheques depends on your landlord).

If the rented property will be in your employer's name, then the landlord needs a copy of the company's trade licence, a passport copy of the person signing the rent cheque, and the rent cheque itself.

It is the landlord's responsibility to register the lease with the relevant municipality. The registering of leases showing rental at less than the real amount is against the law, and it is also a big risk for tenants, who will have no protection in the event of a dispute.

Housing Abbreviations

BR	Bedroom
C A/C	Central air conditioning (usually included in the rent)
D/S	Double storey villa
En suite	Bedroom has a private bathroom
Ext S/Q	Servant quarters located outside the villa
Fully fitted	Includes major appliances (oven, refrigerator, washing machine)
Hall flat	Apartment has an entrance hall (entrance doesn't open directly onto living room)
L/D	Living/dining room area
Pvt garden	Private garden
S/Q	Servant quarters
S/S	Single storey villa
Shared pool	Pool is shared with other villas in compound
W A/C	Window air conditioning (often indicates older building)
W/robes	Built-in wardrobes

The landlord must ensure that the house is in good condition before you move in, so don't sign the lease until he has made the improvements you think need to be done (like painting, filling in wall holes, regrouting bathrooms and servicing the air-conditioning units).

Rent Disputes

It goes without saying that there are distinct advantages to keeping friendly relations with your landlord. There are no hard-and-fast laws protecting the tenant and therefore it pays to stay on your landlord's good side. If you have a disagreement with him that reaches a stalemate, the Ministry of Justice (24 697 699) will assist.

Real Estate Agents

The entire leasing process in Muscat is governed by well-drafted legislation and the lease is prepared on a standard Municipality form. The standard lease, which can have minor changes made to it, is normally for one year (which is automatically renewable unless three months notice is given before expiry by either the landlord or the tenant). Annual rent for villas is often requested in advance in one cheque, although it is sometimes possible to agree with the landlord that six-months' rent is paid upon signing of the lease and the remainder of the amount by post dated cheque. Rent for apartments is usually payable quarterly, or in some cases monthly. In most cases, no security deposit is payable by tenants.

Real Estate Agents		
Al Habib & Co	24 702 666	www.alhabibonline.com
Al Qandeel Real Estate	24 696 519	www.alqandeel.com
Amlak Real Estate	99 337 536	www.amlak-oman.com
Bazaar Propeties	99 205 535	www.bazaarproperties.com
Cluttons & Partners ▶ p.87	24 564 250	www.cluttons.com
Eamaar Real Estate	24 699 733	www.eamaar.com
Gulf Property World	24 697 588	www.gulfpropertyworld.com
Gulf Real Estate	24 814 371	na
Hamptons International ▶ p.83	24 563 557	www.hamptons-int.com
Hay Al Rahbah	24 693 877	na
Hilal Properties ▶ p.85	24 600 688	www.hilalprp.com
Oman Homes	24 488 087	www.omanhomes.com

If you decide to let an agent help you find your new home, you can choose from somebody local or from an internationally recognised agency. The more reputable agencies (see table) will arrange all the paperwork for your tenancy agreement and ensure that the required Municipality procedures are followed. It is worth trying to negotiate over the rent, especially if the market is slow or if you offer to pay in one cheque (rather than three). Many people can organise an estate agent through their company PRO but it is always wise to check that the recommended agent is a registered real estate broker, authorised to conduct leasing in Muscat.

You may find that some agents don't have access to a car and you will have to pick them up to go to viewings. Landlords pay the agent's commission so you should pay nothing to the agent. The other option is to drive around the area you would like to live in looking for 'To Let' signs, which may be agency or private landlord.

Annual Rents ◀

Rents quoted in real estate ads are yearly, not monthly. It is almost unheard of to pay rent monthly, unless you are living in a hotel apartment.

Main Accommodation Options

Your employer may provide a house or apartment for you, but if they provide you with an allowance instead, you will be able to choose what type of accommodation is suitable. The following options are available:

Apartment/Villa Sharing

You can cut your accommodation costs in half by sharing an apartment or villa with colleagues or friends. It's also a great way to avoid those long, lonely nights of feeling homesick and wondering what all your mates back home are up to. Some villas are so big that even if you've got numerous house mates, you should still be able to find a quiet corner. To look for shared accommodation or find a suitable housemate, check the noticeboards outside supermarkets.

Standard Apartment

Apartments are found all over the Muscat area and vary from tiny studio apartments to vast penthouses. Muscat's hilly terrain means that people living on the top floors usually have a great view. Rents are usually between RO 350 and RO 1350 per month.

If you've found the perfect villa but it's a few hundred rials out of your budget, there are a few ways you could try negotiating with the landlord. Paying in one lump sum may help, or offering to undertake maintenance of the villa yourself. If that doesn't work, try to negotiate a longer lease period – often if you sign for two or three years instead of one, the landlord may consider dropping the rent slightly. However, even if you manage to negotiate two or three years, the official lease is only for one year.

Villa

Whether your budget stretches to a luxurious four-bedroom palace overlooking the beach in Qurm, or a more modest villa in outlying areas such as Azaibah or As Seeb, you should find something to fit your budget. If your villa has a swimming pool, central air conditioning, covered parking, electric gates, a big garden or outside maid's quarters, the price will be higher. A garden court is a group of small, semi-detached villas built around a communal garden (often with a swimming pool). There are quite a few of these found in the Madinat As Sultan Qaboos area. Villas currently rent for RO 600 to RO 6000 depending on size and location.

Serviced Apartments

Serviced apartments are fairly expensive and therefore more suited to shorter stays. Some people live in serviced apartments for a month or two until they find the house they want, or while they await the arrival of their family members or furniture shipment. Apartments can be rented on a daily, weekly, monthly or yearly basis and are fully furnished right down to the last detail, with a cleaning and laundry service included. The main contacts for serviced apartments are ASAS Residence (24 571 509), Al Noorah Gardens (24 696 106), and Safeer Hotel Suites (24 691 200).

Other Rental Costs

Apart from your rent (paid annually), you will face additional costs when moving into a new house. These might include:
• A 3% municipality tax
• A security deposit (refundable when you vacate the premises, minus any damages)
• A deposit for your water and electricity accounts
If you are renting a villa with a garden, your water costs will be higher since the grass and plants will need watering every day in Oman's hot climate.

Buying Property

Being able to buy a property in Oman if you are an expat is a new phenomenon – until the relevant change in the law was announced by royal decree in 2006, non-nationals could only rent accommodation. Although the prospect of buying property in Oman was once one that raised certain doubts and concerns, the performance of the freehold property sector in neighbouring Dubai has certainly made it a much more attractive investment. Expats can only buy property within areas designated as 'integrated tourist complexes' or ITCs. ITC licences are granted by the Ministry of Tourism, and have so far been approved for The Wave, Blue City and the Muscat Golf and Country Club. Properties within these complexes can be bought for investment purposes, meaning that you can buy one to let out to a third party. You are also permitted to sell your property at any time after the construction is completed. It is important to note that in the event of the death of a property owner, the laws regarding transfer of ownership are governed by the laws of that person's home country. It is essential to have a valid will in place if you are considering purchasing property in Oman. If no heir applies to inherit the property within one year, the Ministry of Tourism will manage the property for 15 years, after which time ownership reverts to the Government of Oman.

Property Developers		
Al Madina Al Zarqa	24 699 773	www.almadinaalzarqa.com
Muscat Hills Golf & Country Club	24 511 024	www.muscathills.com
Waterfront Investments	24 600 083	www.thewavemuscat.com

Mortgage Providers		
Bank Muscat SAOG ▶ p.77	24 795 555	www.bankmuscat.com
Habib Bank	24 817 139	www.hbl.com
HSBC ▶ p.IFC	24 799 920	www.hsbc.co.om
National Bank of Oman	800 770 077	www.nbo.com.om

Mortgages

Since the government announced that expatriates would be entitled to purchase freehold property in certain developments, some of the banks have started offering mortgage options to expats. Mortgage conditions are different for expats as opposed to locals, especially in terms of how many years you can repay your loan for and how much deposit you have to put down. The mortgage industry is still in its infancy, and as more freehold residential developments near completion, there will be more on offer.

Looking over Bait Al Falaj

Interchange at Bait Al Falaj

White houses of Muscat

House in Kalbuh

A Al Azaiba   p.92   **C** As Seeb   p.94

B Al Ghubrah & Bawshar   p.93   **D** Al Khuwayr Al Janubiyyah   p.95

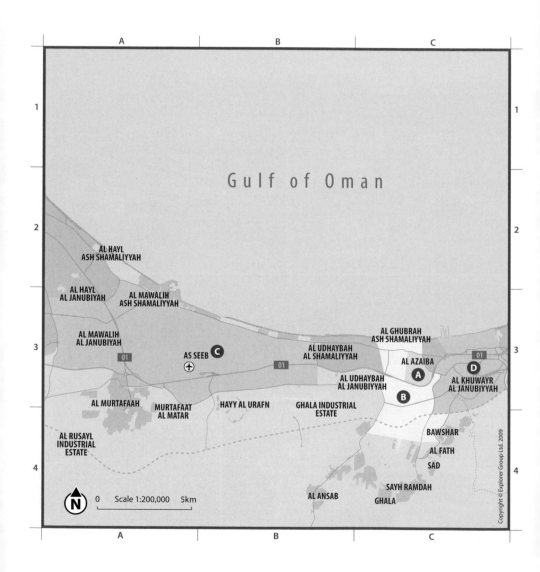

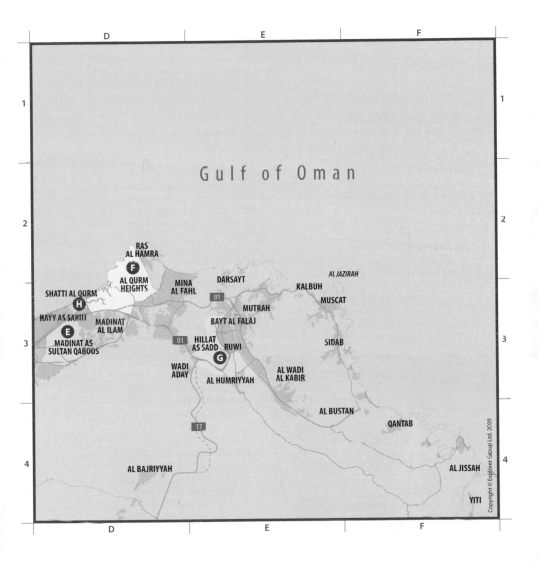

Residential Areas
Other options **Exploring** p.146

Once you have received confirmation that you are relocating to Oman, it can be difficult to choose which residential area you would prefer to live in – especially if your knowledge is still limited. Of course, your budget may affect your decision, and you may decide to live in an area that is a little further out of town and therefore a bit cheaper. You should also consider closeness to schools (if you have children) – the traffic situation in Muscat is currently bearable but you don't want to get stuck in a jam every morning on your school run. Also important is the proximity of entertainment venues – if you've got an exorbitant taxi fare to pay every time you go out anywhere it might deter even the most social of butterflies.

That said, every area of Muscat has its advantages and disadvantages, and with Muscat being a relatively small city you should be able to get to most places in under half an hour, no matter where you live. The following pages will give you some insight into the various residential areas, but remember that nothing beats getting in the car and exploring on your own.

Area **A** C3 p.90
See also Map 6

Al Azaiba

Al Azaiba merges with Al Ghubrah to the east and As Seeb to the west and is mostly a residential area but is fast becoming a business district.

Best Points
The beautiful long stretch of beach is a big plus.

Accommodation

Large villas on the beach are sought after and prices are very steep. Old and new villas are available with gardens or paved areas and maid's accommodation. Some landlords can smell a naive expat a mile away and may quote you an inflated price if they think you don't know better, so do some price comparisons before you agree to anything.

Worst Points
There are not many shops or amenities.

Shopping & Amenities

There are plenty of shops in neighbouring areas to keep you in stock of everything, but nothing of note locally apart from a few large car dealerships and service centres which line the road parallel to the highway, and Al Safeer supermarket.

Entertainment & Leisure

Endless sandy beaches will keep you busy outdoors. There is not much in the way of dining or nightlife in the area, but it is a short drive to some great restaurants in neighbouring areas.

Villas in Al Azaiba

Healthcare

There are no clinics or hospitals to speak of in the area, although you'll find plenty of medical facilities a short drive away.

Education

Nurseries are popping up all over the place.

Traffic & Parking

Al Azaiba is mostly a residential area, so you won't face too much frustration on the roads. Parking is easy to find. However, there is ongoing construction which might lead to diversions and occasional delays.

Safety & Annoyances

Lurking youths 'hanging out' and stray dogs roaming around are the two main annoyances, but as long as you pick your neighbourhood carefully you should be fine. Stray dogs are usually dealt with by the ROP.

Area **B** *C3 p.90*
See also Map 6

Al Ghubrah Ash Shamaliyyah & Bawshar

This area covers a large expanse from the beach to the mountains and is within easy reach of many businesses and the main Sultan Qaboos highway.

Best Points
The scenery in Bawshar is fantastic.

Accommodation

Accommodation is mainly two-storey villas, with a few apartment blocks above the shops and businesses in Ghubrah. Rents are lower in Bawshar and you have the advantage of a spectacular view of the sand dunes and mountains. Oasis Residence has some options for shopping, eating out plus a bakery and health club. The Dolphin Complex is also popular with families because of the leisure club facilities (including pool, tennis court and gym), the safe outdoor play area for kids and licensed restaurant.

Worst Points
Peak-hour traffic congestion and ongoing roadworks make this a hotspot for traffic jams.

Shopping & Amenities

The biggest and best supermarket in Muscat – Lulu Center – is located just off the Bawshar Roundabout, between Bawshar and Ghubrah. There are also a variety of small shops in Ghubrah selling everything from fabrics to fertiliser. While this means you can usually buy essential items at all hours, it also results in a certain amount of traffic congestion, particularly at peak times.

Entertainment & Leisure

There are three hotels in the area: the Bowshar Hotel, Park Inn and Chedi. The Bowshar is basic and not a particularly great haunt for western expats, while the Chedi is spectacular in its understated Zen-like architecture and superbly decadent restaurant. The Chedi also has one of Oman's most popular and luxurious spas. Park Inn is a great business hotel with rooftop pool and several restaurants.

Healthcare

Muscat Private Hospital – the main healthcare choice for expats – is located here. It offers a complete range of in-patient and out-patient facilities, and has a 24 hour emergency room (24 592 600). See p.120 for more information.

Traditional Muscat

Education

There are various Arabic and Indian schools in the area, but no education facilities for western expat children.

Traffic & Parking

The Ghubrah Roundabout has undergone construction to ease the flow of heavy traffic, which usually congests the area. The smaller 'Sail' roundabout is now a junction for the same reason. At peak times (mornings, lunchtimes and evenings) you might find a few traffic backups that could delay you for five minutes or so.

Safety & Annoyances

Construction in Ghubrah can really slow down traffic.

Area **C** *B3 p.90*
See also Map 4

Best Points
Lower rents and larger houses, and some of Muscat's best shopping right on your doorstep.

Worst Points
Out of town location means lots of time in the car and expensive taxi fares.

As Seeb

This is not usually the first choice for expats when looking for a home, mainly due to the distance from the city centre and all the facilities they will probably desire (such as schools and medical services). However, many are now moving to the area due to lack of accommodation in other parts of town.

Accommodation
Rents are a little lower this side of the airport, and villas are spacious with more likelihood of a small garden or paved area outside. If you don't mind travelling a few extra minutes in the car, this is a great opportunity to live in a much bigger villa at a lower price.

Shopping & Amenities
It doesn't get much better than having Muscat's two largest shopping malls right on your doorstep. Markaz Al Bahja (p.296) and Muscat City Centre (p.298)

Fountain on As Seeb Street

have all the large shops you will need, and you will find plenty of smaller local shops in As Seeb town and Seeb souk itself. As Seeb is also home to all the garden centres, which are located in a row on the same street. Park at one end and walk down.

Entertainment & Leisure
There is a cinema in Markaz Al Bahja Centre, as well as a super play area that will keep your kids busy the year round. This is particularly useful during summer, but during the cooler months there is plenty of white sandy beach to have fun on, as well as a beach park. The Golden Tulip Seeb is predominantly a business hotel, although it does have a few restaurants, including one on the roof which is excellent in winter, and some good leisure facilities. The Seeb International Exhibition Centre is nearby.

Healthcare
The area is home to various small clinics offering private outpatient treatment to all nationalities. It is also the location of the Sultan Qaboos University Hospital, which is not usually available to expats unless you require treatment that is not available at one of the city's private hospitals.

Education
Sultan Qaboos University is in the area, and although this is a reputable institution it is only for Omanis. It is, however, an establishment that hires quite a few international lecturers.

Traffic & Parking
Traffic can be busy around the airport area but a new flyover has helped and it is much calmer in As Seeb town and in Al Hayl. The highway can become a bit of a racetrack beyond the airport, so keep your wits about you. Also beware of stray goats crossing in front of you. On the whole though the roads in the area are good.

Safety & Annoyances

The crime rate is reportedly rising here, but is still very low. Be sensible with protecting yourself and your property as you would anywhere else. While you may be able to hear the odd plane taking off at the nearby airport, this should not be too much bother.

Area **D** *C3 p.90*
See also Map 7

Al Khuwayr Al Janubiyyah

Al Khuwayr is fast becoming a desirable place to live. Your neighbours are likely to be Omanis or expats from the subcontinent and tend to keep to themselves, apart from some of the children who will think nothing of using your parked car as a goalpost.

Best Points
The beautiful mountain backdrop and reasonable rents.

Accommodation

Al Khuwayr offers mainly two-storey villas, but also many apartments in the business district which runs along the road parallel to the highway.

Worst Points
Traffic congestion, particularly during peak times.

Shopping & Amenities

There are some big name electrical shops, local home furnishing stores, clothing stores and art supply stores located along the slip road and off the Al Khuwayr Roundabout towards Madinat As Sultan Qaboos.

Entertainment & Leisure

The Radisson Hotel is superbly located in the area with a backdrop of White Mountain and the Taimur Mosque (if you can see past the motorway construction). It houses bars and restaurants, particularly the excellent Tajin Grill (p.322) and a swimming pool to keep you entertained. Opposite the hotel are a number of shisha cafes with their plastic tables and chairs spilling out onto the pavement, and which sell food and fresh juices. These are very popular with locals and expats alike, and a great place to spend a cool evening with friends, watching football or politics on the big-screen TV.

Healthcare

There are many small clinics offering a variety of medical treatments.

Education

Residential street in Al Khuwayr

Al Khuwayr is home to the College of Technology, which seems to be expanding at an alarming rate judging by the number of cars parked within a one-kilometre radius. It is not open to expat students.

Traffic & Parking

Flagrant disregard for parking regulations around the mosque at prayer time can be interesting – it's amazing to see just how far people will go to avoid having to walk any distance. The roundabout becomes a carpark and all roads leading from it are lined on both sides with double-parked vehicles.

Safety & Annoyances

Some of the younger residents and students like to practise 'doughnuts' and other noisy tricks in their cars and beach buggies when most people are trying to sleep.

Area **E** *D3 p.91*
See also Map 11

Madinat As Sultan Qaboos

Fondly known as 'Little Britain', this area is extremely popular with western expats and young families.

Best Points
MSQ is a tranquil, leafy suburb that comes with a great range of amenities.

Accommodation

MSQ has a mixture of older villas with established gardens, swanky new apartment blocks with swimming pools, and garden courts. It is one of the most prized areas sought after by expats, due to its proximity to the British School and American British Academy, and it has soaring rental prices to reflect the fact.

Shopping & Amenities

Worst Points
Traffic in the mornings and around the Home Centre junction, plus escalating rents.

It's all here – there is a large Al Fair supermarket (with a pork room), an off-licence, a travel agent, a vet, a medical centre, huge furniture shop (Home Centre), Tavola, Busy Bees and much more.

Entertainment & Leisure

D'Arcy's and Costa Coffee are popular with ladies of leisure, and there is a Starbucks in the area too. Pavo Real is a lively Mexican hotspot that serves up fantastic margaritas and burritos, and Kargeen Caffé serves food inspired by Arabia in a jungle-themed atmosphere. If all the great dining outlets leave you feeling like you've overindulged, you can burn it all off in Adam's Gym.

Healthcare

The Medident Centre offers general medical care, as well as dentistry and prenatal care. It is staffed by expats.

Education

The British School of Muscat (BSM) follows the English National Curriculum and has been established in Muscat since 1971. Apart from being an excellent educational establishment, BSM also contributes to the community by allowing its facilities to be used for various activities (such as dance classes, karate and singing groups). It is likely that you'll be put on a waiting list. The Scientific Nursery is also popular with expat mums, as are new nurseries like Teddy's.

Madinat As Sultan Qaboos

Traffic & Parking

Parking can get a little busy around Al Fair, but there are other parking areas dotted about so you will never have to walk far. Traffic at the junction near Home Centre can hold you back, so avoid lunchtimes if possible. Drop-off time in the mornings around the schools and nurseries can also be tricky.

Safety & Annoyances

Due to the popularity of the area with young families, there are ladies with prams everywhere so watch your driving.

Area F D2 p.91
See also Map 8

Best Points
*Due to its hilly setting,
Qurm has some
amazing views.*

Worst Points
*The traffic around
Qurm junction can
get quite congested at
peak times.*

Al Qurm (Including Qurm Heights)

Qurm is home to the Petroleum Development Oman complex, which is a private residential area and club for PDO employees and their families. Its high location means it has the benefit of breezes, which can be a godsend on stuffy days. The area is attractive and is home to many different nationalities.

Accommodation

Older villas and palatial mansions wind their way down the hills, often with great views of the beach or the city. Rents are not cheap due to a shortage of PDO housing so very few private villas are available.

Shopping & Amenities

Shopaholics will enjoy living in Qurm, as it is home to four large shopping centres, including Qurm City Centre (p.299) containing some

Contemporary villa in Qurm

big-name brands, a host of fabric shops, a fancy dress shop, a pet shop, a selection of banks and three big supermarkets, including Carrefour in Qurm City Centre.

Entertainment & Leisure

There is no shortage of leisure options in the area. You'll find a selection of restaurants, some of which are in the Crowne Plaza Muscat (which also boasts a health club and a great swimming pool). Kids will be able to spend hours in Al Marah Land (a well-equipped amusement park), and you could spend many a cool evening strolling around the adjacent Qurm National Park. In terms of beaches, you've got Al Marjan beach and the long stretch of beach running from Qurm to Azaiba and beyond.

Healthcare

Qurm is home to the Al Hayat Polyclinic, Al Masaraat Clinic and various smaller clinics.

Education

Muscat Private School, offering an international curriculum to both local and expat children from kindergarten to A-Level, is in Qurm.

Traffic & Parking

There is a healthy amount of free parking around the shopping centres, although in some areas a 50 baisa ticket is required. Traffic can get congested around the Qurm junction.

Safety & Annoyances

The 'PDO Pong' is sometimes noticeable if the wind blows in a certain direction. This is just an odour from the PDO petrochemical plant, and it is harmless.

Area ⑤ E3 p.91
See also Map 12

Ruwi

Ruwi is home to the Central Business District area of Muscat. Ruwi High Street comes alive in the evenings as people throng the streets and the roadside cafes.

Best Points
You can pick up a good range of fake designer items here.

Accommodation

As Ruwi is predominantly a business area, accommodation is mainly in the form of low-cost apartments.

Shopping & Amenities

Ruwi is fantastic for little fabric shops and pirate DVDs. There is also a large Lulu Centre, and many shops selling sunglasses and cheap clothing.

Worst Points
There is a lot of traffic throughout the area.

Entertainment & Leisure

Star Cinema shows Bollywood and Arabic releases and the odd Hollywood movie too. There are plenty of roadside Indian and Arabic restaurants where you can get a decent curry or a tasty shawarma for pocket change. The Golden Oryx (p.312) is an excellent dining venue, serving up Chinese and Thai food in an authentic setting. The Al Falaj Hotel houses Muscat's only Japanese restaurant and a top-floor bar with a fantastic view of the nightlights of the CBD. The Sheraton is currently under construction.

Healthcare

The Badr Al Samaar Hospital is located near Ruwi Church, and there are also several homeopathic clinics, a Chinese herbal medicine clinic and various smaller clinics dotted around the area.

Education

Ruwi is home to the Pakistan International School, but there are no educational establishments offering English or American curriculums.

Traffic & Parking

Traffic is very busy and parking can be a problem. You may find a spot on one of the roads behind Ruwi High Street, or near the Lulu Centre.

Safety & Annoyances

With all the comings and goings of the local businesses in the area, and the resulting traffic, Ruwi can be noisy.

Buildings in the CBD

Area **H** *D3 p.91*
See also Map 8

Shati Al Qurm

Shati is home to the embassies and their staff, and is a highly desirable area near the beach and official offices.

Best Points
The area is close to a beautiful beach and a wide range of leisure options.

Accommodation

Unfortunately, living in Shati Al Qurm is out of most people's leagues. The area is characterised by huge villas with stained glass windows and mature trees, as

Worst Points
The beach gets very congested, especially during low tide.

well as rows of private parking spaces for numerous cars outside. There is an apartment block above Bareeq Al Shatti mall (p.294) but it's on the pricey side.

Shati Al Qurm

Shopping & Amenities

There is plenty here – the Al Sarooj Centre houses a big Al Fair and a selection of smaller shops. Next to the centre there is a Shell petrol station with a large 24 hour convenience store. Bareeq Al Shatti mall (p.294) is a great spot for a coffee while Jawharat Al Shatti is a handy shopping complex with restaurants, a post office, some souvenir shops, a party balloon outlet, a card shop and a nail bar for that all-important manicure.

Entertainment & Leisure

Al Shatti Cinema is popular at weekends – it shows all the current Hollywood releases and is conveniently located next to an icecream shop, which is handy for afterwards. There is also a bowling nearby. The Al Deyar restaurant has a collection of outside tables and offers shisha and snacks late into the night. Future Gym is next door and is well-equipped for both men and women. The beach is a stone's throw away and popular for football, walking and jogging. Starbucks, Costa Coffee and Darcy's Kitchen all have outdoor seating areas that are great for watching the world go by. The InterContinental Muscat (p.31) has an excellent choice of restaurants and bars, as well as one of the best health clubs in the city.

Healthcare

Muscat Eye Centre is nearby and also Emirates Dermatology Clinic and Precision Dental Clinic. If it's cosmetic surgery you're after, Cosmesurge is located in the Al Sarooj Centre.

Education

Al Zumurrud Montessori Kindergarten is located in a bright, modern villa in Shati Al Qurm, just past the Grand Hyatt. The kindergarten has a high staff-to-child ratio.

Traffic & Parking

There are many places for parking near the shops and cinema and also near the hospital. Traffic is not a problem but you may wait a while at roundabouts during rush hour.

Safety & Annoyances

Bad car parking can result in scratched paintwork and there are lots of local youths cruising in their cars which can be intimidating.

Customs ◄

Customs officers may retain certain items such as CDs, DVDs, books and even photo albums, for further investigation. You will get these items back once they have been checked, although it may take several weeks.

Moving Services

Moving house can be stressful, especially if you are relocating to a new country. You can reduce the stress by planning the move well, and enlisting the help of a professional moving service.

When moving your furniture to or from Oman, you can ship it by air or by sea. Airfreight is quick, and is good for small consignments and the essential things you can't live without. But to move a whole houseful of furniture you need to arrange a container by sea, and this will take several weeks. You can get a 20 or 40 foot container, depending on how much stuff you are moving. If you're really lucky and you know someone moving at the same time as you, you could share a container.

Either way, ensure that you use a reputable company to pack your goods and make all the arrangements. If you are unlucky enough to move to Oman in the height of the summer (July or August), your belongings will travel at sustained high temperatures in the container ship, so some of your plastic items may warp and your china might have little surface cracks from the heat. A reputable moving company should be able to offer you advice on how to minimise damage by using proper packaging. A company with a wide international network is usually the best option.

When your shipment arrives in Muscat you may be called to the customs department so that you can be present when your crates are opened. This is done to ensure that you are not bringing anything illegal or inappropriate into the country. Someone from your company (such as the PRO) may be able to stand in for you, and you will only have to go if something suspect is found. The process can be exhausting, because the search can take a few hours, often out in the heat, and you will have to watch your carefully packed boxes being unceremoniously rummaged through.

Relocation Experts

Relocation experts offer a range of services to help you settle into your new life in Oman as quickly as possible. Practical help ranges from finding accommodation or schools for your children to connecting a telephone or information on medical care. In addition, they will often offer advice on the way of life in the city, putting people in touch with social networks to help them get established in their new lives. The Specialists can help you search for a house or school, provide orientation and settling in services, and even help you get to grips with culture shock.

Smooth Moves

- Get more than one quote – some companies will match lower quotes to get the job.
- Make sure that all items are covered by insurance.
- Make sure that you have a copy of the inventory and that each item is listed.
- Don't be shy about requesting packers to repack items if you are not satisfied.
- Take photos of the packing process, to use for evidence if you need to claim.
- Carry customs-restricted goods (DVDs, videos or books) with you: it's easier to open a suitcase in an air-conditioned airport than empty a box out in the sun.

Removal Companies

Eagle Global Logistics	24 495 417	www.circle-muscat.com
Gulf Agency Company (GAC)	24 479 155	www.gacworld.com
Inchcape Shipping Services	24 701 291	www.iss-shipping.com
Khimjis Ramdas (Project & Logistic Group)	24 786 123	www.khimjiramdas.com
Middle East Shipping & Transport Co	24 790 024	www.suhailbahwangroup.com
Yusuf Bin Ahmed Kanoo & Co	24 712 252	www.kanooshipping.com

Furniture Shopping ◄
See the Home
Furnishings table in
the Shopping section
(p.258) for a list of
shops where you can
buy everything you
need to make your new
house a dream home.

Furnishing Accommodation
Other options
Home Furnishing & Accessories p.276,
Second-Hand Items p.285

If you are a new arrival in Oman and moving into a new home, chances are that you will need to buy some furniture. Most properties are unfurnished, and that means not only will you have no furniture, but in most cases you will have no electrical items or white goods either (not even a cooker). Not all villas have fitted wardrobes. Oman is home to several big furniture shops so no matter what your tastes, you'll find something you like. A lot of furniture is locally or regionally made, and is often extremely ornate. Simpler styles can be found in IDdesign (Markaz Al Bahja) and Home Centre (City Plaza). The world famous Swedish furniture store IKEA is just a few hours down the road in Dubai, so you can load your car up with flat-pack furniture.

Tailor in Mutrah

Second-Hand Furniture
The population of Muscat is fairly transitory, with people coming and going all the time. As a result there is quite a busy second-hand furniture market, so keep an eye on the supermarket noticeboards. Look out also for adverts for local garage sales, where families will sell all the stuff they are not taking with them at rock-bottom prices.

Tailors
Other options **Talloring** p.287

There are plenty of tailors in Oman and this comes in handy if you want some curtains or bedding made up for you. Most tailors, even dressmakers, should be able to knock up simple curtains or sheets. However, if you are after something fancy, like swags and tails or furniture upholstery, it's best to look around for someone who specialises in this kind of work. Test a tailor with a small job first.

Tailors		
Ahmed Abdul Rahman Traders	Ruwi	24 787 756
Assarain Textiles	Ruwi	24 830 149
Dress Unique	Madinat As Sultan Qaboos	24 607 136
European Style Tailoring	Al Qurm	24 566 214
Mehdi Store	Ruwi	24 814 200
Mutrah Tailoring House	Ruwi	24 701 960
Raymond Shop	Ruwi	24 561 142
Talia	Al Qurm	24 566 066
Women Today	Al Khuwayr	24 488 580

Household Insurance

As you probably won't own your house in Oman, it's easy to take a more relaxed attitude to household insurance. The sultanate is very safe and the crime rate extremely low, but burglaries do occur and it's predominantly expat residential areas that are the targets. It is a good idea to arrange household insurance against theft or damage. A range of reputable insurance companies are listed below. Many national and international insurance companies have offices in Muscat, offering all the standard services. To take out a policy you will need confirmation of your address, your passport, a list of household contents and valuation, and invoices for any items over RO 250.

Household Insurance		
Al Ahlia Insurance Company	24 709 441	www.alahliaoman.com
ALICO AIG	24 707 827	www.alico-measa.com
Arabia Insurance	24 793 299	www.arabiainsurance.com
AXA Insurance	24 400 100	www.axa-gulf.com
Dhofar Insurance Company	24 423 075	www.dhofarinsurance.com
Oman United Insurance Company	24 703 990	www.ouic-oman.com
Risk Management Services	24 704 004	www.rmsllc.com
Royal & Sun Alliance Insurance Oman	24 478 318	rsagroup.com.om

Laundry Services

Although you will not find self-service launderettes, there are numerous laundries in Muscat. As well as dry cleaning and laundry, they all offer an ironing service. If you have specific cleaning or ironing instructions, make sure these are noted when you drop off your laundry – creases in trousers, for instance, are standard, so speak up if you don't want them pressed into your jeans.

Compensation policies for lost or damaged items vary. But even though some laundries may seem disorganised from the piles and piles of stuff behind the counter waiting to be ironed or collected, losses are rare. Some of the more upmarket laundry chains may offer a pick-up and drop-off service.

Laundry Services		
Al Tayyibat Services	Madinat As Sultan Qaboos	24 695 599
Assem Trading & Contg. Est	Wadi Adai	24 560 926
Grand Sultanate Laundry	Hamriya	24 833 097
Ibn Iqbal Trading Est	Al Khoud	24 540 082
Kwik-Kleen	Al Qurm	24 561 213
	Madinat As Sultan Qaboos	24 604 785
	Wadi Kabir	24 816 749
	Al Khuwayr	24 483 581
Mawa Trading	Wadi Kabir	24 810 535
National Laundry & Dry Cleaners	Salalah	23 226 140
Snowhite Laundry & Dry Cleaners	Bawshar	24 597 088
	Nizwa	25 412 277
	Salalah	23 299 176
	Sohar	26 843 519
	Sur	25 542 319
Wadi Al Khuwair Laundry	Al Khuwayr	24 485 274

A Helping Hand ◀

Moving to Oman is made easier with a helping hand from Sununu Muscat, a relocation and lifestyle management company for corporate and individual clients. Sununu Muscat will short list properties that match requirements, help process school applications, provide orientation and offer useful tips to help you settle with ease. From the ideal home to interior design and even house plants, Sununu Muscat can help make a home away from home. For more info call 99 800 613 or email info@ sununumuscat.com.

Domestic Help

Other options **Entry Visa** p.60

One of the perks of expat life is how common it is for people to have domestic help. Most expat families have some sort of home help, whether it's a full-time, live-in housemaid, or a part-time ironing lady. Most domestic helpers come from India, Sri Lanka, Bangladesh, Indonesia, Pakistan or the Philippines, and the only restriction in terms of nationality is that you are prohibited from employing someone from the same country as you (or someone related to you).

Azooz Manpower (24 831 448) and Friends Manpower (24 478 153) are two domestic help agencies in Oman. When you employ a domestic helper, you must sponsor them and provide accommodation. Most villas have servant's quarters (an independent room, usually fairly small, with a private bathroom). You have a duty of care to your domestic helper, and you must make all the arrangements (and payments) for their residence visa, medical test, and labour card. You are also obliged to pay for their medical bills and provide them with a return flight to their home country every two years.

The visa will cost you RO 20 and the labour card will cost you RO 70. It is up to you what salary you want to pay your domestic helper and there is no stipulated minimum wage. However, part-time helpers (two to four hours per day, five days a week) usually earn RO 70 to RO 100 per month, and full time helpers (eight hours a day, six days a week) usually earn RO 100 to RO 120 per month. If you hire a full-time, live-in helper, you should be clear with them at the beginning what duties they will be responsible for, including any evening babysitting. Part-time helpers usually charge extra for babysitting (RO 1–1.5 per hour).

Sponsoring a maid is a substantial financial commitment so make sure you have the right person. The best way to find a good helper is by word of mouth, so keep your ear to the ground in case a 'friend of a friend' is going back home and leaving behind their loyal, trustworthy maid who is good with pets and kids. You could also look on supermarket noticeboards and in newspaper classifieds, but remember to check references if you are taking on someone unknown. There are several reliable maid agencies who can recommend a good maid and in some cases, help you with the paperwork.

Traditional lamps

Babysitting & Childcare

Childcare – the dilemma facing all working parents. Options are limited and there is no network of childminders like you might find in your home country. If you have a live-in maid, and you trust her with your children, then you have a round-the-clock babysitter. Alternatively you could pay your part-time maid an extra hourly rate (around RO 1.5) to babysit for you when you need her.

Word of mouth is a great way to find a babysitter, whether it's a friend's maid or a responsible teenager needing pocket money. Domestic help agencies may offer babysitting services, although there is no guarantee you will be able to get the same person each time (which means leaving your child with a stranger). You could also try asking at nursery schools – often teaching assistants will babysit in the evenings to make some extra money.

Domestic Services

Having maintenance done in your villa or apartment is usually just a case of making a quick call to the landlord. He is responsible for any plumbing or electrical work (unless otherwise stated in your lease), and will probably use a specific maintenance company every time. This is good if they know what they are doing, but landlords will often go for 'cheaper' rather than 'better'.

If you need some work done that your landlord won't pay for, you can use the services of a plumber, electrician or handyman. The table lists companies specialising in carpet cleaning, carpentry, plumbing, painting and electrical services, although these companies may also offer other services too. Often word of mouth is the best way to find a trustworthy company that shows up on time, does the job that needs doing, and doesn't charge you an arm and a leg.

Domestic Services		
Al Ahid Trading & Contracting	24 817 509	Carpentry
Al Besat Al Hariri	24 692 249	Carpet cleaning & repair
Al Wadi Al Kabir Carpentry	24 812 856	Carpentry
Bahwan Engineering Co	24 597 510	Plumbing
Cape East & Partners	24 496 469	Painters
International Sanitation Co	24 592 351	Plumbing
London Cleaning & Maintenance	24 603 006	Carpet cleaning
National Electrical Contractors	24 571 363	Electrical services
Ocean Centre	24 707 833	Carpet cleaning
Ruwi Furnishing	24 521 118	Curtains & blinds
Shafan Trading	24 692 058	Electrical services
Specialised Technical Contractors	24 788 640	Painters
West Coast Trading	24 535 680	Carpet cleaning

Pets

There is a mixed attitude towards pets in Oman, so if you are an animal lover and have a pet, it is advisable to keep them under strict control at all times. There are cases of animal abuse, mainly caused by a lack of education in the proper care of animals. The Animal Rescue Centre of Oman (ARCO) aims to improve animal welfare in the sultanate. It has a neutering programme to help control the feral cat population, and also rehome unwanted cats and dogs wherever possible. Contact ARCO on 92 501 366 for more information or to report animal abuse.

Cats & Dogs

It is a commonly held misconception that Muslims dislike dogs and this explains why there are some cases of animal cruelty in the Middle East. The Quran forbids the maltreatment of animals, including dogs, so the problem does not have a religious foundation. In the Arab culture in general, however, dogs are not held in high regard and are not usually seen as fluffy, lovable members of the family. On the other hand, there are many dog owners in Oman.

If you are looking for a dog, contact ARCO (Animal Rescue Centre of Oman) on 92 501 366. The centre rescues, cares for and re-homes maltreated and unwanted cats and dogs. All dogs must be registered with the municipality and inoculations must be kept up to date. Puppies should be vaccinated at six weeks old and then annually. It is recommended that cats and dogs are sterilised to stop them from roaming (and adding to the stray population), although this is not compulsory.

Stray cats are a huge problem in Oman – they are often called 'string' cats because they are as thin as a piece of string. Every now and then the municipality has a crackdown where they round up and shoot or gas strays and it doesn't warn when this will happen so best to make sure your pet wears a collar at all times.

If you do adopt a stray, make sure it is vaccinated, dewormed, and sprayed for fleas. Oman is not a rabies-free country, so be very careful. If you are bitten by a stray animal (cats can carry rabies as well as dogs), go to Accident & Emergency at Khoula Hospital in Al Wattayah for an anti-rabies shot (only government hospitals have stocks of the vaccine).

Pet Shops

There is only one pet shop in Muscat, located downstairs in Sabco Centre. They have fish, birds, mice, hamsters, rabbits, dogs, cats and even a snake or two. Conditions in which the animals are kept leave something to be desired and prices are not cheap. You can pay up to RO 400 for a dog and RO 200 for a 'pedigree' cat (sort of Persian or Siamese), but you won't get papers. These cats are locally bred – genuine pedigree animals, with papers, come from Eastern Europe and will cost you twice as much. You can have your cat or dog vaccinated at the pet shop and the first set of jabs is free, but they don't give all the vaccinations your pet will need. It's better to pay a visit to a reputable vet who can provide the essential rabies vaccination and give your new pet a check-up.

Pets Boarding	
Creatures Trading	24 563 721
Dr Khaled	24 562 263
Pet Home	99 324 606

Vets & Kennels

Although there is not a huge number of vets practising in Muscat, you can still find good quality healthcare for your pet. Dr Khaled, located behind the Capital Commercial Centre in Qurm, is well known and offers services above and beyond medical treatment. He can also arrange paperwork and procedures involved in bringing your pet into Oman, having it registered, or taking it home again. He also offers boarding kennels for cats and dogs – handy if you are going away in the summer. Tafani Veterinary Clinic is based in Al Azaiba, but they also offer a mobile vet service run by Louise. If your pet hates travelling in the car, or you'd prefer the vet to come to your home, Louise will pop round to treat your pet.

One of the advantages of having a live-in domestic helper is that they can care for your pets while you are on holiday. Alternatively, you can book your pet into boarding kennels, Dr Khaled offers pet boarding, and Pet Home has a number of fully air-conditioned, spacious kennels for dogs.

Bringing Your Pet To Oman

There are a number of regulations regarding the importing of your pet, and the procedure involves its fair share of paperwork and time. Before you leave your home country, you need to make sure that all your pet's vaccinations are up to date and stamped in its veterinary record booklet (which should be in English). The rabies vaccination, in particular, should be up to date. Ask your vet which other vaccinations are required. You will also need two health certificates from the vet in your home country: one should be dated no more than six months

Requirements For Importing Cats & Dogs

- Dogs and cats must be fully vaccinated, including for rabies, at least one month and no more than 12 months before arrival in Oman.
- The rabies vaccination sticker must be applied to the vaccination card.
- Dogs and cats must be at least 4 months old.
- An import permit must be obtained from the ministry of agriculture before arrival. The permit is valid for one month.
- The original vaccination card and health certificate must travel with the animal, and they must be in English or have an English translation.

before your departure, and one should be obtained 10 days before your pet is due to travel. Check which airlines will carry pets, and book a space for yours.

Veterinary Clinics	
Al Marai Al Omaniya	26 840 660
Dr Fathy A Fadil	24 705 974
Al Hossan Pet Surgery	24 562 263
Dr Marie-Christine Maufrais-Vandi	24 560 459
Royal Vet Royal Stables	24 420 322
Samha for Veterinary Services	26 882 927
Tafani Veterinary Clinic	24 491 971
Veterinary Centre	24 699 079

With the help of your sponsor, you need to get a pet import certificate (RO 5) from the Ministry of Agriculture and Fisheries Animal Health Department (24 696 300). This certificate, along with a copy of the vaccination records and health certificates, should accompany your pet on arrival into Oman. Certificates must be produced at the airport on arrival of the animal to the quarantine office. If the authorities are not satisfied with the certificates, they can quarantine your pet for six months (so it is essential to check with your local vet and the Oman embassy in your home country about the exact requirements).

Clearing your pet at Seeb International Airport will take two to three hours. Although there are no special facilities for animals, they are placed in a special ventilated area where they won't suffer from the high temperatures.

Taking Your Pet Home

When you leave Oman you will need to start the procedure for taking your pet home a few weeks before your departure. Check with your airline about their policy on pets – if your pet is small enough you may be allowed to take it as carry-on luggage, rather than as cargo.

The regulations for exporting your pet depend on the country you are taking them to, so check beforehand. The basic requirements are usually the same though. You will need a valid vaccination card (which should have been issued not more than one year and not less than 30 days before. You need to get a pet health certificate from the municipality or the Ministry of Agriculture and Fisheries (normally issued one week before departure). Contact your airline to find out the best place to get a travel box that meets their regulations (normally it is made of wood or fibreglass).

For more information, a vet or kennels in your destination country, or the airline you are using, can give you more specific regulations such as quarantine rules.

Mosque entrance

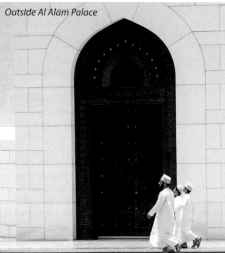

Outside Al Alam Palace

Electricity & Water

Electricity & Water
Electricity and water services are provided by the Omani government, although there are plans to privatise them eventually. The electricity supply is 220/240 volts and 50 cycles and there are few shortages or stoppages. The socket type is the three-pin British system. The mains tap water is purified eight times and is fine to drink but can taste chlorinated. Locally bottled mineral or desalinated water is a cheap alternative and there are many brands available. Bottled water is usually served in hotels and restaurants – make sure the seal on the bottle is unbroken.

Water and electricity services are supplied by the government and are generally efficient and reliable. There is no mains gas service but bottled gas (LPG) is available for cooking. Power cuts – lasting from a few minutes to several hours – occur every now and then but rarely pose a major inconvenience. It helps to have a stock of candles and torches handy, just in case. Utility bills are paid at Oman Investment & Finance Company (OIFC) or through your bank or ATM. To use the ATM service, you have to register your details by phone (the bank will have the number). Once you are registered, it means you can pay your bills outside banking hours, without having to stand in queues. The bank transfer system is slower than paying directly to OIFC so allow a few extra days so that you don't get disconnected. Wherever you pay, make sure your bill is stamped and that you keep it for reference – you may need it for proof of payment at a later date.

Electricity

The electricity supply in Oman is 220/240 volts and 50 cycles. Sockets correspond to the British three-pin plug but many appliances are sold with two-pin plugs, so you will need lots of adaptors (available in any supermarket or corner shop) – better still, change all the plugs.

Water

Though some water comes from natural wells, there is not enough to service the country's needs so most of the supply is from the sea, processed at the desalination plant at Al Ghubrah. The main supply of water is very reliable but not all of Muscat's residential areas are connected to it. If your house is not, you will have to rely on a water bowser to fill up your tank every two or three days. Water trucks for domestic use are blue (the green ones carry non-potable water, for municipal garden watering and industrial use) and they are everywhere – just flag one down or ask your neighbours which 'water-man' they use. You will often see several trucks filling up at one of the water wells dotted around the city. Expect to pay around RO 25 a month for truck water. Global Water Services will deliver 24 hours (24 487 575).
If you are connected to the main supply, keep an eye on your bills and water meter; if you have an underground leak within your property boundary you could be held responsible for a hefty bill, even if you weren't aware of the leak.

In the heat of summer, it's unlikely you'll have the chance to take a refreshing cold shower. Water tanks are usually located on the roof, where they are heated to near boiling point by the

Water Suppliers	
Al Afia Water	25 544 555
Al Bayan	24 594 634
National Mineral Water Company	24 590 095
Oasis Water Company	24 446 392

sun, and you can't even stand under the shower because it's so hot. Between April and October, the only way to get a cool shower is to turn off your water heater, and use the hot water tap.
Oman's water is safe to drink as it is purified eight times. However, it is heavily chlorinated (which affects the taste) so most people prefer to drink one of the many locally bottled mineral waters. Apart from the coffee shops, all restaurants will supply bottled water. If in doubt, ask for a sealed bottle to be brought to your table. You can get 20 litre bottles of purified water for use at home, either with a hand pump or a water cooler. These are available from shops and supermarkets, and you pay a RO 6 deposit per bottle, and refills cost RO 1. Alternatively, get a company to deliver the water to your house.

Gas

Oman doesn't have mains gas but there are many suppliers of bottled gas. Gas canisters are available in various sizes, and you pay RO 15–20 as a deposit, and RO 3 per refill. Gas is delivered to houses by orange trucks

Gas Suppliers		
Al Khabourah Cooking Gas Factory	Sohar	24 811 689
General Contracting & Trading Co	Ghala	24 594 072
Mohsin Haider Darwish	Rusayl	24 446 112
	Ruwi	24 791 205
	Salalah	23 211 605
	Sur	25 545 451
	Sohar	26 846 349
Muscat Gases Company	Rusayl	24 446 030
Oman Industrial Gas Company	Al Wadi Al Kabir	24 813 012
	Ruwi	24 816 134

that drive around residential areas. If you need gas, just flag one of the trucks down; popular times for the gas run are late mornings, early evenings and on Fridays. Once you've found a supplier, get his mobile number and you'll be able to call him whenever you need more gas. Most will deliver any time up to 21:00.

Sewerage

All properties in Oman have septic tanks, which must be emptied regularly by one of the yellow sewerage trucks. The cost for having a septic tank emptied is between RO 10 and RO 14 each time, and you'll probably have to get it done about once a year (you'll know when it's time from the smell). If you need to order a sewerage truck, the easiest way is to call the number on the back of one of the yellow tankers, or ask a neighbour. Alternatively, call Oman Wastewater Services Company (24 693 412). The Oman Wastewater Services Company is currently undertaking a RO 350 million sewerage recycling project.

Rubbish Disposal & Recycling

The rubbish disposal system in Oman is efficient – it has to be, because the health hazards of mounds of domestic waste festering in the sweltering heat would be too great. Large metal containers (skips) are placed at regular intervals along residential streets and you just chuck your daily rubbish bags into them. Skips are emptied regularly by rubbish trucks (although not before the local 'bin cats' have had a good rummage).
There is a landfill site at Al Amerat – previously waste was just dumped in the desert. Unfortunately there are no recycling systems at present, the argument being that it would be too expensive to implement and educate people how to use it effectively.

Telephone

In 2005, Nawras began operating as an alternative mobile phone service provider in Oman, ending the monopoly held by the government-owned Oman Telecommunications Company (Omantel). Friendi Mobile came to the market in 2009, offering great coverage and flexible packages including prepaid recharge cards for amounts as low as 500 baisas. SIM cards start at RO 2 and users can call fellow Friendi customers for 39 baisas 24 hours a day. Customer service is offered in a number of languages including Arabic, English, Malayalam, Hindi, Urdu and Bengali.
Omantel remains the sole provider of landline and internet services, however. The organisation was recently privatised and has invested in the latest technology to enable it to offer an efficient service. The main complaint is the slow speed of internet access, but as the country moves increasingly towards broadband and wireless connection, this is less of an issue. The government's 'access for all' policy keeps prices low, and rates often decrease but hardly ever increase.

Now Offering Fantastic Features

- Flat rates across Oman
- Lowest call rates in the Sultanate
- 33 Bz only for calls to mobiles
- Single bill for phone and ADSL

عمانتل
Omantel

or more information visit your nearest Omantel counter or call 1300

ww.omantel.net.om

Landline Phones

It is unlikely that your accommodation will have an active phone line when you move in. To apply for a landline connection you should submit the following documents to Omantel: a completed application form (in English), your passport (and a copy), your visa, and a copy of your tenancy agreement. Once you have submitted your application it will be one to two weeks before you are connected. Be warned that is has been known to take much longer. If you need additional phone sockets, be sure to ask at the time of application. You pay a deposit of RO 200, and RO 10 per line installation. Quarterly rental is RO 3 and calls are charged according to distance and time, ranging from 3 to 75 baisas per minute (emergency calls are free). Off-peak rates apply on long distance calls all day Friday and on national commercial holidays. Omantel offers many additional services such as call waiting, call forwarding and conference calling. You can also use the Jibreen service – a prepaid phone card that can be used to make local or international calls from any landline or payphone. The card is available in denominations of RO 1.5, RO 3 and RO 5, is valid for 90 days from first call, and is charged at the payphone tariff. For more information and details visit the Omantel website (www.omantel.net.om), which lists services and charges.

Thuraya

Omantel offers the Thuraya system – a satellite-based GSM (mobile phone) service that is valuable for emergency communication when travelling outside standard GSM range. Although Oman's populated areas have GSM network coverage there are still empty spaces with no reception. If you're a regular camper and wadi basher, you may consider it worth buying a Thuraya phone – especially if you travel with small children or need to be accessible at all times for some reason. Thuraya currently provides access to 99 countries in Europe, the Middle East, Africa and Asia. The handset costs around RO 300 and doubles as a GPS receiver.

Mobile Phones

No Mobile When Mobile
It is against the law to use a mobile phone handset while you are driving, so if you like to talk behind the wheel you should use a hands-free kit. Failure to do so can result in you being pulled over and given a spot fine of RO 70.

Mobile phones, commonly referred to as GSMs, are an integral part of Oman life. Everybody has at least one, and they're probably used more than landlines. You can use your own handset or buy one in Oman – handsets are always sold independently of contracts and there's a wide range of brands available at reasonable prices. You'll usually find a good deal on a handset in Carrefour or the smaller mobile phone shops in shopping malls.

For help with your GSM, voicemail, SMS or other mobile services, call 1234 (toll free). Friendi, Oman Mobile and Nawras offer a huge range of services and it might be difficult to choose the provider you like best. The companies usually have information desks in various malls, so go along for a chat with one of their representatives or see www.friendimobile.om, www.omanmobile.om or www.nawras.com.om.

All organisations offer pre-paid and post-paid packages. You do not have to be a resident to get a mobile phone card (but you can only go for the pre-paid option if you are not a resident). If you do use a pre-paid GSM service, you can upload extra credit to your mobile by purchasing top-up cards from supermarkets, petrol stations or the respective kiosks.

If you're just visiting Oman, or still waiting for your residency to come through, you can use prepaid services from the providers. There are no contracts or monthly bills, and it is a popular option among residents too, both local and expat. You can use any GSM handset – just buy a SIM card from Friendi costing from RO 2 and you can make a call as soon as your starter kit is activated. The flexible recharge package allows you

SAIL
ACROSS
THE
SEAS
Connect worldwide
with more than 363
roaming partners
in 153 countries.
OMAN MOBILE

to top up your credit with any amount from 10 baisas, and a physical card isn't always necessary as a dealer can do this for you. Friendi's website also allows you to reserve any available phone number free of charge so you can pick one you've got a chance of remembering! Friendi is available at petrol stations, supermarkets and convenience stores across Oman.

Oman At Your Fingertips
The Omantel Yellow Pages can be accessed online at www.omantel-yellowpages.com.

The Hayyak kit from Oman Mobile (RO 30) includes a SIM card and a RO 5 top-up card. Top-up cards (valid for one year and in denominations of RO 1.5, RO 3, RO 5 and RO 10) are available from supermarkets and smaller shops displaying the Hayyak sign.

The Nawras prepaid service is called Mousbak, and you can buy the sim card (compatible with any GSM phone) from any Nawras outlet or kiosk. Mousbak recharge cards come in the denominations RO 1, RO 2, RO 4 and RO 8, and area available at all Nawras stores as well as at supermarkets and petrol stations.

Once you are a resident you can apply for a GSM contract; you'll need an application form and a copy of your passport, visa and labour/resident card. Both Oman Mobile and Nawras offer GSM contracts, and each has different terms and conditions. Visit their websites for more information (www.friendimobile.om, www.omanmobile.om or www.nawras.com.om).

Missing Mobile

Lost your mobile? Call 1234 to temporarily or permanently disconnect your number. You will have to provide the number of the document that you presented when you applied for your SIM card (probably your passport or labour card). To replace the SIM, you'll need to go to a branch of Oman Mobile with your essential documents in hand and a fee of RO 7. As soon as you have the new SIM card, your old one will be permanently disconnected. You can keep the same telephone number.

Useful Numbers

Frendi Mobile ▶ p.ii-iii, xiv, 54	98 400 000
Mobile phone customer services (Frendi, Oman Mobile, Nawras)	1234
Nawras	95 011 500
Oman country code (landlines & mobiles)	968
Oman Mobile ▶ p.109, 111, 113	24 474 000
Omantel customer services ▶ p.109, 111, 113	24 632 124
Omantel directory enquiries ▶ p.109, 111, 113	1318
Omantel internet help desk ▶ p.109, 111, 113	1313
Speaking clock	1306

Apart from the mobile phone network which has three providers, all other telecommunications are provided by Oman Telecommunications Company (Omantel).

National call charges are based on the area to which the calls are made. International direct dialling is possible to over 170 countries and surprisingly enough the charges are often reduced rather than increased. Rates are published in the telephone directory and the Omantel website (www.omantel.net.om).

All telephone numbers in Oman have changed from six digits to eight. If you see a landline number that is still six digits, simply add 24 before the number if it is in Muscat, 23 for Salalah, 25 for Nizwa or Sur, and 26 for Sohar. If you are still in doubt, call 1318 for directory assistance.

Public pay phones accept phone cards. Cards are available in values of RO 2, RO 3 and RO 5 from petrol stations, supermarkets and some smaller shops.

Internet

Other options **Websites** p.51, **Internet Cafes** p.337

As you'll notice from the quality of many local websites, the internet isn't as popular in Oman as elsewhere in the world. According to 2008 figures only 9.1% of the population are online. The sole internet service provider is Omantel and all sites are accessed through its proxy server. The proxy blocks any sites that are considered offensive to religious, moral, political or cultural sensitivities.

Fastest **Speed.**
Unbeatable **Price.**

The power of speed

or the first time in Oman, you can enjoy downloads at the incredible speed of
Mbps. With Omantel's 8 Mbps ADSL package. It's the ultimate solution if you
e a heavy user with multiple devices including computers, mobiles and gaming
nsoles. What's more, with totally unlimited usage and no traffic charge, you can
ownload at speeds that dazzle, whatever, whenever. Now, which other internet
ovider can promise you more?

so available in 512 Kbps, 1 Mbps, 2 Mbps & 4 Mbps
sit your nearest Omantel counter and get connected today

ww.omantel.net.om

You don't need to be an Omantel subscriber to surf the internet, as there is a 'Log n Surf' system. All you need is a computer with a modem and a regular phone line (visit www.omantel.net.om for more information).

When you sign up for an internet account with Omantel, you will be given an email address. It will be an eight-character user name, along with the omantel suffix (username@omantel.net.om).

There are various Wi-Fi spots around Muscat where you can enjoy high-speed internet access on your laptop without the need for a phone connection. New Wi-Fi sites are being added all the time, and you can find a list of outlets on www.ibhar.omantel.net.om. Wi-Fi is currently available at selected outlets in the Al Bustan Palace InterContinental Muscat, The Chedi, Al Harthy Complex, Capital Commercial Centre, Sabco Centre, MSQ Centre, Zakhir Mall, Jawharat Al Shatti Complex, Oman International Exhibition Centre, Radisson SAS Hotel, and Knowledge Oasis Muscat. You will need to buy a prepaid Ibhar card (available in denominations of RO 3, RO 5 and RO 15) and log in.

You can access the internet from any Omantel landline, using a computer and a 56Kbps modem. To get connected using your own landline (or one in your company's name), you need to apply at Omantel. There are several Omantel Customer Service Outlets in Muscat – check the website for details of the one closest to you. You'll need to hand over a completed application form, copies of your passport, visa and labour/resident card (plus the originals, just in case), and a letter from your sponsor. There is also a registration fee of RO 10. The monthly charge for internet connection is RO 2, and each hour's surfing is charged at 0.180 baisas. You can have one email address – yourname@ omantel.net.om. If you need extra email space, it costs 0.200 baisas per megabyte. If you register for a PIN on the Omantel website, you can also access your Omantel email account from any computer anywhere in the world. Omantel now offers packages for corporate web hosting.

If you need assistance with the internet, you can call 1313 toll free. Broadband (ADSL) is available in many areas of Muscat, and use of broadband services is increasing all the time.

Log & Surf

This facility allows you to surf the internet without a contract or subscription to Omantel. All you need is a computer with a modem, and a phone line. The charge will be billed to the line you are connecting from. To connect, just double click on 'My Computer', then on 'Dial-up Networking' and then on 'Make a New Connection'. Type in 'omantel' for both your username and password, dial 1312 and click connect. Charges are a little higher – 25 baisas per minute from a landline and 50 baisas per minute from a mobile (to access the internet using your mobile you need to subscribe to the data service, for an extra RO 3 per month).

Bill Payment

Telephone bills are sent monthly and include rental charges and call costs. Only international calls are itemised on the bill, although the number of local and mobile calls and text messages is listed. You can pay your landline bill at the Omantel office in Al Khuwayr (behind Al Zawawi mosque, next to the ice rink) which is easy and efficient, and the best way to ensure continuity of service. You can also pay through some banks (such as Bank Muscat or HSBC) or through the ATM, but these services have a processing time of up to 10 days. You can check your GSM and internet bills on Omantel's website. Apply online for a PIN and just log in to find out how much you owe (for more information on paying your landline and mobile bills for Omantel, see their website – www.omantel.net.om). If you do not pay when you receive your bill, Omantel will helpfully send an email reminder. If you ignore that, they will cut you

No Naughty Sites
While using the internet in Oman you will have to do so under the watchful eye of a proxy. Sites that are considered harmful to the political, religious, moral or cultural sensitivities of the country are inaccessible.

off without further warning. Landlines continue to receive calls for several days but outgoing calls will be barred. If you do get cut off, take your bill to the Al Khuwayr office, pay all outstanding debts and a reconnection fee of RO 1, and your service will be reconnected immediately. Always keep your bills and receipts for proof of payment. If you are a Nawras post-paid GSM subscriber, you can pay your bills at certain banks, online, through your ATM, over the phone, or at a Nawras store. See their website (www.nawras.com.om) for more information.

Postal Services

There is no postal delivery service to home addresses, so everyone gets their mail delivered to a post office box. All mail is routed through the Central Post Office and then distributed to post office boxes in central locations. Most people use their company address, but it is also possible to get an individual PO box number – just apply through your local post office

The postal system is fairly reliable and efficient but on occasion parcels will be returned, deemed 'undeliverable' and you'll have to pay to get them back. There is a regular airmail service and an express mail service. Most leading courier services also have branches in Oman

Postal services are provided solely by the government-operated General Post Office (GPO). The GPO is reasonably efficient, with standard airmail letters taking 10-14 days to reach the USA, Europe or Australia. The GPO offers an express mail service (called EMS), and letters posted using the EMS get delivered in half the normal time. It costs 50 baisas to send a postcard anywhere within the GCC, 100 baisas to other Middle East countries, and 150 baisas to anywhere else. Letters cost from 50 baisas internally (15g maximum) and from 250 baisas internationally (10g maximum).

Post office opening times vary, but most branches open at 07:30 and close at 14.00 from Saturday to Wednesday, and most also have a short evening session. They close at 11:00 on Thursdays and do not open on Fridays. The post offices inside the Al Harthy Complex (Qurm) and in As Seeb are open for longer hours.

Post Office Locator

Al Harthy Complex: 24 563 534
07:30-14.30 & 19:00-21:00

Madinat Sultan Qaboos: 24 697 083
08:00-14:00

Al Hamriya: 24 789 311
08:00-14:00 & 16:00-20:00

Muscat: 24 738 547
07:30-14:00 & Thurs 08:00-11:00

Mina al Fahal: 24 565 465
08.00 14:00

Ruwi: 24 701 651
07:30-14:30 & 16:00-18:00

As Seeb: 24 519 922
08:00-15:00 & 17:00-24:00

SQU campus: 24 413 333 ext 3161
8:00-14:00

Jawaharat A'Shati Complex:
24 692 181, 09:00-13:30

Courier Services

The major international courier companies operate in Oman, although some may limit their deliveries to Muscat itself and not the entire sultanate. Aramex (www.aramex. com) provides a 'Shop & Ship' service, which sets up a mailbox for you in both the UK and the US. You pay a small fee to set up the mailbox, and then you can get online purchases delivered there. Aramex will then deliver the contents of your mailbox to you in Oman, at very reasonable rates. The amount you pay will depend on the weight of the shipment, but the rate is $15 for the first half-kilogram, and $9 for every additional half-kilogram. It's a great solution if you're shopping online and the company you are buying from doesn't ship to the Middle East.

Courier Services

Aramex	24 563 668	www.aramex.com
DHL	24 563 599	www.dhl.com
Federal Express	24 833 311	www.fedex.com
TNT	24 489 170	www.tnt.com
UPS	24 700 165	www.ups.com

Radio

Oman has a number of commercial radio stations, broadcasting mostly in Arabic. Hi FM (95.9 FM) is the most popular English-language station, with current music,

competitions and upbeat DJs. You can listen online at www.hifmradio.com, where you can also find the programme schedules and find out more about the station.
The government-owned English language radio station (90.4 FM in Muscat and Salalah) plays a mixture of news, talk shows, classical music and modern music. The station operates daily from 06:00 to midnight and the schedule is printed in the local newspapers. It is also available on www.oman-tv.gov.om. News headlines, weather forecasts and a list of pharmacies on duty are read out frequently on air in between the somewhat limited playlist. If you have broadband you can tune in to various international radio stations on your computer, or even download a pre-recorded 'podcast'. The BBC World Service broadcasts on 15575 Hz. If you want to hear Arabic music, tune in to 89.0 FM and 107.7 FM.

Television

Oman TV (Channel 6 in Muscat and Channel 10 in Salalah) is the only local television channel in Oman. The shows on this channel are mainly Arabic, although you'll get the occasional film or series in English. The daily English news broadcast is at 20:30, and news in Arabic is shown at 11:00, 15:00 and 18:00. It also broadcasts by satellite throughout the world. Go to www.oman-tv.gov.om for the schedule of English programmes.

The Ministry of Information recently granted permission to Oman International Holding Company to set up a private television channel that will broadcast to the entire country.

There is a wider choice of programmes offered by satellite TV, ranging from international entertainment and films to sport, cartoons and current events. Most leading hotels have satellite television for guests, and it is usually quite straightforward for a resident to have it installed (see p.116).

There are several sports bars around Muscat that will show important games (usually of football, cricket and rugby) on their big-screen TVs. Premiership football is shown regularly at Feeney's Irish Pub in the Sheraton Oman Resort (p.340) and in the Al Ghazal Pub inside the InterContinental Muscat (p.339).

TVs are in PAL format (UK standard), so certain videos will not work unless you have multi-system equipment. However, almost any TV, VCR or DVD player you buy in Oman is multi-system and will work anywhere in the world.

Satellite TV

Thank goodness for satellite TV! Satellite offers an enormous choice of programmes and channels, and most expats have at least one satellite provider. You will need to pay for any equipment you need (dish and decoder) as well as installation. You can usually choose from a number of packages depending on what kind of programmes you like to see – the advantage being that you don't have to pay for things you won't use (for example, if you are not interested in watching sport, you can subscribe to a package that does not include any sports channels). There are quite a few 'free-to-air' satellite channels, and to view these you need to get the dish and decoder but then you pay no subscription fees. However, most of these channels are not in English. Equipment can be bought from main dealers or any of the small electrical shops. Second-hand dishes and decoders are often advertised on supermarket noticeboards and in the classifieds. The majority of dealers will offer installation. Many apartment blocks have satellite systems already fitted. If not, ask your landlord about a cost-share system.

Satellite & Cable Providers	
Al As'hab Trading Co	24 837 477
Al Hamli Telecommunication	24 830 550
Mohd & Partners Electronic Store	24 836 413
Orbit Direct	24 482 214
Salim Al Humaidi Trading	24 836 708
Shanfari & Partners (Salalah)	24 292 480
Showtime	+971 4 367 7888
Space star Trading (First Net)	24 834 420

General Medical Care

The general standard of healthcare in Oman is high, both in the public and private sectors. Like in most countries, private healthcare is seen as preferable (English-speaking staff, shorter waiting lists and more comfortable in-patient facilities) which is lucky for expats as they are only permitted to use private hospitals (except in cases of medical emergencies or in instances where private hospitals do not have the necessary facilities for treatment).

There are many private specialist clinics, private and government hospitals, all staffed by qualified professionals. Most people who receive medical treatment in Oman can say their experience was a positive one. However, private medical care is costly, and visitors and non-residents are strongly advised to take out medical insurance.

Although there are no specific health risks facing visitors, it's a good idea to keep your anti-tetanus and hepatitis protection up to date. The most common health threats are heat exhaustion and dehydration. Oman summers are hot and humid and, unless you've lived in this part of the world before, you'll probably underestimate just how hot it can get. Wear a strong sunscreen all year round, especially on your face and neck, and drink plenty of water (a minimum of two litres a day). Take special precautions to protect children from the heat, and make sure they wear UV protected swimsuits and plenty of sunscreen on the beach.

Health Centres & Clinics		
Al Wattayah Hospital	Al Wutayyah	24 571 744
Azaibah Hospital	Al Azaiba	24 497 233
Daushar Polyclinic	Al Qurm	24 593 311
Ghubrah Hospital	Al Ghubrah	24 497 226
Muscat Private Hospital ▶ p.119	Bawshar	24 583 600
Muttrah Health Center	Mutrah	24 711 296
The Royal Hospital	Al Ghubrah	24 599 000
Ruwi Heath Center	Ruwi	24 786 088
Wadi Kabir Hospital	Wadi Kabir	24 812 944

Whenever you can, stay out of the sun – park in the shade where possible and wear a hat. Hotels, restaurants and shopping malls often have arctic air conditioning to combat the heat outside, but constant temperature changes can leave you prone to colds for the first few months.

Omani nationals receive healthcare for a nominal cost at government hospitals, although expats must have a referral from a health centre to receive treatment. Although costly, the walk-in convenience of private medical care is handy. Waiting times are longer at government hospitals, which are very busy. You'll have to wait to get an appointment, and then wait again when you arrive for your appointment; whereas at Muscat Private Hospital you can usually get an appointment almost immediately.

Emergency Services

The ambulance service in Oman is fairly new and the fleet of vehicles with trained staff is still relatively small. Response times are not published so it's difficult to say how reliable a service it actually is. This may be due in part to the fact that other road users do not automatically move out of the way to let an ambulance through the traffic, or are already blocking the emergency lane. Some of the hospitals and clinics have their own ambulance service but again, may take some time to reach you.

The golden rule is never to attempt to move an injured person, but in a place where ambulance response times are slow, you may have to weigh up the risks and decide whether it would be better to transport the victim to hospital in your own car.

Pharmacies

Most pharmacies are open from 09:00 to 21:00, Saturdays to Thursdays. Some do close for lunch between 13:00 and 16:00. Some pharmacies are open on Fridays from 16:00 to 21:00. There is always at least one pharmacy open 24 hours a day - this is done on a rota system so check the daily papers for details. Alternatively, call Muscat Pharmacy (24 702 542) or Scientific Pharmacy (24 566 601).

Health Insurance

Your employer may provide health insurance for you but it may be less than fully comprehensive. It is vital that you arrange insurance for yourself and your family as treatment here can be very costly. Dental and maternity cover are usually optional extras and not provided as standard.

Giving Blood

Like any other country in the world, Oman relies on donations from the public to keep its blood banks topped up. You can give blood at the Central Blood Bank opposite Royal Hospital (24 591 255). You may come across mobile blood banks at supermarkets or in shopping malls.

> **Kick The Habit**   **i**
>
> If you want to quit smoking but need some help, Al Hayat Clinic has a dedicated smoking cessation programme. Call 24 565 941 for more details.

Main Government Hospitals

Government healthcare is reserved for native Omani residents, with the exception of expats requiring emergency treatment that is not available in private hospitals. If you are an expat and you do require treatment at a government hospital or clinic, you will be charged for their services.

Wadi Adai R/A
Ruwi
Map 12 C3

Al Nahda Hospital
24 707 800

Al Nahda Hospital specialises in ENT surgery, eye surgery and treatment, as well as dental surgery, dermatology and diseases of the nervous system. It is Oman's main referral hospital for thyroid gland operations.

Wadi Hatat, Quriyat
Muscat
Map 1 C2

Ibn Sina Hospital
24 577 361

Ibn Sina is a 60 bed modern facility for psychiatric treatment and patient care. The hospital caters for adults, children and adolescents with serious mental and psychiatric problems. Facilities include an electroencephalogram, x-ray, laboratory and two occupational therapy units. Ibn Sina is the only in-patient psychiatry hospital in Oman and is in heavy demand.

Maydan Al Fath St
Al Wuttayyah
Map 9 A4

Khoula Hospital
24 563 625

The Khoula Hospital is the Sultanate's referral hospital for cases from orthopaedic surgery, neurosurgery, cosmetic surgery and burns departments. This 428 bed hospital also has maternity, gynaecology and physiotherapy departments. Khoula is equipped with the latest MRI scanner.

Al Gubrah St off
Al Athaiba R/A
Al Ghubrah
Map 6 D4

The Royal Hospital
24 599 000 | www.royalhospital.med.om

The Royal Hospital has facilities for up to 630 in-patients. There are separate A&E departments for adults and children. Departments include child health, surgery & obstetrics, gynaecology, oncology, paediatric and adult intensive care units, a coronary care unit and a 30 bed special care baby unit. The national oncology unit comprises an out-patient department, daycare chemotherapy, radiotherapy and nuclear medicine. The paediatric and adult A&E departments are open 24 hours, seven days a week.

Live a **Healthy Life**

Muscat Private Hospital, a leader in the Healthcare Industry, provides a wide range of services that covers all the family needs.
Our specialities are:

- Emergency Room (ER)
- Paediatrics
- Women's Health Services
- General Surgery
- Endocrinology & Diabetology
- Nephrology
- Psychiatry
- Rheumatology
- Internal Medicine

- Orthopaedics
- Urology
- Dermatology
- Ear, Nose & Throat (ENT) Surgery
- Plastic and Cosmetic Surgery
- Cardiology and Cardiac Surgery
- Neurosurgery
- Dental Oral & Maxillo Facial Surgery

Other Services
- Physiotherapy
- Medical Imaging
- Pathology Laboratory Services

Main Private Hospitals

There is only one private hospital in Muscat, Muscat Private, providing a full range of treatment options and excellent facilities. There are also numerous other smaller private clinics specialising in particular areas such as fertility treatment and dermatology. Many expats living in Oman choose to make the trip to the UAE or to their home countries if they need any serious, non-emergency medical treatment.

Bausher St
Bawshar
Map 1 B2

Muscat Private Hospital ▶ p.119

24 583 600 | *www.muscatprivatehospital.com*

Muscat Private Hospital is a 72 bed general hospital with out-patient and in-patient facilities. The hospital provides a wide range of services including dentistry, diagnostics, family & ER medicine (24 hours, seven days a week), cardiology, dermatology, psychiatry, paediatrics, physiotherapy, obstetrics & gynaecology, CT scan, MRI and cosmetic surgery. Packages available include Well Baby, Well Woman and Antenatal among others. For emergencies call 24 583 600 (ext 3790 or 3792), or the direct number (24 583 792), 24 hours.

Private Health Centres & Clinics

Al Amal Medical & Health Care Center	Al Khuwayr	24 485 052
Al Lamki Polyclinic	Al Khuwayr	24 489 563/695 543
Al Massaraat Medical Centre	Al Qurm	24 566 435
Al Rimah Medical Center	Ruwi	24 700 515
Atlas Star Medical Centre	Al Ghubrah	24 504 000
Dr Maurice Al Asfour Specialised Medical Centre	Shati Al Qurm	24 605 411
Elixir Health Centre	Al Qurm	24 565 802
Emirates Medical Center	Mina Al Fahal (PDO)	24 604 540
Hatat Polyclinic	Al Wutayyah	24 563 641
Khasab Clinic	Musandam	26 731 088
Lama Polyclinic	Ruwi	24 788 577
Medicare Centre	Shati Al Qurm	24 692 801
Medident Centre	Madinat As Sultan Qaboos	24 600 668
Muscat Eye Laser Center	Al Qurm	24 691 414
Qurum Medical Centre	Qurm Heights	24 562 198
Tahhan Medical Centre	Madinat As Sultan Qaboos	24 694 930

Diagnostics

Al Afaq Medical Diagnostic & Imaging Centre	Ghala	24 501 162
Al Amal Medical & Health Care Center	Al Khuwayr	24 485 052
Al Hassan Medical Center	Al Khuwayr	24 481 135
Al Hayat Polyclinic	Al Qurm	24 565 941
Al Lamki Polyclinic	Al Khuwayr	24 489 563/ 695 543
Al Rimah Medical Center	Ruwi	24 700 515
Apollo Medical Centre	Ruwi	24 787 766
Ibn Sina Hospital	Muscat	24 577 361
Medicare Centre	Shati Al Qurm	24 692 801
Muscat Private Hospital ▶ p.119	Bawshar	24 583 600
Qurum Clinic	Al Qurm	24 563 181
Tahhan Medical Centre	Madinat As Sultan Qaboos	24 694 930

Baby Massage ◄

With just 15 minutes of massage each day, babies tend to cry less, be more alert, gain weight faster, fall asleep faster, are happier, and develop into more sociable children. Janet Wilson is a registered nurse and midwife, as well as a certified infant massage instructor. She teaches techniques to help parents and babies establish closer bonds, as well as showing strokes to relieve trapped wind, colic and teething. For more information, contact Janet on 99 470 593 or email her on mwilson@omantel.net.om.

Maternity

Other options **Maternity Items** p.280

It is possible to have an elective caesarean section if you want to choose your baby's birthday or you can't face the trauma of a natural birth. After a caesarean, you will usually stay in the hospital for up to five days, whereas with a natural birth you only need to stay for two days.

There are no home visits from hospital staff after the birth, although you might be lucky enough to come across some kind expat midwives who will give you a friendly call to make sure you are coping and answer any questions you might have. Muscat Mums is a group of mothers that offer invaluable support by meeting regularly to chat and swap advice – a godsend when you are away from your familiar network of family and friends. Contact them via the website: www.muscatmums.110mb.com.

Hospital staff will usually offer plenty of breastfeeding advice before you leave the hospital, but you can get ongoing help if you need it. Remember that Oman is a Muslim country and therefore you should be sensitive when breastfeeding in public places. On the other hand, local women are encouraged to breastfeed, so you shouldn't have any trouble as long as you are discreet.

Both you and your baby can benefit from going to baby massage – your baby will find it relaxing and comforting, and it can even help ease the discomfort of colic. It is also a great opportunity to meet and socialise with other mums. For more information on baby massage, call 99 470 593. Other baby contacts that you may find useful are: multiple births support group (for twins and triplets aged 3 and over) – 99 264 179 (Heidi); Bumps and Babies group – 92 572 501 (Sandy); Bumps, Babies and Triplets group – 99 313 862 (Teresa); and prenatal yoga classes – 24 694 527.

Many expats choose to give birth in Oman and do so without any problems. The main difference is that you will not have the same choices regarding your birth plan as you would probably have in your home country. You don't have the option of a home birth or a water birth, but straightforward births are expertly handled.

If you do decide to travel home to give birth, you will need to check with your doctor regarding whether it is safe to travel at an advanced stage of pregnancy. Your doctor will usually give you permission to fly up to 34 weeks, but you should check with your airline about their restrictions and requirements for pregnant passengers.

If you give birth in Oman your only choice is to give birth in one of the private hospitals, unless you develop complications that can only be dealt with in a government hospital. In such cases you will be referred to the government hospital

Dermatologists

Abu Musafir Skin Clinic	Ruwi	24 706 453
Al Amal Medical & Health Care Center	Al Khuwayr	24 485 052
Al Rimah Medical Center	Ruwi	24 700 515
Al Shatti Hospital	Shati Al Qurm	24 604 263
Atlas Star Medical Centre	Al Ghubrah	24 504 000
Bio Carre	Ruwi	24 707 444
Emirates Medical Center	Mina Al Fahal (PDO)	24 604 540
Hatat Polyclinic	Al Wutayyah	24 563 641

Maternity Hospitals & Clinics

Hatat Polyclinic	Al Wutayyah	24 563 641
Medident Centre	Madinat As Sultan Qaboos	24 600 668
Muscat Private Hospital ▶ p.119	Bawshar	24 583 600
Qurum Clinic	Al Qurm	24 563 181
Sultan Qaboos University Hospital	Salalah	23 413 355/415 747

Gynaecology & Obstetrics

Advanced Fertility & Genetics Centre	24 489 647
Al Massaraat Medical Centre	24 566 435
Al Rimah Medical Center	24 700 515
Apollo Medical Centre	24 787 766
Atlas Star Medical Centre	24 504 000
Dr Maurice Al Asfour Specialised Medical Centre	24 605 411
Hatat Polyclinic	24 563 641
Medicare Centre	24 692 801
Muscat Private Hospital ▶p.119	24 583 600
Qurum Clinic	24 563 181

by the private hospital or clinic where you have had your prenatal care. Standards of care are excellent at both government and private hospitals, so don't worry if you are referred to a government hospital for your labour.

It is possible to get private health insurance to cover maternity costs, although there is usually a specific time period which must have lapsed before conception – in other words, you usually have to have been on the insurance plan for a year or so before you fall pregnant.

Prices for private maternity packages start from around RO 900 for a standard antenatal, delivery and postnatal package – this may include all your ultrasound scans, blood tests, and any extra tests or procedures you require.

Don't listen to any urban myths about having to go through labour without pain relief – the normal pain solutions such as gas and air, Pethidine and epidurals are common. You will pay extra for Pethidine or an epidural, and if you end up having a caesarean section, that will cost extra too. Your husband is allowed to be in the delivery room with you, and so is an independent doula if you have one.

Once your baby is born you need to have the birth registered within two weeks and then set about getting a passport for him or her from your embassy. The nationality of the child is automatically that of the mother, but there may be extra paperwork if the mother was also born outside of her country of origin or if her embassy is not represented in Oman. For more information on registering a birth, see p.67.

Antenatal Care

If you have your antenatal care in a private clinic, they will refer you to a hospital for delivery. Your gynaecologist will possibly be present at the birth. A doctor must deliver the baby – unlike in some countries where a midwife can perform a delivery in the absence of any complications.

If you are over 35, or you are seen as having a greater chance of having a baby with spinal or neurological birth defects, you will be offered a variety of tests to check for certain problems. Many expats travel to the UAE for these tests, as the standards of equipment and staff training are exemplary and no more expensive than in Oman. You could combine this medical trip with a big shopping spree, as you'll find a lot more variety in Dubai in terms of baby clothes and equipment.

Maternity Packages From Muscat Private Hospital

Type	Full package	24-30 weeks	30-36 weeks	36 weeks+
Ante-natal package	RO 370	RO 220	RO 170	RO 120
Normal delivery package only	RO 495	RO 495	RO 495	RO 495
Normal delivery combined price	RO 865	RO 715	RO 665	RO 615
Elective C-Section	RO 1,135	RO 1,135	RO 1,135	RO 1,135
Elective C-Section Delivery combined price	RO 1,505	RO1,355	RO 1,305	RO 1,255

Postnatal Depression

A relatively high number of women suffer from postnatal depression to varying degrees. In serious cases it can be debilitating and can even result in you or your baby being in danger of injury.

advertising

landscapes

interiors

architecture

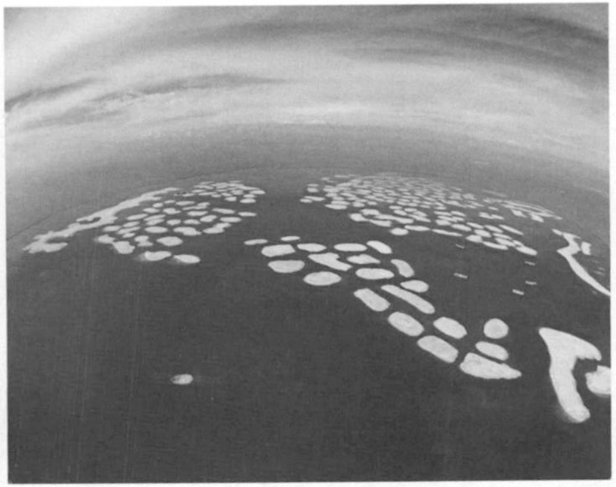

2009 winner-book cover advertising awards PX3 Grand Prix de la Photographie Paris
2008 winner-magazine cover of the year International Printing Awards Moscow

victor romero photographer

+971 50 844 85 64

www.v7photography.com

If you are having your baby in Oman, you will probably be far away from the important emotional support of your family and friends back home, and this can increase your chances of suffering from PND. Although there is no support group dedicated to mothers with PND, your doctor should be able to give you the necessary support and, in some cases, offer medication to help you through the first few weeks.

Maternity Leave

Oman labour law allows working mothers their basic salary, including allowances, for six weeks after the birth. If you have had a caesarean section, you may be granted extra leave depending on your doctor's recommendation. You are also allowed two hours a day for the hilariously titled 'milking time' for the next 12 to 24 weeks, so that you can go home and feed your baby. After that, you will be required to return to work as you did before the birth, unless your doctor has recommended that you take extra time. Paternity leave is at the discretion of your employer, but it is not recognised as a father's right in Oman. Instead, it is common to take some of your annual leave if you want to spend time with your exhausted wife and new baby.

Paediatrics		
Al Lamki Polyclinic	Al Khuwayr	24 489 563
Apollo Medical Centre	Ruwi	24 787 766
Atlas Star Medical Centre	Al Ghubrah	24 504 000
Muscat Private Hospital ▶ p.119	Bawshar	24 583 600
The Royal Hospital	Al Ghubrah	24 599 000
Tahhan Medical Centre	Madinat As Sultan Qaboos	24 694 930

Muscat Mums ◀

Having a baby in a strange town can be taxing, since you've probably left your support network (mum, sister, friends) behind. Muscat Mums is an amazing group that was set up to help new mums find their feet, and they welcome all new members. To find out more visit www.muscatmums. 110mb.com.

Paediatrics

Most hospitals have full-time paediatricians on staff. Many private clinics also have paediatricians – the trick is finding one that both you and your child like. Ask around, call Muscat Mums (p.129) for a recommendation, or just try a few different ones until you find a good one.

Dentists & Orthodontists

Private dentistry in Oman is, like most other private medical services, of a high standard. Various practitioners offer not only general checkups and basic dental care, but also dental surgery and cosmetic dentistry.

Dentists & Orthodontists		
Al Amal Medical & Health Care Center	Al Khuwayr	24 485 052
Al Essa Dental Clinic	Ruwi	24 797 406
Al Ghubrah Dental Clinic & Orthodontic	Ruwi	24 597 708
American Dental Center ▶ p.125	Shati Al Qurm	24 695 422
Amira dental Clinic	Al Qurm	24 565 477
Emerald Dental Clinic	Al Qurm	24 561 641
Emirates Medical Center	Mina Al Fahal (PDO)	24 604 540
Harub Dental Clinic	Shati Al Qurm	24 563 814
Medident Centre	Madinat As Sultan Qaboos	24 600 668
Muscat Dental Specialists	Al Qurm	24 568 565
Precision Dental Clinic	Shati Al Qurm	24 696 247
Qurum Medical & Dental Centre	Shati Al Qurm	24 692 898
Scientific Polyclinic	Al Qurm	24 560 035
Sun Dental Centre	Al Ghubrah	95 961 234
Waneela Polyclinic	Al Khuwayr	24 489 319
Wassan Specialty Dental Clinic	Al Khuwayr	24 489 469

AMERICAN DENTAL CENTER

Muscat

World-Class Care

www.adcoman.com

an operation of:
American Int'l. Dental Consultants Inc. USA

Al Masa Mall, Shatti Qurum, PO Box: 458 PC:133, Muscat, Sultanate of Oman
Tel: +968 24695422, Fax: +968 24695433. e-mail: info@adcOman.com

Prices tend to match the level of service (high), and unfortunately most standard health insurance packages will not cover dental costs (except for emergency treatment required as the result of an accident). Most policies offer the option of paying a higher premium to cover dentistry.

Opticians		
Al Ghazal Opticians	Al Qurm	24 563 546
Al Said Optics	Al Qurm	24 566 272
Grand Optics	As Seeb	24 558 890
Muscat Eye Laser Center	Al Qurm	24 691 414
Oman Opticals	Al Qurm	24 562 981
Yateem Opticians	Al Qurm	24 563 716

Opticians

There are plenty of opticians in Oman, with most outlets selling a range of sunglasses and prescription lenses. Most opticians offer free eye tests if you are ordering your glasses from them. Disposable contact lenses and coloured contact lenses are also available. Look out for special offers where you can get two pairs of prescription glasses for the price of one.

Cosmetic Treatment & Surgery

There are reputable options if you want a little 'touch-up' in the form of cosmetic surgery. Muscat Private Hospital (24 583 600) has resident plastic surgeons, and Emirates Medical Center (24 604 540) offers a huge range of treatments. They also have regular visits by specialists from around the world.

Alternative Therapies

Muscat is a cultural crossroads and many of its residents come from countries where traditional therapies are practised. Consequently, there is a good balance of holistic treatments and orthodox western medicine available. Natural medicine can be very effective and, because the treatments are aimed at balancing the whole person, your therapist will need to know a lot about you. Be prepared to spend up to two hours on the first consultation so that your therapist can build up a picture of your background and medical history. Alternative treatments can cost as much as western medicine. While they rarely offer the quick fix that one expects from orthodox practice, they work slowly and gently with the body's natural processes, so be prepared to stick with it to get a result. As always, word of mouth is the best way to find the most appropriate treatment. Some of the more common disciplines are listed below, but for general advice on a range of alternative medical treatments, contact the Al Kawakeb Complex Ayurvedic Clinic, Qurm (24 564 101 or 99 340 138), or the All Seasons Ayurvedic Clinic, MSQ (24 604 178).

Acupressure & Acupuncture

One of the oldest healing methods in the world, acupressure involves the systematic placement of pressure with fingertips on established meridian points on the body. This therapy can be used to relieve pain, soothe the nerves and stimulate the body, as determined necessary by the therapist. Acupuncture is an ancient Chinese technique that uses needles to access the body's meridian points. The technique is surprisingly painless and is quickly becoming an alternative or complement to western medicine, as it aids ailments such as asthma, rheumatism, and even more serious diseases. It has also been known to work wonders on animals.

Acupressure & Acupuncture		
Acu-Magnetic Treatment Centre	Al Khuwayr	24 487 828
Al Bustan Palace InterContinental Muscat ▶ p.29	Al Bustan	24 799 666
The Chedi	Al Ghubrah	24 524 400
Chinese Medical & Herbal Clinic	Ruwi	24 799 729
Star Salon & Spa	Shati Al Qurm	24 693 436

Homeopathy

This form of treatment has been practised in Europe for 200 years. It is a safe and effective treatment for jump starting the body's formidable self-healing powers. Working at both the physical and emotional levels, it treats the whole person rather than the symptoms, using remedies derived from a variety of natural sources. Practitioners undergo rigorous training and many are also qualified western medical doctors. Homeopathic remedies are not available over the counter in Oman as they are in many countries, but there are several practising homeopaths and clinics.

Homeopathy		
Al Farooj Clinic	Barka	99 726 797
Al Kawakeb Ayurveda Clinic	Al Ghubrah	24 597 977
The Chedi	Al Ghubrah	24 524 400
Raz Hair Studio Beauty Salon	Madinat As Sultan Qaboos	24 692 219
Taimour Ayurvedic Clinic	Ruwi	24 799 689

Reflexology & Massage Therapy

Reflexology is another scientifically detailed method of bringing the body and mind back into balance. Based on the premise that reflex points on the feet and hands correspond to the organs and body systems, and that massaging these points improves and maintains health, reflexology works by stimulating the body's natural self-healing process. When considering reflexology, remember the following safety guidelines: do not eat right before your massage; keep drinking water during the course of your massage; and get your doctor's permission if you suffer from asthma, diabetes, a heart condition, kidney problems, high blood pressure or epilepsy. While many spas and salons offer massage and reflexology, there are those which offer a more focused therapeutic approach to the holistic healing qualities of reflexology and massage.

Reflexology & Massage Therapy		
Acu-Magnetic Treatment Centre	Al Khuwayr	24 487 828
Al Bustan Palace InterContinental Muscat ▶ p.29	Al Bustan	24 799 666
Al Jamal Health Club	Al Azaiba	24 490 526
Al Kawakeb Ayurveda Clinic	Al Ghubrah	24 597 977
	As Seeb	24 543 289
Chinese Massage Centre	Al Ghubrah	99 890 004
Crowne Plaza Muscat ▶ p.25	Qurm Heights	24 660 660
Dar Al Saha Clinic	Al Khuwayr	24 479 141
Grand Hyatt Muscat	Shati Al Qurm	24 641 234
Muscat Beauty Salon	Al Qurm	24 562 541
Physiotherapy & Rehabilitaion Centre	Wadi Kabir	24 605 115
Sama Health Club (Thai Massage)	Al Ghubrah	24 496 191
Star Salon & Spa	Shati Al Qurm	24 693 436

Chakra & Crystal Healing Therapy

Chakras are the seven energy centres of the body and they make up a person's aura. The direction and intensity of the chakras' spin indicate your level of emotional health. Peter Emery Langille provides workshops on request that will teach you how to explore the attributes of each Chakra, how to visually diagnose your own chakras' condition, and how to rebalance your chakras using colour, crystal and light energy, and meditation. Call 92 605 102 for more information, or email lahave@canada.com.

Rehabilitation & Physiotherapy

Many expats lead active lives, working hard and then playing hard. But accidents and injuries do happen, so whether you get roughed up playing rugby, pull something in the gym, or simply trip over the cat, there are some excellent facilities to help you on the road to recovery.

Physiotherapy		
Muscat Private Hospital ▶ p.119	Bawshar	24 583 600
Physiotherapy & Rehabilitaion Centre	Wadi Kabir	24 605 115

Back Treatment

Treatment for back problems is widely available with some excellent specialists. Chiropractic and osteopathy treatments concentrate on manipulating the skeleton in a non-intrusive manner to improve the functioning of the nervous system or blood supply to the body. Chiropractic is based on the manipulative treatment of misalignments in the joints, especially those of the spinal column, while osteopathy involves the manipulation and massage of the skeleton and musculature.

Back Treatment		
1st Chiropractic Centre	Shati Al Qurm	24 698 847
Chinese Medical & Herbal Clinic	Ruwi	24 799 729
Muscat Private Hospital ▶ p.119	Bawshar	24 583 600
Palm Beach Club	Shati Al Qurm	24 680 000

Pilates is said to be the safest form of neuromuscular reconditioning and back strengthening available. Les Mills' Body Training System classes are also extremely effective, particularly BodyPump, BodyBalance and RPM. The Palm Beach Club at the InterContinental Muscat (24 680 660) has five Body Training System licences. A number of clinics offer therapeutic massage for back pain, and word of mouth is a good way to get a recommendation.

Nutritionists & Slimming

Unfortunately, there is no Weight Watchers or similar slimming group in Oman, so if you have a few pounds to shift, you're on your own. You might benefit from the various slimming treatments on offer at Ayana Spa in Shati Al Qurm (24 693 435, www.ayanaspa.com) – depending on your needs they will recommend a combination of treatments such as ultrasonic treatment, lymphatic drainage, body sculpting massage and healthy eating programmes.

Apollo Medical Centre in Ruwi (24 787 766, www.apollomuscat.com) has an obesity clinic aimed at helping you control your weight in a healthy way. While the clinic will focus on your eating habits and give you diet and exercise guidelines to follow, in severe cases of obesity they may prescribe certain medications.

Most gyms have professionally trained staff who can advise you on a healthy eating plan along with an exercise regime. They will monitor your progress until you achieve the results you are after. For a list of health clubs, see p.248.

Counselling & Therapy

In addition to the normal pressures of modern living, expat life can have its particular challenges. Moving to a different culture can be stressful, even for the most resilient personalities. If you have moved to Oman with your spouse and aren't working, time can hang heavy on your hands. Although people are generally friendly here, they have their own busy lives and it can be lonely until you settle in. If you need someone to talk to there are places you can go for support. The Al Harub Medical Center (24 600 750) in Shati has both life coaches and psychotherapists available, while Muscat Private Hospital (MPH), University Hospital and Hatat Polyclinic can put you in touch with counsellors, psychologists and psychiatrists. The hospitals and clinics listed in the table either have excellent practitioners on their staff, or they can refer you to an appropriate counsellor or therapist.

Counsellors & Psychologists		
Al Shatti Hospital	Shati Al Qurm	24 604 263
Bait Al-Salama Polyclinic	Darsait	24 792 698
Hatat Polyclinic	Hillat Al Sud	24 563 641
Ibn Sina Hospital	Wadi Hatat, Quriyat	24 577 361
Muscat Private Hospital ▶ p.119	Bawshar	24 583 600
Sultan Qaboos University Hospital	Salalah	23 413 355/ 415 747

Support Groups

One of the toughest parts of expat life is the loss of your immediate support network back home (friends and family). In 1992, Unicef, together with the Ministry of Health set up CSG (Community Support Groups). With the help of the Omani Women's Association, CSG holds workshops and training to implement support networks throughout the region. In addition, health centres, private clinics and hospitals are good sources of information for finding support groups.

Alcoholics Anonymous: The Oasis Group meets on Saturdays, Mondays and Wednesdays from 19:30 to 20:30 at the Medident Medical Centre. The Candlelit Group meets on Sundays and Tuesdays at the Top Care Medical Centre. Call the 24 hour hotline (99 721 396), email serenity@aa-oman.org, or visit the website (www.aa-oman.org).

American Women's Group: Although it is run by American women, women of any nationality are welcome to join this group. For more information contact Angela Stephenson (99 231 077) or Marilyn Searle (24 594 751).

ANZO: The Australian and New Zealand Organisation puts you in contact with people from your home country; anzo_oman@yahoo.co.uk.

British Businessman's Forum: The BBF arranges networking, social and fund raising events. For more information, contact Chris Green (99 360 263).

Caledonian Society of Oman: They organise Scottish social events and fund-raising activities. Email Moira Cameron on moira@omantel.net.om.

Down Syndrome Support Group: This group is affiliated to the Association of Early Intervention for Children with Special Needs (www.aei.org.om). For more information, call 24 496 960 or email earlyint@omantel.net.om.

European Business Persons' Group: The EBPG holds regular networking and social events. Email ebpgoman@gmail.com.

Multiple Births Group: This informal group of mothers provides support and social interaction for mothers of twins and triplets. Current contact numbers are Teresa (99 313 862, teresavallancey@yahoo.com) and Fiona (99 733 998, fififerrari@yahoo.co.uk).

Muscat Mums: A friendly support group for expectant mums and mums with young children. All nationalities are welcome. www.muscatmums.110mb.com.

Narcotics Anonymous: NA meets at Hatat Polyclinic on Mondays at 19:30 and Thursdays at 19:00, and at the Medident Clinic on Fridays at 19:00; 99 721 396.

Overeaters Anonymous: Meetings take place at Medident Medical Centre on Fridays at 16:00 and Tuesdays at 19:30. Call 92 151 840 or email oainoman@hotmail.com.

Women's Guild: The Women's Guild is open to women of all nationalities and holds events throughout the year plus weekly coffee mornings. For more information contact womensguildinoman2@hotmail.com.

Wadi Al Kabir

Education

Oman, and Muscat in particular, is home to several international schools catering to children of various nationalities. Government schools are for Omani citizens only, so if you are living in Oman as an expat you will have to send your child to a private school. While it is advisable to visit as many schools as you can to get an idea of the academic standards and extra-mural facilities, remember that it makes sense to stick to a national curriculum that fits in with your future plans. For example, if you will probably end up living back in the UK during some stage of your child's education, it is sensible to enrol your child in a school that teaches the English National Curriculum.

If possible, have a chat to other expats to ask for their advice on schools. Try to visit schools during the school day and ask if you can see a class in progress.

You will sometimes find that there are waiting lists for certain schools or nurseries, so register your child as early as you possibly can. To enrol your child in a school, you will need to submit the following:

- School application form
- Passport photos of your child
- Copies of your child's birth certificate
- Up-to-date immunisation record
- Reports from your child's previous school (if applicable)

The school will inform you of any other documents they need, as well as any registration fees.

Nurseries & Pre-Schools

If you have a child of nursery age, you will find quite a lot of choice in Muscat. Facilities and standards vary enormously, as do the fees, so it is worth checking out a few different nurseries before you make your decision. Some nurseries accept children as young as six months, but this is the exception rather than the rule. There are often waiting lists for the more popular nurseries, so put your child's name down early if there is one you have your heart set on.

Nurseries are usually open in the mornings only. Some offer flexibility in terms of how many days per week your child will attend, so if you don't want your child to go to school for a full five days a week, you may be able to choose four, three or even two days a week. Different nurseries have different teaching styles – some encourage learning through play and some have a more structured curriculum. It is up to you to decide what system will be most beneficial to your child. Other factors to consider are child to teacher ratio, staff qualifications, and provision of extra services such as meals and transport.

American-British Academy (ABA)
24 605 287 | www.abaoman.edu.om

The kindergarten programme at the American British Academy accepts children between the ages of 3 and 5. The curriculum follows the IB (International Baccalaureate) system, and covers areas like language and literacy, knowledge and understanding of the world, personal and social development, music and art, and physical education. The advantage is that your child can then progress directly into Grade 1, without changing schools.

Bright Beginnings Nursery
24 699 387 | bbnursery.com

The programme at Bright Beginnings draws on the Montessori methods of education, but also uses other teaching methods to create a happy, caring environment where children learn through interaction and imaginative play. The nursery accepts children from 18 months.

Perfect English
Kings Language School is based in the UK but it offers some excellent online courses in the English language, from beginner to advanced. For more details, call 99 473 709 or visit www. kingslanguage.com.

Al Khuwayr Heights District (Sheikh Khalili Heights)
Madinat As Sultan Qaboos
Map 7 E4

Al Nadhayer St
House 49 (Nr British School)
Madinat As Sultan Qaboos
Map 7 F1

Times may have changed. *Our foundations never will.*

Foundations are built to last. They are laid with the very premise of creating structures that will withstand the course of time.

At Repton, we've built our boarding houses with the sole purpose of creating immovable stability for our students. A place where they are recognised as individuals, nurtured, and motivated by the boarding house staff to become all they can be and more. And it's no different now. Just as this was our ambition 450 years ago, it remains today.

For our boarding houses are more than just residences for pupils – they are part of the foundations that their lives are built on – now and in the years to come.

If a strong foundation – in every aspect – is what you look for in a school, enrol your child today.

REPTON SCHOOL DUBAI IS NOW OPEN. VISIT WWW.REPTONDUBAI.ORG FOR MORE INFORMATION.

Repton
School

Founded UK 1557. Dubai 2007

British School Muscat
Ruwi
Map 7 F1

The British School Nursery
24 600 842 | *www.britishschool.edu.om*
The British School Nursery follows the UK Foundation Stage Curriculum, so there is great emphasis on learning through play. There are two classes holding up to 24 children each, but each class is split into two large rooms so there is only ever a maximum of 12 children in one room at a time. There is one teacher and two assistants per class, and all teachers are UK trained. The school also has a well-equipped playground.

Villa 1045
Way 2414
Al Qurm
Map 8 D3

National Nursery Montessori
24 560 096 | *www.montessorioman.com*
This private Montessori school is based in Qurm and accepts children aged 1 to 6. Their spacious converted villa has an outdoor play area, a garden and a swimming pool, and many excellent indoor facilities too. The school has a full-time music teacher, and music and movement are important parts of the daily curriculum.

Al Khuwayr
Map 6 E4

The Oasis Kindergarten
24 691 348 | *www.ok-oman.om*
The Oasis Kindergarten follows the English National Foundation Stage Curriculum and the emphasis is on providing a secure and happy environment where children can learn through play. The kindergarten takes children aged 3 to 6 years.

Villa 4472
Way 2742
Al Khuwayr
Map 7 E4

Tender Buds Nursery
24 691 055 | *www.nurseriesofoman.com*
Tender Buds is a safe and caring nursery that welcomes children of mixed ages and nationalities. Children are divided into two groups according to their age. The environment is safe and the multi-national staff take vigilant care of the children. Children are given snacks (which you provide) in the kitchen – the school has a strict 'no junk food' policy. Arabic classes are offered twice a week.

Nurseries & Pre-Schools

ABA	Al Khuwayr	24 605 287
Abu Adnan	Madinat As Sultan Qaboos	24 605 704
American International School of Muscat	Ghala	24 595 180
Al Zumurrud Montessori Kindergarten	Shati Al Qurm	92 285 849
Bright Beginnings	Madinat As Sultan Qaboos	24 699 387
The British School Nursery	Madinat As Sultan Qaboos	24 600 842
Indian Nursery	Al Khuwayr	24 486 412
Little Gems	Al Azaiba	24 498 464
National Nursery Montessori	Al Qurm	24 560 096
Oasis Kindergarten	Madinat As Sultan Qaboos	24 691 348
Royal Flight	As Seeb	24 516 330
Teddy's	Madinat As Sultan Qaboos	98 104 245
Tender Buds	Al Khuwayr	24 691 055
TLC	Al Azaiba	99 381 458

Primary & Secondary Schools
Standards of teaching in Oman's schools are usually high and schools tend to have excellent facilities with extracurricular activities offered. International schools will often employ teachers who have been trained in, and have teaching experience from, the country relevant to the curriculum. The curriculum will probably be an important factor in choosing a school for your child – it makes sense to choose a curriculum that

will make it easy for your child to slot back into a school in your home country (or in whatever country you might end up in one day). Be aware that waiting lists can be very long so prioritise this when you confirm the move to Oman. A relocation company like Sununu Muscat (99800 613, sununumuscat.com) can help.

The American International School Of Muscat

Ghala St
Opp Church Complex
Ghala
Map 1 B1

24 595 180 | *www.taism.com*

The American International School follows the American curriculum and is the only school to be sponsored by the American embassy. The school, which opened in 2000, has some great facilities for students to enjoy arts, sports and academic excellence. The school has nearly 400 students, of over 40 nationalities, and teaching is done in English. There are support facilities for special needs children.

American-British Academy (ABA)

Al Khuwayr Heights
District (Sheikh
Khalili Heights)
Madinat As Sultan
Qaboos
Map 7 E4

24 603 646 | *www.abaoman.edu.om*

The American British Academy takes children from 3 years (into the kindergarten), right up until grade 12. The school follows the international curriculum (IB). The curriculum includes languages, social studies, science and IT, arts and music, maths, Arabic lessons and physical education. The school has some excellent facilities including a library, a gym, computer labs, a multi-purpose hall, a swimming pool and a cafeteria. There are also some good sports facilities such as an astroturf football pitch and courts for tennis and volleyball.

Azzan Bin Qais Private School

Boucher St
Ghala
Map 1 B1

24 503 081 | *www.azzanbinqais.com*

Azzan Bin Qais Private School follows an international curriculum and offers teaching in both Arabic and English. Facilities include an auditorium (seating 600 people), sports facilities including an athletics track and an Olympic-size swimming pool, a comprehensive library, science labs and an IT centre, as well as rooms for arts and music. The school also has provisions for special needs children. It is one of only three Omani schools offering international GSCE and AS/A level courses.

Qurm Amusement Park

Omani youth in Mutrah

The British School Muscat ▶ p.135

▶ p.135

Ruwi St
Madinat As Sultan
Qaboos
Map 7 F1

24 600 842 | www.britishschoolmuscat.com

The British School Muscat is one of the most popular schools in the area – so much so that in some age groups classrooms are filled to capacity and a waiting list is in operation. The school is multi-cultural and its students represent over 50 nationalities. All teachers at BSM have UK-recognised qualifications. The school's facilities are superb, and include indoor and outdoor play areas, two libraries, science and IT facilities, arts and drama studios, a sports hall, a swimming pool and an outdoor astroturf pitch. The school accepts children between the ages of 3 and 18.

Indian School Al Ghubrah

4287 Way
Al Ghubrah
Map 6 E3

24 491 587 | www.indianschool.com

The Indian School is mainly for children of Indian expats, although it does accept children of other nationalities too. It takes students from kindergarten to senior secondary level. The school has some excellent academic and sports facilities, but it also offers a unique tutorial system, whereby students are assigned meetings with a teacher on a regular basis, thus providing more focused attention.

Indian School Al Wadi Al Kabir

Al Wadi Al Kabir
Wadi Kabir
Map 13 A4

24 816 633 | www.iswkoman.com

The Indian School at Wadi Al Kabir is linked to New Delhi's Central Board of Secondary Education, and provides English-language education to expat Indian children. The school's facilities include science labs, and IT centre, rooms for arts and music, an audiovisual room and a multi-purpose hall. Hindi is taught as a second language (compulsory). Children can attend the school from KG1 right through until grade 12.

Muscat Private School

Madinat Al Sultan
Qaboos Street
Al Qurm
Map 11 D1

24 565 550

Both Omani and expatriate children can attend this international school (the expat programme follows the English National Curriculum). The school accepts children aged between 3 and 18. It is well established and has some excellent facilities, including two libraries, five laboratories, two computer laboratories, two art rooms, three workshops, three music rooms, an auditorium and a dark room for photography. The sports facilities are just as diverse, with a football pitch, swimming pool, volleyball court, tennis court, gymnasium and an outdoor playground.

Pakistan School

2519 Way
Off Ruwi St
Ruwi
Map 12 C1

24 702 489 | www.pakistanschool.edu.om

The Pakistan School is affiliated to FBISE Islamabad and EDEXCEL International London. A new junior block with 10 extra classrooms was opened in 2004, adding to the schools range of facilities. Other facilities include laboratories, an auditorium, a junior play area, basketball courts and tennis courts. The school also has branches in Salalah, Sohar, Nizwa and Musanah.

The Sultan's School

3117 Way
Al Khawd
Map 3 D1

24 536 777 | www.sultansschool.org

The Sultan's School is predominantly for Omani students. They offer a choice of the Oman National Curriculum or the English National Curriculum. The staff is made up of teachers of many nationalities, although the majority of teachers are from the UK. Facilities include 36 classrooms, six science labs, a cafeteria, art and music rooms, a mosque, football fields, netball and volleyball courts, a sports hall, a gymnasium, a swimming pool and an athletics track.

Calligraphy in Mutrah

University & Higher Education

Oman has signed a five-year deal with the New Zealand Tertiary Education Consortium (NZTEC). The NZTEC provides course content to the Ministry of Higher Education, mainly in the fields of IT, business and English language, for use in Oman universities.

There are several higher-education institutions in Oman, although most of these are for Omani students only. Sultan Qaboos University (www.squ.edu.om) is the largest and arguably the best university, although expatriate students are not permitted to apply.

The Modern College of Business and Science (www.mcbs.edu.om) accepts international students and offers degrees in IT, business, computer science and economics. It is a private college, but is licensed by the Ministry of Higher Education. Due to the lack of choice of higher education, many expat students return to their home countries after finishing secondary school, so that they can attend university. However, there have been huge developments in the higher-education sector in neighbouring Dubai, so expat students living in Oman could always attend university there. For more information, the following websites might be helpful: the American University of Dubai (www.aud.edu), the American University of Sharjah (www.aus.edu), the British University in Dubai (www.buid.ac.ae), Heriot-Watt University in Dubai (www.hwud.com), the University of Wollongong (www.uowdubai.ac.ae) and Knowledge Village (www.kv.ae).

Special Needs Education

There are no dedicated schools in Oman for expatriate children with special needs. Schools with learning support departments may be able to accommodate children with mild difficulties. The American International School of Muscat (TAISM) has a support unit of professionals including a special education teacher. You can contact them on 24 600 374 for more information. In addition, the British School Muscat (see p.134) has a Learning Support Department which provides targeted support for children with a range of learning difficulties such as Dyslexia or Dyspraxia. Teachers and Teaching Assistants plan and deliver targeted programmes of support to enable each child to access the curriculum. The school is not able to meet the needs of children with moderate to severe learning difficulties.

Learning Arabic

Other options **Language Schools** p.236

English is so widely used in Oman that you can get by without having to learn a single word of Arabic. However, some say that to enrich the cultural experience of your time in this part of the world, knowing some basic Arabic is helpful. If you have children there is a good chance they will be learning some Arabic at school, so it can be useful to know a bit yourself.

Learning Arabic		
British Council low cost English classes	24 681 000	www.britishcouncil.org
New Horizons Computer Learning Center	24 600 647	www.newhorizons.com
Polyglot Institute Oman	24 831 261	www.polyglot.org

Don't Drive Dirty

It is against the law to drive a dirty car – if you do then you could be stopped by police and ordered to go and have your car washed, or even risk getting a fine. So after a weekend of off-road adventuring, make sure you roll those sleeves up and get scrubbing, or make a trip to the nearest carwash. The Rainbow carwash at Al Sarooj is excellent, and you can sit and have a coffee while they do all the hard work for you.

Transportation

Other options **Getting Around** p.37, **Car** p.41

In the absence of an extensive public transport system, cars are definitely the most popular way of getting around in Oman. The costs involved in buying, insuring and maintaining a car are very reasonable, and fuel is up to 50% cheaper than in many parts of the world.

Driving standards can be less than perfect, however, and upon your arrival in Oman you may fear that you'll never be able to get behind the wheel. However, the sooner you start driving the quicker you'll get to know your way around your new area. The following section covers leasing, buying and renting cars, registration and insurance for buyers, and fines and accident procedures.

Taxis

Until you feel comfortable driving, you can always use a taxi. Taxis are plentiful and relatively cheap – a 10km taxi ride will cost you around RO 3. It won't be hard to find a taxi, because they will often hoot at you if they see you standing by the side of the road. Keep an eye out for the bright orange-and-white cabs, although if you are a woman you should never use one of these at night if you are on your own. In such cases, it is safer to use a private taxi firm such as City Taxi (24 603 363) or Hello Taxi (24 607 011).

Driving

With cars and petrol both being considerably cheaper in this region than in other parts of the world, you can afford that luxury 4WD vehicle you've always wanted – it may not be as environmentally friendly as a little city car that does over 100km per litre, but you will certainly feel much safer, and you'll realise the importance of this once you see the driving. You can expect lots of overtaking on the inside, dramatic lane-switching manoeuvres, sudden stops, speeding, and surprising levels of aggression. Your first few weeks of driving will be an ordeal, but you will quickly learn to drive defensively and soon that speed demon driving about 30cm behind you and flashing his headlights to tell you to move won't even bother you (well, not much anyway).

Vehicle Leasing

Leasing a vehicle has many advantages over buying. Not only is it a good option for shorter or uncertain periods, but the leasing company will deal with breakdowns, accidents, insurance and registration for you and will offer 24 hour assistance. Cars can be leased on a weekly, monthly or annual basis. You can choose from a range of models from saloon cars to four-wheel drives. Prices vary according to the model and the length of lease, but a one-year lease on a basic saloon car will cost about RO 200 per month. For short-term rental, many of the local and international companies offer daily rates – check the newspapers or the Oman Business Directory for the most competitive. To hire any vehicle, you will need to provide a passport copy and driving licence.

Driving Licence

You must be a resident to apply for a driving licence. Visitors may drive a hired or borrowed car on a valid international or home country licence. Residents from many countries, including the UK and US, may simply exchange their national licence for an Oman one at Death Valley Road traffic police headquarters. To do this, you will have to have an eye test, and pay the fee of RO 20. To apply for an Oman licence, you need your essential documents (p.58), the relevant application form from the traffic police and your original driving licence. Your company PRO should take you to the police station and help you through the process of licence exchange or test booking. Always carry your driving licence when driving; you may be fined if you fail to produce it during a spot check. Driving licences are valid for 10 years and can be renewed at traffic police HQ on Death Valley Road. Roads are policed rigorously by the Royal Oman Police. Drinking and driving is illegal, as is driving while using a mobile phone handset. See p.142 for more information.

Vehicle Leasing Agents

Maha Rent A Car	24 603 376
Al Maskry Car Rentals	24 595 241
Al Miyasa Rent-A-Car	23 296 521
Anwar Al Shaikh Trdg Est	23 298 085
Avis Rent A Car	24 400 888
Budget Rent A Car ▶ p.43	24 683 999
Europcar	24 700 190
Global Car Rental	24 697 140
Hertz	24 566 208
Mark Car Rental & Tours	24 562 444
Payless	24 567 261
Sixt	24 482 793
Thrifty	99 323 619
Unic Rent-A-Car	24 691 108
United Finance Co SAOG	24 565 151
Value Plus Rent A Car	24 597 264
Wattayah Motors	24 562 729
Xpress Rent A Car	24 490 055

Buying A Vehicle

To own a car in Oman you must have a labour or resident card. If you decide to buy a car, you'll find that it is considerably cheaper to buy, maintain and run a car in Oman compared with most other countries. Every expat resident is allowed to own up to three vehicles. Whether you are buying a brand new car or a second-hand one, when it's time to close the deal you'll need to present certain documents. You'll need your essential documents (p.58), a vehicle purchase form (available from the police station or the showroom), plus your valid driving licence and a copy. The vehicle purchase form should be signed by your sponsor or company, and then taken to your insurance provider. In the case of a private sale, the seller should be with you, as the car must be insured in your name before the registration can be finalised. Once the car is registered, you will get a vehicle registration card (a 'mulkia'). You should always have the mulkia with you in the car, although many people keep a copy in the car and leave the original mulkia at home.

New Vehicles

Most new car models are available through the main dealers. Many car dealerships have showrooms between the Al Wattayah and Wadi Adai Roundabouts, although there are others located all along the highway. Some dealers sell several makes of car. Don't forget to haggle – most dealers will offer a discount on the advertised price of a new car. The best time of year to get a good deal is during Ramadan, when all the

New Car Dealers

Al Jenaibi International Automobiles	BMW	24 560 889	www.bmw-oman.com
Al Rumaila Motors	Various	24 490 627	na
Al-Hashar & Company	Various	24 596 434	www.alhashargroup.com
Auto Plus (International Commercial House)	Various	24 478 080	na
Bahwan Automotive Centre	Lexus	24 578 000	na
Mohsin Haider Darwish	Jaguar	24 703 777	www.mhdoman.com
Oman Gulf Enterprises	Various	24 793 072	na
Oman Marketing & Services Co (OMASCO)	Various	24 561 780	www.omasco.com
Sata	Porsche	24 492 544	na
Saud Bahwan Group	Toyota, Lexus & Daihatsu	24 578 000	www.saudbahwangroup.com
Shanfari Automotive Co	JEEP	24 561 482	www.shanfari.com
Suhail Bahwan Automobiles	Nissan, Infiniti, Renault	24 560 111	www.suhailbahwangroup.com
Towell Auto Centre	Mazda	24 564 048	www.towellauto.com
Wattayah Motors	VW, Skoda, Audi, Bentley	24 562 729	www.wattayah.com Zawawi
Trading Company	Mercedes	24 562 077	na
Zubair Automotive	Mitsubishi	24 500 000	www.zubairautomotive.com

dealers have promotions. Some dealers even offer a 'buy one, win one' raffle ticket that gives you the chance to win a second car. You'll also get a good deal if a new batch of cars arrives, as last year's models immediately drop in price.

The dealer will take care of all the paperwork involved in the car purchase on your behalf, including registration and arranging finance. They will also usually offer good warranties and free servicing for the first few years. Unless you are paying cash for the car, you will need to get a bank loan or leave a post-dated cheque for every month of the finance period (typically 12, 24 or 36 months). When you collect your car you will drive with green licence plates until the vehicle registration is complete.

Used Vehicles

With cars being relatively cheap, and expats coming and going all the time, the second-hand car market is thriving. The main areas for used car dealers are Al Wattayah, Al Khuwayr and Wadi Kabir, although you'll find dealers in other locations too. The advantage of buying through a dealer is that they'll arrange the registration and insurance for you. In general, dealers do not offer warranties, unless you are buying a car that is still protected under its 'new car' warranty. Newspaper classifieds offer little in terms of second-hand vehicles for sale, except for Sunday's *Times of Oman* supplement and the classified section of *The Week*. Supermarket noticeboards are a good source of cars for sale, and there is the car souk at the Friday Market. If you do buy a second-hand car privately, it's a good idea to have it checked for major faults and Gonu damage before you buy. Reputable car dealers will perform a thorough check-up of a vehicle for about RO 15.

Used Car Dealers

Al Fajer Cars	Al Ghubrah	99 352 924
Al Itihad Cars Showroom	Al Hayl	24 542 990
Al Jazeera Motors	Madinat As Sultan Qaboos	24 600 127
Al Siyabi Used Cars	Madinat As Sultan Qaboos	24 698 195
Al Wathbah Trading	As Seeb	24 421 828
Auto Plus (International Commercial House)	Salalah	23 211 898
Best Cars (Saud Bahwan Automotive)	Al Wutayyah	24 578 000
General Automotive Co	Al Azaiba	24 500 849
Modern Cars Exhibition	Ruwi	24 786 011
Mohsin Haider Darwish	Ruwi	24 703 777
New Zahra Trading	Ruwi	24 833 953
OK Used Cars	Al Khuwayr	24 691 218
Popular Cars	Al Qurm	24 560 111
Real Value Auto	Ruwi	24 560 508
Wattayah Motors	Al Wutayyah	24 562 729

Ownership Transfer

To transfer a private vehicle into your name you need to fill in a form, which details the buyer's personal information and bears the signatures of both buyer and seller. The seller must appear in person before the Directorate of Licencing at the traffic police department. If the seller still has a loan outstanding on the vehicle the bank must give its approval, and if the loan has been paid the bank will issue a letter of discharge. All transactions related to buying or selling second hand vehicles should go through the Royal Oman Police.

Vehicle Import

If you are importing a vehicle, you need to go with your shipping agent to the port to get the import papers from the port authorities (if you're lucky your shipping agent will do this without you). They'll give you a form with some details of the car on it, such as engine number, chassis number and date of production. Depending on the age of the vehicle, and the mood of the person helping you, you might have to pay tax.

The next thing you need is insurance. Even though the car is not registered, you can insure on the basis of the engine number or chassis number to identify the car. The insurance company will give you a form, all in Arabic, which you'll need for the registration. The insurance company will fill in the form for you. You'll also need a letter from your sponsor to say they approve of you importing the vehicle. The next step is to go to the Ministry of Commerce in Ruwi, behind the Lulu shopping centre. Take the vehicle export papers from the country of origin, the import papers from the shipping agent, the registration form in Arabic from the insurance company, the insurance papers, the sponsor letter, passport copies, your Oman driving licence, a copy of your labour card, and the original ownership papers. To be on the safe side, just take any document remotely connected with the vehicle, plus a few spare copies. After paying a fee of RO 1 you'll be given an approval form. Armed with all your papers, your next stop should be the police station on Death Valley Road to have your car checked in the Annual Inspections section. Once your vehicle has been inspected, collect the inspector's report (from the small office in the inspection area) and proceed to the main office of the police station. Here you'll have to present your documents before being directed to the customs counter (in the same room). After customs, you'll be sent back to the inspector's office and this is when you'll have to pay a fee of RO 20 – remember to keep the receipt. You will then get your licence plates, which you'll take home to affix to your car. The following day you should go back (to the same counter) and hand over the receipt (take all the other papers too, just in case). They will give you the final registration card, which is the same size as a credit card. Finally, go back to the insurance company and give them the registration number and show them the card.

Vehicle Finance

Many new and second-hand car dealers will be able to arrange the finance for you, often through a deal with their preferred banking partner. Strangely, it is unusual to set up a direct debit to cover your monthly car payment, and instead you will have to write out a post-dated cheque for every month of the life of your loan, and submit them all at the very beginning. So if you take a four-year car loan, you will have to write out 48 cheques before you can take ownership of your car.

Always ask about the rates and terms of the loan, and then consider going to a different bank to see if they will offer you a better deal.

Vehicle Finance		
Bank Dhofar	24 790 466	
	23 294 886	www.bankdhofar.com
Bank Muscat SAOG ▶ p.77	24 795 555	www.bankmuscat.com
Bank Sohar ▶ p.49	24 730 000	www.banksohar.net
Habib Bank	24 817 139	www.hbl.com
HSBC ▶ p.IFC	24 799 920	www.hsbc.co.om
National Bank Of Oman (NBO)	24 811 711	www.nbo.co.om
Oman International Bank	24 682 500	
	23 291 512	www.oiboman.com/OIB-Main.html

Vehicle Insurance

You must have adequate insurance before you can register your car in your name. The minimum requirement is third party insurance, but fully comprehensive insurance is advisable. Many insurance companies, both local and international, are listed in the Yellow Pages. To insure your car you need copies of your driving licence, your labour or residence card, and the 'mulkia' for your car. In some cases the insurance company will want to inspect the car first.

It is simple and inexpensive to insure your car for the UAE, should you wish to drive across the border. Remember, your insurance will not be valid if your licence is not valid, or if you have an accident while under the influence of alcohol.

Vehicle Insurance		
Arabia Insurance Company	24 793 299	www.arabiainsurance.com
AXA Insurance	24 400 100	
	26 846 421	www.axa-gulf.com
Dhofar Insurance Company	24 423 075	www.dhofarinsurance.com
Oman Qatar Insurance Company	24 700 067	na
Oman United Insurance Company	24 703 990	www.ouic-oman.com
Risk Management Services	24 704 004	www.rmsllc.com
Royal & Sun Alliance Insurance Oman	24 478 318	rsagroup.com.om

Registering A Vehicle

All cars must be registered and the registration must be renewed annually. The registration document is called the mulkia, and should be carried with you in the car whenever you drive.

Along with your essential documents (p.58) the following documents are also required:
• New registration form filled in by the applicant or their representative and stamped by the sponsor.
• Insurance certificate
• Proof of purchase certificate
• Copy of a valid driving licence

There is a detailed list on the ROP website (www.rop.gov.om) of all required documents when registering your vehicle. Regulations can change overnight, so it is always a good idea to check what the requirements are before you go. Additional documents are needed if you have imported your car or bought it at an auction.

The Process

If you are buying your car from a dealer, they will usually do this for you. If you have bought a vehicle privately, you can do it yourself or pay a local to do it for you – many advertise their services on supermarket noticeboards (they'll probably charge around RO 10 to RO 15 – well worth it).

If you decide to do it yourself, collect the necessary documents (and some spare copies, just in case), and head down to the police headquarters on Death Valley Road. Across the road from the station you'll see a group of Omanis fitting registration plates – approach one and wait your turn (it's usually less busy in the afternoons).

It is at re-registration that you find out if you've picked up any traffic fines, so take extra money with you in case you have to pay your fines. You can find out if you've been caught by checking your licence plate number on the ROP website before you go (www.rop.gov.om).

If your car is 10 years old or more, it will need to pass a roadworthy test. This involves an inspection to check that the chassis and engine numbers match those on the mulkia, that the lights and brakes work, that there are no smoke emissions, and the paintwork is not damaged or fading. Once the car has passed the test, you can proceed with registration. If your car fails the test, you must first fix any problems then start the process again.

Traffic Fines & Offences

Police
Station Location
To register your car, head for the ROP station on Madinat Qaboos Street. There is also a traffic police branch in As Seeb, which is open 24 hours a day.

If you are caught driving or parking illegally, you will be fined (unless the offence is more serious, in which case you may have to appear in court). Around Muscat, there are a number of police-controlled speed traps, fixed cameras and mobile radar traps, which are activated by cars exceeding the speed limit by nine kilometres or more. Fines start at RO 10 and go up in increments of RO 5. All traffic fines should be paid at the traffic fines section of the Death Valley Road police station. Your fines are 'banked' and you only have to pay them once a year when you renew your car registration, but you can check whether you've received any fines online at www.rop.gov.om/trafficfine.

Breakdowns

In the event of a breakdown, you will usually find that passing police cars stop to help you, or at least to check your documents. It is important to keep water in your car at all times – the last thing you need is to be stuck on the side of the road with no air conditioning and no water while you wait for assistance.

If you can, pull your car over to a safe spot. If you are on the hard shoulder of a busy road, pull your car as far away from the yellow line as possible, display your red warning triangle and step away from the road until help arrives.

You can call the Arabian Automobile Association (AAA), a 24 hour breakdown service (similar to the AA in the UK). If you break down for any reason (even a flat tyre or if you run out of petrol), they will send a mechanic out to you as soon as possible. The number is 24 605 555 and often the operator on duty won't speak great English so be patient.

Traffic Accidents
Other options **Car** p.41

Traffic
Traffic is not a huge problem, even in Muscat. You will find traffic back-ups at certain hotspots during rush hour, but even these little traffic jams are no where near as bad as the gridlock you would face in other countries.

Oman has a relatively high rate of road accidents, and the figures of death and injury on the roads increases every year. The government started a big road safety campaign to educate drivers about safe driving standards and how to reduce accidents. The name of the campaign is 'Salim and Salimah, Safe and Sound' (www.salimandsalimah. org), and the website contains a great deal of excellent information on accidents and road safety.

If you have an accident, don't move your car until the police arrive, even if you are causing a major road blockage. The police will usually arrive pretty quickly. In case of an accident, call 24 560 099 (don't call 9999, it is reserved for the Fire Department and emergency cases only). Expect a crowd of rubberneckers to gather around the accident – at least you'll have someone there who can translate from Arabic to English when the police arrive. The police will decide (on the spot) which party is responsible for the accident, and then all involved parties should go to the nearest police station. If your car can't be driven, the police will arrange for it to be towed away. When you get to the police station you might have to wait around for quite some time, so be patient. You'll need to present your driving licence and mulkia (registration card). If any of your documents are invalid you will immediately be blamed for the accident. If your company has a PRO, it's a good idea to get him to come down to the station to help you translate and fill in the many forms. If there is a fine to be paid, the police will hold your licence until you've paid it.

The police will fill in an accident report and you will be given a reference number. The car must be sent to a garage that is approved by your insurance company. The garage is not allowed to carry out repairs to any vehicle without the police report.

If you are in an accident where someone is hurt or killed, and the case goes to court, you will not be allowed to leave the country until the case is settled.

Vehicle Repairs

By law, no vehicle can be accepted for repair after an accident without an accident report from the Traffic Police. Usually, your insurance company will have an agreement with a particular garage to which they will refer you. The garage will carry out the repair work and the insurance company will settle the claim. Generally, there is a RO 100 deductible for all claims, but confirm the details of your policy with your insurance company.

Besides accidents and bumps, you may also have to deal with the usual running repairs associated with any car. Common problems in this part of the world can include the air conditioning malfunctioning and batteries suddenly giving up the ghost. If your air conditioning is not working well it is usually a case of having the gas

Vehicle Repairs		
Al Khuwair Auto Maintenance	Al Khuwayr	24 602 393
Balqees Trading & Contracting	Wadi Kabir	24 815 161
East Arabian Establishment	Wadi Kabir	24 815 961
Four Wheel Drive Centre	Wadi Kabir	24 810 962

topped up, which is a fairly straightforward procedure. However, if something more serious goes wrong it can be very costly to fix, mainly due to labour charges as the mechanic has to remove your dashboard to get access to the air conditioning.

Car batteries don't seem to last too well in the heat, and it is not uncommon to come back from your holidays to find your car won't start.

Sunset in Riyam

Sculpture in Bait Al Falaj

Exploring

Exploring

Fort Permits ◀

Forts are plentiful in Oman and you will find a brief selection of some of the better ones in this section. However, if forts take your fancy most hotels provide leaflets and booklets or you can get hold of a copy of the book Forts of Oman. *You will need a permit for Quyiyat Castle, available free of charge from the Ministry of Culture & National Heritage (24 641 300) in Muscat. The ministry is located next to the Natural History Museum, or you can phone the Department of Forts on 24 641 524.*

Exploring

Oman, the fabled land of Sindbad the Sailor, has been a place of great attraction to explorers for centuries. During his expedition, Marco Polo visited the region of Dhofar in the late 13th century, and then sailed up to the coast of Qalhat, once a city of high prosperity. Fifty years later he was followed by the Moroccan explorer Ibn Battuta, who started his pilgrimage to Mecca in 1325. Twenty-nine years later Ibn Battuta had seen the whole of Arabia, referring to Oman as 'the coast of the fish eaters' (not surprising as he arrived in Oman by sea at Sur). The more recent desert explorations of Britain's Wilfred Thesiger are most fondly remembered in Oman and the UAE today. Thesiger crossed the Rub Al Khali (Empty Quarter) twice between 1946 and 1948, both times disguised as a Syrian Bedouin.

Nowadays there are still countless reasons to visit Oman. The Gulf of Oman's rich sea life, the variety of unspoilt landscapes, the vast deserts, the rugged mountains, the numerous forts, the wildlife and, last but not least, the friendly Omani people are all things that you will remember fondly. Fortunately, the Omanis treasure their past and therefore abundant remains of ancient cities can be admired with some excellent museums (p.171) to educate residents and visitors alike. Adventure seekers will enjoy activities like desert driving, wadi bashing, diving and trekking. Other local attractions include a visit to the souks or the camel races, and are a perfect opportunity to mingle with the locals and get a taste of everyday Omani life. All in all – there's something for everyone in Oman.

Also known as the Pearl of Arabia, Muscat still lies embedded in a traditional culture. With all its greenery, beaches, museums, the famous Mutrah Souk (p.292) and other commercial centres (including modern malls), visitors should take at least a few days to discover this friendly city, getting adjusted to the lifestyle and pace. The driving also might take some patience. The modern city of Muscat has grown and developed and there are now many separate areas making up the whole, which is usually referred to as the Greater Muscat area. Hence, there is no one place which you can visit to get a 'feel' of Muscat – the areas are divided by low craggy hills and each part has its own distinctive character.

After Muscat, it is time to take off to other, more rugged regions of the country. Travelling north will bring you to the cities of Barka, Nakhal and Sohar. If time allows, the Musandam peninsula (p.166) to the north-west is highly recommended, with its main cities of Khasab and Bukha, and with scenery totally different from the rest of Oman. It features beautiful fjords and lagoons and is becoming an increasingly popular tourist destination.

Travelling inland leads you to Rusayl, Rustaq, Nizwa, Bahla, Jabrin and also to the mountains of Jebel Shams, an experience not to be missed if you enjoy the surroundings of rocky mountains and total tranquility. Going south via the interior route, you will pass the cities of Fanja, Sumail, Ibra, Al Mudayr, Al Mintrib, Sur and Ra's al Hadd. On the coastal route Tiwi village is worth a stop, as is the ancient city of Qalhat, if only for the fact that this historical city, nowadays in ruins, was of such particular interest to Marco Polo and Ibn Battuta.

The southern province of Dhofar, with its capital Salalah, provides a welcome change in climate in the hot summer months. While the rest of Oman is paralysed by heat, the monsoon (khareef) blowing off the Indian Ocean ensures a high percentage of rainfall in this area, resulting in cool weather and beautiful greenery. Salalah attracts international as well as local visitors for its peace and tranquility.

Apart from the major regions to visit in Oman, this section also includes its largest island, Masirah, which is off the south-east coast.

Tuck Into Omani Food

Enjoy the taste of Omani food, as well as the traditional customs involved in the Omani way of eating. The menu varies from spicy to mild, and has delicious fish, meat and vegetarian options. Dishes are usually served with rice, and lunch is often the main meal of the day.

Cruise On A Dhow

Watch these traditional boats being built by hand in the dhow yard in Sur. The building process can last for up to 12 months, but once finished the boats can last for more then 100 years. If you would like to make a trip on a traditional dhow, find out from Tour Operators (p.194) where you can arrange a dhow cruise.

Watch For Dolphins & Whales

When you head out to the open waters of the Gulf of Oman, it is very common to bump into a school of playful dolphins. Dolphin experts may even spot several different species. While the chance of spotting a whale is much smaller, keep your eyes peeled and your patience might be rewarded.

Take To The Water

The beautiful Gulf of Oman has some amazing diving and snorkelling spots, best pointed out by one of the dive centres. Many hotels and major tour operators (see p.194) run activities including surfing, sailing and fishing. See the Activities section (p.211) for more information on independent operators.

Marvel At The Turtles

One of the major attractions in Oman is a trip to see the nesting turtles. Watching these huge creatures lumber up the beach to lay their eggs, then make their way back into the sea is to experience nature at its most miraculous. You are virtually guaranteed a sighting at Ras Al Jinz.

Go Mountain Biking

Avid mountain bikers will love pedalling along the tracks that wind their way through Oman's rocky mountains, the wadis and along the coastline. Even the most hardcore bikers will find routes to test their skills. There are also some easier tracks for beginners. See Mountain Biking (p.239)

Hike The Peaks

The spectacular mountain scenery of Oman, with its miraculous staircases criss-crossing the peaks, is paradise for those who like exploring the country by foot. The climate in these higher areas is usually perfect, which can be a relief after the heat of the plains and coastal areas.

Go Underground

Oman's caves provide a mystical underground world containing glittering stalactites and stalactites, white gypsum crystal and underground lakes. These underground treasures are there for you to explore, but remember to respect and preserve them, since they are part of Oman's natural heritage. See Caving in the Activities section (p.218).

Get Twitching

Oman has a good variety of birds, thanks to its varied landscapes and habitats, from lush green slopes, open sea and beaches, to the tidal mudflats, coastal lagoons and arid desert plains. Oman's birdlife will please any keen twitcher. See Activities (p.211) for more information.

Shop The Souks

Experience the sounds, smells, sights and tastes of Oman at the local markets. It's the ideal opportunity to mingle with the local people, practise your bargaining skills and sample the local street cafe cuisine. Even if you just go 'for a look', you'll probably leave with at least one bag full of souvenirs.

Go For Gold

The city of Muscat is full of examples of gilt-inspired architecture, and as you wander through the city streets you'll find many buildings with a golden glow. Take for example the Oman International Bank in Al Khuwayr – its huge front doors are plated in 24 carat gold.

Ride A Camel

This is a chance for you to ride on the back of the traditional 'ship of the desert'. The experience of being atop an ungainly, yet surprisingly graceful, camel is one you won't forget in a hurry. If you'd prefer to keep your distance, get involved in the competitive camaraderie as a spectator at a camel race (p.170).

Follow The Frankincense Trail

In ancient times, frankincense was more valuable than gold because of its aromatic fragrance and relative scarcity. Oman was a major frankincense producing country, and you can follow the historical tracks of this heritage in the Dhofar region, or sample the product itself in one of the souks.

Carrying On Camping

Nature lovers and happy campers will adore Oman, where you can pitch your tent just about anywhere for a night out under the stars. Choose from the white beaches, the rocky mountains or the desert dunes, set up camp, and then just relax and enjoy your surroundings.

Drive The Wadis

Oman's wadis (dry gullies carved through rock by rushing water) are often filled with running water, and offer spectacular driving opportunities for off-road enthusiasts. You'll find some hard navigating along narrow rocky tracks, but if you need to take a break you can have a swim in one of the freshwater pools.

Go On Safari

Experience the adventure of driving up and down golden sand dunes, ride a camel, watch the unique desert sunset, dance along with the belly dancers, sleep under the stars and wake up to a sunrise in total tranquility. Refer to Tour Operators for more information (p.194).

Bask On The Beach

Oman has a long coastline and many beautiful beaches. Qurm Beach in particular is a very popular, very long stretch of beach that spreads from the Crowne Plaza Muscat to Azaiba and beyond. Most of the beaches are public, although the five-star beach hotels (such as The Chedi and the Al Bustan Palace InterContinental Muscat) have their own private beaches.

Take In A Museum

The Natural History Museum in Muscat is fascinating for adults and kids, featuring an informative tour around the wildlife of Oman. For an insight into the traditions and lifestyles of the Omanis, a trip to the Bait al Zubair Museum offers a glimpse into the past. See Museums, Culture and Heritage (p.171).

Visit The Sultan Qaboos Grand Mosque

The grandeur of the Sultan Qaboos Grand Mosque strikes you as you drive along Sultan Qaboos Road, and inside it is magnificent. It is one of the largest in the Arab world and also one of the highest, with its highest minaret reaching almost 100m. The mosque is open to visitors between 08:30 and 11:00, Saturday to Thursday.

Discover Nizwa

Once the capital of Oman and the centre for trade between the coastal and interior regions, Nizwa is still one of the largest towns in the interior. Embedded in a beautiful palm oasis, with its surprisingly large fort and a variety of souks, visiting Nizwa is an absolute must.

Search For Sindbad

While you're in Oman you just can't miss out on a trip to Sohar, the birthplace of the legendary Sindbad the Sailor. The Sohar Fort Museum, located in the fort, is the ideal place to learn all about Sohar's history. The museum touches subjects on from geology and anthropology to historic trading.

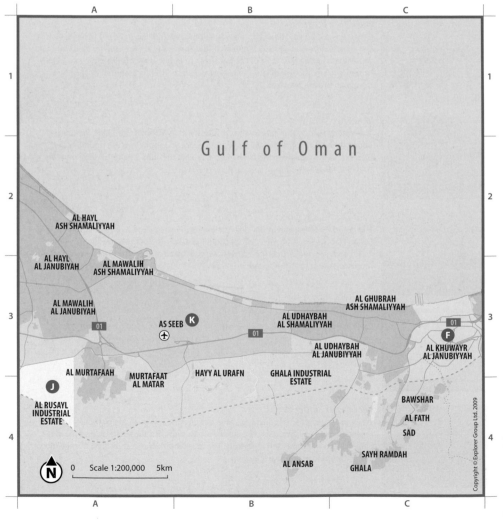

Gulf of Oman

AL HAYL
ASH SHAMALIYYAH

AL HAYL
AL JANUBIYAH

AL MAWALIH
ASH SHAMALIYYAH

AL MAWALIH
AL JANUBIYAH

AS SEEB **K**

AL GHUBRAH
ASH SHAMALIYYAH

AL UDHAYBAH
AL SHAMALIYYAH

AL UDHAYBAH
AL JANUBIYYAH

F

AL KHUWAYR
AL JANUBIYYAH

AL MURTAFAAH

MURTAFAAT
AL MATAR

HAYY AL URAFN

GHALA INDUSTRIAL
ESTATE

J

AL RUSAYL
INDUSTRIAL
ESTATE

BAWSHAR

AL FATH

SAD

SAYH RAMDAH

AL ANSAB   GHALA

0   Scale 1:200,000   5km

Copyright © Explorer Group Ltd. 2009

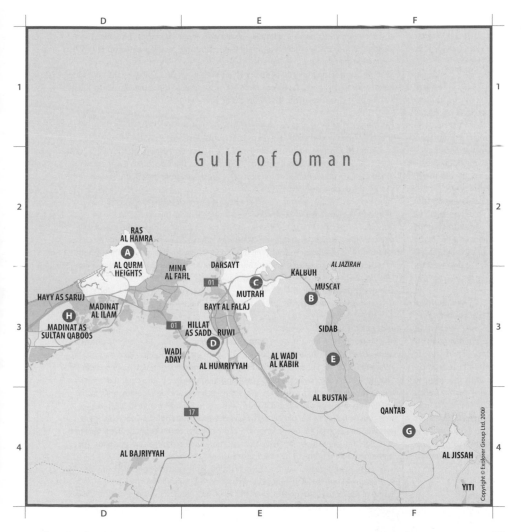

Area **A** *D2 p.151*
Map 8

Al Qurm

The area known as Qurm (meaning 'mangrove' in English) lies in the centre of the greater Muscat area, stretching along the coast north of Madinat As Sultan Qaboos and Ruwi. It is divided into two districts – Qurm and Shati Al Qurm – each with quite different characteristics.

Qurm Must-Dos

Crowne Plaza Muscat is perched on the edge of a clifftop and therefore has some of the best views in the area. Pull up a comfy chair and enjoy a sundowner at The Edge. Alternatively, take a long walk along the Beach Promenade – if it's low tide when you get there, you'll be able to walk from the Crowne Plaza Muscat to the Hyatt Regency.

The Good
Qurm offers some beautiful parks and beaches for when the weather is cool enough, and some amazing shopping and great restaurants when summer's high temperatures drive you indoors. It's the perfect destination, no matter what time of year.

Residential

Qurm is home to a mixture of residential and commercial buildings, and it is safe to say that this is one of the most desirable areas in which to live (and the most expensive). Qurm features mainly large villas set amid a range of undulating slopes, and therefore your chances of landing a villa with a view are high. This is also the location of the Petroleum Development Oman housing compound (complete with its private leisure facilities).

Shati Al Qurm is the epitome of luxury living, with huge white villas spaced out along quiet suburban streets. However, unless you are a foreign diplomat, a wealthy local or an overpaid chief executive, it may be out of your budget.

The Bad
One of Qurm's main attractions, the Beach Promenade, can be uncomfortably crowded during the last few hours before sunset. You'll have to look pretty hard to find yourself a spot in between all the informal football games and out of the way of passing joggers and walkers.

Retail

One of Muscat's main shopping areas is in Qurm. Just near the Qurm Roundabout you'll find four of the main shopping malls: Al-Araimi Complex (p.294), SABCO Centre (p.299), Capital Commercial Centre (CCC) (p.300) and the new Qurm City Centre (p.299). All are pleasant places to shop with a wide range of goods and services and plenty of free parking.

The Jawharat A'Shati Centre in Shati Al Qurm is mainly a coffee-drinkers' hangout, thanks to the presence of Starbucks, Costa Coffee (across the road) and the very popular D'Arcy's Kitchen (they have a superb menu if you're after more than just a cup of coffee). However, Jawharat A'Shati also houses a few shops, notably Megastar for music and DVDs, Gecko for home decor, Eye Candy for designer clothes, Totem for unique greetings cards, Persian Carpet Bazaar, Turtles Bookshop and the Oman Heritage Gallery, which sells traditional, hand-made Omani crafts.

The newly opened Bareeq Al Shati is a great destination for dining, with Ubhar, Abala Cafe and B+F Roadside Diner, plus a foodcourt and several coffee shops.

The Lowdown
Excellent shopping, great restaurants and arguably the best beach in Muscat: Qurm offers the whole package. It is home to some of the top hotels, all of which have superb leisure facilities. You'll find plenty of expats living here, or wishing that they did.

Places Of Interest

The largest park in Muscat – the Qurm National Park & Nature Reserve – is one of the main attractions of this area. The park incorporates a large boating lake, a fountain (Waterfall Hill), the Sultan's rose garden and many meandering pathways to wander around. During the cooler months you'll find many people in the park in the early evening; some strolling, some striding, some reclining and some enjoying a picnic. In 1999 the Ministry of Regional Municipalities and Environment established a mangrove nursery in the park, which has since provided thousands of mangrove seedlings every year for transplantation in other parts of the country. The aim is to stimulate the growth of mangrove trees, as mangrove-rich areas are good for fish breeding and are home to rare bird species.

While it may be smaller than the Qurm National Park, Qurm Heights Park (next to the Gulf Forum Hotel) is still an enjoyable grassy, shady respite from city life.

Some of Muscat's major hotels are in this area, including the InterContinental Muscat (p.31), the Crowne Plaza Muscat (p.30) and the Grand Hyatt Muscat (p.31). All have great leisure facilities and between them they offer an excellent range of food and beverage outlets. The Beach Hotel (p.26) is perfectly situated in the heart of Shati Al Qurm, and offers clean and functional three-star accommodation at a reasonable price.

Old Muscat

Area ⓘ E3 p.151
Map 10

Muscat (Old Town)

The old town of Muscat is situated on the coast at the eastern end of the Greater Muscat area between Mutrah and Sidab. It is a quiet and atmospheric place, based around its sheltered port which was historically important for trade.

The Good

Culture vultures and history buffs will love the museums in the area; Muscat Gate House Museum, Bait Al Zubair and the Omani French Museum all offer fascinating insights into Oman's colourful history and heritage.

Residential

While the old town of Muscat is an interesting place to visit, it can't really be seen as a popular residential area, especially for expats. You will find many Omani families living there in houses that have stood for generations.

Retail

Apart from a shop or two inside the museums, and the odd cornershop selling essential supplies like bread and milk, this area is not considered a rich hunting ground for shopaholics. However, it is just a stone's throw away from the famous souk in Mutrah (p.292).

The Bad

The old town of Muscat has a confusing one-way street system and on your first visit you might find it impossible to get out. If the weather permits, this is an area that is easier to explore on foot.

Places Of Interest

The striking Alam Palace, home of Sultan Qaboos, was built on the waterfront in the 1970s and dominates the area. While you can't get into the palace, you can walk right up to the gates to marvel at the distinctive gold and turquoise exterior, and you should be able to take photos without anyone hassling you. The palace is flanked by two forts overlooking the harbour: Jalali Fort and Mirani Fort. Both forts were built when Oman was under Portuguese control. The forts are rarely open to visitors due to their proximity to the palace and the fact that they are still in use by authorities. However, you are allowed to take photos of the exteriors.

The Lowdown

A fantastic area to explore, particularly to get a glimpse into the past. You'll see many old houses that must have been there for generations and are still being used by Omani families today.

The city wall of Muscat connects to mountain hills behind the old town of Muscat, along the natural bay. You can walk from the bay to the front side of the palace by passing the beautiful Al Zawawi Mosque, then turn left into Qasr Al Alam Street. Evidence of the city walls can still be seen – these walls used to completely surround the old town. You can also still see the three gates that were closed to protect the city from intruders. At one of these gates you'll find the Muscat Gate House Museum, which opened in 2001 and offers, among other attractions, a great view over the town from its roof. Within the old city walls you'll also find the Omani French Museum (Bait Fransa), and the Bait Al Zubair Museum is located just outside the walls on Al Saidiya Street. Bait Al Zubair is well worth a visit to find out how life was for Omanis centuries ago (it was a lot harder than it is now).

Mutrah

Area **G** E3 p.151
Map 9

Mutrah

Mutrah rests between the sea and a protective circle of hills, and is neighboured by Qurm, Ruwi and the old town of Muscat. It has grown around its port, which today is far more vibrant than the port of the old town.

The Good

For a relatively small area, Mutrah packs a lot in. The souk is essential for any visitor, and you'll find plenty of little street cafes where you can grab a bite to eat for pocket change. The fish and produce markets at the northern end are great if you want to buy your groceries in a more traditional way, and you could easily spend a relaxing hour watching the ships in the port.

Residential

As with the old town, there is not much in the way of residential accommodation in Mutrah, save for a crop of old houses that belong to Omani families. There are a few budget hotels along the corniche.

Retail

One of Muscat's most famous shopping experiences lies in Mutrah: the Mutrah Souk. It is always buzzing with activity and is renowned as one of the best souks in the region. It has recently undergone a bit of a facelift and some might say that this has diminished its authenticity; however it is still well worth a visit for the sheer choice of goods on offer. You'll find all the usual things like pashminas and tacky souvenirs, household goods and scented oils. But you'll also find plenty of tiny shops stacked to the ceilings with dusty Omani silver (a good rummage through might result in a lucky find). Look out for the place with barrels of silver and beads as you'll also find photos of supermodel Kate Moss taken in the shop trying on the wares. There are shops selling some rare Omani antiques too, such as pots, leatherwork, silver scrolls and khanjars (traditional daggers).

The Bad

Parking can be hard to find along the main road, and most parking is metered. It's a good idea to keep some loose change handy. If you visit the fish market, leave those with sensitive stomachs at home; the smell can be overwhelming.

Places Of Interest

Mutrah Corniche shows how far Oman has come since the early 1970s. It runs for about three kilometres along the harbour, and is lined with pristine gardens, parks, waterfalls and statues. At the northern end, the old traders' houses and the Lawati Mosque showcase traditional architecture, complete with windtowers designed to capture the slightest whisper of breeze. You'll also find the fish market on the edge of the dhow harbour, where you can witness the hustle and bustle of the local fishing industry. Small fishing boats start returning with their catches at around 06:30, so get there early if you can.

The Lowdown

You won't find many expats living here but it is fantastic for visitors. You can experience traditional shopping at the Mutrah Souk (bargaining is compulsory) and watch Omani fishermen drag their catches into the busy harbour.

Right next to the fish market is an excellent fruit and vegetable market with a colourful range of exotic produce. With some good bargaining skills you should be able to save yourself some money compared with buying your produce in the supermarkets.

When the weather is not too hot it is a pleasant walk from the souk area along the corniche to Mutrah Fort. Unfortunately it is rarely open to visitors since it is still used by the authorities, although you are permitted to take photos.

Further east you'll find the Al Inshirah restaurant and Riyam Park, where a huge incense burner sits on a rocky outcrop. Just behind Al Inshirah is an ancient watchtower overlooking Mutrah. The view at the top is lovely and well worth the steep climb.

Mutrah Must-Dos

A wander through the Mutrah Souk should definitely not be missed – if you're after some silver jewellery and you've got some time on your hands, rummage through the massive bowls full to the brim with rings and bangles. You'll find them in most souvenir shops, and you might walk away with an amazing find.

Area D E3 p.151
Map 12

Ruwi

Less than 30 years ago, the valley (Wadi Kabir) in which Ruwi lies was completely undeveloped. Today it is the bustling commercial district of Muscat, commonly referred to as the central business district (CBD).

The Good

Although it is not traditionally an expat area, a good exploring session around Ruwi could result in some excellent finds, particularly if you are on the lookout for fabrics, souvenirs or a cheap Indian meal.

Residential

There is plenty of low-cost accommodation in Ruwi's many apartment blocks. However, for various reasons (the main one being that there are other quieter, more picturesque residential areas), Ruwi is not an area where you'll find an abundance of western expats living.

Retail

Apart from the very large Lulu Centre, which is excellent, there are no real shopping malls in Ruwi. However, you could spend hours exploring all the little backstreet shops selling fabric, household goods and a variety of knick-knacks. There is also a weekend market on Ruwi High Street that it well worth a visit.

The Bad

Ruwi is the central business district and therefore is quite busy; expect to meet with frustrating traffic delays around peak times. Parking can also be problematic.

> ### Ruwi Must-Dos
>
> It is well worth the trip into Ruwi to experience the traditional Chinese and Thai cuisine served up at the Golden Oryx restaurant (p.312). This restaurant has been a major attraction in Ruwi for over 25 years, and standards are still as high as ever. For a real treat, try the Mongolian Barbecue, where you select your meat or seafood and vegetables, and the chef stir-fries it before your eyes on a special flat wok.

Places Of Interest

Wadi Kabir is like the main artery of Ruwi, since all the main buildings are found alongside it. Although there are plenty of modern buildings in the area, building regulations are restrictive and you won't find any obscenely tall skyscrapers. In fact, the tallest building is the Sheraton Oman, which is cuurently closed for refurbishment. Although Ruwi may not be a tourist hotspot, It is worth a wander around for the charming little shops and all the streetside restaurants selling excellent Arabic and Indian food at cheap prices.

A good point to begin your exploration of Ruwi is at the GTO Tower next to the main post office (almost in the centre of the CBD). On the south side you'll find Sultan

The Lowdown

Ruwi is notable for its modern architecture, particularly along Bank Street which is home to the headquarters of both the Central Bank of Oman and Bank Muscat. Although it is a business area, there is also a healthy supply of low-cost accommodation in apartment blocks.

Qaboos Mosque on Al Jaame Street, as well as the central bus and taxi stations and the clock tower. On the northern side of the GTO Tower, the Bait Al Falaj (in the army base) houses the Sultan's Armed Forces Museum.

The National Museum can be found in Al Noor Street, in the north-west part of Ruwi. The Ruwi Souk (also known as Ruwi High Street) is the place to go for anything from souvenirs to diamond rings.

Ruwi

Area **E** *E3 p.151*
Map 13 & 15

Al Bustan & Sidab

The villages of Al Bustan and Sidab provide an interesting diversion from the main Muscat areas. Heading south along Al Bustan Street out of Ruwi, the spectacular mountain road takes you over the rise from Wadi Kabir, where you can see the village of Al Bustan nestled at the base of the hills with the sea in the background.

On Al Bustan Roundabout at the foot of the hills is the Sohar dhow. In 1980, it set sail on an eight-month journey from Sur to Canton, captained by Tim Severin. This journey was made to commemorate a voyage made by an adventurous trader, Abu Ubaida bin Abdullah bin Al Quassim, in the eighth century. The dhow was constructed at the Sur dhow yard and is made in the traditional manner, entirely from local materials and with no nails, and sits at 24 metres in length.

Just past this landmark is the Al Bustan Palace InterContinental Muscat, one of the most famous hotels in the Gulf. You can spend a leisurely day drifting around the hotel and grounds, having a cocktail on the beach or dinner in Vue by Shannon Bennett (p.322). The surroundings are beautiful and the service is five star. Even if your budget doesn't stretch to a night's stay in this luxury hotel, you should still experience the royal treatment with the gorgeous weekend breakfast buffets and relax at the outdoor tables near the lawns and swimming pool.

From the Al Bustan Roundabout you can head up the coast towards the old town of Muscat, where along the way you will find the scenic harbour area of Sidab. Fishing is the lifeblood of this area and traditions have been passed down through the generations. The Marine Science and Fisheries Centre is an academic institution that undertakes studies of different fish stocks, but it also has a very interesting public aquarium and library where you can learn more about the area's aquaculture. On your way to Sidab you will pass Marina Bandar Al Rowdha and the Capital Area Yacht Club, both offering a chance to get closer to the ocean with all manner of marine activities for members and guests.

Area **F** *C3 p.150*
Map 7

Al Khuwayr

Heading towards central Muscat from As Seeb, Al Khuwayr is on the south side of the main road. It is home to a few ministry buildings as well as some banks and embassies. There are some very impressive buildings to be seen in the area, most notably the head office of the Oman International Bank. The front doors are 10 metres high and plated in 24 carat gold, and the interior is just as impressive. If you pass by early enough, you'll see the doors being polished every day. The architecturally splendid Zawawi Mosque is also found in this area, just off the main road.

Al Khuwayr has its fair share of shopping opportunities, although there are no big shopping malls. Al Zakher Centre has an Al Fair and a range of small shops, and there are plenty of other independent shops scattered around the area. Al Khuwayr Commercial Centre is billed as the area's obligatory souk, although it is more of a shopping centre.

Area **G** *F4 p.151*
Map 15

Bandar Al Jissah & Qantab

Further down the coast from Al Bustan, the mountains increase in height and the landscape gets more rugged. However, this rocky coastline hides a number of beautiful secluded coves. These bays, mostly reachable by the road winding over the mountain, are home to the beaches of Qantab and Jissah, the Oman Dive Centre (p.225) and the Shangri-La's Barr Al Jissah Resort (p.24).

Many of the bays in this area have stretches of sandy beach sheltered by the rocky cliffs, and crystal clear waters that are perfect for snorkelling, diving and fishing. At Qantab Beach you'll find a number of friendly local fishermen offering to take you out fishing (for a price, of course).

Capital Area Yacht Club

A little further south is the Oman Dive Centre, regarded as one of the top dive centres in the world. It offers dive training in a customised dive pool, and organises dive trips for certified divers. There are two daily dives in the morning and it costs RO 2 for a guide per dive if you have less than 20 dives experience. For RO 3 (RO 1.5-2 on weekdays), you can get a day pass to the Oman Dive Centre and make use of their facilities. They have the dive pool, which you can use when there are no lessons in progress, as well as a special kids' pool. Both pools are shaded. You can also use their private beach. The dive centre has an excellent in-house restaurant and if it isn't too hot you can sit on their shaded terrace and enjoy a delicious lunch. They also have a number of barasti chalets on their beach that are available for hire if you want accommodation with a difference.

To get there, when following the road from Ruwi and Wadi Kabir to Al Bustan, you will see the village of Qantab signposted to the right just past the top of the hill. Take this right turn and follow the road until you reach the new roundabout, where you can turn left for Oman Dive Centre or go straight for the Barr Al Jissah Resort at the end of the road.

The Shangri La's Barr Al Jissah Resort (p.24) opened in phases from the end of 2005. The resort has three distinct hotels: Al Bandar, the focal point of the resort; Al Waha, the largest of the hotels and the one that focuses on family fun and entertainment; and Al Husn, the ultimate luxury destination offering six-star service. The resort also offers some amazing food and beverage outlets in a beautiful setting.

Area **H** *D3 p.151*
Map 11

Madinat As Sultan Qaboos

On the other side of the main Sultan Qaboos highway is the leafy suburb of Madinat As Sultan Qaboos, which is also referred to as Madinat Sultan Qaboos, Madinat Qaboos, or most commonly by the abbreviations 'MSQ' and 'MQ'. It is here that you will find a high concentration of villas inhabited by expats, particularly British expats. Perhaps part of the reason is that this is the location of the renowned British School Muscat, one of Muscat's best schools (www.britishschoolmuscat.com). The British School provides high quality education for children from the age of 3 right up to A-levels, and follows the English National Curriculum. It is also a community meeting point for all kinds of activities from Scottish dancing to karate.

MSQ is home to a few embassies and the British Council, which holds a range of English language courses for non-English speakers. The British Council also offers CELTA courses for people wishing to teach English as a second language.

There is a small but friendly shopping centre in the area, the main attraction of which is a big Al Fair supermarket (with a lively community noticeboard). Also in this centre are an excellent branch of Family Bookshop (24 600 084), a Pizza Hut, a Starbucks, a travel agent, a laundry, another branch of D'Arcy's Kitchen (p.334) and an interesting restaurant with local flavour and a jungle setting: Kargeen Caffé. You've also got a great Mexican restaurant in the centre – Pavo Real (24 602 603) is an authentic and lively venue that has all the right ingredients (tequila included) for a fabulous night out. Apart from the lively Mexican atmosphere on offer any night of the week, Pavo also hosts a legendary karaoke night on Mondays.

Just across 'Death Valley Road' is the superb ladies' salon Diva (24 693 011) and the Iranian Kabab House (24 605 515).

Area **J** *A4 p.150*
Map 2

Rusayl

Rusayl is located to the south-west of As Seeb, and doesn't hold too much of interest. However, it is home to one of the world's most renowned perfume factories, owned by Amouage LLC (24 540 757). Amouage produces the 'most valuable perfumes in the world', and the guided tour explains the production process as well as allowing visitors to test the fragrances. Tours are available for groups or individuals, although they can only accommodate a maximum of 30 people at any one time. The tour can be done in English or Arabic, and there is no charge. People taking the tour are served with traditional Omani coffee and dates, and if you buy any Amouage product after the tour, you will be given a valuable gift. See www.amouage.com for the latest products.

Well-known Amouage fragrances include Silver Cristal and Salalah, as well as Ubar (named after the mysterious city hidden deep in the Arabian desert), which was launched in 1995 to commemorate Oman's Silver Jubilee.

The factory opening times are from 08:30 to 17:00, from Sundays to Thursdays but you must phone ahead to book before visiting. It is closed on Fridays and Saturdays.

Area **K** *B3 p.150*
Map 2

As Seeb

You might think that As Seeb is just a bit too far out of Muscat, but from Qurm it should take you less than 30 minutes to get there. At some point or another every Muscat resident has to head for As Seeb, since it is the location of the airport.

As Seeb is located on the main road from Muscat to the UAE, about 35km from the main commercial areas of the city. The area has become a lot more popular since the openings of two of Muscat's biggest shopping malls: Muscat City Centre (p.298) and Markaz Al Bahja (p.296). Both malls have some major tenants, such as Carrefour, Monsoon, Mothercare and Early Learning Centre in Muscat City Centre, and Al Fair, Marks & Spencer, Toys R Us and ID Design in Markaz Al Bahja. If it's too hot to play outside, kids will enjoy the excitement of the huge indoor play area in Markaz Al Bahja, and there is also a cinema in this mall.

Perhaps because of its proximity to the airport, As Seeb is where many business travellers end up. The Oman International Exhibition Centre (www.omanexhibitions. com) hosts many interesting trade and consumer exhibitions throughout the year. The Golden Tulip Seeb Hotel is right next door.

As you travel from As Seeb to Muscat, you'll see the Grand Sultan Qaboos Mosque on the right hand side of the road just after As Seeb. Apart from being a breathtaking example of Islamic architecture, it also offers non-Muslims a rare opportunity to enter a working mosque. Tours of the mosque are available between 08:30 and 11:00, Saturday to Thursday. It is one of the largest mosques in the Arab world, with the point of its highest minaret reaching almost 100 metres, and it is well worth visiting. If you do go on the tour, make sure that your clothing is appropriate – men should wear long trousers and women should be modestly dressed (trousers or long skirts, and long-sleeved, loose-fitting blouses). There have been reports of women being turned away if there is any danger of their long, flowing skirts blowing up in the wind.

Al Dhahirah Region

With a name meaning 'the back', the Al Dhahirah region lies in Oman's interior, to the west of the Hajar mountains and bordering the UAE and Saudi Arabia. Due to the harsh environment, characterised by huge sandy plains, Al Dhahirah is sparsely populated and there is not much in the way of modern-world comforts. Water is transported from the mountains to the towns using the age-old falaj system, which is deceptively sophisticated.

This is an area where you will get to see Omanis living their lives as they have done for centuries, and if you are fortunate you may get to see displays of traditional dances and crafts. It is also a great place for exploring old forts, ancient tombs and caves. In fact, it is home to the famous beehive tombs in Ibri (also called the Bat tombs), which have been listed as a Unesco World Heritage site. While there is some debate as to whether these were actually used as tombs or whether they were rudimentary homes for small families, it is widely accepted that the tombs date back to early civilisations that lived in the region over 5,000 years ago. Ibri was historically a critical stopping point on the overland trading route.

Buraimi

The Buraimi governance is the part of the Buraimi Oasis that falls on the Oman side of the border; the part of the oasis that falls on the UAE side is called Al Ain. Although it spans what is in effect an international border, there are no checkpoints within the town itself and the official Oman-UAE border is located about 50km east of Buraimi. Non-GCC residents travelling from Oman will need a road permit (see p.44). Like Ibri, Buraimi can trace its history back to its strategic position at the intersection of various

As Seeb

caravan routes to and from Oman. There is an extensive falaj system that keeps the region fertile. Buraimi is an oasis and therefore is pleasantly green with plenty of date palm plantations. It also benefits from a cooler, less humid climate than coastal regions, making it a popular destination during the summer months.

It is home to a famous mud fort, Hisn Al Khandaq, which has been extensively restored and is open to visitors. There is also a must-see camel souk where the merchants will happily explain the differences between one camel and another, and may even make a serious attempt at convincing you to buy one. Watching the camels being loaded onto their new owners' pick up trucks is a show in itself. You might find there is more to do in neighbouring Al Ain, although hotels are generally cheaper in Buraimi itself. A word of warning: UAE taxi drivers will cruise for passengers in Buraimi although they may refuse to use the meter, so it is up to you to negotiate a price before you get in the cab.

Ibri

Ibri lies 300km to the west of Muscat, between the foothills of the Hajar Mountains and the vast Rub Al Khali desert. With its central location, it was a historically important stopover for merchants travelling between the different regions of the Arabian Peninsula and trading remains active today. The bustling souk sells an range of merchandise including locally produced woven palm goods. The most fascinating sight though is the auction which takes place every morning, where residents, farmers and traders from the town and surrounding villages come together to haggle over dates, fruit and vegetables, livestock, camels and honey. The souk is situated near Ibri's impressive fort, which is notable for the large mosque set within its walls.

Al Wusta Region

In contrast to Oman's other regions Al Wusta has few sites of historical interest, and is often only seen from a car window as people make the long drive between Muscat and Salalah. However, the region does boast areas of natural beauty, a mild summer climate and an abundance of wildlife. Al Wusta also has around 170km of coastline, which includes some rocky beaches but also some amazing long stretches of white sandy beaches.

The Jiddat Al Harasis region in Al Wusta is where Arabian oryx were last recorded in the wild, and a sanctuary for these magnificent desert creatures has been established there. The sanctuary is supported by the World Wildlife Fund, and it has been remarkably successful – thanks to some careful breeding programmes, the first herd of Arabian oryx was released back into the wild in 1992. For more info on the sanctuary and the various facilities in it (including camping facilities), see www.oryxoman.com.

Batinah Region

With a coastline stretching north-west from Muscat to the UAE border, Batinah has a collection of beautiful coastal towns and villages that are worth visiting. The most populated area after Muscat, Batinah has 12 wilayats: Awabi, Barka, Khabura, Liwa, Musanaa, Nakhal, Rustaq, Saham, Shinas, Sohar, Swaiq and Wadi Mawail. Inland towards the Western Hajars there are dramatic peaks and wadis, and numerous areas of historical interest.

Carry On Camping

The *Oman Off-Road Explorer* has all the information you need on off-road adventuring and camping helping you make the most out of living in the region.

Barka

Barka is a small coastal town, approximately 75km west of Muscat. It makes an interesting daytrip from Muscat or as a stop off on a visit to Sohar further along the coast. It is famous for its fortnightly bullfights and large central fort, located only a few hundred metres from the shore of the Gulf of Oman. Barka is still home to craftsmen practising traditional trades including weaving. The historical fort Bait Naa'man, the Ostrich Breeding Farm (see p.190) and Al Nahda Resort & Spa are attractions worth exploring while in Barka.

Nakhal

Nakhal is 30km inland from Barka and about 100km from Muscat. The town has an imposing restored fort set on a hill, and if you climb to the top of the watchtowers you'll be rewarded with magnificent views of the surrounding countryside and town. Inside the fort visitors can see the prison, kitchen, living quarters of the Wali (leader) and the male and female majlis.

The area is also well known for the Al Thowarah hot springs which can be found a few kilometres beyond the fort. The natural spring water is channelled into the falaj system to irrigate the surrounding date plantations, and you can dip your toe or have a paddle in the run-off water. There's a carpark and picnic facilities in addition to Nakhal Fort Museum (www.omanet.om), making it a popular destination for locals and tourists.

Rustaq

In the middle ages, Rustaq (or Rostaq) was the capital of Oman. However, today it is best known for its large and dramatic fort, which has been extended over the years.

Get into high spirits. Get high on water.

Sometimes all you need to get on a high is water! Yes, just water will do. After all, the enchanting pools and streams at Al Nahda will leave you spellbound. As you take a dip in the pool, you'll loose yourself to the beauty of the coconut palms around playing tag with the wind.

What's more, the invigorating aroma of the green grass, chirpings of some rare species of birds, verdant greenery around the pool, cool breeze throughout the day of the year, will all mesmerize you and take you to an enthralling world. So the next time you feel like getting on a high, head straight to Al Nahda, and let the spirits soar high!

Al Nahda
Resort & Spa
Five star.... Naturally
www.alnahdaresort.com

For reservations please call 800 73525 or email stay@alnahdaresort.com

Rustaq is located in the Western Hajar Mountains about 170km south-west of Muscat. The fort has been restored and the main watchtower is believed to be of Sassanid origin. It was well placed to withstand long sieges since it has its own water supplies. Apparently at one time there was a tunnel connecting this fort to the nearby fort in Al Hazm.

There is a small souk near the fort, selling a variety of items. Not far from there you'll find the hot springs that Rustaq is famous for. The water in these springs are believed to have healing powers – it has a high sulphur content, which is supposed to provide relief for sufferers of arthritis and rheumatism.

About 20km north of Rustaq is the village of Al Hazm, which has an interesting fort. It was built in around 1700AD and the original falaj system is still in working order today. There is also an excellent view of the countryside from the watchtower.

Sohar

Sohar lies about halfway between Muscat and Dubai, 200km north-west of the capital. Situated on the Batinah coast, it was once the maritime capital of the country and an important distribution centre for locally produced copper. Sohar is renowned for its fort with an in-house museum, the lively Fish Souk (located just off the corniche), and for being the birthplace of the legendary Sindbad the sailor. As with the rest of Oman the people here are very friendly, although in Sohar they do tend to be less used to visitors and cameras, but this is changing as the country becomes more popular.

Dakhiliya Region

Despite being isolated from the sea, Dakhiliya was historically important as many trade routes between the coast and the interior passed through the region. The Sumail Gap is a valley that divides the Eastern and Western Hajars. It is the home of Jabal Akhdar. Also in this region is the ancient town of Nizwa which was once Oman's capital and a popular destination for exploring.

Bahla

The ancient walled city of Bahla is only two hours' drive away from Muscat, and just 40km from Nizwa. It has a small population of around 60,000, and contains 46 separate villages. While it is not yet on the mainstream tourist map (although efforts are being made to attract more tourists to the area), archaeology buffs and history enthusiasts will find that it is well worth a visit. It is believed to be one of the oldest inhabited regions in Oman, and archaeologists have found artefacts here dating back to the third century BC. It was historically a strategic stopover on the old trading route from Muscat to other parts of the Arabian Peninsula.

Apart from the historical buildings and the traditional way of life, Bahla also has a rich and diverse ecology – a balanced mixture of fertile land, mountains, wadis and desert. The productive soil, fed by a continuous supply of water from Jabal Akhdar, has in the past yielded crops of wheat, barley, cotton and sugar cane, and today it is still home to many viable date plantations. The town is characterised by its many winding roads, some so narrow that you have to pull over to let an oncoming car pass. Whether you explore the town of Bahla on foot or by car, you will find an eclectic balance of the new, functioning town, the ancient, fascinating ruins, and the many date plantations that are perfect picnic spots.

Bahla is enclosed by a protective, fortified wall that stretches for 12km around the town. Although large sections of the wall are still standing, parts of it are in ruins and earmarked for eventual reconstruction.

Need Some Direction?

The *Explorer Mini Maps* pack a whole city into your pocket and once unfolded are excellent navigational tools for exploring. Not only are they handy in size, with detailed information on the sights and sounds of the city, but also their fabulously affordable price means they won't make a dent in your holiday fund. Wherever your travels take you, from Europe to the Middle East and beyond, grab a *Mini Map* and you'll never have to ask for directions again.

Forts & Ruins

The Bahla Fort, situated on Balhool Mountain, is one of the main attractions in Bahla. It is included on Unesco's list of World Heritage sites, and has undergone careful and extensive renovation under Unesco's sponsorship and supervision. The ruins of the fort tower 50m above the village, and although its famous windtowers have been almost totally destroyed over time, they were once thought to be the tallest structures in Oman. In the area around the fort you can wander through deserted mud-brick villages, the largest of which is Al Aqar. You can explore the ancient houses at your leisure, and in some houses you can go up to higher storeys and look through the old window frames for a unique perspective. It is a fascinating glimpse into the past, showing you what life was like in Oman's olden times. The ruins of the mosque are particularly interesting. The Jabrin Fort, which is a very short drive from Bahla, has been extensively restored and redecorated. The Imam Bilarab originally built it in the 1600s as a grand country residence. His tomb is still located within the fort, to the left of the main entrance. It is believed that Jabrin Fort was home to one of the first schools in Oman, way back in the 17th century.

Updated Routes

Log on to www.liveworkexplore.com/off-road for updates from Explorer staff and fellow readers to off-road routes throughout Oman.

The Souk

There is no better place to rub shoulders with the friendly people of Bahla than at the traditional market or 'souk'. Locals gather here to trade in livestock and socialise under the shade of a huge central tree. Goats are tethered to this tree before being bought or sold. In the alleyways leading away from this central livestock trading area, you'll find many small shops that sell traditional crafts, Omani antiques (a particularly good spot to hunt for a genuine antique khanjar), rugs, spices and nuts. You can watch the local silversmith at work, repairing khanjars and jewellery in the same way it has been done for generations. The souk also has sections for fruit and vegetables, all of which are locally produced, and the locally grown dates are delicious.

You can't visit the area without buying some distinctive Bahla pottery to take home with you. Bahla is a good source of high quality clay, and there are many skilled potters in the area (all male – it is only in the southern regions of Oman that you'll find female potters). You can see them working at the traditional pottery site, which is just past the souk. There is also a pottery factory, built by the government in the late 1980s, and the Alladawi clay pots workshop that boasts four industrial kilns each able to produce around a hundred pots each month. While you will probably buy a piece of pottery for ornamental purposes (plant pots, vases, incense burners or candle holders), clay pots are still used for practical purposes in Bahla, such as carrying and cooling water, and storing food and dates.

Fanja

The picturesque village of Fanja is situated next to an extensive palm grove that runs alongside Wadi Fanja. It is around 70km from Muscat, and the approach is one of the most scenic views that Oman has to offer. The village has a dramatic tower perched on top of a hill offering spectacular views of the surrounding scenery and the wadi below. Fanja is renowned for its pottery and visitors can wander round the market bargaining for locally produced pots, local fruits and vegetables, honey and woven goods made from palm leaves.

Nizwa

About 140km from Muscat, Nizwa is a popular destination for tourists and residents of Oman alike. In the sixth and seventh centuries, Nizwa was the capital of Oman and the centre for trade between the coastal and interior regions. It is still the largest and most important town in this area of the interior. Historically, the town enjoyed a reputation as a haven for poets, writers, intellectuals, and religious leaders, and for centuries it was considered the cultural and political capital of the country. Positioned as it is alongside two wadis, Nizwa is a fertile sea of green with an oasis of date plantations stretching eight kilometres from the town. Its two notable attractions include Nizwa's 17th century fort and the magnificent Jabrin Fort, renowned for its wall and ceiling decorations and its secret passageways and staircases. Many ancient ruins such as Bahla Fort and mud brick villages can be seen among the date palm plantations and the wadis.

The Nizwa Souk is an interesting and atmospheric place where visitors will find many examples of the local silversmiths' art, especially ornately engraved khanjars.

Sumail

The town of Sumail (or Samail) sits in the Sumail Gap, a natural valley that divides the Hajar Mountain chain into the Eastern and Western Hajars. As the most direct path between the coastal regions and the interior of the country, this route has always been an important artery. Irrigated by countless wadis and man-made falaj systems, the area is green and fertile, and the dates produced here are highly rated.

Dhofar Region

Dhofar is the southernmost region of Oman, bordering Saudi Arabia and the Republic of Yemen. Dhofar frankincense is regarded as the finest in the world and once made this area immensely wealthy and important. Visitors still flock to the coast to enjoy the lush greenery and cool weather.

Salalah

Salalah is the capital of Dhofar, the southernmost region of Oman, and is over 1,000 kilometres from Muscat. It is possible to get there by road, but the drive is long and boring, with little of interest to see or do along the way. You may therefore prefer to fly, and Oman Air operates three flights a day from Muscat. Salalah has a museum, and the souks are worthy of a visit; especially the Al Husn Souk (next to the Palace) where you'll find silverware, frankincense and locally made perfume.

There are also a number of beautiful beaches to be found along the coast. The landscape features plenty of trees, mainly at the border of the desert at the lower reaches of the jebels. You'll also find an impressive grouping of trees in Wadi Qahshan that runs through the mountainous backdrop of the Mughsayl-Sarfait road which links Salalah with the Yemen border. This is where frankincense trees grow and are farmed by local villagers. They cut into the trunks and allow the sap to seep out and harden into lumps that are then scraped off and traded in bulk.

The Khareef

The coastal region is subject to weather conditions quite different from the rest of the country, and as such the scenery is completely different to that in many areas further north. From June to September the monsoon rains (or khareef), active in the Indian Ocean, clip southern Dhofar and the countryside comes alive in an explosion of greenery, featuring lush green fields, swollen rivers and beautiful waterfalls. The foothills of the mountains, a few kilometres inland, are often covered with thick fog during this time. The rain and fog cause a significant temperature drop, making Salalah a popular destination for residents of other Gulf countries trying to escape the summer heat.

Frankincense

The Dhofar region was historically the centre of the frankincense trade, with the local trees producing what was (and still is) considered the best frankincense in the world. As a result the area grew prosperous as this precious commodity was exported by sea to

India and by land throughout Arabia and as far as Europe. Locally produced frankincense is still widely available in the local souks. The Frankincense Souk is packed with merchants selling incense, perfumes and traditional artefacts. The Land of Frankincense site opened in Salalah in 2007 and features trees and the remains of a caravan oasis.

Ubar

The legendary lost city of Ubar (referred to as Iram in the Quran) is said to have been a wealthy trading post at the junction of numerous caravan routes, where merchants would come from afar to buy much sought after incense. At the crossroads of these ancient trade routes, traders to Ubar would sell pottery, spices and fabric from India and China in return for the unique silver frankincense of Oman. The trade made Ubar a city of unrivalled wealth and splendour and those who visited it referred to it as 'paradise'. According to the Quran the wickedness of the inhabitants led Allah to destroy the city and all roads leading to it, causing it to sink into the sand. For a thousand years the city's location remained unknown until the 1990s when British explorer Sir Ranulph Fiennes, in a 20 year search using modern satellite technology, discovered the city of Ubar beneath the shifting sands of the Oman desert near Shisr, north of Salalah. Excavations have revealed the thick outer walls of a vast octagonal fortress with eight towers or pillars at its corners, and numerous pots and artefacts dating back thousands of years. Debate continues as to whether this is indeed Ubar, but the site is fascinating nonetheless for being the location of what was surely an important desert settlement many years ago. Tour companies offer full day tours to Ubar through the Qara Mountains and stunning landscape.

Red Tide ◀

Throughout several months of 2008 and 2009, large parts of Oman's coastline were affected by 'red tide', where a specific type of algae turned the water red and cloudy. Swimming in affected water is not recommended, as it can cause a rash and sickness.

Musandam Region

Other options **Weekend Break Hotels** p.209

The Musandam peninsula is an Oman enclave to the north, which is divided from the rest of Oman by the United Arab Emirates. It has only recently been opened to tourists and is a beautiful, largely unspoiled area. The capital is Khasab, a quaint fishing port mostly unchanged by the modern world. The Strait of Hormuz lies to the north, with Iran just across the water, the Arabian Gulf is to the west and the Gulf of Oman lies to the east; hence the area is one of great strategic importance.

Musandam is dominated by the Hajar Mountains, which also run through the UAE and into the main part of Oman. It is sometimes referred to as the Norway of the Middle East, since the jagged mountain cliffs plunge directly into the sea, and the coastline features many inlets and fjords. The views along the coastal roads are stunning. Just a few metres off the coast you'll find beautiful and fertile coral beds, with an amazing variety of sea life including tropical fish, turtles, dolphins (a common sight) and, occasionally, sharks. Inland, the scenery is equally breathtaking, although you will need a 4WD and a good head for heights to explore it properly.

You can reach Musandam from Muscat by air, sea (via ferry) or by road. The flight takes around 90 minutes. Oman Air (24 531 111) offers internal flights and holiday packages from Muscat to Musandam; a return flight costs RO 40 and flights leave daily from Saturday to Wednesday. The National Ferries Company (98 111 162) offers deals including accommodation at the Golden Tulip Resort Khasab starting from RO 75 per person for ferry tickets, two nights in the hotel and breakfast based on two people sharing. Visitors travelling in Oman do not need an additional visa.

To drive to Musandam from Oman you need to travel through the UAE. GCC nationals and Omanis are free to travel this route without needing any travel documents, but non-GCC residents of Oman need to apply for a road permit. Entry into Musandam by expatriates can only be made at the Ras Al Khaimah border post, and not at Dibba. Visitors to Oman carrying a single-entry visa may not be allowed back into Oman once they have left. Check with your nearest Oman embassy for updated information.

Bukha

Bukha is located on the western side of the Musandam peninsula, with a coastline on the Arabian Gulf. The area borders the UAE emirate of Ras Al Khaimah and is 27km north of Khasab. This small town is overlooked by the ruin of an old fort, but there is little to see other than the remains of one watchtower. The Bukha Fort is more impressive, however, and is by the side of the main road just metres from the sea. It was built in the 17th century, restored in 1990, and it is certainly the town's biggest landmark. Traditionally, fishing and boat building have been the occupations of Bukha's residents, and the town has a harbour for a small number of vessels. There is also a pleasant strip of sandy beach with a number of shelters. The village of Al Jadi, about three kilometres north of Bukha, is picturesque and has a couple of fortifications, two of which are restored watchtowers.

Khasab

Khasab, the capital of the Musandam region, is surrounded by imposing and dramatic mountains that dominate the entire area, with some peaks above 2,000m. The town of Khasab is relatively spread out and has numerous date palm plantations. There is a small souk and a beach, but the port is the main area of interest. The town relies on fishing, trade (mostly with ports in Iran) and agriculture for subsistence, and produces a range of fruit and vegetables. In fact khasab is the Arabic word for 'fertile'.
At one end of the bay is the restored Khasab Fort which is open to the public. There's not that much to see inside, but its setting against the mountainous background is spectacular. Kumzan Fort is just outside Khasab. It was built in about 1600AD by the Imam but little is left of it today, apart from the two watchtowers.
About 10km west of Khasab is the village of Tawi where there are prehistoric rock carvings of warriors, boats and animals.
One of Khasab's biggest draws is the diving opportunities. These waters are not recommended for beginners, but experienced divers can enjoy spectacular underwater cliffs and an abundance of marine life at sites just a short boat ride away.

Sharquiya Region

Sharquiya is a region of contrasts. The coastline features numerous fishing villages and ports, and the area's beaches are home to some of the most important turtle breeding grounds in the world. Inland, you'll find a combination of breathtaking wadis and dramatic expanses of sand dunes.

Masirah Island

Masirah Island lies 20km off the south-east coast of Oman and is the Sultanate's largest island. It is about 80km long and 18km wide, with hills in the centre and a circumference of picturesque isolated beaches. The island is off the coast of the Barr Al Hikman area, and can be accessed by taking a ferry from Shana'a – but only during high tide. The ferry leaves regularly but there are no set times and it seems to set off when full or when the ferry from the other side arrives. You can cross with your car, and the crossing takes around 90 minutes. There is a military base on the island, and the main town of Hilf, with its 8,000 residents, has a hotel, some shops, and a couple of restaurants, but otherwise the island is relatively undeveloped.
The highest point of the island is Jebel Hamra at 275m, and a network of graded roads connects parts of the island.

Beaches ◀

The beaches of Masirah Island's east coast offer some of the best surfing in the region, with waves of seven or eight feet on a good day. The summer months are also a good time for windsurfing, but the strong winds that lash the island during this time can be unpleasant and make camping on the beach quite uncomfortable. The beaches are also a great location for camping, and you'll find yourself sharing your habitat with the donkeys, camels, goats and gazelles that roam the island. Conchologists will be in their element here as the beaches are home to a vast range of shells, some of which are quite rare. If camping is not for you, the other option is to stay at Masirah Hotel in Hilf (25 504 401) which has 29 rooms.

Turtles

Masirah's beaches are internationally recognised for their importance as turtle breeding grounds. Four species of turtle come ashore to lay their eggs here – green turtles, hawksbill, olive ridley and loggerheads. Masirah is thought to be home to the world's largest nesting population of loggerhead turtles, estimated at 30,000 females.

Sur

Sur is an old fishing and trading port 300km south-east of Muscat. For centuries the town was famed for its boatbuilding and became quite prosperous as a result. Its fortunes did decline somewhat with the advent of more modern vessels and construction techniques, but Sur is enjoying something of a revival, and with its pretty corniche, forts and interesting Marine Museum the town is definitely worth a visit, as is the Sineslah Fort which overlooks the town, offering breathtaking views of the area and coast.

The Arabic word Sur means a walled fortified area and there is evidence of the ancient defences throughout the town. As the first port of call in Arabia for traders from the Far East, it is believed that trading with the African coast dates back to as early as the 6th century AD.

From Muscat there are two roads to Sur. The Sur highway (Route 23) is the best option if you're looking for a smoother ride. The 300km single tarmac road, leading through the mountains and crossing some wadis, will take you to Sur in between three and four hours. Alternatively, you can take the coastal road (direction Quriyat-Sur) which is under construction so be alert. In terms of distance this route is much shorter (only about 150km), but it takes at least four hours to navigate. In Quriyat turn right to Sur at the roundabout, then follow the asphalt road and keep following the signposts to Sur (not Tiwi). Before long the tarmac changes to gravel.

There are a few highlights along this route: Bimmah Sinkhole is located six kilometres after Dibab Village, just 500 metres off the road on your right. Tiwi Beach (also known as White Sand Beach) makes a perfect stop for some snorkelling or relaxing (just don't go on public holidays, especially if you don't like crowds). Wadi Shab, one of the most stunning wadis in Oman, is just past Tiwi Village. The end of the coastal road is marked by an oasis and the ancient city of Qalhat, which is famous for its dry stone walls, the remains of ancient water cisterns and the scattered headstones of a cemetery. There is also a shrine to a saintly woman known as Bibi Miriam, although it is in poor repair. From here you progress into the mountains, where you will encounter some steep slopes and hair-raising descents.

You will eventually reach the enormous LNG plant (liquefied natural gas). Head south for around 15km to get into Sur. If you came along the Muscat-Sur highway, you will first pass Sur Bilad, a suburb of Sur. This is where you can visit the very impressive Bilad Fort.

Tiwi

Tiwi is a small fishing settlement about 30km up the coast from Sur, situated in a little cove between two of the most beautiful and picturesque wadis in the area – Wadi Tiwi and Wadi Shab. These verdant green oases are a must-see for anyone visiting the area, for their crystal clear pools and lush vegetation including palm and banana plantations. The residents of Tiwi are spread across nine small villages and there are endless opportunities for walking and exploring. In Wadi Shab you can start your walk with a trip across the water courtesy of a small boat operated by locals. Further along the wadi you can swim through pools and access a cave that has a waterfall inside. Tiwi Beach, also known as the White Sands Beach, is located on the way to Fins and is a tranquil spot to rest for a while.

Amusement Centres

Muscat City Centre
As Seeb
Map 3 E2

Magic Planet

This amusement centre is popular with kids of all ages. It has a small carousel, a mini train and bumper cars as the main attractions. It is located next to the foodcourt in Muscat City Centre. RO 30 gets you an unlimited ride pass. Magic Planet has a party zone area that can be booked for private parties.

Al Harthy Complex
Al Qurm
Map 11 E1

Sindbad's Wonder Centre

24 794 677 | sindbad1@omantel.net.om

There is a host of fairground rides to amuse children here, and because there are rides for all age groups, there is no age limitation. It also has computer and video games. You can bring your own food or get Sinbad's to cater in the separate dining area. Children will love the carousel, bumper cars, magic carpet train ride and spinning teacups. Parents can relax while the kids wear themselves out. There are other Sindbad Parks in Al Khuwayr (opposite SABCO supermarket), Al Masa Mall, Wadi Kabir and in As Seeb (near Al Khud Roundabout).

Al Hoota Cave
Al Hoota Cave is located at the foot of Jebel Shams. It is over five kilometres long and was previously reserved for experienced cavers only. The cave is a treasure trove of stalactites, stalagmites and crystals. Parts of the cave are only accessible by electrical train and tickets are available from the ticket office in the visitor centre. The visitor centre also has some restaurants and heritage shops plus a museum. Admission costs RO 5.5 for adults, RO 3 for children aged 6 to 12 and is free for those under 6. Call 92 404 444 or see p.185 for further information.

Archaeological Sites

Archaeological excavations in south-eastern Arabia only started in the 1950s. It was then that Danish archaeologists found settlements and temples of the city-state of Dilmun, dating back over 4,000 years, in the grave mounds of Bahrain. Some time later, these archaeologists were surprised by an unexpected discovery on the island of Umm An Nar off Abu Dhabi (UAE) of another previously unknown culture contemporary with Dilmun. Encouraged by the discoveries at Dilmun and Umm An Nar, Danish archaeologists excavated 200 single-chambered burial cairns in 1961 near Jebel Hafeet in Al Ain, just on the Oman-United Arab Emirates border, showing a culture even earlier than Dilmun and Umm An Nar. In literature, sites are often referred to as either the Umm An Nar or Hafit Periods. Umm An Nar is well known for its large, circular tombs – these were used by families for collective burials over several generations. In some cases, archaeologists have found the remains of more than a hundred people buried in one tomb. The Hafit period is characterised by smaller cairns, originally with a beehive-like appearance, designed for one or two burials.

It is only recently that the Oman tombs have been 'discovered' by the outside world, although of course local people have always known their whereabouts and had their own stories about their origin.

To find out about other interesting archaeological sites in Oman, see Bat & Al Ayn Tombs, Shir Tower Tombs, Halban Tombs and the Lost City of Ubar.

Art Galleries

Other options **Art** p.264, **Art & Craft Supplies** p.264

Art is valued highly in the Arab world, so galleries in the region tend to stock art of high quality and in various styles. Although Oman has no art museums, its art galleries do offer peaceful surroundings where you can browse or buy. Most of the galleries also offer a framing service.

For information on art galleries found in the main areas of Muscat, see the Omani Society for Fine Arts (p.213), Bait Muzna Gallery (p.170), and Al Madina Art Gallery (p.169).

Villa 1691
Road 2
MSQ
Map 7 F1

Al Madina Art Gallery

24 691 380 | almadgal@omantel.net.om

The Al Madina Art Gallery is a one-stop shop for many different forms of art in Oman. It has regular exhibitions of watercolours and oil paintings, and also hosts many special events throughout the year. If you have some time to kill, have a browse through the ample selection of prints – you could be rewarded with an attractive piece of art for a lot less than you would pay for an original. Al Madina also stocks some interesting jewellery made from unconventional materials such as freshwater pearls or desert diamonds. And if a genuine Omani wooden chest is on your shopping list, this is the place to go if you want to make sure you are buying an original and not one that has been made in India.

Opp Bayt Al Zubair
Saidiya Street
Al Qurm
Map 10 D4

Bait Muzna Gallery
24 739 204 | www.omanart.com
This gallery first opened in 2000. Set in a traditional house that was originally built as a home for a member of the royal family, it showcases the work of local talent and organises a number of workshops for both Omanis and expats. Workshops are offered periodically (check website) and are provided by a number of qualified teachers, some of whom are successful international artists themselves. The gallery sells fine arts and antiques, and offers a framing service.

Bull Fighting
Unlike Spanish bullfighting, the Oman version is bloodless and the animals suffer little or no injury during fighting. This is not a gory sport, but rather a contest of strength between two powerful animals. The Brahmin bulls used in fighting are often pampered family pets. At the beginning of a fight, two bulls of similar size are led into the centre of the ring to lock horns for battle. The fight is over when the weaker of the two either gives up and runs away, or is forced out of the ring. Each fight lasts just a few minutes, and usually the worst injury suffered is a bruised ego on the part of both the losing bull and its owner! There is no prize money, although sometimes the owner of the winning bull receives a token amount.
This historical form of entertainment is loved and treasured by Omanis, and you'll find that half the fun is watching the locals cheering for their favourite bull, and trying to recapture it at the end of the fight.
Bullfights are held in several places along the Batinah coastline; usually on Friday afternoons at around 16:30. Barka and As Seeb are the two main bullfighting sites, and a smaller ring is located in Al Sawadi. There is also a well-known bullfighting ring in Sohar. Entrance is free, and visitors are welcome. Fights are not held during the hottest summer months and Ramadan.

Camel Racing
Other options **Camel Rides** p.186

Camel racing is a popular traditional sport and you shouldn't miss the chance to see it up close. The camels are bred specially for the track, and it is still Bedouin families who raise and train them. The racing season runs from August to April, and races are held mainly at weekends, and on Saturdays and public holidays during the winter months. Races start at around 06:00 and continue until 09:00, so you may have to forsake your lie-in. Announcements for camel races appear mostly in the Arabic newspapers, but if you are keen to go you can find out details from one of the tour operators. Race tracks can be found all around the country, including As Seeb (the main location) in the north and Salalah in the south. In the interior you'll find many other racing tracks, sometimes clearly signposted, along the main roads. A visit to any of these might give you the opportunity to see the camels being trained, although only usually before 08:00. For a list of camel race locations and dates, plus information on events and festivals visit www.omantourism.gov.om.

Forts & Castles

The mud brick and stone architecture of Oman's many forts is a constant reminder of the country's past. Whether you travel the interior, the coast or the mountains, you are sure to happen across the remains of a fort, each with its own story to tell of Oman's defensive history. The Oman government takes great care of these national treasures, and many of the forts are either heavily restored or in the process of restoration, sometimes against the wishes of archaeologists who would rather see the forts in their original states.

While forts were built primarily as structures for military defence, they also served as points of convergence for political, social and community activity. Therefore, some forts have palatial, luxurious interiors hidden behind their stark exteriors.

Despite there being official opening times, it is not uncommon to arrive at a fort and find it is closed off for restoration. To avoid disappointment, you can check with the Ministry of Tourism (www.omantourism.gov.om) or the Ministry of National Heritage and Culture (24 641 300, www.mhc.gov.om) in Al Khuwayr beforehand.

Oman is renowned for its forts and there are literally hundreds around the country. The list below is a brief selection of some of the best forts around Oman but for more information on other forts, most hotels have leaflets and booklets from the Oman Tourist Board or you can check out *Forts of Oman*, available in bookshops. If you are planning to visit some specific forts in Oman, see also Barka Castle, Bilad Sur Castle, Jabrin Castle, Khasab Castle, Kumzan Fort, Sohar Fort, Sunaysilah Fort, Jalali Fort & Mirani Fort and Mutrah Fort.

Museums

Other options **Art** p.264, **Places Of Worship Tours** p.190

The Oman government plays an active role in preserving the country's history, and museums are an important way of doing this. You can spend hours learning about the achievements of Oman's ancestors, most of which are impressive considering the often harsh circumstances they lived in, and in the process you'll gain valuable insight into the history of life in each specific area.

Outside Muscat there are only a few museums, but those that do exist make interesting excursions for history fans. Entrance to museums costs very little, and you will generally find that information on exhibits is given in both English and Arabic. Opening times often change during summer, Ramadan (typically 09:00 to 13:00 Saturday to Wednesday), Eid and on public holidays, so try to call in advance to avoid a wasted journey. The Ministry of Tourism website (www.omantourism.gov.om) now lists opening times for museums in the region.

Museums within the main areas of Muscat include: Children's Museum (p.234), Muscat Gate Museum (p.172), Omani French Museum (p.173), National Museum (p.172), and The Sultan's Armed Forces Museum (p.174). Museums within other areas of Muscat include the Natural History Museum (p.173) and Omani Museum (p.173).

Al Saidiyah St
Al Qurm
Map 10 D4

Bait Al Zubair

24 736 688 | *bazubair@omantel.net.om*

A collection rather than a museum, Bait Al Zubair offers a fascinating insight into the Omani lifestyle and traditions, mixing ancient and modern. It is located in a beautiful restored house in Muscat, and each display is accompanied by excellent explanations and descriptions. There are knowledgeable and helpful staff on hand. The four major displays cover men's jewellery, khanjars and male attire; women's jewellery and female attire; household items including kitchenware, incense burners and rosewater sprinklers; and swords and firearms. There is a central photo gallery showing fascinating pictures from the 1920s up until the present day which are great for everyone from children to history enthusiasts. Outside you'll find full-size recreations of stone-built Omani homes, a small souk, fishing boats and a flowing falaj. There is also a gift shop which sells a variety of items and paintings, custom-made miniatures of the pieces on display and other museum souvenirs. Opening hours are 09:30 to 13:30, Saturday to Thursday and entry costs RO 1.

Nr Qurm Ntl Park
Al Qurm
Map 8 C4

Children's Museum

24 605 368 | www.omantourism.gov.om

Kids of all ages will enjoy this interactive science museum. Solidly built displays clearly explain holography, lasers, the human body, energy, faxes, computers and many other fascinations of daily life. There is ample opportunity for children to indulge in button-pressing, handle-turning, pedalling, balancing or jumping and there is lots of running space so kids can exhaust themselves before lunch. This museum is popular and can get crowded on Thursdays. Entrance is free for children under 6, but costs 100 baisas for children aged 6 to 12, and 300 baisas for those aged 12 and over. The museum is open from 09:00 to 13:00, Saturday to Wednesday and 09:00 to 13:00 on Thursdays (closed on Fridays).

Nr Marina Bander
Al Rowdha
Sidab
Map 13 F4

Marine Science & Fisheries Centre (MSFC)

24 736 449

The Marine Science & Fisheries Centre was set up in 1986 near Sidab, on the coast near Muscat, with the support of Unesco. In cooperation with the Sultan Qaboos University, the centre is intended to develop sea-based aquaculture on a large scale. It has a public aquarium that displays local aquatic flora and fauna, and a modern library, both of which are interesting exhibits for visitors. You can view loggerhead, hawksbill and green turtles up close in the turtle pool. The Centre shares an entrance road with Marina Bander Al-Rowdha (p.184), near the Al Bustan Palace InterContinental Muscat. Entrance is free.

Al Bahri Rd
Inside City Gates
Map 10 D4

Muscat Gate Museum

Located in one of the fortified gates of the old city walls, the Muscat Gate House is the newest museum to open its doors to visitors. It illustrates the history of Muscat and Oman from ancient times right up to the present day with a special display on the city's springs, wells, underground waterways, souks, mosques, harbours and forts. The awe-inspiring view from the roof over the old town of Muscat is almost worth the visit alone.

Way 3123
Nr Al Falaj
Mercure Htl
Ruwi
Map 12 D2

National Museum

24 701 289 | www.omantourism.gov.om

This is a small but fairly comprehensive museum showing silver jewellery, ladies' costumes from around Oman, pottery, a selection of scale-built dhows, crockery, coffee pots, and guns. Additionally, there is a selection of unique items of furniture from the old palace in Muscat, clothes, pictures and medals from the Zanzibar rulers; as well as correspondence and pictures of the last five sultans in the Al Said Dynasty.
You will be provided with an English-speaking guide who will probably offer you the chance to sample the legendary Omani hospitality, by inviting you to have some traditional kahwa (coffee), halwa and dates afterwards. The museum is open Saturday to Wednesday 08:00 to 13:30 and Thursday 09:00 to 13:00. Entry costs 500 baisas for adults (or 300 baisas if they are with their family), 200 baisas for children and kids under 6 get in free.

Natural History Museum

Al Wazarat St
Al Khuwayr
Map 7 B2

24 641 374 | www.omantourism.gov.om

This museum, housed within the Ministry of National Heritage & Culture, is a fascinating and informative collection of exhibits relating to Oman's wildlife. You can see stuffed animals in their different natural habitats, many of which are unique to Oman and the Gulf region (such as the oryx and the Arabian leopard). The 'Oman Through Time' exhibition follows the history of Oman through fossils, and includes the development of oil and gas reserves. The separate Whale Hall should not be missed – it is dominated by the suspended skeleton of a 25 year old sperm whale. The quiet blue hall is filled with the sounds of whale and dolphin calls, and offers a wide range of information about the unique selection of whale species found off Oman's coast. The dolphin and whale skeletons that are displayed in the Whale Hall have all been recovered from Oman's beaches.

If you visit during the winter months, you can tour the botanical gardens next to the museum. These carefully tended gardens feature indigenous trees, shrubs and flora, including frankincense, desert rose, henna and aloe. Entrance costs 500 baisas for adults, 200 baisas for children between 6 and 12 and 100 baisas for children under 6.

Oil & Gas Exhibition Centre

Seeh Al Maleh St
Nr Gate 2
Mina Al Fahal (PDO)
Map 8 F3

24 677 834 | www.pdo.co.om

The Exhibition Centre was given to the Omani people as a gift from Petroleum Development Oman (PDO), the largest oil and gas production company in the country. It is a well designed interactive journey through the development, discovery, extraction and use of fossil fuels in Oman. Kids will love the interesting displays that include seismic computer games, nodding donkeys, and gigantic rotating drill bits. There is a cafe serving light meals and refreshments, as well as a computer playground featuring familiar computer games. In 2000, a planetarium was built. It is open Saturday to Wednesday 07:00 to 15:45 and Thursday 20:00 to midnight. Admission is free. To find out more about the Oil & Gas Exhibition Centre, visit the www.pdo.co.om and click on the 'PDO & Community' link.

Omani French Museum

Nr Police Station
Al Alam St
Map 10 E4

24 736 613 | www.omantourism.gov.om

This museum is on the site of the first French Embassy, which is a carefully preserved example of 19th century Omani architecture. It celebrates the close ties between France and Oman over the past few centuries. Although the museum exhibits have French captions, there are usually brief English translations. The ground floor of the museum features exhibitions on early French contacts, the history of Omani-Franco trade and on HM Sultan Qaboos' visit to France. Upstairs you'll find records, furniture, clothes and photographs of early French diplomats. One room holds not just regional Omani women's clothing, but also some antique French costumes. The museum is open from 09:00 to 13:00, Saturdays to Thursdays. Entrance costs 500 baisas for adults and 200 baisas for children aged 6 to 12. Children under 6 enter free.

Omani Museum

Al Alam St
Way 1566
Nr Ministry
of Information
Madinat As Sultan
Qaboos
Map 11 A1

24 600 946 | www.omantourism.gov.om

The Omani Museum sits on top of Information Hill and is almost worth visiting for the view alone. It is run by the Ministry of Information, and although it is fairly small, it is very informative. It is the only museum in the capital city of Muscat that offers detailed archaeological information and artefacts. It also has displays on agriculture, minerals, trade routes, architecture, dhows, arts and crafts, jewellery and weaponry. The museum is open Saturday to Wednesday 08:00 to 13:30 and Thursday 09:00 to 13:00. Admission costs 500 baisas for adults (300 if with a family), 200 baisas for children aged between 6 and 12 and is free for children under 6 and school groups.

Bait Al Falaj Fort
Mujamma St
Ruwi
Map 12 E1

The Sultan's Armed Forces Museum

24 312 657 | www.omantourism.gov.om

This showcase of Oman's military history is set in the main building and grounds of the beautiful Bait Al Falaj Fort, which was built in 1845 to be the garrison headquarters for Sultan Said bin Sultan's armed forces. It features descriptions of the origins of Islam in Oman, tribal disputes and the many invasions of the coast by foreign powers. While these exhibits are a little on the dry side, the more recent military history is lavishly represented with uniforms, antique cannons, early machine guns, weapons confiscated from the rebels in Dhofar, models of military vehicles and planes, instruments, medals and even an ejector seat and parachute.

Outside you'll find exhibits of military hardware such as planes, helicopters, boats, rough terrain vehicles and the first car owned by HM Sultan Qaboos when he became Sultan – a Cadillac with inches-thick bulletproof glass. You can also have a wander around wartime field headquarters and a military hospital. A representative of the army, navy or airforce will guide you around the museum, which is a definite must-do for military enthusiasts. The museum is open Saturday to Wednesday 07:30 to 14:00, Thursday 08:30 to 12:00 and 15:00 to 18:00 and Friday 08:30 to 11:00. Admission costs RO 1 for adults and is free for children up to 18 years old.

Museums – Out Of Muscat

An Nahdah St
Salalah
Map 1 F3

Salalah Museum

23 294 549 | www.omantourism.gov.om

The museum is the cultural centre of Salalah and offers visitors an extended display of traditional literary works, ancient scriptures and coins dating back to the 11th century, pottery dating back to the middle ages and traditional irrigation tools and manuscripts. In the lobby there is an exhibition of Wilfred Thesiger's photographs of Salalah and other parts of Arabia in the 1940s and 1950s. Entrance is free. The museum is open Saturday to Wednesday from around 08:00 to 14:00.

Sohar Fort
Sohar
Map 1 B2

Sohar Fort Museum

26 844 758

This small museum, situated in one of the towers of the Sohar Fort, provides an interesting insight into Oman's geology, geography and ancient history. It includes an extended display on the copper trade, which was once very important for Oman. You can also see the tomb of Sayyid Thuwani bin Said bin Sultan al-Busaid, the ruler of Oman from 1856 to 1866. On the first floor, the history of Oman's notable forts is illustrated. A walk up to the roof of the fort gives you beautiful panoramic views of Sohar and the sea. To get there, take the city centre exit off the Muscat-Dubai road, and after two kilometres turn right at the second roundabout. The museum is open Saturday to Wednesday 08:00 to 13:30 and 16:00 to 18:00 and Thursday 09:00 to 13:00. Admission costs 500 baisas for adults, 200 baisas for children aged 6 to 12 and is free for under 6s.

Al Orouba Youth
Sports Club
Opp Sineslah Fort
Sur
Map 1 C1

Sur Maritime Museum

99 387 155

The local youth sports club in Sur runs this small marine museum. It gives you an idea of what life is like at sea and the importance of fishing and trade to the area. Highlights include old photographs, wooden models and maritime artefacts, as well as examples of local weaving and fabrics embroidered with silver. The museum is located on the premises of the Al Orouba Youth Sports Club, near the main entrance of Sineslah Fort. The small white building that houses the museum is identified by a ship's wheel on the wall. If you are planning to visit the museum, it is advised to call Mr Abdullah M. Al-Araimi (99 387 155). He is the secretary of the sports club, and he will gladly open the museum for you if it is closed, and give you the grand tour. Please note: the best times to call Mr Abdulla are 08:00 to 13:00 and 16:00 to 20:00, Saturday to Thursday. Please do not disturb him on Fridays or during prayer times. Entrance to the museum is free.

Showjumping

Various Locations

Oman Camel Federation
www.omantourism.gov.om
The primary aim of this organisation is to hold various camel races throughout the year in different areas of Oman. However, they also hold showjumping events, although these tend to take place only during the cooler months. Keep your eyes on the local papers, as this is where you'll find details of upcoming events. Alternatively you can contact the federation for a schedule, although a good understanding of Arabic is needed as they don't speak much English.

Various Locations

Oman Equestrian Federation
24 490 424 | www.omaneqf.org
This federation organises a variety of equestrian races. Showjumping used to be a regular fixture, although there are not currently any showjumping events scheduled. Events are published in the newspapers, or you can get more information by calling the federation.

Muscat Gate

Children's Museum

Beach Parks

Other options **Parks** p.180

Ar Rowdah St
Nr Markaz Al Bahja
As Seeb
Map 2 F3

Seeb Beach Park

Seeb Beach Park opened in 1997, on the lovely stretch of sandy beach in As Seeb. In terms of size and facilities, this park is only outshadowed by the magnificent Qurm National Park (see p.182). In Seeb Beach Park, children can paddle in the sea and play on the specially created children's playgrounds. There is also an artificial lake and various watersports are available. The park is an official venue for events held during the Muscat Festival (p.52).

Beaches

Other options **Beach Clubs** p.248, **Parks** p.180, **Swimming** p.246

With over 1,700km of coastline it is hardly surprising that Oman offers some wonderful stretches of sandy beach. Many of them are unspoilt areas where you will find seclusion and isolation. The following are some of the main beaches near Muscat that are popular with visitors and residents alike.
Beaches within the other exploring areas of Oman include: Ras Al Hadd Beach (p.177), Dibad – Tiwi Coast (p.168), and Bandar Jissah (p.176).

Nr Civil Aviation
Recreation Ctr
Al Azaiba
Map 5 B1

Azaiba Beach

Also known as Aviation, Strabag or Shell beach (or as Seeb beach further up the coast), this long stretch of beach is backed by dense bushes that act as a good windbreak. It's a popular camping spot. Access is mainly by 4WD, although if you don't mind a short walk you can get there in a normal car. It is not the best beach for snorkelling, as there is no coral, but it is a good windsurfing site. Because it is a quiet beach, it is suitable for taking your dogs for a run – just make sure you don't disturb the fishermen, as this is still a working beach and they can get a bit grumpy if you get in their way. But on the other hand they are usually more than happy to sell you some fish, show you how their nets work and teach you how to cast sardine nets. Because of construction on the Wave development, access to the beach changes frequently. Make your way to the Civil Aviation Recreation Centre (map 5-C1) and the most recent tracks in the sand will guide you onto the beach.

Nr Oman Dive Ctr
Al Jissah
Map 15 D3

Bandar Al Jissah

While this beautiful (although quite short) stretch of beach can be very busy on Fridays, its attraction is twofold – firstly it is accessible by two-wheel drive car, and secondly it is the best place to catch a sea taxi. Sea taxis are the small fishing boats you see loaded up with fresh fish during the week, and at weekends they go for much bigger fish – tourists. For a very small fee they will transport you and all your gear to one of the secluded beaches such as Khayran, and leave you there until a specified time when they will come and pick you up. It is widely understood that you need not pay the fee until you have been picked up. Snorkelling gear is recommended as the marine life here is stunning. A new market has opened up for them since the opening of the Shangri-La's Barr Al Jissah Resort – they are offering half-hour or one-hour trips around the bay to get a glimpse of this luxurious trio of hotels from a completely different perspective. With a bit of hard bargaining you should be able to get yourself a half-hour trip for around RO 3-5.
To get to the beach, head towards the Al Bustan Palace InterContinental Muscat from Wadi Kabir – you will see the village of Qantab signposted to the right as you reach the top of the hill. Take this right turn and follow the road until you see a signpost for Oman Dive Centre – Bandar Jissah is at the end of this road.

Nr Hyatt Regency
Shati Al Qurm
Map 8 A4

Beach Promenade

In the hour or two before sunset the beach and shoreline stretching from the Hyatt Regency Muscat to the InterContinental Muscat becomes a lively promenade. People come here to walk, jog, jetski, play football and barbecue, and it is a pleasant spot to relax and watch the world go by as the sun goes down. Don't be confused by the concrete wall that you'll see about half way down – while this appears to be the end of the beach it is possible to walk out onto a concrete ledge and continue further. During low tide it is possible to cross the small inlet and walk all the way to the cliffs near the Crowne Plaza Muscat.

Nr Ras Al Hamra Club
Qurm Heights
Map 8 D1

Majan Beach

This small and quiet beach, which is easily accessible, is ideal for snorkellers as it has superb coral reefs. On good days you can see parrot fish, rays and turtles. The beach is equipped with man-made sunshades and barbecue pits.

To get there, go past the Ras Al Hamra Recreation Club, keeping it on your right, and continue over the slight rise for another 150 metres. Parking for the beach is on the opposite side of the road.

60km from Sur
Nr Turtle
Beach Resort
Sur
Map 1 C1

Ras Al Hadd Beach

The beaches around Ras Al Hadd are famous for nesting turtles especially during June and July. They are also popular with visitors who like the relaxing atmosphere and tropical surroundings. The Turtle Beach Resort (99 007 709 or 25 543 400), located at the end of a beautiful turquoise bay, is a good choice for those who like to combine simplicity with a little bit of luxury. The resort has an outdoor dhow-shaped restaurant where you can have a drink overlooking the bay. Lunch and dinner are also served. You don't need to pack your tent, since the resort offers 32 sleeping cottages (RO 42 for two people which includes dinner and breakfast), each one supplied with two beds and an air ventilator. You should definitely take your snorkelling or diving gear; this is a prime spot to see turtles, rays, moray eels and a colourful range of fish. The resort has a small motorboat and on request they will take you out to see the turtles in the summer season.

New Developments
A scientific centre and museum is being set up as part of a tourism drive in the region. The centre, due for completion by 2010, will be located at the entrance to the turtle sanctuary p.168.

The drive from Muscat will take you between four and five hours, so many people make a weekend trip of it. To get there from Sur, follow the signs to Ras Al Hadd. After about 60km you'll reach a T-junction, where you should turn left. Turn left again after about three kilometres, following the sign for Turtle Beach Resort.

Nature Reserves

There is significant emphasis on the care and protection of the Omani environment, such as conserving biodiversity and promoting ecotourism. Nature reserves have been established to prevent damage to the natural habitat of many different species, including leopards, oryx and various birds and fish.

Jiddat Al Harasis
Map 1 D2

Arabian Oryx Sanctuary

24 693 537 | www.oryxoman.com

This reserve is located in the isolated area of Jiddat Al Harasis, the home of Arabia's last true nomads. The environmental resources in this area (flat plains, sand dunes, high hills and rocky slopes) support a unique desert ecosystem that benefits diverse species of flora and fauna. The Arabian Oryx is a medium-sized antelope that is well adapted to its desert existence, particularly because it has the capacity to conserve water. Unfortunately, wild Oryx died out in 1972, but thanks to the efforts of HM Sultan Qaboos, the first Oryx from a captive herd was successfully released into the wild. An entry permit for the sanctuary is available from the Office of the Adviser for

Conservation of the Environment, Diwan of Royal Court (24 693 537). To get there from Muscat, follow the main Salalah highway about 500km to Hayma, and then follow the Duqm graded road to the Habab Junction. Head north on a secondary graded road for a further 23km, and then head due east following a desert track for another 23km. It is recommended that you travel in a convoy with at least two 4WD vehicles.

As Saleel Natural Park

Al Kamil Al Wafi
Sur
Map 1 C1

The As Saleel Natural Park in Al Kamil Al Wafi, approximately 55km south-west of Sur, is divided into three vegetation areas; alluvial plain covered with acacia woodland, wadis in the higher mountains, and sparsely vegetated hills and rocky outcrops forming the northern boundaries. These zones provide good habitat for some of the medium-sized wildlife species in Oman, such as gazelles, wild cats, wolves and foxes. The park has been designated for the future development of wildlife education and tourism, protecting the wildlife in its own habitat. Unfortunately unrestricted access in the past has made the animals quite shy, so a visit to this park is no guarantee of a sighting.

Damaniyat Islands Nature Reserve

Seeb/Barka
As Seeb
Map 1 B1 & 2

The Damaniyat Islands are a cluster of nine islands along the coast of As Seeb and Barka. They are surrounded by rocks and shallow seas, and can only be reached by boat. The islands are of great environmental importance, as they are home to some endangered species and the nesting sites for several species of migratory birds. The islands themselves are off limits to visitors. You can anchor just off the islands and dive or snorkel in the surrounding waters, although you need to get permission to do this. The waters feature an abundance of marine life and the greatest diversity of corals in the region. Each year, 250 to 300 hawksbill turtles nest on the islands – this species is the most endangered of all marine turtles, and they usually nest in small numbers over a large geographical area. Therefore, this congregation of such a large group on such a small cluster of islands is of global importance.

Jebel Samhan Nature Reserve

66km past Tawi Atayr
Dhofar
Map 1 E3

The immense Jebel Samhan Nature Reserve is in Dhofar and stretches from Marbat in the south to Shuwimiya in the northeast. The limestone highlands, scalloped mountain peaks, wadis and canyons, and the 1,500m high escarpment overlooking foothills and the coastal plain between Marbat and Sadh, provide ideal habitat for the last-known wild population of Arabian leopard. Other wildlife present in the area includes nubian ibex, Arabian gazelle, striped hyenas, caracal, wild cats, foxes and wolves. Whales can sometimes be seen along the coast between Hadbin and Shuwaymiya. Green and loggerhead turtles also nest on the sandy beaches, and the adjacent cliffs provide a resting place for migrating birds. To get there, turn left at the signpost marked Tawi Atayr (32km before you reach Taqah). In Tawi Atayr, turn left following the signpost for Khis Adeen. Turn right after one kilometre, and then drive along the graded road for about 66km, at which point you will reach the plateau on top of Jebel Samhan.

Khors Of The Dhofar Coast

Nr Taqah Village
Dhofar
Map 1 E4

The Dhofar coast khors are valuable resources with an abundance of wildlife. One of the most important reasons for protecting the khors is their use by large numbers of migratory birds for food and rest during their annual migration – over 200 species of birds have been recorded in this area. The khors were traditionally used by the local people to water and graze their livestock, while the marine life provided rich fishing territory. With the increase in population and the expansion of the Salalah area, some of the khors' resources became threatened by over-utilisation. Hence, the Oman government has proclaimed these valuable resources as protected areas. To witness

Something
for the
Weekend...

From idyllic beach getaways to activity-packed city breaks, this guide is the ultimate resource for pepping up your downtime.

Supported by:

The Wave
MUSCAT

Weekend
Breaks
Oman & UAE

EXPLORER

The Wave

some of the khors' beauty go to Khor Rouri Beach, a few kilometres east of Taqah Village (east of Salalah).

Ras Al Hadd
Sur
Map 1 C1

Ras Al Jinz Sea Turtle & Natural Reserve ▶ p.181

96 550 606 | www.rasaljinz.org

Turtle nesting sites on the coast of Oman have been recorded on over 275 beaches along the coast, from the Musandam in the north to near the border with Yemen in the south. Five out of the seven recognised species of marine turtle are found in Oman's waters, while the green turtle, the loggerhead, hawksbill and olive ridley are known to come ashore and nest. The giant leatherback turtle, which can weigh up to a ton, feeds in the waters off Oman's coast, but does not regularly nest here. Turtles face many threats to their survival, not least being caught in fishing nets and having their nesting sites destroyed by man. Green turtles are estimated to lay up to 60,000 egg clutches each year in Oman; the effort of about 20,000 female turtles. While they nest all along the coast, the majority of nest sites are along a 45km stretch of coastline around Ras Al Hadd (the most eastern point of the Arabian Peninsula). Here, the government has set up a reserve to allow the public to view the amazing spectacle of nesting females and newborn hatchlings. The area has been limited to the beaches at Ras Al Jinz, with access to the other beaches being prohibited. To visit the turtle reserve at Ras Al Jinz you must get a permit. However, you no longer have to apply to the Directorate General of Nature Protectorates, because you can now get one directly from the Ras Al Jinz gate. Places are limited to about 60 people and it is advisable to book well in advance if you can. A fee of RO 1 is charged for adults and 100 baisas for children. You will need to supply names and nationalities of all visitors, plus a contact phone number, visit date and your car registration number. The permit allows you to stay on the government campsite at Ras Al Jinz and to have access to the beach. When you receive the permit you will also get an information pack on using the campsite and watching the turtles.

Nr Tawi Atayr
Dhofar
Map 1 E3

Tawi Atayr & Wadi Darbat

The Wadi Darbat Natural Park in the Dhofar region has stunning views of waterfalls, lakes, mountains and lush vegetation. There are also caves to explore (rich in stalactites and stalagmites) and a wide range of wildlife. During the khareef season (in summer), there is a monsoon waterfall that is 100 metres high. To get there from Taqah, drive towards Marbat and after 32km you'll find the turn-off for Tawi Atayr (famous for its 'Well of Birds' – a natural sinkhole that is over 100 metres wide and 211 metres deep, and which is home to many species of birds, particularly during the khareef). From the Tawi Atayr turn-off, turn left after a few hundred metres to get onto the track that will lead you down into Wadi Darbat.

Parks

Other options **Beaches** p.176

In 'desert' countries such as Oman, the lack of lush greenery is something that you might miss from back home. Fortunately, Oman has a good selection of parks and gardens that are welcome patches of green. Parks are well looked after by the municipality, and usually include lawns, sandy play areas and playground equipment for children, and maybe a water feature or two. Before you load your bicycle, rollerblades or dogs into the car, check the park's policy on these – some might allow certain activities, while others don't. Entry to many of the parks is free. Muscat has some beautiful parks to explore – see Kalbooh Park (p.182), Naseem Park (p.182), Qurm Park & Nature Reserve (p.182), and Riyam Park (p.182).

Ras al-Jinz - Oman
Crossroads for life

At the edge of the Arabian Peninsula lies one of the Indian Ocean's largest nesting areas for Green Turtles: Ras al-Jinz. It's part of the Ras al-Hadd Nature Reserve, which also contains some of the most important archaeological sites in Oman.

Ras al-Jinz
crossroads for life

The Ras al-Jinz Scientific and Visitor Centre offers a unique ecotourism experience: an encounter with sea turtles in their natural environment. It also houses a marine biology and archaeology research centre.

Kalbooh Park

Kalbooh
Mutrah
Map 10 D3

Situated along the coast by the village of Kalbooh, this small park is a picturesque spot for an evening stroll. It features paved walkways and a grassed amphitheatre. A selection of kiosks and a small Pizza Hut sell snacks and drinks. The views are amazing, with the sea to one side and sheer, rocky hills to the other. In the daytime there is a beautiful view along the coast of Mutrah.

Naseem Park

Past Seeb Airport
As Seeb
Map 1 B1

This large park, opened in 1985, is located on the highway leading to the Batinah area, about 30km from Seeb International Airport. There is a train ride that goes round the park, a mini falaj system, a jasmine maze and well-tended Arabic and Japanese gardens, built to commemorate the strong ties between Japan and Oman. A cafeteria selling drinks, icecreams and snacks is situated in the centre of the park.

Beach Parks

Get the best of both worlds at Seeb Beach Park (p.176). The large area combines lush greenery with the beauty of the beach.

Qurm Heights Park

Nr Crowne
Plaza Hotel
Qurm Heights
Map 8 C2

This small park is perched high on the cliffs in Qurm, next to the Gulf Forum Hotel. Its grassy lawn is surrounded by shady trees and plenty of plants and shrubs. At one end of the park is a collection of stone benches on a small paved area – the perfect spot for a few minutes of contemplation at the end of the day. This tranquil park is very popular in the evenings with people living in the area.

Qurm Park & Nature Reserve

Al Qurm St
Al Qurm
Map 8 D4

This sprawling park and nature reserve runs from the side of the main coastal road right down to the public beach. It is Muscat's main park, and features large lawns, a boating lake, water fountains and shady pergolas. It is the home of the Sultan's rose garden, a tranquil, fragrant area that is full of rose varieties from around the world. The large fountain shoots water up to 30 metres into the air, and it is even more impressive at night when it is lit up. The park incorporates a nature reserve, which is made up of tidal wetlands and mangroves. It's a great place for spotting migratory birds, and you can expect to see sooty gulls, white-cheeked terns, crested terns and, at low tide, various herons and waders. There is also a mangrove nursery, which yields thousands of valuable mangrove tree seedlings every year. Children will enjoy the playground (no entry fee) and light refreshments in The Rose Garden Cafe. The park is also home to the City Amphitheatre, which seats up to 4,500 people and is a popular venue for events. Open Saturday to Wednesday 16:00 to 23:00; Thursday, Friday and public holidays 09:00 to midnight.

Riyam Park

Mutrah Corniche
Mutrah
Map 10 C3

Riyam Park is located on Mutrah Corniche and offers pretty views of the harbour. You can't miss it if you drive along the corniche – it's the one with a gigantic white model of an incense burner perched on top of a hill. It is usually possible to climb up to the top of the incense burner but at the time of writing it was closed for renovation so the view from the summit will have to suffice. It's a fairly steep climb but it is worth it for the spectacular views of the harbour, sea and cliffs. Riyam Park is great for kids, with lots of playground equipment and a small funfair (usually open from 16:00, depending on the season). There is plenty of shade and a pond.

Muscat's parks

Tour-Tastic
If you are booking
a tour for family or
friends who are visiting
you in Oman, make
sure you ring around
to get the best price.
Tour operators can spot
a naive tourist miles
away, but they will
often drop the prices for
savvy expats who know
what things cost in
rials. Just remember it
is all about putting on
the charm, not being a
cheeky customer.

Tours & Sightseeing

As you might expect from a country with such breathtaking scenery and rich history, Oman has numerous tour operators offering an exciting range of city, desert and mountain trips. The following are descriptions of the most popular (and most general) tour itineraries available, but remember that if you have something specific in mind, many operators can tailor-make a tour for you.

When booking your tour, it is useful to book three or four days in advance if possible. Some operators will request a 50% deposit. Tours usually depart from set pick-up points, such as major hotels. As a general guideline, wear cool, comfortable clothing, and don't forget your hat and sunglasses. Desert and mountain tours require strong, flat-soled shoes, and if you're going into the desert in the cooler months, take a jacket as the temperature can drop after sunset. And don't forget your camera!

One last word on desert and mountain tours: these trips often involve some pretty extreme driving over sand dunes or through wadis. If you are pregnant, elderly, sick, are travelling with young children or you suffer from motion sickness, inform your tour company and they will arrange a gentler route for you.

Boat Tours & Charters
Other options **Dhow Charters** p.186

**Marina Bandar
Al Rowdha**
Mutrah
Map 13 F4

Al Khayran
24 737 286 | *www.alkhayran.com*
A new addition to the Oman exploring scene, Al Khayran is a semi-submersible boat to take you beneath the ocean without getting wet. Trips leave four times a day, seven days a week, from Marina Bandar Al Rowdha where a speedy passenger boat zips you along the coastline past the Al Bustan Palace InterContinental Muscat and Shangri-La to the waiting vessel. Venture down the stairs and you'll find yourself in a submarine boasting windows onto the underwater world. Informative posters help you spot species of fish and even turtles if you're lucky. The two-hour trip includes soft drinks and costs RO 25 for tourists and expats or RO 6 for Omanis.

Sidab St
Sidab
Map 13 F4

Marina Bandar Al Rowdha
24 737 288
Marina Bandar Al Rowdha is located on the western coast of Oman, and is one of the best launch spots for fishing, diving and sailing. It has a total of 400 berths, and is fully equipped for launch, recovery, service and marine control. The marina can organise tours for whale and dolphin watching, watersports, diving and fishing. For a more relaxing excursion, you can go for a cruise on a traditional dhow, or be transported to a secluded beach for an afternoon's sunbathing. The marina has its own restaurant, the Blue Marlin (p.330), which does a great alfresco breakfast and, not surprisingly, good fish pie.

**Nr Grand
Hyatt Muscat**
Shati Al Qurm
Map 7 E1

Moon Light Dive Centre
99 317 700 | *www.moonlightdive.com*
The Moon Light Dive Centre can deliver a customised cruise package to meet your requirements. It offers trips for groups (from four people to 10) in one of its three boats, which are based on the beach in Shati Al Qurm, next to the Hyatt Regency Muscat.

A typical cruise heads south along Muscat's spectacular coast, visiting rocky islands out at sea, secluded beaches or even marina cafes for breakfast or refreshments. Time can be allocated for other activities as per your requirements, such as fishing, snorkelling, sunbathing or watersports. For a three-hour trip, expect to pay around RO 25 per person with discounts for groups.

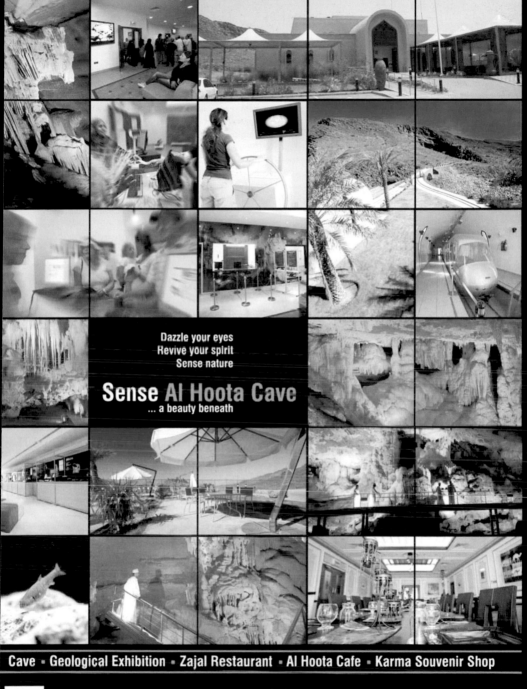

Dazzle your eyes
Revive your spirit
Sense nature

Sense Al Hoota Cave
... a beauty beneath

Cave ▪ Geological Exhibition ▪ Zajal Restaurant ▪ Al Hoota Cafe ▪ Karma Souvenir Shop

For reservations: Tel: +968 92 404444
Email: reserve@alhootacave.com
Website: www.alhootacave.com

Member:
International Show Cave Association

ISO 9001
ISO 14001
BUREAU VERITAS
Certification
IND91097A IND91097B

Managed by:

Camel Rides
Other options **Camel Racing** p.170

A visit to this part of the world is hardly complete unless you've been up close and personal with a 'ship of the desert'. A ride on a camel is hard to forget – you will generally mount the camel when it is lying down, and then you need to hang on for dear life when your humped steed unfolds its gangly legs to stand up. Once you're up though, it's fairly smooth riding and you can lose yourself in your 'Lawrence of Arabia' fantasies. Don't forget to take a photo!

Many tour operators incorporate a short camel ride on their desert safaris. Alternatively, for a unique adventure, you could try a camel ride into the spectacular sand dunes. Your guide will lead you to a Bedouin camp, where you can enjoy a well-deserved rest and some refreshments. Don't forget to take your camera, so you can remember this unique experience long after the aches subside.

Wahiba Sands
Bidiyah
Ibra
Map 1 C1

Desert Camp
99 311 338 | info@desert-camp.com
Desert Camp offers a variety of desert activities, including camel rides or desert cycles for kids. Based 220km from Muscat, you can accessorise your camel adventure with dune bashing, sand surfing and trips to nearby encampments at Wadi Bani Khalid and Ras Al Jinz (p.180) on the coast, where you may even get to watch turtles coming ashore.

Nr Radisson BLU
Al Khuwayr
Map 7 C3

Muscat Diving & Adventure Centre
24 485 663 | www.holiday-in-oman.com
The centre offers two main tours by camel, which are operated along eco-tourism lines. The company works with Bedouin families of the Northern Region Sands (Wahiba) in the Sharquiya, and it runs expeditions in the Rub Al Khali in Dhofar. Camel trips or 'safaris' can vary in length from a short day ride to a 14 day trek across the sands. This is one of Oman's most authentic tours and it allows you the opportunity to see and engage in the Bedouin way of life with an overnight stop at a Bedu campsite.

Dhow Charters
Other options **Boat Tours & Charters** p.184

Salahuddin Rd
Sharjah
Map 1 A3

Al Marsa Tours
+971 6 544 1232 | www.musandamdiving.com
Al Marsa has four purpose-built dhows that are suitable both for divers and tourists. You can relax on the sundeck for a day trip and discover fishing villages or you can go on anything up to a seven-night voyage and explore Oman's fjords. The dhows are equipped for diving and other watersports. Prices start at Dhs.370 for divers and Dhs.300 for non-divers. Based in Sharjah, the company operates along the eastern coastline of the UAE and Oman.

Nr Al Maha
Gas Station
Mussandam
Map 1 A2

Hormuzline Tours & Cruises
26 731 616 | www.hormuzlinetours.com
Hormuzline offers excursions and accommodation packages tailored to your needs. The dhow cruise options range from one-day trips exploring the Khasab on a traditional wooden dhow, to an overnight tour that includes a dhow cruise. It also offers the opportunity for you to sail into the Strait of Hormuz, to swim with dolphins, snorkel around islands and to explore laidback, sleepy coastal villages.

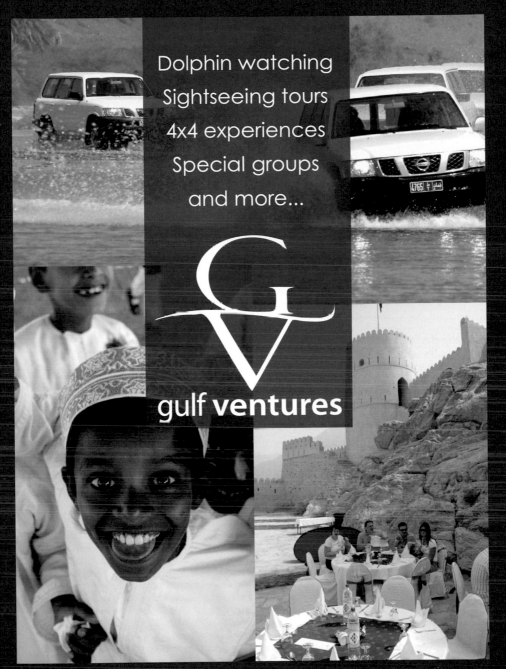

Dolphin watching
Sightseeing tours
4x4 experiences
Special groups
and more...

gulf ventures

Marina Bandar
Al Rowdha
Mutrah
Map 13 F4

Ibn Qais & Partners

24 487 103 | omandhow@omantel.net.om

Ibn Qais owns the Lubna, a traditional dhow that's available for charter to any of the islands in Oman. The company provides everything you need while onboard, and even tailor-make packages for special occasions. So, if you want a celebration with a difference, you can set sail on the Lubna for an evening of good food and entertainment. Sunset cruises set sail every Thursday and Sunday from 16:00 to 18:00.

Fishmarket/Port
Dibba
East Coast
Map 1 A3

Khasab Dhow Charters

+971 4 266 9950 | www.khasabtours.com

Khasab Dhow Charters arranges one, two or three-night fishing and diving trips along the Musandam coastline. Large, independent groups can charter a traditional wooden dhow that sleeps about 40. Facilities are fairly basic and it's advisable to take camping equipment and arrange for the dhow to stop along the coast at night, although it is possible to sleep on board. You'll also need to take your own food and water, but there are ice lockers onboard. During the day you can go ashore to visit a village or walk in the mountains. Alternatively, Khasab Dhow Charters has an air-conditioned and luxurious dhow, Sindabad, that accommodates up to 50 passengers. It's mostly used for day trips to the fjords of Musandam and the price of RO 20 per person includes swimming and snorkelling around Telegraph Island, and lunch and refreshments. Sindabad also has eight cabins for overnight cruises, and shower facilities.

Musandam
Nr Khasab Airport
Khasab
Map 1 A2

Khasab Travel & Tours

26 730 464 | www.khasabtours.com

Khasab Travel & Tours has a traditionally decorated Omani dhow on which to take you exploring in the fjords. It's decked out with cushions and carpets for you to lounge on while enjoying the passing scenery. The dhow will also stop and allow you to explore the villages of the Strait of Hormuz, and a session of swimming or snorkelling around Telegraph Island. Refreshments and a buffet lunch are also included.

Musandam
Khasab
Map 1 A2

Musandam Sea Adventure Tourism

26 730 069 | www.musandam-sea-adventures.com

With its dramatic fjords, the Musandam area is often referred to as 'the Norway of the Middle East'. Take a dhow cruise and experience the area's rocky topography where mountains jut up out of pristine waters. Every now and then you can land and explore remote Omani villages, and then stop at Telegraph Island for a leisurely picnic. Cruises vary from half-day to three-day options, and prices range from RO 15–150 per person, with children under 3 free and under 10s half price. The company takes care of transportation, food and lodging, and creates comfortable but adventurous, tours.

Dolphin & Whale Watching

There are more than 20 species of whales and dolphins either living in or passing through the seas off the coast of Oman. Although no tour operator can guarantee a sighting of these beautiful sea creatures, the odds are definitely high that you will get to see a school of dolphins swimming alongside your boat and playing in its wake. Many tour operators will tentatively rate your chances of seeing dolphins at 85% to 90%. Whales are not so frequently seen – these gentle giants travel in smaller groups and stay under the surface for a lot longer, so you have to be a little bit more patient. Early mornings and evenings, when the seas are at their calmest, are the best times for whale sightings. It is possible to see them from the shore (usually in cliff areas, such as Musandam) but it is better to be out at sea in a boat, where the experience is closer and infinitely more exciting.

Working hard to monitor and protect these magnificent mammals is the Whale & Dolphin Research Group, part of the Environment Society of Oman (ESO). This is a group of volunteer scientists and other interested parties who work together to collect and disseminate knowledge about Oman's cetaceans (whales & dolphins). The group's activities include emergency rescue services for whales and dolphins, collection of cetacean bones, skulls and tissue samples, maintenance of a database of cetacean sightings and strandings, cooperation with local tour operators to promote responsible whale and dolphin watching activities, dissemination of information through articles in local and international publications to promote awareness of Oman's cetaceans and the need to protect their environment. For further information, see www. whalecoastoman.com or contact: Andy Wilson (95 920 461), Iain Benson (95 035 988), Louise Waters (99 473 140) or the main office (24 696 912).

Arabian Sea Safaris

InterContinental Muscat
Shati Al Qurm
Map 8 A4

24 693 223 | *www.arabianseasafaris.com*
Watching wild dolphins is a thrilling way to start the day, and if you are extremely lucky you may even come across one of the many species of whale that can be found just a few kilometres off Muscat's coastline. Not every trip guarantees a sighting, but the trip out to sea is enjoyable in its own right and you will learn more about the region's fascinating marine life. Boats depart daily, with trips lasting two hours and costing RO 25 including breakfast.

Gulf Leisure

Nr Jawharat Al Shati Mall
Al Bustan
Map 15 A1

99 013 424 | *www.gulfleisure.com*
There are more than 20 species of dolphins and whales in Oman, and one of the best ways to see them is on Oman's only glass-bottom boat, the 'Gulf Vision'. You can see the stunning coral reefs and tropical marine life along the coastline from a unique perspective. Your bilingual Omani guide provides fascinating commentary peppered with his account of local legends and folklore. When the boat anchors in one of the many sheltered reefs, you can swim or snorkel in complete safety or remain on board. Dolphin sightings are more common either early morning or just before sunset. Cruises on Gulf Vision depart daily from Marina Bandar Al Rowdha. An adult trip costs RO 20, under 12s are RO 10, under 5s sail for free and all prices include soft drinks.

Marina Bandar Al Rowdha

Sidab St
Sidab
Map 13 F4

24 737 288
The Marina Bandar Al Rowdha offers dolphin tours a short distance off the coast of Muscat and is the leaving point for the Al Khayan semi-submersible boat (p.184). For more information on the marina, see p.184.

Muscat Diving & Adventure Center

Nr Radisson BLU
Al Khuwayr
Map 7 C3

24 485 663 | *www.holiday-in-oman.com*
This upbeat tour operator can take you out to sea to spot dolphins, and they estimate the chance of a sighting at around 80%. The most common species seen are common, spinner and bottlenose. There are two boats which seat up to 15 and 20 people. Daily departures are at 07:00 and 10:00. The cruises last for three to four hours, and the cost per person is RO 20 (which includes soft drinks).

Oman Dive Center

Bandar Al Jissah Qantab
Al Bustan
Map 15 D3

24 824 240 | *www.omandivecenter.com*
Every morning, the Oman Dive Center organises a boat trip to go and spot dolphins off the coast of Muscat. Your chances of seeing dolphins (usually common, spinner,

bottlenose or Indo-Pacific species) are high at any time of year and estimated at around 95%. Your chances of seeing whales are not as high, although they have been spotted from time to time (usually from October to May). The boat trip includes breakfast served onboard.

Farm & Stable Tours
Other options **Horse Riding** p.232

Nr Majan
Water Factory
Barka
Map 1 B2

Ostrich Farm

The Ostrich Breeding Farm in Barka is surprisingly interesting. Visitors can see the 100 adult birds or the eggs being incubated and also chicks between February and June. The farm started in 1993 when the eggs were imported from South Africa. They were the first ostriches to have been hatched in Oman since early last century when the birds became extinct in this region.

The ostrich is farmed for a variety of reasons and the aim of the farm is to sustain a 300 bird breeding group to meet the ever-increasing demands for healthy meat, fine leather and exquisite feathers. Ostrich meat is considered an excellent alternative to beef, since it is low in cholesterol, but has a very similar consistency and texture. The farm is also home to about 30 crocodiles.

Entrance to the farm costs 500 baisas per adult and 300 baisas per child. The timings are 07:00 to 12:00 and 15:00 to 18:00, seven days a week.

To get there, turn on to Nakhal Road from the Barka Roundabout, and after four kilometres you'll see the Majan Water Factory on the right. Turn right into the private road just before the factory, and the ostrich farm is the first farm on your left.

Places Of Worship Tours
Other options **Museums** p.171

As Sultan Qaboos St
Al Khuwayr
Map 6 D4

Sultan Qaboos Grand Mosque

This beautiful example of Islamic architecture provides a wonderful insight into the cultural heritage of Oman. It is also one of the few mosques that allow entry for non-Muslims. Apart from being a place of worship, this huge mosque is a centre for scholars and houses an Islamic reference library containing over 20,000 sources of information on Islamic sciences and culture. The mosque is lavishly decorated, and features a 263m prayer carpet, 35 crystal chandeliers (the central one is 14 metres high and eight metres wide), and a floor entirely paved with marble. The tour takes you into the men's

Sultan Qaboos Grand Mosque

and women's prayer halls, where you are even allowed to take pictures. There are strict rules governing entry of non-Muslims into the mosque – you have to take your shoes off before entering, and both men and women should wear conservative clothing (women should be covered up, including their hair), and children under 10 are not permitted. The hours for the tour are strictly between 08:30 and 11:00 from Saturday to Thursday.

Safari Tours

Dune Dinner

There are a range of dune dinners on offer, but on a typical tour you will be collected in the mid-afternoon, when you will be driven inland towards the Hajar mountains and then off-road through the lush green scenery and freshwater pools of Wadi Abyad. Then you'll head for the undulating dunes of the nearby Abyad desert for some exciting dune driving, before stopping to watch the sun set over the sands. After a sumptuous barbecue, you'll head back to Muscat.

Full-Day Safari

This trip combines a visit to one of Oman's most spectacular wadis, Wadi Bani Khalid, with the breathtaking expanse of the Wahiba Desert. Different tour operators have different itineraries, but on the way from Muscat you will visit places such as the ruined fort of Mudairib, Shab Village and the town of Sur. Some of the unforgettable sights you may see on the way are traditional mud-brick homes clinging to steep valley walls, clear streams carrying fresh water into deep pools, and manmade irrigation systems called 'falaj'. As you leave the mountains you'll head for the Wahiba desert for an exhilarating ride over the dunes, some of which are 200 metres high.

Mountain Safari

The height and extent of Oman's mountain ranges surprise many visitors. Mountain safaris either head into the highest range, Jebel Akhdar, or up to Jebel Shams, which is Oman's highest peak at over 3,000m. On the way, you'll pass through towns (such as Nizwa) and remote villages set on terraces cut into the mountains. Ancient irrigation channels bring water to the villages to feed the crops. The top of Jebel Shams feels like the top of the world, with the entire mountain range and the awe-inspiring 'Grand Canyon' of Oman (a rocky canyon dropping thousands of metres from the plateau), way below.

Overnight Turtle Watching

Many tour operators offer trips to the famous Ras Al Jinz Turtle Sanctuary, where you can watch the rare sight of turtles coming onto the beach to lay their eggs. On your way to Ras Al Jinz you'll pass Quriyat, Wadi Shab, and the town of Sur, home to the most skilled dhow builders in Oman. After arriving at the Turtle Sanctuary, you'll be served a beach barbecue before night falls and the turtles come lumbering onto the beach to lay their eggs and bury them in the sand. After a few hours sleep, you'll return to the beach and watch the mass of tiny hatchlings struggle out of their eggs and make their journey into the sea. On your return journey to Muscat you will get to see more of the countryside and historical settlements.

Wadi Drive

An off-road tour through the wadis can either be half-day, full-day or overnight, camping in the peaceful surroundings of the rocky wilderness. You'll get to see falaj irrigation channels, in place for centuries, bringing water from underground springs to irrigate palm plantations and vegetable terraces. Natural streams run all year round in several wadis, transforming the dry, rocky landscape into fertile areas of lush greenery and clear rock pools that are often home to fish, frogs and other wildlife. Hidden villages in the mountains, seemingly trapped in time, illustrate how people used to subsist in times gone by.

Safari Savvy
Off-road driving is exhilarating but extreme, and people who suffer from motion sickness may not enjoy the experience very much. You may rest assured that your driver is a skilled professional and knows exactly what he is doing. However, remember that you are the client and have the right to request him to slow down or tackle less challenging routes, if you feel the ride is too bumpy. Most drivers will take an easier route if you are with children, elderly people or people with special circumstances. Note that it may not be safe for pregnant women to go on an off-road tour.

Wahiba Desert
The Wahiba Desert stretches all the way from the coast to the mountains. This tour travels into the middle of seemingly endless dunes of red and white sand. Dune driving is a must-do; a ride up and down the steep slopes, courtesy of a very skilled driver, is like a natural rollercoaster. A visit to a traditional Bedouin homestead for Arabic coffee and dates usually follows, as well as the chance to try camel riding, the oldest form of desert transport.

Overnight Desert Safari
Leave the noise of the city behind you and experience the peace of the desert for a night. After an exhilarating drive through the dunes you will set up camp in a remote area of Wahiba, where Bedouin tribes have lived traditionally for thousands of years. At sunset, enjoy a camel ride while a barbecue is prepared and then relax in comfortable surroundings under the starlit sky. In the morning, after a leisurely start, visit the flowing wadis to see the greenery and rugged mountain landscape, which form a complete contrast to the desert sights of the previous day.

Tours Outside Muscat
Other options **Beyond Muscat** p.159

East Salalah Tour
Leaving from Salalah and travelling east, this tour visits many historical sites and places of interest along the picturesque coast including the fishing village of Taqa with its watchtowers and castle. Further on is Khor Rouri, a freshwater creek now separated from the sea. It is the site of the ancient city of Samharam, known for its frankincense and for being the former capital of the Dhofar region. Also on the tour is Mohammed Bin Ali's Tomb, the Ayn Razat ornamental gardens, the Hamran Water Springs and the historical trading centre of Mirbat.

West Salalah Tour
Venture inland from Salalah to the northern part of the Qara Mountains, where the road winds up hairpin bends and eventually leads to the border with Yemen. The tour goes to the Tomb of the Prophet Job, a place visited by many Islamic pilgrims, and the wadis and green pastures where they grow the finest frankincense in the world. Returning from the mountains, you will head to the spectacular Mughsail Beach where, at high tide, seawater gushes through natural blowholes in the limestone, reaching dizzying heights. On the way back to Salalah, common stops are the bird sanctuary and Mina Raysut.

Nizwa
Nizwa is the largest city in Oman's interior, and this full-day tour explores the fascinating sights and heritage of this historically significant place. After driving deep into the Hajar mountains, you'll come to the oasis city of Nizwa, home to the Nizwa Fort (which dates back to the 17th century) and the magnificent Jabrin Fort, notable for its wall and ceiling decorations and secret passageways. Many ancient ruins, such as Bahla Fort and various mud-brick villages, can be seen among the date palm plantations and wadis.

Taste Oman ... Naturally

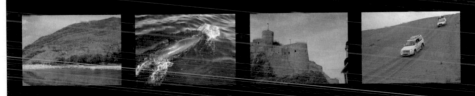

Let Alwan Tourism take you to an unforgettable experience and journey of a lifetime.

We also offer Airport Transfer Services, Rent a Car Services, Organized Tour Services.

ألوان السياحة
Alwan Tourism

ALWAN TOURISM

P.O. Box 202 Al Harthy Complex, Muscat, Post Code 118, Sultanate of Oman
Tel: +968 24594002, Fax: +968 24594003, E-mail : talal@alwantour.com, Website : www.alwantour.com

Rustaq & Batinah

Batinah, the north-west region of Oman, has always been an important area for its abundant agriculture and strategic position as the trading centre between the mountains and the coast. It is home to many forts including the oldest and largest in the country, Al Kersa Fort. En route you will also visit the ancient souks, hot springs and sandy beaches, all amid spectacular mountain scenery. See also Batinah Region, p.160.

Ubar

The discovery of the 'Lost City of Ubar' in the early 1990s caused great excitement in the archaeological world. This full-day tour takes you through some stunning scenery as you drive through the Qara mountains to the site of Ubar. This ancient city was at the crossroads of significant trade routes, making it a place of unrivalled wealth and splendour – when Marco Polo visited Ubar, he called it 'paradise'. However, at the height of its glory it sank into the desert sands, leaving no trace of its existence. Legend had it that to punish the residents of Ubar for their greed and lavish lifestyle, God caused the sand to swallow the city. When the lost city was uncovered, less than 20 years ago, it was discovered that a huge limestone cavern underneath Ubar had collapsed, causing the city to sink into the sand.

After leaving Ubar you'll continue off-road as the tour ventures into the famous sands of Rub al Khali (the Empty Quarter), for some dune driving.

Tour Operators

The following guidelines are just to give you an outline of how tour operators do business. Each operator may offer something different, and tour itineraries, timings and prices will vary from one operator to the next. Most companies have head offices in Muscat, although they all offer tours both in and out of the capital. When booking a tour it is normal practise to do so three or four days in advance. In some cases bookings can be made on shorter notice. You usually pay a 50% deposit when you make the booking, with the remainder payable when you are picked up at the start of the tour. Cancellation policies differ from company to company; although cancelling your tour without an appropriate notice period may result in the loss of your deposit. Tours are often priced per vehicle rather than per person, although some tours offer fixed individual rates for tours and do not stipulate minimum numbers.

Tour Operators

Al Ebda	99 661 527	na
Al Ghadeer Tours	24 425 557	na
Alwan Tours ▶ p.193	24 594 002	www.alwantour.com
Elite Travel & Tourism	24 485 020	www.eliteoman.com
Global Tours	24 695 959	www.globaltoursoman.com
Mezoon Travel	24 796 680	www.mezoontravel.com
National Travel & Tourism	24 660 300	www.nttoman.com
Nomadic Explorer	99 316 507	www.nomadic.biz
Oman Discovery	24 706 424	www.oman-discovery.com
Oman United Agencies	24 700 326	na
Orient Holidays	24 478 902	www.visitingoman.com
Orient Tours Oman	24 485 066	www.orienttours.ae
Premier Tours	24 700 272	na
Shanfari Holidays	24 786 916	www.shanfari.com
Sidab Sea Tours	24 737 885	na
United Tours	24 787 448	www.ajitkhimjigroup.com
Zahara Tours	24 400 844	www.zaharatours.com

On the day of your tour you will be picked up either from your hotel, residence or an agreed meeting point. Tours usually leave on time, and no-shows do not get a refund. At most times of year it is advisable to wear cool, comfortable clothing such as shorts and T-shirts. Hats and sunglasses are also recommended. If you are going on a desert or mountain tour, you should wear strong, flat-soled shoes as there is usually some walking involved. You might want to take sun protection, a camera and money (in case there's a chance to buy souvenirs).

Main Tour Operators

Jawaharat
A'Shati Complex
Shati Al Qurm
Map 8 A4

Al Azure Tours

99 856 888 | *www.alazuretours.com*

The team at Al Azure Tours provides camping tours with tailor-made itineraries, high quality equipment and expert knowledge to help you experience the countryside and culture of Oman. Tours include day trips and sea tours (dhow cruises, diving, water sports, glass bottom boat, chartering a yacht), but the most exciting and popular option involves camping. These customised tours, ranging from one overnight stay (starting at RO 175 per person) to several weeks, are perfect for a country made for outdoor living. Due to high quality camping accessories (roof tents and tents with beds are available, and even a shower tent is included) and the energetic team, you shouldn't feel tired even after weeks of travelling around Oman. All tours are guided and offered languages include English, Arabic, German, French and Hungarian.

InterContinental
Muscat
Shati Al Qurm
Map 8 A4

Arabian Sea Safaris

24 693 223 | *www.arabianseasafaris.com*

Arabian Sea Safaris was founded in 1996 and is dedicated to the provision of outstanding tourism services. The staff are experts on dolphins and whales in Oman, thanks to founder Mohamed Al Riyami – he was a senior official at the Ministry of Information for over a decade, and his main function there was showcasing Oman's tourism treasures to visiting dignitaries, journalists and television teams from around the world. The role took him throughout Oman's varied terrain, from mountain settlements and Bedouin campsites to the modern cities of Muscat and Salalah, and it is this experience that he shares with his clients. Visit Arabian Sea Safaris at the InterContinental Muscat to learn more about their leisure and entertainment tours. Apart from tours to some of Oman's most beautiful places, a range of activity tours including bicycle tours and watersports are also offered. See also p.239 and p.222.

Way 4852
Al Azaiba
Map 1 C1

Desert Discovery Tours

24 493 232 | *www.desert-discovery.com*

Desert Discovery offers a range of activity and sightseeing tours under the guidance of officially appointed Omani guides. From camping in the Wahiba Sands and desert driving, to camel riding and turtle watching, Desert Discovery can organise an itinerary for you. For a unique chance to explore Oman off the beaten track, you can book a tour in one of the mobile camping units. Each unit has a large entertainment tent and several smaller sleeping tents, equipped with campbeds and sleeping bags. The GPS coordinates for the Al Areesh Camp are N 22°29.767, E 058°41.200, and for the Al Naseem Camp (Turtle Beach) N 22°16.112, E 059°47.357.

Various Locations

Eihab Travels

24 683 900 | *www.omanvalueholidays.com*

Eihab Travel has been in business for 25 years and provides extensive tourism services throughout Oman. It offers 'Oman Value Holidays', a range of sightseeing and shopping tours, as well as camping and diving trips. While on these tours and trips, you can partake in activities such as rock climbing, camel trekking or off-road driving. You can do a daytrip through Muscat, around the forts, or to the amazing coast of Batinah. Off-road daytrips include excursions to the Wahiba sands, the Hajar mountains and to Oman's stunning coast. If water tours are more your thing, it can arrange dolphin-watching trips and sunset dhow cruises. Experience more by extending your tour into an overnighter: Eihab offers overnight trips to the Wahiba sands, to Ras Al Jinz for turtle watching, and to the Hajar mountains.

Various Locations

Empty Quarter Tours
99 387 654 | *www.emptyquartertours.com*
Experienced Omani guides (who speak both English and Arabic) will lead you in the tour of your choice, be it crossing the Rub Al Khali (Empty Quarter), watching nesting turtles lay their eggs on the beach, spending the night in a traditional Bedouin campsite with a Bedouin family, or camel trekking over the Wahiba Sands. Empty Quarter Tours can customise tours for special occasions such as weddings, birthdays or Christmas parties, and educational trips for schools and scientific expeditions. If you are arriving in Oman by plane, an airport meet and greet service can also be arranged. The company's Nahar Tourism Oasis (near Ibra), offers accommodation with the added bonuses of a restaurant and pool.

Oman Mobile Bld
Al Khuwayr
Map 7 C2

Golden Oryx Tours
24 489 853 | *www.goldenoryx.com*
Golden Oryx prides itself on being not too big and not too small – it promises to serve every client on an individual basis where possible. With your input it can tailor-make an itinerary that will suit your needs. Some of the activities you can choose from include dune driving, paddling in a tranquil oasis, tours of historical monuments, and watersports. The company offers a range of packages which include breakfast, accommodation and transport and it can also provide a guide who speaks French, German, Spanish and Japanese.

Shati Al Qurm
Map 8 B3

Grand Canyon Of Oman Tours
92 605 102 | *lahave@canada.com*
This tour operator specialises in tours of Oman's 'Grand Canyon'. Over a two-day period you will get the chance to see mountain pools, a prehistoric sea bed, three spectacular canyons, a range of breathtaking mountain peaks, some wild and wonderful wadis, a variety of mountain villages that are virtually untouched, and much, much more. Tours are hosted by Peter Emery Langille. Prices starts at RO 60 per person, which includes dinner and breakfast, beverages and snacks, transport in a 4WD vehicle, overnight accommodation, a cultural event at Jebal Shams, all taxes and amenities, and all entrance fees. The tour departs from Shati Al Qurm or Muscat on Thursday morning, and returns late on Friday evening.

Nr The Chedi
Al Ghubrah
Map 6 E2

Gulf Ventures Oman ▶ p.187
24 490 733 | *www.gulfventures.ae*
With an impressive 120 years' experience, Gulf Ventures is well established and very knowledgeable about culture, history and the lay of the land. It offers a great variety of exciting and informative tours over a wide area of the UAE and Oman including Bedouin camps, tours around the UAE East Coast, and a wide range of city tours, plus creek cruises, fishing, polo, and hot-air ballooning which are run from its Dubai office (+971 4 404 5880).

Nr Al Maha
Petrol Station
Mussandam
Map 1 A2

Hormuzline Tours & Cruises
26 731 616 | *www.hormuzlinetours.com*
Explore the magnificent landscapes of Khasab and the Musandam peninsula with Hormuzline Tours & Cruises. The main office is in Oman but there is also a smaller office in Dubai. Some of the services offered include dhow cruises through the beautiful fjords of the Musandam, mountain safaris in Khasab, city tours that explore history and heritage, diving and snorkelling tours, and camping trips (with all equipment and meals provided). Daytrips and overnight tours are available and all trips can be customised according to your preferences.

Khasab Travel & Tours

Musandam
Nr Khasab Airport
Khasab
Map 1 A2

26 730 464 | www.khasabtours.com

Khasab Travel & Tours was founded in 1992 by Abdul Khalique Ahmed, a native of Khasab. The company can customise an amazing holiday package to Khasab, helping you discover all the natural beauty, history and culture of this breath-taking area. Depending on requirements, tours can include a multilingual tour guide, car rental, and transfers to or from Khasab. Some of the activities available are 4WD adventure safaris, dhow cruising, camping, fishing, snorkelling, kayaking, trekking, wildlife safaris and cultural tours. For further details and prices, check the website.

Muscat Diving & Adventure Center

Nr Radisson BLU
Al Khuwayr
Map 7 C3

24 485 663 | www.holiday-in-oman.com

The Muscat Diving & Adventure Center (MDAC) specialises in diving tours and adventure activities for the energetic tourist. It offers a comprehensive and personal service during your stay in Oman, including airport pickups, transport from your hotel to the centre, car rental and customised tours. Accommodation at MDAC's guesthouse is also available. The centre organises various land and water activities, such as kayaking, game fishing, dolphin watching, climbing, trekking, abseiling, caving, mountain biking, sandboarding, quadbiking and birdwatching. In addition, desert safaris, wadi tours, and 4WD self-drive holidays are on offer. The centre specialises in diving, and can arrange diving tours according to your requirements. There is a shop onsite, selling diving and climbing equipment.

Outreach Arabia

Nr the Corniche
Sidab
Map13 E2

99 352 990 | www.outreachoman.com

Outreach Arabia offer desert safaris, 4WD dune driving, trekking, camping, birdwatching excursions and trips to historical sites. It specialises in eco-tours and practices environmentally responsible tourism aimed at preserving Oman's natural ecology and heritage so you can explore with a clear conscience. Diving, snorkelling, dolphin watching and boat trips can be arranged through Outreach's sister company Scuba Oman (p.225).

Sunny Day Tours, Travel & Adventures

Opp Lulu
Supermarket
Al Grubrah
Map 6 F3

24 490 055 | www.sunnydayoman.com

Whatever your passion or interest, Sunny Day Tours, Travel & Adventures offers an extensive list of services to cater for your needs. From overnight historic tours and turtle watching excursions, to luxury hotel stays, half and full day wadi, mountain and city tours, or a combination of all of the above, Sunny Day will tailor your trip to suit your exact needs and wishes. The experienced chauffeurs will show you the best of Oman creating an unforgettable trip. Car rental and chauffeur services are also available through Sunny Day (p.197).

Treasure Tours Land & Sea Adventure

Bank Of Muscat Bld
Al Khuwayr
Map 7 B2

99 349 399 | treasure@omantel.net.om

Whether you have a few hours, a few days or even longer, Treasure Tours can arrange a special tour for you. It is accredited and fully licensed with the Ministry of Tourism and is dedicated to ensuring that your trip runs smoothly from start to finish. With a fleet of trusty 4WD vehicles and experienced drivers you can experience some of the best off-road locations in Oman. Choose from a wadi or desert safari, a city tour, dolphin watching, snorkelling and coral reef diving, as well as fishing trips and dhow cruises. Ideal for a special weekend trip or when you have visitors in town.

Visa On Arrival

UAE Overview

Citizens of the following countries can get a visa on arrival in the UAE: Andorra, Australia, Austria, Belgium, Brunei, Canada, Cyprus, Denmark, Finland, France, Germany, Greece, Hong Kong, Iceland, Ireland, Italy, Japan, Liechtenstein, Luxembourg, Malaysia, Malta, Monaco, The Netherlands, New Zealand, Norway, Portugal, San Marino, Singapore, South Korea, Spain, Sweden, Switzerland, United Kingdom, United States of America and Vatican City.

The United Arab Emirates borders the Sultanate of Oman to the north-west. It is a small country covering an area of 83,600 square kilometres, with a population of 4,490,000 at the end of 2007. Made up of seven emirates, with Abu Dhabi as the capital, the Emirates also incorporates Ajman, Dubai, Ras Al Khaimah, Sharjah, Umm Al Quwain and Fujairah, which is the only emirate entirely on the east coast of the peninsula. Each emirate was once an independent state, but they united in 1972 on the withdrawal of the British from the region.

The UAE is generally seen as the most relaxed and westernised country in the Gulf. Dubai, in particular, is a shopper's paradise and is well set up to cater for a large tourist industry with plenty of hotels, shopping centres and sports activities, as well as an amazing array of restaurants, bars and nightclubs.

Abu Dhabi is about five hours by car from Muscat, while Dubai is about four hours. There are two crossing points by road into the UAE which are open to expatriates – one at Hatta and one at Buraimi. Dubai, Abu Dhabi and Al Ain have excellent airports and flights from Muscat are frequent. The exchange rate hovers at around RO 1 to Dhs.10.

Visas

Visa requirements for entering the UAE vary greatly between different nationalities, and regulations should always be checked before travelling, since details can change with little or no warning. All visitors, except Arab Gulf Co-operation Council nationals (Bahrain, Kuwait, Qatar, Oman and Saudi Arabia), require a visa. However, citizens of the countries listed in the margin automatically get a visit visa stamp in their passport upon arrival. In most cases this will be valid for 30 days. If you plan to extend your stay you will either need to renew this visit visa for a charge of Dhs.620, or get a new one by leaving and re-entering the country.

Residents of other nationalities who meet certain criteria may obtain a non-renewable 30 day visa on arrival. Residents of Oman, of certain nationalities, may enter the UAE on a free-of-charge entry permit.

Tourist nationalities (such as eastern European countries, China, South Africa and members of the former Soviet Union) may obtain a 30 day, non-renewable tourist visa sponsored by a local entity, such as a hotel or tour operator, before entry into the UAE. The fee is Dhs.100 for the visa and an additional Dhs.20 for delivery. The visa must be applied for before the visitor enters the country.

Other visitors may apply for an entry service permit (for 14 days exclusive of arrival/ departure days), valid for use within 14 days of the date of issue and non-renewable. Once this visa expires the visitor must remain out of the country for 30 days before re-entering on a new visit visa. The application fee for this visa is Dhs.120, plus an additional Dhs.20 delivery charge.

For those travelling onwards to a destination other than that of original departure, a special transit visa (up to 96 hours) may be obtained free of charge through any airline operating in the UAE. Companies may levy a maximum of Dhs.50 extra in processing charges for arranging visas.

Visit visas are valid for 30 or 60 days, not one or two calendar months, and as the arrival and departure dates are counted in this number it is safer to consider the length as 28 or 58 days. If you overstay, there is a Dhs.100 fine for each day plus a Dhs.100 fee. If you overstay a significantly long time, the matter may go to court where a judge will decide the penalty. Also, Israeli nationals or travellers whose passports bear Israeli stamps will be denied a visa.

A multiple-entry visa is available to visitors who have a relationship with a local business, meaning they have to visit that business regularly. It is valid for visits of a maximum of 14 days each time, for six months from the date of issue.

Abu Dhabi Emirate

GCC Easy As ABC
While Oman certainly has its charms, other GCC countries are worth visiting too while you live in the neighbourhood. Whether you want to catch up with developments in Qatar, check out the colourful history of Kuwait, join in the excitement of the grand prix in Bahrain or Abu Dhabi, or spend a glamorous weekend (and a small fortune on a shopping spree) in luxurious Dubai, there's a whole load of exploring to be done just a short haul away. Pick up a copy of the respective Explorer visitors' guide, and make the most of your trip.

Although its neighbour, Dubai, is glitzier and perhaps a more obvious choice for tourists, Abu Dhabi is the capital of the UAE and has its own collection of merits. Oil was discovered in Abu Dhabi before Dubai (1958 compared to 1966) and today accounts for 10% of the world's known crude oil reserves. No surprise then that Abu Dhabi is the richest emirate in the UAE and its main city has the skyline to prove it. In recent years there has been a greater commitment to tourism with a number of developments attracting a greater number of tourists. It has a slightly slower pace than Dubai, which makes for a more relaxing stay. The city itself lies on a scorpion-shaped island connected to the mainland by causeways. It is home to numerous internationally renowned hotels, a selection of shiny shopping malls and a sprinkling of culture in the form of heritage sites and souks. The Abu Dhabi Tourism Authority website (www. visitabudhabi.ae) has some useful information on the city. Shoppers may be pleasantly surprised to find the malls much less busy than in Dubai, and goods and services are a little cheaper too. There are often good deals to be had on hotel breaks too, and quite a few restaurants offer 'all you can eat and drink' deals for much less than you might pay in Dubai.

Abu Dhabi is marketed as the cultural capital of the UAE and is home to an annual jazz festival, a film festival, a music and arts festival, and hosts numerous exhibitions throughout the year. Find out more from the Authority for Culture & Heritage (www adach.ae). There is also a new Formula 1 circuit for sports fans.

In the cooler months the newly renovated and extended corniche is a lovely spot for a stroll, and on weekend evenings the area comes alive with families meeting up to enjoy a barbecue and shisha.

Liwa Oasis

A few hours south of Abu Dhabi by car lies the Liwa Oasis, which is situated on the edge of the famous Rub Al Khali desert (also known as the Empty Quarter). Covering parts of Oman, Yemen, a good chunk of Abu Dhabi emirate and most of southern Saudi Arabia, the Rub Al Khali is actually the largest sand desert in the world. If you appreciate spectacular scenery and enjoy a spot of camping, a trip into the dunes here is possibly one of the most rewarding experiences in the country. The scale is hard to describe, but imagine standing at the top of a 300 metre-high dune (if you can reach the top!) and looking out over a 'sea' of sand that stretches to the horizon in every direction. It's desolate and remote, but quite breathtaking and thoroughly recommended. The driving is hard and should only be attempted by experienced off-roaders, in groups, with all the necessary equipment. If you're not up to the challenge yourself, many Omani and UAE-based tour companies can organise the trip for you.

Al Ain

Al Ain is Abu Dhabi emirate's second city. It lies on the border with Oman and shares the Buraimi Oasis The shady oasis is a pleasant stretch of greenery among the harsh surroundings, and the palm plantations have plenty of examples of the ancient 'falaj' irrigation system. Al Ain has a variety of sights and attractions to interest visitors and the zoo is particularly popular. Hili Archaeological Garden is the source of many ancient finds, most of which are now displayed in the Al Ain Museum. The museum is worth a visit, with displays of traditional Bedouin life and photographs showing how much the area has changed. The camel market is also a must. Arrive early to see the traders haggling over these grunting ships of the desert. Jebel Hafeet, around 15km to the south of Al Ain, is a rather dramatic mountain that rises abruptly from the surrounding flat terrain. A silky smooth road allows you to reach the very top and survey Al Ain and the desert beyond. At the base of the jebel is the surprising sight of Green Mubazzarah,

Liwa

a landscaped park of rolling grassy hills, trees, hot springs, and waterfalls. Accommodation is available here in chalets, either within the park, or around a man-made lake where you can even rent pedalos. Reservations can be made by ringing +971 3 783 9555, and prices range from around RO 50 a night for a one-bedroom chalet during the week, to RO 100 for a two-bedroom at the weekend.

Ajman Emirate

Ajman is the smallest of the seven emirates, its centre being about 10km from Sharjah, although the two towns merge along the beachfront. Ajman also has two inland enclaves, one at Masfut on the edge of the Hajar Mountains and one at Manama between Sharjah and Fujairah. Ajman is known for having one of the largest dhow building centres in the region; a visit here is a great chance to see these massive wooden boats being built with rudimentary tools, using skills passed down through the generations. The old souk too, is another traditional reminder of a slower pace of life. This quiet emirate has some great beaches and a pleasant corniche, and an increasing number of facilities to tempt the visitor, including the Ajman Kempinski Hotel & Resort, and the Ajman City Centre mall offering a good selection of retail outlets and a cinema. Find out more at www.visitajman.org. The developers are making their way up the coast too, with Al Ameera Village – a project featuring heritage-styled residential buildings, a mall, and a hotel, located on Emirates Road.

Ajman Museum

Ajman Museum (+971 6 742 3824) is interesting and well arranged, with displays described in both English and Arabic. The museum has a variety of exhibits, including a collection of passports (Ajman used to issue its own) and depictions of ancient life, but it's the building itself that will most impress visitors. Housed in a fortress dating back to around 1775, and a former residence of the ruler of Ajman, the museum is a fascinating example of traditional architecture, with imposing watchtowers and windtowers. The fortress served as a police station before becoming the museum in the early 1980s. Entrance fees: adults Dhs.5; children under 6 years Dhs.3; students Dhs.3. Timings: 08:00 to 13:00 and 17:00 to 20:00. Closed on Saturdays.

Dubai Emirate

Dubai is the second largest emirate and the most important of the northern emirates. With limited natural resources, it has founded its wealth on trade, and more recently, tourism.

Originally a small fishing settlement based around a creek, Dubai was taken over by a branch of the Bani Yas tribe from the Liwa Oasis around 1830. The Maktoum family led the takeover and descendants of this family still rule the emirate. The booming modern city has grown up around the creek, which makes it an excellent starting point for any exploration.

The city is growing at an incredible rate, with much of the construction taking place around the Abu Dhabi–Dubai highway. The city stretches all the way to Jebel Ali, the largest man-made port in the world and the original free zone.

Dubai's reputation as a progressive place is not undeserved, and it's great for a night out. Renowned as the 'shopping capital of the Middle East', it is the ultimate place for a shopaholic with a healthy credit limit. The enormous Ibn Battuta Mall, the even bigger Dubai Mall, and Mall of the Emirates (the one with the ski slope), are all easily accessible from the highway.

Just be aware – the driving in Dubai can be pretty hair-raising. Speeding is common as is changing lanes at random without signalling. Defensive driving is not an option – it's a must, and you'll find yourself longing for the calm roads of Oman.

The emirate's emergence as a tourism hotspot is enhanced by an exciting calendar of sporting events and festivals that draws visitors from near and far. For the inside track on this vibrant city, check out the latest edition of the *Dubai Explorer*.

Discover Hatta ◄
To find out more about Hatta and the various attractions it offers, contact Dubai Tourism on +971 4 223 000 or visit www. dubaitourism.ae

Hatta

Hatta is a small town nestled at the foot of the Hajar Mountains, about 100km from Dubai city and 10km from the Dubai-Oman border. Hatta is still within the Dubai emirate though, and is home to the oldest fort in the emirate, built in 1790. You'll also see several watchtowers on the surrounding hills. On the drive you'll pass row after row of carpet shops, great for practising your bargaining skills or picking up a new rug. The town of Hatta has a sleepy, relaxed feel about it and apart from the ruins and the Heritage Village, there is little to see or do unless you fancy a good lunch or a round of mini golf at the Hatta Fort Hotel. However, past the village and into the mountains are the Hatta Pools, where you can see deep, strangely shaped canyons that have been carved out by rushing floodwater.

The Hatta Fort Hotel is great as a weekend destination. Spacious bungalow-style luxury rooms sit in tranquil gardens with a mountainous backdrop – it's the perfect antidote to city living. A good range of sports and leisure facilities will leave you refreshed and relaxed.

A little way past Hatta on the way to Dubai is the famous 'Big Red' sand dune. Estimated to be over 100m high, it's a popular spot for practising dune driving in 4WDs or on quad bikes, as well as attempting sandskiing (although the number of Landcruisers and Patrols hitting the hill on a Friday may make you think twice about the skiing). Alternatively, take a walk (if you have the energy) to the top for a great view. For further information on the area around Hatta, refer to *UAE Off-Road Explorer*.

Ras Al Khaimah Emirate

Ras Al Khaimah (RAK) is the most northerly of the seven emirates, but thanks to the new Emirates Road extension you can make the trip from Dubai in less than an hour. With the majestic Hajar Mountains rising just behind the city, and the Arabian Gulf stretching out from the shore, RAK has possibly the best scenery of any city in the UAE. A creek divides the city into the old town (Ras Al Khaimah proper) and the newer Al Nakheel district.

If you're visiting for the day you should make time to visit the souk in the old town and the National Museum of Ras Al Khaimah, which is housed in an old fort. Manar Mall is a large shopping and leisure complex, housing a cinema complex, family entertainment centre and watersports area. The town is quiet and relaxing, and is a good point from which to explore the surrounding countryside and visit the ancient sites of Ghalilah and Shimal. Also worth quick stops are the hot springs at Khatt or the camel racetrack at Digdagga. The town of Masafi, inland towards the east coast, is the source of the bottled water of the same name.

Although relatively unknown and undiscovered, RAK is in the process of reinventing and rebranding itself with the aim of becoming a popular tourism destination in the coming years. Projects such as Al Hamra Village, Al Marjan Island, Port Arabia (aka Khor Qurm), RAK Financial City, Mina Al Arab and the Jebel Jais Mountain Resort will add five-star hotels, sports, business and leisure facilities and a host of dining and

entertainment options, in addition to freehold housing available for purchase by foreigners. Take a look at www.raktourism.com for details and updates.

National Museum Of Ras Al Khaimah

Housed in an impressive fort, the former home of the present ruler of Ras Al Khaimah, this museum mainly has local natural history and archaeological displays, plus a variety of paraphernalia from pre-oil life. Upstairs you can see an account of the British naval expedition against Ras Al Khaimah in 1809, a model of a 'baggala' (a typical craft used in the

UAE East Coast

early 1800s), and excellent examples of silver Bedouin jewellery. Look out for fossils set in the rock strata of the walls of the fort – these date back 190 million years. The building has battlements, a working windtower, and ornate carved wooden doors. Entrance is priced at Dhs.2 for adults and Dhs.1 for children. A photography permit costs an extra Dhs.5. Contact the museum on +971 7 233 3411, or visit the website (www.rakmuseum.gov.ae) for up-to-date visitors' info, including opening times.

Hit The Road ◀

When leaving Oman by road, you need to ensure you have the correct exit permit for your vehicle. See p.44 for details.

Sharjah Emirate

Before Dubai's rise to prominence as a trading and tourism hotspot, its neighbour, Sharjah, was one of the wealthiest towns in the region, with settlers earning their livelihood from fishing, pearling and trade. Sharjah is the only emirate with coastline on both the Arabian Gulf and the Gulf of Oman. The highway, which links the two coasts, heads through the spectacular Hajar Mountains, and it takes less than two hours to cross the country. The east coast towns of Dibba, Khor Fakkan and Kalba are all part of Sharjah.

In 1998, Unesco named Sharjah the cultural capital of the Arab world, due to its commitment to art, culture and preserving its traditional heritage. A monument to commemorate this award has been built opposite the Sharjah Natural History Museum on Al Dhaid Road. One place you shouldn't miss is the Heritage Area; the museums here are definitely worth a look as they cover everything from traditional domestic life to the emirate's maritime history and the intricacies of Arabic calligraphy. The nearby Arts Area, with galleries and more museums, is a treat for art lovers.

Sharjah is built around Khalid Lagoon (popularly known as the creek). The Buheirah Corniche surrounding the lagoon is a popular spot, especially for an evening stroll. Small dhows can be hired from various points on the lagoon to see the lights of the city from the water.

Another must is Al Qasba (06 556 0777, www.qaq.ae); the kilometre-long canal linking Al Khan Lagoon and Khalid Lagoon has lots of attractions and eateries along its banks. The emphasis is on culture, with an ever-changing calendar including Arabian poetry and film (with English subtitles), art exhibitions and classes, musical events and theatrical performances, either in the dedicated venues or outdoors on the walkways beside the canal. The Tent of Wonders is a permanent 'big top' featuring shows by performers from around the world. Motorised abras provide boat tours up and down the canal, but perhaps the biggest draw, and certainly the most visible, is the Eye of the Emirates – a 60 metre high observation wheel with air-conditioned pods offering amazing views over Sharjah and across to Dubai and beyond. See Al Qasba website for details of events.

The city's latest attraction is Sharjah Aquarium (06 556 6002, www.sharjahaquarium. ae). Another worthy weekend stop-off is the Sharjah Desert Park (06 531 1411, www. sharjahmuseums.ae). For further information on Sharjah, see the Sharjah section of the *Dubai Explorer*. For a photographic tour of the stunning architecture of the emirate, pick up a copy of *Sharjah's Architectural Splendour*, published by Explorer Publishing.

The Dibba Dead

A vast cemetery on the outskirts of town is said to be the last resting place of over 10,000 rebels who died in a great battle fought in 633AD, when the Muslim armies of Caliph Abu Baker were sent to suppress a local rebellion and to reconquer the Arabian Peninsula for Islam.

Umm Al Quwain Emirate

Umm Al Quwain is the second smallest of the Emirates, and has the smallest population. Nestled on the coast between Ajman and Ras Al Khaimah, it's a quiet place where not much has changed over the years, giving visitors an idea of how life in the UAE was a few decades ago. The main industries are still fishing and date cultivation. The emirate has six forts and a few old watchtowers around the town, and the lagoon, with its mangroves and birdlife, is a popular weekend spot for boat trips, windsurfing and other watersports. Umm Al Quwain has not escaped the attention of the developers though, and a project currently underway will see over 9,000 homes and a marina emerge on the shore of the Khor Al Beidah wildlife area. What impact this will have on the delicate ecosystem and abundant plant and animal life remains to be seen. The area north of the lagoon is known for being the 'activity centre' of the region, with a variety of distractions to suit all tastes. Umm Al Quwain Aeroclub (www.horizonuae. ae/uaqaeroclub) offers flying, skydiving, and pilot training, and can also arrange 10 minute air tours, either in a Cessna or a microlight, at very reasonable prices. The Emirates Car & Motorcycle Racing Club hosts all types of motorsport events, including the Emirates Motocross Championship that takes place here on a specially built track. One of the most popular attractions here is Dreamland Aqua Park – see details below.

Dreamland Aqua Park

With over 25 water rides spread across 250,000 square metres of green, landscaped grounds, Dreamland Aqua Park (+971 6 768 1888, www.dreamlanduae.com) is one of the largest water parks in the world. Adrenaline junkies will not be disappointed with rides such as the Twister, the Kamikaze, and four 'Twisting Dragon' slides. For a more leisurely experience there's the lazy river, a wave pool, and a high-salinity pool allowing you to float as if you were in the Dead Sea. The Aqua Play area has a range of games and attractions, and if you prefer not to get wet you can burn rubber on the 400 metre go-kart track. There are cafes and a restaurant, as well as a licensed pool bar, and you can even camp overnight on the premises.

UAE East Coast

Even of you're only in the UAE for a short time, a trip to the east coast is worth the effort. It's really easy to get there from the Oman-UAE border near Hatta, and the drive takes you through the interesting scenery of the rugged Hajar Mountains. The east coast and the desert and mountains inland provide plenty of opportunities for sampling the great outdoors, from camping and off-road driving to snorkelling and scuba diving. The diving off the east coast is considered better than that off Dubai, mainly because of increased visibility. Snoopy Island is a favourite spot for snorkelling, where you're guaranteed to see a host of exotic fish species, and perhaps turtles and small sharks if you're lucky. The scuba diving is good too, and many diving schools operating out of Dubai actually head east with their students.

In 2008 and 2009, the east coast was periodically affected by a 'red tide'. While this is a naturally occurring phenomenon, caused by blooming algae turning the water a rusty colour, it isn't particularly pleasant to swim in and you may find diving and snorkelling trips are cancelled due to reduced underwater visibility. It's worth calling an east coast hotel or tour operator to check that there's no red tide before you set off from Muscat.

Badiyah

The site of the oldest mosque in the UAE, Badiyah is located roughly half way down the east coast, north of Khor Fakkan. The mosque is made from gypsum, stone and mud bricks finished off with white washed plaster and its design of four domes, supported by a central pillar, is considered unique. The building is believed to date back to the middle of the 15th century. Officially called Al Masjid Al Othmani, it was restored in 2003, but it must be said that the restoration was more of a renovation, and this ancient mosque now looks quite smart and new. The mosque is still used for prayer, so non-Muslim visitors have to satisfy themselves with a photo from the outside. Built into a low hillside with several recently restored watchtowers on the hills behind, the area is now lit up at night with lovely sodium coloured light. The village of Badiyah itself is one of the oldest settlements on the east coast and is believed to have been inhabited since 3000BC.

Bithna

Set in the mountains about 12 km from Fujairah, the village of Bithna is notable mainly for its fort and archaeological site. The fort once controlled the main pass through the mountains from east to west and is still impressive. The village can be reached from the Fujairah-Sharjah road, and the fort through the village and wadi. The archaeological site is known as the Long Chambered Tomb or the T-Shaped Tomb, and was probably once a communal burial site. It was excavated in 1988 and its main period of use is thought to date from between 1350 and 300BC, although the tomb itself is older. Fujairah Museum has a detailed display of the tomb that is worth seeing, since the site itself is fenced off and covered against the elements. The tomb can be found by taking a right, then a left hand turn before the village, near the radio tower.

Dibba

Located at the northern-most point of the east coast, on the border with Musandam (part of Oman), Dibba is made up of three fishing villages. Unusually, each part comes under a different jurisdiction: Dibba Al Hisn is part of Sharjah, Dibba Muhallab is Fujairah and Dibba Bayah is Oman. The three Dibbas share an attractive bay, fishing communities, and excellent diving locations – from here you can arrange dhow trips to take you to unspoilt dive locations in the Musandam. The Hajar Mountains provide a wonderful backdrop, rising in places to over 1,800 metres. There are some good public beaches too, where your only company will be the crabs and seagulls, and where seashell collectors may find a few treasures. Since the RAK border crossing closed, going via Dibba is the only way to access the stunning gorge drive through Wadi Bih.

Fujairah Emirate

Fujairah was actually part of Sharjah until 1952, making it the youngest of the seven emirates. Its independence makes it the only emirate located entirely on the east coast, and with its golden beaches bordered by the Gulf of Oman on one side and the Hajar Mountains on the other, it's definitely worth a visit. The town is a mix of old and new; overlooking the atmospheric old town is the fort, which is reportedly about 300 years old, and has been fully restored. The surrounding hillsides are dotted with ancient forts

Weekend Breaks

Downtown Al Ain

Dubai skyline

UAE East Coast

Sheikh Zayed Grand Mosque, Abu Dhabi

Sharjah

and watchtowers, which add an air of mystery and charm. Most of these also appear to be undergoing restoration work. Fujairah is also a busy trading centre though, with a modern container port and a thriving free zone attracting major companies from around the world.

Off the coast, the seas and coral reefs make a great spot for fishing, diving and watersports. It is also a good place for birdwatching during the spring and autumn migrations since it is on the route from Africa to Central Asia. The emirate has started to encourage more tourism by opening new hotels and providing more recreational facilities. Since Fujairah is close to the mountains and many areas of natural beauty, it makes an excellent base to explore the countryside and discover wadis, forts and waterfalls; you can even find natural hot springs located at Al Ain Madhab Gardens. An excellent tourist map has been produced by the Fujairah Tourism Bureau (+971 9 223 1554). To get a copy of this map, visit the Tourism Bureau at Fujairah Trade Centre, 9th Floor, Office #901, on Sheikh Hamad Bin Abdullah Rd (call ahead for opening times, as these are subject to change). The tourist bureau's website (www.fujairah-tourism.gov. ae) has some helpful, if limited, information.

Fujairah is one of the fixtures on the world power boat racing championship circuit and races are hosted annually in winter. For dates and further info, contact the race hosts, Fujairah International Marine Club, on +971 9 222 1166 or fujfimc@emirates.net.ae.

On Friday afternoons during winter, crowds gather between the Hilton Hotel and the Khor Kalba area to watch 'bull butting'. This ancient Portuguese sport consists of two huge bulls going head to head for several rounds, until after a few nudges and a bit of hoof bashing, a winner is determined. It's not as cruel or barbaric as other forms of bullfighting, but animal lovers may still want to avoid it. A new wire fence protects spectators from angry runaways.

Al Hisn Kalba

As you drive along the coast road in Kalba town, you come to the restored house of Sheikh Sayed Al Qassimi (+971 9 277 4442), overlooking the sea. The house is located at the end of a large grassy expanse with swings and small rides for children. On the opposite side of the road is Kalba's Al Hisn Fort, which houses the town's museum and contains a limited display of weapons.

Desert Rangers

A canoe tour by Desert Rangers (+971 4 340 2408) is an ideal opportunity to reach the heart of the Kalba reserve and you can regularly see over a dozen kingfishers on a trip. There is also the possibility of seeing one of the region's endangered turtles. The reserve is a unique area so please treat it with respect.

Kalba

Just to the south of Fujairah you'll find Kalba, which is part of the emirate of Sharjah and renowned for its mangrove forest and golden beaches. It's a pretty fishing village that still manages to retain much of its historical charm. A road through the mountains linking Kalba to Hatta has recently been completed, creating an interesting alternative to returning to Dubai on the Al Dhaid-Sharjah road.

Khor Kalba

South of the village of Kalba is Khor Kalba, set in a beautiful tidal estuary (khor is the Arabic word for creek). This is the most northerly mangrove forest in the world, the oldest in Arabia and a 'biological treasure' – home to a variety of plant, marine and birdlife not found anywhere else in the UAE.

The mangroves flourish in this area thanks to the mix of saltwater from the sea and freshwater from the mountains, but worryingly they are receding due to the excessive use of water from inland wells. For birdwatchers, the area is especially good during the spring and autumn migrations when special species of bird include the reef heron and the booted warbler. It is also home to the rare white collared kingfisher, which breeds here and nowhere else in the world. There are believed to be only 55 pairs of these birds still in existence.

Khor Fakkan

Khor Fakkan lies at the foot of the Hajar Mountains halfway down the east coast between Dibba and Fujairah. It is a popular and charming town, set in a bay and flanked on either side by two headlands, hence its alternative name 'Creek of the Two Jaws'. It is a favourite place for weekend breaks or day trips and has an attractive waterfront and beach. The iconic 70s style Oceanic Hotel (www.oceanichotel.com) is a popular choice, and there are plenty of good fishing and diving sites nearby. Khor Fakkan is part of the emirate of Sharjah, and above the Oceanic Hotel the Ruler of Sharjah's Palace is visible high up on the hilltop. The town has a modern port, and its position on the Gulf of Oman means visiting ships don't have to undergo a further 48 hour journey through the Strait of Hormuz to the west coast. The nearby old harbour is an interesting contrast to the modern port. There are some great dive sites just a few minutes from Khor Fakkan, including Shark Island, Martini Island, and the Car Cemetery. See the *UAE Underwater Explorer* for more details. Set inland in the mountains is the Rifaisa Dam built to contain flood water and feed the towns below. Local legend has it that when the water is clear, a lost village can be seen at the bottom of the dam.

Fujairah Heritage Village

This 6,000 square metre heritage village depicts life in the UAE as it was before oil was discovered, with displays of fishing boats, simple dhows, clay, stone and bronze implements and pots, and hunting and agricultural tools. The heritage village is close to Ain Al Madhab Gardens, which are situated in the foothills of the Hajar Mountains just outside Fujairah City. The gardens are fed by mineral springs and this warm sulphur laden water is used in two swimming pools (separate for men and women). Private chalets can be hired on a daily basis.

Fujairah Museum

This interesting museum offers an insight into Fujairah's history and heritage, which despite being less colourful than its neighbouring emirates is interesting nonetheless. You can see permanent exhibitions on traditional ways of life including the not so distant Bedouin culture. There are also artefacts found during archaeological excavations throughout the emirate. Some of the items uncovered by local and foreign archaeologists include weapons from the bronze and iron ages, finely painted pottery, carved soapstone vessels and silver coins. Call +971 9 222 9085 for opening times. The museum is closed on Saturdays.

Bahrain

For a change of pace, head to nearby Bahrain. It is just a 50 minute flight away and small enough to be explored in a weekend. With traditional architecture, miles of souks, excellent shopping and some truly outstanding bars and restaurants, you can choose from a cultural escape or fun-packed break. Formula One fans won't want to miss the Grand Prix that usually takes place in March or April, with hotels booked up months in advance – see the *Bahrain Mini Visitors' Guide* for more on what to do there.

Off Shk Hamad Causeway
Manama

Novotel Al Dana Resort

+973 1729 8008 | *www.novotel-bahrain.com*

This city beach resort in Bahrain offers three restaurants, a lounge bar, a large outdoor pool, a small private man-made beach, indoor and outdoor play facilities for children and a health club including a steam room, sauna, and Thai and aromatherapy massages. Watersports equipment available for hire on the beach includes jet skis, water skis, banana boat, windsurfers and kayaks.

Seef
Manama

The Ritz-Carlton Bahrain Hotel & Spa

+973 1758 0000 | www.ritzcarlton.com

This hotel has one of the best beaches in Bahrain, in a man-made lagoon surrounded by lush gardens. The 600 metre private beach sweeps round the lagoon with its own island and private marina. It has nine quality dining venues and comprehensive business facilities. Hotel residents have access to all of the club facilities, including the racquet sport courts, the luxurious Ritz-Carlton Spa and watersport activities.

Kuwait

Kuwait is not always immediately considered as a weekend break destination (no alcohol, don't forget), but the colourful (and somewhat tainted) heritage of this small, yet rich, country means it is still worth a visit. Kuwait may be one of the world's smallest countries but its 500 kilometre coastline has long golden beaches that remain refreshingly tranquil. From the Grand Mosque to the Kuwait Towers there are many architectural splendours to explore, while Al Qurain House, which still shows the scars of war with its bullet holes, gives you a fascinating insight into the troubled times of the Iraqi invasion. There is also Green Island, an artificial island linked by a short bridge and home to restaurants, a children's play area and a great alternative view of Kuwait's shoreline. For more information and inspiration, check out the *Kuwait Explorer*.

Coast Rd
Manqaf

Hilton Kuwait Resort

+965 225 6222 | www.hilton.com

Located in Mangaf, this resort has one of the best beaches and health clubs in the country. There are 143 rooms, four suites, 80 chalets, 61 studios and apartments, 52 Presidential Villas and 12 Royal Villas, plus four restaurants, two cafes, one coffee shop and two poolside bars. The resort also has a watersports pavilion and a dive centre.

Fahed Al-Salem St
Kuwait City

Le Meridien Tower (Art + Tech)

+965 831 831 | www.lemeridienkuwait.com

Built in 2003, the Art + Tech hotel takes modern hospitality to another level with cutting edge amenities perfect for business travellers. All of the 70 rooms feature interactive plasma screen TVs, DVD, VCD and CD facilities, and high speed internet access. Hotel facilities include a restaurant, lobby lounge, health club and outdoor swimming pool.

Qatar

Qatar once had something of a sleepy reputation, but things are changing fast. The amount of development and investment in the country means it is becoming increasingly popular with visitors. With an attractive corniche, world-class museums and cultural centres, and plenty of hotels with leisure and entertainment facilities, the capital Doha makes a perfect weekend retreat. The Doha Asian Games in 2006 attracted thousands of visitors and put Qatar firmly in the spotlight; many new hotel, retail, leisure and entertainment projects were built especially for the event. Away from the city, the inland sea (Khor Al Udaid) in the south of the country also makes a great day trip, usually as part of an organised tour. See the *Qatar Mini Visitors' Guide* for more details.

Corniche Rd
Doha

Mövenpick Hotel Doha

+974 429 1111 | www.moevenpick-hotels.com

This modern hotel boasts the breathtaking corniche as its vista, where guests can enjoy a morning jog or afternoon stroll. Popular with business travellers, this boutique-style hotel also attracts tourists with its excellent restaurants and leisure facilities which include a swimming pool, whirlpool and steam bath.

Corniche West
Bay Lagoon
Doha

The Ritz-Carlton Doha

+974 484 8000 | *www.ritzcarlton.com*

The opulent Ritz-Carlton is a perfect stop-off point if you are sailing in the region, with its 235 slip marina and clubhouse. You can expect five-star touches as standard at this resort, which takes opulence to another level. All of the 374 rooms and suites have breathtaking views over the sea or marina. The beach club provides a great selection of watersports while the luxurious spa offers every imaginable pampering treatment. You'll be spoilt for choice with nine restaurants all serving a range of excellent international and local cuisine, and you can finish the night off with either a cigar at Habanos or a cocktail at the Admiral Club.

Weekend Break Hotels

Other options **Hotels** p.24

Below is a list of hotels that are suitable for short trips. For more information get hold of a copy of *Weekend Breaks in Oman & the UAE*, a gorgeous book packed with essential information on UAE and Oman destinations, complete with hotel reviews and glossy photos. Hotels in this region almost always give discounts, and during the summer there are often promotions and price cuts. When making a reservation, check whether the taxes and service charges are included – these can add a whopping 20% to your bill otherwise.

Weekend Break Hotels

Abu Dhabi	Beach Rotana Hotel & Towers	+971 2 697 9000	www.rotana.com
	Hilton Abu Dhabi	+971 2 681 1900	www.hilton.com
	InterContinental Abu Dhabi	+971 2 666 6888	www.intercontinental.com
	Le Meridien Abu Dhabi	+971 2 644 6666	www.starwoodhotels.com/lemeridien
	Mafraq Hotel	+971 2 582 2666	www.mafraq-hotel.com
	Sheraton Abu Dhabi Hotel & Resort	+971 2 677 3333	www.sheraton.com
Al Ain	Al Ain Rotana Hotel	+971 3 754 5111	www.rotana.com
	Hilton Al Ain	+971 3 768 6666	www.hilton.com
	Mercure Grand Jebel Hafeet	+971 3 783 8888	www.mercure.com
Dubai	Al Maha Desert Resort & Spa	+971 4 303 4222	www.al-maha.com
	Al Qasr Hotel	+971 4 366 8888	www.madinatjumeirah.com/al_qasr
	Bab Al Shams Desert Resort & Spa	+971 4 809 6100	www.jumeirahbabalshams.com
	Jumeirah Beach Hotel	+971 4 348 0000	www.jumeirahbeachhotel.com
	Mina A'Salam	+971 4 366 8888	www.madinatjumeirah.com
	The Palace at One&Only Royal Mirage	+971 4 399 9999	www.oneandonlyroyalmirage.com
	The Ritz-Carlton, Dubai	+971 4 399 4000	www.ritzcarlton.com
Fujairah	Fujairah Rotana Resort & Spa	+971 9 244 9888	www.rotana.com
	Le Meridien Al Aqah Beach Resort	+971 9 244 9000	www.le-meridien-alaqah.com
Hatta	Hatta Fort Hotel	+971 4 852 3211	www.jebelali-international.com
Jazira	Golden Tulip Al Jazira Hotel & Resort	+971 2 562 9100	www.goldentulipaljazira.com
Sharjah	Millennium Hotel	+971 6 556 6666	www.millenniumhotels.com
Ras Al Khaimah	Al Hamra Fort Hotel	+971 7 244 6666	www.alhamrafort.com
	Hilton Ras Al Khaimah	+971 7 228 8888	www.hilton.com
	Ras Al Khaimah Hotel	+971 7 236 2999	www.rakhotel.net
Umm Al Quwain	Flamingo Beach Resort	+971 6 765 0000	www.flamingoresort.ae
	Imar Spa	+971 6 766 4440	www.imarspa.com

You'll never really leave

Whether it's skiing, snowboarding, tobogganing or just plain fun, you'll find it all at Ski Dubai. With over three-football fields of snow, Ski Dubai will leave a lasting impression. What won't be so easy is getting the experience out of your head.

Tel: 04 409 4000 | www.skidxb.com

an unforgettable snow ex.

Activities

Activities

Sports & Activities

Oman is a land of opportunity when it comes to getting involved in sports and activities, or taking your pursuits to new levels. The rugged mountains, unspoilt wadis, the sea and the vast desert sands provide beautiful surroundings in which to try a range of outdoor pastimes, particularly in winter when the weather is warm but not blistering. Typically, residents of Oman spend their winter weekends camping on the beach, swimming, or tackling the dunes of the Wahiba sands in a 4WD and trying out sandskiing. Even the heat of the summer doesn't stop some hardy sports enthusiasts from spending their leisure hours sailing the Gulf or hitting the greens. Alternatively, if you stay in Oman during the summer, you can always retreat to the mountains or to Salalah during its refreshing rainy season, where you can enjoy cooler weather. In Muscat there is always the air-conditioned gym option, or the opportunity to take up a new hobby or complete a short course.

As in most places, word of mouth is one of the best ways to get details and information about your favourite pastime. An assortment of sports and activities are available in Oman so you will be well-rewarded if you hunt around. Good luck and enjoy!

Aerobics

Other options **Dance Classes** p.221, **Sports & Leisure Facilities** p.248

Aerobics is an excellent way to keep fit throughout the year, no matter what the temperature is like outside. Classes are available in most of the hotels and you can choose from different disciplines and timings to suit you. Most health clubs around Muscat offer classes in aerobics, with costs per class ranging from RO 1.5 – 2.5 for members and RO 2.5 – 3.5 for non-members.

Aqua aerobics is an excellent way to combine aerobic activity with the chance to splash about in water. It's great for people of all ages and body shapes, and with various medical conditions, as the water provides protection for the joints. Many of the local health clubs offer aqua aerobics, see the Health Club table (p.249) for more information.

Activity Finder

Art Classes

Other options **Art Galleries** p.169, **Art & Craft Supplies** p.264

Nr Qurm Park
Al Qurm
Map 8 D3

Classic Music & Arts Institute

24 560 025 | *musictec@omantel.net.om*

The institute offers an array of art classes for children and adults. Take your pick from silk painting, mosaic work, glass painting and pottery. Instruction is given in English and each course requires at least four members to sign up. Sessions are sociable and coffee and tea is served during the class. An hour-long lesson costs RO 4 for children and RO 12 for adults.

Way 2235
House 1756
Block 222
Al Qurm
Map 8 D3

Daat Art Centre

daatart@omantel.net.om

The Daat Art Centre focuses on drawing, painting and oil painting. It offers classes for everyone, whatever your level of expertise may (or may not) be. It has also recently introduced art classes for children aged 5 to 6. Adult classes cost around RO 20 for four lessons and each lesson is two hours long. Children's classes cost RO 5 and last for an hour.

Shati Al Qurm
Map 7 E1

The Omani Society For Fine Arts

24 694 969 | *www.omaniartsociety.org*

The Omani Society for Fine Arts was established in 1993 to encourage fine art and photography in the country. The group organises a number of activities and initiatives to support artists in Oman and participates in various international exhibitions and events. One of the society's aims is also to encourage and support youngsters and hobbyists.

Basketball

The Oman Basketball Federation (www.asia-basket.com) is an active association, and you can call it on 24 793 802 to find out where the nearest courts are to you, and how you can join any of the league teams. It runs regular competitions and is part of the Eurobasket.com global network, which means it keeps on top of basketball events and developments happening across the world and can bring you up to date on all the tournament news.

Birdwatching

Other options **Birdwatching** p.213, **Environmental Groups** p.225

Oman is an extremely interesting country for the bird watcher. Because of its location at the junction of three bio-geographical areas, the keen observer can see Palaearctic and African bird species, as well as others from further east. It doesn't require much to take yourself on a birding expedition – as long as you follow the usual rules of not heading off-road without a guide and all the necessary equipment. But to find out more about birding in Oman and what books are available, log on to www.birdsoman. com which is updated on regular basis.

Some tour companies offer birdwatching trips. The Muscat Diving & Adventure Centre, Gulf Leisure and African Sea Safaris (see their entries under Main Tour Operators on p.195) are among those that do.

Birdwatchers in Oman can take advantage of the fact that the country lies on the migration path for thousands of exotic birds doing the long haul flight between Asia and Africa. The beaches and lagoons along the coastline are good places to spot a rich variety of marine birdlife, from storks and herons to flamingos and ducks.

For a detailed introduction to the birdlife in Oman, the *Birdwatching Guide to Oman*

(Hanne & Jens Eriksen and Panadda & Dave E. Sargeant) is invaluable. You'll find other publications and recent photographs on www.birdsoman.com. You can also contact the Oman Bird Group via the Natural History Museum, and the Muscat Diving & Adventure Center (see below). Gulf Leisure (p.213) also offers birdwatching trips, as does Arabian Sea Safaris (www.arabianseasafaris.com, 24 693 223), which runs birding tours for RO 30 per person.

Muscat Diving & Adventure Center

Nr Radisson BLU
Al Khuwayr
Map 7 C3

24 485 663 | www.holiday-in-oman.com

This company does birdwatching tours throughout the week (upon request). You'll be collected from your hotel and accompanied by an experienced birder who will help you to identify your sightings and fill you in on all the details about Oman's birdlife, from the little green bee-eater to the huge lappet faced vulture. A half-day tour costs RO 140 per car (up to four people) and you need to book a place on a tour 24 hours in advance.

Bowling

City Bowling Centre

Markaz Al Bahja
Seeb
Map 2 D4

bowling@omantel.net.om

The City Bowling Centre is a one-stop shop for fun and games, whether it's bowling, snooker, billiards or video games that interest you. This bowling alley has eight computerised Brunswick lanes, boasts a very active league, and organises regular tournaments and social events. It also has a junior club of about 25 members. The alley caters to everyone, from serious bowlers to people who want to hold a birthday party or a corporate event. And you won't go hungry either – there's a Cyber Cafe on site where you can refuel between games. Games cost RO 2 per person and RO 0.5 for shoe rental, with discounts sometimes offered for social events. If you want to avoid the crowds and work on your game, go on weekday afternoons.

Oman Bowling Centre

Opp Holiday Inn
Al Khuwayr
Map 7 A3

24 480 747

This large bowling centre has 10 computerised lanes and a good set-up that includes a coffee shop where you can get refreshments while relaxing and watching everyone working on their game. It is open between 10:00 and 02:00, and the very reasonable price of RO 1.50 per game includes shoe hire.

Bridge

Muscat Bridge League

PDO RAH Club
Ras Al Hamra
Map 12 D2

99 354 467 | mukherji@omantel.net.om

Dedicated bridge players in Oman have been organising weekly bridge sessions every Saturday evening for over 20 years. Attendance ranges from five to seven tables and the game is played over 22 to 24 boards. There is a nominal table charge. Full-day sessions are occasionally held here. The game is friendly, with varying degrees of competence, and visiting players are always welcome. In an effort to popularise the game further, Muscat Bridge League is planning to hold sessions to teach the game to those interested.

Muscat Ladies Bridge Club

Crowne Plaza
Muscat
Qurm Heights
Map 8 C3

24 600 306

The Muscat Ladies Bridge Club plays duplicate bridge twice a week, on Sunday and Wednesday mornings at the Crowne Plaza Hotel. Sessions start at 08:45 and run until

12:45. A nominal fee is charged but this includes refreshments. More competitive players have the opportunity to flex their tactical muscle at two tournaments each year. An annual membership costs RO 6 per person. For more information call the above number or 99 471 014.

Camping
Other options **Outdoor Goods** p.282, **Off-Road Driving** p.240

Other options **Outdoor Goods** p.282, **Off-Road Driving** p.240

Camping is a great way to experience and explore Oman's varied landscape. Many expats pack their 4WDs with camping gear and food and set out for a weekend, particularly during the winter months when you can sleep under the stars. You can set up your tent wherever the mood takes you, as long as it's not too close to the villages.

For most campers, basic equipment will be enough for a successful trip. The following items are usually necessary:

- Tent
- Lightweight sleeping bag or light blankets and sheets
- Thin mattress or air bed
- Torches and spare batteries
- Coolbox for food
- Water (always take too much)
- Camping stove, or BBQ and charcoal if preferred
- Firewood and matches
- First aid kit including personal medication, insect repellent and antihistamine cream
- Sun protection – hats, sunglasses, sunscreen
- Warm clothing for cooler evenings
- Spade
- Toilet rolls
- Rubbish bags (ensure you leave nothing behind)
- Navigation equipment – maps, compass, GPS

There are many wadis (dry riverbeds) within two to three hours' drive of Muscat and some of the more popular sites, such as Wadi Shabs and Wadi Tiwi, are along the coastal road from Quriyat to Sur. Down the coast beyond Quriyat and after Dibab are a number of beaches between rocky outcrops. The most popular is Mokallah, also known as White Beach, where the snorkelling is excellent. Those who prefer the desert have the whole of the Wahiba Sands (Ramal Al Wahaybah) to cross, all the way to the coast. Oman has plenty of official camping grounds with full amenities. You can also camp outside the grounds, but there are no facilities (and you are not allowed to cook). In Jaaluni, just over six hours' drive from Muscat, you can camp in the Arabian Oryx Sanctuary. Facilities are very basic and you should check the website in advance to get a better idea of what is available (www.oryxoman.com).
On the more luxurious side, several tour operators have established their own permanent or rolling campsites in the Wahiba Sands, equipped with air-conditioned huts and refrigerators. Apart from the camping, you'll also get an Omani barbecue under the stars, as well as the opportunity to try dune bashing and camel riding.

Carry On Camping
The *Oman Off-Road Explorer* has all the information you need on off-road adventuring and camping helping you make the most out of living in the region.

Wahiba Sands
Ibra
Map 1 C1

Al Areesh Camp
99 328 858 | www.desert-discovery.com
The campsite at the Al Areesh Resort in the Wahiba Sands allows you to get away from it all in a peaceful 'back to nature' environment, while still enjoying a good level of luxury, certainly by most campers' standards. The camp consists of 12 tents with camp-style beds. Meals are prepared on site and cooked over open fires.

Al Naseem Camp

Nr Turtle Beach
Ras Al Jinz
Map1 C1

99 328 858 | *www.desert-discovery.com*

This is a great base camp if you plan to go turtle watching because it is just four minutes away from the Ras Al Jinz nature reserve. And it's even greater if you're the type of camper who needs running water, flushing toilets, and hot showers nearby – Al Naseem has all of these, as well as electric lighting, soft mattresses (single beds only), and continental breakfasts. What makes it really special is the spacious entertainment area, covered in palm fronds, where you can dine and lounge on carpets and cushions in true Omani style.

Al Raha Tourism Camp

Ibra Muscat Sur Rd
Al Ghabbi
Wilayat Bidiya
Ibra
Map 1 C1

99 343 851 | *www.alrahaoman.com*

This desert camp in the Wahiba Sands offers visitors a chance to sample a tourist-friendly version of Bedouin life – as well as to dabble in some dune buggy driving, dune bashing in 4WDs, sandboarding and, of course, go on a camel ride. Accommodation is in clean but basic concrete rooms with an attached toilet, or Bedouin-style tents with communal bathrooms. The meals are generally buffets, set out beneath the stars in an open courtyard that is also the venue for live music and entertainment.

Desert Camp

Wahiba Sands
Wilayat Bidiyah
Ibra
Map 1 C1

99 311 338 | *info@desert-camp.com*

Desert Camp lies about 220km from Muscat and is a good spot to get a taste of Omani hospitality. You can choose to sleep in a Bedouin tent, but there are single bedrooms and rest rooms for men and women available too. Breakfast and dinner is included for RO 20. Dinner usually takes place under the stars where you're often treated to traditional music for an authentic desert experience. Various activities available in the camp include dunebashing, camel rides, desert cycles for the kids, or even a desert crossing on foot with an experienced guide.

Empty Quarter Tours

Various Locations

99 387 654 | *www.emptyquartertours.com*

Operating out of the Nahar Farm in Ibra, 30 minutes from the famous Wahiba Sands, Empty Quarter Tours has a comfortable Bedouin-style camp. Accommodation is in fixed barasti (palm frond) shelters with modern conveniences, including showers, toilets and a swimming pool, surrounded by palm trees. Delicious Omani meals are served in a date palm garden or in dining areas fitted out with authentic Arabian carpets and cushions. Traditional performances by dancers and musicians can be arranged. Empty Quarter Tours also offer camping at a 'back to nature' 1,000 Nights Camp in the Wahiba Sands.

Hormuzline Tours & Cruises

Nr Al Maha
Petrol Station
Musandam
Map 1 A2

26 731 616 | *www.hormuzlinetours.com*

Hormuzline offers camping in a tent or, for an alternative take on the theme, nights on a dhow, where you sleep under the starry skies. The company offers various sightseeing and activity tours but call to arrange a few nights of camping on the Musandam Peninsula.

Hud Hud Travel

Jebel Akhdar
Nizwa
Map 1 C2

95 694 330 | *www.hudhudtravels.com*

This is no ordinary camping experience. Hud Hud Travel offers, quite simply, the very best. From Egyptian cotton sheets and European chefs to highly qualified tour guides and evening entertainment, guests will enjoy luxury in the desert. The camp at Nizwa is in the foothills of the Jebel Akhdar mountains, only half an hour from the town, making it a perfect location to explore the surrounding attractions including the souk, fort and date plantations. It operates from October to April. Tents are furnished with comfy beds, rugs and lanterns, and each has a veranda with maximum privacy ensured. Bathrooms benefit from full facilities and you can enjoy dinner under the stars before reclining with a book, game or some shisha.

Khasab Travel & Tours

Musandam
Nr Khasab Airport
Khasab
Map 1 A2

26 730 464 | www.khasabtours.com

Khasab Travel & Tours does precisely that, but it also offers camping options around Musandam Peninsula. You can either do the dhow sleepover, or you can camp on terra firma. The company will set everything up for you – from tents, mattresses and sleeping bags to basic toilet and shower facilities and lighting. You'll receive three meals a day and soft refreshments, and the evening meal is typically a chicken or fish barbecue. It can cater for a minimum group of six, but can accommodate up to 100 people at a time and can arrange entertainment if you want. There are camping locations at Hiyut Beach on the west coast and Hablein on the east coast.

Turtle Beach Resort

Ras Al Hadd
Map 1 C1

25 540 068 | www.surtoursonline.com

A few kilometres from Ras Al Hadd, Turtle Beach Resort offers no-nonsense accommodation and facilities, as well as varied activities, all at reasonable prices. Guest rooms consist of 22 traditional barasti huts, which are small and basic but perfect for rolling out of bed straight onto the beach. There's also a large restaurant and dining area built in the shape of an old boat. The big drawcard though is the resort's programme of activities which includes turtle watching at Ras Al Jinz, dolphin and bird watching around Ras Al Hadd, snorkelling (you will need to bring your own equipment), diving trips, and dhow cruises aboard its own vessel.

Canoeing

Other options **Outdoor Goods** p.282

There may not be any rivers or lakes in Oman, but its coastline is fantastic for canoeing and kayaking enthusiasts. The coast is littered with inlets and sheltered bays to discover, many of which have isolated beaches that make for excellent picnic spots. Paddling allows you access to otherwise hidden places of natural beauty and it's a good way to appreciate the country's abundant bird and marine life. Adventurous canoeists with sea-going canoes can tour the stunning waterways of Musandam (p.166), where you'll see some spectacularly rocky coastlines with fjord-like inlets and towering cliffs – some of which reach heights of 1,000m. Many hotels and adventure centres hire out sea kayaks, or you can bring your own.

Muscat Diving & Adventure Center

Nr Radisson BLU
Al Khuwayr
Map 7 C3

24 485 663 | www.holiday-in-oman.com

If you are going to take to the waters, a good way to do so is in a kayak and with a guide. You've got over 1,700km of rugged coastline to explore and you can stop at any of the small fishing villages in between. Muscat Diving & Adventure Center hires out single and double sea-kayaks. Renting a kayak costs RO 20 for a double and RO 59 for a single (with a guide). You'll need to put down a credit card deposit – presumably to prevent you from sailing off into the sunset.

Canyoning

Other options **Hiking** p.231

Oman's interesting topography makes canyoning a popular activity here. It's not for the timid though as it's often challenging and treacherous and involves using various methods, such as abseiling, scrambling and swimming, to ascend or descend a canyon. There are some awesome treks in the country including Wadi Shab, Snake Canyon, Wadi Hajir, Wadi Haylayn and Wadi Qashah, each with its own individual challenge and beauty and each with opportunities for canyoning.

There are risks associated with scrambling or abseiling down uneven and slippery surfaces so it's really advisable that you go as part of a group and ensure that you have at least basic knowledge of first aid. Dress lightly, take sun protection along and always expect to get wet.

Although canyoning is an activity more commonly enjoyed by experienced groups, some tour companies do offer adventurous treks.

Caving

The caving network in the Hajar Mountains of Oman is extensive, and much of it has yet to be explored and mapped. The area includes what's believed to be the second largest cave system in the world. The most famous cave in Oman, and the most stunning in terms of size, is the Majlis Al Jinn. Entering it is not for the fainthearted as it starts with a 180m abseil from the entrance in the roof. Caving here ranges from the fairly safe to the extremely dangerous. Even with an experienced leader, it's not for the casual tourist or the poorly equipped. It's important to understand the dangers. Make sure you take plenty of water and basic first aid equipment. Some of the cave exploration here is among the most hair-raising in the world and should only be attempted by experienced, fit cavers, preferably accompanied by someone who has traversed the caves before.

The Al Hotta Cave (also seen as Al Hotti or Hoti Cave) can be found at the foot of Jabal Shams in Tanuf Valley. At over five kilometres long, Al Hotta was previously one of the most challenging caves in Oman, with its one entrance being strictly for experienced cavers equipped with ropes, safety equipment, and a guide familiar with the cave. However, the Oman Ministry of Tourism has recently completed an overhaul of the caves, making them safer and transforming them from an adventurous location reserved only for experienced cavers, into a fascinating ecotourism attraction.

The first entrance to the cave can be found near the village of Al Hotta (about 1,000m above sea level), and the other is near the town of Al Hamra (about 800m above sea level). Inside the cave, you can see an amazing collection of crystals, stalactites and stalagmites, but perhaps the most interesting sight is the underground lake in the main cave. The lake is inhabited by thousands of blind, transparent fish, who rely on floods to carry in nourishment from the outside world.

The lower cave can only be reached in a train that transports visitors through a tunnel near the main entrance. You will be able to see the underground lake from a special viewing balcony (monitors are provided so that you can get a more close-up view). After you have toured the caves, spend some time in the visitor centre (this, by the way, is where you will get your ticket for the cave tour). A natural history museum was still under construction at time of going to print, but the visitor centre has a couple of restaurants and some heritage shops where you can buy locally made pottery, silver and carpets.

To get to the caves, head for Nizwa, and when you reach Nizwa old town take the road for Al Hamra. When you get to Wadi Tanuf, turn right and head for Al Hotta. The cave is approximately a 20 minute drive from Nizwa. Please note that the main cave is closed during July and August. See www.alhottacave.com for more information.

Proud To Be A Trekkie

Discover some of Oman's most breathtaking sights in the comfort of your hiking boots. The *Oman Trekking Explorer* details 12 spectacular hiking routes printed on handy cards, and comes with detailed maps as well as a trekking handbook.

One of the largest sinkholes in the world, Teyq Cave, is located between Taqa and Mirbat. The two wadis in the sinkhole keep it topped up with water when it rains. Sultan Qaboos University houses an active Earth Sciences Department, and this is a good source of information on the sinkhole (www.squ.edu.com).

Gulf Leisure

Jawharat A'Shati
Shati Al Qurm
Map 8 A4

99 819 006 | *www.gulfleisure.com*

With some of the largest, most complex and even the most recently discovered caves in the world, Oman is a playground for people who are fascinated by caves. While you can't go charging in where you have no experience or local knowledge, tour groups like Gulf Leisure allow even the least experienced of cavers to enjoy what the sultanate has to offer. Gulf Leisure will take care of all the technicalities and all your requirements, so that you can enjoy a safe and memorable excursion into the depths of the earth.

Muscat Diving & Adventure Center

Nr Radisson BLU
Al Khuwayr
Map 7 C3

24 485 663 | *www.holiday-in-oman.com*

Try caving with the skilled guides and instructors of the Muscat Diving & Adventure Center. Among the hot spot destinations is the second biggest cave in the world, Majlis Al Jinn. The company offers a two-day experdition through the cave that includes a compulsory four-session training course before the trip. The session will ensure that you're familiar with the skills, techniques and equipment you will need and the guides will assess your confidence and skill levels at the same time. The breath-taking abseil in and out of the 180 metre deep chamber is not to be missed. Prices start at RO 250 per person which includes equipment, transport, training sessions and a two day trip.

Climbing

First-time climbers in Oman need to get used to the nature of the rock – most climbs are on fairly soft and brittle limestone that's not always reliable. Rock that looks strong can easily flake and become detached when pulled too hard, so climbing in Oman is often more subtle than athletic, requiring balance and patience. The friction though is superb, and invites delicate moves using pressure and counter pressure.

Apart from the quality of the rock, Oman's hot climate is another limiting factor and during the summer months of May to September the temperatures can reach 50ºC. For the dedicated climber it is possible to climb through the summer, if you pick your crag carefully. North-facing crags are usually in the shade in the afternoon. The usual climbing equipment will be sufficient, but you'll have to bring your own gear as there are no dedicated shops in Oman selling it. The Muscat Diving & Adventure Center (listed below) can supply you with equipment and also guide you to the best climbs.

Muscat Diving & Adventure Center

Nr Radisson BLU
Al Khuwayr
Map 7 C3

24 485 663 | *www.holiday-in-oman.com*

The centre has qualified instructors who will show you the ropes of climbing and help you discover a more adventurous side of Oman. The routes include some good, large walls and the instructors have been busy bolting more sports routes. The instructors offer tuition on an individual or group basis. Apart from climbing, the centre also offers activities such as abseiling, canyoning, caving, kayaking and trekking. All equipment is provided, and prices start at RO 5 per person per hour.

Cookery Classes

Several of the premier hotels in Muscat offer gourmet nights. These special evenings provide food lovers the opportunity to create the works of a renowned chef. Naturally, tasting and sampling is absolutely unavoidable in the course of the class, but the real

Impromptu cricket

treat comes right at the end when the feast is laid out for all to enjoy. Most of the chefs allow you to walk away with their recipes in hand, so you're all set to create your own in-home fine dining. Contact the food and beverage departments of the major hotels to find out if they hold gourmet nights.

Cricket

With the large numbers of expats from cricket loving nations living in Oman, as well as an increasing number of Omanis entering the sport, there is plenty of opportunity to get yourself in a team here. There are currently 60 teams registered with the Oman Cricket Association (www.omanicricket.com), but many organisations have their own teams for inter company competitions and the sport is also becoming more popular in schools. The Oman national team is also the current Gulf Cup Cricket title holder after beating Bahrain in the final.

If you want to start your own team and play in the various leagues and regional competitions, you can register with the Oman Cricket Association. The only conditions are that you have at least one Omani in your team, and that he bats in the top five. If you don't have an Omani on your team, you have to play with only 10 men.

Nr Haffa House Htl
Ruwi
Map 12 D2

Oman Cricket Association

99 314 348 | *www.omanicricket.com*

The Oman Cricket Association has been organising league tournaments since 1979. There are currently 60 teams, divided into eight divisions. Every team must register with the association to play in the league. The cricket season begins in September and lasts until March, with tournaments beginning some time in April. If you're interested in playing please contact Madhu Sampat or Jesrani.

Cycling

Other options **Sports Goods** p.287, **Mountain Biking** p.239, **Bicycle** p.265

Oman has tremendous scope for cycling, with many routes that run both along the beautiful coastline and through the rugged hills and mountains. Cycling is a great way to get to know Muscat too – you can ride along the corniche at Mutrah, weave through old Muscat, and scale the roads through the spectacularly rocky mountains to Al Bustan and Qantab.

While riding in traffic requires caution in any country, it requires particular attention in the Middle East. Drivers are not very sympathetic towards cyclists and don't allow them much space or time. You need to be particularly careful in the busy parts of town, especially at junctions and roundabouts. On the plus side, road surfaces are decent and punctures are a rarity. Joining a cycling club will quickly introduce you to the routes and safety issues of cycling in and around Muscat.

Most of the main roads in the city have a hard shoulder that provides a fairly safe lane for cyclists. Although bikes are not allowed in most of Muscat's parks, there are some nice rides through the quieter, residential, and pleasantly green areas of the city.

Various Locations

Muscat Cycling Club

99 324 594 | oabmkt@omantel.net.ae

The Muscat Cycling Club welcomes both road and off-road cyclists, so whether you prefer speeding down the highway or bumping your way over rocks, it will happily accommodate you. The quickly growing group has over 80 riders and meets regularly for weekend rides with off-road routes on Thursdays and road cycling on Fridays. The Muscat Cycling Club has an active social schedule and always welcomes new members, regardless of initial skill level.

Dance Classes

Other options **Music Lessons** p.239

Nr Qurm Park
Al Qurm
Map 8 D3

Classic Music & Arts Institute

24 560 025 | musictec@omantel.net.om

The institute offers a wide variety of dance classes for both adults and children. Ballet classes are given by a trained ballerina, but you also have the option of modern dance, ballroom and salsa which appeal to many adults. Individual classes cost RO 14 (you'll get a discount if you book multiple sessions). Other classes are booked as required and prices start at RO 3 per person. The institute also provides a venue for flamenco, belly dancing and Indian modern dance groups, and there are often line dancing and tap dancing sessions held in the small dance studio too. If you're interested in taking up any of these, give the institute a call to find out about timings and costs.

Grand Hyatt
Shati Al Qurm
Map 7 E1

Grand Hyatt Club Olympus

24 641 155 | www.muscat.hyatt.com

Proving that getting fit isn't all about gym apparatus and reps, the Grand Hyatt's health club also offers a variety of dance classes. Children aged 8 and older can sign up for modern dance classes, while adults can choose from salsa, belly dancing and Latin dance. Some of these classes are mixed. Call the hotel to find out about timings and when the next course will begin.

Various Locations

Peter Emery Langille

92 605 102 | peter@divineconnections.ca

Feel like trying something completely different? Peter Emery Langille offers English and Scottish country dancing as well as traditional Sri Lankan Sinhalese dancing. He welcomes everyone to his classes, whether you're a dancer or not – all you need is plenty of energy and the willingness to try something new. All the dances are taught to the appropriate music, which is often half of the evening's fun. They are also usually quite social affairs. He will teach a class or dance workshop wherever there are eight or more people who want to learn, and his regular classes are held at various venues in the Al Batinah region, Muscat and Barka. You don't need a partner, but couples are welcome. For the latest venues and times, or to enquire about demonstrations or a specific class, email him on the above email address.

Desert Driving Courses

Other options **Off-Road Driving** p.240

Nr the British Council
Madinat As
Sultan Qaboos
Map 7 D1

National Training Institute

24 472 121 | www.ntioman.com

If you'd like to learn how to put your 4WD through its paces off-road, or for some expert advice on desert, wadi or mountain driving, sign up for one of NTI's courses. You will learn the theoretical side of driving off-road, followed by plenty of hands-on practise in the vehicles. Topics covered include how to control skids, brake safely on sandy or rocky surfaces, and driving in the desert. Instructors also offer advice on safety precautions, emergency procedures and what to do when things go wrong. There is also a two-day defensive driving course to help you cope with the roads and other drivers in Oman.

Diving

Other options **Snorkelling** p.244

If you are fortunate enough to live in Oman, year-round diving is one of its most breathtaking pleasures. Oman has a long coastline and a variety of underwater treasures – coral reefs and shipwrecks provide a multitude of dwellings for an array of marine life. The quantity and variety of sea life in what is still a quiet diving destination will keep even the most jaded diver enthralled. While you're underwater it won't be other divers you bump into, but turtles, cuttlefish, stingrays, moray eels – the list is endless.

While Oman's waters suit novice and advanced divers alike, experienced divers with a penchant for more adventure will find cave diving a unique experience. Please be aware that all divers must have a diving permit from the ROP to dive in the waters off Oman, and most obtain their permits through the club or dive centre they are diving with (it is usually included in the dive price).

Night dives are very popular, and provide the opportunity to see many nocturnal marine creatures that you wouldn't normally see. The phosphorescence in Oman's waters is more visible after dark and this green-blue substance, released by plankton as a result of chemical reactions from their vigorous movements, makes for an amazing underwater display.

If all this sounds wonderful but you've never dived, don't worry – there are plenty of centres that provide training in PADI or BSAC, depending on your preference. PADI's Open Water Certification is ideal if you're on holiday here or want to get into the sea without too much delay, and your skill levels are easily added to with a variety of Advanced and Specialist courses. BSAC training courses are of a longer duration and especially good for the novice diver who wants to take it slowly and thoroughly.

Below is a list of a just a few of the most popular dive sites in Oman, but keep in mind that each site is extensive and you could spend years exploring every nook and cranny.

Fahal Island – Located in Muscat's Qurm region. This island has around 10 dive sites and is good in a variety of weather conditions, so even if you head out on a particularly windy day, there's usually at least one area of the island that will offer perfect diving conditions. Diving depth is from three to 42 metres. Around Fahal Island are isolated reefs, a swim-through cave, and artificial reef balls. The most notable fish in the area are angelfish, trigger fish and large broom-tail. Also look out for diamond-shaped stingrays (who enjoy backflipping out of the water), honeycomb eels and a few friendly sharks. The islands also sport a large variety of corals. Non-divers will find good snorkelling on the western side of the island.

Bander Khayran – Located near Muscat, 20 to 30 minutes by boat or 40 minutes by 4WD. This area consists of a small fjord system littered with inlets. The diving depth here ranges between one and 30 metres. It's known for diverse and beautiful corals – table, bush, boulder, brain, hedgehog, cauliflower, and pore corals, often all intermixed and always in a variety of colours. Of course all that coral means a wide variety of marine life is attracted to the area too.

Al-Munassir Naval Shipwreck – Located near Bander Khayran. In April 2003 the Royal Navy of Oman sank this naval ship to create an artificial reef in Omani waters. It lies at a depth of about 30 metres and spans a length of 84 metres. All the ship's canons and guns were removed before it was sunk, and the rooms in the ship have been opened up for divers to penetrate them easily. Making your way through the ship's engine, dining and

Water Treat

Oman has some amazing dive sites, but right next door in the UAE you'll find many more. For more information on various underwater adventures grab a copy of the brand new edition of the handy *UAE Underwater Explorer*, which contains details of 64 different dive sites.

other rooms is an excellent opportunity for divers to learn orientation. It's also a great site to watch marine life go about its daily business within and around the vessel.

Daymaniyat Islands – The Daymaniyat Islands span approximately 20 kilometres from Seeb to Barka and consist of nine islands, named numerically from D1 to D9. The Oman government has designated the islands and their surrounding reefs as a national nature reserve, and access to the islands is controlled. This has allowed for the growth of an extensive coral reef and abundant sea life, and the islands are well known for the magnificent diving. The diving depth of the islands ranges from one to 30 metres.

Arabian Sea Safaris

InterContinental
Muscat
Shati Al Qurm
Map 8 A4

24 693 223 | *www.arabianseasafaris.com*

Arabian Sea Safaris offers dive trips on board spacious vessels. It will take you to most of Oman's more spectacular sites – such as the Damaniyat Islands, which are famed for their clear waters and healthy marine life. It also offers a variety of other watersports out of its base, the Arabian Boat House (Bait Al Bahar).

Blu Zone Water Sports

Marina Bander
Al Rowdha
Sidab
Map 13 F4

24 737 293 | *www.bluzonediving.com*

Blu Zone is a family-run PADI Gold Palm IDC five star dive centre with experienced instructors and guides. The company offers daily dive trips as well as courses from beginner to instructor level. For those wanting to hone specific skills, it offers wreck, deep, navigation, search and recovery, peak performance and night diving speciality courses too. The Bubblemaker course is available for children aged 8 to 10 and there's a Junior Open Water Diver course available for children aged 10 years and older who are keen to get underwater. Non divers can go on dolphin watching cruises and snorkelling trips. The centre also has a swimming pool, kids' pool, restaurant and a Jacuzzi for you to relax in after a dive.

Capital Area Yacht Club

Sidab
Map 13 F3

24 737 712 | *caycoman@omantel.net.om*

CAYC Divers offers a variety of activities including diving, snorkelling and wreck dives. The club also offers PADI courses for those who want to learn how to dive, and for divers who want to specialise or advance their skills. CAYC is a members-only club but members are welcome to bring guests along. Dive boats go out every day of the week.

Daymaniyat Divers

Al Sawadi Beach
Resort
Barka
Map 1 B2

26 795 545 | *www.alsawadibeach.com*

With a recently refurbished dive centre, Daymaniyat Divers offers good facilities for people to take dive courses, as well as trips to the famous islands the company is named after. The dive centre has new equipment for 15 divers and 50 snorkellers, a classroom with space for four students, and a library full of the latest PADI videos and DVDs. It offers a range of PADI courses from Bubblemaker and Discover Scuba for kids, all the way to Dive Master for adults. Its dive excursions go out to 17 distinctly different sites around the Daymaniyat Islands.

Global Scuba

Al Azaiba – Civil
Aviation Club
Madinat As Sultan
Qaboos
Map 5 C1

24 692 346 | *www.global-scuba.com*

Global Scuba's dive centre is conveniently located just 25 to 30 minutes away from the Daymaniyat Islands by boat, and it also offers dive trips to Fahal Island. It runs a range of PADI courses, from beginner to advanced and in a range of specialities. There are also dolphin watching and snorkelling trips for those who prefer to keep their heads above water.

Jawharat A'Shati
Shati Al Qurm
Map 8 A4

Gulf Leisure

99 819 006 | www.gulfleisure.com

For qualified divers, Gulf Leisure has a range of dive trips, all aimed at showing you the underwater paradise of the waters off Muscat and around the Daymaniyat Islands. It also runs snorkelling expeditions where you can happily kick off, secure in the knowledge that the boat will be anchored nearby in a safe and beautiful spot. Gulf Vision is Oman's only glass bottom boat and if you really want to see what's happening down under, this is the ideal way to view the spectacular reefs without getting wet. Soft drinks and snacks are provided.

Nr Al Maha
Petrol Station
Musandam
Map 1 A2

Hormuzline Tours & Cruises

26 731 616 | www.hormuzlinetours.com

Among the range of activity tours that Hormuzline offer are also plenty of options for avid divers. You can book yourself on a single day or even an overnight cruise on a dhow and spend your time snorkelling. You can also try scuba diving off the beaches and islands of Khasab for RO 50. Speak to the company if you have specific needs and requests and it will organise an expedition according to your needs and wants.

Nr Khasab Airport
Khasab
Musandam
Map 1 A2

Khasab Travel & Tours

26 730 464 | www.khasabtours.com

With the diving in the UAE and surrounding areas being fairly limited, a dive trip off the Musandam peninsula is a welcome addition to your log book. Diving here has been described as being an 'experienced diver's dive' because of strong currents and some large fish. That said, the area offers a variety of sites, some more sheltered and shallow, which are perfect for beginners. Khasab Travel & Tours will take out groups with a minimum of two adults to enjoy the good visibility and the excellent marine life.

Nr Grand
Hyatt Muscat
Shati Al Qurm
Map 7 E1

Moon Light Diving Centre

99 317 700 | www.moonlightdive.com

This is a five-star dive centre situated on the public beach next to the Grand Hyatt Muscat. The activities on the menu range from PADI dive courses, to dolphin watching, sunset cruising and fishing trips. If it's something more relaxing you're after, you have a choice of boat trips along the coast and its secluded bays, or superb snorkelling in some of the best waters in the Middle East. The centre also does equipment rental and repairs, and will even arrange hotel accommodation and land tours for you.

Golden Tulip
Resort Khasab
Khasab
Map 1 A2

Musandam Extra Divers

26 730 501 | www.extra-divers.li

Musandam Extra Divers has a dive centre in Khasab on the Musandam peninsula. A relatively new operation, the facilities include equipment hire, a compressor, tanks, dive shop and a dry room. Staff offer instruction for SSI and courses in German, English and French. The company runs daily two-tank dives for RO 47 from 09:00 to 15:00. This charge includes equipment, soft drinks, fruit and biscuits.

Nr Radisson BLU
Al Khuwayr
Map 7 C3

Muscat Diving & Adventure Center

24 485 663 | www.holiday-in-oman.com

Catering to all of your water sports needs, the Muscat Diving & Adventure Center takes full advantage of the vast beauty and abundance of fascinating sea life that Oman has to offer. Experienced and proficient instructors are on hand to teach Discover Scuba courses, or to organise trips for snorkellers and more experienced divers. A two-dive trip with full equipment costs RO 48. The boat goes out from 08:00 to about 14:00.

Nr Harbour
Al Biah
Dibba
Map 1 A2

Nomad Ocean Adventures

+971 50 885 3238 | www.discovernomad.com

Nomad Ocean Adventures is a UAE based company that can organise excursions to your specifications. In addition to offering diving and snorkelling, it can also arrange for you to go on a dhow cruise, to go deep sea fishing, trekking or stay overnight in a traditional Arabian campsite. For qualified divers a single dive, with all equipment, starts at Dhs.200, while a weekend package at a guesthouse with two dives and full equipment costs around Dhs.600. For more details, call Christophe on the UAE mobile number above or email him on chris@discovernomad.com.

Bandar Al
Jissah Qantab
Al Bustan
Map 15 D3

Oman Dive Center

24 824 240 | www.omandivecenter.com

Popularly known as ODC, this centre is set in the picturesque and sheltered bay of Bandar Al Jissah. The bay is perfect for snorkellers and for novices to practise their new skills in before venturing out to the ocean. The training facilities here have been awarded five-star PADI status, and it runs the full range of courses, including first aid. Activities include day and night diving, snorkelling, underwater photography and wreck diving. Day trips to the Daymaniyat Islands, the Quriyat wreck, and a new wreck dive at Al Munnassir, can be arranged for divers and snorkellers, and ODC provides accommodation in luxury barasti-style huts on the beach.

Sidab Beach
Nr Al Bustan Palace
Sidab
Map 15 B1

Scuba Oman

24 737 545 | www.scubaoman.com

Scuba Oman offers diving and snorkelling trips, PADI courses, dolphin watching and more. The company can take underwater fans to the depths at over 100 dive sites, with all levels of experience catered for. A range of courses are available, including discovery dives and specialities like rescue and open water sessions. Beginners can benefit from 'dive holidays' which start from RO 169 for three days (four nights) and includes accommodation, breakfast, airport pick up, dive permits, equipment and two dives.

Drama Groups

Various Locations

Muscat Amateur Theatre

24 562 511 | kezar157@hotmail.com

The Muscat Amateur Theatre group was formed in 1980, and to date it has put on 50 plays by a wide variety of playwrights. Its repertoire ranges from Neil Simon to Shakespeare, so you're sure to find a play to suit your theatrical tastes. The group performs at various venues in Muscat's hotels, including the InterContinental Muscat.

Environmental Groups

Other options **Voluntary & Charity Work** p.74

Oman is fortunate to have some beautiful natural assets together with a government that is interested and active in environmental issues, always making them a high priority. There are currently three nature reserves where there is a facility for controlled tourism – the Damaniyat Islands, the Ras Al Jinz turtle reserve and the Arabian Oryx Sanctuary. You may need a permit to visit these fascinating reserves; to find out more information about them, refer to their entries in the Exploring chapter (Damaniyat Islands Nature Reserve, p.178; Ras Al Jinz Turtle Reserve, p.191; and Arabian Oryx Sanctuary, p.177).

In addition to the government's efforts to promote protection of the environment, there are also several interest groups and environmental organisations in Oman. The sultanate is a member of the International Whaling Commission, and although it is not yet a signatory to CITES (Convention on International Trade in Endangered Species), it follows the guidelines laid down by CITES, such as stopping trade in endangered species. On a more everyday level, there are increasing numbers of bottle/can recycling points around Muscat. These are sponsored by various local companies, and are mainly located near shopping centres.

Various Locations

ESO Whale & Dolphin Research Group
24 696 912 | *www.whalecoastoman.com*

Part of the Environment Society of Oman (ESO), this is a group of volunteer scientists and other interested parties who collect and disseminate knowledge about Oman's dolphins and whales. They are independent researchers whose work is recognised and approved by local Ministries, and they work closely with the Oman Natural History Museum, the Ministry of Agriculture and Fisheries, and the Raysut Marine Laboratory. The group's primary activities include emergency rescue services for whales and dolphins, maintenance of a database of sightings and strandings, and cooperation with local tour operators to promote responsible whale and dolphin-watching activities. If you are interested in volunteering or just want to find out more about local whales and dolphins, check out the website or call Rob Baldwin on 99 045 109.

Various Locations

The Historical Association Of Oman
24 563 074 | *www.hao.org.om*

The Historical Association of Oman is a non-profit making organisation, established in 1971, with the aims of documenting and distributing information about Oman's history, whether natural, national, linguistic or cultural, and to encourage research. In addition to the usual activities including lectures, trips and publishing, the HAO conducts research and assists researchers from within and outside the country. The most recent projects embarked upon are two documentation projects of old settlements in Bawshar and Manah funded by the US Ambassadors Fund for Cultural Preservation. Meetings are held twice a month on Monday evenings from 20:00, with venues varying; call for more details.

**Nr Oil & Gas
Exhibition Ctr**
Mina Al Fahal (PDO)
Map 9 A3

PDO Planetarium
24 675 542 | *www.pdo.co.om*

Astronomers of all ages can gaze up at the twinkly dome of the PDO Planetarium, which opened in 2000. Since then, seven different shows have been presented, three of which have been locally produced. On Wednesdays at 19:00 and Thursdays at 10:00 shows are held in English, and on Wednesdays at 16:00 and Thursdays at 11:00 shows are held in Arabic. All last about an hour and are free of charge. The planetarium also hosts guest lecturers, conferences and workshops and can arrange special social gatherings when astronomical events occur. Booking is required in advance. For more info see the website.

First Aid

Various Locations

Kibara Technical Services
99 445 969 | *www.ktsgroup.org*

Kibara Technical Services is an international organisation that provides first aid training in 82 different countries, including Oman. Instruction is given in English and Arabic and the course teaches practical skills. Courses include emergency first aid, basic first aid and advanced trauma and life support. Courses can be carried out in convenient locations with timings to suit you. The National Training Institute (p.221) also offers first aid courses.

Bandar Al
Jissah Qantab
Al Bustan
Map 15 D3

Oman Dive Center
24 824 240 | www.omandivecenter.com

While first aid will be covered briefly in some of the dive training it does, the Oman Dive Centre also offers a general introductory first aid course aptly called the Emergency First Responder. This course is suitable for everyone, not just divers, and can be taught either at the dive centre, or at a location of your choice.

Fishing

Other options **Boat Tours & Charters** p.184

Coastal Fishing

The Sultanate of Oman boasts some of the best surf fishing in the world. The coastline from Al Khaluf down to Salalah is home to a variety of species belonging to the warm waters of the Indian Ocean. Depending on where you've chosen to cast your line, the species you're likely to catch include blue fish, trevally, shark, black bream, rays, grouper and spotted grunter. Blue fish will range from five pounds upwards, and ray and shark anywhere between 10 and 200.

Light and heavy tackle combos are a must for fishing these waters. All the various species tend to take turns in feeding during the day and night. Ensure your secondary tackle supplies are plentiful as you will often experience toothy beasts taking your bait. Fishing along these coastal coves is seasonal due to the severe weather conditions caused by the monsoon.

The coastline of Oman beyond Al Khaluf can be taxing on both vehicles and supplies. This is not the place for a jaunt down to the beach with rod in hand and, in fact, most people choose not to travel the roads with their boats in tow, but rather to sail from one harbour to the next. The villagers along the coastline of Oman are very friendly and always happy to help, but do remember that you're in a Muslim country and have respect for their traditions and religious beliefs. Maps of the Oman coastline are available and it will be very helpful to have one on your first few trips at least.

Big Game Fishing

The season from October to April is best for big game fishing. The rest of the year tends to be slow, as the fish move further south to avoid the higher waters in summer. The true Indian Ocean meets the Gulf of Oman off Ras Al Hadd and you'll clearly see the difference between the colours and surface textures of these two bodies of water.

The most common big game fish during the high season is yellowfin tuna. A tricky fish to hook by nature, successful fishermen sometimes land them in weights exceeding 100 pounds. Although much larger specimens are available to offshore anglers, these are usually only caught south of Muscat or much further out than the average fisherman cares to venture. On rare occasions yellowfin tuna close to the 250lb mark have been caught within 10km of Muscat's coast.

Sailfish dominate the waters off Muscat during September and October, and it's thought that they migrate through the region on their way to the Arabian Gulf for breeding. They're often caught close to shore and vary in weight from 60 to 110lb.

Mal mai or dolphin fish are found in abundance from the end of July to September. Travelling in schools, these fish make for some fast, light-tackle action. They average about 15lb, but you might occasionally land something in the 35-45lb range.

Black marlin sometimes travel into the coastal waters off Muscat but there's only been one confirmed capture to date – and that one weighed in at a whopping 400lb. Reports that marlin can be found in greater abundance off the coastal area of Ras Al Hadd have been confirmed by the local commercial fisheries who estimate that an average of 10 marlin a day are brought in by their boats. The season is typically from November to April. The length of the Oman coastline is met by underwater mountain ranges and drop-offs that go down to 300m and more in some areas. Due to the deep water ridges rising up into the warm coastal shallows, an abundance of game species are found feeding on the bait fish, that in turn thrive on the nutrients brought up from the depths – an excellent example of the natural food chain.

InterContinental
Muscat
Shati Al Qurm
Map 8 A4

Arabian Sea Safaris

24 693 223 | *www.arabianseasafaris.com*

Arabian Sea Safaris is dedicated to arranging memorable fishing trips for you in its luxurious, fast and comfortable Sport Fisherman boats, which are each rigged with a shaded seating area, fish finder and outriggers. The company offers a wide variety of activities, ranging from wildlife tours to sightseeing cruises and active day trips, so if there's something you want to do, it will probably have just the thing you want. The staff will certainly be happy to take you exploring Oman's unspoilt waters by any combination of fishing, swimming, diving or snorkelling. Keen anglers can go game fishing, or you can try your hand at traditional tuna fishing, beach casting or bottom fishing under the guidance of Arabian Sea Safaris.

Jawharat A'Shati
Shati Al Qurm
Map 8 A4

Gulf Leisure

99 819 006 | *www.gulfleisure.com*

Mike Harris of Gulf Leisure is an experienced game fishing charter skipper who gained success in the 2006 and 2007 IGFA Middle East world qualifier. The company's fishing charter boat, Gulf Catch, is fully equipped with radar, chartplotter, fishfinder, fighting chair and outriggers including the latest Penn rods and reels. It is therefore well-equipped for the Middle East's premier game fishing destination, which happens to be the Gulf of Oman, where marlin, tuna, barracuda and dorado are found. Half-day (four hours) charters (RO 170) and six hour charters (RO 220) are available for a maximum of four people. Full day (10 hour) charters (RO 300) are available for a maximum of six people.

Nr Al Maha
Petrol Station
Musandam
Map 1 A2

Hormuzline Tours & Cruises

26 731 616 | *www.hormuzlinetours.com*

With its main office in Khasab on the Musandam Peninsula, Hormuzline will be happy to organise excursions to your specifications. If your interest in fishing is more leisurely you can get a good insight into the traditional lifestyle of Omani fishermen and the Bedouin from its dhow cruise fishing tours. You'll share the early morning hustle and bustle of life in the fishing harbour and visit a number of different villages for a glimpse of a way of life that hasn't changed much over the years. If you want to actively fish while you're out on one of its dhow charters, have a chat with the company about what it can organise for you.

Nr The Corniche
Sidab
Map 13 E2

Sidab Sea Tours

99 655 783 | *sidabseatours@hotmail.com*

While there will always be tales of the one that got away, and some days when all of them do, you're almost guaranteed an end to the tall stories when you've got a local skipper who knows the waters like the back of his hand. Sidab Sea Tours organises four-hour professional game fishing excursions for RO 120 (for four people), with barracuda, tuna, marlin and sailfish as the intended targets. For a more relaxed experience you can try traditional handline fishing 'Omani style'. Whatever you choose as your bait, all tackle and equipment is provided and soft drinks are available on board.

Marina Bandar
Al Rowdha
Mutrah
Map 13 F4

Water World Marine

24 737 438 | www.waterworldoman.com

Water World Marine established its presence in Oman in 1997 by stocking premium angling gear and the top brands in all the gadgets a fisherman needs. If you want to benefit from its expertise, you can charter one of its specialist sports fishing boats for the day and go looking for tuna (boats sail from the outlet in Marina Bandar; call Mr Provi on 99 319 468). The less predatory can simply go on a leisure cruise around Muscat's bays and beaches. A full day charter (eight hours) costs RO 320. All charters are fully catered – just bring yourself, a hat and a towel. The operating hours are from 07:00 to 13:00 and 16:00 to 18:00, Saturday to Thursday. The Sidab outlet opens from 08:30 to 12:30 and 16:00 to 20:00 Monday to Saturday.

Football

As in most places in the world, you don't have to travel far to see a game of football in Oman. Rural villages usually have a group knocking a ball around on the local sand and rock pitch – and you could probably join in if you wanted. There are also often teams kicking about on the beaches, particularly at the InterContinental beach strip. There's a semi-professional football league in Oman that teams such as the Oman Club, Sidab and Quriyat participate in. A maximum of two expatriate players are allowed to join each of these clubs, so the majority of expat football fans play in the weekly social soccer games at the grounds of the Oman Club. The main teams include Loan Service, Deuch PDO, Aerworks, British PDO, Royal Flight and the Sultan Qaboos University Squad. Unfortunately, all of the above teams only accept players from within their own organisations, making it difficult for newcomers to get into the game. So you could always start a team of your own, either via your company or group of friends – if it turns into a regular event give Explorer a call and we'll give you a mention in the next edition of the *Oman Explorer*.

The schools have taken charge of the footie scene for children. The PSSL schools soccer league has five age categories, ranging from under 9s to under 19s. The students play from September to December, with the Irishman's cup for the under-13s a fitting climax to the season. The Al Sahwa school and PDO Elementary usually fare well in the youngest age group, while the American British Academy (ABA) and Indian School Wadi Kabir tend to dominate the under 11s. The ABA and the Indian School Muscat are strong in the under 13 sector, while Muscat Private School, British School and ISM are the main rivals in the under 15s category. In the older age groups, Royal Guard and Sultan School tend to be the dominant forces. Touch football is also played at the PDO Elementary playing field Sunday and Tuesday evenings from 17:30 till 19:00 – you simply need to turn up.

Football on the beach

Golf

Golf in Muscat has a healthy band of supporters who play on 'brown' (sand) courses. The lack of green courses though is improving. Muscat's first green golf course, the Muscat Golf & Country Club, has been built behind the Seeb Novotel. The unique 18 hole tournament-grade course has been designed by top golf course designer David Thomas to challenge the best golfers in the world. The completion of Oman's first green golf course is hoped to boost the country's tourism sector, and put the sultanate on the golfing world map.

There are several golf tournaments on Oman's annual calendar, such as the Oman Ladies' Open Championship, the Men's Oman National Championship and the Ras al Ghala Trophy.

Those who have never played golf in the Middle East should be warned that the game here can be more physically demanding than elsewhere in the world – even acclimatised golfers avoid playing in the heat of the day during the summer months. It's always wise to carry plenty of drinking water and wear a sun hat.

Golf in Oman

Ghallah Wentworth Golf Club

Nr As Sultan
Qaboos Mosque
Ghala
Map 6 D4

24 591 248

This is a fair challenge for any level of player. The club has a driving range built on concrete tee boxes and a few sets of clubs for hire. Players should bring their own Astroturf mats for teeing off. There are two separate golf seasons; an 18 hole season in winter, and a nine hole season in summer, and competitions in these two categories are organised accordingly. Lessons are available upon request.

Marco Polo Golf Course

Crowne Plaza
Resort Salalah
Salalah
Map 1 F3

23 235 333 | www.cpsalalah.com

A relative newcomer on the Oman golfing scene, this is a grass course that includes a driving range, putting green and training area. The course itself is an unusual nine hole, par three set in a coconut grove. You can hire golf clubs if you wish, and even benefit from the assistance of a professional golf instructor on request.

Muscat Hills Golf & Country Club

Nr Golden Tulip Hotel
As Seeb
Map 1 B1

24 511 024 | www.muscathills.com

The Muscat Hills Golf & Country Club has been carefully carved into the jebels, with great care taken to maintain the natural beauty of the surrounding landscape and wadis. It opened in March 2009 and is the first 18 hole par 72 championship grass course in the Sultanate of Oman. In addition to the golf course, the Muscat Golf & Country Club offers members and residents tennis and squash facilities, a swimming pool, gymnasium and a spa. When completed, the very smart clubhouse will boast restaurants, a conference room, a pro shop and lounges.

Hashing

Other options **Running** p.242

Sometimes described as drinking clubs with a running problem, the Hash House Harriers form a worldwide family of social running clubs. The aim of running in this setup is not to win, but to merely be there and to take part. The first hash club was formed in Kuala Lumpur in 1938, and it's now the largest running organisation in the world, with members in over 1,600 chapters in 180 countries.

Hashing consists of running, jogging or walking around varied courses, often cross-country, laid out by a couple of hares. It's a fun way to keep fit and meet new people, as clubs are very sociable and the running is generally not competitive.

Various Locations ◀
Jebel Hash House Harriers
994 436 012 | www.omanshash.com

Founded in 1985, the Jebel Hash is a social, non-competitive running club that forms part of the worldwide Hash House Harriers family. There are always two trails to follow – one for those who prefer to walk, and a longer one for the more energetic. A social gathering follows each run, so be prepared; running fit may not be all the fitness you need. The Jebel Hash runs take place anywhere within Muscat and its surroundings. Apart from meeting new people, it's a great way of seeing some places you might have otherwise missed.

Various Locations ◀
Muscat Hash House Harriers
99 619 320 | www.hasher.net/muscat_hhh.htm

More familiarly known as the Muscat Hash, this group meets every Saturday evening at various locations around Muscat, depending on where the hare has set the run. Meeting times also vary in accordance with the changing times of dusk and there's an RO 1 fee for each meeting you attend. Celebrations of various international holidays are always lively.

Hiking
Other options **Outdoor Goods** p.282, **Canyoning** p.218

Whether you go for a stroll on the beach or an ascent of Jabal Shams, one of the country's highest peaks, Oman has plenty to offer hikers. Check out the *Oman Trekking Explorer* for 12 hiking routes printed on handy cards. The land's ancient geological history has created inspiring gorges, wadis, peaks, ridges and plateaus. The terrain is heavily eroded and shattered due to the harsh climate, but there are many excellent routes to be enjoyed. These range from short easy walks to spectacular viewpoints, to longer, more arduous treks up high peaks. Many of the paths follow ancient Bedouin and Shihuh trails through the mountains. Some of these are still used today as the only means of access to remote settlements.

The main mountain area, shared in part with the United Arab Emirates, is the Al Hajar Range, which splits into the Northern, Eastern and Western Hajar. The highest peak in this range, at just over 3,000m, is Jabal Shams in the west (in Arabic 'jabal' means mountain and 'shams' means sun). In the south, near Salalah, are the Dhofar Mountains, whose highest point is Jebel Samhan. Many of the mountains here are over 2,000m, providing excellent walking and fabulous views. The spectacular 'Grand Canyon of Oman' is also in this area, and a demanding, but very beautiful, walk around the rim of the canyon is well worth the effort.

There are many documented treks in Oman that are rated according to difficulty. But whatever your hiking skills or fitness, Muscat is full of easily accessible local walks that you can do on your own or as part of a group.

If you prefer to venture further afield, Jabal Shams has numerous hikes. One of the shorter, less rigorous hikes, at four hours, is the Balcony Walk along Jabal Shams Plateau. Incredible canyon views and a trek through an abandoned village will delight everyone who summons up the energy to try it out. Adventure trekkers looking for a more challenging experience will be inspired by the Al Hawb to Jabal Shams summit. This hike requires good climbing abilities and an

Taking in the scenery

overnight camp. It may take up to 12 hours to reach the summit and the trek is a 20 hour round trip, depending on the descent path you choose, but the views at the top are the ultimate reward for all that hard work.

Be sure that on any hike, short or long, you consider the weather conditions in Oman. Always carry plenty of water and snacks, check your routes before setting out, notify a friend as to your whereabouts and your itinerary, and wear light boots and appropriate clothing. Take a compass or GPS and check the customs and conditions of the area before taking on any long trips. Be warned: no mountain rescue services exist, and anyone venturing out into mountains should be reasonably experienced, or be with some one who knows the area. As long as you are properly prepared your trek will be an outstanding experience leaving you with nothing but fond memories… and possibly a pair of sore feet.

Various Locations

Donkey Trekking
99 348 440 | *www.trekkingoman.com*

Donkey Trekking offers trips along Oman's fairly new hiking trails in the spectacular Hajar Mountains. Donkeys carry your luggage, freeing you up to enjoy the views. The trails take you into remote areas of the mountains, near the village of Misfat Al A'briyeen where you can sleep under the stars, eat traditional food and get into the local culture. Trips can be custom designed, depending on your requirements, to include trekking without donkeys and desert camping. Call Ahmed for more details or email thestars200@yahoo.com.

Musandam
Nr Khasab Airport
Khasab
Map 1 A2

Khasab Travel & Tours
26 730 464 | *www.khasabtours.com*

One of the most peaceful ways to visit the mountains of Musandam is to trek through them. Khasab Travels & Tours offers a number of routes, the favourite being one that takes you on a crossing from Sham Fjord to Kumzar. Your trail winds past an abandoned village with old pottery and derelict houses, and includes an overnight stop in the mountains. The views over the Gulf of Arabia and Gulf of Oman are amazing and have to be experienced. Groups must consist of at least 10 adults.

Nr Radisson BLU
Al Khuwayr
Map 7 C3

Muscat Diving & Adventure Center
24 485 663 | *www.holiday-in-oman.com*

Thanks to Oman's varied terrain, your trekking adventure can be as easy or as difficult as you want it to be. Whether you decide on little more than a brisk walk through a pleasant wadi, or a challenging hike through harsh rocky desert, the Muscat Diving & Adventure Center has a number of different routes for you. Each tour has a minimum group size of four.

Horse Riding
Other options **Farm & Stable Tours** p.190

Qurm Park &
Nature Reserve
Al Qurm
Map 8 D4

Al Fursan Stable
99 386 978

Al Fursan Stable (also known as Shah Mohammed Khalili's stables) caters for riders of all ages and levels, from beginners through to competent riders. In addition to riding and show-jumping lessons given by its qualified trainers, the company also offers pleasure trips to Qurm Garden, Qurm Nature Reserve, the Creek, and the breathtaking beach in Shati Al Qurm, all accompanied by a guide, for RO 15 per hour.

Qurm Park &
Nature Reserve
Al Qurm
Map 8 D3

Qurm Equestrian School
99 339 222
mhhmm@omantel.net.om
Located in the beautiful Qurm Park, the Qurm Equestrian School is open 16:00 to 18:00 every day and teaches everyone from beginners to advanced riders. The school offers beach rides, carriage rides and carriage rental for weddings or special events. There are five instructors who provide one-hour lessons in riding and show jumping, for those who just want to ride for enjoyment or those who want to ride competitively. The school has

Waiting to saddle up

four donkeys for small children to ride, and it has introduced a Pony Club (RO 45 for 10 classes) for kids every Monday. Call the number above, or Mohammad on 99 832 199.

Ice Hockey
Other options **Ice Skating** p.233

Ice Skating Centre
Al Khuwayr
Map 7 B2

Muscat Oryx Hockey
24 489 492 | *mikefern@omantel.net.om*
This ice hockey club has a number of teams for players of various ages and skill levels, from teenagers to adults and from beginners to advanced; new members are always welcome. Practise nights are on Tuesdays, beginning at 17:00 for 7 to 10 year olds. You must provide your own equipment. The rink is only a third of the regulation size, so it's only used for practise sessions, but the teams participate in tournaments in the UAE. The season runs from September to May. For more information, call the centre on the number above or Michael on 99 346 029.

Ice Skating
Other options **Ice Hockey** p.233

Ice Skating Centre
Al Khuwayr
Map 7 B2

Figure Skating School
24 489 492 | *mikefern@omantel.net.om*
If you've ice-skated in the past and spent the whole time tottering around the rink or clinging onto the side bar, it might be time to get professional help. Ice-skating classes at the Figure Skating School are available privately or in groups. A course runs for six lessons and group students also get six free practise sessions. Your final class involves a test and you're given a proficiency badge at the end of it. Prices per course are RO 33 for Pre-Alpha to Delta Freestyle 1 to 10. Private lessons cost RO 42 for six half-hour sessions, including a test in the sixth week.

Nr Zawawi Mosque
Al Khuwayr
Map 7 B2

Ice Skating Centre
24 489 492 | *mikefern@omantel.net.om*
Ice skating is the perfect way to keep cool – and active – during the hot summer months. The Ice Skating Centre will gladly accommodate requests for professional training for beginners and competitors alike. You can join a group or have private lessons. And once you've mastered the techniques you can take part in the figure skating and hockey competitions that are also held here.

Jetskiing
Other options **Beach Clubs** p.248

Much of Oman's coastline is open and accessible and jetskiing is becoming a more popular pastime here, especially along the coast of Muscat. Be wary of fishermen and swimmers; it's a good idea to remain 500m from the shore. In the past riders have been prosecuted for accidents involving jetskis. Most hotels and resorts hire out jetskis for about RO 7 to 10 for half an hour. Make sure you get a life jacket and a helmet with the jetski rental.

Kids' Museums
Other options **Museums – Out Of Muscat** p.174, **Museums** p.171

Children's Museum
Nr Qurm Ntl Park
Al Qurm
Map 8 C4

24 605 368 | www.omantourism.gov.om

The Children's Museum is a delightful place for young children to play and gain knowledge at the same time. The dome-like building is filled with numerous activities to foster inquisitiveness and inspiration as well as feed hungry minds and fuel imagination. Children will love it and parents will be thrilled to see their kids having fun while they learn. The facility encourages school groups to benefit from these educational opportunities and charges just a minimal entrance fee.

Kids' Activities
Finding activities to keep your kids occupied could end up keeping you very busy. Fortunately there are a few options available. Avid skateboarders who have PDO membership can go to the PDO skate park. Kids here are usually aged from 5 to 14, and they meet a few times during the week to skate together, show off new tricks and swap tips. The park has a specially constructed half-pipe, ramps and rails. Unfortunately, skaters without membership to PDO will have to stick to skating on the streets.

The British School Muscat also runs a few kids' activities and is the venue for meets for the 1st Cubs and Beavers and the 4th Muscat Brownies. You can call the school on 24 600 842 to find out more details.

Al Sawadi Beach Resort (p.30) has some excellent facilities for children in use throughout the year, including a kids' pool and a huge playground. During the summer the resort has a special kids' festival, where children can take part in arts and crafts, sports, and games while you relax around the pool.

Little Town (below), an indoor playground in Bareeq Al Shatti mall (p.294), opened in early 2009 to provide a space for kids to burn off energy while parents browse the shops or enjoy a coffee in one of the nearby cafes. It is open from 09:00 to 22:00.

Kids' Rest
Capital Commercial
Centre (CCC)
Al Qurm
Map 8 F4

92 358 583

Kids' Rest is a children's play area situated on the first floor of CCC (p.300). It's very popular with mothers of young children who can leave them here while they go off and do their shopping. Apart from a huge range of colourful, clean and safe toys, Kids' Rest also has a soft-play area for tiny tots.

Little Town
Bareeq Al Shatti
Shati Al Qurm
Map 8 A4

24 643 898

This play area in new shopping mall Bareeq Al Shatti (p.294) is a welcome addition to the area. It offers an indoor play area for kids aged up to 7, has a coffee shop for parents and is open from 09:00 to 22:00.

Name:
Carmen Soto

Occupation:
MSF Doctor

Dependants:
2800

MÉDECINS SANS FRONTIERES
أطباء بلا حدود

Kitesurfing

Other options **Beaches** p.176

Other options **Beaches** p.176

Kite surfing is one of the fastest growing extreme water sports not only in Oman, but in the region as a whole. With plenty of uncrowded beaches and superb wind conditions, kite surfing is definitely on the rise. The sport involves surfing the waves on a wakeboard while holding on to and steering a large kite that powers you along. You'll find a small group of kite surf enthusiasts who gather on Thursday and Friday afternoons at Azaiba Beach. This is a relatively quiet and sandy spot that offers perfect kitesurfing conditions when winds exceed 10 knots. Be careful of the occasional car or group of people wandering across the beach, especially in the early evenings – you wouldn't want to become entangled in them.

During summer, hardcore kitesurfers escape the relatively light conditions of Muscat and head for the east coast, where the winds often reach 15-30 knots.

At present there is no kite surf school or kite surf shop in Oman, but if you have a chat with any one of the regulars they will be able to offer advice about where to buy equipment and how to get started.

Dubai Kite Club
Dubai has an active kitesurfing club with an interesting website that lists some good contacts and places to get gear. For more information visit www. dubaikiteclub.com.

Language Schools

Other options **Learning Arabic** p.136

Other options **Learning Arabic** p.136

British Council

24 681 000 | www.britishcouncil.org/oman

The British Council in Muscat offers a variety of services with the main focus on education. The Teaching Centre provides English courses for adults and young learners, IELTS preparation courses, teacher training courses and special courses for contract clients. The Council's Education Information Centre also has a wide selection of information for anyone considering further education and training in Britain. Contact the Examinations staff for queries concerning British exams, copies of rules and regulations and syllabus details.

Al Inshirah Rd
Madinat As Sultan
Qaboos
Map 7 E2

Omani French Language Centre

24 697 579 | cfomct@omantel.net.om

This centre offers tuition in French at all levels (with official diplomas available from the French Ministry of Education), as well as classes in Arabic. A group of highly qualified instructors teach courses for beginner, intermediate and advanced students. Courses are run mainly in the evenings, although there are some morning ladies' classes, classes for children, and special tailor-made classes. Each course costs RO 30 for children, RO 40 for Omanis and RO 45 for other nationalities. To get a class schedule or more information about the courses, contact the above number. The Centre also has branches in Salalah (23 211 105) and Sohar (26 842 530).

Nr British Council
Madinat As Sultan
Qaboos
Map 7 E2

Polyglot Institute Oman

24 831 261 | www.polyglot.org

The Polyglot Institute Oman was established in 1975 and offers English and Arabic language courses as well as courses in translation services, commercial subjects, management seminars and training, computer tuition and national vocational qualifications. All programmes are approved by the Ministry of Manpower, Labour and Vocational Training. All Polyglot staff have qualifications and experience relevant to their own teaching subject, and English language teachers are all native speakers. The institute has another branch in Al Surror Street, Al Hayl, 24 541 545 (next to Omantel).

Nr Wadi Aday R/A
Hillat Al Sud
Map 12 C3

Libraries

Other options **Books** p.50, **Second-Hand Items** p.285

Biblioteque Francaise

French Embassy
Shati Al Qurm
Map 7 B1

24 681 874

This is a lending library and information resource for French books and videos. Biblioteque Francaise carries a wide selection of fiction and non-fiction literature by French and foreign authors, as well as magazines, French videos and children's books. Books are lent for a two-week period. The library is open from 16:00 to 17:30 Saturday to Wednesday.

British Council Library

Al Inshirah Rd
Madinat As Sultan
Qaboos
Map 7 E2

24 681 000 | www.britishcouncil.org/oman

Membership of this lending library allows you to access its electronic database and to use the internet facilities here, as well as, of course, to borrow books, DVDs and CDs. You may borrow two books per person for up to two weeks, and one DVD or CD per person for up to one week. Membership costs RO 80 per person per year. The library is open from 07:00 to 19:30 from Saturday to Wednesday, and from 09:00 to 12:00 on Thursday.

Knowledge Public Library

Nr PDO main gates
Mina Al Fahal (PDO)
Map 8 F3

24 673 111 | www.publiclibrary.gov.om

This library contains over 14,500 volumes, with a balanced split between Arabic and English. The subjects covered are mainly in the areas of science and technology, but there are also materials covering topics in the humanities and social sciences, such as environmental issues and Omani history. You'll find general encyclopaedias, language resources, dictionaries and atlases here too, and a video collection has been added to the library's resources.

Oman Chamber Of Commerce & Industry

CBD
Ruwi
Map 12 E2

24 707 684 | www.chamberoman.com

This small but well-stocked library has a range of reference books, periodicals, newspapers, trade and industrial catalogues and directories. Most are in Arabic, but there is a small collection of English books on business or trade-related subjects, such as economics, accounting, management and finance. An internet facility is available at a nominal charge and there are a number of CD-ROMS and business-related videos. You may borrow books from the library but you must pay a bond of RO 10 for Arabic books and RO 20 for English books, plus 500 baisas per book. The library is open from 07:30 to 14:30 from Saturday to Wednesday and from 07:30 to 13:00 on Thursday.

US Information Service Resource Centre

American Embassy
Shati Al Qurm
Map 7 C1

24 643 400 | muscat.usembassy.gov

This highly informative reference library specialises in US policy, legislation, trade data and social and cultural issues. In addition, the IRC offers students and researchers access to the internet and computer databases. There is also a reading section – the IRC carries around 20 periodicals in hard copy, including *Time, Newsweek, Business Week, National Geographic, Fortune* and *Harvard Business Review* so you can keep updated without paying the high cover prices of imported titles. Full text versions of more than 200 online journals and magazines are available. There are many books on American states, literature, art, social history and science, as well as information on Oman.

Martial Arts

Al Falaj Hotel Muscat
Ruwi
Map 12 D1

Black Stallion Martial Arts

24 702 311 | jonjuaguillons@yahoo.ca.com

Black Stallion offers a variety of martial arts classes for children and adults. Options include karate, taekwondo kicks, aikido, judo, nun-chacko, kick-boxing, Philippine arnis and gymnastics. Classes cost from RO 15 for children and RO 20 for adults per month, or RO 2 per session. Timings are from 17:00 to 21:00, Sunday to Thursday. Whatever your skill or fitness levels to begin with, these classes can help increase both your physical prowess and mental well-being.

Hummer Gym
Darsayt
Map 9 D4

Fit & Tough

99 629 490

Fit & Tough holds classes at the New Generation Fitness Club in Darsayt. The company teaches students at all levels and provides one-on-one coaching with street combat expert Jess Beltran. The classes will help you to gain confidence, develop strength (of the mental and physical sort) and improve your physique.

British School
Of Muscat
Madinat As Sultan
Qaboos
Map 7 F1

Oman Karate Tenshinkan Center

24 487 092 | www.tenshinkan.com

The Oman Karate Tenshinkan Center is affiliated with the Japan Karate Tenshinkan Federation. It's run by Hussam Nasser, a black belt fifth dan karate instructor who has trained in Japan and been well-placed in Arab championships. Classes are held on Sundays at the British School Muscat.

Motocross

Other options **Motorcycling** p.238, **Quad Bikes** p.241

Nr Golden Tulip Hotel
As Seeb
Map 5 A4

Oman Automobile Club

24 510 239

The Oman Automobile Club operates under the umbrella of the Oman Automobile Association (OAA) and offers many activities, one of which is motocross. The OAC has an excellent one-kilometre sandy motocross track complete with hills, jumps, twists and turns. It's terrific for learning on or sharpening your skills. Membership of the club is required and you need to provide your own bikes and equipment, although there is an area where you can store your bike for a fee. The OAC hosts a number of local and international rallies throughout the year, with off-road rallies held once a month.

Motorcycling

Other options **Motocross** p.238

Nr Golden Oryx Rest
Ruwi
Map 12 D1

Bikers Oman

24 789 680 | www.bikersoman.com

If you're a biker or a bike enthusiast looking to indulge your passion, or at least share it with other petrol heads, check out www.bikersoman.com. By joining this online biking fellowship you'll be one of the first to know about what's new in town, any planned bike rides, who's selling their lean mean machine, and you'll even score special discounts at outlets that sell biking gear, parts, accessories and souvenirs. New bikers can find out more about the tests involved and are able to hire a bike through the website for RO 5. Email contactus@bikersoman.com for more information.

Nr Zakher Mall
Al Khuwayr
Map 7 D2

Harley Owners' Group – Muscat Chapter

24 489 428 | www.hogmuscat.com

When the Harley Davidson showroom opened in 1998, the Muscat chapter of the Harley Owners' Group commenced its activities. The Harley Owners' Group (HOG), which includes expats and Omanis, meets at the 'HOG Pen' (coffee shop) in the showroom regularly and arranges activities, rides and events for Harley Davidson enthusiasts and their families. Rides are usually held on Tuesday evenings and Friday mornings and an overnight ride is organised at least once a month (in the cooler months). For more information visit the Harley Davidson showroom or check out the website above.

Mountain Biking
Other options **Cycling** p.220

Muscat has some great mountain biking routes – due to its location amid the rocky mountains along the coast, the city offers rides virtually from your door. There are many off-road tracks winding their way through the quiet areas, wadis and along the coast. The Bawshar dunes are close to the city and offer some great rides, as do Sayh Ad Dhabi or the route from the InterContinental Muscat to the desalination plant.
Riding in the mountains is adventurous and generally rocky, technical and challenging. There are many tracks to follow and the terrain is on a par with the classic trail areas of Utah and Arizona in the USA. Those who are just getting into mountain biking should start on the tracks in the gentler hilly areas. For hardcore mountain bikers there is a good range of topography, from highly technical rocky trails to mountain routes that can take hours to climb and minutes to descend. Be prepared and sensible – the sun is strong, you'll need far more water than you think and it's very easy to get lost or to have an accident.
Muscat Diving & Adventure Center (24 485 663, www.holiday-in-oman.com) now offers mountain biking trips. For more information on biking in Oman, or to get together with other mountain bikers, contact Muscat Cycling Club (see Cycling, p.221).

Music Lessons
Other options **Dance Classes** p.221, **Singing** p.244, **Music, DVDs & Videos** p.282

Al Ghubrah
Map 6 E4

Associated Board Of The Royal Schools Of Music

99 440 441 | www.abrsm.org

The Associated Board of the Royal Schools of Music was established in 1889, as part of an agreement between the Royal Academy of Music and the Royal College of Music. The board acts as an examining body for local music examinations and aims to improve the standard of musical education. It offers a scheme of examinations suitable for candidates at different stages of ability in all orchestral instruments, as well as in music theory. It also maintains a database of music teachers in Oman.

Nr Qurm Park
Al Qurm
Map 8 D3

Classic Music & Arts Institute

24 560 025 | musictec@omantel.net.om

The institute's team of fully trained musicians offers a wide range of lessons in piano, vocals, cello, Arabic violin and beginner oud, and classical and acoustic guitar. There are often other visiting musicians, and the institute is happy to connect musicians with teachers in the area. Costs are kept reasonable and children are encouraged to use their skills in ensemble work. Lessons are available for children aged 7 and above. Each child receives a report from their teacher and regular concerts are arranged for the institute's aspiring musicians.

Way 2235
House 1756
Block 222
Al Qurm
Map 8 D3

Daat Art Centre

daatart@omantel.net.om

The Daat Art Centre teaches basic musical skills for children in classes that cover listening, singing, playing the recorder, moving and creating. Children are grouped according to age and the classes are for 3 to 7 year olds. Adults can take piano lessons at the centre, as long as they have access to a practise piano. Lessons last for half an hour once a week and are taught on an individual basis for a fee of RO 7. Participants would typically sign up for a trimester.

Way 1952
Darsayt
Mutrah
Map 9 D4

Melody Music Centre

24 782 834

The Melody Music Centre opened in the mid 90s. Since then, it has obtained recognition from the UK's Associated Board of the Royal Schools of Music to teach both a theoretical and practical syllabus. Examinations take place for different grades, ranging from Preparatory Grade One to Grade Eight levels. It also offers classes in piano, keyboard, guitar, drums, conga drums, violin, carnatic vocal and classical dance (Bharatanatyam). The centre has another location in Al Khuwayr (24 486 647).

Netball

PDO Recreation
Centre
Ras Al Hamra
Map 8 E1

PDO Netball Club

99 536 596 | netball@yahoo.co.uk

Members of the PDO Netball Club include everyone from beginners to long-term players, residents and expats. Training and matches take place on an indoor air-conditioned court on Sunday nights from September to June. Sessions begin at 18:30 and run until 20:00. During the season, players are invited to represent Oman in the annual Inter-Gulf Netball Tournament, which features teams from Abu Dhabi, Bahrain, Dubai, Kuwait, Oman, and Saudi Arabia. It is best to contact the club by emailing the above address.

Off-Road Driving

Other options **Tour Operators** p.194, **Desert Driving Courses** p.221, **Camping** p.215

With vast areas of virtually untouched wilderness in Oman, wadi and dune bashing are activities many residents enjoy immensely. Most off-road journeys are on existing tracks to protect the environment from any damage – the sandy dunes and rocky wadis support a surprising variety of flora and fauna that exist in a delicate balance. Dune bashing, or desert driving, is one of the toughest challenges for both car and driver – it's also a great deal of fun once you've mastered it. The golden rule is never to go alone. If you're new to this activity it's essential to go with an experienced off-roader. Driving on sand requires very different skills to road driving.

Useful equipment to take with you includes shovels, strong tow ropes, a pressure gauge, foot pump or compressor, matting or planks of wood, a full tool kit for the car, a spare tyre in good condition, a car jack (with an extra piece of wood to prevent it from sinking in the sand), extra petrol and plenty of water for both cars and passengers.

If you don't think your driving skills are up to scratch, you could try dune bashing through any of the major tour companies (see Tour Operators, p.194). All offer a range of desert and mountain safaris.

Driving in the wadis is usually more straightforward. Wadis are (usually dry) gullies, carved through the rock by rushing floodwaters, following the course of seasonal rivers. The main safety precaution to take when wadi bashing is to keep your eyes open for developing thunder storms – the wadis can fill up quickly and you will need to make your way to higher ground smartly to avoid flash floods.

It is always advisable to go off road with at least two vehicles. If anything goes wrong, you'll be glad of an extra pair of hands and a tow. Although it requires marginally less skill than in the desert, when you drive in the mountains and wadis you still need to use your common sense and forward planning (you need to think ahead about choice of gears for the hills and river crossings).

Close to Muscat are the Bawshar dunes. Although this is a small area, it has numerous criss-cross tracks through the sand that provide you with an easy introduction to this challenging sport. When you're ready for more serious stuff, head for the Wahiba Sands, just over two hours from Muscat, for endless stretches of undulating desert. Or try The Empty Quarter (Rub Al Khali), which is spectacular in its seclusion, remoteness and the impressive size of the dunes.

The Hajar Mountains offer amazing drives through rugged mountain scenery. You'll pass remote mountain villages and freshwater rock pools as the rough tracks take you to incredible views up to 3,000m above sea level.

The better-known wadis are often over-visited, especially by tour companies. This is not necessarily because they're the best but because they are the easiest to get to. If you are more adventurous and are prepared to travel further, you can find some amazing, almost untouched places

For further information and tips for driving off road, check out the *Oman Off-Road Explorer*. This fabulous book features detailed routes, stunning satellite imagery, information on outdoor activities, striking photos and a useful off-road directory.

Quad Bikes
Other options **Motocross** p.238

The rough terrain and dunes of Oman's remote areas attract all kinds of motor sports enthusiasts. If you're into motorbikes, quads or dune buggies, and you have your own, it's easy to take yourself and a few friends for a fun day out – you don't run the risk of bumping into anyone else and you can explore at will. The Bawshar Sands, just outside Muscat, are very popular and it is a great place to fly your bike or quad off a dune. If you don't have your own quad, you can rent one at many of the hotels and beach resorts. Unlike dune buggies, quad bikes have no roll cages and therefore extra care should be taken. Where possible get training and wear protective gear to make the most of your thrills and spills adventure.

Exploring 4WD style

Rollerblading & Rollerskating
Other options **Parks** p.180, **Beaches** p.176

Rollerskating is an exciting sport that is such fun you often don't notice that you're getting a great workout too. Though it's not very common in Oman, it is growing in popularity and the good weather in winter makes it the perfect season to get outdoors. A good spot for rollerblading at night is the Embassies area, since it's fairly quiet and the road surfaces are smooth. Muscat's parks have long, wide walkways, although these often have interlocking tiles that make roller blading more difficult. Helmets, knee and elbow guards are highly recommended since falls can be hard.

Rugby

Salalah Youth
Sports Complex
Salalah
Map 1 F3

Dhofar Nomads Rugby Club
andrewlumley102@hotmail.com

Based in Salalah, this is a friendly club for players from anywhere in the Dhofar region. Membership is open to beginners and seasoned players over 18 years old who are interested in getting fit and keen to play seven-a-side rugby. It's a great way to meet people from all walks of life, and although small, the club still enters a team into the Dubai 7s every year. Training takes place at 17:00 on Saturdays.

Nr American
British Academy
Al Khuwayr
Map 7 E4

Muscat Rugby Club
99 821 782 | www.muscatrfc.com

Located next to the American British Academy, the Muscat Rugby Club is both a sporting facility and social centre. The club currently has over 100 members and they all enjoy free use of the facilities and free flights to away games for playing members. The club takes part in the Arabian Gulf Rugby League and several other tournaments, including the Bahrain 10s and the Dubai 7s. The season runs from September to April, adults play on Sundays and Wednesdays at 18:00, children aged 7 to 16 play on Mondays from 17:00. There is also a big social scene connected to the rugby club with regular events for all ages. Call Carl on the above number for further information.

Running

Other options **Hashing** p.230

Various Locations

Muscat Road Runners
www.muscatroadrunners.com

Muscat Road Runners meet twice a week and run competitively every Tuesday, with a designated race organiser responsible for timekeeping and results. Social runs take place every Sunday, where a member of the group hosts a run and provides refreshments afterwards. Summer runs tend to be short (usually not longer than five kilometres) due to the temperatures. Winter runs are longer, culminating in the half marathon in late February.

Bait Al Falaj St
Ruwi
Map 9 E4

Oman Athletics Association
99 359 802 | omanaa@omantel.net.om

The OAA's main role is to train the national Omani team in track and field events, preparing them for national and international competitions. The organisation also arranges local competitions – in activities from running to marathons – which are open to everyone. There are categories for adults and children and medals are awarded for first, second and third positions. The OAA maintains a list of contacts for all sporting activities, so if you would like details about a particular event or interest, email omanaa@omantel.net.om.

Sailing

Other options **Boat Tours & Charters** p.184

Sailing off the coast of Muscat is a wonderful experience, both in winter when temperatures are perfect for watersports, and in the summer when it offers a great escape from the scorching heat inland. Unfortunately, much of the club sailing in and around Muscat is closed to outsiders and the facilities are limited to employees of particular companies. That said, sailing regattas are held regularly and the people at Marina Bander Al Rowdha (24 737 288) and Capital Area Yacht Club (24 737 712) can give you more information on these. There is also the Oman Laser Association (p.243). This is definitely a sport where word of mouth is the best way to get information. Many companies will take you out for a pleasure or fishing cruise, either for a couple of hours or for a full day. Arabian Sea Safaris (24 693 223) and Muscat Diving & Adventure Center (24 485 663) both offer a wide range of activities. There are also companies from which you can charter your own boat – whether you take it for a single day or several weeks is up to you.

Various Locations

Oman Laser Association
24 678 759

The Laser is a popular one-man sailing boat, and in Oman Laser sailing is represented by the Oman Laser Association. The OLA has been promoting the interests of laser sailing and small boat sailing in general here for over 20 years. It organises around 10 competitions annually. The races are competitive yet friendly affairs, where the more experienced sailors readily share tips and techniques with others. Most races are held at the RAH Recreation Club, with occasional events in Sawadi Resort or the Marina Bander Al Rowdha. There are occasionally co-organised events aimed at expanding the Omani Laser fleet that include instruction for beginners and organised races. Races are organised at places like Al Sawadi Beach Resort, Civil Aviation Beach Club, Capital Area Yacht Club and Marina Bander Al Rowdha.

Ruwi
Map 12 E2

Oman Offshore Sailing Owners' Group
99 732 035 | clarkd@omantel.net.om

As the name would suggest, the Oman Offshore Sailing Owners' Group is an owners' network that has been formed to promote offshore sailing in the country. Based near Muscat, the group has an active fortnightly racing programme and plenty of social gatherings for owners and crew.

Sand Boarding & Skiing
Other options **Tour Operators** p.194

Head out to any stretch of desert in the interior of Oman, find yourself some big dunes and feel the rush of the wind as you take a fast ride down the sandy slopes. It's an easy sport to learn, it doesn't hurt when you fall, and you'll feel a real sense of achievement when you master it and glide to the bottom. Most people tend to use old snowboards, but you'll even find the odd skier taking to the sandy slopes. Standard snowboards or skis can be used. The best places for sandboarding and skiing are where you'll find the biggest dunes – the Wahiba Sands area or the massive dunes of the Empty Quarter in the south-west of the country. Many tour companies and camps provide equipment and direction. One of these is the Desert Camp at Wahiba Sands, which offers sandskiing or surfing from its permanent campsite. Call 99 311 338 for more information.

Scouts & Guides

British School
Of Muscat
Madinat As Sultan
Qaboos
Map 7 F1

1st Muscat Guides
dorothyhulse@hotmail.com

This group is a member of the British Guides in Foreign Countries, which is in turn a division of the United Kingdom Guide Association. The group caters for girls wishing to continue their Guiding while living overseas. The groups are open to all nationalities, but there is sometimes a waiting list and priority is given to girls who have been members in their own country. All of the packs base their programme on the British system to provide continuity.

British School Of
Muscat
Ruwi St
Madinat As Sultan
Qaboos
Map 7 F1

British Scouts

99 242 078 | www.omanbga.org

The Scout Association started in Oman in 1975 and acts under the auspices of British Groups Abroad. There are different groups for different ages: Beavers (ages 6 to 8), Cubs (ages 8 to 11), and Scouts (ages 11 to 16). The association focuses on outdoor activities such as camping, map reading, astronomy, cycling, first aid and conservation, and members can earn a variety of challenge badges. For more information, contact Sonia on the number above.

Singing

Other options **Music Lessons** p.239

Meeting the fish

British School
Of Muscat
Ruwi St
Madinat As Sultan
Qaboos
Map 7 F1

Muscat Singers

99 330 604 | kateclarkeoman@hotmail.com

One of the longest established choirs in Muscat, this group welcomes new singers from all backgrounds and nationalities. The choir covers a broad spectrum of music ranging from classical and light opera through to folk and jazz. Much of the singing is in parts and there is always a need for new members of all singing styles. The ability to read music is not essential but previous experience of choral singing is an advantage. The minimum age is 15 years, but there is no upper limit. The choir meets on Saturday evenings (starting from 19:30) at the British School Muscat. For more information contact Philip Brierley on the above number.

Snorkelling

Other options **Diving** p.222

A mask and snorkel are all you need for a fabulous view of Oman's awesome marine life. The number and variety of underwater sea creatures are incredible and the seas are pristine. You don't need much to get into this activity: a mask, snorkel, a pair of fins to motor you along and plenty of sun protection (a rash vest is a very good investment). Most hotels or dive centres will rent out equipment, and you can buy good gear at dive shops. Costs vary greatly so shop around.

Social Groups

Other options **Support Groups** p.129

Various Locations

American Women's Group

www.awgoman.com

AWG is an international social organisation which has been serving the women of Muscat for 30 years. It boasts almost 1,000 members representing over 45 nationalities. Meetings are held in local hotels and each one features a short programme, announcements of interest to the members, sign-up sheets for the various activities, and the opportunity to meet and talk with other women. See the website for the latest meeting times. For membership details and information please contact the Membership Chair by email.

Various Locations

Caledonian Society Of Oman
99 433 829 | www.britishschool.edu.om/caledoniansociety.htm

The Caledonian Society of Oman is one of the oldest expatriate societies in Oman, having been founded in the early 1970s. It's the only British society in Oman that's officially registered with the British Embassy, but it is also possibly one of the least known societies here. This could be because it doesn't hold regular monthly meetings, unlike the American Women's Group and the Women's Guild of Oman. What the society does is arrange annual events, some of which are purely for fun and others that are money-raisers. For more information, visit the website or contact Bill Henry on the number above.

Various Locations

The National Association For Cancer Awareness
24 498 716 | www.ocancer.org.om

Cancer survivor Ms Yuthar Al-Rawahy promised herself while she was under active treatment that if she were to survive her third bout of cancer, she would develop a patient advocacy group in Oman. The association's aim is to create awareness about cancer, teaching self-examination in order that early diagnosis can be made, and to help people to accept their diagnosis and work towards successful treatment. The association has met with much support from cancer patients, their friends and relatives and it is the first patient advocacy group in the country.

Qurm Information City
Madinat Al Ilam
Map 11 B1

Royal Omani Amateur Radio Society
24 600 407 | roars@omantel.net.om

ROARS was founded in 1972 and its membership currently stands at 188 people. The Society offers courses, limited to Omanis, who want to obtain amateur radio licences, and classes are held on Sunday and Tuesday evenings. Anyone of any nationality may join, as long as they have a current amateur radio licence from their home country. Membership costs RO 15 per year and the society holds seminars, expeditions, trips and social gatherings several times a year.

Various Locations

Women's Guild In Oman
24 516 433 | www.womensguildinoman.org

The Women's Guild has an excellent reputation in Oman for distributing funds to charities in the country. While fundraising for charities is an important part of the guild's aims, it also sets out to provide an opportunity for women to meet and enjoy a varied programme of speakers and events (including weekly coffee mornings and the popular Crystal Ball annual fundraiser) and to offer its members fellowship. Membership is open to women of all ages and nationalities and it currently boasts over 1,000 members. The regular newsletter is an invaluable resource for events around Muscat, containing news and classified adverts.

Softball

Oman Automobile Club
As Seeb
Map 5 A4

Muscat Softball League
99 337 593 | john_a_chappell@hotmail.com

The Muscat Softball League organises all softball games and tournaments in Oman. There are two divisions with women's, men's and mixed teams, and a children's league. The teams play on Sunday nights at 19:00. There are two seasons, one from September to January and one from January to May. All games are played on the fields at the Oman Automobile Club, which is equipped with changing rooms, a children's play area and a place to buy something to eat. Whenever possible the MSL also sends teams to participate in one international tournament each year.

Squash
Other options **Sports & Leisure Facilities** p.248

Shati Al Qurm
Map 7 E1

Grand Hyatt Muscat
24 641 155 | www.muscat.grand.hyatt.com
The Grand Hyatt's Club Olympus Fitness Centre has squash courts that are available for both games and coaching. If it's lessons you're interested in, call Mr Yousaf on 99 705 449 for more details – he will happily arrange coaching for players of all ages and skill levels. Lessons cost RO 15 for 45 minutes.

Summer Camps & Courses
During the hot summer months, it's very important to be able to keep your children active – and their minds off the heat. There are a number of summer camps and short courses available, but you should also check out what's happening at the hotels near you.

Nr Qurm Park
Al Qurm
Map 8 D3

Classic Music & Arts Institute
24 560 025 | musictec@omantel.net.om
The Classic Music & Arts Institute has dance, music and art classes for children all year round, but during the Easter and summer breaks it also puts on holiday camps. Its motto is to learn something new and have fun – and if there's an activity it doesn't offer, speak to the staff about it and they will see what they can do. It can also arrange birthday parties for kids, with dancing, art, and even DJ lessons.

Surfing
Other options **Kitesurfing** p.236, **Beaches** p.176

The idea of surfing in Oman may not inspire images of Hawaii style waves, but you'd be surprised by how popular the sport is here. And really, you generally have all the ingredients you need for a good day's surfing. Although it might not be one of the world's great surf spots, Oman is certainly one of the better places to catch a wave in the Gulf because part of its coast lies on the Indian Ocean. Surfers in other Gulf countries, like the UAE, often make regular trips to Oman to get their fix. While there are currently no major surf clubs in Oman, the Dubai surfers' group has an excellent website that gives information on surfing in the UAE, the Arabian Gulf and in Oman (www.surfersofdubai.com).
The eastern side of Masirah Island is one of the better surfing spots. It's easily reached by ferry from Sana on the mainland, followed by a short drive to the other side of the island. Ferry times depend on the tide. Wave sizes vary with the seasons, but the average is around four to six feet.

Swimming
Other options **Beaches** p.176, **Sports & Leisure Facilities** p.248

Most hotels have swimming pools that are open for public use. Day charges range from RO 2 (at Al Falaj) to RO 10 at the five-star hotels), but expect to pay a bit more at the weekends and keep in mind that the beach clubs tend to be more expensive. You can also swim off the beaches, whether at a public beach or hotel beach club. Remember to be modest in your choice of swimwear and to wear it only on the beach. The tides and currents here can be surprisingly strong, so do not underestimate them. With this in mind, take due care when swimming on quiet beaches. For your own safety it's better to choose somewhere with a few people around.

In summer, jellyfish can be a problem, both in the water and when washed up on the beach. All varieties can sting but one particular species, the box jellyfish, can be lethal. Stone fish and sea snakes are also not creatures you want to tangle with, but they're shy, retiring types and do tend to keep well away from the more populated areas. Swimming lessons are widely available and prices of these will vary.

Tennis

Other options **Sports & Leisure Facilities** p.248

Tennis is popular in Oman and you'll find courts available for public use at hotels, or courts belonging to private organisations that are only open to members. Many hotels have floodlit courts to allow play in the evenings, when temperatures are a bit lower. Prices for hiring courts vary between about RO 3 and RO 6.

The Oman Tennis Association oversees the national Omani team in tournaments at home and abroad. The association also organises a variety of annual local tournaments. These are mainly held at hotels and are usually for a mixture of standards, but some are for professionals only. You can get more information if you email bhingpaguyo@yahoo.com. Coaching is available at the hotels by freelance coaches and again prices vary. Expect to pay between RO 11 and RO 20 for an hour-long private lesson. Fathi provides coaching for groups, individuals and kids at the Grand Hyatt (24 641 155).

Crowne Plaza Muscat
Qurm Heights
Map 8 C3

Cliff Club

245 660 660 | www.cpmuscat.com

Resident tennis professional Vafu (92 35 22 04) offers coaching at reasonable rates for both members and non-members at the Cliff Club. A one-hour private lesson will cost RO 11 for members and RO 12 for non-members, or you can buy a package: five lessons for RO 85 (RO 90 for non-members); 10 lessons for RO 150; 20 hours for RO 330 (RO 350 for non-members). Group lessons are also available for groups of two to seven people.

Triathlon

Surprisingly, considering the extreme heat, training for and participating in triathlons is popular here. Clearly, enthusiasts of this sport enjoy a good challenge and Oman certainly provides one. Hash House Harriers clubs (p.230) are good sources of information regarding triathlon schedules. Events are also usually well advertised at hotels and in local newspapers.

Volleyball

The Bawshar Club has been leading the way for sport-loving women in Oman. It was the first Omani club to start a woman's football team and has now organised a women's volleyball tournament, in conjunction with the Oman Women Sports Development Committee (OWSDC). The tournament covered football, volleyball and basketball and was open to girls between 12 and 19. Call the Oman Volleyball Association for more information (24 705 567).

Game with a view

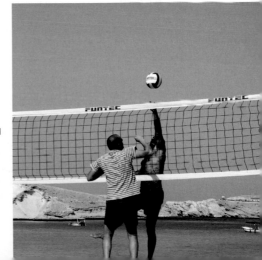

Sports & Leisure Facilities

Muscat's health and beach clubs are one-stop fitness and leisure shops. They are mainly located in hotels and include access to the beach facilities, the hotel health club and various activities. You can expect to find specialised instructors for everything from aerobics to salsa, and swimming to tennis. Many health clubs have separate facilities for men and women, as well as 'ladies only' times. Shop around to see which clubs offers timings and facilities that are best suited to you.

Beach Clubs

Other options **Health Clubs** p.249, **Beaches** p.176

Beach clubs offer a similar range of facilities to health clubs (see opposite) but with the added bonus of beach access. They are very popular with families at weekends, and offer a peaceful environment in which you can swim, play sports or just lounge in the sun. Most include some excellent food and beverage outlets, so people tend to stay for the day. Generally, beach clubs require you to be a member before you can use their facilities, although many also have day guest rates.

Club Membership Rates & Facilities

OMAN

Beach Clubs	Location	Area	Map Ref	Phone
Beach & Country Club ▶ p.29	Al Bustan Palace InterContinental	Al Bustan	15 A1	24 799 666
Cliff Club ▶ p.25	Crowne Plaza Muscat	Qurm Heights	8 C3	24 660 660
Club Olympus Fitness Centre	Grand Hyatt Muscat	Shati Al Qurm	7 E1	24 641 155
Palm Beach Club ▶ p.344	InterContinental Muscat	Shati Al Qurm	8 A4	24 680 000
Sheraton Resort Health Club	Sheraton Qurum Resort	Shati Al Qurm	8 A4	24 605 945
Health Clubs				
Al Falaj Health Club	Al Falaj Hotel Muscat	Ruwi	12 D1	24 702 311
Al Safa Health Club	Ramada Qurum Beach Hotel	Shati Al Qurm	8 A4	24 603 555
Beach & Country Club ▶ p.29	Al Bustan Palace InterContinental	Al Bustan	15 A1	24 799 666
Fontana Health Club ▶ p.321	Radisson BLU Muscat	Al Khuwayr	7 C3	24 487 777
Future Health Club	Opp Shati Cinema	Shati Al Qurm	7 F1	24 600 030
Health Club	Golden Tulip	As Seeb	4 E4	24 510 300
Health Club	Haffa House Hotel	Ruwi	12 D2	24 707 207
Health Club ▶ p.29	Holiday Inn Muscat – Al Madinah	Azaibel	7 A2	24 529 700
Horizon Fitness Centre	Moosa Abdul Rahman Complex	Al Qurm	11 D1	24 571 337
Sheraton Health Club	Sheraton Oman Hotel	Ruwi	12 F2	24 772 772
Out Of Muscat				
Bodylines	Al Sawadi Beach Resort	Barka	1 B2	26 795 545
Health Club ▶ p.29	Crowne Plaza Resort Salalah	Salalah	1 F3	23 235 333
Health Club	Sohar Beach Hotel	Sohar	1 B2	26 841 111
Hilton Fitness Centre	Hilton Salalah	Salalah	1 F3	23 211 234

For listings of rates, facilities and the contact details of Muscat's beach clubs, see the table below.

Health Clubs

Other options **Beach Clubs** p.248

Most health clubs offer workout facilities such as machines and weights, plus classes in anything from aerobics to yoga, while some also have swimming pools and tennis or squash courts. Many of the beach clubs also offer some sports and gym facilities so are worth considering if you want the added bonus of the beach. In addition to these, the Ras Al Hamra Club offers a wide variety of activities for PDO employees, and members are sometimes allowed to sign guests in for specific occasions or events.

Remember that when using the changing rooms of your health club, some people may feel uncomfortable if you do not use the private cubicles. Respect the modesty that prevails in any Islamic country, and always remain as covered up as possible.

For listings of Muscat's main health clubs, see the Health & Beach Club Table.

| Membership Rates | | | | | Gym | | | | | | Activity | | | | Relaxation | | | | |
Male	Female	Couple	Family**	Non-Member	Treadmills	Exercise bikes	Step machines	Rowing machines	Free weights	Resistance machines	Tennis courts	Swimming pool	Squash courts	Aerobics/Dance	Massage	Sauna	Jacuzzi	Plunge pool	Steam Room
–	–	–	2000	–	2	2	4	1	✓	✓	4FL	✓	–	✓	✓	✓	✓	–	✓
425	425	525	645	10	4	5	1	2	✓	✓	2FL	✓	2	✓	✓	✓	–	✓	✓
670	670	000	950	10	11	1	2	1	✓	✓	3FL	✓	1	✓	✓	✓	✓	✓	✓
750	750	930	1030	10	8	4	2	3	✓	✓	6FL	✓	2	✓	✓	✓	✓	✓	✓
180*	180*	300*	353*	7	2	4	1	1	✓	✓	–	✓	–	–	–	–	–	–	✓
230	230	300	400	4	8	4	4	1	✓	✓	1FL	✓	1	✓	✓	✓	✓	✓	✓
160	160	250	350	5	9	6	2	3	✓	✓	2FL	✓	–	–	✓	✓	–	–	✓
7	600	600	1000	–	–	2	2	4	✓	✓	4FL	✓	–	✓	✓	✓	✓	–	–
250	250	320	420	6	4	4	2	–	✓	✓	–	✓	–	✓	✓	✓	–	–	✓
195	195	290	440	4	3	3	1	–	✓	✓	–	–	–	✓	–	✓	✓	–	✓
250	250	350	350	3	3	4	2	1	✓	✓	2FL	✓	–	–	✓	✓	–	–	✓
150	150	200	200	–	–	–	–	–	✓	✓	–	✓	–	–	–	–	–	–	–
125	125	150	150	6	4	3	1	1	✓	✓	1FL	✓	–	✓	✓	–	–	✓	✓
130	130	365	400	5	8	5	3	–	✓	✓	–	✓	–	✓	✓	✓	–	✓	✓
280	280	380	450	5	9	6	2	3	✓	✓	2FL	✓	–	✓	✓	✓	–	✓	✓
250	250	400	520	5	3	2	1	1	✓	✓	2FL	✓	1	✓	✓	✓	✓	–	–
200	200	250	300	5	3	2	1	–	✓	✓	1FL	✓	1	–	–	✓	✓	✓	✓
200	200	250	250	–	3	2	–	1	✓	–	1FL	✓	–	–	–	✓	✓	–	–
180	180	230	280	5	3	2	2	3	✓	✓	2FL	✓	–	–	✓	✓	–	–	–

* Membership for 6 Months
** Family rates are based on two adults & two kids under 12

Well-Being

For some, it takes little more than the soothing sound of the sea to relax mind and body. Even if that doesn't quite do the trick, mental and physical well-being is easily obtainable in Oman. Whether you choose to set the tone of your day with a morning yoga session, or you want to fix your weight, skin or hair, there are a number of centres that can help.

Beauty Salons

Other options **Perfumes & Cosmetics** p.238, **Health Spas** p.252

Beauty salons in Oman offer a wide variety of treatments and one of the more unique experiences is to have your hands and feet painted with henna. This is a traditional art, mainly done for weddings or special occasions. The intricate patterns fade after two to three weeks. You can easily identify which salons offer henna painting by the pictures of patterned hands and feet displayed in their shop windows.

All the major hotels have their own in-house styling salons, which are open to both guests and the general public. Some of the more popular salons are listed below.

As Sarooj St
Shati Al Qurm
Map 7 E1

Angels Beauty Centre
24 695 811

One of the best salon experiences you'll have, Angels offers facials, body scrubs and wraps, crystal peeling, manicures and pedicures, waxing – the list goes on. The skin treatments use the Environ range of products and professional make-up and hairdressing are also available. The bridal packages are an excellent option for wedding parties. A must-try is the Moroccan bath, a long hot soak in water scented with various herbs.

Jawaharat A'Shati
Complex
Shati Al Qurm
Map 8 A4

Beauty Centre
24 602 074

The Beauty Centre is a salon that offers a range of treatments for your hair, face and body. Try it for facials, waxing and hairdressing. A manicure and pedicure (that includes a foot scrub) will cost you around RO 14, and a haircut and blow dry will cost RO 15 to 18.

Opp Capital
Commercial Centre
Al Qurm
Map 8 E4

Beauty Today
24 568 991

This beauty salon has an extensive menu of services, including facials, massages, and manicures and pedicures. The salon also cuts, colours, styles and blow-dries hair. It offers a range of bridal packages, perfect for the bride and all her attendants (and mum, of course). Beauty Today is open daily from 09:30 to 20:30, except on Fridays when it opens at 16:00.

Al Khandaq St
Salalah
Map 1 F3

Crowne Plaza Resort Salalah
23 235 333 | www.cpsalalah.com

Crowne Plaza Resort Salalah has now opened a five-star hair and beauty salon. Located within the hotel's health club, the salon is open from 09:00 to 19:00 daily. The treatments on offer include hairdressing (with advice on haircare if you wish), manicures, pedicures, herbal face packs, facials, body cleansing and other special body treatments, all administered by a highly qualified Chinese beautician.

Street 2333
Madinat As
Sultan Qaboos
Map 7 F2

DIVA
24 693 011

DIVA is one of the most established salons in Oman and, as a result, it's always busy. It is located just outside Madinat Sultan Qaboos, and offers a wide range of treatments and therapies to suit all requirements. All the stylists are trained to the highest of standards and offer the latest cutting and colouring techniques. Complementing the popular hair salon is a serene and relaxed beauty treatment area. Booking is essential.

Hana's Hair & Skincare Centre

MSQ Shopping Centre
Madinat As Sultan Qaboos
Map 7 F2

24 698 138 | maftrdg@omantel.net.ae

Hana's offers all the typical beauty treatments as well as extended services such as a skincare clinic, semi permanent makeup and hair treatments. Hana's also runs a slimming centre with a focus on weight loss, spot area reductions and figure corrections without harsh diets or gruelling exercise. Similar services for men are available in a separate part of the salon.

Hollywood Beauty Centre

Nr Qurm Private School
Al Qurm
Map 8 D3

24 568 292

This salon, located in the rolling hills of the Qurm area, offers a comprehensive range of services for everyday beauty and for special occasions such as weddings. It does hair, makeup, facials, manicures, pedicures, waxing and massage, and also offers Moroccan bath treatments.

Lucy's Beauty Salon

Al Asfoor Plaza
Al Qurm
Map 8 E4

24 571 757 | Lucysalon2003@yahoo.com

Lucy's is a quaint salon with experienced and capable staff. Nail and beauty treatments are available in a comfortable environment and the salon is conveniently located, so you can finish off your shopping or have a quick coffee before starting your treatment. Call ahead for an appointment, or you can try your luck and just drop in.

Muscat Beauty Salon

SABCO Centre
Al Qurm
Map 8 E4

24 562 541

The international and experienced team at this top hair and beauty salon will ensure that you get the very latest in cuts, colour and highlights. Meanwhile, its beauticians specialise in non-surgical facelifts, luxury Decleor facials, luxury manicures and pedicures, acrylic nails and much more. There are also treatments on offer such as hot stone massage and reflexology.

Nails

Jawharat A'Shati
Shati Al Qurm
Map 8 A4

24 699 440

As the name would suggest, this beauty salon specialises in hands and feet and offers a range of luxurious treatments from basic manicures and pedicures to luxurious spa treatments for your fingers and toes. You can have acrylic nails applied here, and if you're feeling ultra-glam, you can decorate your fingertips with real Swarovski crystals. It also offers massages so you really can put your feet up.

Raz Hair & Beauty Studio

Nr Centrepoint
Madinat As Sultan Qaboos
Map 8 D4

24 692 219

The proficient and well-trained team of international therapists at Raz Hair & Beauty Studio offers a full range of beauty and hair services. You'll find Guinot facial treatments and home care products plus exceptionally good nail extensions, along with the more routine salon treatments. The hair studio is a L'Oreal appointed centre and the full range of Kerestase home use products are available for purchase. Hair extensions, pieces and wigs are available to order. It has also added aromatherapy massage and the latest Diamond Medlift face and body treatment to its list of services.

Jawharat A'Shati
Shati Al Qurm
Map 8 A4

The Spa Bar For Men

24 698 681

This is the sultanate's first, and to date only, masculine oasis. At The Spa Bar For Men, the team is dedicated to offering excellent skin care and hand and feet treatments in a very upmarket setting, designed to appeal to all those men who see taking care of their appearance as part of their success. A manicure and pedicure costs RO 14 with facials around RO 24. A very relaxing environment in which to be pampered.

Hairdressers

Oman has a wide range of options for getting your hair done – at one end of the scale there are small barber shops where men can get a haircut and relaxing head massage for under RO 2 (if you're feeling brave, opt for a cut-throat razor shave for a few hundred baisas more).

For ladies, there is a choice of basic cuts in a beauty salon (a standard cut without blow dry should cost around RO 5 or less), and top-of-the-range haircare in a swanky hairdressers, where you could spend RO 30 or more.

Hairdressers

Al Hana Saloon	Qurm Heights	24 561 668
Angels Beauty Centre	Shati Al Qurm	24 695 811
Beauty Centre	Shati Al Qurm	24 602 074
DIVA	Madinat As Sultan Qaboos	24 693 011
Modern Barber Stores	Ruwi	24 561 704
Princess Beauty Center	Al Khuwayr	92 764 499
Raz Hair & Beauty Studio	Madinat As Sultan Qaboos	24 692 219
Wadi Centre Beauty Salon	Shati Al Qurm	24 563 321

Health Spas

Other options **Massage** p.253, **Sports & Leisure Facilities** p.248

Way 4429
Villa 2081
Al Azaiba
Map 6 C3

Al Jamal Health Club

24 490 526 | advantagecards@hotmail.com

Al Jamal offers a range of body treatments, but it specialises in massage. For more information, see its entry under Massage on p.253.

Al Kawakeb Medical
Complex
Al Ghubrah
Map 6 D2

Al Kawakeb Ayurveda Clinic

24 597 977 | ayurveda_oman@yahoo.com

The essence of Ayurveda is to preserve and enhance health, and to prevent disease through the use of herbs and natural therapies that have no side-effects. All branches of Al Kawakeb have separate treatment rooms for men and women. Here, trained masseurs work under the supervision of experienced Ayurvedic consultants to provide the best of massages and herbal beauty care. It also offers treatment for asthma, bronchitis, sinusitis, diabetes and skin and gynaecological disorders, as well as slimming therapies. There is also a branch of the clinic in Al Khoud (24 543 289).

Off As Seeb Street
Barka
Map 1 B2

Al Nahda Resort & Spa ▶ p.161

26 883 710 | www.alnahdaresort.com

This new, luxurious resort and spa in Barka is a haven of pampering for weary souls in need of some care. Whether you want to improve your fitness, lose some of those extra pounds, or just spend a few days of blissful relaxation away from the stresses of everyday life, Al Nahda's expert team of fitness and health specialists will be able to help. After you check into your beautiful villa or room on the resort, you can start your wellness programme and take the first step towards a better you. While at the resort, you can enjoy a healthy menu of spa cuisine, although a glass of wine or a big slice of chocolate cake is available too, in case you lose your resolve. A minimum stay of three days is recommended (but not compulsory).

Well-Being

Al Sarooj Plaza
Shati Al Qurm
Map 7 F1

Ayana Spa

24 693 435 | www.ayanaspa.com

Looking and feeling good is taken to a whole new level here. The Balinese-inspired decor, with its water features and soft background music, puts you in the mood for some soothing pampering. You have a range of personalised spa treatments for body and hair to choose from (and they'll just happen to do wonders for your mind too), plus the usual manicures, pedicures and massages. Treatments from the Institute of Biologique Recherché care for every skin type and condition, while the slimming programmes are executed by an expert team of professional aestheticians and therapists, using state of the art endermology, ultrasound and electrolypolisis machines.

The Spa at The Chedi

Shangri-La's Barr Al Jissah Resort & Spa
Al Jissah
Map 15 E3

Chi ▶ p.309

24 776 666 | www.shangri-la.com

Chi, the spa at the Shangri-La, offers Muscat dwellers a chance to get out of the city for a holistic, relaxing escape. The therapy rooms are dotted around the private grounds so guests walk through gardens and past fountains before reaching the relaxing villas. Don't forget to enjoy the Chi Water Oasis, before or after your treatment, complete with hydro pool, herbal steam room, tropical showers, ice fountain and lounge area. The hammam is particularly recommended but there is an extensive choice of signature treatments and half-day rituals to choose from, including hot stone massage, reflexology wraps and body polishes. Men are also well catered for with specialised facials. Appointments are essential.

The Chedi
Al Ghubrah
Map 6 E2

The Spa

24 524 400 | www.chedimuscat.com

As you'd expect from one of the most luxurious hotels in Muscat, The Spa at The Chedi is truly a retreat. Indulge in Asian-inspired rituals including the Himalayan crystal body polish, Balinese bathing ceremony and jade massage, or simply book yourself in for a pedicure. It's on the pricy side but guests of the serene spa will enjoy an utterly relaxing experience from the warm welcome to the iced mint tea. Open 10:00 to 22:00.

Massage

Other options **Health Spas** p.252, **Reflexology & Massage Therapy** p.217, **Sports & Leisure Facilities** p.248

One of the best ways to pamper yourself is to have a massage. Whether it is a regular weekly treat, or an occasional indulgence, it is a surefire way to relax body and mind. Health clubs and spas offer a variety of techniques to soothe your aches and pains, and the cost of a full body massage ranges from about RO 10 to RO 30 for one hour. Some of the hotel health clubs offer massages for members and non-members (at different rates). A 60 minute Thai or Swedish massage at Club Olympus, at the Grand Hyatt Muscat (24 641 155), for instance, will cost members RO 18, while non-members are charged RO 20.

Villa 2081
Way 4429
Al Azaiba
Map 6 C3

Al Jamal Health Club
24 490 526 | advantagecards@hotmail.com

This health club offers a Thai traditional massage for healthy bodies that want to keep themselves healthy and in top condition. Treatments cost around RO 10 for an hour. It also does Thai and Indian oil, foot and facial massages. You can also add a Thai herbal and salt scrub or a herbal steam bath to your selection of treatments.

Al Kawakeb Medical
Complex
Al Ghubrah
Map 6 D2

Al Kawakeb Ayurveda Clinic
24 597 977 | ayurveda_oman@yahoo.com

The Al Kawakeb Ayurveda Clinic specialises in getting everyone into excellent health. Among its range of massage therapies is a body slimming massage which costs RO 170 for one hour every day for two weeks, or RO 14 for a single visit. The massage uses special herbal powders, and it is claimed that you can expect weight loss of around five to six kilograms in three weeks. It also does fabulous head massages with herbal oils and luxurious facial massages using exotic creams. Other location: As Al Khoud, 24 543 289.

Pilates
Other options **Yoga** p.254

InterContinental
Muscat
Shati Al Qurm
Map 8 A4

Palm Beach Club ▶ p.29
24 680 000 | www.intercontinental.com

Pilates is a method of exercise that works on building your core stability and strength. It involves the use of apparatus or work on mats. The Palm Beach Club offers Pilates classes every Wednesday. The classes are one hour long and start at 09:30. They cost RO 2 for members and RO 3 for non-members, and booking is essential.

Reiki
Reiki (pronounced ray-key) is a hands-on healing art developed in Japan in the early 1900s by Mikao Usui. The word reiki comes from the Japanese words rei and ki, meaning universal life energy, and is used to describe both the energy and the Usui system of using it. The technique is based on the belief that energy can be channelled into a patient by means of touch and converted into 'universal life force energy', which has a healing effect. Like meditation, reiki can emotionally cleanse, physically invigorate and leave you more focused. You can learn the art of reiki to practise on yourself or others, directly or remotely. Reiki master Peter Emery Langille does all levels of attunements and is available for individual appointments, classes, group sessions and distant healing work as well. You can call him on 92 605 102 for information or to make an appointment, or email him on peter@divineconnections.ca.

Yoga
Other options **Pilates** p.254

Yoga is a form of exercise that benefits body and mind. A class usually consists of a series of postures and ends with a meditation session, leaving you feeling a bit like putty – stretched and relaxed. In Oman, you'll be able to sign up for classes at some of the hotel health clubs and one or two other organisations.
At the Grand Hyatt (24 680 000) you can attend classes on Wednesdays from 17:30 to 18:30 and Saturdays and Wednesday from 08:30 to 10:00. Members pay RO 2.5 and non-members are charged RO 3. The Palm Beach Club (24 680 660), at the InterContinental Muscat, offers stretch and tone classes on Sunday and Tuesday at 09:30, and Monday and Wednesday at 18:45. Muscat Oasis Health Club (99 320 466) also offers classes on Saturday and Tuesday 17:00 to 18:30.

The No. 1 off-road guide to Oman

The ultimate accessory for any 4WD, *Oman Off-Road Explorer* helps drivers to discover this region's 'outback'. Just remember your 4WD was made for more than just the school run.

Oman Off-Road Explorer
What your 4WD was made for

MAGIC CHOICE OF BOOKS

EXCITING CHOICE
OF *B*OOKS

Phenomenal choice of books

UNBEATABLE CHOICE OF BOOKS

IN FULL COLOUR

SPECIAL CHOICE of books

THRILLING CHOICE OF BOOKS

Encyclopedic choice of Books

BALANCED CHOICE OF BOOKS

FANTASTIC
CHOICE OF BOOKS

BORDERS ®

YOUR PLACE FOR KNOWLEDGE AND ENTERTAINMENT

Shopping

Shopping

Muscat is the shopping capital of Oman and offers a cosmopolitan range of shops and goods. From expensive boutiques to handicraft stalls and everything in between, shoppers are never far away from finding what they want. The fact that goods are tax-free means that items like carpets, textiles and gold are often cheaper than they are in other countries, while many imported goods fetch prices similar to what they do elsewhere. The key to shopping like a pro in Muscat is to bargain where possible or to wait for the sales when prices can be cut up by up to 70%.

Oman has some of the liveliest, most authentic and colourful traditional markets (souks) in the region. Distinguished old men in their dishdashas sit behind the counters in small shops, while bejeweled women in their abayas haggle with authority. Modern shopping centres, replete with global brands and ample parking, are pivotal social settings. They provide air-conditioned entertainment for a mix of nationalities that are there to see and be seen, shop or just pass the time.

Wednesday, Thursday and Friday nights are the busiest shopping times and it can get a little too crowded, even for the serious shopper. During Ramadan, some shops are open until midnight, supermarkets are packed to the brim with unbelievable amounts of food, and the queues are long, especially in the evenings. Many shops have sales during the annual Muscat Festival in January and in the months around the two Eid holidays, and there are invariably numerous promotions and raffles up for grabs.

This section covers the shopping areas around Muscat and Salalah, and some towns

Refund Policies

Some of the larger shops display their refund policies clearly (for example, underwear is non-returnable) and only allow exchanges for a limited period (usually seven days from date of purchase). Many international department stores are more proactive with their customer service policies, so it may be best to stick with the big name shops when you're looking to buy larger, more expensive items.

What & Where To Buy – Quick Reference

Alcohol	p.262	Flowers	p.272	Musical Instruments	p.282
Art	p.264	Food	p.273	Outdoor Goods	p.282
Art & Craft Supplies	p.264	Gifts	p.274	Party Accessories	p.283
Beachwear	p.264	Handbags	p.275	Perfumes & Cosmetics	p.283
Bicycles	p.265	Hardware & DIY	p.275	Plants & Gardens	p.284
Books	p.265	Health Food	p.275	Second-Hand Items	p.285
Camera Equipment	p.266	Home Furnishings & Acc	p.276	Shoes	p.285
Car Parts & Accessories	p.268	Jewellery & Watches	p.277	Souvenirs	p.286
Cards & Gift Wrapping	p.268	Kids' Clothing & Toys	p.278	Sports Goods	p.287
Carpets	p.268	Lingerie	p.279	Stationery	p.287
Cars	p.269	Luggage & Leather	p.280	Tailoring	p.287
Clothes	p.270	Maternity Items	p.280	Textiles	p.288
Computers	p.271	Medicine	p.281	Wedding Items	p.288
Electronics & Home App	p.271	Mobile Phones	p.281		
Eyewear	p.272	Music, DVDs & Videos	p.282		

in the interior noted for their traditional markets, telling you where you can find what you're searching for and how to stretch your rial to the max.

Refunds & Exchanges

In general, you'll have no problem in trying to exchange goods that are faulty or that you've changed your mind about as long as they are unworn, unused, still in their original packaging if possible, and you have the receipt. However, most retailers will only either exchange the item or give store credit; very few will refund you.

Shop assistants are always willing to help and exchanging goods is generally easy enough. However, if you insist on a refund it's best to ask to see the manager or to leave your number and ask the assistant to call you once they've discussed your case with their supervisor. It's likely to require some chasing up but with a bit of persistence you can sometimes get your money back. Getting angry rarely works; it's better to remain unfailingly polite. If you really feel you've been unfairly treated read about consumer rights below.

Consumer Rights

Taking a retailer to court in Oman is likely to be a very lengthy and costly procedure and will probably cause you a great deal more stress than the original problem did. Instead, try to sort things out with a compromise. Perhaps you can have an item exchanged, or a service upgraded? The key is to remain calm and, if you're not getting anywhere, you could try to involve an Omani friend in your negotiations. If the problem cannot be resolved, try the Oman Association for Consumer Protection. Its offices are at the Al Harthy Complex in Al Qurm or you could try calling 24 81 / 013. You might struggle to get through, but once you do they may be able to help you sort out your problem.

Go Big
It's easier to arrange for a whole houseful of goods to be shipped, rather than just a couple of boxes. What a great excuse to buy more!

Shipping

Sending purchases abroad can be a tedious business but there are many shipping and cargo agencies that make it easier. Items can be sent by sea freight (the least expensive option), air freight or courier. You'll find companies that offer this service under Courier Services, Cargo Services or Shipping Companies in the Omantel telephone directory, or in the newspapers' classified ads.

Shop & Ship

If you want to get goods shipped from overseas to Oman, check out the 'shop & ship' service offered by Aramex (www.aramex.com). It gives you a UK or US mailbox, and then ships the contents of your mailbox to you at competitive rates.

Most airlines also have a cargo service division, but your chosen destination may not necessarily be on their list of routes.

When buying carpets or furniture, some shops may arrange shipping for you. You should always ask what this will cost first – that antique wooden chest may not seem like such a bargain after adding in the shipping costs. Shops will sometimes issue a certificate stating that the item is worth less than it is to save you money on import duty. This is highly illegal, of course, but they seem to have no qualms about doing it.

How To Pay

International credit cards like Visa, MasterCard, Diners Club and American Express are widely accepted by established retailers in Muscat and Salalah. Small traders in the souks and local convenience stores only take cash, but some jewellery shops in the Mutrah Souk will accept credit cards. You might be able to pay with postdated local cheques when buying expensive items like cars, but this depends on your credentials and the vendor's reputation.

There seems to be a fairly relaxed attitude to accepting foreign currency and in many places you can pay with dollars, sterling or one of the GCC currencies (the UAE dirham is accepted almost everywhere). However, it's always good to carry some local currency with you, and there are plenty of money exchanges (see p.48).

Bargaining

Other options **Markets & Souks** p.291

Although bargaining can feel alien and uncomfortable for many visitors, it's a time-honoured tradition in this part of the world, one that both parties invariably get enjoyment from.

Outside of the souks or the stores in Ruwi, bargaining is less common and involves more subtle hinting than overt haggling. You can politely enquire if the price is 'before discount', or mention that you're paying cash. Sometimes even if you don't ask for a discount, the assistant will pass it on to you anyway, which can be a welcome surprise.

In the souk though you're expected to haggle and if you're paying cash you'll

Bargain Fair

After greeting the vendor, ask the price of the item. Whatever price he gives you, offer half and work your way up from there. Always remain polite – never use aggression as a bargaining tool. If the vendor won't budge on a price, try walking out of the shop; sometimes he will follow you with a better offer. Once you've agreed on a price, make sure you buy the item – you'll face an irate vendor if you don't.

find vendors will often drop the price substantially. In contrast to other countries in the region where you may be badgered into buying something after accepting a glass of mint tea, bargaining in Oman is less stressful and it can be fun if you relax and take your time. Sellers remain polite and don't normally push for a sale. The key is to decide on how much you want to pay for the item (scout out other shops to get an idea) and to be prepared to walk away if you don't get it for that.

Mutrah Souk

AMOUAGE

THE GIFT OF KINGS

EPIC

LEGENDS OF THE SILK ROAD ON WWW.AMOUAGE.COM

What & Where To Buy

You can get most of the things you need in Muscat although the shopping areas are rather scattered across the city and you'll need a car or taxi to move from one to another. The following pages cover the main categories of items to be found in Oman, and where you can find them.

Alcohol

Other options **Liquor Licence** p.66, **Drinks** p.338, **On The Town** p.338

Anyone over 21 can buy alcohol at licensed bars, restaurants and some clubs, for consumption on the premises. However, to buy alcohol for home consumption you need a liquor licence. You have to have your employer request a licence, which looks like a mini passport, on your behalf, and not all companies will assist with this – it depends what kind of business it is and their attitudes towards alcohol.

> ### Drinking
> Drinking alcohol in public places is not allowed and there are stiff penalties for drinking and driving. If you do decide to take a few drinks with you on your next wadi trip, be discreet about it and stay well away from any villages.

Muslims are not allowed to apply for a liquor licence. For more information on how to get your licence, see p.66 in the Residents section.

Alcohol is not sold in supermarkets but there are a number of bottle stores in Muscat. These are usually hidden away and there's no indication on the outside that these shops sell alcohol. Look for names like Onas, African & Eastern, Gulf Supply Services, and Oman United Agency, or ask around.

You can buy alcohol on the black market but it's a dodgy move and not recommended. And besides, the cheaper the tipple, the worse the hangover.

It's illegal to transport alcohol unless you're taking it from the shop or the airport duty free to your house (even then you should make sure you have a receipt in case you are stopped by the police).

Live. Work. Explore.

Log on to www. liveworkexplore.com for more reviews, competitions, offers, an online shop and a forum where you can share the best (and worst) about living in Oman with your fellow residents.

Alcohol		
African & Eastern ▶ p.263	Al Khuwayr	24 486 513
	Salalah	23 467 817
	Ruwi	24 799 045
	Madinat As Sultan Qaboos	24 602 121
	Magan	26 751 068
Gulf Supply Services	Al Hayl	24 422 199
	Al Khuwayr	24 483 122
	Madinat As Sultan Qaboos	24 696 869
	Wadi Kabir	24 810 709
	Wadi Kabir	24 815 678
Oman United Agency	Madinat As Sultan Qaboos	24 603 892
	Ruwi	24 704 031
	Ghala	24 504 109
Onas	Sohar	26 843 434
	Al Qurm	24 565 467
	As Seeb	24 538 401
	Ruwi	24 817 669
	Ghala	24 592 675

Oman's 5 most desirable locations.

HIGHWAY RUWI
BOBWAR R/A
HOLIDAY INN
Traffic Signal
AL MAHA PETROL PUMP

Al Khuwair
Tel: 24483050
Fax: 24483050

RADISSONS

AL FAIR
PIZZA HUT
CITY PLAZA
SHELL
Al Khuwair R/A

Madinat Al Qaboos
Tel: 24602121
Fax: 24602121

Al Hatat Hotel
POLICE STATION
TAXI STAND
SHAH NAGARDAS
KFC
From Bait R/A   From Ruwi R/A

Ruwi
Tel: 24799045
Fax: 24799045

SOHAR PORT   SOHAR BEACH
SOHAR IND AREA
MAGAN TOWN SHIP

Magan
Tel: 26751068
Fax: 26751068

AIRPORT
BAR1 R/A
AIRPORT R/A
HILTON ROAD
OMAN TEL
KFC
MUSCAT ROAD
LULU CENTER
24 JULY STREET
NBO SIGNAL
NBO SALALAH

Rafo Salalah
Tel: 23467817
Fax: 23467817

You'll find that apartments and villas close to african+eastern stores are particularly sought after. This maybe because we offer some the World's finest beers, spirits and wines. Or perhaps it's because people want easy access to our service and knowledge Saturday to Thursday, 9am to 1pm and 5pm to 9pm. Or possibly it's the fact that we can help explain how to obtain or renew alcohol licenses. Whatever the reason, whenever you see an african+eastern store, you know you've found just the right part of town.

african+eastern
drink. taste. enjoy.

P.O. Box 3022, P.C. 112 Muscat, Oman
Tel: (968) 24486496 Fax: (968) 24486514

Art

Other options **Art Galleries** p.169, **Art Classes** p.213, **Art & Craft Supplies** p.264

Muscat has a reasonable selection of galleries. These sell paintings, mainly, and a few selected pieces of sculpture, jewellery and pottery, often created by local or expatriate artists. Foreign artists and photographers with an interest in Omani culture and landscapes often hold exhibitions in museums and galleries; check the local papers or *The Week* for details of upcoming events. The Mutrah Souk, Capital Commercial Centre and Al Harthy Complex, the Omani Fine Arts Society, and the Bait Muzna Gallery are treasure troves of local and Arabian art. For more information, see Art Galleries (p.169).

Art			
Al Jawahiz Gallery	Al Qurm	92 154 827	na
Al Madina Art Gallery	Madinat As Sultan Qaboos	24 691 380	na
Bait Muzna Gallery	Al Qurm	24 739 204	www.omanart.com
The Omani Society For Fine Arts	Shati Al Qurm	24 694 969	www.omanartsociety.org
Raj Relics	Al Ghubrah	24 493 131	www.rajrelics.com
Yiti Art Gallery	Al Qurm	24 564 297	na

Art & Craft Supplies

Other options **Art Galleries** p.169, **Art** p.264, **Art Classes** p.213

Shah Nagardas Manji carry basic art supplies like oil paints, acrylics, pastels, brushes and drawing paper, and you'll find stores in Al Qurm and Ruwi. Serious artists are better off bringing their materials from home or ordering on the internet though as specialised supplies are hard to come by. When you're ready to display your work, the many framing shops in Ruwi High Street provide quick, professional and inexpensive service.

Art & Craft Supplies			
Office Supplies Co	Al Qurm	24 563 033	www.omzest.com
The Omani Society For Fine Arts	Shati Al Qurm	24 694 969	www.omanartsociety.org
Shah Nagardas Manji & Co	Al Qurm	24 562 656	na
	Ruwi	24 702 772	na

Keeping Under Wraps

Wearing a bikini on a public beach isn't illegal, but you may find yourself drawing some unwelcome attention. If that's going to irritate you then keep the bikini for the private beach clubs or hotels and stick to a one-piece in more public areas. A shirt or a sarong is always useful for a quick cover-up too.

Beachwear

Other options **Sports Goods** p.287, **Clothes** p.270

The beachwear you'll find in Muscat veers towards the no-nonsense, one-piece styles for competitive swimmers rather than teeny-weeny numbers for lounging around the pool. Bhs, Marks & Spencer and Monsoon have good ranges, but if it's something unique you're after you'll have more luck looking abroad or online. Sports shops carry a limited range of swimwear for kids and adults. You can get inexpensive Thai sarongs and fashionable imitation swim shorts for men in Mutrah Souk and on Ruwi High Street.

Beachwear		
Bhs	Al Qurm	24 562 456
Marks & Spencer	Markaz Al Bahja	24 536 035
Monsoon	Muscat City Centre	24 558 902
SLT Beach Shop	Al Khuwayr	24 489 303
Sun & Sand Sports	Muscat City Centre	24 558 355

Bicycles

Bicycles		
Al Muianee Trading	Al Amrat Road, Wadi Hattat	24 878 887
Babyshop	City Plaza, Nr Qaboos Signal	24 698 988
Sun & Sand Sports	Muscat City Centre	24 558 355
Toys R Us	Markaz Al Bahja	24 540 360

It's probably not wise to pedal down the Sultan Qaboos Highway, but there are plenty of quieter roads that are safe for cyclists. Mountain biking (p.239) is popular and a ride around the steep hills of the Qantab area will certainly give your legs a workout.

Books

Other options **Second-Hand Items** p.285, **Libraries** p.237

Due to the laws of supply and demand, the range of imported books and magazines available in Muscat is relatively limited. To bring a title into the country, it must first be checked for its content. Books that are deemed to be against the religious, cultural, political or moral sensitivities of the country will be banned. Of course, books can be ordered from www.amazon.com but packages are often opened and examined first.

Foreign newspapers and magazines are flown in regularly but are expensive. Magazines that contain illicit material are censored with the aid of a black marker pen, as opposed to being banned completely. Subscription magazines may take longer to reach you, as someone has to go through all the racy pictures of scantily clad women and dress them up with black ink.

Latest releases aside, there are some beautiful coffee table books full of inspired photographs of Oman and its people. These are really good for taking home to show people you don't live in a country filled with nothing but sand.

Prices for paperbacks are almost the same as in other countries. The large branches of Borders are very popular for their new releases, great non-fiction sections plus magazines and stationery. The Family Bookshop, Al Manahil and Turtle's cater primarily for English speakers, but also stock Arabic titles, and they both have a good selection of children's books.

Al Batra Bookshop stocks mostly reference books, hobby books, some children's books and older fiction titles. Most of the larger hotels have small bookshops that stock a limited range of fiction, travel books and books on Oman. Supermarkets like Carrefour,

Books		
Al Batra Bookshop	SABCO Commercial Centre	24 568 460
	Al Wadi Commercial Centre	24 563 662
Al Fair	Shati Al Qurm	24 561 905
Al Marifa Bookshop	Mutrah	24 713 607
Borders	Muscat City Centre	24 558 089
	Qurum City Center	24 470 491
Family Bookshop ▶ p.267	Salalah	23 290 027
	SABCO Commercial Centre	24 564 391
	Madinat Al Sultan Qaboos Centre	24 600 084
New Academic Bookshop	Ruwi	24 830 006
Sultan Center	Al Qurm	24 567 666
Turtle's Bookshop	Al Bandar	24 776 682
	Seeb Int'l Airport Holding Lounge	24 519 762
	Seeb Airport Arrivals	24 510 478
	Al Waha Hotel	24 776 820

Al Fair and The Sultan Center also carry a reasonable selection of books and magazines. If you can't find what you're looking for, you can order books online, although make sure you take into account the extra fee – the cost of postage may double the price of the book.

One particularly interesting bookshop is House of Prose in Al Qurm. A second-hand bookshop that stocks mainly fiction, travel and biographical titles, it has a buy-back policy that refunds half the price you originally paid for any of its books if you return it in good condition and can show the receipt.

The store's 'look-out list' is useful if you have a request for a particular title. The shop stocks about 20,000 books in Muscat and another 20,000 in its Dubai store, and books can be sold back to either store. Alternatively, the American Women's Group holds periodic second-hand book sales and exchanges.

Camera Equipment
Other options **Electronics & Home Appliances** p.271

Those who enjoy photography, whether as an amateur or a pro, will find a reasonable selection of cameras in Muscat. You may not find all of a brand's models in the range, but you'll have a fair bit of choice and prices are comparable to what you pay in duty-free stores.

Camera Equipment		
BOSCH	Al Qurm	24 566 557
Capital Store	Capital Commercial Centre (CCC)	24 562 254
	City Plaza	24 699 723
	SABCO Commercial Centre	24 563 542
	Salalah	23 297 910
	Markaz Al Bahja	24 545 532
Khimjis Megastore	Al Qurm	24 560 419
	Nizwa	25 410 415
	Ruwi	24 708 075
	Sur	25 540 214
	Salalah	23 295 671
	Sohar	26 840 232
OHI Electronics	Al-Araimi Complex	24 561 459
Photocentre	Capital Commercial Centre (CCC)	24 565 305
	Zakher Shopping Mall	24 479 296
Salam Studio & Stores	Al Qurm	24 564 071
Shah Nagardas Manji & Co	Ruwi	24 702 772
	Al Qurm	24 562 656
	Madinat As Sultan Qaboos	24 600 532
	Salalah	23 292 354

For the average holiday snapper there are plenty of choices. Most electronics shops sell a variety of film and digital point-and-shoot cameras. Sales staff are generally helpful and patient with even the greatest of technophobes. There is never any harm in trying to haggle over the price a little – you never know, it might just work, and you could get a reduced price or an extra or two thrown in for good measure. Most department stores also usually have some kind of photography section, with cameras from the likes of Nikon, Pentax, Olympus and Samsung. Professional photographers or serious hobbyists should check out Salam Stores in Al Qurm. The store carries medium format cameras, lenses and camera accessories, like Manfrotto tripods. The staff will also help you set up your darkroom, supply you with a Durst enlarger and train you in its use.

Foto Magic (now in Qurm City Centre) is a reliable outlet for buying and developing film and downloading images from digital cameras, and it has branches in most shopping areas. You can also ask the store to print pictures on greeting cards, mugs or T-shirts if you're looking for a personalised gift for someone.

A BOOK

IS A PRESENT

YOU CAN OPEN
AGAIN
A N D
AGAIN

Car Parts & Accessories

Cars are one of the best buys in Oman, with prices usually much lower than in your home country. This could be your only chance to drive a really luxurious petrol guzzler, rather than something more practical. It is almost de rigueur to own a four-wheel drive, even if the closest you get to off-roading is parking on the pavement. See the lists of new and used car dealers on p.138. Wherever there are cars, there will be accessories for them. Hypermarkets like Carrefour sell ranges including steering wheel covers, rubber mats, sheepskin seat covers and even little vacuum cleaners that you can plug into the cigarette lighter. The other outlets listed in the table are the places to go if you need tyres, spare parts, or if you want to transform your car to look like something from MTV's *Pimp My Ride*.

Car Parts & Accessories		
Al Aitibar	Wadi Kabir	24 814 115
Car Care Centre	Wadi Kabir	24 542 745
Carrefour	Muscat City Centre	24 558 140
Hisin Majees Trading	Wadi Kabir	24 811 442
Ibrahim Essa Al Sheti	Sohar	26 840 720
Opal Marketing & Industry	Marbella	24 453 044
Ramal As Sawadi Trading	Wadi Kabir	24 813 599
Sadween Trading	Wadi Kabir	24 837 570
Saied Mohd Al Naibi	Wadi Kabir	24 810 025
Scrap Collection Co	Wadi Kabir	24 811 600
Star Spare Parts	Wadi Kabir	24 812 376

Cards & Gift Wrapping

Other options **Art & Craft Supplies** p.264, **Books** p.265

The larger supermarkets like Carrefour, Sultan Center and Al Fair carry a good supply of English greeting cards, wrapping paper and stationery while specialist shops such as Carlton Cards can be found in the Al Harthy Complex, SABCO, Zaher Mall and City Centre. Birthdays and most holidays (Christmas, Easter, Mother's Day) are catered for and you can surprise your friends back home with special cards for Eid. The offerings here may be a little soppy or sentimental so if it's a wider range or a humorous card you're looking for you could try Carlton Cards or the Sultan Center. For some witty cards imported from New York, check out the stand outside Totem in Jawahrat A'Shati Complex. Cards with Omani themes, created by local artists, can be found in museum gift shops and at

Cards & Gift Wrapping		
Al Fair	Shati Al Qurm	24 561 905
Al Fikri Centre	Al Khuwayr	24 478 870
Carlton Cards	SABCO Commercial Centre	24 562 799
	Muscat City Centre	24 558 887
Carrefour	Muscat City Centre	24 558 140
Marks & Spencer	Markaz Al Bahja	24 536 035
Murtada AK Trading	Mutrah Souk	24 711 632
Sultan Center	Al Qurm	24 567 666

Murtada AK Trading in Mutrah Souk. Apart from costing less, they are good quality and make original alternatives to standard greeting cards. Creative expat Lucie Cruickshank (99 479 618) also creates hand-made cards for every occasion. While postcards can cost as little as 100 baisas, greeting cards and wrapping paper are more expensive.

Carpets

Other options **Bargaining** p.260, **Souvenirs** p.286

Weaving is one of Oman's major handicrafts and the skills have been passed down through the generations. Camel and goat hair, sheep wool and cotton are all used in weaving, either in their natural state or coloured with plant dyes or murex shells. Designs are usually simple stripes and occasionally geometric figures. *Traditional Spinning and Weaving in the Sultanate of Oman* is worth reading if you want to learn more about this art.

Carpet shopping can be a minefield for those who know little about it, so it's a good idea to read up about it first and to browse around a number of shops before committing yourself to buying so that you can get an idea of designs and cost. The price reflects the quality of the carpet, with silk being more expensive than wool or cotton. There's also a significant difference between hand-made and machine-made carpets – hand-made carpets will have some imperfections in the design and weaving, and are usually more expensive. The more knots per square inch, the better the quality of the carpet and the higher the price.

Carpets from Turkey, Iran, Pakistan, Central Asia and China are easy to find in Muscat. All of the shopping centres have at least one carpet shop, which is good news for those people who like to shop in an air-conditioned environment, and many of them sell authentic antique carpets from Iran or Afghanistan and will provide you with a certificate stating its age and value. It's not that easy to find good imported carpets in other areas of Oman, although Salalah and Nizwa may have a few stores.

You can find local carpets in the Omani National Heritage Gallery in Shati Al Qurm, or you can buy them directly from the weavers on the long, winding road to Jabal Shams. A 1.5m x 2.5m rug of sheep wool will cost around RO 30.

Bargaining is expected and you'll disappoint the seller if you don't even try (see Bargaining, p.260). The seller with elaborately roll out countless carpets for you to view, but don't let this make you feel obliged to buy. Once you reach an agreed price though, you're committed. Some shops will let their regular customers take a carpet home for a few days to 'try it out' with your furniture.

Carpets		
Al Azad Trading	Al Harthy Complex	24 561 645
Al Shabiba	Capital Commercial Centre (CCC)	24 565 552
Carpet Bazaar	Jawaharat A'Shati Commercial Complex	24 696 142
Gulf Shell Trading	Al-Araimi Complex	24 571 630
ID Design ▶ p.297	Markaz Al Bahja	24 536 638
Majid Carpets	Al Harthy Complex	24 565 750
Oman Heritage Gallery	Jawaharat A'Shati Commercial Complex	24 696 974
Oriental Carpets & Handicrafts	Al Wadi Commercial Centre	24 564 786
Persian Carpets	Al Wadi Commercial Centre	24 562 139

Car Dealers
See p.138 for a list of new and used car dealers.

Cars

Other options **Buying A Vehicle** p.138

New residents in Oman are generally pleasantly surprised to find that cars are much cheaper here than in their own countries due to very low import duties. All the major car manufacturers have their own enormous showrooms showing the latest and most expensive models and it's not uncommon for sales reps to pay you a visit at your new company, shortly after you arrive in Oman, to try to persuade you to buy a car from them. The dealers can take care of all the headaches, such as financing and registration, and can have you on the road before the ink on your signature is dry. Prices are never final so be firm if you're determined to close the sale. Remember, the dealer has paid the original owner a fraction of the price he is now asking you to pay. Good discounts are given towards the end of the year when next year's model is due in the showroom and during Ramadan. Japanese brands are popular and have an excellent resale value. Most of the big garages have a second-hand car section. When buying a used car, make sure you see the car's service history and check that it hasn't been in any major accidents or was damaged during Gonu. You can pay an independent garage around RO 30, depending on the model, to check the car for any mechanical faults. If you decide to avoid the dealership route, keep an eye on supermarket noticeboards or in the newspapers for used cars. Take an Arabic-speaking friend to the car market in Wadi Kabir on Fridays and you may be lucky enough to find a used Porsche or 4WD at a bargain price. Strangely, people occasionally stop each other at traffic lights or garages to ask if they want to sell their car – there's no harm in trying this if you see something you really want.

Clothes

Other options **Tailoring** p.287, **Beachwear** p.264, **Lingerie** p.279, **Shoes** p.285, **Sports Goods** p.287, **Kids' Clothes** p.278

Your fashion options in Muscat have expanded substantially over the last few years. This is largely thanks to the new Qurm City Centre (p.299) home of H&M, Monsoon and Next, and Muscat City Centre (p.298). This large mall is located quite far out of town past the Seeb Airport but with its array of shops that you may well recognise from home – Mango, Fat Face, Gap, Promod, Forever 21, Splash and Zara – it's worth the trip.

Clothes		
Bench	Muscat City Centre	24 558 048
Bhs	Al Qurm	24 562 456
Carrefour	Muscat City Centre	24 558 140
Giordano	Muscat City Centre	24 558 139
Hang Ten	Muscat City Centre	24 558 870
Jazz	Jawharat A' Shati Complex	24 695 965
Landmark Group (City Plaza)	Madinat As Sultan Qaboos	24 698 988
Lulu Hypermarket	Ruwi	24 811 449
Mango	Muscat City Centre	24 558 244
Marks & Spencer	Markaz Al Bahja	24 536 035
Monsoon	Muscat City Centre	24 558 902
Moustache	Jawharat A' Shati Complex	24 693 392
	SABCO Commercial Centre	24 562 589
Next	Muscat City Centre	24 558 801
Pepe Jeans	Al-Araimi Complex	24 571 162
Promod	Muscat City Centre	24 558 240
Safeer Hypermarket	Al Azaiba	24 496 019
Sana Fashions	Ruwi	24 810 289
Splash	City Plaza	24 698 988
	Muscat City Centre	24 558 981
Taalali	Mutrah	99 655 525

Stores here receive new stock every four to six months. Markaz al Bahja, past City Centre, has a Marks & Spencer and a few smaller shops where you can pick up some good bargains. Some of the places will do alterations if items don't quite fit. The Sultan Center has a small range of sportswear and hypermarkets like Lulu and Carrefour also have clothing sections where you can pick up a few bargains.

The Al Qurm shopping area contains five shopping centres and numerous shops within walking distance of each other. The Landmark Group stocks fashions for all ages and sizes and has a reasonably-priced accessories department. It also runs frequent sales.

There isn't yet a range of designer boutiques for women although men have been able to shop for designer suits, jackets and casuals at places like Tahani, Cerutti, Jazz and Moustache in SABCO for some time. Moustache sells a variety of men's designer gear including Armani Jeans, Damat, Dolce & Gabbana, Ferre, Trussardi, Tween and Iceberg. Jazz has begun to cater for ladies and now stocks Miss Sixty, Cerutti and Indian Rose. Capital Store carries men's suits by Loewe and you'll find Hugo Boss at Salam Stores.

Sana Stores and Ruwi High Street are good places to pick up textiles, saris and salwar kameez, but for something different call Taalali in Mutrah Souk for an appointment. Florence Rusconi, a French designer, reworks traditional Omani clothes into tops. Accessories are also available. You could also enlist the services of a tailor. Workmanship can vary but generally the quality is very high for the amount you pay. If you take along your fabric and a photo, drawing or sample of what you want, a tailor will copy it. Good sales are generally held during Ramadan and the Eid holidays, but also in January and September/October when shops are clearing old stock. Discounts of 70% are not uncommon, but be prepared to sort through a rack of odd sizes and last season's styles.

Computers
Other options **Electronics & Home Appliances** p.271

You'll find plenty of computer shops with stock up to the ceilings and knowledgeable staff in Muscat. The best of these are in Al Wadi Centre in Al Qurm, Computer Street in Ruwi and Carrefour in Qurm City Centre (p.299) which often has good deals on laptops. You'll also find E-Max at Muscat City Centre (p.298) which is fairly cheap and there are authorised dealers for Apple in Al Harthy Complex, and Dell Computers on the Al Khuwayr slip road.

Computers		
Al Morsad Trading Est.	Al-Araimi Complex	24 562 118
Carrefour	Muscat City Centre	24 558 140
Computer Point	SABCO Commercial Centre	24 565 848
Computer Xpress	Ruwi	24 835 631
Faisal Al Alawi Trading	Ruwi	24 702 812

Prices aren't bad, but you must bargain before agreeing on a price. You can also strike a deal where a vendor will get you a PC, printer, scanner, desk and chair (depending of course on what you want), bring it all round and install it for you. Getting computers fixed is easy and usually cheap, but you may get frustrated at deadlines that aren't met.

Outside Muscat you won't find much in terms of technology and may have to wait a long time for anything you've ordered.

The Omani government has been clamping down on the sale of pirated software since it became a member of the World Trade Organisation. However, you can still find copies of PC and Playstation games in small shops in Ruwi and Al Qurm for as little as RO 1 if you're happy to turn a blind eye.

Electronics & Home Appliances
Other options **Computers** p.271, **Camera Equipment** p.266

Electronics & Home Appliances		
Capital Store	City Plaza	24 699 723
	As Seeb	24 545 532
	Salalah	23 297 910
	Al Qurm	24 562 254
	Al Qurm	24 563 542
Carrefour	As Seeb	24 558 140
Lulu Hypermarket	Al Khuwayr	24 504 504
	Ruwi	24 701 401
Muscat Electronics Co	Ruwi	24 796 243
OHI Electronics	Al Qurm	24 561 459
Salam Studio & Stores	Al Qurm	24 564 071
Salman Stores	Mutrah	24 796 925
	As Seeb	24 422 213
	Al Qurm	24 566 286
	Al Qurm	24 560 135
	Salalah	23 293 146
Sony	Al Qurm	24 564 485

Muscat's shops stock a reasonable selection of electronics and home appliances, from well-known brands to knock-offs. Prices are competitive and can be brought down even further by bargaining. Wide screen televisions and home theatres are bargains compared to back home, although it's still smart to shop around.

The branches of Carrefour in Muscat and Qurm City Centres have a wide range of inexpensive items, which is great for people furnishing a house without a company allowance, but prices here are fixed. Larger appliances such as washing machines and fridges are delivered and installed free of charge and a 12 month warranty is given on most items. Ruwi High Street is good for browsing and comparing prices as all the showrooms are here. If you don't see what you're looking for, ask, as it may be hidden in the back room.

If you live in Salalah you can usually find good deals on appliances in town, so there's no need to go all the way to Muscat. Warranties, after-sales service, delivery and installation should all be discussed before you buy. If you're intending to take anything overseas with you, confirm its compatibility with the power supply. Check noticeboards or classifieds for second-hand items. Expats who are leaving often sell things at reasonable prices in order to clear them quickly. This is especially good if you're looking for large appliances or air conditioners.

Eyewear

Other options **Opticians** p.126, **Sports Goods** p.287

Life in Oman is definitely easier with a pair of sunglasses. The strength of the sun, the days at the beach and the long drives mean you're going to want to protect your eyes. All kinds of sunglasses are available in the malls, in Ruwi and in the souk, from designer eyewear to rip-offs and everything in between. Prices range from a few rials to many hundreds but as competition is fierce you can often find a good bargain in designer shades. Make sure they offer 100% UVA and UVB protection and are large and dark enough to protect your eyes from the sun's glare. Polarised lenses are particularly good if you spend a lot of time on the water. Shopping centres have opticians that will make prescription eyeglasses, prescription sunglasses and contact lenses (hard, soft, gas permeable and thoric). They usually offer free eye tests if you order from them. Disposable contact lenses and coloured contact lenses are also available. You'll find lens cleaning solutions at opticians and pharmacies.

Eyewear		
Al Ghazal Opticians	SABCO Commercial Centre	24 563 546
Al Said Optics	Capital Commercial Centre (CCC)	24 566 272
Grand Optics	Muscat City Centre	24 558 890
Gulf Eyes	Al Harthy Complex	24 560 867
Gulf Optical Centre	Al Harthy Complex	24 565 261
Hassan Opticals Co	Al Harthy Complex	24 565 499
Oman Opticals	Al Khamis Plaza	24 562 981
Ridwan	Capital Commercial Centre (CCC)	24 564 027
Yateem Opticians	Al Khamis Plaza	24 563 716

Flowers

Other options **Plants & Gardens** p.284

Given Oman's desert climate, flowers are a real luxury – which means they make a really nice present for a special occasion or for someone you love. There's a reasonable selection of florists in Al Qurm – ones worth mentioning are Caravan in the Al-Harthy Complex and The Flower Shop in SABCO. Bella La Rose in Capital Commercial Centre specialises in (you guessed it) roses, and a stunning arrangement of 10 roses sprinkled with gold dust is reasonably priced at around RO 8. Simple bouquets can be bought at Sultan Center, Al Fair and Carrefour, and cost between RO 2 and RO 7, depending on the number and kind of flowers included.

It's usually cheaper and quicker to send flowers internationally via the internet than to use a local florist.

Flowers		
Al Fair	Shati Al Qurm	24 561 905
Angel Flowers	Ramada Qurum Beach Hotel	24 605 158
Bella La Rose	Capital Commercial Centre (CCC)	24 566 766
Caravans	Al Harthy Complex	24 566 795
Carrefour	Muscat City Centre	24 558 140
The Flower Shop	SABCO Commercial Centre	24 560 043
La Bonita	Markaz Al Bahja	24 535 197
Sultan Center	Al Qurm	24 567 666

What & Where To Buy

Food

Other options **Health Food** p.275

Oman has a good range of supermarkets and grocery shops that cater to its multinational population's culinary needs. Although there are some speciality items that you won't find, most things are available somewhere if you look hard enough or ask your friends. Prices vary considerably, even among supermarkets. Imported items are sometimes double what they would cost in their country of origin, and locally made equivalents are much cheaper and just as good.

Carrefour (Qurm and Muscat City Centres), the Sultan Center, Lulu Hypermarket and Al Fair are the biggest and most popular supermarkets. The smaller ones, like Al Jadeed, Pic n Save and Family Supermarket, might not be as well laid out, but they do carry a wide range of goods that's sometimes even cheaper than you'll find in the hypermarkets. During Ramadan, mountains of food, both fresh and tinned, are on sale. They seem to specialise in feeding large families; products are bundled up with sticky tape and sold for a rial so it's a good time to stock up on non-perishables.

Carrefour, the well known French hypermarket, sells everything from laptops and French cheeses to shoes and stationery. It has an excellent selection of fresh fruits, vegetables, meats and seafood and a good bakery where

Food		
Al Fair	Zakher Shopping Mall	24 482 047
	Markaz Al Bahja	24 543 243
	Capital Commercial Centre (CCC)	24 561 750
	Madinat As Sultan Qaboos	24 698 174
	Ruwi	24 702 246
	Shati Al Qurm	24 561 905
Al Jadeeda Supermarket	Al Khuwayr	24 601 010
Carrefour	Muscat City Centre	24 558 140
Family Shopping Centre	Ruwi	24 799 635
Godiva Chocolates	SABCO Commercial Centre	24 562 367
Lulu Hypermarket	Al Ghubrah	24 504 504
	Sohar	26 843 040
	Al Khuwayr	24 504 504
	Ruwi	24 811 449
Patchi	Muscat City Centre	24 558 032
Pic n Save	Al Khuwayr	24 479 211
Spinneys	Al Sarooj Commercial Centre	24 607 075
Sultan Center	Al Qurm	24 567 666

croissants, baguettes, European style breads, cakes, and Arabic and Indian sweets are made on the premises. It also stocks a small selection of Filipino and Indian foods. Al Fair supermarket, with branches in Al Qurm, Madinat Sultan Qaboos, Al Sarooj and Zakher Mall, is favoured by expats for its British, European and Asian foods. It's the only supermarket that sells frozen pork and pork products like paté, proscuitto, salami and ham. Al Fair also has a 'Monday Market' when special items are on sale. The Lulu Hypermarket in Al Ghubrah has a good fresh produce section selling fresh Thai herbs and grated coconut.

There are plenty of local convenience stores in residential areas, some of which have a small produce section with onions, garlic, ginger and a small range of vegetables. Petrol stations have also entered the market with their own forecourt shops – these little shops sell necessities from quick, hot snacks to washing powder, and some are open 24 hours a day. Look out for Select shops at Shell stations, and Souk shops at Al Maha.

Fruit & Vegetables

A lot of fresh fruits, vegetables and herbs are used in Middle Eastern cuisine, and produce coming from this region can be amazingly cheap. A box of Jordanian oranges, for example, costs as little as one rial – a bonus for people who love freshly

Chatting in the souk

squeezed orange juice. Excluding imported fresh produce, fruits and vegetables are, in general, very affordable, especially if bought from places like the fruit and vegetable markets in Wadi Kabir in Ruwi, Mutrah and Al Mawaleh on the road to Nizwa.

Fish

If you get to the Mutrah fish souk early in the morning you'll find the freshest catches straight off the boat. A browse among the stalls reveals an amazing variety of fish and seafood, some still squirming or struggling to get out of the baskets. Fishermen in the Azaiba beach area may also sell their daily catch to you. The larger supermarkets carry fresh seafood and fish (whole, filleted or in steaks), in slightly less-smelly surroundings.

Vegetarians

Vegetarians shouldn't have too much difficulty finding suitable products in Oman. Fresh and imported fruits and vegetables are widely available and cheap, especially in open-air markets. Spices and nuts imported from all over the world are sold by the scoop in large supermarkets. Al Fair also carries some soya based products, but the choice is limited.

Gifts

Most expats enjoy a high standard of living in Muscat, with more disposable income to spend on gadgets and luxuries for themselves. Therefore it can be quite a challenge to find gifts for your expat friends who already seem to have everything. Fortunately, there are plenty of unusual items to choose from, whether you choose something modern that you could find anywhere in the world, or whether you go for something traditionally Arabian.

It is much easier to buy gifts for your friends and family back home, since you can go for the souvenir-type items that are always a hit. For something particularly special, you could buy a beautiful hand-crafted piece of Omani silver jewellery or a genuine silver khanjar dagger.

Most shops issue gift vouchers, and it is also possible in some malls to get shopping mall vouchers that allow you to use the vouchers in any outlet within that mall. Enquire at the information desk. Of course, if you can't find what you're looking for in the many shops of Oman, you can always go for the online gift-shopping option. The advantage is that sites like www.amazon.com and www.giftexpress.com will take care of delivery for you if you are buying something for someone back home.

Gifts

Gifts		
Carlton Cards	SABCO Commercial Centre	24 562 799
	Muscat City Centre	24 558 887
China City	Ruwi	24 799 506
Claire's Accessories	Muscat City Centre	24 558 846
Godiva Chocolates	SABCO Commercial Centre	24 562 367
Gulf Shell Trading	Al-Araimi Complex	24 571 630
JK Enterprises	Alasfoor Plaza	24 560 977
Lifestyle	Muscat City Centre	24 558 981
Majid Trading	Al-Araimi Complex	24 563 098
Marks & Spencer	Markaz Al Bahja	24 536 035
Next	Muscat City Centre	24 558 801
Silver World	Mutrah Souk	24 714 373
Tiffany & Co	Salalah	23 211 976
	Jawahir Oman	24 565 301

Handbags

Handbags		
Capital Store	Salalah	23 297 910
	City Plaza	24 699 723
	SABCO Commercial Centre	24 563 542
	Markaz Al Bahja	24 545 532
	Capital Commercial Centre (CCC)	24 562 254
Carrefour	Muscat City Centre	24 558 140
Lifestyle	Muscat City Centre	24 558 981
Mango	Muscat City Centre	24 558 244
Marks & Spencer	Markaz Al Bahja	24 536 035
Monsoon	Muscat City Centre	24 558 902
Next	Muscat City Centre	24 558 801
Salman Stores	Mutrah	24 796 925
	Al-Araimi Complex	24 566 286
	Capital Commercial Centre (CCC)	24 560 135
	Salalah	23 293 146
	As Seeb	24 422 213
Splash	Muscat City Centre	24 558 981

Local ladies love their accessories– the humble handbag has become a major status symbol, especially since it is often the only item visible when dressed in the long black abaya. As a result, you can get some amazing creations (both in terms of craftmanship and price) at various exclusive boutiques around town plus stores like Zara, Forever 21 and Accessorize. For the less label conscious, handbags are sold in most fashion, luggage and accessories shops, and even in supermarkets like Carrefour – so keep your eyes peeled for fab bags next time you're doing your grocery shopping. Capital Store sells a range of Givenchy handbags.

Hardware & DIY

Other options **Outdoor Goods** p.282

DIY enthusiasts will find Honda Street in Ruwi a veritable paradise. It's one long street of nothing but hardware, tools, paints and construction materials, from washers to entire bathroom suites in marble. Parking can be a problem, particularly on

Hardware & DIY		
Carrefour	Muscat City Centre	24 558 140
Durrat Al Sahil Est.	Al Ghubrah	24 592 232
Lulu Hypermarket	Al Ghubrah	24 504 504
	Ruwi	24 701 401
Safeer Hypermarket	Al Azaiba	24 496 019
	Al Azaiba	24 591 677
Souk Al Khuwayr	Al Khuwayr	na
Sultan Center	Al Qurm	24 567 666

Thursdays. Carrefour, Sultan Center, Safeer and Lulu Hypermarket also have some good DIY equipment, but the smaller shops are sometimes better because you can negotiate the price. The shops have counters directly inside the door, so you have to ask for what you want rather than browse around for it. If you are not inclined to put up your own shelves, enquire at the shops and someone will come round and do it for a couple of rials. DIY furniture bought in Home Centre is assembled in your home for free.

Health Food

Other options **Health Clubs** p.249, **Food** p.273

Health Food		
Al Fair	Shati Al Qurm	24 561 905
	Capital Commercial Centre (CCC)	24 561 750
General Nutrician Centre (GNC)	Muscat City Centre	24 558 222
Muscat Pharmacy	Ruwi	24 814 501
Sport One	Capital Commercial Centre (CCC)	24 563 230
Sultan Center	Al Qurm	24 567 666

While you won't find quite the same range of organic, bio and health foods that you'll find in your home country, things are improving in Oman. Al Fair has some non-dairy, low fat, low calorie products but these are usually mixed in with the regular items. The Sultan Center also has a very limited range in its dietetic section.

GNC in Muscat City Centre stocks a comprehensive range of nutritional supplements and alternative remedies – it also offers a membership option where for just RO 3, you'll get a card which gives you 20% discount on all purchases during the first week of every month. Muscat Pharmacy, and The Health Store in the Capital Commercial Centre, also stock nutritional supplements and gym enthusiasts who swear by protein and food supplements should check out Sport One, also in CCC. The supermarkets have a limited selection of multivitamins for kids and adults, but it's good to check the sell-by dates.

Home Furnishings & Accessories
Other options **Hardware & DIY** p.275

It is possible to furnish a house quite cheaply in Oman although you may have trouble finding what you want if your tastes run to the minimalist or modern.
A great new addition is Gecko in Jawaharat A'Shati mall, where you'll find pieces imported from Bali, in addition to gorgeous fabrics from Designer's Guild and the ever-popular Fatboy beanbags in a range of sizes and styles.
On the Al Khuwayr service road, parallel to Sultan Qaboos Street, you'll find vast stores selling what Europeans call 'Arabic style' furniture, although confusingly Arabs call it 'European style'. Regardless of what it's called, think statuesque horses and mirrors looming over you on your headboard and bright sofas with silver lion-claw legs. You can dilute the gaudiness of these pieces by ordering them in different colours or sizes to those on display in the showroom. These shops also stock curtains and orthopaedic mattresses.

Home Furnishings & Accessories

Al Batna Commercial Centre (Antiques)	Capital Commercial Centre (CCC)	24 560 284
Bartech	Jawharat A' Shati Complex	24 601 280
Bombay	Markaz Al Bahja	24 545 658
Duniya Stores (Antiques)	Capital Commercial Centre (CCC)	24 561 609
Fahmy Furniture	Al Khuwayr	24 489 812
Furniture Village	Ruwi	24 481 701
Gecko	Jawaharat A'Shati Commercial Complex	24 461 181
Home Centre	Centrepoint, City Plaza	24 698 988
Hyat Furniture	Al Khuwayr	24 478 664
ID Design ▶ p.297	Markaz Al Bahja	24 536 638
International Golden Furniture (IGF)	Salalah	23 293 225
	Madinat As Sultan Qaboos	24 604 533
Lifestyle	Muscat City Centre	24 558 981
Maathir	Al-Araimi Complex	24 562 585
Marina Gulf Trading Co	Al-Araimi Complex	24 562 221
Najeeb Alla Baksh (Antiques)	Capital Commercial Centre (CCC)	24 564 415
The Shuram Group	Jawharat Shopping Complex	24 600 919
Tahani Antiques	Al Khuwayr	24 601 866
Tavola	Sultan Madinat Qaboos	24 605 630
Teejan Furnishing	Nizwa	25 410 292
	Al Hayl	24 535 195
	Ruwi	24 835 825
	Al Khuwayr	24 489 490
United Furniture Co	Madinat As Sultan Qaboos	24 603 416
Villeroy & Boch	Muscat City Centre	24 558 001

Home Centre, Centrepoint and a Danish shop, ID Design, in Markaz al Bahja that sells Scandinavian furniture are all popular. These large stores generally have good sales during Ramadan and around September. While Muscat doesn't have its own IKEA yet, there is a huge store in Dubai and you'll be amazed at how much flat-pack furniture you can fit into one carload.

There are also some excellent shops selling wooden furniture but don't be taken in by the 'antiques' label; most of the items here are mass-produced in India and artificially aged. There are a few furniture stores in Al Qurm around Al-Araimi and SABCO. Marina

Traditional carved antiques

In Al-Araimi and Bombay in Markaz al Bahja have lovely Anglo-Indian colonial pieces, and prices are fixed so you don't have to worry about haggling.

The many excellent wood and metalworking shops in Wadi Kabir in Ruwi will make any piece of furniture you want for a reasonable price. Ruwi is also a good place to find readymade furniture and home furnishing shops – try Al Baladiyah Street and Ruwi High Street up to the Al Hamriyah Roundabout. You can reduce prices by bargaining. Stock isn't always unlimited though and things can disappear if you don't buy it there and then, so if you see something you love grab it while you can.

Every area has shops that make curtains and blinds. You'll probably have to wade through books and books of fabric samples, but the end result (custom made curtains that fit your windows perfectly) will be worth it. While these places will be able to offer advice on styles, it will make it easier and quicker if you go with something specific in mind, and even a picture if possible.

Jewellery & Watches
Other options **Markets & Souks** p.291

Living in Oman means access to a wide range of well-priced watches and jewellery, particularly gold. Apart from the obvious 'bling' factor, quality watches and jewellery are good investments too (tell that to your man if he whinges). Gold is sold by weight and priced according to the international daily gold rate published on the internet or in the local papers. In Europe, 18 carat gold is more common, but here 22 or 24 carat gold is more popular. In addition to being priced by weight, there is also a price for workmanship which varies according to the intricacy of the design. As the international gold price is fixed, it's the workmanship fee that you can negotiate.

Jewellery comes in many forms, from traditional Omani silver to cultured pearls from Japan and ethnic creations from India. More modern designs can be found in exclusive jewellery shops. If you're a serious gold shopper, check out the Mutrah Souk and Ruwi High Street where you can find every design at all prices and for all tastes.

A word of advice: do a thorough shop around until you're certain you've found just the thing – if you buy something you're not sure about, you might regret it when you turn the corner see your dream piece on display in the next shop. You can also design your own jewellery, or have a copy made from a drawing or photograph.

Jewellery & Watches

Al Asala Jewellery	Al Wadi Commercial Centre	24 560 654
Al Felaiij Jewellers	Muscat City Centre	24 558 518
Al Qurum Jewellers	SABCO Commercial Centre	24 562 558
Alukkas Jewellery	Muscat City Centre	24 558 034
Damas	Salalah	23 297 744
	Muscat City Centre	24 541 766
	Crowne Plaza Muscat	24 563 673
	Ruwi	24 788 946
	Al Khamis Plaza	24 563 723
	Sur	25 541 498
	Sohar	26 846 384
	Bawshar	24 584 340
	Barka	26 882 657
Future Jewellery	SABCO Commercial Centre	24 565 637
Hamdam Hasan Swaid Al Jimi	SABCO Commercial Centre	24 565 167
Himat Jewellers	Muscat City Centre	24 558 088
Jewellery Corner	SABCO Commercial Centre	24 563 946
Khimjis Watches	Ruwi	24 703 142
Mouawad	Al Khamis Plaza	24 560 945
Muscat Watch Centre	SABCO Commercial Centre	24 562 459
Ruwi Jewellers	Al Khamis Plaza	24 565 977
Tiffany & Co	Jawahir Oman	24 565 301
	Salalah	23 211 976
Watch House	Muscat City Centre	24 558 838
	SABCO Commercial Centre	24 567 638

Silver

Omani silverwork has been held in such high regard in Gulf countries that many 'antique' pieces of silver today are labelled Omani to enhance their value and reputation. Silver was used not only to make necklaces, anklets, rings, bracelets and other forms of wedding jewellery, but also to decorate weapons and create everyday objects such as coffee pots, pipes, thorn-picks and ear-cleaners. Each region in Oman has its distinctive designs. If you are a serious collector of Omani silver, the books *Silver, the Traditional Art of Oman* and *The Craft Heritage of Oman* are indispensable.

A short walk around the souks of Muscat and the interior will reveal a variety of dusty, black looking silver that will look great with a bit of polish. There are small boxes used to hold kohl, and huge earrings which might terrify you on first sight but that are actually hooked over the top of the ears and not for pierced ears. A lot of this is wedding jewellery and although it might look ancient, it's unlikely to be very old. Traditionally, a woman's wedding jewellery was melted down and sold or refashioned on her death, but inherited pieces are not uncommon. Bedouin women may also sell their silver jewellery as Eid approaches in order to have some cash for celebrations; the souk in Sinaw is a good source. You may also see Maria Theresa dollars (or thalers) which were the legal currency in Oman until the 1960s. Take your time to browse and you can dig up some real treasures.

Watches

As with jewellery, watches are cheaper here than in Europe. Supermarkets stock cheap to medium-priced watches, while dedicated watch showrooms stock pieces priced from average to outlandish.

Kids' Clothing & Toys
Other options **Clothes** p.270

You won't have any trouble shopping for children's clothes in Muscat. From the moment your baby is born right up until they are too cool for kids' clothes, there is a huge range available. The presence of some popular stores from your home country will be comforting such as Marks & Spencer, Mexx, H&M, Pumpkin Patch

Kids' Clothing

Adams	Muscat City Centre	24 558 914
Babyshop	City Plaza, Nr Qaboos Signal	24 698 988
	Muscat City Centre	24 558 981
Bhs	Al Qurm	24 562 456
Carrefour	Muscat City Centre	24 558 140
Hang Ten	Muscat City Centre	24 558 870
Kids' Corner	Capital Commercial Centre (CCC)	24 560 560
Lulu Hypermarket	Ruwi	24 701 401
	Al Khuwayr	24 504 504
Marks & Spencer	Markaz Al Bahja	24 536 035
Monsoon	Muscat City Centre	24 558 902
Mothercare	Al Qurm	24 562 456
Next	Muscat City Centre	24 558 801
Pumpkin Patch	Muscat City Centre	24 558 085
Safeer Hypermarket	Al Azaiba	24 496 019
Sana Fashions	Ruwi	24 810 289

Kids' Toys

Babyshop	Muscat City Centre	24 558 981
	City Plaza, Nr Qaboos Signal	24 698 988
Carrefour	Muscat City Centre	24 558 140
Lulu Hypermarket	Al Khuwayr	24 504 504
	Ruwi	24 701 401
Mothercare	Al Qurm	24 562 456
Pumpkin Patch	Muscat City Centre	24 558 085
Safeer Hypermarket	Al Azaiba	24 496 019
Smart Kids Toys	Al-Araimi Complex	24 564 898
The Toy Store	Muscat City Centre	24 558 381
Toys R Us	Markaz Al Bahja	24 540 360

and Next, and you'll be able to kit your kids out in exactly the same clothes their friends back home are wearing (although maybe with a slight time delay). However, clothes in these outlets are often quite pricey compared to what you'd pay at home. If you're looking for cheap, cheerful clothing that you don't mind getting muddy or covered in paint, you'll find some bargains at Carrefour, Sana Fashions or Lulu Hypermarket. While some of the stock may seem a bit garish at first glance, a good rummage often yields some great results and it is not unknown to make brand-name discoveries. If you are stocking up on clothes for a new baby, head for Mothercare, Adams and the Baby Shop, where you'll find most of the things you'll need.

Muscat is a child-friendly city, and you'll find plenty of shops selling toys for your little angels. There is something for everyone, from hi-tech baby learning laptops to cheap plastic tat (which your kids will probably prefer, despite your best intentions). Remember that not all toys conform to international safety standards though. All this means is that you will need to make a judgement call and ensure your kids only play with the dodgy toys under constant supervision.

Dangerously Cheap
Be aware that soft toys and other kids' items sold in souks and cheaper shops may not conform to world safety standards for very young children.

Toys R Us, Baby Shop, and The Toy Store in City Centre carry everything from dolls to computer games, perfect for one-stop shopping. The supermarkets also stock good ranges of toys and Ruwi High Street is excellent for lower priced items. Mothercare, Babyshop and Adams are where to head if you're looking for soft toys suitable for newborns and infants.

If you're looking for second-hand items like prams, cots and large toys, keep an eye on supermarket noticeboards. Some churches and societies lend out baby equipment too, so ask around or contact Muscat Mums (p.124).

Lingerie
Other options **Clothes** p.270

Lingerie is big business in the Middle East and you might be surprised by what's lurking under some of those conservative clothes. A browse around a specialist lingerie shop, like Triumph and Inner Lines (both in City Centre) and High Lady in Al Wadi Centre, can be eye opening.

Lingerie		
Bhs	Al Qurm	24 562 456
Carrefour	Muscat City Centre	24 558 140
High Lady	Al Wadi Commercial Centre	24 567 134
Inner Lines	Muscat City Centre	24 558 228
Lulu Hypermarket	Al Khuwayr	24 504 504
	Ruwi	24 701 401
Mango	Muscat City Centre	24 558 244
Marks & Spencer	Markaz Al Bahja	24 536 035
Next	Muscat City Centre	24 558 801
Sana Fashions	Ruwi	24 810 289
Splash	Muscat City Centre	24 558 981
	City Plaza	24 698 988
Women's Secret	Muscat City Centre	24 558 452

If you're looking for something a bit more everyday and functional, you can try old favourites Next, Marks & Spencer or Bhs, all of which have a good cotton range to suit the climate. Prices can be inflated compared to in the UK, but you could always wait for the sales and stock up then. Carrefour and Lulu Hypermarkets have good lingerie sections, as do Woolworths Lingerie, Splash, Next, Calvin Klein (all in Muscat City Centre) and Sana Fashions in Wadi Kabir. You'll find plenty of affordable underwear and nightwear at the Mutrah Souk and Ruwi High Street, if you're not particular about colours or cotton content.

Luggage & Leather

There's nothing like a full range of Louis Vuitton luggage to show off with in airports, and since you'll probably be travelling back home once or twice a year, you may as well do it in style. Head for Capital Stores, Salam Stores, Salman Stores or Khimjis Megastore for a range of luxury luggage at luxury prices. If you'd rather spend your money on holidays than hand luggage, there's a lane off Ruwi High Street that specialises in budget suitcases and bags in every colour and size. Somehow word of what you're looking for travels as you walk along the street, so by the time you reach the end traders will be offering you a 'small black air cabin bag, madam?' Lulu Hypermarket also sells some suitcases and laptop bags. Carrefour and the

Luggage & Leather		
Capital Store	Salalah	23 297 910
	SABCO Commercial Centre	24 563 542
	Markaz Al Bahja	24 545 532
	City Plaza	24 699 723
	Capital Commercial Centre (CCC)	24 562 254
Carrefour	Muscat City Centre	24 558 140
Khimjis Megastore	Khimjis Megastore	24 796 161
	Al Qurm	24 560 419
	Salalah	23 295 671
Muscat Trading	Ruwi	24 831 440
Salam Studio & Stores	Al Qurm	24 564 071
Salman Stores	As Seeb	24 422 213
	Salalah	23 293 146
	Capital Commercial Centre (CCC)	24 560 135
	Al-Araimi Complex	24 566 286
	Mutrah	24 796 925
Sultan Center	Al Qurm	24 567 666
Wala Trading	Ruwi	24 703 488

Sultan Center have functional bags and suitcases, similar to those you'd find in the souk. Copies of designer handbags can be found in some shops, and these make good presents, although some are of better quality than others.

If you're looking for a leather jacket, you can try men's clothing stores in Al Qurm and City Centre. Non-branded leather jackets from Pakistan are also found in the small souk in the Capital Commercial Centre in Al Qurm.

Maternity Items

Maternity Items		
Marks & Spencer	Markaz Al Bahja	24 536 035
Mothercare	Al Qurm	24 562 456
Next	Muscat City Centre	24 558 801

While fashion conscious mums-to-be won't find a huge choice of maternity clothing in Oman, a few of the big name stores do have selections. And if Marks & Spencer, Max and H&M don't deliver the goods in terms of flair and individual style, you could always ask a tailor to whip up something for you.

Medicine

Other options **General Medical Care** p.117

A green cross or what looks like a snake wrapped around a glass on a shop sign indicates a pharmacy (or chemist), and you'll find them all over Oman. Many drugs that you need a prescription for in other parts of the world can be bought over the counter without a visit to the doctor. Pharmacists are willing to listen to your symptoms and suggest a remedy, but will not prescribe antibiotics. They can also recommend a cheaper alternative of the same drug.

On your first attempt to buy a medicine that you regularly use in your home country, try taking an empty packet or the package insert with you if possible. The medicine you use may not be available here, but the pharmacist will be able to tell you of a suitable alternative. Remember to check the expiry date of the medicine before buying it.

Pharmacies also carry beauty products, sunscreen, baby care items and perfumes, usually at a set discount. Opening hours are usually from 09:00 to 13:00 and 16:00 to 20:00. The following pharmacies are open 24 hours a day: Scientific Pharmacy in Qurm (24 566 601) and Ruwi (24 702 850); Muscat Pharmacy in Ruwi (24 702 542) and Al Sarooj (24 695 536). A list of the pharmacies on 24 hour duty can be found in daily newspapers, and on 90.4 FM radio and the English Evening News on Oman TV. If you need over the counter medication for fever, a sore throat or muscle pain, try the larger supermarkets like Sultan Center and Carrefour.

Medicine		
Abu Al Dahab Clinic & Pharmacy	Salalah	23 291 303
Muscat Pharmacy	Ruwi	24 814 501
	Al Ghubrah	24 497 264
	Ruwi	24 702 542
	Muscat City Centre	24 558 704
	Al Sarooj Commercial Centre	24 695 536
	Al Khuwayr	24 485 740
Muscat Pharmacy (24 hour)	Al Mawalih	24 537 080
	Ruwi	24 833 323
	Al Hayl	24 535 977
	Salalah	23 291 635
	Sohar	26 840 211
Scientific Pharmacy	Ruwi	24 702 850
	Al Qurm	24 566 601

Mobile Phones

Other options **Telephone** p.108

A mobile phone (often known as GSM in Oman) is considered an essential accessory and most shopping areas and malls have at least one outlet selling a range of models. There are some specialist stores, while all of the major electronic stores such as Jumbo and E-Max sell mobiles, as does Carrefour.

Mobile Phones			
Bahwan Electronics	Ruwi	24 831 187	na
Carrefour	Muscat City Centre	24 558 140	www.carrefouroman.com
Cellucom	Muscat City Centre	24 558 264	www.cellucom.com
Lucky Phone	Capital Commercial Centre (CCC)	24 566 704	na
Nokia	Muscat City Centre	24 558 859	www.nokia.com
Oman Telecommunications Company ▶ p.109, 111, 113	Al Azaiba	24 632 816	http://omantel.net.om

Music, DVDs & Videos

There are no megastores that sell music or movies in Oman, but there are many smaller outlets within the shopping centres that stock current releases on CD, DVD and video. Carrefour and Sultan Center also carry a small range.

The latest offerings by international musicians are available on CDs and sometimes cassettes. You can also get a reasonable range of Arabic, Bollywood and classical music. New releases tend to sell out quickly. If you can't find what you are looking for, some shop owners might be able to order certain titles for you; or you can order on the internet if you're prepared to pay the postage (try www.amazon.com). Censorship is alive and well and there may be some films that you can't get in Oman; or films that you can get but that have been cut. If you order online your package will usually be held at the post office until you go there in person to oversee a search. If anything in it is deemed to be offensive, it will be confiscated or censored.

Of course there are the usual pirated DVDs and VCDs doing the rounds – just remember that the chances are high that you'll get a poor quality copy.

Music, DVDs & Videos		
Carrefour	Muscat City Centre	24 558 140
Gulf Eyes	Al Harthy Complex	24 560 867
Megastar	Jawaharat A'Shati Commercial Complex	24 693 888
New Age Music	SABCO Commercial Centre	24 568 858
Sultan Center	Al Qurm	24 567 666

Musical Instruments

Other options **Music, DVDs & Videos** p.282, **Music Lessons** p.239

Musicians will find it hard to get what they want in Oman as there are a limited number of shops that sell instruments. Musiq Souq in the Al Wadi Centre and Tunes on the Al Khuwayr service road have the widest range and they also offer music lessons. ElectroCity in the Al-Araimi Complex has drum kits and Yamaha pianos.

Sheet music is not widely available and you might want to order it from the internet or buy some on your next trip abroad.

Musical Instruments		
ElectroCity	Al-Araimi Complex	24 568 806
Musiq Souq	Al Wadi Commercial Centre	24 562 237
Tunes	Majan House, Al Khuwayr	24 698 775

Outdoor Goods

Other options **Sports Goods** p.287, **Hardware & DIY** p.275, **Camping** p.215

Oman is a perfect location for outdoor activities, and weekend breaks in a wadi or in the desert are popular. The mild temperatures and low humidity make the winter months of November to March the best time for camping, picnics, diving, kite surfing, climbing, trekking, caving, or just sitting on your porch with a sundowner. Even in the summer, outdoor activities can be pleasant if you go to the mountains or south to Salalah during the 'khareef' or monsoon season, or spend an evening on the beach (although the humidity can be taxing). Omanis enjoy a good evening of chilling out, singing and barbecuing fresh seafood.

Most of the supermarkets carry basic outdoor gear such as cooler boxes, barbecue stands, folding chairs and tables, gas stoves, tents and even portable toilets and showers. You can kit yourself out cheaply at

Outdoor Goods		
Carrefour	Muscat City Centre	24 558 140
Home Centre	Centrepoint, City Plaza	24 698 988
Khimjis Megastore	Al Qurm	24 560 419
	Nizwa	25 410 415
Lulu Hypermarket	Al Khuwayr	24 504 504
	Ruwi	24 701 401
Marina Bander Al Rowdha	Sidab St	24 737 288
Sultan Center	Al Qurm	24 567 666

Carrefour and Sultan Center while Ruwi High Street and the Mutrah Souk are good for plastic mats. If your idea of enjoying the outdoor life is limited to your patio or garden, take a trip to the Landmark Group (formerly City Plaza) or Ruwi High Street for plastic chairs and tables.

Party Accessories

Large formal or themed parties aren't that common in Oman, where garden parties and casual barbecues are more popular. Supermarkets and stationery shops stock basic party needs and Toys R Us has a good kids' party selection. While there are no independent party organisers in Oman, the larger hotels might be able to help you plan a special event.

Party Accessories		
Al Fair	Capital Commercial Centre (CCC)	24 561 750
	Madinat As Sultan Qaboos	24 698 174
	Markaz Al Bahja	24 543 243
	Zakher Shopping Mall	24 482 047
	Muscat	24 544 350
	Shati Al Qurm	24 561 905
	Ruwi	24 702 246
Carrefour	Muscat City Centre	24 558 140
Lulu Hypermarket	Ruwi	24 701 401
	Al Khuwayr	24 504 504
Safeer Hypermarket	Al Azaiba	24 496 019
Sparks	Jawharat A' Shati Complex	24 692 010

Fancy Dress & Costumes

There are no specialist costume shops here, so if you're going to a fancy dress party and don't sew, head straight to a tailor. Explaining your design to them could be amusing as it will be something rather different from their usual requests. Factor in time before the party to try it on and have it refitted if necessary.

Oudh ◀

Oudh is highly valued in the Middle East and can fetch astonishing prices. The perfume is made from the resin of Aloeswood trees and is imported from India, Cambodia and Malaysia. It's worn on the clothes and the skin and usually only on important occasions such as Eid, weddings, funerals or to celebrate the birth of a child.

Perfumes & Cosmetics

Other options **Markets & Souks** p.291

Many of the raw materials used in perfumes such as jasmine, frankincense and musk, originate in the Middle East, and this is reflected in the vibrant array of perfumes available in Oman. Small bottles of perfume essence that you can pick up at souks and perfume shops are excellent buys; just a drop of these pure perfumes on a scarf will last for days. The souks have hundreds of fragrances and making a choice may prove difficult. If you don't like strong perfume avoid 'oudh', or apply it carefully as it's an acquired taste.

In shopping malls and duty free shops you'll find all the latest international fragrances as well as stronger Arabic perfumes in extravagant bottles. Amouage, 'the world's most valuable perfume', is made in Oman and you can visit the Amouage perfume factory in Rusayl, past Seeb. If you buy any Amouage perfume from the factory, you will receive a special gift. Each perfume is individually packed and attached to the product is a card bearing the name of the person who packed your perfume. See www.amouage.com. Maathir Perfumes in Al-Araimi Complex has a good range of fragrances as well as some interesting solid perfumes – great for packing in your suitcase without having to worry about bottles breaking. Ajmal specialises in reasonably priced Arabic perfumes from RO 5 to RO 10, and it's well worth visiting its branch in the Al-Araimi Complex.

Many perfume shops also sell diluted fragrance in white plastic spray bottles. These only cost a couple of rials and are used for refreshing furniture, carpets and curtains. The effect is subtler than incense.

All luxury brands and some of the less plush names are widely available in Oman. They're not always cheaper than you would find them at home, so shopping at duty free shops, on your way in or out of the country, is a good bet.

You'll find The Body Shop and MAC at Muscat City Centre.

Incense

Oman is home to the world's finest frankincense. Luban (frankincense in resin form) is a good purchase and the fragrance lasts for a long time. Oudh is made from flakes of perfumed wood, and it has a very strong smell. It's expensive but you only need a small piece to burn on top of a bit of charcoal to enjoy the effect. You can buy the small blocks of charcoal from incense shops, supermarkets, corner shops and souks.

Perfumes & Cosmetics

Ajmal	Al-Araimi Complex	24 562 359	www.ajmalperfume.com
Al Bustan fragrances	Al Harthy Complex	24 798 241	www.perfumesofoman.com
Amouage ▶ p.261	As Seeb	24 534 800	www.amouage.com
	Muscat City Centre	24 558 581	
	SABCO Commercial Centre	24 560 533	
Areej	Muscat City Centre	24 558 752	www.al-tayer.com
The Body Shop	SABCO Commercial Centre	24 571 108	www.thebodyshop.com
	Muscat City Centre	24 558 237	
Capital Store	Salalah	23 297 910	www.csoman.om
	Capital Commercial Centre (CCC)	24 562 254	
	City Plaza	24 699 723	
	Markaz Al Bahja	24 545 532	
	SABCO Commercial Centre	24 563 542	
Maathir	Al-Araimi Complex	24 562 585	na
MAC	Muscat City Centre	24 558 842	www.maccosmetics.com
	Qurm City Centre	24 470 581	

Plants & Gardens

Other options **Flowers** p.272, **Hardware & DIY** p.275

Gardening in the Oman heat requires passion and dedication, but if you have these then you'll find everything you need to garden away. You'll find good roadside garden centres on the way to Seeb Town. They open in the morning until about 13:00 and again from 16:00 to 21:00. The staff can offer good advice and plants are not expensive.

There are also some nurseries in Muscat that sell indoor plants, bougainvilleas, border plants and colourful seasonal plants. The Sultan Center and Al Fair have a fair range of potted plants too.

You can also buy glazed and unglazed clay pots from Bahla, some of which seem too decorative to merely put plants in. Garden furniture in many styles can be found upstairs at the Landmark Group (formerly City Plaza), and inexpensive plastic garden furniture can be bought in The Sultan Center, Carrefour and on Ruwi High Street. Again, look on the supermarket notice boards because expats who are leaving often don't take their outdoor furniture with them.

Plants & Gardens

Al Fair	Capital Commercial Centre (CCC)	24 561 750
	Shati Al Qurm	24 561 905
Alaas Services & Trdg	Al Khuwayr	24 482 070
Bahjat Ghala Trading	Ghala	24 502 988
Carrefour	Muscat City Centre	24 558 140
Fahmy Furniture	Al Khuwayr	24 489 812
Home Centre	Centrepoint, City Plaza	24 698 988
Landmark Group (City Plaza)	Madinat As Sultan Qaboos	24 698 988
Palms Garden Centre	Opp Markaz al Bahja	24 546 349
Sultan Center	Al Qurm	24 567 666
Truckoman	Al Wutayyah	24 565 248
Wadi Adai Garden Centre	Ruwi	na

Online Oman Auctions

If you fancy a bit of competition when it comes to buying (or just like to get a real bargain) then visit www.omanbay.com. This website allows sellers to post items as diverse as shoes and boats for buyers to bid on. There are also occasionally properties to rent listed too and it's a great site for picking up cheap books in the '1 Rial Shop' section.

Second-Hand Items
Other options **Cars** p.269, **Books** p.265

Churches and charity groups will take your unwanted clothes, toys and appliances off your hands as donations for people in need. The Catholic Church in Ruwi operates a charity shop, which is worth a visit for its abundant selection of nearly new clothing and home furnishings. For second-hand baby equipment contact Muscat Mums (p.124) who host garage sales and send out a weekly email newsletter with goods advertised. If you want to make a few rials out of the stuff you no longer need, you can put a notice up on supermarket noticeboards or book a classified ad in one of the local newspapers. There is a row of shops behind the Polyglot Institute at the Wadi Adai Roundabout that sell second-hand furniture. They offer a delivery and assembly service for large items. House of Prose at Al Wadi Commercial Centre buys and sells used books and if you do buy one you can sell it back for the half the original price if it's in good condition and you have the receipt.

Frankincense
Trade in frankincense resin once made the southern region of Dhofar one of the wealthiest in the world. It's estimated that around the second century AD over 3,000 tons of incense were traded each year between southern Arabia and Egypt, Greece and Rome. According to the Bible, the three kings presented gifts of frankincense and myrrh to the baby Jesus, and at the time these were considered more valuable than gold. Incense is a serious industry in Dhofar and entire alleys of the Salalah souk are devoted to incense shops.

Shoes
Other options **Sports Goods** p.287, **Beachwear** p.264, **Clothes** p.270

From knee-high boots to plastic flip-flops, you'll be able to find the shoes you need in Muscat, although the range is not quite as good in other parts of Oman. Most sizes are available; just be sure to specify to the sales assistant whether you mean the UK or US size. Sports stores are best for trainers and running shoes, as staff will be able to advise you on fit and support. Shoe City, which has branches in the Landmark Group and Muscat City Centre, has a wide range of shoes for the whole family. You'll find good quality leather shoes in various outlets in Muscat and Qurm City Centres and in World of Shoes in the Al Khamis Plaza.

Shoes		
The Athlete's Foot	Al-Araimi Complex	24 567 438
Carrefour	Muscat City Centre	24 558 140
Charles & Keith	Al Arami Mall	24 567 428
	Muscat City Centre	24 558 011
Clarks Shoes	Al Khamis Plaza	24 560 992
Khimjis Ramdas	Ruwi	24 795 901
Marks & Spencer	Markaz Al Bahja	24 536 035
Milano	Muscat City Centre	24 558 834
Nine West	SABCO Commercial Centre	24 561 872
	Muscat City Centre	24 558 312
Orange	Muscat City Centre	24 558 148
Pretty Fit	Muscat City Centre	24 558 855
	Al-Araimi Complex	24 568 640
Shoe City	Muscat City Centre	24 558 342
	City Plaza	24 601 002
Spring	Muscat City Centre	24 558 049
World Shoes	Al Khamis Plaza	24 565 259

Clay Pots

Incense burners are usually small pots of clay in which various items are burned to give off a distinctive fragrance. Different regions of Oman have their own distinctive incense burners, like the colourfully painted burners of Dhofar. Pair them up with a packet of frankincense or 'oudh', and these burners make excellent gifts.

Souvenirs

Other options **Carpets** p.268

Shopping for presents in Oman is really tough because you always want to buy one for yourself as well. And why shouldn't you? If you're worried about your baggage allowance, find out how to ship goods home on p.259.

Traditional Arabic items make good gifts and ornaments. Popular items include the traditional coffee pot and small decorated cups used for drinking kahwa (Arabic coffee), incense burners, wedding chests and traditional Omani khanjars (daggers). Khanjars are almost always sold encased in an elaborately wrought sheath, and are arguably the most recognisable symbol of Oman. If you do buy one though, make sure you pack it in your suitcase rather than your hand luggage.

Embroidered Omani hats

Other souvenirs that should evoke memories of your time in Arabia are miniature dhows crafted from wood or silver, Quran holders, pottery camels, the traditional hat worn by Omani men (a 'kumah'), clay pots and jars from Bahla, woven milking baskets with leather bottoms, and even ancient rifles.

Heavy silver Omani wedding jewellery is another wonderful souvenir and occasionally you'll find a rare piece or collector's item.

Many souvenir items are made in India but sold as the real thing and it's not always easy to spot the fakes. Although the souks generally offer the best buys, it may be difficult to tell how genuine and old articles are unless you're an expert in Omani crafts. The Oman Heritage Gallery, near the InterContinental Muscat in Shati Al Qurm, is a government-run shop that sells genuine craft items. It was established to keep traditional skills such as pottery and weaving alive and the staff will be able to tell you about the various items, where they come from and how long they took to make. The goods are more expensive than in other places, but they are genuine – and you're helping to keep these traditions alive and providing an income for the artisans.

If you want a comprehensive reminder of Omani crafts, you can pick up the hefty, highly informative and beautifully illustrated *The Craft Heritage of Oman*, a two-volume coffee table book that covers everything on the subject.

If you love humorous 'kitsch', you'll have a field day in the souks where you'll find singing camels (choose from the Macarana or Habibi for a more authentic feel), T-shirts featuring the adventures of Tintin and Snowy in Oman, or the famous mosque alarm clock, that wakes you up with the call to prayer. Don't leave Oman without one.

Souvenirs

Oman Heritage Gallery	Jawaharat A'Shati Commercial Complex	24 696 974
Raj Relics	Villa 1094, Way 3616, Nr Chedi	24 493 131
SABCO Souk	SABCO Commercial Centre	24 566 701
Silver World	Mutrah Souk	24 714 373

Sports Goods

Adidas	Muscat City Centre	24 558 900
Magic Cup Sports	Ruwi	24 786 683
Marina Bander Al Rowdha	Sidab St	24 737 283
Muscat Sports	Al-Araimi Complex	24 564 364
	Markaz Al Bahja	24 537 708
	Ruwi	24 790 241
Oman Dive Center	Bandar Al Jissah Qantab	24 824 240
ScubaTec	Al Wadi Commercial Centre	24 562 322
Sports For All	SABCO Commercial Centre	24 560 086
Sun & Sand Sports	Muscat City Centre	24 558 355
Supa Sportsman	Ruwi	24 833 192
Water World Marine	Sidab	24 737 438

Sports Goods
Other options **Outdoor Goods** p.282

Most shopping centres have sports shops that stock a good range of sports clothing and equipment. You'll easily find racquets, balls and exercise equipment, although prices may be a little steeper than you would like. Diving equipment is easy to track down; there are shops at the Oman Dive Centre near Qantab and at ScubaTec in the Al Wadi Centre.

Stationery

Whether you're looking for a pencil sharpener or professional standard plotting paper, there are stationery shops all over the city. Hypermarkets like Carrefour and Lulu carry all the basics, including huge ranges of back-to-school supplies. While they may be cheap, you might find that to get the best deals you have to buy a pack of 20 identical pencil sharpeners or banded packs of pencils. Of course if you're looking for quality not quantity, head for Mont Blanc where you can offload hundreds of rials on a single pen.

Stationery

Carrefour	Muscat City Centre	24 558 140	www.carrefouroman.com
Lulu Hypermarket	Al Khuwayr	24 504 504	www.luluhypermarket.com
	Ruwi	24 701 401	
Montblanc	Muscat City Centre	24 558 079	www.rivoligroup.com
Office Supplies Co	Al Qurm	24 563 033	www.omzest.com
Souk Al Khuwayr	Al Khuwayr	na	na

Tailoring
Other options **Souvenirs** p.286, **Clothes** p.270, **Tailors** p.101, **Textiles** p.288

In Europe, having an outfit made to order is a luxury few can afford, but in Oman it's cheap and easy. The many fabric shops sell such a vibrant range of material that you'll be spoilt for choice, but once you've made your selection you're then ready to find a tailor. There are many tailors in Oman, some good, some not so good, and word of mouth is the best way to find one of the good ones.

In Muscat, most of the tailors are located in little shops in the back streets of Ruwi, the Mutrah Souk, or in the Al Wadi Centre or Al Khuwayr Souk.

The process is an interesting one and may test your patience in the beginning. The best results come from bringing a picture or an original garment for the tailor to copy, or the shop might have a few

Tailoring

Ahmed Abdul Rahman Traders	Ruwi	24 787 756
Assarain Textiles	Ruwi	24 830 149
Dress Unique	Madinat As Sultan Qaboos	24 607 136
European Style Tailoring	Al Qurm	24 565 214
Mehdi Store	Ruwi	24 814 200
Mutrah Tailoring House	Ruwi	24 701 960
Raymond Shop	Ruwi	24 561 142
Souk Al Khuwayr	Al Khuwayr	
Talia	Al Harthy Complex	24 566 066
Women Today	Al Khuwayr	24 488 580

magazines for you to browse through. Sometimes the language barrier is problematic, but that's where the power of pictures comes in useful. When trying a tailor for the first time, order just one garment so you can check the quality of the work. Confirm the price before you leave the shop, and make sure you're clear about what the price includes (such as lining, zips or buttons) – and feel free to negotiate. Always try the garment on when you pick it up, so that you can have alterations made if necessary. In this case alterations are usually free of charge.

Textiles

Other options **Souvenirs** p.286, **Tailoring** p.287

Textile shops in Oman are excellent and you can buy just about any fabric in any colour, although pure cotton can be difficult to find as it's not that popular among Arab customers. Even the smallest towns have fabric shops selling material by the yard. Shop assistants can advise you on how much fabric you need for the garment you have in mind.

In Muscat, you'll find textile shops in all the major malls and on Ruwi High Street. In Ruwi, you can buy cheap saris that make interesting curtains and tablecloths. The Al Khamis Plaza in Al Qurm has two stores, Abu Hani

Textiles		
Abu Fahmy Textiles	Ruwi	24 750 414
Abu Hani Al Jimi Trading	Al Khamis Plaza	24 571 609
Al Bawab	Al Harthy Complex	24 563 756
Beauty Textile	Ruwi	24 782 194
Gulab Bhai Dwarkadas & Co	Mutrah	24 712 409
Instyle	Al Khamis Plaza	24 563 242
Silky Textiles	Ruwi	24 793 730
Talia	Al Harthy Complex	24 566 066

and InStyle, that stock a huge range of silk and linen, and a basement store that sells printed Indian cushions and bedspreads at reasonable prices. Abu Hani sells a range of printed cotton for making bedding and quilts.

Wedding Items

Wedding Items		
Marks & Spencer	Markaz Al Bahja	24 536 035
Monsoon	Muscat City Centre	24 558 902

While it is not common for expats to get married in Oman, if you decide to do so you should be able to find almost everything you need to plan the perfect wedding. See p.68 for more details regarding help with planning your wedding – if you get yourself a good banquet organiser at one of the top hotels, they will probably have an army of contacts ready to follow your instructions.

Scarves for sale

A bit of bargaining

Places To Shop

The following section on places to shop in Oman covers Muscat's main shopping centres as well as the main shopping streets or areas in Muscat and beyond.

Areas To Shop

South-west of Muscat
Nizwa
Map 1 F3

Nizwa

Nizwa is a great place for souvenir shopping. This atmospheric, historical town is just a 90 minute drive from Muscat, and once you are there it is quite easy to find your way around. Getting there involves a scenic drive, with impressive mountains all along the way. After a visit to the fort (see p.171) you can sample the shopping that Nizwa has to offer, particularly the souk. The people here call themselves the 'real Omanis' and pride themselves on being friendly and helpful. The pace of life is much slower here and a day trip is a relaxing break from Muscat's hustle and bustle. Try to get there early (around 07:00) on Thursday and Friday mornings to witness the goat market which takes place next to the main souk.

**Left at Ruwi R/A
then 1st right**
Ruwi
Map 12 E3

Ruwi Souk Street

Better known as Ruwi High Street, this is a very long, double-laned street that starts at the Al Hamriya Roundabout. It's the place to go for anything from toilet seats to diamond rings, state of the art hi-fi systems to Delsey luggage and everything else in between. While most of the shops cater to lower-income families, expats of all nationalities come here for the excellent and inexpensive picture framing shops and tailors, and to buy textiles, appliances and gold. Shops are generally open from 09:00 to 13:00 and from 16:30 to 21:00.

There are various textile shops, electronics stores and jewellers along the main road, with many official dealerships for international brands of watches, cameras and white goods. Bargaining is encouraged, and if you can out-haggle the shopkeeper then you can walk away with a bargain.

Several smaller roads branch off the high street, and these are home to speciality shops and occasional temporary markets. Honda Road, for example, is devoted to building and construction materials. Smaller shopping areas down the side roads will yield fake designer jeans, Tin Tin T-shirts and the tacky gifts that have made this area famous. There are plenty of coffee shops in the main street, offering mostly battered Indian snacks, masala tea, coffee or fresh coconut juice. You'll also find some small but excellent restaurants serving Filipino, Chinese, Indian, Sri Lankan, Arabic and Turkish food.

Salalah
Map 1 F3

Salalah

Salalah may be Oman's second biggest city, but it retains the feel of a small village. This means that it doesn't have the range and variety of shops that Muscat has, but for the dedicated shopper there's still bargain hunting to be done, particularly for perfume, incense, oils and incense burners. There are no shopping malls as such, but there are streets lined with shops selling clothes, textiles, groceries, appliances and stationery. No one seems to know the exact location of things so you may have to ask a few people and be prepared to get lost – eventually you'll find what you're looking for.

The Lowdown

Salalah is much more conservative than Muscat and it's advisable for women to wear long sleeves and a long skirt or loose trousers when you're out in public. Most people speak at least a little English and are approachable and helpful. As a rule, men should ask men for directions and women should ask women.

The length of Al Haffa Street is lined with small shops, most of which sell women's clothes and accessories. This is where Dhofari women buy brightly coloured lengths of cotton mix fabric (usually imported from Thailand) to make the traditional Salalah dresses ('thobe Dhofari' or 'Abu Dhail' which means 'one with a tail'). These are basically a big square with a hole cut in the middle for the neck and the back cut longer than the front to create a train; they make really comfortable house dresses for the summer. Dhofar City Centre has a little bit of everything under one roof, but sells mainly clothes and accessories for the whole family.

Salalah's semi-tropical climate has given rise to an agricultural industry that supplies Oman with fresh produce such as bananas, coconuts, tomatoes and beans. Locally grown foods are cheap and bountiful. Look out for the small stalls along the beaches or back streets where you can buy finger-sized sweet bananas straight off the trees and drink milk right out of the coconut.

Department Stores

Various Locations

Capital Store

Capital Store is the ultimate shopping destination if you like luxury. Head here if you're looking for a Mont Blanc watch or pen, branded luggage, Dior sunglasses, or jewellery by Misaki and Nina Ricci. Capital also stocks a fantastic range of crystal and china, tableware, appliances and homeware, plus one of Oman's widest ranges of perfumes and cosmetics. The store also stock Pentax and Samsung digital cameras, and a range of accessories. There are six Capital Store branches around Oman: SABCO Centre (24 563 542), Qurm (24 560 973), Markaz Al Bahja (24 545 532), Capital Commercial Centre (24 562 254), Landmark Group (24 699 723) and Salalah (23 297 910). With such a great range of products, and a personal touch, Capital offers a great shopping experience.

Various Locations

Khimji's Megastore

Megastore in this case doesn't mean vast: it means mega-exclusive. The fact that you have to be buzzed in to enter is quite understandable once you see which brands are housed in this compact chrome and marble store. It's a veritable who's who of well known upmarket names like Chanel, Jaeger, Paco Rabanne, Samsonite, OshKosh and Cross, to name a few. The watch department boasts some of the world's finest timepieces, including Rolex and Cartier, so bring your credit card. Other brands include Bvlgari, FCUK, Nikon, Nina Ricci, Ralph Lauren, Ray-Ban and Swarovski.
There are branches of Khimji's in Ruwi (24 796 161), Qurm (24 560 419), Sohar (26 840 232), Nizwa (25 410 415), Sur (25 540 214) and Salalah (23 295 671).

Markaz Al Bahja
As Seeb
Map 2 D4

Marks & Spencer

M&S (as it is fondly known by British expats) is one of the UK's best-known and most-trusted brands. It sells a range of quality men's, women's and children's clothes and shoes, as well as a teeny-tiny range of food items (mainly sweets and chocolates, but it's enough to remind you how brilliant the M&S foodhalls are back home). One thing that you should definitely keep a look out for whenever you are passing by is its book section: it is very small but it often has some great children's classic titles at surprisingly reasonable prices. Marks & Spencer is famous for underwear – it has some lacy numbers, practical cotton whites and a lovely range of sleepwear. Ladies of unconventional sizes will be pleased to discover that not only does it have a petite range, but its clothes range goes up to size 20 and in some lines, even larger.
You'll also be able to shop here for purses and handbags, home furnishings (it does stock a small range of household items like candles, cushions, cookware and utensils), and a fantastic selection of makeup and toiletries.

Salman Stores

Salman Stores was founded in 1953 as a retailer of quality kitchen and home products. Just over 50 years later, the group has grown into a leading importer, distributor and retailer in Oman and its range of products has expanded dramatically. This is the place to go if you're looking for tableware, glass and crystal items, porcelain and china, cutlery, and electrical appliances. Salman also stocks a range of luxurious linen and luggage. Only well-known brand names are good enough for Salman Stores, so you can expect to find Tefal cookware, Luminarc crystal, Singer sewing machines, Helios flasks and Giorcano watches, to name a few. Salman Stores has branches in Capital Commercial Centre (24 560 135), Al-Araimi Complex (24 566 286), Mutrah (24 796 925), Seeb (24 422 213) and Salalah (23 293 146).

Markets & Souks

Other options **Bargaining** p.260

Souk is the Arabic word for a place where all variety of goods are bought, sold or exchanged. Traditionally, dhows from the Far East, Africa, Ceylon and India would discharge their cargo and the goods would be bargained over in the souks adjacent to the docks. Over the years, the items on sale have changed from spices, silk and perfume to include electronic goods and the latest consumer trends. However, the atmosphere of a bustling market with noisy bargaining and friendly rivalry for customers remains. Souks are lively, colourful and full of people from all walks of life – so they're well worth a visit, even in you're not buying.

Oman's souks are some of the most fascinating in the Arab world, having retained the traditional way of doing business that has been lost in many places elsewhere. Apart from the obvious commercial purpose they serve, they're also a focal point for social interaction. In the interior, Bedouins come in from the desert and villagers from the mountains to meet other tribes or catch up on the latest news.

Every important town in Oman has at least one souk. The biggest and most famous of these are in Mutrah, Nizwa, Sinaw and Salalah and there's a women-only souk in Ibra every Wednesday morning. In addition to the permanent souks, pre-Eid markets known as 'habta' souks spring up overnight in places like Fanja, Samayil, Suroor, Nafa'a and Nizwa.

Visiting the souk is a fascinating experience at any time, but it's best to go in the late afternoon or early morning when it is cooler. Business begins at 07:00 (except for Mutrah souk, which starts at 09:30) with a break for midday prayers from 12 30 or 13:00 until 16:30. By 19:00 everything starts to close. On Fridays the souks only open in the afternoon and Thursdays and Fridays are the busiest – the best time to see the souk at full throttle and to take an active part in it.

Al Dhalam Market

This intriguing market starts at the Al Lawatiya Mosque and runs to Khour Bimba. Al Dhalam means 'darkness', an appropriate name for this area since the narrow alleyways receive little sunlight. When the market was originally built from mud and barasti, shoppers used lamps to find their way around. Today it is slightly more modern and there are paved alleyways and lanterns on the walls to light the way. The Al Lawatiya quarter was previously closed to foreigners (even non-Lawati Muslims). However, now you are free to wander around to your heart's content, browsing through the silver jewellery, traditional Omani ornaments, textiles and spices. Please note that you should dress appropriately (this is an area where modesty is required), and leave your camera behind

Salalah
Map 1 F3

Gold Souk

People unfamiliar with Arabic gold may think it's of a poorer quality, but the reverse is usually true. Most of the gold sold in the region is 24 carat, and often softer and better quality than gold bought elsewhere in the world. However, it is very yellow and you may find that the designs are a bit gaudy, depending on your tastes.

A visit to the Salalah Gold Souk may give you an opportunity to see young Dhofari girls choosing their wedding gold. You can shop around for a traditional Dhofari design, or design your own piece and have it made. This souk shouldn't be confused with the gold souk in Souk Al Haffa – the Salalah Gold Souk is situated in the Salalah Centre (after Pizza Hut, turn right 50 metres before the traffic lights).

Nr Fish R/A
Mutrah
Map 10 A3

Mutrah Fish & Vegetable Market

The fish market at the Mutrah end of the Corniche is one of the few places in Muscat where you can still witness the true hustle and bustle of an Arabic market. Smelly, muddy and bloody, it is an unforgettable experience and one best sampled by those who aren't squeamish. It's also the best place to buy fresh seafood at low prices, but you'll have to get there early to score the catch of the day. From 06:30 the small fishing boats are dragged up the beach next to the market to unload their trophies. There always seems to be at least one of everything the Indian Ocean has to offer on display – tuna, hammour, kingfish, bream, octopus and prawns.

Once you've wandered round the stalls and selected your fish, you can have it cleaned and gutted in the area at the back and to the left of the market. It's fascinating to watch and the service costs only a few baisas.

On the left of the fish market is a very good fruit and vegetable section. The wide variety of locally grown and imported produce is cheap, especially considering the huge quantities you go home with. At the entrance to the vegetable market are a row of meat shops selling fresh cuts of beef, mutton and camel.

Mutrah Corniche
Mutrah
Map 10 A3

Mutrah Souk

One of the most interesting souks in the Gulf, this warren-like covered market is still a source of many Omani families' daily household supplies, as well as a draw for souvenir-hunting tourists. The main entrance is on Mutrah Corniche but there are many small streets in the village behind the Corniche that lead into the souk.

The main thoroughfare is primarily for household goods, shoes and ready-made garments. Further inside, you can enjoy the mixed scent of frankincense, perfume oils, fresh jasmine and spices. The real excitement lies in exploring the side streets. The layout is confusing, but keep walking and you'll invariably end up either at the

Mutrah Souk

Corniche or at the main thoroughfare. Wander down any of the side alleys and you'll discover a selection of tiny shops full of dusty Omani silver, stalls of gleaming white dishdashas and embroidered kumahs, vivid cloth, multi-coloured head scarves, Omani pots, paintings, hookah pipes, framed khanjars, leatherwork and incense. There are plenty of bargains and no price is fixed. When you get tired, you can stop at the juice bar before tackling the next section.

Most of the shops here open from 09:30 to 13:00 and 16:30 to 19:00 daily, but are closed on Friday mornings and on Eid holiday weekends.

There is paid parking al along both sides of Corniche Road from the Fish Roundabout, although it does get quite congested in the evenings.

Town Centre
Nizwa
Map 1 C2

Nizwa Souk

In the centre of Nizwa, close to the fort and mosque, the souk lies hidden behind imposing sand-coloured walls. Enter through one of the enormous carved wooden doors and you'll find a small village of traditionally designed buildings, each labelled to indicate the products they sell – such as Silver Souk, Fish Souk and Meat Souk. Although these buildings are all clean, well lit and renovated, the place remains full of atmosphere and traders conduct business as they have done for centuries. The souks are well laid out and vibrant with local colour, especially in the early morning. The shop owners are an unintrusive bunch and are happy to sit and drink coffee while you browse.

In the silver and craft souk, you'll find a mixture of old and new items made locally such as Bahla pottery, old wooden chests, silverwork from the different regions of Oman, antique rifles, and frankincense, as well as modern imports from India. You can watch silversmiths hammering intricate patterns into the hilts of khanjars and join the many antique silver dealers who come here from Muscat in search of treasure for their stores. Although prices are rising as tourism increases, with hard bargaining you can sometimes get a better price than in Muscat.

The Goat Souk is the scene of a lively animal market early on Friday mornings from 07:00 where cows, goats and sheep are auctioned. It's an open-air market located close to the entrance on the left, and worth visiting, especially just before the religious holidays when farmers sell their livestock for the festivities.

Btn Wahiba Sands
& Empty Quarter
Sinaw
Map 1 C2

Sinaw Souk

About two hours' drive from Muscat is Sinaw (at the crossroads of Routes 33 and 27), a busy outpost town set between the Wahibah Sands and the edge of the Empty Quarter. Behind mud-coloured walls and through green metal doors in the middle of the town is the souk, which is where Bedouins gather to do business and to socialise. It's all go around the outside walls, where camels, goats and young cattle are auctioned off. Loading the animals into trucks is a tricky business and the camels in particular can deliver knockout kicks and need at least six men to push them in. Despite the indignity of it all, they manage to maintain their haughty demeanour.

Fruits and vegetables are sold in the central covered area. Bedouin women in their metallic face masks ('burqa') happily trade next to men – quite unusual – and joke with you as you try on one of their masks. Around the covered area are small shops selling jewellery where you can watch old silver being melted down to fashion new jewellery. Sinaw is a good place to find increasingly rare Bedouin silverwork, especially in the weeks approaching Eid when many come to trade livestock or old silver for little luxuries. The souk is closed on Eid holidays.

Al Hafah
Salalah
Map 1 F3

Souk Al Hafah

Set in the coconut groves of the Al Hafah area, three kilometres from Salalah, this is the best place in Oman to buy frankincense and incense powders. There are dozens of buckets sitting around with different qualities and compositions of perfumes and you can either ask a local to explain the differences to you, or just buy the one you like best. The scents are generally quite potent and a little goes a long way. Frankincense is poured into a bag and weighed, while incense comes in little silver or copper pots. Remember to buy some charcoal for burning the incense and some brightly painted clay Dhofari burners to put them in. You can also buy textiles, gold and silver, Indian and Arabic dresses and some traditional souvenirs. Local coffee shops serve snacks such as hummus and mishkak (Omani style barbecued meat).

Main Shopping Malls

Al Qurm
Map 8 E4

Al-Araimi Complex

24 566 180 | alaraimi@omantel.net.om

This bright and spacious complex boasts over 70 shops and is one of the more upmarket centres in Al Qurm. The first floor is devoted mainly to sophisticated clothes shops, while the basement holds many electronics and computer shops, appliance stores, a sports shop and an Oman Mobile outlet. In addition to electronics and some household appliances, ElectroCity stocks Canon cameras and musical instruments, including Yamaha pianos and Zildjian drum kits.

Al-Araimi is quite a handy mall in terms of services. You can sign up to the GSM network at the Oman Mobile shop, and if you are asked to submit a passport copy that's no problem since there is a Xerox Colour Photocopying shop within the centre. If you need passport photos, or you just want to get your holiday snaps developed, the mall has two choices: Photocentre and FotoMagic.

If it's money you're after then you're in luck: Al-Araimi has its very own branch of National Bank of Oman, which is handy if you need to withdraw cash from the ATM or apply for an emergency personal loan to cover all your shopping. And if you are poor in rials but you've got wads of foreign currency in your pocket, the Bin Jadid Exchange will gladly change it for you.

The big parking lot is nearly always full as it's one of the last free parking areas in the Al Qurm shopping area. If you can't find a parking space there, the adjacent car parks offer pay parking at reasonable rates. This is one of three main malls in the vicinity, and therefore you can expect the area to get incredibly busy at peak shopping times. However, check your watch if you go there and the car park is deserted – most shops inside Al-Araimi close down for the lunchtime shift (usually 13:00 to 16:00).

Outlets include: Ajmal, Al Felaij Watches, Al Qurum Shoes, Al Raid Jewellery, Al Shabab, Anne Optician, Arabian Oud, Bosch, Dgal, ElectroCity, Giordano, Golden Gate Café, Golden Pearl Jewellery, Gulf Shells, H. FLo, Hang Ten, House of Aoud Amber & Perfumea, L'Artisan, Levis, LG Electrical, Maathir Perfumes, Majid, Marina, Millennium Music, Modern Capital Optical, MS, Muscat Sports, My Jewellery, New Gift Centre, Nice Lady, OHI Electronics, Perfect Woman Fashions, Photocentre, Pretty Fit/ Bata, Raymond Shop, Riyam Cosmetics, Salman Stores, Scarlet Plus Size, Sheetal, Silk Island Trading, Smart Kids Toys, The Athlete's Foot, Trendz.

Opp Beach Hotel
Shati Al Qurm
Map 8 A4

Bareeq Al Shatti

24 643 898 | www.bareeqalshatti.com

One of the newest shopping spots in Muscat, Bareeq Al Shatti is situated below a popular residential block opposite the Beach Hotel in Shati. It offers some great one-off shops and restaurants in addition to essentials such as a dental clinic, mini supermarket, hair salons, optician and a pharmacy. It's also a good choice for a quick bite with several coffee shops and a foodcourt. Kids will be entertained at Little Town, an indoor play area, while adults can use some free time at the beauticians and even a specialised eye lash salon. Arabic fusion restaurant Ubhar (24 699 827) is particularly recommended with its stylish interior, extensive menu and tasty choices for lunch and dinner, or just a juice with friends. Meanwhile, hungry teenagers and families are flocking to B+F Roadside Diner (24 698 836) with its retro menu of burger and shakes served in a modern interior.

Bareeq Al Shatti's shops are open 10:00 to 22:00 Saturday to Thursday and 14:00 to 22:00 on Fridays, with the various restaurants closing later depending on the day.

Outlets include: Aballa Cafe, Afnan Dental Clinic, Ajmal International, Al-Farsy Pharmacy, Al-Qandeel Travel & Tourism, Ammar Saloon, Automatic Restaurant,

Places To Shop

Jawaharat A'Shati

Shopping and social hubs

SHAM Optix

A stroll through the souk

Open all hours

AL NAFEESA

SILKY TEXTILES

Qurum City Centre

Bread Talk, Buffet Restaurant, Bugatti, Candy Bouquet, Caribou Coffee, Colombian Aroma Café, Costa Coffee, The Cream & Fudge Factory, German Eye Centre, Grand Spa, Home House, Little Beauty Center, Little Town, Oman Arab Bank, Porsche Design , Pure Gold, Second Cup, ShamOptix, Shoe Palace, Supa Sportsman, Tips & Toes , Triple Time, Xtreme Lashes.

Jawaharat A'Shati Commercial Complex

Nr
InterContinental
Muscat
Shati Al Qurm
Map 8 A4

24 692 113 | www.jascomplex.com

Jawaharat's lively atmosphere and beachfront location attracts visitors from all over the city. Shops are arranged on either side of a carpark that's a little too small to cope with the weekend crowds. Lunchtime and weekday evenings are more relaxed.

You'll find some unusual items on sale here, like hand-rolled cigars, Turkish icecream, chocolate covered dates, Italian coffee and Omani handicrafts, to mention a few. Totem sells unique clothing and footwear (plus Havaianas) while Pomegranate boasts a great selection of witty cards. For delightful home decor head to Gecko where you'll find gorgeous Balinese pieces and Designer's Guild fabrics and wallpapers. A browse around The Oman Heritage Gallery is like spending time in a museum, and you can buy some beautiful, traditional crafts, all handmade by local artists. Nails, Muscat's only salon devoted purely to pampering your hands and feet, is hidden behind red and pink glass walls on the first floor, and a new addition is a Spa Bar for men. If you're shopping for furniture you'll find Shuram, the sole agents for IKEA in Oman, here and Marina. There's also Sparks for balloons and party goods, a florist, Bartech with everything you need to create your own bar and Moustache which sells designer gear for men. Women are taken care of by the Eye Candy boutique which sells a stunning mix of designer clothing from the likes of See by Chloe, Essa and Paul & Joe plus sunglasses by Tom Ford. It is also the only Oman stockist of popular Australian makeup brand Becca. The main attraction though, is food. The centre is home to several restaurants, nearly all of which have open areas where you can watch the sun set over the sea. The Sheraton Qurm Resorts' Sushi Night buffet on Thursdays is always popular, the O Sole Mio Italian restaurant at the carpark entrance is highly regarded, and D'Arcy's Kitchen serves hearty international food from breakfast to dinner and is popular with expats. And if your life is empty without your huge cup of cappuccino, you have the choice of Starbucks or Costa Coffee. Pizza Express and nearby Motif Beach Cafe are great for lunch or dinner, while Pane Caldo's Italian dishes (and antipasti platters) are particularly recommended.

On a practical level, there's a post office, a barber and a brokerage house on the top floor of the right hand building, and a car rental agency on the opposite side. An Oman Arab Bank ATM is located outside the Casa del Habano cigar shop.

Outlets include: Al Batra Bookshop, Armani Jeans, Beauty Centre, Card Store, European Jewellery, Eye Candy, Foto Magic, Gecko, Jazz, Kwik Kleen, Light Moon for Herbals, Megastar, Muscat Pharmacy, Muscat Pharmacy Perfumes & Cosmetics, Persian Carpet Bazaar, Totem and Tahani Co.

Markaz Al Bahja ▶ p.297

Al Seeb St
As Seeb
Map 2 D4

24 541 952 | www.markazalbahja.com

This enormous three-storey shopping mall is quite quiet, probably because it's located a bit out of town towards As Seeb. However, it's well worth the trip – it's a spacious mall with plenty of entertainment and free underground parking.

The main attractions are Marks & Spencer and Toys R Us, both of which are on the top floor. Danish furniture chain ID Design is also here and it has a corner coffee shop where delicious crepes and pastries are served. In Shop & Shop you can find quality kitchen gadgets, office accessories and mugs, all priced at RO 10 or under. There are a few clothes

shops but these cater more to Arab customers and specialise in abayas and dishdashas. The foodcourt is vast, but limited to a few fast food joints including an Indian outlet and Glacier Express, where you can get icecream and Belgian waffles. There's a Baskin Robbins on the ground floor, next to a perfume shop.

Of all the malls in Muscat, Markaz al Bahja has the most to offer in terms of family entertainment. The basement has an eight-lane bowling alley, complete with billiards and internet cafe. There's a four-screen cinema, a well-stocked Al Fair supermarket and a bakery with a coffee shop. Next to the foodcourt on the top floor is a games centre and amusement park, complete with mini rollercoaster and bumper boats in a huge tank of water.

Outlets include: Ajmal, Al Faisal, Al Jamil Optical, Al Lubahna, Asdaf, Baqa Fashion, Bank Muscat, Black Net Abayas, Bodum, Bombay, Capital Skin Care Centre, Capital Store, Computer Book Shop, Clothes & Accessories, Elle, Eyewear, Fancy World, Film and Audio World, Fulla Fashions, Golden Pearl Jewellery, Haider Stores, Happy Saloon, Ibn al Naamani, ID Design, La Bonita, Laura, Lujaina Fashions, Marks & Spencer, Mohd. Sharief Stores, Muscat Bakery Stores, Muscat Pharmacy, Muscat Sports, Muscat Watch Center, National Fanar, Perfect Woman Fashion, Rado Tissot, Shoe Palace International, Shop & Shop, Snowhite, Stones, Toys R Us, Yazin Mobil and Zone.

As Seeb
Map 3 E2

Muscat City Centre

24 558 888 | www.citycentremuscat.com

This is currently the busiest, biggest and most modern mall in Oman. Not even its location past Seeb Airport deters people who come from far and wide to shop here. At weekends the huge parking area is heaving with cars and you'll be lucky to find an empty space.

The main shop in City Centre is the French hypermarket, Carrefour. It is a great first stop for people setting up home in Oman – here is where you can buy all the things you need for a new house, like brooms, mops, ironing boards, towels, pots and cooking utensils. On the food side, you can buy delicious French breads and pastries as well as other European products. Carrefour is open from 09:00 until midnight and is busiest at weekends and during Ramadan, when there are instore promotions.

If a mega shopping trip around this gigantic mall leaves you feeling peckish, the L-shaped foodcourt has the usual fastfood places, as well as Arabic, Indian, Italian and Chinese cuisine, Baskin Robbins and Subway. The eating area has separate sections for families and non-smokers. Next to the foodcourt there is a Magic Planet amusement centre for children, and a strategically placed toy shop.

There is a coffee shop at each end of the mall – one Starbucks and one Costa Coffee – great for resting weary legs and watching the world go by. Art Cafe upstairs next to Borders is also good for a quick bite but the smoky atmosphere means it isn't great for families.

Other shops in the mall sell fashion, shoes, jewellery and even special items such as Omani halwa, chocolate covered dates and local handicrafts.

The mall is open from 10:00 (except for Carrefour, which opens an hour earlier) to 22:00. None of the shops close for lunch.

Outlets include: Adams, Adidas, Al Felaij Jewellers, Alukkas, Amouage, Anoosh, Arabian Oud, Areej, Baby Shop, Borders, Carlton Cards, Carrefour, Claire's, Colange, Damas, Early Learning Centre, Fat Face, Forever 21, Foto Magic, Gap, Gasoline, Grand Opticals, Himat, Hour Choice, Lakhoos Money Exchange, MAC, Mango, Mikyojy, Milano, Millenium Games, Misako, Monsoon, Mont Blanc, Mothercare, Muscat Pharmacy, Nawras, Next, Nine West, Oman Mobile, Pretty Fit, Promod, Pumpkin Patch, Splash/Lifestyle, Sun and Sand Sports, Swatch, The Toy Store, The Watch House, Women's Secret, Woolworths and Zara.

Qurum City Centre

Nr Muscat Private School
Al Qurm
Map 11 D1

24 470 700

Qurum City Centre is one of the newest malls in Muscat, offering some of the same stores as its sister destination near the airport (p.298). It is anchored by an enormous Carrefour which is a welcome addition to the area and packed at weekends. Other shops include Jumbo Electronics, Monsoon, H&M, Next, Mango, L'Occitane, Early Learning Centre, Aldo, Bose, Borders and Adidas. In addition, you will also find telecom provider outlets, a pharmacy, National Bank of Oman, Foto Magic and Magrabi Opticals. The large foodcourt includes all the usual suspects such as KFC, Pizza Hut, McDonald's, Cinnabon, Magic Wok, Starbucks, Costa and Coffee Republic plus a branch of Italian restaurant Biella.

Customer service facilities include 1,000 parking bays, taxi drop-off and pick-up areas, ATMs, information desks, toilets, prayer rooms and wheelchairs for the elderly or people with disabilities.

Qurum City Centre is open from 10:00 to 22:00 Saturday to Thursday, 14:00 to 22:00 on Fridays and Carrefour is open 09:00 to midnight throughout the week.

Outlets include: Accessorize, Adidas, Aldo, Bendon, Biella, Body Shop, Borders, Bose, Bossini, Carrefour, Cellucom, Cinnabon, Claire's, Coffee Republic, Cold Stone Creamery, Costa Coffee, Damas, Early Learning Centre, Fillings, Foto Magic, GeeKay, Giordano, Gulf Greetings, H&M, Hatam, Hour Choice, Inglot, Jumbo, KFC, Kipling, L'Occitane, MAC, Magic Wok, Magrabi Opticals, Mango, McDonald's, Monsoon, Mothercare, Muscat Pharmacy, National Bank of Oman, Nawras, Next, Nokia, Oman Mobile, Osh Kosh, Pablosky, Pierre Cardin, Pizza Hut, Porsche Design, Promod, Pure Gold, Rado, Shamiana, Starbucks, Steve Madden, Sun Spot, Swatch, Tap a L'Oeil and Zahara Tours.

SABCO Commercial Centre

Al Qurm
Map 8 E4

24 566 701 | www.SABCOgroup.com

This was one of the first true shopping malls in Oman, and while there are some who prefer the more modern, glitzier malls, SABCO retains a loyal following of shoppers who love it because it is tried and trusted, and they know where everything is. It is usually quite quiet, so perfect if you hate the frantic sardine-like atmosphere of the busier centres. Another plus point is its central location in Al Qurm, with lots of parking. Shopping here is a relaxing experience thanks to the gardens and a soothing indoor waterfall, and plenty of wooden benches on which to flop down when you've exhausted yourself with a marathon shopping trip. They are also great for a bit of people watching.

You can buy yourself a bottle of the world-famous (and locally made) Amouage perfume in Amouage's shop, Oman Perfumery, which is near the entrance. The jewellery shop upstairs is excellent for repairing jewellery, as well as for manufacturing pieces according to your own designs. SABCO is also home to upmarket outlets like Godiva, Cerruti, Raymond Weil and Philippe Charriol, and the only pet store in Al Qurm, Creatures Pet Shop (the owner of the pet shop also runs a fancy dress shop in a basement across the road, and he will open it up for you if you ask). There's a busy coffee shop in the lobby, and an HSBC ATM. Raffles are held frequently and the grand prize is usually a luxury car.

The authentically decorated souk in the corner of the centre is an Aladdin's cave of old Omani silver, local handicrafts, souvenirs and pashminas from India. Bargaining is allowed, making the prices competitive with Mutrah souk.

Outlets include: Abu Mehad Money Exchange, Al Batra Bookshop, Al Felaij Jewellers, Al Felaij Watches, Al Gazal Opticians, Al Khamis, Al Qurum Jewellers, Al Raid, Amouage Oman Perfumery, Capital Store, Carlton Cards, Cerruti, Elle, Foto Magic, Future Jewellery, Gardini, Godiva Chocolates, Jazeera Electronics, Jazz, Jewellery Corner, Le

Carat, Modern Electronics, House, Moustache, Muscat Beauty Salon, Muscat Pharmacy, Perfumes, Muscat Pharmacy, Muscat Watch Centre, New Age Music, Nine West, Philippe Charriol, Rana Abdulrahim, Raymond Weil, Samsung, Silver Jewel Box, Snowhite Laundry, Sports For All, Tahani, The Body Shop, The Flower Shop and Video Centre.

Other Shopping Malls

Nxt to Sultan Centre
Al Qurm
Map 11 E1

Al Harthy Complex
24 564 481 | *ahcmpx@omantel.net.om*

This stand-alone building beside the bustling Sultan Centre looks either like a giant space rocket or a futuristic mosque. Whatever your interpretation, the mall is an impressive landmark, especially at night when the lattice roof and the blue dome are lit up. One of the calmer malls in terms of shopping and parking, it's popular for its internet cafe, Muscat Pizza and Kargeen Cafe. The complex also provides a good range of services – a post office, key cutting kiosk, a barber and a few tailors. The Oman Association for Consumer Protection has an office on one of the upper floors, and it's worth a visit if you have a complaint you haven't been able to resolve.

At The Gallery you'll find paintings by Omani artists, while Cards Store has a fair selection of humorous greeting cards, toys and souvenir T-shirts. Fresh and dried flowers can be ordered from Caravans, and the Modern Technical Computer Centre sells Apple computers and accessories. The first floor is almost entirely made up of shops for women and young girls, including the biggest branch of Muscat Pharmacy Perfumes and Cosmetics.

Also within the mall is a shop run by the Association for the Welfare of Handicapped Children where you can buy cheap accessories, cosmetics and T-shirts – and shop as much as you like because it's all in the name of charity!

A small amusement park in the basement will keep the kids occupied.

Outlets include: Abu Ayat, Ajmal Perfumes, Al Felaij Jewelers, Al Mira Mobil Phones, Al Sulaiman Jewellers, Aman, Gift Store, Happy Salon (for children), Health & Beauty Natural Herbs Centre, Horia Ibra Shoes, Italian Jewellery, Muscat Apollo Photoshop, North Oasis Tailoring, Oman Perfumes Centre, Oman Trading, Patchi, Qurum Textiles, Rahela Trading, Steps and The Unique Corner.

Nr Safeer
Supermarket
Al Qurm
Map 8 E4

Al Khamis Plaza
24 562 791

The medium-sized Al Khamis Plaza in Qurm is spread over three floors and the top floor is a shoe shopper's heaven. There's a branch of Clarks, and a World of Shoes where you can buy brands like Sebago, Caterpillar and Dockers and Arabic-style sandals for men and women.

Other drawcards are the textile shops that have an amazing range of Indian silks, men's shops with suits from Pierre Cardin and Lanvin, and the elaborate and exclusive Mouawad Jewellery. The fountain next to the pleasant Café de Lotus provides the soothing sound of running water. Parking is free, but demand is high.

Outlets include: Abu Hani Textiles, Al Fahid, Al Shaza, Anakah, Arabian Oud, Crystal Gallery, Damas, Dunya Stores, Fashion House, Hamood al Hadhramy, Indian Art Palace, Instyle Fashion Textiles, Kwik Kleen, Oman Optical, Oxygen, Risail Sports, Ruwi Jewellers, Savtalfan, Suhool Al Qurm, Tareti and Yateem Optician.

Way 667
Al Qurm
Map 8 E4

Capital Commercial Centre (CCC)
24 563 672 | *cccqurum@omantel.net.om*

Looking like a sprawling Omani fort, complete with flags and enormous, carved wooden doors guarding the Al Fair supermarket, CCC is a gathering place for locals and expats of both sexes. It is also popular with families who take the kids to Kids Rest (p.234), the play area upstairs.

The opening of Canadian coffee shop chain, Second Cup, over the road has resulted in a definite surge in customer traffic. It serves gourmet coffee and tea, lovely desserts and snacks in modern, comfy surroundings, and it's probably one of the few places where a single female can enjoy coffee and a book without being stared at.

To the left of the main entrance is a small souk where you can pick up a wide range of leather goods, trinkets and Omani handicrafts. The Al Fair Supermarket, which sells western food products (including pork) occupies one wing of CCC. The check-out counters sell stamps, and just past them is a small area that stocks inexpensive clothes and lingerie. Just outside Al Fair is an Oman International Bank ATM and a semi-permanent car exhibition.

The other half of CCC is a shopping centre with the usual range of jewellery, phone, carpet and perfume shops under a beautiful stained glass ceiling. Health nuts will love this centre. The Health Shop carries multivitamin protein drinks, Scholl foot products, orthopaedic cushions and pillows and blood pressure monitors. Island Natural Herbs has a wall of dried bark and herbs guarded by two old Omani men who can presumably concoct anything for what ails you, as well as 'natural' slimming products for women. Sport One is full of huge plastic jars of food supplements for those looking to increase their body mass.

There's a small amusement park for kids, a key cutter, and an internet cafe. The centre's outside walls enclose a gigantic parking lot bordered by small shops and food outlets, including Bollywood Chaat, Pizza Hut, McDonald's, Baskin Robbins and Nando's. CCC's opening hours are 08:30 to 21:00 but individual shop hours may vary.

Outlets include: Ad'dirham, Al Basim, Al Batna, All Felaij Watches, Al Khamis, Al-Marooji Travel & Tourism, Al Nazim, Al Raid, Al Shabiba, Ameera Oud, Bella La Rose, Capital Store Perfumes, Cards Store, Damas, Daraah. Foto Magic, Gardini, Gulf Jewellers, Hamood Textiles, Jazeera Electronics, Kids' Corner. King of Perfumes, Kwik Kleen, Le Carat, Mobile Phone City, Modern Music, Muscat Watch Centre, Nafaf, Najeeb Technical, Nine West, Philippe Charriol, Raymond Weil, Reham Beauty Centre. Ridhwan Opticals, Riyam, Roses. Salman Stores. Sony, Sports For All, Tahoos, The Body Shop, Waleed Pharmacy and Yiti Art Gallery.

Souk Al Khuwayr

Al Khuwayr
Map 7 C3

Also known as the Al Khuwayr Commercial Centre, this is not a souk in the traditional sense, but rather a collection of small shops in one huge block in the middle of Al Khuwayr. It offers a range of goods and services including tailors, furniture makers, second-hand electrical shops, hardware shops, one-rial shops, launderettes, a bakery, a pharmacy and a few coffee shops. Cheap household items and fabrics are the main draws, but you can also have film developed here. and there's a government-run fruit and vegetable market where you can get good fresh produce for a fraction of supermarket prices.

Zakher Shopping Mall

Al Khuwayr
Map 7 D2

24 489 884

A small shopping centre, Zakher has the usual selection of shops found in other malls and an internet coffee shop. The shops cater mostly to Arabs so if you're looking for dishdasha or Arabic art, it's a good destination. You can also buy Bang & Olufsen and G Hanz audio and video equipment at Photocentre on the ground floor, and it boasts a CD and video store and a full colour copy centre. There's a National Bank of Oman ATM at the entrance.

Outlets include: Ajmal Perfumes, Body Shop, Emerald Jewellery, Hallmark Cards Store, Muscat Pharmacy, My Fashion, Optic Bazaar and Snow Star Sweets and Gifts.

TIME TO MIX BUSINESS
WITH PLEASURE

Recognized as Doha`s preferred business hotel, the Doha Marriott Hotel comprises two buildings which include a total of 190 Standard Rooms, 119 Executive Rooms, 51 Executive Suites and 2 Presidential Suites. Located on the East shore of Doha Bay, the Hotel overlooks the marina and the beautiful Corniche with it`s ministries and main business center. The Hotel is 5 km distance from the Doha International Airport and 5 km from the City Center. The Doha Marriott features an innovative Food & Beverage concept with 6 themed restaurants and a Lounge. The Spa offers an extensive range of facilities, including a unique Turkish bath, Jacuzzi, cold plunge and steam room.

Events by Marriott tailor make any event from business functions, small gatherings, international seminars, conferences and cocktail receptions to lavish dinners.

Doha Marriott Hotel | Ras Abu Aboud Street | P.O. Box 1911 | Doha | Qatar | Phone: +974 429 8888 | www.dohamarriott.com
For reservation please call **+974 429 8502**, fax: **+974 435 8327**, email us at **dohmc.reservations@marriotthotels.com**
or visit **www.dohamarriott.com**

DMH909090

Going Out

Going Out

Oman offers a wide variety of dining experiences, and while the majority of visitors to Salalah, Nizwa, Sohar, Sur and other areas outside Muscat tend to dine in the hotel they're staying in, there are interesting independent Arabic restaurants to be found if you take the time to explore. This section, however, concentrates on places to discover in Muscat as the majority of visitors and expats use the capital to explore their culinary tastes and find a surprising variety of restaurants, bars and cafes here. It might not be Dubai, but with tourism being actively promoted in Oman, the nightlife is constantly improving. So whatever your scene, you should find something to fit your appetite and budget.

The following chapter has been divided into two; restaurants are listed under Eating Out (p.304), while cafes, bars, pubs, nightclubs and 'cultural' entertainment such as theatre, cinema and comedy clubs, are discussed in On The Town (p.338).

Eating Out

Oman's multicultural heritage and population is reflected in the variety of international cuisine you'll find here. From Arabic to Mediterranean to Polynesian and everything in between, you'll have a fine time exploring.

Eating out is a time-honoured Arabic pastime; it's seen as an opportunity for friends and family to exchange news, gossip and argue the merits of any thing from a foreign leader to the latest mobile phone. Most restaurants open early in the evening, around 19:00, but generally don't get busy until about 21:00. Lunchtimes can vary between 12.00 and 15.00 so check before you arrive. Many of the places we've covered here are very popular, so if you want to dine out at the weekend, particularly if there's a group of you, it's best to book a table.

A large number of Oman's restaurants are situated in hotels, especially in Muscat, but there are also many independent restaurants throughout the town, some of which are licensed. (If you want to have a tipple with your meal, check for the Alcohol Available icon in individual reviews). While the licensed restaurants are popular for obvious reasons, there's a vast number of excellent independent restaurants around town that shouldn't be ignored just because they are 'dry'.

The more upmarket restaurants tend to specialise in one or two types of cuisine, while the smaller outlets will often entice you with a variety so it's not uncommon to find an Indian restaurant also offers Thai and Chinese dishes. Many also have theme nights featuring different types of cuisine, such as seafood, Italian or sushi. Some have weekly buffet nights when you can eat, and sometimes drink, as much as you like for a good value, all-inclusive price. Easy on the purse strings but hard on the waist band…

Planning Your Getaway?

Whether your idea of a weekend getaway involves a relaxing spa stay, an activity-packed city break, or a camping trip in the wilderness, *Weekend Breaks in Oman and the UAE* is the ultimate resource for pepping up your downtime.

Cuisine List – Quick Reference

American	p.308	Mongolian	p.325
Arabic & Lebanese	p.308	Moroccan	p.325
Chinese	p.311	Omani	p.326
Far Eastern	p.312	Pakistani	p.328
Filipino	p.312	Persian	p.328
Indian	p.314	Pizzerias	p.328
International	p.318	Polynesian	p.328
Italian	p.322	Portuguese	p.328
Japanese	p.323	Seafood	p.330
Latin American	p.324	Spanish	p.331
Mediterranean	p.324	Steakhouses	p.331
Mexican	p.325		

Delivery & Takeaways

Most fastfood cutlets, including Burger King and Pizza Hut, offer free home delivery, but you can also order dishes from your favourite local eatery and have them deliver too. So you can get shawarmas, sweet and sour noodles or butter chicken delivered to your doorstep, and enjoy all the comfort of eating in – without the washing up that usually goes with it.

Hygiene

Don't be fooled by the appearance of some of the outlets you come across in Oman. Many are probably not as bad as they might look. Then again, some of them are, so use

Cafe culture

your judgment. The local authorities are clamping down on hygiene so many places have bucked up their ideas and started to follow procedures and guidelines as laid out by the municipality.

Tipping

Tipping is up to you. The service charge is not generally passed on to the waiting staff and it applies regardless of whether the service was excellent or lousy. So if you would like to reward the waiting staff directly, a 10% tip will be much appreciated. Try to hand it directly to the person you'd like to thank, as at some establishments tips go straight into the till. Most people tend to leave their change as a tip, particularly in cafes.

Restaurant Listing Structure

Considering the size of Muscat, the choice of places to eat is good – the many listed outlets in this chapter will definitely keep you busy for a while and there are some that you'll want to revisit time and again.

Each restaurant review is written to give you an idea of the food, service, decor and ambience, and those venues that really excel have earned a yellow star. The restaurants have been categorised by cuisine (in alphabetic order). If you want to plan your evening out – perhaps you have guests in town and want to dine in a hotel nearby – then simply turn to the index at the back of this book. Each of the hotels will have a list of each of its outlets and their cuisine category.

When selecting an establishment there are a number of factors that will affect your choice. If you want to enjoy a drink with your meal then look out for the icon that indicates that alcohol is available, but bear in mind that the hotel restaurants may be a little more expensive than the independent venues. Also, don't forget that there also exists a wide variety of non-licensed establishments that offer delicious Arabic fare for excellent value.

In order to avoid confusion concerning a particular restaurant's listing, as a rule, non-English names retain their prefix (Al, Le, La and El) in their alphabetical placement, while English names are listed by actual titles, ignoring prefixes such as 'The'. Bon appetit!

Brunch

Friday brunch is perfect for a lazy start or end to the weekend, especially once the really hot weather arrives. Popular with all sections of the community, it provides Thursday night revellers with a gentle awakening, while for families it's a very pleasant way to spend the day together. Many of the venues put on a variety of fun activities for the kids, allowing parents to relax and concentrate on the fine food and drinks. Different brunches appeal to different crowds; some have fantastic buffets, others are in spectacular surroundings, and some offer amazing prices for all you can eat. A number of the four and five-star hotels offer an incredibly enticing spread as well as use of their pool, gardens or beach as part of the deal. Ask around and find out who does what, where and for how much and make a day of it.

Street Food

Other options **Arabic & Lebanese** p.308

Roadside stands throughout the city sell shawarma, rolled pita bread filled with lamb or chicken carved from a rotating spit, and plenty of salad. Costing about 300 baisas each, these are inexpensive, well worth trying, and offer an excellent alternative fast food to the usual burger. The stands generally also sell other dishes, such as falafel, ta'amiya (small savoury balls of deep-fried beans), or foul (a paste made from fava beans).

While most shawarma stands offer virtually the same thing, there are some that stand out from the rest, and sometimes, surprisingly, it's the smallest, most low-key place that you only happen on by chance. You'll find that regulars are often adamant that their particular favourite serves the best falafel in town. You'll find your favourite too – often the very first place you eat at when you come to Oman. Even if it's superb though, you should make the effort to look around as every restaurant has its own way of doing things.

Quick Reference Icons	
🌫	Alfresco Option
😊	Happy Hour
🚫	No Credit Cards Accepted
👶	Kids Welcome
🎵	Live Music
🍸	Serves Alcohol
🚚	Will Deliver

Vegetarian Food

Vegetarians will probably be pleasantly surprised by the range and variety of vegetarian cuisine offered in Muscat's restaurants. Arabic food, although dominated by meat in the main course, offers a staggering range of mostly vegetarian mezze, and the general affection for fresh vegetables provides enough variety to satisfy even the most ravenous veggie diner. Also, due to the large number of Indians who are vegetarian by religion, you'll find numerous Indian restaurants that offer vegetarian dishes in a range of cooking styles.

A word of warning: if you are a strict vegetarian, confirm that your meal is completely meat-free when ordering. Some of the restaurants cook their 'vegetarian' selection with animal fat, or on the same grill as meat dishes. Also, in some places you may need to check the ingredients of seemingly vegetarian dishes.

Special Deals & Theme Nights

Some places, usually hotels, hold occasional promotions with various themes – the InterContinental Muscat (p.31) and Al Bustan Palace InterContinental (p.28) are particularly recommended. These offers also run alongside special nights, such as ladies' nights, which are usually held weekly. The weekly and monthly entertainment publications and the venue itself will be able to update you on the latest promotions. Events like quiz nights tend to be hosted by a bar or pub and can attract quite a following, with Feeney's Irish Pub (p.340) particularly popular.

**THE MORE CARDS YOU SEND,
THE MORE LIVES YOU CHANGE.**

There are millions of children who need the things we take for granted everyday.
This holiday season, you can help make a difference in a child's life
by simply buying UNICEF cards.
To view the collection of cards and gift items, please go to www.unicef.org/gao and contact
us to place your orders. Remember, every card you buy goes towards helping a child in need.

unicef

unite for children

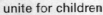
Tel. +971.4.3680703 E-mail: rasfour@unicef.org

aramex
delivery unlimited

American

Muscat City Centre
As Seeb
Map 3 E2

Chili's

24 558 815 | *www.chilisme.com*

A real family favourite, Chili's has a great menu, a fun atmosphere and helpful, amiable staff. The menu caters to all tastes – even those who are counting the calories, with 'guiltless' and 'low carb' options. Chilis' burgers are famous and the lunchtime specials of soup and salad combos are popular, but to really get your taste buds going, try the steak and fish dishes. Shame there are no guilt-free versions of the sinful molten chocolate cake. Children are well catered for with activities and they get colouring pencils and sheets to keep them occupied and a varied menu to fill them up. It is also a good spot for kids' parties.

Arabic & Lebanese

Other options **Moroccan** p.325, **Persian** p.328

Beach Hotel
Shati Al Qurm
Map 8 A4

Al Barouk ▶ p.vi

24 604 799 | *www.omanbeachhotel.com*

Al Barouk is a good option if you're in Shati Al Qurm and fancy Lebanese for lunch or dinner. The interior is simple yet thoughtfully decorated and the atmosphere conducive to a relaxed meal. A Lebanese musician and singer play gentle tunes on Monday nights. If you want to dine alfresco, the best spot is by the hotel pool – perfect for relaxing, taking in the view and enjoying some shisha. The menu includes all the Lebanese favourites as well as a few extras, although prices aren't much more than at a regular takeaway joint, and Al Barouk is licensed to serve alcohol.

Madinat Al Sultan
Qaboos Centre
Madinat As Sultan
Qaboos
Map 7 E2

Al Madinat

24 696 515

This corner of the Madinat Al Sultan Qaboos Centre is always buzzing, and it's fabulous at night when it's lit up with candles and fairy lights. Adjacent to the ever popular Kargeen restaurant is Al Madinat, where you can sit yourself down on comfy majlis cushions inside, or enjoy the fresh air under the trees outside. The friendly staff will offer you a selection of sandwiches, salads, pastries and fresh juices, and the Arabic mezze is great for sharing with friends.

Al Bandar
Shangri-La's Barr Al
Jissah Resort & Spa
Al Jissah
Map 15 E3

Al Tanoor ▶ p.309

24 776 565 | *www.shangri-la.com*

Al Tanoor is the Arabic venue at Shangri-La and a cut above a regular hotel buffet restaurant. The lofty interior is decorated attractively and stylishly in a contemporary design with tall colourful display cases, screened ceilings and 'shaded' tables, alongside traditional Omani items on display such as an alcove filled with coffee pots. Tables also spill out onto the sablah area by the fountains. At the various stations spread through the restaurant, is an impressive spread of Arabic food, starting with a top quality mezze selection, Omani dishes such as ouzi, arsiya, harees and seafood and a shawarma stand. A great place for beginners to Arabic cuisine, with the chance to try all the usual favourites alongside less common items such as ouzi – a dish normally reserved for special occasions. There is also a salad bar and show kitchens offering Indian food and even pasta. After all this, if you've still got room, the dessert section is packed to make the table groan, if not your stomach, with delicious pastries, awesome umm ali and delicious traditional Arabic sweets. Whatever your taste, everyone will leave completely sated.

RESERVED

for you...

...so you can savour exceptional fare from Oman, delectable Moroccan cuisine, stunning seafood spreads, authentic Asian dishes, fine Italian dining and exotic Latin American menus. Drop in today and savour the flavours of a myriad of dishes from around the world in one of our 19 award-winning restaurants, cafés and bars.

...only at

Shangri-La's

منتجع برالجصة.سلطنة عمان
Barr Al Jissah Resort & Spa
SULTANATE OF OMAN

For reservations call: (968) 24 776 565 | Email: fbreservation.slmu@shangri-la.com | www.shangri-la.com

Arabic Oven
24 797 276

Located in the heart of the CBD, making it convenient for office workers, Arabic Oven is a nice change from the usual sandwich at your workstation. The giant water feature on the wall makes for tranquil background noise while you enjoy biryanis, curries, and shawarmas, or pay per plateful for buffet salads. The salads from the main menu are great low-fat, carb-free lunch options (in other words, they're not drowning in dressing). For those who couldn't care less about carbs, the home baked Omani bread with hummus or moutabel is delicious.

CBD
HSBC Junction
Ruwi
Map 12 D2

Automatic
24 561 500

Automatic has established itself as the benchmark for fast Arabic food, among locals and expats alike. It's all about fresh juices, mezze and large portions for very reasonable prices. The waiters are efficient and the food quick to your table. Those with large appetites will be well-pleased with the four daily specials, while the range of traditional starters, salads, grilled meats and locally caught seafood should keep everyone happy. Friday brunch here is also a must. Other locations: Al Khuwayr, 24 487 200; As Seeb, 24 424 343.

Nr SABCO
Al Qurm
Map 8 E4

Fish Village
24 480 918

It's not quite a village, but it is a great little restaurant that is worth a visit for the view alone. It is located opposite the Radisson BLU, looking out over the Taimer Mosque and on towards 'White Mountain'. The outside seating area is large and merges with the other restaurants on either side. It's a bustling area, with lots of locals congregating over shisha and a shawarma. If your appetite permits, treat yourself to spicy squid, shish tawook or a sizzling tajin.

Nr Automatic
Restaurant
Al Khuwayr
Map 8 E4

Green Cedar
24 602 844

This may just be a drive-through, nestled between Al Fair Supermarket and the petrol station, but the food is good enough to savour. There are a few tables outside if you wish to linger a little longer to fully appreciate your snack. You'll find the usual shawarma stand favourites like chicken or mutton sandwiches wrapped up with spicy sauce, in local bread. The real jewel though is the falafels, which are particularly tasty with lots of tahina sauce and crunchy vegetables. If you're lucky you may even come across a french fry in your sandwich – a local delicacy!

Nr Al Sarooj Centre
Shati Al Qurm
Map 7 F1

Jenin
24 696 049

Head up a flight of stairs to an airy and spacious restaurant that serves a selection of traditional Arabic dishes. You can sit at the more formal tables, or lounge on comfortable sofas and gaze out at the jebels through arched windows. Choose from a selection of kebabs and grills accompanied by Arabic salads, all at a reasonable price.

Nr Ramada
Qurum Beach Htl
Shati Al Qurm
Map 7 F1

Kargeen Caffé
24 692 269 | www.kargeencaffe.com

This is a quaint, tented cafe, full of quirky ornaments and furniture, which could easily be part of someone's home. The menu comprises hearty soups, salads and Arabic appetisers, as well as burgers, pizza and steak for mains and a range of cakes, desserts and fruity drinks. This outdoor cafe is a delightfully unusual way to enjoy a leisurely

Madinat Al Sultan
Qaboos Centre
Madinat As
Sultan Qaboos
Map 7 E2

coffee-and-cake session or a complete meal within a great setting. Other locations: City Plaza, 24 694 048; Al Harthy Complex 24 560 531.

Chinese

Other options **Far Eastern** p.312

**Al Bustan Palace
InterContinental**
Al Bustan
Map 15 A1
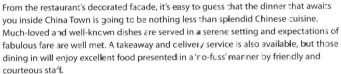

China Mood ▶ p.29

24 799 666 | www.albustanpalace.com

Acknowledged locally as one of the finest Chinese restaurants in Muscat, China Mood excels on many levels. For a start, the atmosphere is decadent and the staff superbly attentive, ensuring that your plate is consistently filled with fabulous colours, tastes and textures. The meat dishes are tender and juicy and the vegetables perfectly cooked and refreshingly free from the usual greasy oil slick. A fantastic place to enjoy a Far Eastern meal, although an early reservation is essential if you want to bag a table.

**Capital Commercial
Centre (CCC)**
Al Qurm
Map 8 E4

China Town

24 567 974 | www.goldenspoongroup.com

From the restaurant's decorated facade, it's easy to guess that the dinner that awaits you inside China Town is going to be nothing less than splendid Chinese cuisine. Much-loved and well-known dishes are served in a serene setting and expectations of fabulous fare are well met. A takeaway and delivery service is also available, but those dining in will enjoy excellent food presented in a 'no-fuss' manner by friendly and courteous staff.

Nr Centre Ice Rink
Al Khuwayr
Map 7 B2

Chinese Garden

24 489 414

Although a tad garish in design, the Chinese Garden serves tasty and satisfying food in a no-frills, no big bills manner. Attached to Oman's only ice rink, in Al Khuwayr, the atmosphere within the small restaurant is friendly and the service is quick – the epitome of cheap and cheerful Chinese cuisine. It's a great place for a laidback supper but you can just make out the low rumblings coming from the generators that power the ice rink.

**Opp Sheraton
Oman Htl**
Ruwi
Map 12 F2

Chinese Palace

24 812 223 | joldway@omantel.net.om

Office workers in Muscat know the Chinese Palace well for its delicious RO 1 office lunch boxes, but it's well worth a visit for dinner too. The private dining rooms are popular in the evenings although if you dine here at lunch you may find you're the only customer. All the classics appear on the menu, with a good selection for vegetarian diners, the service is quick and the portions are large. Be prepared to make your own noise though as it can be eerily quiet.

**Madinat Al Sultan
Qaboos Centre**
Madinat As Sultan
Qaboos
Map 7 E2

Golden Dragon

24 697 374

An upmarket and attractive Chinese restaurant in the quiet part of the Madinat Qaboos Shopping Centre, Golden Dragon has an extensive menu of Chinese and Thai dishes. Its interesting specialities are highly recommended – try the Dragon Boat, which consists of a range of starters served on a miniature wooden boat, or the sizzling dishes from the Chinese oven. This is the place to go for good value, fine Chinese cuisine served by friendly, experienced staff.

Al Burj St
Ruwi
Map 12 D1

The Golden Oryx ▶ p.313

24 702 266 | *www.thegoldenoryx.com*

The Golden Oryx is situated in the heart of the CBD. It's a bit of a drive, so the restaurant's popularity is a credit to the chefs. The decor is sumptuous and the service is impeccable, right down to the free water throughout your meal. The menu is Chinese, Thai and Mongolian, and the Chinese crispy duck in plum or barbecue sauce is a particular favourite. Make sure someone in your party orders the Thai chicken satay starters (and that you get a bite) – they're delicious, with loads of crunchy, decadently rich sauce. Not to be missed.

Nr SABCO
Al Qurm
Map 8 E4

Silk Route

24 561 741 | *harishchamder@rocketmail.com*

Silk Route is not inexpensive, but it is one of the better Chinese restaurants in Muscat. It draws fans from both the local and expat communities so you can expect it to get really busy in the evenings, particularly at the weekend. It's a great family restaurant too, so book in advance. Once there, the varied menu of Chinese, Cantonese and Szechwan cuisines, includes delicious dim sum and a particularly good crispy aromatic duck. There is also a Thai menu. Service is friendly and helpful and the atmosphere is warm and welcoming.

Far Eastern

Other options **Mongolian** p.325, **Filipino** p.312, **Japanese** p.323, **Polynesian** p.328, **Chinese** p.311

Al Qurm Resort
Shati Al Qurm
Map 8 A4

Jade Garden

24 605 945

Even though it's located at the Sheraton on Qurm Beach, the Far Eastern restaurant just misses out on a sea view. Fortunately, the food is well worth your full attention. Choose from a selection of Chinese, Thai and teppanyaki dishes and all the takeaway classics, including lemon chicken and seafood noodles. The typical oriental puddings, from lychees to delicious ice creams, are fabulously indulgent. Service is prompt between courses and the atmosphere is peaceful, however Thursdays are sushi nights and very popular.

Grand Hyatt Muscat
Shati Al Qurm
Map 7 E1

Marjan Poolside Restaurant

24 641 234 | *www.muscat.hyatt.com*

Set to the side of a beach that overlooks the Arabian Gulf, the Marjan Poolside Restaurant is set in the Grand Hyatt's beautifully landscaped garden courtyard. But the real treat here is the fact that you get to select your fish, decide how it should be cooked – whether it's to be grilled, fried or steamed in a banana leaf – and then pick your sauces and settle down to a superb meal. A great venue for either a romantic meal or a rowdy dinner with pals.

Filipino

Other options **Far Eastern** p.312

Nr Ruwi R/A
opp OCC
Ruwi
Map 12 D3

Palayok Restaurant

24 797 290

It's a bit of a challenge to find Palayok, which is tucked away in Ruwi, but once you do you'll agree that the hunt was worth the effort. It looks a little dull on the outside but opens up into a bright, cheery little place. Mr Marlon will make you feel at home and offer you some excellent suggestions regarding the menu. Fresh vegetables, fish and

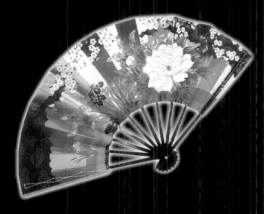

So authentic, that you can
literally feel the whoosh of the oriental fan

At Golden Oryx, the experience tantamounts to a gastronomic voyage to the Orient with its delicate seasoning, subtle flavours, beautiful garnishes and culinary sophistication. The ambience that reflects the Zen-like oriental tranquility might even let you experience the whoosh of the oriental fan.

THE GOLDEN ORYX

P.O.Box 1136, Ruwi, PC 112, Sultanate of Oman. Tel: 24702266, 24706128 E-mail: goryx@omantel.net.om

www.thegoldenoryx.com

meat are perfectly seasoned and dressed in delicious sauces to create some of the finest Asian eating in Muscat. Whether you decide to eat-in or take advantage of the home-delivery option, Palayok should be on your must-try list.

Indian
Other options **Pakistani** p.328

Capital Commercial Centre (CCC)
Al Qurm
Map 8 E4

Bollywood Chaat
24 565 653 | *khimjis@omantel.net.om*
This vegetarian restaurant has a Bollywood-themed menu of light meals and snacks, in a bright fastfood-style setting. The heart-shaped potato cutlets (kajol cutlet) and the sweet and sticky dumplings (moon moon gulab jamun) are two dishes not to be missed. The fact that everything's so reasonably priced makes a meal here that little bit more special. Service is prompt and cheery and the staff willing to explain the ingredients of the dishes on offer.

CBD Area
Ruwi
Map 12 D2

Copper Chimney
24 706 420
Behind the imposing copper door lies an impressive interior and a fabulous kitchen. Best of all, the fine Indian fare served perfectly meets the expectations the decor raises. A high, domed ceiling, complete with great copper lamps, means you eat your meal in an airy, spacious room. And once you've ordered from the mouthwatering selection of dishes, you can watch your meal being cooked in the vast clay oven in the kitchen. For excellent Indian food in a grand setting, with reasonable prices, look no further than the Copper Chimney.

Way 317
Bld 1360
Al Wutayyah
Map 12 A1

Curry House
24 564 033 | *curryhouseom@hotmail.com*
Food eaten with your fingers always seems to taste better. While you don't have to eat with your fingers, the Curry House near the Al Wattayah Roundabout, is a truly authentic North Indian dining experience. The service is some of the best you'll find in Oman, and the delicious and cheap buffet has a superb selection of Indian cuisine. Many of the curries are served in 'karahi', lovely copper bowls imported from India, and all are accompanied by beautifully fragrant vegetable pilau. This is a cheap and very cheerful spot.

Nr Zawabi Mosque
Al Khuwayr
Map 7 B2

Golden Spoon Restaurant
24 482 263 | *www.goldenspoongroup.com*
This is a popular casual spot for good, inexpensive Chinese and Indian food. The decor is a bit dark, but the attentive and friendly staff more than make up for it. The menu is extensive and there are always excellent daily specials to be had. Servings are very generous and each dish is full of flavour. It's tempting to make a meal of the sweet and sour soup, but don't – save room for tasty dishes like the murj masala. There is another branch in As Seeb (24 424 214).

Nr City Plaza
Al Khuwayr
Map 7 D2

Grill House
24 603 660
At the Grill House, just a stone's throw from the Al Khuwayr Roundabout near Madinat Qaboos, the service comes faster than usual and with a smile. You'll feast on well-prepared dishes of the Indian, Chinese or Thai ilk and leave thrilled at the tiny total on your bill. An enjoyable experience from start to satisfying finish. You'll find another Grill House in As Seeb (24 541 502).

Named after a Persian queen, serving Indian cuisine, in Oman.

It's not food of the world, it's out of the world food.

INDIAN SPECIALTY RESTAURANT

For table reservations, banquets and outdoor catering,
Call (+968) 24605907, 24605979
or E-mail: mmtzrest@omantel.net.om

CBD Area
Mutrah
Map 12 D2

Khyber

24 781 901 | khyberrest@omantel.net.om

Khyber serves an extensive range of Indian food with some Chinese options, and boasts two licensed bars and separate dining areas. Its location, near the Central Bank of Oman in Ruwi's busy CBD, means it's well-placed to meet the demands of hungry business executives and it offers excellent specials that reflect this. Specialities include delicious Indian sweets and homemade frozen and fried icecream. The restaurant also boasts a mobile tandoori oven for outside catering events.

Above Qurm
National Park
Al Qurm
Map 8 D3

Mumtaz Mahal ▶ p.315

24 605 907 | mmtzrest@omantel.net.om

Mumtaz Mahal is one of the most interesting dining experiences to be had in Muscat. Costumed waiters will ply you with baskets of poppadoms and dips (try the date chutney is a must try) while you're making your choice. Vegetarians will be very happy here – there are plenty of paneer and spicy vegetable dishes on the menu – while meat lovers will be equally impressed and satisfied. During peak season a traditional Indian band plays to the room and the atmosphere is lively and relaxed.

Nr Hatat House
Al Wutayyah
Map 12 B3

Passage To India

24 568 480 | mohavi99@omantel.net.om

Passage To India is one of Ruwi's finest. Located at the back of Hatat House, it's a truly special evening out. For most of the evening traditional Indian music plays quietly in the background while you eat excellent food, but every now and then, dancers in exquisite costumes come out and perform beautifully synchronised dances from all over India. More than just a meal out, the combination of the relaxing ambience, efficient service, superb food and good value makes this an exceptional experience.

Nr Zawawi Mosque
Al Khuwayr
Map 7 B2

Prince's Restaurant

24 482 213

Despite the rather gloomy interior, Prince's Restaurant serves up a wide and appealing range of Mughlai, Tandoori, Chinese and continental dishes at an appealing price. The decor is eclectic but the interior is comfortable and the service quiet and efficient. The smells from the kitchen encourage you to concentrate on the Indian specialities, such as the tandoori from the clay oven, which is delicious and filling. For a low price you can have a banquet fit for a prince.

Al Rusayl Centre
Rusayl
Map 3 E4

Spicy Village

24 510 120

With three outlets in Muscat, the Spicy Village in Rusayl serves authentic Indian and Chinese cuisine. It may lack atmosphere and a licence to serve alcohol, but its no frills approach offers customers generous portions of Asian food at very reasonable prices. Unfortunately, 'no frills' extends to the decor, atmosphere and ambience, but for cheap fare, this is the place. Other locations: Ruwi, 24 700 175; Nizwa, 25 431 694.

Nr Europcar Bld
CBD Area
Ruwi
Map 12 D2

Woodlands ▶ p.317

24 700 192 | woodlands@ajitkhimjigroup.com

This place hits all the right spots: service with a genuine smile, fabulously large portions of delicious south Indian cuisine, and an easy on your wallet bill to top it all off. If you're having difficulty in deciding what to order, allow one of the friendly waiters to talk you through the menu, but if you're not a fire-eater beware those brutal south Indian chillies and spices. A good place for an easy night out. There is another branch at Salalah Airport (23 204 280).

Authentically South Indian

WINNER.

BEST SERVICE

The Ghatam is a typically south Indian music instrument whose resonant sounds are the perfect accompaniment to finger licking sounds made at Woodlands.

Woodlands

Muscat: 24700192, Sohar: 26843741/46, Salalah: 23204280

International

Al Aktham

Nr Oman Int Bank
Al Khuwayr
Map 7 D2

24 489 292 | www.alaktham.iscentre.net

Behind a rather run-down exterior hides a surprisingly large restaurant with an even larger menu. At Al Aktham you can choose from Arabian, Indian, Chinese and Filipino dishes or, if none of that appeals to the tastebuds, there's Continental too. It's a good place for a private dinner party in one of the screened rooms and you're sure to have an excellent value meal, served by polite and friendly staff. For lunch or dinner, Al Aktham is a hidden gem.

Al Daleh Restaurant

National
Hospitality Institute
Ruwi
Map 12 E4

24 813 141 | www.nhioman.com

There are a couple of things that make this place an ideal choice for lunch. The portions are big and the prices are small, and then there's the opportunity to experience the talents of the town's latest up and coming chefs. As friendly as the waiters are, they aren't quite on top of their game, but you'll still leave full to bursting and very happy. Wednesday's lunch buffet is only RO 2.5 and the regular fast track two-course lunch is RO 2.5.

Al Falaj Coffee shop

Al Falaj Hotel Muscat
Ruwi
Map 12 D1

24 702 311 | www.omanhotels.com

If you work in the throbbing business district of Muscat or want a place to meet someone for a quiet lunch, the Al Falaj Coffee Shop in the Al Falaj Hotel Muscat does the trick. You can tuck into the small lunch buffet or choose from a variety of seafood and Indian fare on the a la carte menu while overlooking the hotel swimming pool. There's not much in the way of ambience, but the service is good and friendly and it's a popular stop for the locals, which is a recommendation in itself.

Al Khiran Terrace ▶ p.29

Al Bustan Palace
InterContinental
Al Bustan
Map 15 A1

24 799 666 | www.albustanpalace.com

A bright and open space with fantastic views of the garden and the beautiful bay is only the beginning – this is perhaps one of the friendliest restaurants in Oman. In addition to alfresco breakfasts, it serves up some of the most mouth-watering themed buffets in Muscat, but there's also an Italian a la carte menu available every night for those who prefer more restrained dining. The staff are attentive and will ensure your evening is one to remember.

Al Nouras

Ramada Qurm
Beach Hotel
Shati Al Qurm
Map 8 A4

24 603 555 | www.ramadamuscat.com

Hungry but not entirely sure what you want? Then head down to the Ramada Hotel's Al Nouras dining area where you'll find Indian, Arabic, Chinese and international cuisine. The diversity of the menu is impressive, but like so many other places that try to be everything, overall quality and taste leaves a little to be desired. Sit on the terrace and you'll be tucking into your meal overlooking the car park and some of Muscat's flashiest cars.

Alauddin Restaurant

Khalil Bldg
nr Traffic Lights
Al Khuwayr
Map 7 D2

24 600 667

You'll be hard pushed to find someone who lives in Muscat and hasn't enjoyed food from Alauddin, whether eating in or taking away. It is, and deservedly so, an enduring favourite. Don't expect the decor to knock your socks off, and you're not

here for the booze either, because this place is not licensed. but do arrive with high expectations of a gastronomic good time. Excellent Indian, superb Arabic, mouth-watering Chinese and tasty international cuisine is all available and all served to deliciously high standards. A Muscat must.

Al Rusayl Centre
Rusayl
Map 3 E4

Bellapais
24 521 100
This unpretentious gem of a restaurant is well worth the 40km drive from downtown

The Chedi Poolside Cabana

Muscat Don't be put off by the decor – the quality of the food surpasses all initial impressions. Known for the authentic moussaka, baked lamb, steaks and seafood, it also offers Chinese and Indian dishes. Try the mezze to start – it's an ideal introduction to your gastronomic journey, whichever route you choose to continue on. Bellapais comes alive at lunchtimes, is quieter in the evenings but no one has been known to leave hungry.

The Chedi
Al Ghubrah
Map 6 E2

The Chedi Poolside Cabana
24 524 400 | *www.chedimuscat.com*
This is one of those places you're unlikely to find unless someone has told you to look for it – and it's worth noting the tip. The Cabana at the glamorous Chedi hotel is a tranquil and intimate place to enjoy a cool evening breeze and a choice of set menus. The small number of tables ensures that each receives efficient service. The flavour is Mediterranean with an emphasis on seafood, served with finesse. An evening isn't complete without one of its wickedly decadent puddings. It's not a cheap night out, but it's definitely worth the splash.

Haffa House Hotel
Ruwi
Map 12 D2

Four Seasons
24 707 207 | *www.haffahouse.com*
Four Seasons has an a la carte menu, but it's the favourably priced buffet that draws the diners in time and again. The choice of fare is international and simple but tasty. You'll be offered a soup starter, the choice of four or five salads, five main courses and a couple of desserts. It certainly makes for good value, but the ambience and setting is more business, less pleasure.

Sheraton Oman Hotel
Ruwi
Map 12 F2

Green Mountain
24 772 772 | *www.ichotelsgroup.com*
Green Mountain's formal exterior – rather reminiscent of a 1970s Dallas skyscraper – doesn't hint at the laidback, all-you-can-eat buffet money saver that lies within, but it's definitely there. An international buffet (there's also an a la carte menu available) keeps diners happy throughout the week. On Wednesdays however, it makes way for a highly recommended seafood extravaganza that costs RO 13.75 per person. Vegetarians will be pleased with the variety of dishes on offer and those with a sweet tooth are also catered for with some delicious sweets and puddings.

Sultan Center
Al Qurm
Map 11 E1

Jean's Grill
24 567 666

Located within the Sultan Centre supermarket, Jean's Grill may seem an unlikely destination for lunch or dinner. However it offers an exciting international spread that's well worth stopping by for. Your choices begin with soups and salads, and carry on through to pasta, curries, grilled meats, fish and even braised duck. Tuck into pastries from around the world, unlimited soft drinks, tea and coffee and enjoy it all for a very reasonable set price. All-in-all the perfect pit stop after a mammoth shopping excursion.

Majan Continental Hotel
Al Khuwayr
Map 6 D4

Khaboura Cafe
24 592 900 | www.majanhotel.com

This is a European-style cafe, fairly plain but clean and welcoming. The range of food is good; Arabic, Asian, Chinese and Continental cuisine with prices around RO 1 to RO 5 – very reasonable for good grub. There's a buffet offered every evening but diners also have an a la carte option. The cafe is not licensed but serves a good selection of juices and coffees. Although it advertises 24 hour service, in reality Khaboura seems to stay open until 01:00 or whenever it's empty enough to warrant closing the doors.

Grand Hyatt Muscat
Shati Al Qurm
Map 7 E1

Mokha Cafe
24 641 234 | www.muscat.hyatt.com

Sharing its enormous domed ceiling and elegant surroundings with the lobby of the hotel, Mokha Cafe lacks identity, but benefits from the hotel's terrace that overlooks the gardens and sea. The cafe offers an a la carte menu and an extensive buffet of freshly-prepared international cuisines, ranging from sushi and salads to meat and seafood. Discerning diners will be well-satisfied and vegetarians will find a good array of options. The staff are attentive, service is good and as this cafe caters for children, it's an ideal venue for Friday brunch.

Radisson BLU Hotel Muscat
Al Khuwayr
Map 7 C3

Olivos Coffee Shop ▶ p.321
24 487 777 | www.radissonblu.com/hotel-muscat

Olivos is more of a restaurant than a coffee shop and overlooks the hotel's swimming pool and gardens. It provides a nice enough, shaded setting for dining alfresco with themed nights and buffet style catering (although a wide range of international dishes is available off the a la carte menu too). With great service in a relaxed atmosphere, Olivos is a good value for money restaurant and the ideal location for a relaxed dinner with friends.

Al Husn
Shangri-La's Bar Al Jissah Resort & Spa
Al Jissah
Map 15 E2

Sultanah ▶ p.309
24 776 666 | www.shangri-la.com

Perched high above the Shangri-La's bay in Al Husn, Sultanah offers first-rate dining, fantastic views and impeccable service. Following the theme of a cruise ship visiting different ports every night, the international menu offers choices from locations such as New York, Singapore and Paris. Creative, contemporary international cuisine at its finest, the menu includes gamey choices such as rabbit, with fish and seafood. The dining room affords panoramic views of the bay from large windows, while the covered terrace and open patio overlook the resort from the edge of the cliff – a jazz trio also play here in the evenings. The stunning views get more romantic at night when the twinkling lights of the resort provide the perfect accompaniment to your meal. Sultanah has to be in the running for best restaurant in Oman.

Awaiting
your arrival

Unwind at the Radisson Blu Hotel, Muscat after a long day's sight seeing or
a full business morning. Indulge yourself with choices, from Italy's finest blends
at The Grind Floor, to exclusive cocktails & mocktails at the Lazy Lizard.
Dine at the highly acclaimed Al Tajin Grill or the Olivos coffee shop.
relax at the Coral Bar or dance the night away at the Cellar.

Radisson Blu Hotel
P.O.Box 939, P.C 133, Muscat, Sultanate of Oman
Tel: +968 2448 7777, Fax: +968 2448 7778
reservations.muscat@radissonsas.com
radissonblu.com/hotel-muscat

HOTEL, MUSCAT

Radisson BLU
Hotel Muscat
Al Khuwayr
Map 7 C3

Tajin Grill ▶ p.321

24 487 777 | www.radissonblu.com/hotel-muscat

Eating at Tajin is simple: just choose a succulent steak, some fresh fish or seafood, and then pick a sauce, a side order (baked potato, rice, fries, vegetables and more), and one of Tajin's flavoured butters, and your tailor-made main course arrives at your table a short while later. The chefs do a brilliant job of cooking everything to your liking, and the friendly waiters are happy to help you choose by making recommendations. The price you pay for your main course includes starters and desserts from a small but adequate buffet table. Overall, Tajin is definitely a special-occasion restaurant, but without the sky-high prices.

Crowne Plaza
Muscat
Qurm Heights
Map 8 C3

Tropicana ▶ p.25

24 660 660 | www.cpmuscat.com

Located at the poolside of the Crowne Plaza hotel in Qurm, Tropicana has an international menu ranging from Oriental (with unlimited sushi and dim sum), Indian and Mediterranean classics to the good old American burger, and theme nights on Wednesdays and Thursdays. Lunchtimes see a loaded buffet and this tastefully decorated restaurant is well frequented in the afternoon hours. Appetising dishes arrive in generous proportions, accompanied by excellent service and a reasonable price tag. The poolside location offers a pleasant view, and outside seating is available.

Al Bustan Palace
InterContinental
Al Bustan
Map 15 A1

Vue By Shannon Bennett ▶ p.29

24 764 133 | www.albustanpalace.com

Hot Australian chef Bennett has brought his slick, international cuisine to the Middle East with Vue. Set in the stunning Al Bustan Palace InterContinental, this is one of Muscat's finest restaurants, from the warm welcome to the petit fours. While the atmosphere is sophisticated, there is no snobbery, with charming staff happy to talk guests through the menu and wine list. Particularly enjoyable is the tasting menu (with wine matching) for RO 40 which features a black truffle risotto perfectly paired with a crisp, cold Madeira and a wagyu beef dish so delicious you'll hope it never ends. Of course, starting an evening with a glass of champagne is always lovely but the pleasure continues through the seven courses, with extra touches like hibiscus and dry ice palate cleansers and frozen kiwi lollipops. With delicate portions you'll have room for desserts which are a delight, including a feather-light chocolate and pistachio soufflé with crème anglaise. The menu changes every two weeks and lunch specials are available with two courses for RO 10 or three courses for RO 13.

Italian

Other options **Pizzerias** p.328, **Mediterranean** p.324

Al Bandar
Shangri-La's Barr Al
Jissah Resort & Spa
Al Jissah
Map 15 E3

Capri Court ▶ p.309

24 776 565 | www.shangri-la.com

Located in Al Bandar Hotel at the end of bay, below the towering cliff from where Al Husn presides over the resort, dining at Capri Court is not about the view outside, it's about the stunning Italian cuisine. Issuing forth from the kitchen, which is presided over by the chef from Sicily, are some very special and beautifully presented dishes. Starters such as baked aubergine combine ingredients seamlessly, while mains such as the squid ink linguine with sauteed lobster is spectacularly served in half a lobster shell. Portions are perfect – there's no scrimping with size – but also allow space for dessert. Which is just as well, as the crowning glory to your meal could well be the tiramisu, which is outstanding. Daily menus have four course specials with wines matched to each course.

Crowne Plaza
Muscat
Qurm Heights
Map 8 C3

Come Prima ▶ p.25

24 660 660 | www.cpmuscat.com

Inside, or out, this establishment has some of the best views in town. Top these with garlic bread like it should be – hot, fresh, and very, very moreish – a traditional Italian menu with homemade pasta, pizza, meat and seafood dishes and you have yourself the making of an excellent night out. (And if you find yourself craving mamma's cooking during the day, it offers delivery at lunch time). Food is served at a relaxed pace, allowing time for plenty of chatting. Come Prima is not the most hip restaurant in town, so come here to enjoy the food and your friends – not to be seen.

Sheraton Oman Hotel
Ruwi
Map 12 F2

La Mamma

24 772 772 | www.starwoodhotels.com

La Mamma offers casual Italian dining in the heart of Muscat's CBD. It's all an Italian restaurant should be, right down to the rather garish red and white chequered curtains and the plaits of garlic. The menu consists largely of simple but delicious Italian fare including classic antipasti, a variety of pastas and a selection of main courses. Friendly and attentive service rounds the evening off.

Jawaharat A'Shati
Commercial Complex
Shati Al Qurm
Map 8 A4

O Sole Mio

24 601 343 | jasco@omantel.net.om

An award-winning restaurant, O Sole Mio is ideal for a candlelit dinner for two or an informal dinner with friends, thanks to its lively atmosphere, musical entertainment and delicious Italian food. The menu is extensive, with plenty of grilled options for the health-conscious, and servings are ample. The staff are attentive and offer quick, efficient service. O Sole Mio's popularity stems from its prime location and its ability to deliver good food at reasonable prices, making it advisable to book in advance.

Jawaharat A'Shati
Commercial Complex
Shati Al Qurm
Map 8 A4

Pane Caldo

24 698 697

This family-friendly restaurant errs just on the right side of bright, without being garish. The handy location next to Jawahat A'Shati Commerical Complex attracts customers, but the super thin pizzas, fantastic antipasti platters and fresh pastas keep the interest of food fans. With reasonable prices, lunch and dinner opening hours, and friendly service, Pane Caldo is a reliable Italian that you'll revisit again and again.

Grand Hyatt Muscat
Shati Al Qurm
Map 7 E1

Tuscany

24 641 234 | www.muscat.hyatt.com

Voted Best Italian Restaurant of 2005 by *Oman Today*, Tuscany delivers an authentic Italian dining experience, complete with Romanesque pillars and a fountain. The menu is extensive and offers all the classic Italian dishes but if your favourite isn't there, just ask the chef. The food is superb and the service impeccable. The restaurant maintains that perfect blend of formal dining with a relaxed atmosphere – and it's clear that it's sought-after, so be sure to reserve a table.

Japanese

Other options **Far Eastern** p.312

Al Falaj Hotel Muscat
Ruwi
Map 12 D1

Tokyo Taro

24 702 311 | www.omanhotels.com

This place is vibrant with the smells and sounds of authentic Japanese food being prepared. Meat, vegetables and seafood sizzle at the teppanyaki bar and the green tea is on tap. If you're in a group you can book one of the private dining rooms and sit at

a traditional banquet table to enjoy your meal. The setting is serene and convincing enough for you to imagine that you actually are in the land of the rising sun. Dining here affords you a tantalising – and delicious – glimpse of Japan.

Latin American
Other options **Mexican** p.325

Al Waha
Shangri-La's Barr Al Jissah Resort & Spa
Al Jissah
Map 15 E3

Samba ▶ p.309
24 776 565 | www.shangri-la.com
The South American theme has touched on all aspects of this restaurant, from the terracotta tiled floors, to the splashes of vibrant colour, and of course, the food. The

The Restaurant

adventurous can try the cactus and date salad on the buffet or spicy seafood from the a la carte menu. While you can expect to be seated among families at Samba, the alfresco seating option is spacious and the service is excellent. Combined with a tequila bar, this can make for a very enjoyable evening.

Mediterranean
Other options **Italian** p.322, **Spanish** p.331

InterContinental
Muscat
Shati Al Qurm
Map 8 A4

Musandam Cafe & Terrace ▶ p.344
24 680 000 | www.intercontinental.com
A real winner for breakfast or brunch, the Musandam Cafe & Terrace is less of a sure thing for dinner, particularly during the off-season when you can expect typical hotel buffet fare. However, for a Friday family brunch, this is the spot. Fresh fish and salads, roast meats, an egg station and pancake making make this an ideal venue for a young and hungry family. On Fridays, children can have their faces painted and watch magic shows while you fill up at the buffet. And at this casual eatery, no one minds gaudily-daubed children running amok between the tables.

The Chedi
Al Ghubrah
Map 6 E2

The Restaurant
24 498 035 | www.ghmhotels.com
The Restaurant boasts a fusion of contemporary Arabic and Far Eastern decor, aptly reflecting its menu. You can choose from sushi, tajin, fish or curries from one of the open kitchens, but leave room for the puddings, cakes and macaroons. You'll appreciate the warning as these are the best you'll ever taste in Muscat. Prices are high, especially for alcohol, but the wine list is extensive. After an excellent meal you can stroll around the tranquil garden or along the beach and enjoy your after-dinner coffee alfresco.

InterContinental
Muscat
Shati Al Qurm
Map 8 A4

Tomato Restaurant ▶ p.344
24 600 500 | www.intercontinental.com
When it comes to restaurants with the most tranquil settings, Tomato is the leader of the pack. It is situated deep in the beautiful gardens of the InterContinental Muscat, and getting there requires a picturesque walk along the palm-tree-lined pathways near the swimming pool. All tables are located on a deck and there is no option of dining inside, making this a venue to be enjoyed when the weather is not too sticky. The food is the perfect combination of simple, wholesome classics and innovative flavours, and the funky cutlery and dazzling range of crockery wouldn't be out of place in any cutting-

edge European eatery. The breakfasts are particularly pleasant, and you can choose from three options – healthy, American or continental – while you enjoy another beautiful Muscat morning under the shade of a huge cream canopy. However, with live music, ambient lighting and some delectable Mediterranean fare, dinners are good too.

Mexican

Madinat Al Sultan Qaboos Centre
Madinat As Sultan Qaboos
Map 7 E2

Pavo Real

24 602 603 | pavoreal@omantel.net.om

Muscat is perhaps the last place in the world you'd expect to find a slice of real Mexico, but that's exactly what you get when you walk through the doors of Pavo Real. Don't over indulge in the complementary taco chips and salsa because you'll need room for the fabulous food and must-have margaritas (which are also available in non alcoholic form). Pavo Real offers you all the ingredients for a great night out – awesome ambience, friendly service, absolutely delicious food and live music. Monday nights are for karaoke; the singers are pretty good and some take it very seriously. Oddly, dancing is only allowed by special licence. Still, you'd better book your table and your song early as the place fills up quickly.

InterContinental Muscat
Shati Al Qurm
Map 8 A4

Senor Pico ▶ p.344

24 680 000 www.intercontinental.com

An expat favourite, Senor Pico is nestled in the back corner of the InterContinental Muscat and is always busy with hotel guests and Muscat's legion of Mexican food fans. At first glance it's quaint and conducive to conversation, but don't be fooled. Come 22:00 and the arrival of the band, this is one of the most happening restaurants in the city. The decor is cool Aztec, the cuisine is hot Mexican – fajitas, enchiladas, and the most fantastic, must-try nachos. The hot, sweet and spicy tomato and saffron soup is an amazing way to start your meal. You will also find an excellent selection of succulent grills. The food is hearty, well presented and deserves to be complemented with the best margarita in Muscat.

Mongolian

Other options **Far Eastern** p.312

Golden Oryx
Ruwi
Map 12 D1

Mongolian Barbecue

24 706 128 | www.thegoldenoryx.com

At first glance the menu seems limited, but after the choice of soup or starter (the latter at an additional cost), you are presented with a large bowl and invited to create your own meal. Once you've selected your choice and combination of ingredients, you can then watch it all being cooked. And if you manage, somehow, to keep each serving small enough, you can return again and again, sampling any number of combinations of meat, vegetables and delicious sauces. Mongolian Barbecue is a relaxed venue with reasonably priced, potentially excellent food (depending on your own culinary combining).

Moroccan

Other options **Arabic & Lebanese** p.308

Shangri-La's Barr Al Jissah Resort & Spa
Al Jissah
Map 15 E3

Shahrazad ▶ p.309

24 776 565 www.shangri-la.com

From the shimmering walls of fabric dividing the tables to the splendid mosaic lanterns above, the Shahrazad experience is the definitive in decadent dining. A simple but excellently prepared menu offers the pick of Moroccan cuisine and a wine list to match.

The friendly staff are the real thing, authentic from their knowledge down to their attire and they cannot do enough to help and serve. Try the tajine for melt-in-the-mouth meat, with a side order of fluffy couscous to soak up the delicately spiced juices. Worth making the trip for a special occasion.

Omani

Al Sawadi Beach
Resort
Al Sawadi
Barka
Map 1 B2

Al Khanjar
26 795 545 | *www.alsawadibeach.com*
Set in a traditional Omani majlis, on a beautiful unspoilt beach, this restaurant's great location makes it a fabulous place to come and enjoy the legendary Omani shuwa. Shuwa is an Omani delicacy that entails elaborate and well-planned preparation. It usually consists of beef or goat that's been marinated in a special, spicy mix and then roasted for up to two days in a special pit oven. The staff are welcoming and very friendly, and the band and the enthusiastic belly dancer add a certain spark to your evening's entertainment. The more than reasonable prices ensure that Al Khanjar is a great venue, whether it's an intimate dinner you're having, or a casual get-together with a group of friends.

Nr Shell
Al Khuwayr
Map 7 A2

Bin Ateeq
24 478 225 | *binateeq@omantel.net.om*
One of the friendliest and most welcoming restaurants in Muscat, Bin Ateeq serves Omani food at its best. The takeaway queue is testament to the popularity with the locals but dining in is worth the experience. The cane-clad walls are reminiscent of a jungle hut, but air-conditioned huts, with TVs in every private dining room. Simply spiced meat, chicken and fish, all still on the bone, and mountains of fried fluffy rice are brought to you as you recline on your majlis cushion. Prepare to get messy.
Other locations: Ruwi, 24 702 727; Nizwa, opposite Friday Market, 25 410 466; Salalah, nr Souk Hafa, 23 292 380; nr Al Saada Public Park, 23 225 652.

Nr Shell
Al Khuwayr
Map 7 A2

Ofair Public Foods
24 482 965
Dining at Ofair is an experience, one where you'll sit on majlis cushions and have a myriad of Omani dishes served to you with pride. If you go in a group you'll be able to enjoy the experience in a private dining room. It's worth visiting for the traditional atmosphere, as long as you can ignore the TV, and remember that you will need to respect local customs. This means that women should cover their arms and legs. The food is pretty basic but for the price you pay, it will definitely fill a hole, not only in your stomach but also in your list of cultural experiences.

Al Bustan Palace
InterContinental
Al Bustan
Map 15 A1

Seblat Al Bustan ▶ p.29
24 799 666 | *www.albustanpalace.com*
At Seblat Al Bustan you'll be treated to dinner in a Bedouin tent that's set out under the stars, between swaying palm trees on the hotel grounds. Traditional music and folk dancing, bread making, henna and handicrafts make this more a cultural experience than just a meal which, incidentally, is very tasty. And since you've come this far into the culture, be sure to try the shuwa, an Omani dish of slow-cooked meat. Finish the evening with traditional coffee and dates. Dinner is held every Wednesday night from September to May, from 19:30 to 23:00. A shuttle bus will take you from the hotel entrance to the tented village where your dinner awaits.

Restaurants

Shiraz

Nando's

China Mood

Golden Oryx

Bait Al Eahr

Al Khiran

Pakistani

Other options **Indian** p.314

Karachi Darbar

24 479 360
www.goldenspoongroup.com

This is a fantastic fastfood joint and perfect if your lunch hour allows you just enough time to grab something quick and tasty. A good sign is its popularity with the local community, particularly later in the day and around dinner time. The menu is limited and consists of curries and grilled dishes, but everything is delicious and the tandoori chicken is exceptional. Karachi Darbar is great value for money and casual dining – definitely one to try.

Pizzerias	
Come Prima	24 660 660
O Sole Mio	24 601 343
Pane Caldo	24 698 697
Papa John's Pizza	24 503 333
Pizza Express	99 114 210
Pizza Hut ▶ p.329	24 822 500
Pizza Muscat	24 565 618
Tuscany	24 641 234

Persian

Other options **Arabic & Lebanese** p.308

Shiraz ▶ p.25

24 660 660 | www.cpmuscat.com

Shiraz offers a hearty menu of Iranian favourites. A tented ceiling and open bread preparation area add to the already-plush setting. It's definitely advisable to take along a huge appetite for the generous, and complimentary, portions of cheese, salad and Arabic bread you'll be given before your meal. Shiraz's starters and desserts are a particular treat, while the main courses, sadly, are a tad bland by comparison. During the cooler months, day and evening diners will enjoy eating on the terrace with its views of the coastline and the mountain backdrop.

Polynesian

Other options **Far Eastern** p.312

Trader Vic's ▶ p.344

24 680 000 | www.intercontinental.com

A popular venue, Trader Vic's is a dream for the indecisive diner. You'll find Caribbean cocktails, a Cuban band, an international menu and dishes prepared in a gigantic Chinese clay oven, all under one roof. It might sound like a bit of a mish mash but it's actually great and you would probably want to head here for the cocktail list alone. The service is excellent and, if nothing else, this is one of the only places that do a good Irish coffee. Dining here isn't cheap, but for a good night out, it's worth it.

Portuguese

Nando's

24 561 818 | www.nandos.com

Put simply, at Nando's good food is served quickly. Diners enjoy something different, from main meals you eat with your hands, to the legendary chicken espetada, your appetite will be nicely satisfied. Nando's speciality is the marinated chicken, butterfly grilled on a naked flame and then spiced with the seasoning of your choice – from mild and lemony to hot-lips chilli. For a warm greeting at the door, rustic decor, the chance to watch your food being cooked and value prices you just can't go wrong.

Pizza Hut

Share the good times !

OUTLETS IN MUSCAT:

Qurum	MBD	
CCC	Airport	
MSQ	Al Khuwair	24 822 500
Al Khoud	Ghala	
Mabella	Qurum City Centre	

OTHER CITIES:

Salalah	23 29 03 03
Sohar	26 84 11 55
Nizwa	25 41 20 96
Sur	25 54 53 88
Tharmad	26 81 00 36
Wajaja	26 84 99 40

Seafood

Al Waha
Shangri-La's Barr Al Jissah Resort & Spa
Al Jissah
Map 15 E3

Bait Al Bahr ▶ p.309
24 776 565 | www.shangri-la.com

If you fancy sampling some local delights from the nearby sea, Bait Al Bahr is a perfect choice. Standing alone from the main hotels, a stop off the lazy river route running throughout the resort, you are made to feel as unique as the location you are sitting in. Bag a table on the veranda and cool off in the ocean breeze while you select from the mouth-watering menu. Obviously the emphasis is on succulent seafood, but there are some vegetarian choices too. Your chosen dish is presented to you by elegantly dressed waiting staff. Portions are on the small side, but decadently rich.

Al Bustan Palace
InterContinental
Al Bustan
Map 15 A1

Beach Pavilion ▶ p.29
24 799 666 | www.albustanpalace.com

The seashore location of the Beach Pavilion makes this a delightful place to enjoy a light lunch, watching the waves crash onto the shore as you tuck into good food. Home-baked rolls supplement smallish portions and the staff are only too happy to adjust a dish to suit your needs. Service can be slow at weekends and holidays – in fact, it's so popular that you'll be lucky to get a table at all, so make sure you book in advance. Newly rebuilt, this restaurant now serves fresh seafood, and comforting dishes like risotto, year round.

The Chedi
Al Ghubrah
Map 6 E2

The Beach Restaurant
24 524 400 | www.chedimuscat.com

The path to this glamorous beachside spot follows a candlelit walkway through the grounds of the Chedi, towards the sound of crashing waves. You are greeted by elegant staff and can choose from outdoor dining or a table inside with its high ceilings, Colonial-style fans, modern wooden screens and accents of rich burgundy silk. The well-chosen wine list allows you to order by the bottle or glass (try the delicious gavi di gavi white) but take your time while trying the bread basket served with dipping sauces and unique rock salts. The Beach Restaurant's menu is exclusively seafood boasting chilled and cooked dishes with an undeniably Asian feel; think mussels in a spicy coconut broth and yellowfin tuna with a chili and garlic risotto. The exotic flavours continue through to dessert with chocolate and coconut cheesecake served with Malibu sorbet. While undeniably at the more expensive end of the scale, you're bound to leave this stunning spot feeling sated, de-stressed and spoilt. Note: The Beach Restaurant is closed from mid-June to mid-August.

Marina Bander
Al Rowdha
Sidab
Map 13 F4

Blue Marlin
24 737 288

A haven of tranquility, intimacy and serenity, the Blue Marlin at Marina Bander Al Rowdha makes the most of the fact that it has one of the most picturesque locations in Muscat. The alfresco breakfasts by the pool (including full English and buffet options) are incredibly popular at the weekend and booking is recommended, especially in the cooler months. Come evening, a sundowner watching the boats come in is also particularly enjoyable. The modern European fare is fantastically prepared and presented, surpassed only by the service. The menu offers a good selection of seafood with a bit of a twist (the fish pie is fantastic), as well some unusual variations on non-fish dishes. This is one of the few restaurants where as much care is taken with the presentation as with the food itself. Blue Marlin is a great lunchtime favourite that, due to its location, is often under-utilised as an evening destination.

Spanish

Other options **Mediterranean** p.324

Al Bandar
Shangri-La's Barr Al
Jissah Resort & Spa
Al Jissah
Map 15 E3

Tapas & Sablah ▶ p.309

24 776 666 | *www.shangri-la.com*

Spread around the attractively lit and atmospheric 'Sablah' square outside Al Bandar Hotel, the alfresco Tapas & Sablah is open every evening for the only chance to sample Spanish cuisine in Muscat. The range of dishes is good, all tasty and pretty authentic, and for some international twists on the tapas theme, they are complemented by some Arabic mezze and Asian tapas-style dishes. There are also often specials such as paella on offer, and the house sangria is worth sampling. Portions are generous – order less than you might normally, and top them up if your appetite keeps going. For vegetarians, the selection of tapas is great, and the vegetable paella is one the best you'll find anywhere. This restaurant is a perfect spot for a pleasant evening, either for couples or for groups.

Steakhouses

Other options **American** p.308

Grand Hyatt Muscat
Shati Al Qurm
Map 7 E1
🚫 🍷

Rooftop Grill House

24 641 234 | *www.muscat.hyatt.com*

With a spectacular backdrop of the sea, and overlooking the pool, the Grill House is only open during the cooler months (October to May) to allow diners to make the most of the view. As the name would suggest, dishes here range from steaks to lobster, all grilled. There are also fresh salads and assorted side-dishes as well as soup and desserts. It also offers a set menu from RO 13 – an excellent deal as it includes beer, wine and a few other selected beverages. Great for a party night out.

Beach Pavilion

The Beach Restaurant

Cafes & Coffee Shops

Other options **Afternoon Tea** p.336

Muscat's cafe scene is thriving, due in part to the split shifts with long lunch breaks, and to the generally laidback feel to the place. The many cafes around the city vary greatly. There are those that will serve you a three-course meal, and those that offer a doughnut or sandwich to go with your coffee. For relaxed business lunches, lazy evening hang outs or just good coffee and a dose of people watching, cafe culture is a fabulous way to pass the time. The major international coffee house chains are all here, with branches of Costa, Second Cup and Starbucks across Muscat.

Bowshar
Hotel Deluxe
Al Khuwayr
Map 6 F3

Al Mas
24 491 105 | *www.bowsharhotel.com*
Al Mas is located in the Bowsher Hotel, just north of the Ghubrah/Bowsher roundabout. The sleek hotel decor sets the pace for this fabulous little eatery. Open most hours, this is more of a restaurant than a quick coffee stop, and its menu is bursting with Indian, Chinese and Arabic dishes that will tempt you into staying longer. Those wanting just a quick coffee stop can choose from the small menu of snacks and quick bites. The staff are friendly and convivial and the prices are surprisingly reasonable.

SABCO Commercial
Centre
Al Qurm
Map 8 E4

Barista
24 571 531 | *www.sabcogroup.com*
If you need a hit of good Italian coffee then Barista is the place. Situated in the SABCO Centre it's a bright, airy spot for a cup of caffeine with a pastry or some cooling icecream. The milkshakes are particularly good. It's a popular spot in the evenings and it is open from 09:00 until 22:00 throughout the week, with a later opening time of 16:30 on Fridays.

Al-Araimi Complex
Al Qurm
Map 8 E4

Café Ceramique
24 566 617 | *www.cafeceramique.com*
Children and adults alike can unleash their inner artist at Café Ceramique, with a huge range of pottery pieces just waiting to be painted and glazed. Simply choose from the selection (which includes everything from dinner plates to jewellery boxes), pick your paints and get creative. Even if you're not in the artistic mood, Café Ceramique's extensive and well-priced menu, with an emphasis on healthy quick bites, makes it a worthwhile trip. The fantastic staff are on hand to recommend dishes while serving up great advice for your work of art, or showing customers the painting and firing process. The light, bright space is complemented by a large room downstairs for parties and events, making this a popular destination for birthdays and unique corporate days out.

Getting creative at Café Ceramique

The No. 1 off-road guide to the UAE

The ultimate accessory for any 4WD, *UAE Off-Road Explorer* helps drivers to discover this region's 'outback'. Just remember your 4WD was made for more than just the school run.

UAE Off-Road Explorer
What your 4WD was made for

Includes Dhs.200 voucher for Off-Road Zone

Supported by:

Capital Commercial
Centre (CCC)
Al Qurm
Map 8 E4

Cafe Glacier
24 489 245
This spacious cafe is a welcome pitstop on a day of shopping, and it's long been a favourite of families and weary shoppers. Well-presented dishes and generous portions satisfy a hungry crowd. Free popcorn appeals to kids, and high chairs are available. As well as serving Rombouts coffee, there are herbal teas, fruit smoothies and a menu that includes breakfasts, pasta, salads, soups, sandwiches and pancakes, all served by friendly and efficient wait staff. There is another branch at Zakher Mall, Al Khuwayr (24 694 245).

Haffa House Hotel
Ruwi
Map 12 D2

Cafe Samaharam
24 707 207 | www.halfahouse.com
Far enough away from Muscat's bustling CBD to be relatively peaceful, Samaharam is still a convenient retreat for a lunch break from the office or a leisurely informal evening meal. The food is simple but tasty and quick to arrive. The grills, pasta, sandwiches and fruit juices all make for filling fare. After your meal indulge in a headily pungent shisha, or sniff at the one being smoked near you.

Al Masa Mall
Al Sarooj
Map 7 E1

CinnZeo Bakery Cafe
www.cinnzeo.com
The smell of freshly baked cinnamon rolls will draw you into this bakery cafe. Not only does it have a lovely atmosphere, but you can watch the bakers at work in the open kitchen. Try the world-famous cinnamon rolls with different toppings, or splash out (calorie-wise) on one of the decadent chocolate twists. All of these naughty-but-nice delights come straight from the oven – you can choose fruity sauce instead of chocolate or caramel if you want to kid yourself that you are being healthy. It's perfect for a yummy sugar fix, a good cup of coffee and friendly service in comfortable surroundings.

Jawaharat A'Shati
Commercial Complex
Shati Al Qurm
Map 8 A4

D'Arcy's Kitchen
24 600 234
Overlooking the sea, this sunny cafe in the buzzing Shati Al Qurm area is a welcome stop for a late breakfast, lunch or a light dinner. Step inside and you'll feel as though you've walked into a farmhouse – a theme that's matched by the size of the servings. The interesting menu includes special salads, soups and burgers served with a selection of delicious fruit smoothies by friendly staff. Whether you pop in for a light meal or just a coffee, D'Arcy's treats you well. There is also a new branch in Madinat Al Sultan Qaboos with a some extra dishes and fairy-lit outdoor area.

Al-Araimi Complex
Al Qurm
Map 8 E4

Golden Gate Cafe
24 571 644
There's nothing fancy at the Golden Gate Cafe, but don't let that stop you from trying it out. The inexpensive food comes quickly and the venue is a good getaway from the hustle and bustle of Qurm. Located downstairs in the Al Araimi Complex, it has a fairly wide selection of quick meals to refuel the diehard shopper. Try the soup served inside a massive crusty roll. The service has to be beckoned but it comes with a smile.

Nr Grand Hyatt Htl
Shati Al Qurm
Map 7 E1

Le Mermaid
24 602 327 | alhamidint@hotmail.com
In the shadow of the Grand Hyatt you'll find one of the coolest cafes in Muscat. With a large outside seating area complete with majlis tents, shisha and great sea views, this popular cafe has people dropping by from all over town. Dishing up a wide range of seafood, grills and snacks, Le Mermaid is a hidden treasure. Indulge in a refreshing fruit cocktail or choose from the range of coffees and local hot drinks.

The Chedi ◀
Al Ghubrah
Map 6 E2
🍸

The Lobby Lounge
24 524 400 | www.ghmhotels.com

Another string to the bow of the tranquil haven that is The Chedi, is the Lobby Lounge. Situated just beyond the majlis area at the entrance, the cafe is an intimate arrangement of comfy seating areas in a brightly sunlit room. At night it's perfect for sundowners or after-dinner drinks. Guests spill outside to bag one of the sought-after tables around the giant gas fires in heavy black planters. You'll need to hover about to claim one – people don't give them up easily.

InterContinental Muscat ◀
Shati Al Qurm
Map 8 A4
🔥

Majlis Al Shams ▶ p.344
24 680 000 | www.intercontinental.com

A relaxing light lunch or an indulgent coffee and cake session are on offer at this cafe in the InterContinental Muscat. Despite its grand surroundings, it's a surprisingly peaceful and intimate spot, and you could happily while away time here, musing over the range of delectable cakes and pastries. It also has freshly made sandwiches, fresh juices, and a selection of teas and coffees. The service is extremely friendly and this, coupled with the comfortable sofas and chairs, means an afternoon here slips away very easily.

Nr Crowne Plaza Htl ◀
Qurm Heights
Map 8 C3
🚫

Marina Cafe
24 567 825

This is a great little place right on the Shati beachfront with a sister outlet a little further along. The architecture is contemporary and the curved walls lead you into a cool and comfortable cafe, or up to the next floor where you can eat under the stars. Serving a range of seafood and salads, snacks and juices, the Marina is popular with both locals and expats. Service is slow but portions are big and worth waiting for.

Beach Hotel ◀
Shati Al Qurm
Map 8 A4
🚫 🔥

Motif Beach Cafe ▶ p.vi
24 696 601 | www.omarbeachhotel.com

Motif is a cafe serving great food, a range of juices and coffees, and as much shisha as you can smoke, in an Omani-inspired setting. Seafood, steaks and sandwiches are all on offer between noon and 02:00 and there is even a big screen TV outside so patrons can catch that crucial football match while kicking back on the sofas.

Capital Commercial Centre (CCC) ◀
Al Qurm
Map 8 E4
🔥

Second Cup
24 566 616

Customers love the warm, friendly ambience and the contemporary coffee-shop setting in Second Cup. However, any fears that it is more about style than substance are quickly laid to rest when you sample the range of coffees, teas and fruit drinks, all of which are expertly prepared. To complement your choice of drink, Second Cup offers a delectable variety of delicious desserts that are freshly made each day. It's a great place to meet friends for a sociable 'coffee and cake' date, and if you're alone, you can keep busy by reading through the latest newspapers and magazines provided.

Motif Beach Cafe

Icecream Cafes

Nr Zawawi Mosque
Al Khuwayr
Map 7 B2

Tropical Juices & Ice Cream

24 482 476 | *www.goldenspoongroup.com*

With tall glasses of freshly squeezed juices, home made icecream, milkshakes and sundaes that melt in your mouth a trip to this icecream and juice bar is a treat. This is an ideal after-dinner stop when you'll find it frequented by families, couples and groups of friends looking to round off a good night out. Other locations: Capital Commercial Centre, 24 560 473; Ruwi, 24 799 884.

Shisha Cafes

Other options **Arabic & Lebanese** p.308

Shisha cafes are common throughout the Middle East, and they offer you a relaxing place in which to smoke a shisha pipe (aka 'hubbly bubbly' or 'narghile') in a variety of aromatic flavours. Traditionally the preserve of local men who meet here to play backgammon and gossip, the cafes are also places where locals and visitors meet, and hang out, especially in the cooler evenings of winter. Most shisha cafes offer a basic menu, generally consisting of Arabic dishes plus coffees, teas and fresh fruit juices. If you get 'hooked' (pun intended), and wish to have your own shisha at home, you can purchase one from some of the larger supermarkets or at Mutrah Souq.

Shisha Cafes		
Al Barouk ▶ p.vi	Beach Hotel	Shati Al Qurm
Al Deyar	Nr Shati Cinema	Shati Al Qurm
Al Madinat	MSQ Centre	MSQ
Automatic	Nr Sabco Centre	Al Qurm
Fish Village	Nr Radisson BLU	Al Khuwayr
Kargeeen Caffe	MSQ Centre	MSQ
Layali Al Hilmya	Nr Zakher Mall	Al Khuwayr
Le Mermaid	Nr Grand Hyatt	Shati Al Qurm
Marjan Poolside	Grand Hyatt	Shati Al Qurm
Seblat Al Bustan ▶ p.29	Al Bustan Palace	Al Bustan

The flavoured tobacco and coals you need to burn it, are also quite widely available. Despite the obvious health risk, it's an activity you should try at least once but be aware that smoking shisha for 40 minutes is estimated to be the equivalent of smoking 40 cigarettes.

Afternoon Tea

Other options **Cafes & Coffee Shops** p.332

Al Bustan Palace
InterContinental
Al Bustan
Map 15 A1

Atrium Tea Lounge ▶ p.29

24 799 666 | *www.albustanpalace.com*

You'll be hard pressed to find a better way to take in the splendour of the palatial Al Bustan than with high tea at the Atrium. Relax under the magnificent dome and imposing crystal chandelier with a coffee or tea and one of the delicious cakes or pastries. The friendly service, plush surroundings and the gentle music issuing from the piano makes it terribly easy to linger in the lap of luxury.

Grand Hyatt Muscat
Shati Al Qurm
Map 7 E1

Sirj Tea Lounge

24 641 234 | *www.muscat.hyatt.com*

Comfortably furnished in Arabian style, the Sirj Tea Lounge offers you the choice of taking your tea in a tented or open area. The traditional English afternoon tea consists of finger sandwiches, homemade scones with clotted cream and jam and a large slice of the cake of your choice. There is a good selection of fresh juices to choose from and you may be lucky enough to have the resident pianist treat you to light music while you sip away your afternoon.

Internet Cafes

Internet cafes or shops can be found in most areas of Oman, generally in shopping centres, but also in small shops. Not surprisingly, Muscat has more internet cafes than the rest of Oman, especially in Ruwi. Prices range from 400 to 700 baisas per hour, with different rates during the evenings and at weekends. Many places allow you to pay per quarter of an hour.

You should shop around for a cafe that suits your needs – not all have broadband, printers, scanners or webcams. The best value shop is Mamoon Internet Services in Al Khuwayr (24 692 369). It has the cheapest rates and the best service and equipment. First Internet Cafe in CCC Shopping Centre is the most expensive at 700 baisas per hour (no broadband).

Bakeries

In addition to bread, Arabic bakeries offer a wonderful range of pastries, biscuits and Lebanese sweets. Look out for 'borek', which are flat pastries, baked or fried with spinach or cheese, or the biscuits filled with ground dates. All are delicious, and must be tried at least once. Omani halwa is a sticky concoction of sugar, ghee (clarified butter), rosewater and saffron. It's made in huge batches and served in little dishes with a spoon.

Fruit Juices

Other options **Cafes & Coffee Shops** p.332

A variety of fresh juices are widely available, either from shawarma stands, juice shops, coffee shops or cafes. They are uniformly delicious, healthy and cheap, and made on the spot from fresh fruits such as mango, banana, kiwi, strawberry, watermelon and pineapple, and the mixed fruit cocktail is a blessing for the indecisive. Fresh lemon mint juice is also very popular (ask for no sugar if you prefer), as is the local milk, laban, a heavy, salty buttermilk that's best drunk on its own (but doesn't go well in tea or coffee). Arabic mint tea is available, but it's probably not drunk as widely here as it is in other parts of the Arab world; however, Arabic coffee (thick, silty and strong) is extremely popular and will have you on a caffeine high for days.

Getting stuck into a shawarma

On-street eating

On The Town

Life in Muscat is led at a relatively sedate pace, which is good for the stress levels but this does also mean that there's less chance of a wild night on the town here than in other cities in region, like Dubai or Manama. Places tend to wind down quite early but, considering its size, Muscat has a reasonable variety of restaurants and bars. The following section covers cafes, bars, pubs and nightclubs as well as 'cultural' entertainment such as theatre and comedy. A lot of Muscat's social scene may appear a little exclusive to a newcomer, with cliques that seem to have limited memberships. However, once you're in, you're in and the expat community is in fact very friendly and welcoming. As there isn't a huge range of places to go out to, you will start to see familiar faces out and about.

Dress Code

Most bars have a reasonably relaxed attitude to their customers' dress sense. Some places, however, insist on no shorts or sandals, while others require at least a shirt with a collar and no jeans. Nightclubs generally have a dressier approach, so dress to impress. As Oman's reputation as a trendy tourist destinations grows, the dress code will no doubt get stricter.

Many people socialise at home, particularly after the bars and nightclubs have closed and especially during Ramadan. In addition, much of the nightlife centres around the hotels, which generally organise events throughout the year. Special nights are arranged about a month in advance, so it is a good idea to have your name added to their mailing lists to receive information on what's happening. They will usually email, fax or mail you details of forthcoming events.

If you're after a bar scene, check out some of the places listed in the Restaurants section on p.308. Some restaurants also function as a bar, and a few even have a dancefloor so you can eat, drink and be merry.

Throughout the week, some of the bars and restaurants hold special nights and promotions to attract custom. Wednesdays and Thursdays are the busiest nights out as, depending on what working week you follow, they are the start of the weekend. Most bars and nightclubs close between midnight and 01:00, especially those in hotels, while the occasional bar will stay open until 03:00.

Door Policy

Some of the cooler hang outs implement a members only policy that allows them to control the clientele frequenting the place. At quieter times though, non-members may have no problem getting in, even if unaccompanied by a member. Basically, the management uses the rule to disallow entry if they don't like the look of you or your group, in which case they will point to their sign and say 'sorry'. Large groups of men are often refused entry, so breaking up your group by recruiting some friendly ladies is a worthwhile tactic. Getting irate really won't get you anywhere, so if you're refused entry your best bet is to move on and find somewhere else that's more accommodating.

Drinks

Other options **Alcohol** p.262

While Oman is a Muslim country, it has a relatively liberal attitude towards the consumption of alcohol by non-Muslims. Alcohol is generally available in hotel restaurants and bars that have the appropriate licence. However, drinking alcohol in these establishments can be an expensive pastime – nearly double what you are probably used to paying.

Non-Muslims can apply for an alcohol permit that allows them to purchase alcohol from a liquor shop. You're not likely to find a huge selection in your local off-licence, and wine can cost three times more than you usually pay, but spirits are cheaper.

Local bottled water is produced either in Oman or the neighbouring Emirates and is of a high quality, even compared to premium-imported brands. So instead of paying for an international label, try the local water which should go down well at around 200 baisas for a 1.5 litre bottle.

Bars

Muscat has a reasonable number of bars. Most are located within hotels and the 'in' places are a hive of after hours activity. In addition to the bars reviewed here, there are plenty of others (usually in the smaller hotels), that may not attract the regular crowd but which are still worth popping in to, if only for a change of scenery.

InterContinental Muscat
Shati Al Qurm
Map 8 A4

Al Ghazal Pub ▶ p 344

24 600 500 | www.intercontinental.com

Set within the five-star InterContinental Muscat, this pub offers a traditional pub experience that's second to none. With a friendly atmosphere, a huge selection of beverages, delicious pub grub and live entertainment, what more could you want? Tables are screened so diners can enjoy a meal of steak or fish and chips, or just a light sandwich, in privacy. Good food, drinks, service and reasonable prices ensure this pub is nearly always crowded with regulars.

Majan Continental Hotel
Al Khuwayr
Map 6 D4

Al Khaima

24 592 900 | www.majanhotel.com

While you could debate whether this is a club or a pub, what is clear is that this Arabic venue is exclusively male and is likely to remain so. The room resembles a small theatre with seats and tables facing a circular performance area in the centre. The band – two musicians and five ladies – pumps out Arabic tunes at a deafening volume to a limited audience. A belly dancer also makes an appearance at some point in the evening. Al Khaima is well suited to large groups of men out on a stag night but definitely not a romantic evening.

Majan Continental Hotel
Al Khuwayr
Map 6 D4

Barrio Fiesta

24 592 900 | www.majanhotel.com

This space-age 1970s themed bar, named after a famous village near Manila, has something of an identity crisis but it's still an experience. The resident band is a Russian quintet that plays a mixture of Arabic, Russian and European hits. If you buy them a garland they will dance with more enthusiasm in your direction. Despite the inordinate number of men, this isn't really the place for a ladies' night out, but it is worth a visit for the novelty of it all.

Radisson BLU Hotel Muscat
Al Khuwayr
Map 7 C3

Cellar Bar ▶ p.321

24 487 777 | www.radissonblu.com/hotel-muscat

Cellar by name, cellar by nature. Located below the efficiently run Radisson BLU is Muscat's only sports bar. The long bar entices and the food, which is provided by Olivos Coffee Shop (p.320), is always good and tasty. This, together with the cocktail list, means your night is made. It's advisable to choose your night though as weekdays tend to be quiet unless there's a big footie game or a themed night on. But being the early bird can have its perks as the earlier you arrive, the cheaper the drinks. Ladies night is on Tuesdays and this is a good venue to start your night off with… or to wind it down.

Majan Continental Hotel
Al Khuwayr
Map 6 D4

The Chambers

24 592 900 | www.majanhotel.com

Chambers maybe small in size but it's big in stature. With a pool table, large screen TV and a few gaming machines, it draws a regular crowd of local and Eastern European men. You won't find any draft beer here, but the rest of the beverage selection is very reasonably priced. An African band plays nightly and you'll receive friendly-enough service from the staff. The overall impression is one of a working man's pub

Ruwi Hotel
Ruwi
Map 12 D2

Club Bar

24 704 244 | www.omanhotel.com

Situated in the heart of the Ruwi business district, this is a small, no-frills hotel bar designed to serve the many businessmen in the area. It's friendly, low-lit and decked out in standard British pub paraphernalia but its identity as an unassuming bar gets a jolt when the lively Russian band starts up. The service is quiet and efficient and while the menu is fairly standard, the food is good.

Grand Hyatt Muscat
Shati Al Qurm
Map 7 E1

Club Safari

24 641 234 | www.muscat.hyatt.com

Club Safari has really taken its jungle theme to heart with ethnic African decor galore. Faux animal skins, African masks and bamboo adorn the walls and ceiling creating an atmosphere that's a little over-the-top but still kind of appealing. The Safari Pub, on the middle level of this three-floor extravaganza, has a distinct party atmosphere and regulars range from sports fans who come for the multitude of TV screens to party princesses who strut their stuff and sip the (not cheap) exotic cocktails.

Radisson BLU
Hotel Muscat
Al Khuwayr
Map 7 C3

Coral Bar ▶ p.321

24 487 777 | www.radissonblu.com/hotel-muscat

This is a piano bar with acts that change every few months and fabulous underwater themed murals. The staff are very friendly, and the beers, spirits and wines are sold at standard hotel prices. There's always a selection of nibbles at your elbow to keep you thirsty. Coral Bar is popular with local businessmen and hotel guests, and appeals to the slightly older customer or someone who's happy for a chilled-out evening of something to drink and conversation.

Crowne Plaza
Muscat
Qurm Heights
Map 8 C3

Duke's Bar ▶ p.25

24 560 100 | www.cpmuscat.com

Given enough dark wood panelling, brass fitting and cosy leather seats, you can knock up an English theme pub almost anywhere. But only Duke's has the evocative rocky seascape view, framed by a giant picture window. The regulars here are a diverse bunch: locals and expats of many nationalities, kept busy with quiz nights, ladies' nights and various live music acts. The food is typical pub-grub and can be enjoyed on the terrace outside if you can secure a sought-after table.

Al Qurm Resort
Shati Al Qurm
Map 8 A4

Feeney's Irish Pub

24 605 945

If you're in the area this is a comfortable little stop for a drink and perhaps some decent pub grub. It's small inside but it somehow manages to pack a lot in – head for one of the tables if you're eating, or prop yourself up at the bar for a few friendly drinks. Feeney's hosts a popular quiz night on Tuesdays and is has live music every weekend. And if you're looking for somewhere to watch the big game, major Premiership football matches are also shown here.

Grand Hyatt Muscat
Shati Al Qurm
Map 7 E1

John Barry

24 641 234 | www.muscat.hyatt.com

This five-star piano bar was designed to recreate the feeling of being on board the ill-fated SS John Barry that sank off the coast of Dhofar. The theme is carried through all the way to rusty rivets, sea chest tables and waiters dressed as sailors. It still manages to be a low-key, sophisticated bar that serves a good range of alcoholic and non-alcoholic cocktails, spirits, beers, soft drinks and good house wine by the glass. Snacks are also available so it's good place for a pre-dinner drink or a quiet beer after work.

Al Falaj Hotel Muscat
Ruwi
Map 12 D1

Le Pub

24 702 311 | www.omanhotels.com

Le Pub is situated on the eighth floor of Muscat's second oldest hotel. Being so high up means you get the chance to drink in spectacular views over the Ruwi area, especially at night, if you're lucky enough to get one of the two window booths. The bar is very quiet, frequented mainly by the hotel's guests and local men. There's live entertainment nightly and if you're peckish, you can order light snacks.

Above Qurm
National Park
Al Qurm
Map 8 E3

Left Bank

24 693 699
www.emiratesleisureretail.com

Perched above Qurm National Park (p.182) is one of the hottest bar-restaurants in Muscat, with the slickest interior in town. Left Bank has a fantastic reputation for serving up high quality fare and imaginative cocktails – and the applause is well deserved.

Left Bank

The burgers, fish dishes and pastas are particularly recommended, as are the desserts which are a one worth the trip. While it's not a huge menu, each dish earns its place and everyone from gourmands to steak and veg fans are kept happy. The drinks list deserves special mention, with delicious martinis and a credible wine list just waiting to be sampled. It gets busy at weekends so reservations are essential if you want one of those coveted booths.

Al Bandar
Shangri-La's Barr Al
Jissah Resort & Spa
Al Jissah
Map 15 E3

The Long Bar ▶ p.309

24 776 666 | www.shangri-la.com

Long Bar has one of the best spots in Oman to enjoy a happy hour. Although it is a little out of the way, it is worth the drive to enjoy a beachfront sunset from the terrace as you work your way through the martini menu and tropical cocktails. Be sure to pack your dancing shoes when you visit Long Bar, which transforms into Xyro Nightclub later in the evening, a very popular dancing venue with expats and locals.

Sheraton Oman Hotel
Ruwi
Map 12 F2

Oliver

24 772 772 | www.ichotelsgroup.com

Oliver makes a good attempt at recreating a traditional English pub, from its dimly lit tables and alcove seating, to the memorabilia dotted around the place. If you're feeling homesick this will go down a treat, and even if you're not, it's a good place to while away an afternoon. It's a quiet pub, ideal for catching up with a few mates or just getting away from it all. The service is friendly and the bar tenders are only too happy to 'lend an ear', in the traditional sense.

Al Bandar
Al Jissah
Map 15 E3

Piano Lounge ▶ p.309

24 776 666 | www.shangri-la.com

Soft lighting, carpets, couches and cushions, the piano lounge makes an elegant addition to an evening out at the Shangri-La Barr Al Jissah Resort (p.214). The bar doesn't serve meals, but does offer first class service and front row seats to the pianist every night from 20:00 to 23:45. The drinks menu has reasonably priced wine by the glass, beer and spirits, but this is definitely the place to treat yourself to a bottle of Moet or an aged malt whisky on the rocks.

Opp Golden
Oryx Restaurant
Ruwi
Map 12 D1

Uptown
24 706 020

The decor at Uptown is an unusual fusion of south-east Asian and European, but still sports the swanky touches you expect of a bar – the dim lighting and sofa seating. The latest sporting events play out on a large screen TV in one corner of the bar and the simple but moreish bar snacks will keep you ordering from the reasonably priced drinks menu. There's live entertainment every night and a happy hour. In other words, you've got all the ingredients for a good night out.

Ramadan Timings

During Ramadan, opening and closing times of restaurants change considerably. Because eating and drinking in public is forbidden during daylight hours, many places only open after sunset then keep going well into the early hours. Restaurants in some hotels remain open, but will be screened off from public view. Live entertainment is not allowed, so while some nightclubs remain open, all dancefloors are closed.

Nightclubs

The nightclub scene in Muscat is somewhat limited, which means that the few places available are invariably busy, even on weekdays. The music is an eclectic mix of upbeat Arabic dance music through to funky R&B and smooth soul. The club-savvy may be a little disappointed at the variety of venues on offer, but the plethora of people watching opportunities make up for it.

Though they are growing in number, there are still only a few nightclubs in Muscat. More often than not you'll come across bars that have a dancefloor and a club vibe. Live entertainment is popular and often gets the party going. Of these bar/clubs, the ones that are particularly worth trying are Club Safari, Uptown, Duke's Bar, Left Bank and Pavo Real (see Bars, p.339).

Grand Hyatt Muscat
Shati Al Qurm
Map 7 E1

Copacabana
24 641 234
www.muscat.grand.hyatt.com

One of the liveliest nightclubs in Muscat – especially if people-watching is high on your agenda. The music is an eclectic mix of the good, the bad and the ugly and features anything that's hit the playlists in the last 15 years or so. The target clientele is mainly couples, but local males seem to dominate the dance floors. Service is friendly and efficient, with the staff dressed in frilly rhumba style outfits, wandering between giant fake palm trees and the long, well-stocked bar. Noisy but nice.

Piano Lounge

Cinemas

Cinemas			
Al Bahja Cinema	Nr Seeb Airport	24 540 855	1 B1
City Cinema Ruwi	Ruwi	24 831 809	12 E3
City Cinema Shatti	Nr Ramada Hotel	24 692 656	7 F1
Ruwi Cinema	Nr Mansoor Ali Centre	24 780 380	12 E3

Cinemas

A trip to the movies is a popular pastime in Omar and film lovers who want to see the latest Bollywood, Hollywood and Arabic releases are reasonably well catered for. There are two English language cinemas and a few smaller ones that show mainly Hindi and Arabic films. Show timings are printed (sometimes inaccurately) in a few of the local daily papers and release dates vary considerably. Films don't tend to hang around for long and are well attended, so put a trip to the movies off and you may miss your chance.

Concerts & Live Music

Classical music concerts are held in Muscat every now and again, but there are no regular or long-term fixtures. It's best to keep an eye on the local newspapers and magazines to find out what new shows are happening – details are usually only available about a month before the event. Some of the hotels, particularly the Grand Hyatt Muscat (p.31) and the Al Bustan Palace (p.28) also arrange events where for example, the Royal Oman Symphony Orchestra might perform. There's no regular pop or rock concert scene, but you might be able to catch a few performances: keep an eye (or ear) out for announcements in newspapers, email newsletters and on the radio.

DVD & Video Rental

Because most people have sate lite TV, DVD and video rental shops are not as booming as they used to be. And then of course there is the easy access to cheap and nasty DVDs – the fact that they are illegal doesn't seem to deter many people and the salesmen do a roaring trade. However, there are times when rental places still come in handy – especially when it is too hot to go outside and there is nothing good on TV. Video Club in Al Khuwayr (near Home Centre) usually has a good selection of fairly recent releases (24 600 079).

Theatre

Other options **Drama Groups** p.225

Theatre in Muscat is limited, but there are occasional professional performances. The amateur theatre companies always welcome new members, either on stage or behind the scenes. The Muscat Amateur Theatre (p.225) is one of these and there are regular performances at the InterContinental Muscat (p.31) which usually includes a buffet dinner. There are also occasional murder mystery dinners where you're encouraged to display your thespian skills by being part of the performance.

Caterers

A popular and easy way to put on a party, special occasion or business lunch, in-house catering allows you to relax and enjoy yourself, without worrying about the cooking. A number of companies offer this service, so decide on the type of food you want, be it Indian, Chinese, Lebanese or finger food, and ask your favourite restaurant or cafe whether they do outside catering. Most of the larger hotels have a catering department that's usually capable of servicing extravagant five-star functions.

You're not confined to the house – how about throwing a party in the desert or on a dhow? Depending on requirements, they will provide anything from the meal to crockery, waiters, furniture and even a clearing up service. Costs vary according to the number of people and food. Check the Yellow Pages for details and look out for flyers.

Comedy

The regular comedy scene in Muscat is unfortunately rather limited, but shows are held on an ad hoc basis. The Green Can Laughter Factory makes a regular return to Muscat (part of the Laughter Factory, a comedy promoter based in Dubai) and is very well received. Keep an eye out in the local press and at the hotels or get your name on hotel mailout lists – a regular venue is the Radisson BLU hotel (p.32).

MAKE YOUR BUSINESS TRIP TO MUSCAT A REJUVENATING EXPERIENCE.

InterContinental Muscat, located in the heart of Muscat's Diplomatic area, is set in 35 acres of landscaped gardens with the Gulf of Oman on one side and the majestic Hajar mountains on the other.

With 6 restaurants and bars, a fully equipped health club and stunning pool there are plenty of leisure options to ensure that your business trip is not all work and no play.

For more information or reservations log on to intercontinental.com or call on +968 24680680 or email muscat@icmuscathotel.com

Do you live an InterContinental life?

INTERCONTINENTAL®
MUSCAT

intercontinental.com

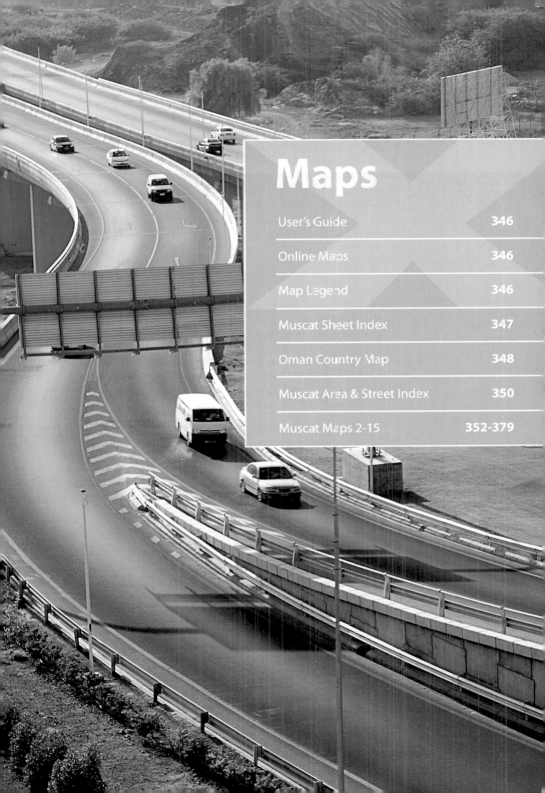

Maps

Maps

User's Guide

This section contains maps enabling you to quickly find your way around town. The Muscat Overview Sheet Index (opposite) shows which areas are covered by the maps. Map 1 illustrates the whole of Oman, showing the different regions and highlighting major cities, towns and roads. Maps 2 to 15 show the various areas of Muscat at a scale of 1:30,000, meaning one centimetre on the map is equivalent to 200m.

To assist you further, information such as main roads, roundabouts, hospitals, schools, and landmarks have been marked on these maps. Many places that are listed throughout the book, such as shops, hotels and restaurants, have a map reference – turn to that map to see precisely where you need to go.

Mapophobia!
Many people have an irrational fear of all things cartographical, but there's really nothing to be afraid of. The street maps in this section are good for getting your bearings – main roads and landmarks are all marked to help you work out where you are. And if you're still panicking then you can find a list of taxi companies on p.44.

Need More?

This book will provide you with all you need to know to get the most out of Muscat and Oman, but for when you need something a little more convenient in size, reach for the *Muscat Mini Map*. The whole city can slot in your back pocket, handy for when you need to travel light but still navigate your way around. It's part of a series of Mini Maps that includes a range of cities as diverse as London, Amsterdam, New York and Beijing. If you require something bigger, pick up a copy of the *Muscat Map* or *Oman Road Map* from any petrol station, bookshop or www.liveworkexplore.com. The all-encompassing detail makes them a necessity for any glove box. Finally, if you're a real off-road nut, you'll love the *Oman Off-Road Explorer*. Complete with 26 routes, photos and GPS points, it will become an indispensible partner when you're exploring the dunes and wadis.

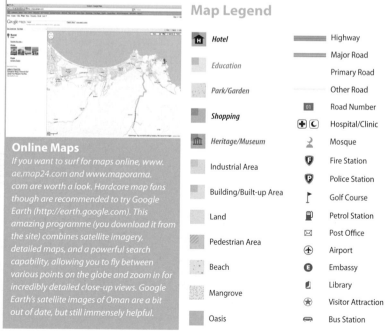

Online Maps

If you want to surf for maps online, www.ae.map24.com and www.maporama.com are worth a look. Hardcore map fans though are recommended to try Google Earth (http://earth.google.com). This amazing programme (you download it from the site) combines satellite imagery, detailed maps, and a powerful search capability, allowing you to fly between various points on the globe and zoom in for incredibly detailed close-up views. Google Earth's satellite images of Oman are a bit out of date, but still immensely helpful.

Map Legend

Hotel		Highway	
Education		Major Road	
Park/Garden		Primary Road	
Shopping		Other Road	
Heritage/Museum		Road Number	
Industrial Area		Hospital/Clinic	
Building/Built-up Area		Mosque	
Land		Fire Station	
Pedestrian Area		Police Station	
Beach		Golf Course	
Mangrove		Petrol Station	
Oasis		Post Office	
		Airport	
		Embassy	
		Library	
		Visitor Attraction	
		Bus Station	

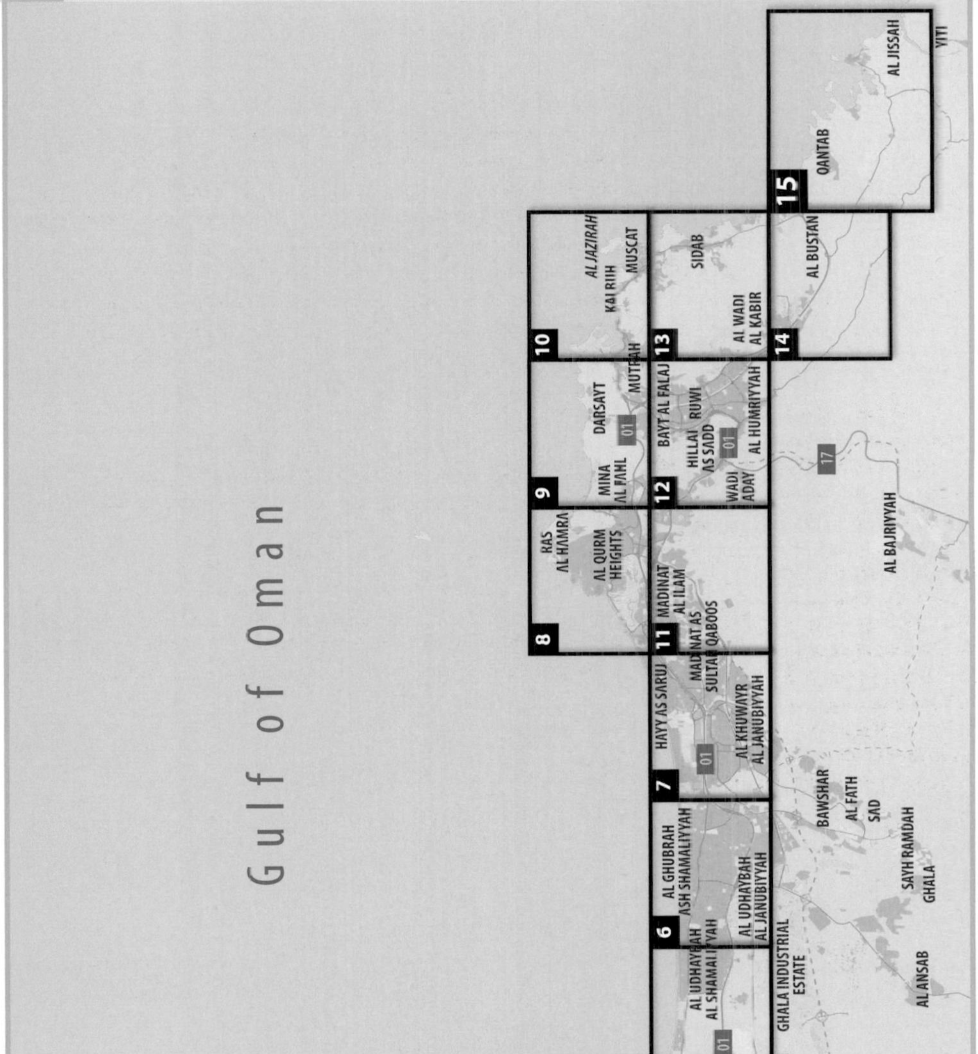

Gulf of Oman

15 QANTAB
AL JISSAH
YITI

10 AL AZIRAH
KAI RIH
MUSCAT

13 SIDAB
AL WADI AL KABIR

14 AL BUSTAN

9 MINA AL FAHL
DARSAYT
MUTRAH
01

12 BAYT AL FALAJ
HILLAT RUWI
AS SADD
01
WADI ADAY
AL HUMRIYYAH

8 RAS AL HAMRA
AL QURM HEIGHTS

11 MADINAT AL ILAM
MADINAT AS SULTAN QABOOS

7 HAYY AS SARUJ
AL KHUWAYR AL JANUBIYYAH
01

17

AL BAJRIYYAH

6 AL GHUBRAH
ASH SHAMALIYYAH
AL UDHAYBAH AL JANUBIYYAH

BAWSHAR
AL FATH
SAD
SAYH RAMDAH
GHALA'

AL ANSAB

5 AL UDHAYBAH AL SHAMALIYYAH
01
GHALA INDUSTRIAL ESTATE

HAYY AL URAFN

4 MURTAFAAT AL MATAR

AL MURTAFAH

AL RUSAYL INDUSTRIAL ESTATE

2 AL HAYL ASH SHAMALIYYAH
AL HAYL AL JANUBIYYAH
AL MAWALIH ASH SHAMALIYYAH

3 AL MAWALIH AL JANUBIYYAH
01

2.5km

Map **1**   Oman Country Map

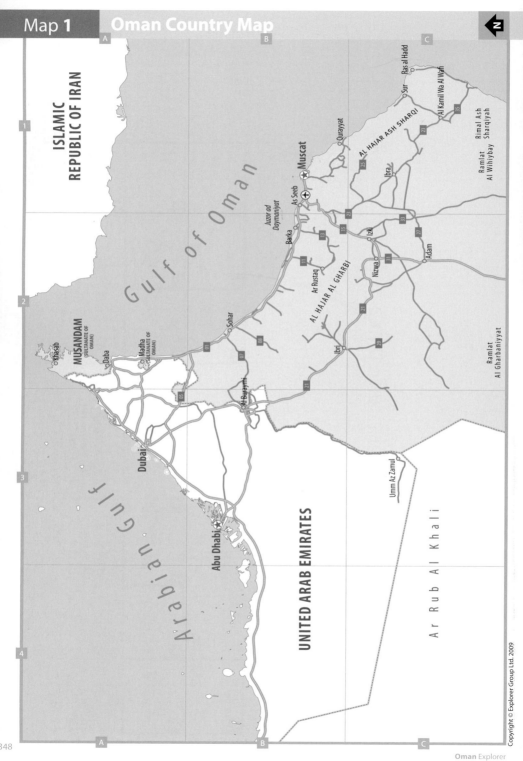

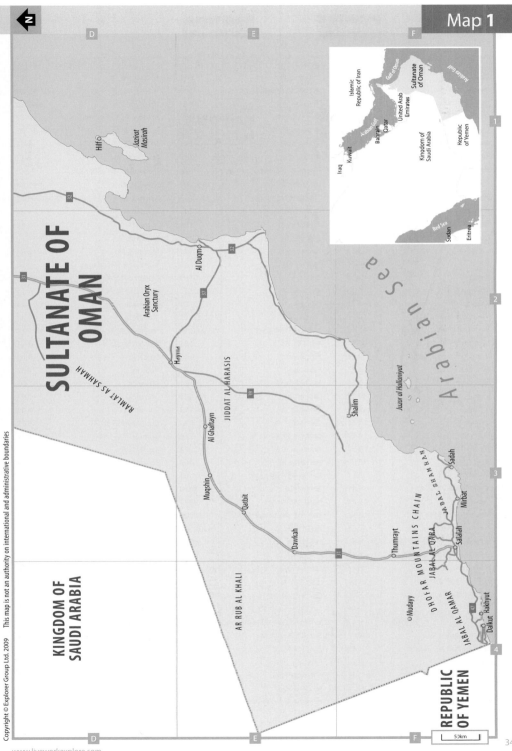

Map 1

N

SULTANATE OF OMAN

Islamic Republic of Iran
Gulf of Oman
Sultanate of Oman
United Arab Emirates
Qatar
Bahrain
Arabian Gulf
Kuwait
Iraq
Kingdom of Saudi Arabia
Republic of Yemen
Arabian Gulf
Red Sea
Sudan
Eritrea

Hilf
Jazirat Masirah

Al Duqm

Arabian Oryx Sanctuary

Haymā

JIDDAT AL HARASIS

RAMLAT AS SAHMAH

Al Ghaftayn

Muqshin

Qatbit

Dawkah

Shalim

Juzur al Hallaniyat

Arabian Sea

Sadah
Mirbat

JABAL SHAMHAN

DHOFAR MOUNTAINS CHAIN

JABAL AL QARA

Thumrayt
Salalah

KINGDOM OF SAUDI ARABIA

AR RUB AL KHALI

Mudayy

JABAL AL QAMAR

Dalkut Rakhyut

REPUBLIC OF YEMEN

50km

Fugro **MAPS**

Fugro MAPS is the leading provider of geospatial products and services in the Middle East and Africa. Utilizing the latest state-of-the-art technologies in airborne and satellite imaging, LiDAR, ground based collection systems and customized GIS software solutions; Fugro MAPS serves all land-use and natural resource industries in the region.

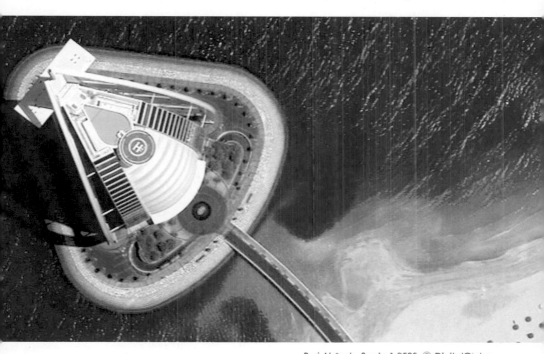

Burj Al Arab, Scale 1:2500 © DigitalGlobe

Fugro MAPS is a Master Distributor of DIGITALGLOBE imagery for the Middle East and Africa.

Corniche Plaza 1, P.O.Box 5232, Sharjah, United Arab Emirates

T : + 971 6 5725411 • F : + 971 6 5724057 • E : info@fugromaps.com

w w w . f u g r o m a p s . c o m

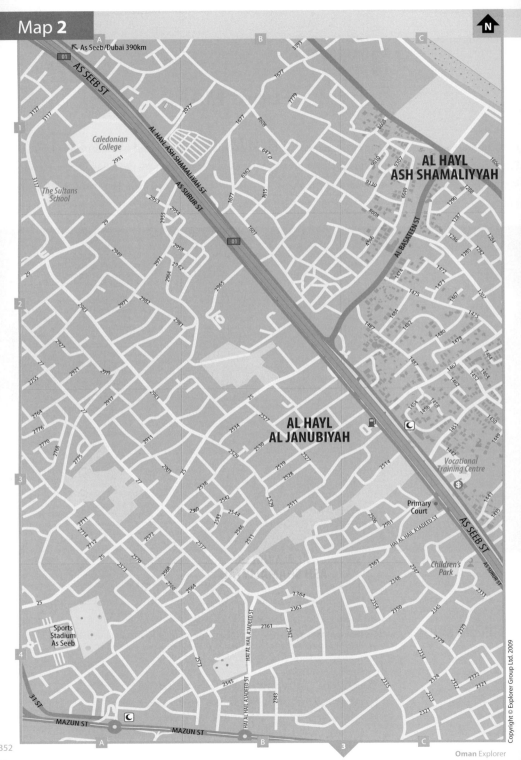

Map **2**

N

As Seeb/Dubai 390km

AS SEEB ST

01

A

B

C

3127
3117

AL HAYL ASH SHAMALIYYAH ST

AS SURUR ST

Caledonian
College
2931

The Sultans
School
3117

1677
1677

1027

8608
647 0
6367
7815
1677
1603

7779

3393

AL HAYL
ASH SHAMALIYYAH

8608
9810
9307
9130
6649

AL BASATEEN ST

1806

1288
1790
1287
1286
1285
1282
1384
1474
1472
1471
1207
1475
1484
1492
1480
1478
1475
1487
1464
1467
1453
1464
1462
1454
1459
1453
1450
1449
1442

01

8608
4366

29
2953
2955 2954
29
2949
2971 2958
2962
2964
2965

2993
2971 2982
2981

2927
27 2921 2919
2755

2983

25

2577

2534

AL HAYL
AL JANUBIYAH

2519
2529
2511

2590

2528

2514

Vocational
Training Centre

$

1441
1435

2764
2776
2770
2768
2775

2917
2911
2903
2538

2542
2363
2544
2546
2557
2511

2290

Primary
Court

2506
2501

2363
2348
2354
2347
2345
2350

Children's
Park

2313
2339

2711
2714 2712
25

2972
2570
2588
2566
2564

2571

2573

HAIL AL HAIL A'JADEED ST

2364
2363
2361
2367

2345
2323
2329
2322
2321

HAIL AL HAIL A'JADEED ST

2324

2335

25

Sports
Stadium
As Seeb

2345
2343

AS SEEB ST

AS SURUR ST

HAIL AL HAIL A'JADEED ST

311 ST

MAZUN ST

MAZUN ST

A

B

C

3

Oman Explorer

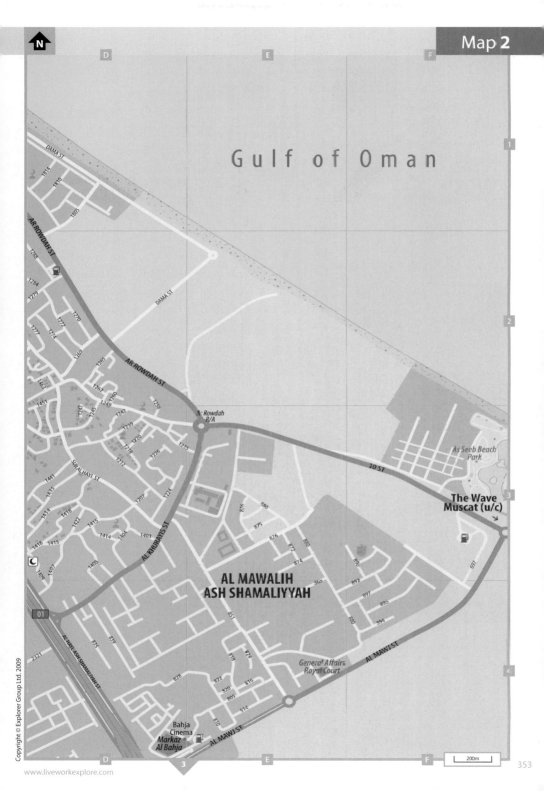

Map **2**

N

D   E   F

Gulf of Oman

DAMA ST

1814
1810
1805

AR ROWDAH ST

1288
1284
1279
1270
1277 1274
1269
1265
1263
1262 1260
1249
1245 1247
1239
1270 1256
1218 1220
1212 1226

DAMA ST

AR ROWDAH ST

1451
1463

SUR AL HAYL ST

1441
1435
1434
1418
1472
1415
1416 1414 1404
1415 1403

AL KHUBAYS ST

1409 1408
1407

1224
1207

1225

Ar Rowdah
R/A

876
980

875
876
872 890
874

863

892

851

897
895
894

890

10 ST

As Seeb Beach
Park

**The Wave
Muscat (u/c)**

691

**AL MAWALIH
ASH SHAMALIYYAH**

2321

AL HAWL ASH SHAMALIYYAH ST

855
859

828

875
879
878
827
820 816
805
810

General Affairs
Royal Court

AL MAWJ ST

AL MAWJ ST

Bahja
Cinema
*Markaz
Al Bahja*

01

C

200m

Map **3**

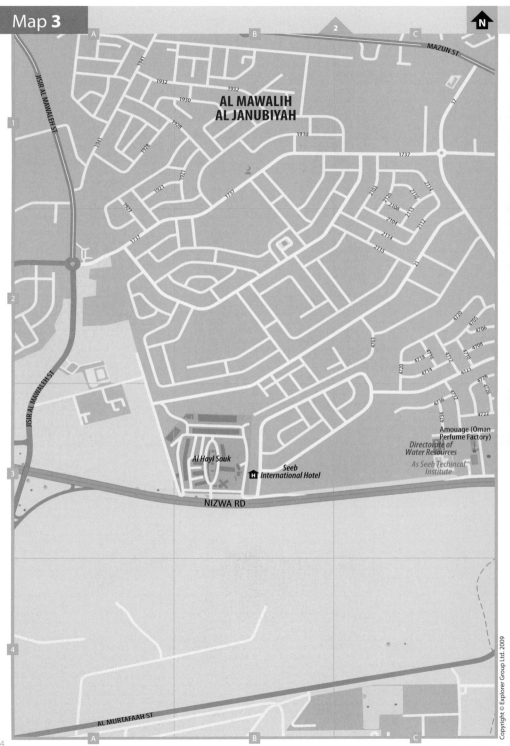

AL MAWALIH
AL JANUBIYAH

MAZUN ST

JISIR AL MAWALEH ST

JISIR AL MAWALEH ST

NIZWA RD

Al Hayl Souk

Seeb
International Hotel

Amouage (Oman
Perfume Factory)

Directorate of
Water Resources

As Seeb Techincal
Institute

AL MURTAFAAH ST

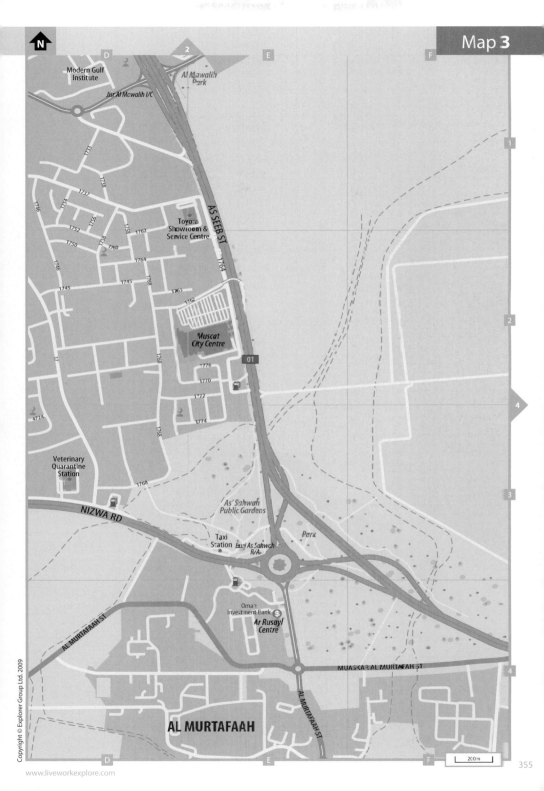

Map **3**

N

D   2   E   F

Modern Gulf
Institute

Al Mawalih
Park

Jisr Al Mawalih I/C

1733

1738
1737
1754
1746   1756
1752   1758   1762
1750   1758   1760
1746   1764
1745   1768
1745   1763
17   1764

AS SEEB ST

Toyota
Showroom &
Service Centre

1769

Muscat
City Centre

01

1776
1770
4724   1772
1768   1774
1768

Veterinary
Quarantine
Station

1768

NIZWA RD

As Sahwah
Public Gardens

Taxi
Station   Burj As Sahwah
R/A

Park

Oman
Investment Bank $

Ar Rusayl
Centre

AL MURTAFAAH ST

MUASKAR AL MURTAFAAH ST

AL MURTAFAAH ST

AL MURTAFAAH

1

2

4

3

4

200m

Map **4**

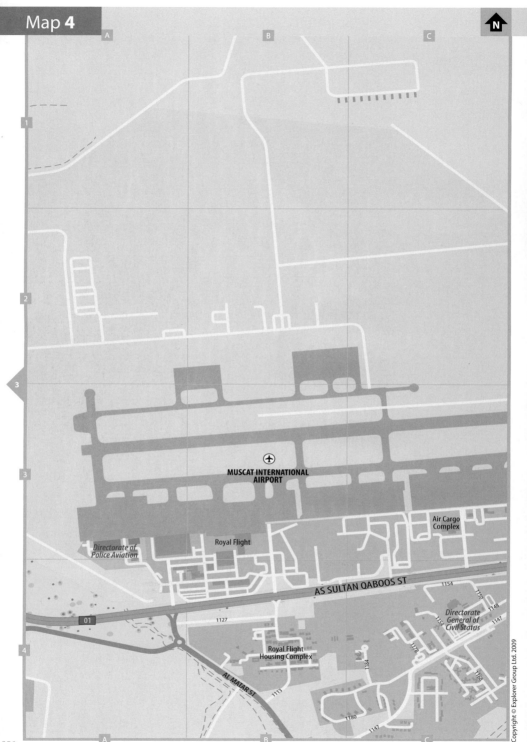

MUSCAT INTERNATIONAL
AIRPORT

Air Cargo
Complex

Royal Flight

Directorate of
Police Aviation

AS SULTAN QABOOS ST

1154

1150

1148

1147

Directorate
General of
Civil Status

01

1127

1154

1178

Royal Flight
Housing Complex

1184

1168

AL MATAR ST

1113

1180

1147

Map **4**

N

D   E   F

Azaiba
Beach

18TH NOVEMBER ST

1

2

5

3

MUSCAT INTERNATIONAL
AIRPORT

Airport   Oman Air
Terminal   Engineering

AS SULTAN QABOOS ST

Oman Air
Catering

Pizza Hut

AL MAARIDH ST

Majlis
Ash Shura

Directorate
General of
Traffic

Directorate
General of IT

Golden
Tulip Seeb

Oman Intl
Exhibition
Centre

Directorate
General of
Customs

Oman
Air

Food Control &
Environment
Centre

Oman Tourism &
Hospitality
Academy

Royal Oman
Police -Traffic
Director General

4

AL MATAR ST

99

Fire & Safety
Engineering College

Muscat Golf &
Country Club

D   E   F

200m

Map **5**

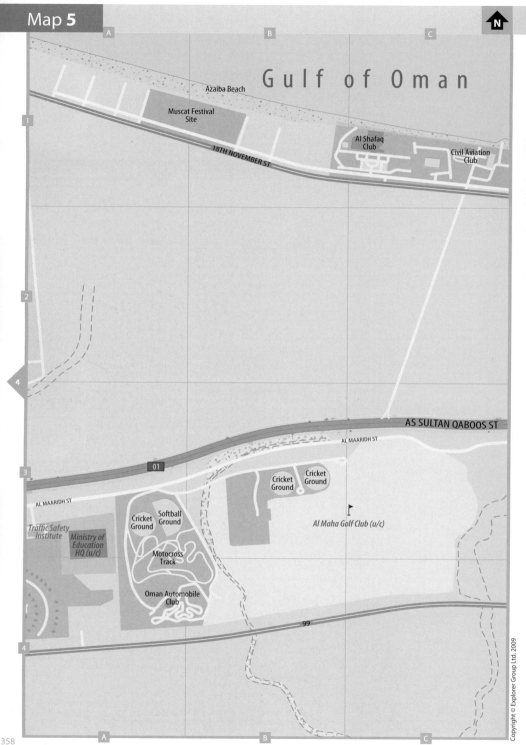

Gulf of Oman

Azaiba Beach

Muscat Festival Site

Al Shafaq Club

Civil Aviation Club

18TH NOVEMBER ST

AS SULTAN QABOOS ST

AL MAARIDH ST

01

Cricket Ground

Cricket Ground

AL MAARIDH ST

Cricket Ground

Softball Ground

Al Maha Golf Club (u/c)

Traffic Safety Institute

Ministry of Education HQ (u/c)

Motocross Track

Oman Automobile Club

99

Map **5**

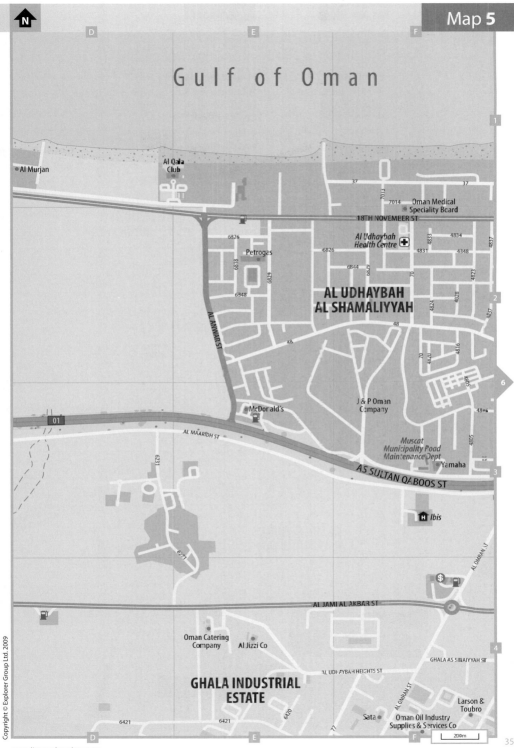

Gulf of Oman

Al Murjan

Al Qala Club

37   37

7014   Oman Medical
        Speciality Board

18TH NOVEMBER ST

6826

Petrogas

Al Udhaybah
Health Centre

6826

4833   4834

4831   4348

4837

6818

6829

6844   6829

70

4823

6348

**AL UDHAYBAH
AL SHAMALIYYAH**

4824   4028

4837

AL ANWAR ST

48

4816

48

70

4824

4805

01

McDonald's

J & P Oman
Company

48 66

AL MAARIDH ST

Muscat
Municipality Road
Maintenance Dept

4805

Yamaha

AS SULTAN QABOOS ST

6231

H *Ibis*

6221

AL OMRAN ST

$

AL JAMI AL AKBAR ST

Oman Catering
Company   Al Jizzi Co

AL OMRAN ST

GHALA AS SINAIYYAH ST

AL UDHAYBAH HEIGHTS ST

**GHALA INDUSTRIAL
ESTATE**

6421   6421   6420

77

Sata

Larson &
Toubro

Oman Oil Industry
Supplies & Services Co

200m

Map **6**

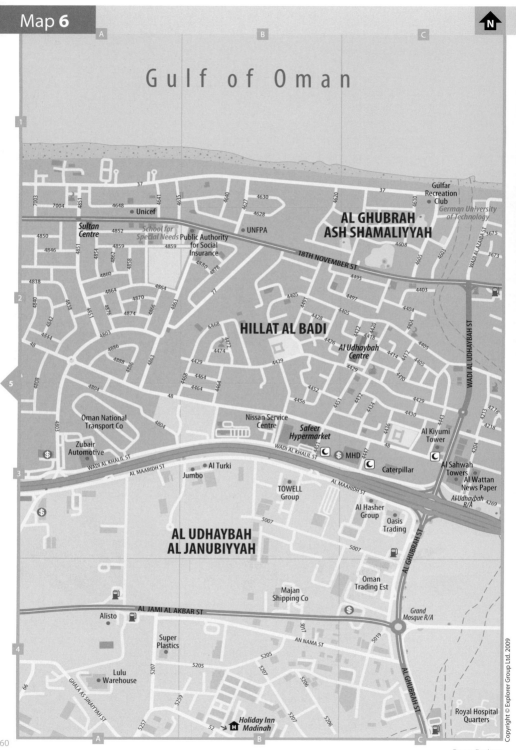

Gulf of Oman

**AL GHUBRAH
ASH SHAMALIYYAH**

HILLAT AL BADI

**AL UDHAYBAH
AL JANUBIYYAH**

Gulfar Recreation Club

German University of Technology

Unicef

UNFPA

Sultan Centre

School for Special Needs

Public Authority for Social Insurance

18TH NOVEMBER ST

WADI AL AZAIBA ST

WADI AL UDHAYBAH ST

Al Udhaybah Centre

Oman National Transport Co

Zubair Automotive

Nissan Service Centre

Safeer Hypermarket

MHD

Caterpillar

Al Kiyumi Tower

Al Sahwah Towers

Al Wattan News Paper

Al Udhaybah R/A

WADI AL KHALIL ST

WADI AL KHALIL ST

AL MAARIDH ST

Al Turki

Jumbo

AL MAARIDH ST

TOWELL Group

Al Hasher Group

Oasis Trading

AL GHUBRAH ST

Majan Shipping Co

Oman Trading Est

Grand Mosque R/A

AL JAMI AL AKBAR ST

Alisto

Super Plastics

AN NAMA ST

GHALA AS SINAIYYAH ST

Lulu Warehouse

Royal Hospital Quarters

Holiday Inn Madinah

Map **6**

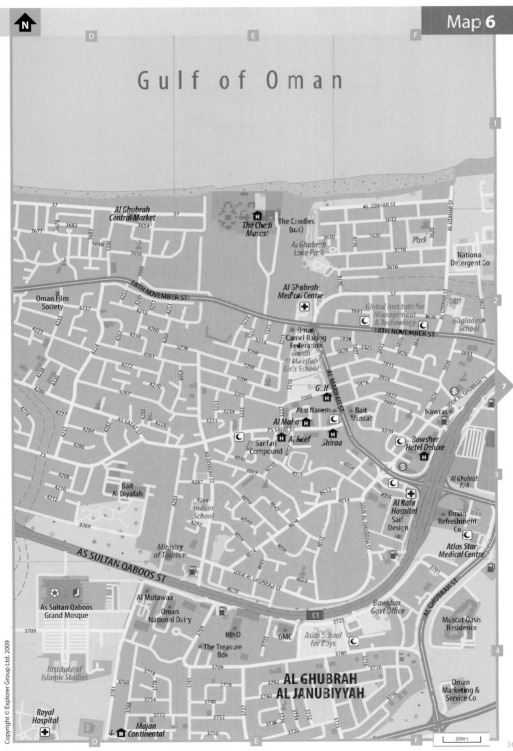

Gulf of Oman

Map **7**

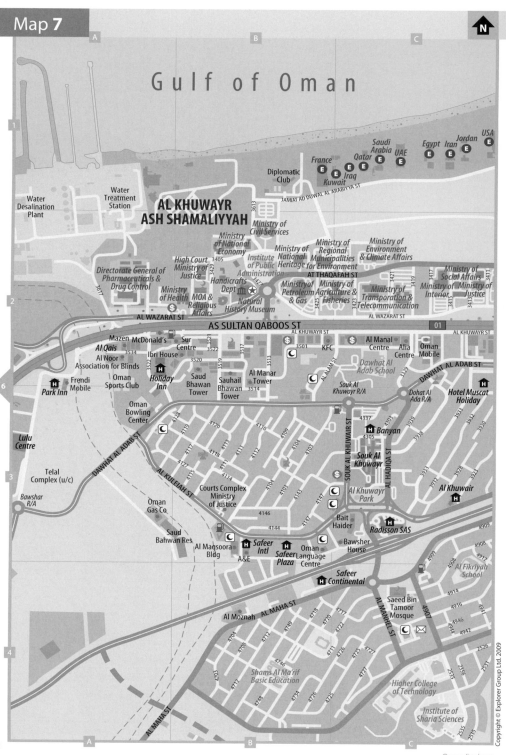

N

Gulf of Oman

AL KHUWAYR ASH SHAMALIYYAH

Water Desalination Plant

Water Treatment Station

Diplomatic Club

France **E**
Kuwait **E**
Iraq **E**
Qatar **E**
Saudi Arabia **E**
UAE **E**
Egypt **E**
Iran **E**
Jordan **E**
USA **E**

JAMIAT AD DUWAL AL ARABIYYA ST

Ministry of Civil Services

Ministry of National Economy

Ministry of Regional Municipalities

Ministry of Environment & Climate Affairs

High Court
Ministry of Justice
Institute of Public Administration
Ministry of National Heritage for Environment

Directorate General of Pharmaceuticals & Drug Control

Ministry of Health

MOA & Religious Affairs
Handicrafts Dept
Natural History Museum

AT THAQAFAH ST

Ministry of Petroleum Agriculture & Gas
Ministry of Agriculture & Fisheries
Ministry of Transporation & Telecommunication
Ministry of Social Affairs
Ministry of Interior
Ministry of Justice

AL WAZARAT ST
AL WAZARAT ST

AS SULTAN QABOOS ST
01
AL KHUWAYR ST
AL KHUWAYR ST

Mazen
McDonald's
Sur Centre
KFC
Al Manal Centre
Alia Centre
Oman Mobile

Al Qais
Ibri House

Al Noor Association for Blinds

Holiday Inn

Saud Bhawan Tower
Sauhail Bhawan Tower
Al Manar Tower

Dawhat Al Adab School

DAWHAT AL ADAB ST

Park Inn
Frendi Mobile
Oman Sports Club

Souk Al Khuwayr R/A

Dohat Al Ada R/A
Hotel Muscat Holiday

Lulu Centre

Oman Bowling Center

Banyan

Souk Al Khuwayr

SOUK AL KHUWAIR ST
AL HADIQA ST

Al Khuwair

Telal Complex (u/c)

DAWHAT AL ADAB ST

AL KULEIAH ST

Courts Complex Ministry of Justice

Al Khuwayr Park

Bawshar R/A

Oman Gas Co

Bait Haider

Radisson SAS

Saud Bahwan Res

Al Maqsoora Bldg

Safeer Intl
A&E
Safeer Plaza
Oman Language Centre
Bawsher House

Al Fikriyah School

Safeer Continental

Saeed Bin Tamoor Mosque

AL MANHEL ST

Al Moznah
AL MAHA ST

Shams Al Ma'rif Basic Education

Higher College of Technology

AL MAHA ST

Institute of Sharia Sciences

Oman Explorer

Map 7

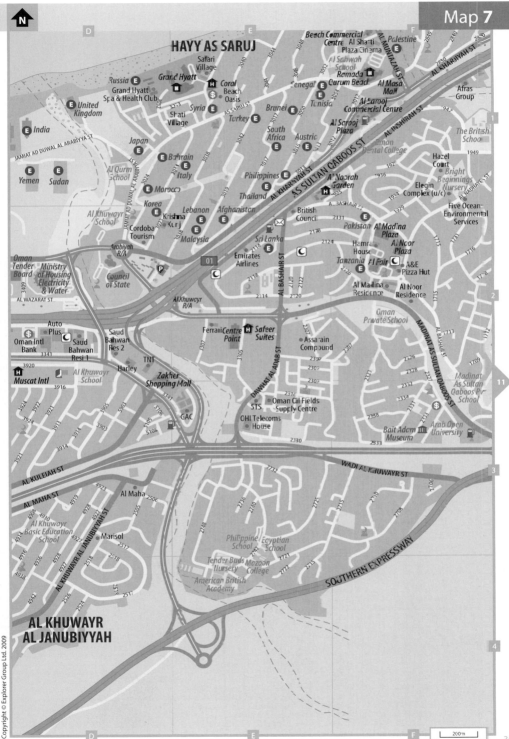

HAYY AS SARUJ

AL KHUWAYR
AL JANUBIYYAH

Map **8**

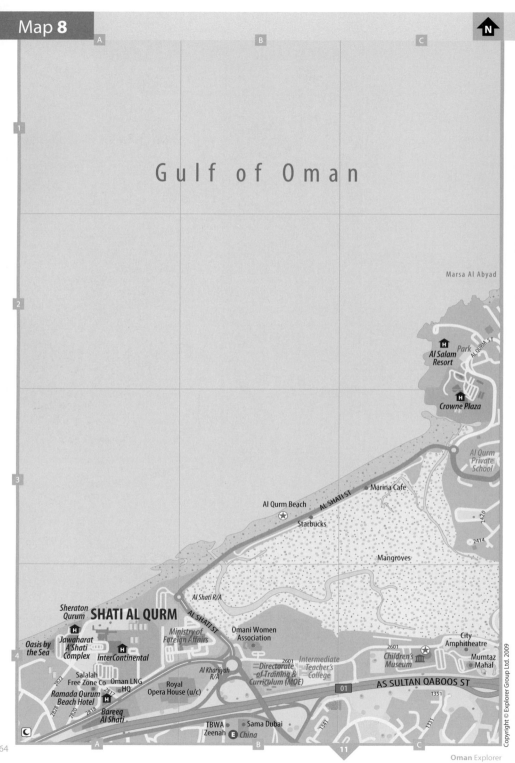

Gulf of Oman

Marsa Al Abyad

Park

Al Salam Resort

AL QURM ST

Crowne Plaza

Al Qurm Private School

2420

Marina Cafe

2414

AL SHATI ST

Al Qurm Beach

Starbucks

Mangroves

Al Shati R/A

AL SHATI ST

Sheraton Qurum

SHATI AL QURM

Omani Women Association

City Amphitheatre

Oasis by the Sea

Jawaharat A Shati Complex

Ministry of Foreign Affairs

Children's Museum

Mumtaz Mahal

InterContinental

2601

Intermediate Teacher's College

Salalah Free Zone Co

Al Khariiyah R/A

Directorate of Training & Curriculum (MOE)

2601

2602

Oman LNG HQ

AS SULTAN QABOOS ST

1351

Ramada Qurum Beach Hotel

2617

Royal Opera House (u/c)

01

2818

Bareeq Al Shati

TBWA Zeenah

Sama Dubai

China

2020

1341

1331

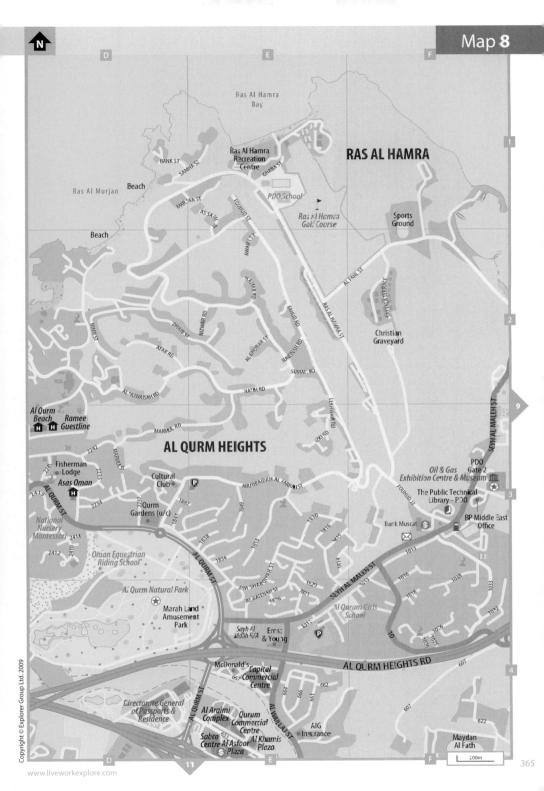

Map **8**

N

RAS AL HAMRA

Ras Al Hamra Bay

BANK ST

SAMMA ST

Ras Al Hamra Recreation Centre

GHABA ST

Ras Al Murjan   Beach

MAR'AH ST

AS SAFA ST

FOUHUD ST

PDO School

Ras Al Hamra Golf Course

Sports Ground

Beach

AWAFI ST

SALMA RD

AL FAHL ST

SHIYALA TERRACE

NIZWAR RD

FAHUD RD

RAS AL HAMRA ST

NIMR ST

DHAIB ST

AFAR RD

AL GHUBAR ST

SUMEINAH RD

Christian Graveyard

AL YUWAISAH RD

VATHI RD

SUMAT RD

SEYH AL MALEH ST

LEKHWAIR RD

9

IZKI RD

Al Qurm Beach   Ramee Guestline

MARMUL RD

AL QURM HEIGHTS

PDO Gate 2

MARMUL ST

2242

Fisherman Lodge   Asas Oman

2235

Cultural Club

2237

ABUOBAIDAH AL JARRAH ST

Oil & Gas Exhibition Centre & Museum

Qurm Gardens (u/c)

1897

FOUHUD ST

The Public Technical Library – PDO

2419

AL QURM ST

2234

1884

1849

1530

1816

1815

Bank Muscat

BP Middle East Office

National Nursery Montessori

2411

1838

1853

1834

Oman Equestrian Riding School

2412   2410

AL QURM ST

ASH SHARQIYAH ST

1814

1013

1016

1022

1025

1033

Al Qurm Natural Park

Marah Land Amusement Park

1836

AL BATENAH ST

1821

1813

SEYH AL MALEH ST

Al Qurum Girls School

1013

1018

1046

10

1025

1016

1032

McDonald's   Capital Commercial Centre

Sayh Al Malih 5/A

Ernst & Young

AL QURM HEIGHTS RD

607

4

Directorate General of Passports & Residence

662

664

666

641

607

622

Al Araimi Complex

Qurum Commercial Centre

AL WAHLAJ ST

AIG Insurance

Sabco Centre   Al Asfoor Plaza

Al Khamis Plaza

Maydan Al Fath

200m

Map **9**

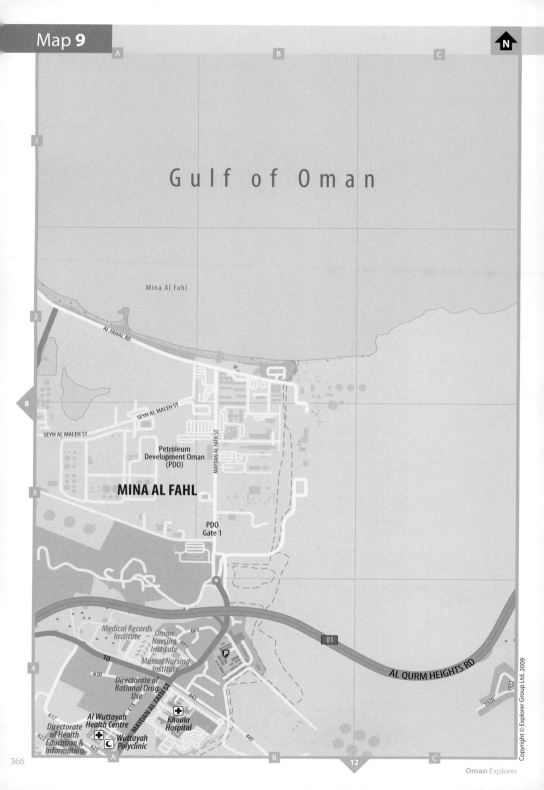

Gulf of Oman

Mina Al Fahl

AL FAHAL RD

SEYH AL MALEH ST

SEYH AL MALEH ST

MAYDAN AL FATH ST

Petroleum
Development Oman
(PDO)

MINA AL FAHL

PDO
Gate 1

Medical Records
Institute

Oman
Nursing
Institute

603

605

Muscat Nursing
Institute

10

610

Directorate of
Rational Drug
Use

445

AL QURM HEIGHTS RD

01

1920

1922

618

MAYDAN AL FATH ST

617

Al Wuttayah
Health Centre

Khoula
Hospital

622

Directorate
of Health
Education &
Information

625

Wuttayah
Polyclinic

445

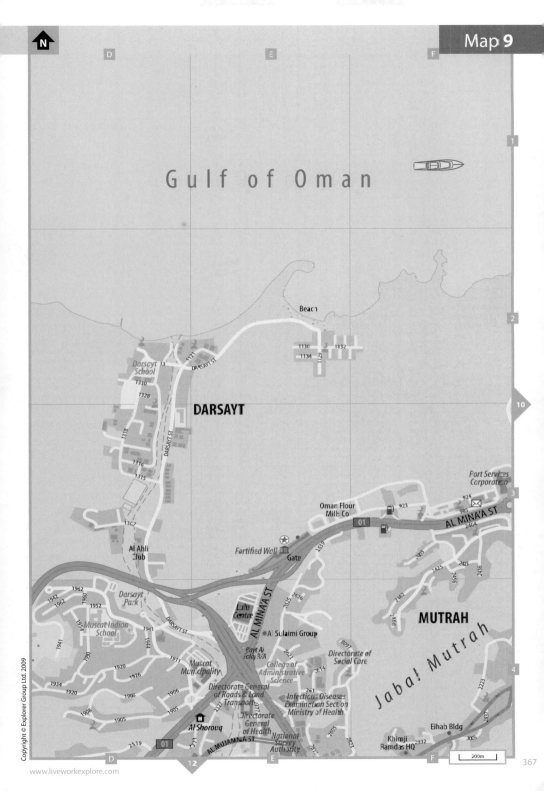

G u l f   o f   O m a n

Beach

1130   1132
1134

Darsayt
School
1330
1328

1121

DARSAYT ST

DARSAYT

1318

DARSAYT ST

1316
1315

1307

Al Ahli
Club

Port Services
Corporation

924

Oman Flour
Mill Co

923

905

AL MINA'A ST

2464

01

903

Fortified Wall
Gate

1639

925

2426

2436

AL MINA'A ST

2626

2462

2456

1962
1962
1960
1952
1941

Darsayt
Park

DARSAYT ST

1944

Lulu
Centre

2999

MUTRAH

1942
1962

1954

Muscat Indian
School

1920
1926

1911

Muscat
Municipality

1941

A Sulaimi Group

8697

Jabal Mutrah

2223

1920

1905

1906

1905

Bayt Al
Falaj R/A

2521

College of
Administrative
Science

Directorate of
Social Care

2C14

2837

1934
1920

1908

1905

Directorate General
of Roads & Land
Transport

1332

2517

Al Shorouq

Directorate
General
of Health

261

Infectious Diseases
Examination Section
Ministry of Health

2605

National
Survey
Authority

2823

Khimji
Ramdas HQ

2332

Eihab Bldg

3005

2519

01

2577

AL MUJAMMA'A ST

12

200m

Map **10**

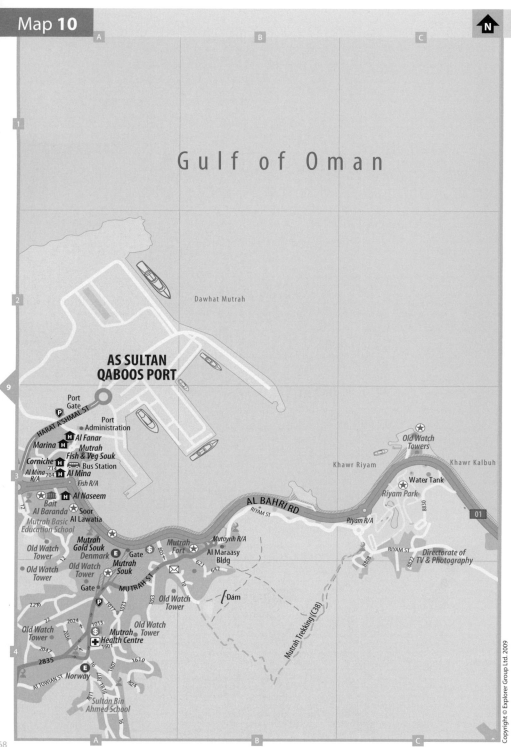

N

Gulf of Oman

Dawhat Mutrah

AS SULTAN
QABOOS PORT

Port
Gate
Port
Administration
Al Fanar
Marina
Mutrah
Fish & Veg Souk
Corniche
Al Mina
R/A
Bus Station
Al Mina
Fish R/A
Al Naseem
Bait
Al Baranda
Mutrah Basic
Education School
Soor
Al Lawatia
Mutrah
Gold Souk
Denmark
Old Watch
Tower
Old Watch
Tower
Gate
Mutrah
Fort
Gate
Mutrah
Souk
Old Watch
Tower
Old Watch
Tower
Mutrah
Health Centre
Old Watch
Tower
Norway
Sultan Bin
Ahmed School
Al Maraasy
Bldg
Mutayrih R/A
Dam
AL BAHRI RD
RIYAM ST
Riyam R/A
RIYAM ST
Khawr Riyam
Old Watch
Towers
Water Tank
Riyam Park
Khawr Kalbuh
Directorate of
TV & Photography
Mutrah Trekking (C38)

2835

Oman Explorer

Map **10**

N

Gulf of Oman

Lighthouse

AL JAZIRAH

Kalbuh Park

Khawr Muscat

KALBUH

AL BAHRI RD

9559

RIYAM ST

Royal Yacht

AL MIRANI ST

Muscat
Gate Museum

Al Mirani
Fort

MUSCAT

Al Jalali
Fort

BAB AL MUTHAIB ST

Council of
The Ministers

9541 ST

KASIB ST

Diwan
of Royal Court

ALAM ST

Al Alam
Palace

P

Bayt Miznah
Gallery

Omani French
Museum

Royal
Estate

Diwan
Clinic

Muscat
Health
Centre

Bayt Az Zubair
Museum

BAD WAL AT ST

Zahra School
Zohour
School

AL BAREED ST

Al Saidiya
School

8259

Cabinet of
The Deputy
Prime Minister

Directorate of
Information
Systems

State Audit
Institution

Ministry of
Finance

8261

9119

8613

2

13

D

E

F

200m

Map 11

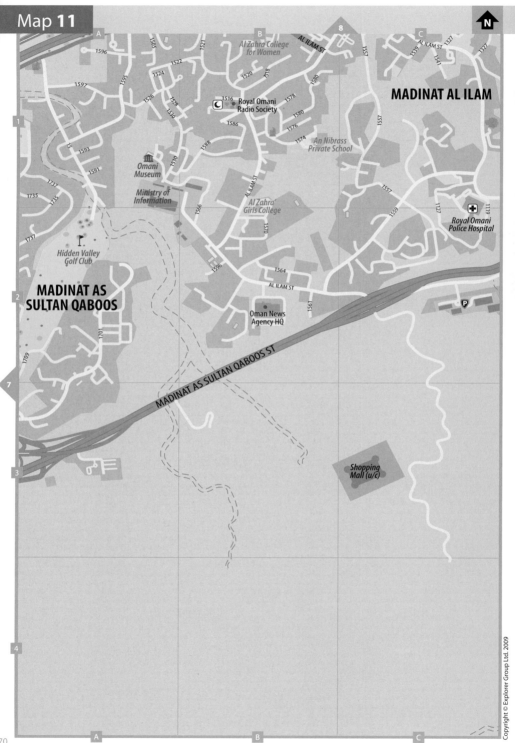

MADINAT AL ILAM

Al Zahra College
for Women

AL ILAM ST

Royal Omani
Radio Society

An Nibrass
Private School

Omani
Museum

Ministry of
Information

AL ILAM ST

Al Zahra'
Girls College

Royal Omani
Police Hospital

Hidden Valley
Golf Club

MADINAT AS
SULTAN QABOOS

AL ILAM ST

Oman News
Agency HQ

MADINAT AS SULTAN QABOOS ST

Shopping
Mall (u/c)

Map **11**

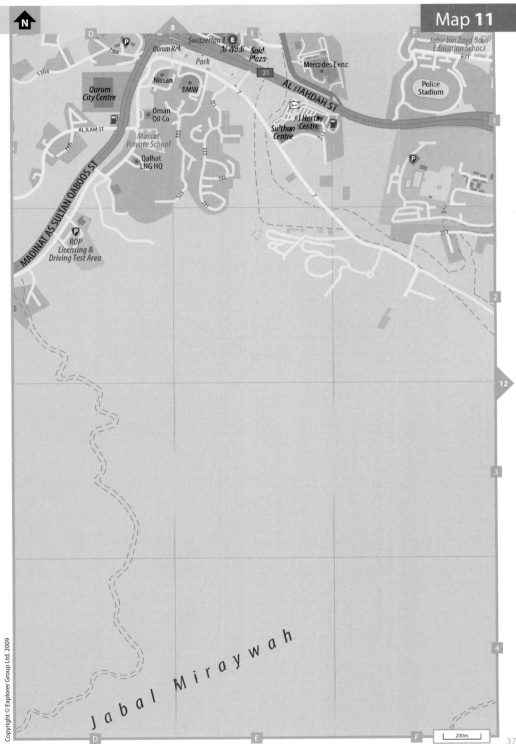

D

P
7-04
1304

Qurum
City Centre

AL ILAM ST

MADINAT AS SULTAN QABOOS ST

1105

P

ROP
Licensing &
Driving Test Area

Qurum R/A

Park

Nissan

BMW

Oman
Oil Co

Muscat
Private School

Qalhat
LNG HQ

551

551

551

551

51

3

Switzerland
Al Wadi

E

Said
Plaza

01

Sultan
Centre

AL HAHDAH ST

Mercedes Benz

Al Harthy
Centre

7

7

7

Jabir bin Zayd Boys
Education School

631

Police
Stadium

P

351

1

2

12

3

4

D   E   F

200m

Map 12

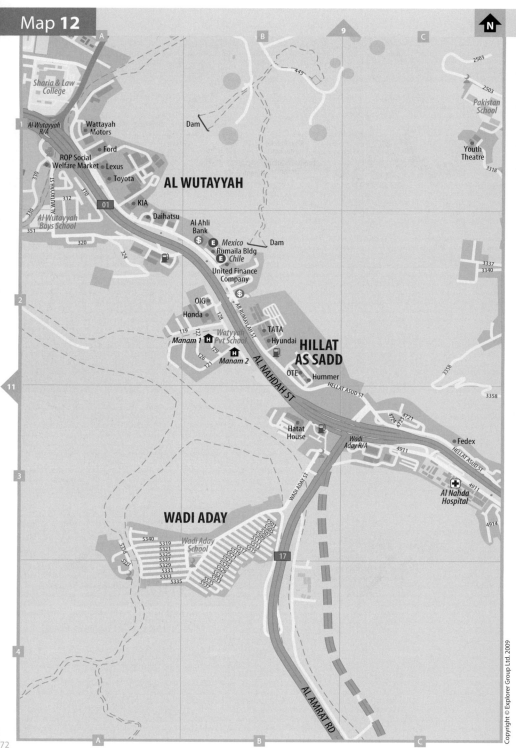

N

Sharia & Law College

2503

2503

Pakistan School

Dam

445

Youth Theatre

3318

Al Wutayyah R/A

Wattayah Motors

Ford

ROP Social Welfare Market

Lexus

Toyota

KIA

Daihatsu

AL WUTAYYAH

01

Al Wutayyah Boys School

330

330

351

312

310

320

324

Al Ahli Bank

Mexico

Rumaila Bldg

Chile

United Finance Company

Dam

3337
3340

OIG

Honda

Watyyah Pvt School

Manam 1

Manam 2

128

119

122

123

126

127

TATA

Hyundai

HILLAT AS SADD

OTE

Hummer

AL NAHDAH ST

HELLAT ASUD ST

3358

3358

AR RUMAILAH ST

Hatat House

Wadi Aday R/A

4720

4721

4911

Fedex

HELLAT ASUD ST

WADI ADAY

Wadi Aday School

5340

5319

5321

5325

5327

5329

5331

5333

5335

5336

5337

5501

Al Nahda Hospital

4911

4914

WADI ADAY ST

17

AL AMRAT RD

Oman Explorer

Map 12

N

Nuzha

BAYT AL FALAJ

Al Hadow
ONEIC
MUTRAH ST
Lima House
Oman House
Mutrah

Ministry of Higher Education
Ministry of Education

Al Walid Ibn Abi-Al Malik Basic School

Armed Forces Museum

Church

Al Falaj

AL MUJAMMA ST

Hindu Temple

AL WASHAL ST

Bayt Al Falaj Stadium

Muscat Water Service Office

Communication Tower

Al Burj R/A

Ministry of Sports Affairs

AL BURJ ST

Turtles

Semiramis

Ruwi Health Centre

Sultan

Al Masa Hall

Supasave

Star Cinema

Omanzel

Bait Sohar

HSBC

Al Amal Basic Education

Al Burj Intl

National Museum & Islamic Library

White Nile

CNB

CBN

Central Bank of Oman Currency Museum

Maryam Bldg

Bait Hour

L&T Oman (Zubair Towers)

Najila Complex

Fatima Shopping Centre

Saudi Airlines

AL NUR ST

RUWI

Oman Air India

Salam Centre

Oman Trade Net

Ikram House

Ruwi Boys Secondary School

Canada

Renaissance Chamber of House
Commerce & Industry

Oman Sheraton

OTE Group

AL FARAHIDI ST

Sarco

Directorate General of Health Affairs

Ministry of Commerce & Industry

Muscat Intl Centre

Haffa House

Gulf Air

Al Wafa

AL JAAME ST

Clock Tower
Muscat Securities Market

Hala

Ruwi

Ead- Al Samaa Poly Clinic

KFC

Centrepoint
Directorate General of Tax

Sweden

OCIPED

Ruwi R/A

Oman Commercial Centre

AL FURSAN ST

Safeer Mart

A&E

Bait Al Ahlam

RUWI ST

Al Raha

Family Shopping Centre

Ministry of Manpower

Bait

Danube

BAYT AL FALAJ ST

Muscat Gold Souk

KM Trading Mall

Naai Al Kabir GHS School

Shopping & Saving Co

Intl Printing Press

International Medical Centre

01

Al Madharah Basic Education School

Al Nas Cinema

AL BALADIYAH ST

Toyota Service Centre

Oman Financial Services Company

Dar Al Hamriyah

Makha Business Centre

ROP Complex

AR ROBI BIN HABIB ST

Makha

Royal

Al Hamriyah

Germany

Ariaf Nizwa

SOUK RUWI ST

Ruwi Comm Centre

AL SALADIYAH ST

AL FURSAN ST

Al Humriyah R/A

Spring

Najiyah Bint Amer School

SOUK RUWI ST

AL HUMRIYYAH

YITI ST

200m

Map **13**

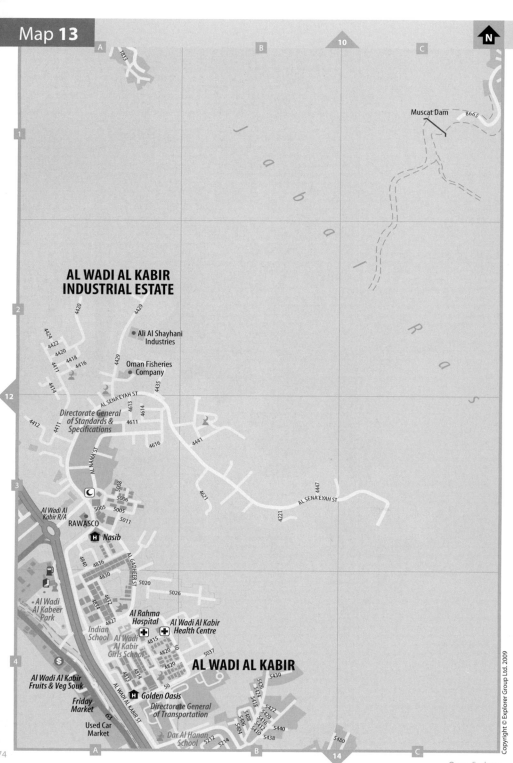

AL WADI AL KABIR
INDUSTRIAL ESTATE

Ali Al Shayhani
Industries

Oman Fisheries
Company

Directorate General
of Standards &
Specifications

Al Wadi Al
Kabir R/A

RAWASCO

Nasib

Al Wadi
Al Kabeer
Park

Indian
School

Al Rahma
Hospital

Al Wadi
Al Kabir
Girls School

Al Wadi Al Kabir
Health Centre

AL WADI AL KABIR

Al Wadi Al Kabir
Fruits & Veg Souk

Friday
Market

Used Car
Market

Golden Oasis

Directorate General
of Transportation

Dar Al Hanan
School

Muscat Dam

Oman Explorer

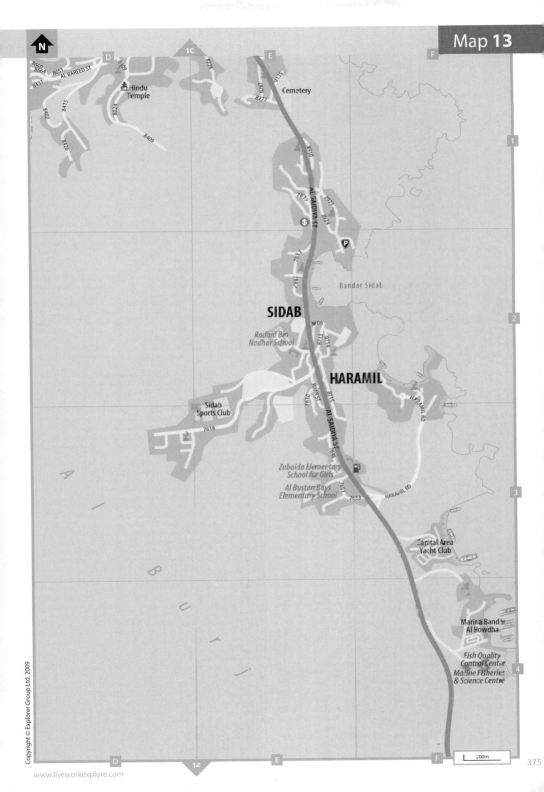

Map **13**

N

AL BAREED ST

Hindu
Temple

Cemetery

AL SAIDIYA ST

$

P

Bandar Sidab

SIDAB

Radhid Bin
Nedhar School

HARAMIL

Sidab
Sports Club

HARAMIL RD

Zubaida Elementary
School for Girls

Al Bustan Boys
Elementary School

HARAMIL RD

A   L   B   U   R   J   I

Capital Area
Yacht Club

Marina Bandar
Al Rowdha

Fish Quality
Control Centre
Marine Fisheries
& Science Centre

1

2

3

4

D

1C

E

F

200m

Map **14**

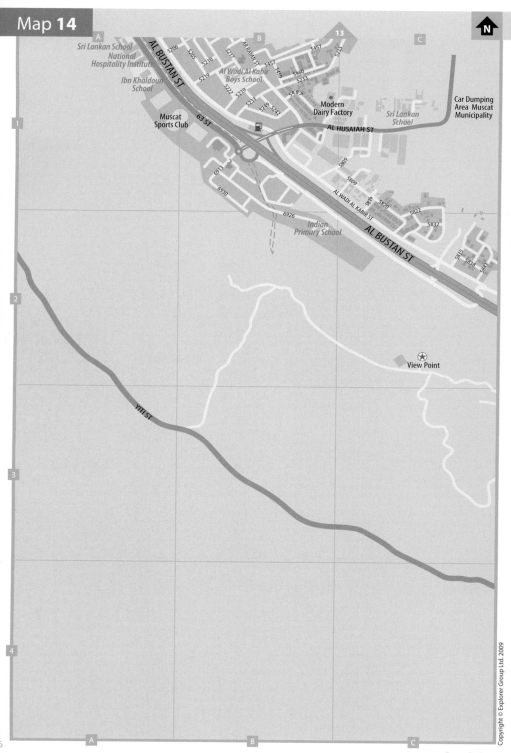

Sri Lankan School
National
Hospitality Institute

Ibn Khaldoun
School

AL BUSTAN ST

5206
5205
5210
5219
5217
5222
5219
5233
5249 5242

AB RAVAN ST
5217
5457
5459
5460
5233
5483

Al Wadi Al Kabir
Boys School

13
5457
5233

Muscat
Sports Club

63 ST

6913

6930

6926

Indian
Primary School

Modern
Dairy Factory

AL HUSAIAH ST

Sri Lankan
School

Car Dumping
Area Muscat
Municipality

5809

5809

5816

5820

AL WADI AL KABIR ST

AL BUSTAN ST

5822

5832

5835

5838

5831

View Point

YITI ST

Oman Explorer

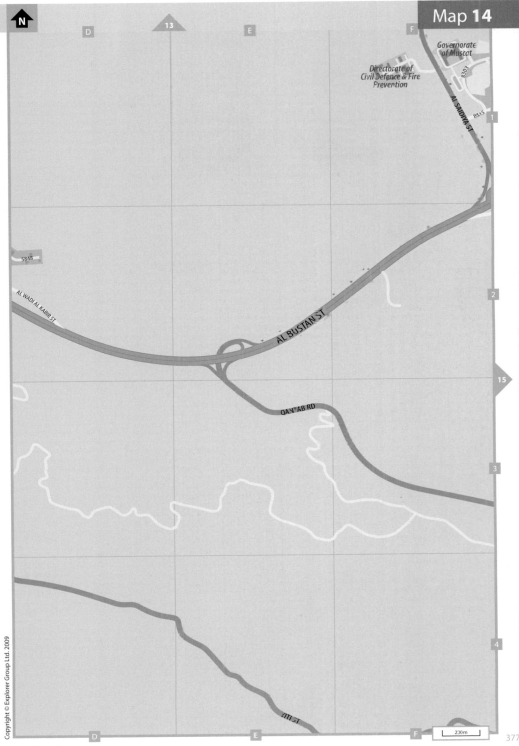

Map **14**

N

13

D

E

F

Governorate
of Muscat

Directorate of
Civil Defence & Fire
Prevention

8303

AL SAIDIYA ST

8315

1

5848

AL WADI AL KABIR ST

AL BUSTAN ST

2

15

QARYAB RD

3

ATI ST

4

200m

D

E

F

Map **15**

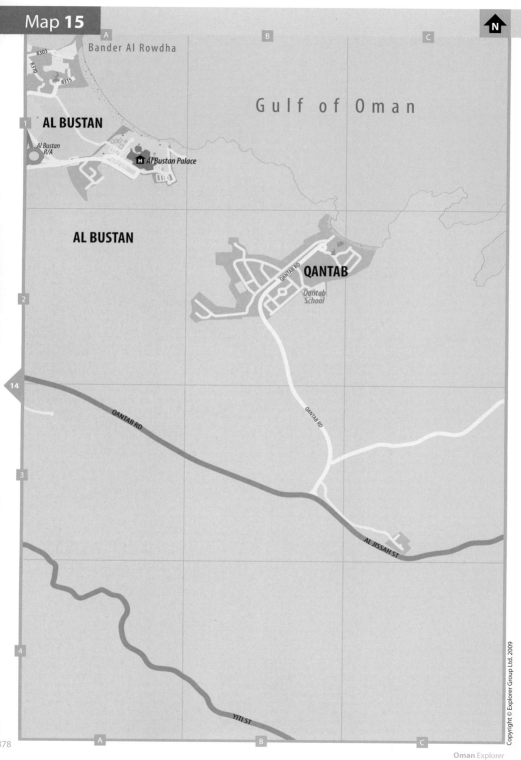

Oman Explorer

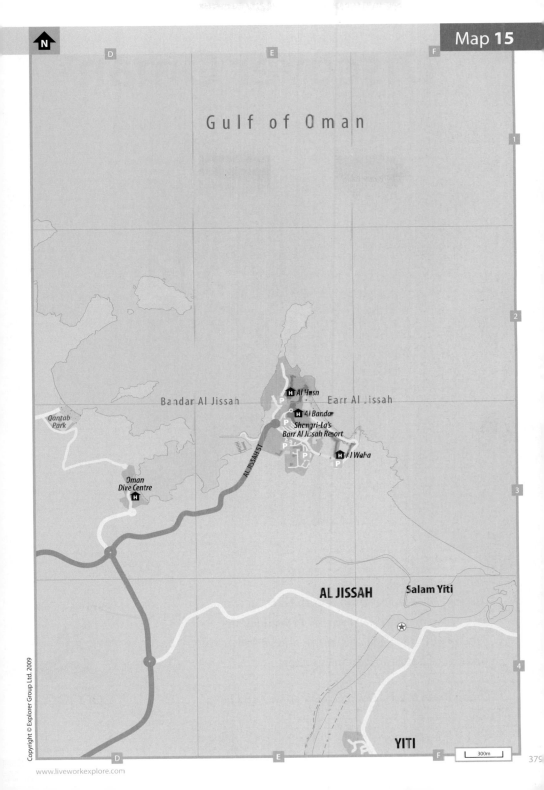

Map **15**

Gulf of Oman

Bandar Al Jissah

Barr Al Jissah

Qantab
Park

Al Hisn

Al Bandar

Shangri-La's
Barr Al Jissah Resort

Al Waha

AL JISSAH ST

Oman
Dive Centre

AL JISSAH

Salam Yiti

YITI

300m

Discover Oman

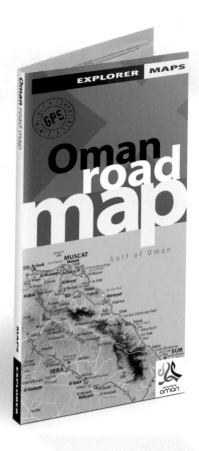

This fold-out map of Oman uses the most accurate, up-to-date mapping available. Also included is a directory of the main cities, towns and villages, roads, landmarks, hotels and useful numbers.

Oman Road Map – We've Got Oman Covered

Supported by

SULTANATE OF
oman

Index

Index

Oman Explorer

Residents' Guides

Mini Guides

Mini Maps

Photography Books

Maps

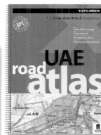

Activity and Lifestyle Guides

Check out
www.liveworkexplore.com/shop

Quick Reference

Public Holidays (2010)

New Year's Day (1)	1 Jan ^{Fixed}
Prophet Muhammad's Birthday (2)	26 Feb ^{Moon}
Lailat Al Mi'Raj (1)	09 July ^{Moon}
Renaissance Day (2)	23 July ^{Fixed}
Eid Al Fitr (3/4)	11 Sep ^{Moon}
Eid Al Adha (3)	17 Nov ^{Moon}
National Day (2)	18 Nov ^{Fixed}
Islamic New Year (2)	18 Dec ^{Moon}

Taxi Companies

Allo Taxi	24 697 997
City Taxi	24 603 363
Hello Taxi	24 607 011

Embassies & Consulates

Australia (Saudi Arabia)	+966 1488 7788
Austria	24 694 127
Bahrain	24 605 074
Canada	24 791 738
China	24 696 698
Czech Republic (Saudi Arabia)	+966 1450 3617/9
Denmark	24 526 000
Egypt	24 600 411
France	24 681 800
Germany	24 832 482
India	24 684 500
Iran	24 696 944
Ireland	24 701 282
Italy	24 695 131
Japan	24 601 028
Jordan	24 692 760
Korea (South)	24 691 490
Kuwait	24 699 627
Lebanon	24 695 844
Mexico (Saudi Arabia)	+966 1480 8822
The Netherlands	24 603 706
New Zealand	24 794 932
Norway	24 703 289
Pakistan	24 603 439
Philippines	24 605 140
Qatar	24 701 802
Russia	24 602 894
Saudi Arabia	24 601 744
Singapore (Saudi Arabia)	+966 1480 3855
South Africa	24 694 793
Spain (Saudi Arabia)	+966 1488 0606
Sri Lanka	24 697 841
Sweden	24 708 693
Switzerland	24 568 202
Thailand	24 602 684
United Arab Emirates	24 400 000
United Kingdom	24 609 000
United States of America	24 643 400

Useful Numbers

Directory Enquiries (Omantel)	1318
Electricity Holding Company	24 698 818
Explorer Publishing's Dubai office (from overseas)	+971 4 340 8805
Mobile Phone Customer Services (Frendi, Oman Mobile, Nawras)	1234
Municipality Emergency	150
Muscat Municipality	800 777 222
Oman Area Code	24
Oman Country Code	968
Oman Power & Water Procurement Company	24 508 400
Payphone Faults & Complaints	1307
Police Emergency	9999
Salalah Area Code	23
Telephone Faults & Complaints	1300

Airport Information

Oman Air	24 519 031
Muscat International Airport:	
Flight Information	24 519 223/519 456
Baggage Services	24 519 662
Customer Service	24 518 977
Salalah Airport:	
Flight Information/Customer Service /Baggage Services (Oman Air)	23 294 237

Banks

Bank Dhofar	Muscat	24 790 466
	Salalah	23 294 886
Bank Muscat SAOG ▶ p.77	Muscat	24 795 555
Bank Sohar ▶ p.49	Muscat	24 730 000
Banque Banorabe	Muscat	24 704 274
Central Bank Of Oman	Muscat	24 702 222
Habib Bank	Muscat	24 817 142
HSBC ▶ p.IFC	Muscat	24 799 920
National Bank Of Abu Dhabi	Muscat	24 761 000
National Bank Of Oman (NBO)	Muscat	24 811 711
Oman Arab Bank	Muscat	24 706 265
	Salalah	23 292 005
Oman International Bank	Muscat	24 682 500
	Salalah	23 291 512
Standard Chartered Bank	Muscat	24 773 666

Hospitals With Emergency Rooms

Main Government Hospitals	
Al Nahda Hospital	24 707 800
Ibn Sina Hospital (Wadi Hatat)	24 577 361
Khoula Hospital	24 563 625
The Royal Hospital	24 599 000

Main Private Hospitals	
Al Shatti Hospital	24 604 263
Muscat Private Hospital ▶ p.119	24 583 600